BUILDING AN INTRANET

Tim Evans

201 West 103rd Street
Indianapolis, Indiana 46290

Building an Intranet *is dedicated to C²E, and is in memory of my father, Jim Evans, who taught me the value of work.*

Copyright © 1996 by Sams.net Publishing

FIRST EDITION

International Standard Book Number: 1-57521-071-1

Library of Congress Catalog Card Number: 95-72941

99 98 97 96   4   3   2   1

Interpretation of the printing code: the rightmost double-digit number is the year of the book's printing; the rightmost single-digit, the number of the book's printing. For example, a printing code of 96-1 shows that the first printing of the book occurred in 1996.

Composed in AGaramond and MCPdigital by Macmillan Computer Publishing

Printed in the United States of America

President, Sams Publishing	*Richard K. Swadley*
Publisher, Sams.net Publishing	*George Bond*
Publishing Manager	*Mark Taber*
Managing Editor	*Cindy Morrow*
Marketing Manager	*John Pierce*

Acquisitions Editor
Beverly Eppink

Development Editor
Fran Hatton

Software Development Specialist
Merle Newlon

Production Editor
Johnna VanHoose

Copy Editors
Kathy Ewing, Faithe Wempen, Joe Williams

Technical Reviewer
John Nelson

Editorial Coordinator
Bill Whitmer

Technical Edit Coordinator
Lynette Quinn

Formatter
Frank Sinclair

Editorial Assistants
Carol Ackerman
Andi Richter
Rhonda Tinch-Mize

Cover Designer
Tim Amrhein

Book Designer
Alyssa Yesh

Copy Writer
Peter Fuller

Production Team Supervisor
Brad Chinn

Production
Michael Brumitt, John Carroll, Michael Dietsch, Lisa Daugherty, Judy Everly, Jason Hand, Sonja Hart, Michael Henry, Natalie Hollifield, Ayanna Lacey, Clint Lahnen, Louisa Klucznik, Steph Mineart, Angel Perez, Laura Robbins, Bobbi Satterfield, Craig Small, Laura A. Smith, Andrew Stone, Chris Van Camp, Mark Walchle, Todd Wente, Colleen Williams

Overview

Contents

Acknowledgments

Although *Building an Intranet* was not a DuPont-supported project, I'm indebted to several people at the DuPont Company for important moral and other support in the writing of the book. First, Hank Morneau encouraged the basic idea of the book and allowed early versions of the manuscript to appear on the DuPont-Wide Web. Dr. David Pensak, as always, leads by encouraging people to explore, knowing the benefits of the exploration will provide value both to the DuPont Company and to its people. Karen Bloch provided valuable help with the material on the *Khorosware* training course in Chapters 21 and 23. Wade Rogers put up with, and invariably (whether he wanted to or not) contributed to, my verbal brainstorming. Last, but by no means least, Cristy provided a great deal of support from cover to cover, but in particular with respect to Chapter 15.

I also owe thanks to a number of people at the Social Security Administration for their support in years past. These include Ben Dean, Joe Dorsey, Billy Lewis, and John Sabo. Without their help at yet another career turning point, I'd still be pushing paper.

At Sams.net, Bevery Eppink, Fran Hatton, and Johnna VanHoose helped with the authoring and editing process under difficult time pressures, under which the author was not always as gracious as they.

About the Authors

Author of Que Publishing's *10 Minute Guide to HTML* and *10 Minute Guide to Netscape for X Windows*, Tim Evans is a UNIX system administration and network security consultant. Employed by Taratec Development Corporation, his full-time contract assignment for the past four years has been at the DuPont Company's Experimental Station in Wilmington, Delaware, home of the company's Central Research and Development Department. He pioneered development of DuPont's own world wide web, known as DuPont-Wide Web, or DW2, widely used within the company for information sharing via its worldwide network. Previously, Tim worked for the U.S. Social Security Administration in various staff jobs for more than 20 years. In 1991, before the Internet got hot, he brought that government agency onto the Internet. At both DuPont and the SSA, he provided support for large numbers of UNIX users, running UNIX on a variety of computer systems, ranging from PCs to workstations to mini-computers.

Born too early for the Designated Hitter Rule, and because he couldn't run, field, or throw, he had to pursue alternative careers to baseball. A native of Missouri, Tim has therefore been a carny, auto assembly line worker, janitor, bureaucrat, and bartender. His degrees in history show a liberal arts education can qualify you for almost any job, depending on what you do afterwards. Tim also is a produced playwright with an extensive background in community theatre, both on and off stage. His favorite role was that of James in Jason Miller's *That Championship Season*, though he really, really wants to do Professor Harold Hill in *The Music Man*. His three produced stageplays were presented at a theatre on a street named Broadway. He lives with his wife and best friend, Carol, and their Irish Setter, Judy! Judy! Judy!, in Delaware, just three hours from their vacation home in Chincoteague, VA. He can be reached via Internet email as tkevans@tkevans.com.

Billy Barron (billy@metronet.com) is currently the Network Services Manager for the University of Texas at Dallas and has an MS in Computer Science from the University of North Texas. He writes and edits such books as *Tricks of the Internet Gurus*, *Education on the Internet*, and *Accessing Online Bibliographic Databases* as well as writing for periodicals.

Lay Wah Ooi (ooi@pobox.com) is a Computer Systems Engineer at Titan Spectrum Technologies. She graduated with a Computer Science degree from the University of North Texas. Lay Wah has contributed to Sams.net Publishing's *Internet Unleashed* and was also a technical editor for *Java Unleashed*.

Introduction

You've used Netscape, Mosaic, or another World Wide Web browser and found many wondrous things. Hypertext documents with hyperlinks, colorful graphics, and multimedia technology allow you to jump here, there, and yon around the world on the Internet, following your interests and your impulses just by clicking your mouse buttons. Vast information resources—useful knowledge, interesting trivia, and electronic garbage, in possibly equal amounts—are at your fingertips. With a Web browser's intuitive interface, all these resources are accessible even to novice computer users.

Institutions, businesses, and individuals have created (or are rushing to create) Web pages as a means of marketing products or services or of distributing some kind of information about their organization or people. Maybe your company already has a Web site online. Web technology and Web technology companies are in the news on a daily basis. Netscape Communications Corporation's wildly popular initial public stock offering is already a Wall Street legend, and the stock's prices continued to soar throughout 1995. Even high-tech behemoths like Microsoft and IBM have jumped into the whole Web/Internet world with all the weight of a couple of 800-pound gorillas. Rumor has it the next release of Microsoft Windows (that is, the one coming *after* Windows 95) will look and work more like a Web browser than like the Windows you know and love.

Clearly, the World Wide Web is an enormous success: Even if the rumor about Windows 96 (or Build 999, or whatever it's to be called) is just a rumor, the very idea that the World Wide Web interface, developed in just the past two years and given away, can replace the world's most popular commercial computer interface, somehow doesn't seem the least bit farfetched.

How Can You Use The Web To Do Your Company's Work?

You and millions of others have found the Web irresistible, most often for recreational and personal reasons. Even the most commonly used buzzword describing how people use the Web— surfing the Net—is a recreational term. It's gotten so that managers worry about just what it is their employees are doing when they're supposed to be working. Are they really searching for work-related resources, or just surfing? And, more importantly, what does or can this phenomenon mean to my business?

Once the novelty of the Web has worn off a bit, you'll wonder about its potential value as a business or educational tool. Can this slick, seductive technology be put to work inside your company, organization, or institution, to some useful, real-work end? Can you capture the enthusiasm with which your employees surf the Web and channel it into their daily duties? Can you share information about your organization with its members—employees, students, and other insiders—using this glamorous and easy-to-use mechanism? The answer to those questions is an unqualified "Yes" in all cases, and the nuts and bolts of doing so is what this book is all about.

Setting up a corporate Intranet requires you to look under the surface of the Web for new and meaningful ways it can be used. Despite its glamour and accessibility for many users, the Web is essentially a passive experience. People use their Web browsers to look at things—documents, images, movies, and the like. For the most part, however, there's very little a Web surfer can actually do with what he sees. Yes, Web pages can be saved or printed, and there's potential value in doing so. Many Web pages contain valuable information and pointers to other information. The information obtained from reading a Web page can often be used for some work-related purpose. Still, the whole Web experience remains passive: people look at static, unchanging things. You may have wondered why this attractive and easy-to-use interface can't somehow be put to work doing something active and real in a corporate or organizational environment that somehow contributes to the realization of the organization's mission.

You're not alone in asking these questions. In a recent survey by Business Research Group, reported in the *Wall Street Journal* (November 7, 1995), nearly a quarter of 170 medium- and large-sized companies surveyed are already setting up corporate Intranets using World Wide Web technology, while another 20 percent are actively considering doing so. The author is personally involved in a growing corporate Intranet of more than 50 Web servers inside chemical giant E.I. du Pont de Nemours & Company. DuPont-Wide Web servers are located inside the corporate network Firewall, isolated from the Internet at large, world wide. This Intranet's main server shows an average of 50,000 accesses per week, all from within the company. While this sort of access count is trivial for Web servers that are accessible to the Internet at large, it's a significant one for a single company, even one as large as DuPont.

What This Book Is Not About

This book is not another *Surfing-the-Web-for-Cool-Sites* book. The author believes, and the phenomenal growth of corporate Intranets confirms, the real value of Web technology is in how it can be put to work, not in recreation. Nor is this book another *How-To-Set-Up-a-Cool-Web-Site* book. There are many such books on this very crowded market, and little reason for more of either type. These often-excellent books are full of useful information about the Web, and even provide great instruction in making information available using Web technology, including how to use the Web as a marketing and public relations tool for an organization's goods and services. But you didn't buy this book to read this sort of information.

What This Book Is About

Organizations do more than sell the goods and services they produce, however. Commercial ventures have to produce the goods or services they sell and they also have to manage production processes of some kind or other in doing so. All organizations, even noncommercial ones, have to manage themselves, buying supplies, running a physical plant, managing employees and their benefits, and otherwise keeping organizational house. None of these other Web-related books pay much attention to how Web technology can be directly used by a company or other organization in fulfilling these missions. Usually, they provide a few simple examples of some kind or other, then trail off with vague statements (or even small-print footnotes) to the effect that the reader should be able to use her imagination to come up with ways to apply the books' examples to her own organization.

This book is about how commercial and noncommercial organizations can put Web technology to work inside their organization to do their real, everyday work.

This book will show how Web technology and related TCP/IP networking technology can be used to create information resources that can be actively used in the daily operation of a business, an educational institution, or any other organization. We'll provide concrete examples, ranging from simple everyday office tools to complex scientific and technical ones, and step-by-step instructions that show you exactly how to implement useful Web features you can use in your daily work, or in the daily work of your company. Once you have set up your Intranet, your users will be able to use their Web browsers and other applications to perform their regular work duties.

Zona Research projects the Intranet software market will more than double in the next two years, from $488 million in 1995 to $1.2 billion in 1996 (*Wall Street Journal*, November 7, 1995). IBM has just upgraded its Lotus Notes groupware package to add Web capabilities, a defense against companies using the Web as a poor man's Notes for collaborative purposes. Netscape Communications Corporation has acquired Collabra Software, Inc., makers of another groupware package, and plans to integrate it into its flagship Netscape Navigator Web browser.

Using Web Technology To Create Your Intranet

WWW technology can provide a familiar, user-friendly front end to a wide range of information ranging from libraries of personnel and technical documents to data warehouses full of corporate statistics, to scientific and technical data. This data not only can be accessed with Web browsers, but also can be actively manipulated as needed. Web technology can provide front ends to commercial database applications, with both search/query and data-entry capabilities. Custom computer application programs can be wrapped up inside an easy-to-use Web interface, with Web-based online help a mouse click away. Users can collaborate with others on work-related projects and share scientific data and other information, again using familiar Web technology. Because Web browsers have built-in support for many kinds of network services, you'll be able to extend your Intranet to include many other facilities. Most of these facilities are based on no-cost software (much of which is available on the Intranet CD-ROM), and they provide strong and inexpensive alternatives to commercial groupware packages like Lotus Notes. These value-added services will be useful in your organization, providing facilities that can be accessed using a Web browser via simple point and click. Once you begin to implement them, that rumor about Windows 96 will seem a lot more reasonable.

What's Assumed About You

This book assumes you have some experience in the use of computers and networks, specifically including some knowledge of TCP/IP networking. While it's assumed you already have a World Wide Web server in place, installing and configuring one on a PC or UNIX system will be briefly outlined in Appendix A, "Setting Up a Web Server." Setting up and maintaining a Web server requires a not-inconsiderable amount of technical experience with computers, but this is not rocket science; moderately experienced computer users should have no trouble with the basic material in the book. (Some of the skills you'll need are outlined in a good deal of detail in Chapter 5, "Skills Sets.") You should also have experience in some computer programming language if you want to create Web server scripts to extend your Intranet and make it more interactive. Mostly, though, you will need the imaginative breadth to visualize how the material in the book can be adapted to your own organization's special needs and circumstances. While the examples in this book are highly specific and detailed and some of them directly usable in your Intranet, examples in a book can never be exactly suited to every organization. You best know your organization and what it does and are therefore in the best position to decide what works for you.

Having read the book, you will be able to set up and maintain a Web server, create basic documents using the HTML markup language, configure the server and clients to use new helper applications, and set up information resources using Web and related TCP/IP networking technology for your Intranet. Further, you'll be able to implement other network services that will be accessible to your users with their Web browsers, extending your Intranet to include more services.

The book focuses on freely available World Wide server software for UNIX systems and Windows. Examples use the NCSA Mosaic and Netscape Navigator Web browser for Windows, Macs, and UNIX systems. In addition, the book uses examples that utilize common application programs such as word processors, spreadsheets, database packages, and so on, along with some more exotic examples with scientific, technical, and other software applications.

How To Use This Book

Organized in six major sections, this book guides you through the process of designing and implementing your Intranet.

- ◆ *Intranet Basics* includes an introductory chapter; a chapter on designing and administering your Intranet; chapters on infrastructure, content development, and people skills; and a chapter on getting a Web server up and running quickly as a foundation for your Intranet.

- ◆ *Getting Set Up* introduces critical World Wide Web server configuration information, which serves as the basis for opening your Intranet to a wide variety of uses; shows you how to add value to your Intranet by including additional network services; and explains the importance of Web server security.

◆ *Setting Up Common Office Applications for Your Intranet* builds on the earlier sections and shows you how to use your everyday word processor, spreadsheet, database manager, and other desktop tools as a vital parts of your Intranet.

◆ *Advanced Applications for Your Intranet* ventures further, into the worlds of indexing and retrieving data, accessing corporate databases, and scientific and technical applications.

◆ *Sample Applications* gives you specific examples of the kinds of things you can do on your Intranet, using the information and techniques explained in the previous sections.

◆ *New Intranet Possibilities* introduces fast-moving, cutting-edge developments, like Java and the Virtual Reality Modeling Language, and how they may provide new ways for you to extend your Intranet, then focuses on collaboration in a Web environment.

In addition, two appendixes to the book provide quick references to setting up a web server and to the HyperText Markup Language, respectively. The appendixes are relatively short, but references to book-length treatments of these subjects are included.

The Intranet CD-ROM

You'll find the Intranet CD-ROM bound into this book. The CD-ROM contains copies of the free- and shareware programs mentioned as examples in the book. Be sure to read and follow installation instructions and all licensing/copyright restrictions.

Conventions Used in This Book

Throughout this book I have adopted a few standard conventions to assist you in recognizing important pieces of information. These include special highlighting methods for information displayed by your computer and for information you need to type in yourself.

Typographical conventions used in this book.

Typeface	Meaning
Computer Type	There are a number Internet addresses, directory paths, and World Wide Web URLs defined throughout this book that are printed in computer type to make them easier to recognize
Bold Computer Type	Text printed in bold computer type represents information you need to type at your keyboard while working with the various programs discussed in this book.
Italic	When you encounter words printed in italic, this indicates that you are about to examine a new concept and should pay close attention to what is being discussed.

Note: Information printed in Note boxes provides you with additional points of interest relating to the topic currently being discussed.

Tip: Tips offer additional suggestions about the use of programs and services.

Warning: Warning messages are designed to make you aware of important issues that may affect set up of your Intranet or general Internet issues.

PART

I

Intranet Basics

Introduction to the World Wide Web

By now it's hard to imagine how anyone could have missed learning at least something about the World Wide Web and the Internet. Mass-circulation newspapers and magazines and broadcast media feature the Internet regularly. You often see Web page addresses (known as *Uniform Resource Locators*, or URLs) in television commercials and printed advertisements. The story of the meteoric rise of Netscape Communications Corporation on the stock market jumped from the financial page to the front page. Univerities, businesses, and other organizations have rushed to "get on the Web," while entrepreneurs have moved equally quickly to take advantage of this rush by setting up shop on the shoulders of the Information Superhighway, hawking everything from Internet connections to Web-page authoring to Web-related conferences.

You probably bought this book because you've been using the Web and want to use its technology to build your own Intranet.

> **Note:** We assume you know what Web URLs, such as `http://www.somecompany.com` mean. If not, you'll probably want to pick up an overall reference to the Web, like *The World Wide Web Unleashed*, by John December and Neil Randall, also published by sams.net. For information about this and other sams.net books, visit the Macmillan Information SuperLibrary at `http://www.mcp.com/`.

This chapter is an overall introduction to the Web, and it lays a foundation for the rest of the book. Because you've probably seen similar introductory material before, I'll put a particular spin on the whole subject in this chapter by pointing to some of the things you'll be able to do on your Intranet. As you read the chapter, think of using your Web browser within your company to view your own company information instead of outside Web pages. Your corporate Intranet, then, is the implementation of World Wide Web services within your organization.

Chapter Objectives

As with the rest of the chapters in this book, let's begin by laying out some chapter objectives. This will help you get oriented to the material to be presented; you may want to refer back to this list as you work your way through the chapter. In this chapter, you'll

- ◆ Gain an overview of the World Wide Web and the Internet
- ◆ Learn about World Wide Web client software, which this book calls *browser* software
- ◆ Learn about World Wide Web servers and their software
- ◆ Learn about the client/server relationship between Web browsers and Web servers
- ◆ Learn how the Web fits into the worldwide TCP/IP Internet
- ◆ Learn about related TCP/IP networking technologies and how they can be made a part of your Intranet

Overview of the World Wide Web and the Internet

The explosion of interest in the Internet is being driven by an even more explosive growth of the Web. Nevertheless, and this isn't meant merely in a pedantic sense, the Internet was here first and has been for more than 20 years. While Chapter 3, "Tools for Implementing an Intranet Infrastructure," presents a brief history of the Internet, it can be defined as those computers and networks worldwide that are interconnected using TCP/IP (Transmission Control Protocol/Internet Protocol) networking.

> **Note:** The term *network protocol* may be unfamiliar to you, so let's draw an analogy. Math equations consist of symbols from a universally agreed to set of symbols. New symbols are not allowed and the rules for using them are very specific. Network protocols work the same way. Like mathematicians, computer programs use a specific, agreed to grammar and set of symbols—protocols—to ensure precise communications.

Most people are familiar with the general idea of a computer network; several computers in an office or other common environment are connected together with wires to enable sharing of printers and files and to otherwise allow communication among them. The idea of the Internet is much the same, only a lot bigger, but it also has an important extra element. TCP/IP networking allows not only the connection of local computers to each other, but also permits networks to be connected to other networks. These connections create *internets* (purposely not capitalized here), in which it appears to users that the computers on all the connected networks are part of a single, large *internetwork*. The same capabilities of sharing devices and communicating data between computers exists, but the sharing has been extended from just the computers on one network to all the systems on all the connected networks.

Interconnected networks need not be in the same location or building; they can be physically remote from each other with connections using special-purpose data lines, satellite radio, infrared radio links, cable TV wiring, or even ordinary telephone lines and modems. Remote computers appear to become local, allowing file transfers, electronic mail, printer and disk sharing, and many other features, including, of course, access to the World Wide Web.

As previously stated, before there was a Web there was already an Internet (now capitalized), a worldwide network of networks interconnected using TCP/IP networking. Some of the major features of the *ante*-Web Internet include

◆ Internet *electronic mail* for sending messages between users on remote computers

◆ *File transfers* between remote computers using the file transfer protocol (FTP)

◆ *Remote login services* (telnet) allowing users to log in to remote computers and use them as if they were local

◆ *Remotely searchable indices* of information, free software, and other data

◆ *USENET News*, the mother of all computer BBSs (bulletin board systems)

Besides these major Internet services, many others have developed over the lifetime of the Internet, some of which use combinations of the above services. Using an Internet search tool called *archie*, for example, you can search a database of free software and find its location on the Internet just by sending a specially worded e-mail message to a special address. Return e-mail services transfer files to you, much like fax-back services, when you request them via e-mail. Special-interest electronic mailing lists have developed for like-minded people who want to discuss subjects ranging from computers and networks themselves to spelunking and men's rights.

Each of these (and many other) Internet services are useful and powerful tools, and all are still widely used. Even before the existence of the Web, the need for electronic mail capabilities was driving substantial growth in the Internet. Each *ante*-Web Internet service, however, has its own particular user interface to be learned. Many of these interfaces are less than friendly to non-technical users. Figures 1.1 and 1.2 show a raw archie search for a software package called ImageMagick (used to capture many of the screenshots in this book), while Figures 1.3 and 1.4 show the same search using a Web browser and fill-in form interface to the archie service.

```
/users/tkevans $ telnet archie.sura.net
Trying 192.239.16.130 ...
Connected to kadath.sura.net.
Escape character is '^]'.


SunOS UNIX (kadath.sura.net)

login: archie
                                Welcome to Archie!
                                    Version 3.3

                            BBN Planet Southeast Region

For Information or questions about this archie server,
please send mail to:

            archie-admin@sura.net


# Bunyip Information Systems, Inc., 1993, 1994, 1995

# Terminal type set to 'xterm 24 80'.
# 'erase' character is '^?'.
# 'search' (type string) has the value 'sub'.
archie> prog imagemagick
# Search type: sub.
# Your queue position: 1
# Estimated time for completion: 5 seconds.
working... =

Host harbor.ecn.purdue.edu    (128.46.128.76)
Last updated 02:52 19 Dec 1995

    Location: /pub
        FILE    -rw-r--r-- 8368504 bytes  18:00 20 Apr 1995  imagemagick.tar.gz


Host csustan.csustan.edu    (130.17.1.70)
```

Figure 1.1. *Raw interface to Archie Internet search service.*

```
Host ftp.warwick.ac.uk    (137.205.192.14)
Last updated 01:59 22 Oct 1995

    Location: /pub/linux-oflo/tsx-11-mirror/binaries/usr.bin.X11
        FILE    -rw-rw-r--  659835 bytes  19:00 15 Nov 1992  ImageMagick-2.0.bin.tar.Z


Host hpcsos.col.hp.com    (15.255.240.16)
Last updated 02:16 21 Sep 1995

    Location: /mirrors/linux/binaries/usr.bin.X11
        FILE    -r--r--r--  659835 bytes  05:00 15 Nov 1992  ImageMagick-2.0.bin.tar.Z


Host ftp.lth.se    (130.235.20.3)
Last updated 02:42 30 Sep 1995

    Location: /pub/netnews/alt.sources/volume92/nov
        FILE    -r--r--r--   13507 bytes  18:00 10 Nov 1992  ImageMagick.2.1.part.1.gz
        FILE    -r--r--r--   17084 bytes  18:00 10 Nov 1992  ImageMagick.2.1.part.10.gz
        FILE    -r--r--r--   16127 bytes  18:00 10 Nov 1992  ImageMagick.2.1.part.11.gz
        FILE    -r--r--r--   14020 bytes  18:00 10 Nov 1992  ImageMagick.2.1.part.12.gz
        FILE    -r--r--r--   16074 bytes  18:00 10 Nov 1992  ImageMagick.2.1.part.13.gz
        FILE    -r--r--r--   15807 bytes  18:00 10 Nov 1992  ImageMagick.2.1.part.14.gz
        FILE    -r--r--r--   18567 bytes  18:00 10 Nov 1992  ImageMagick.2.1.part.15.gz
        FILE    -r--r--r--   19065 bytes  18:00 10 Nov 1992  ImageMagick.2.1.part.2.gz
        FILE    -r--r--r--   16250 bytes  18:00 10 Nov 1992  ImageMagick.2.1.part.3.gz
        FILE    -r--r--r--    2619 bytes  18:00 10 Nov 1992  ImageMagick.2.1.part.4.gz
        FILE    -r--r--r--   19300 bytes  18:00 10 Nov 1992  ImageMagick.2.1.part.5.gz
        FILE    -r--r--r--   21110 bytes  18:00 10 Nov 1992  ImageMagick.2.1.part.6.gz
        FILE    -r--r--r--   24069 bytes  18:00 10 Nov 1992  ImageMagick.2.1.part.7.gz
        FILE    -r--r--r--   18719 bytes  18:00 10 Nov 1992  ImageMagick.2.1.part.8.gz
        FILE    -r--r--r--   18111 bytes  18:00 10 Nov 1992  ImageMagick.2.1.part.9.gz
        FILE    -r--r--r--   21108 bytes  18:00 10 Nov 1992  ImageMagick.2.1.part.gz

    Location: /pub/netnews/alt.sources/volume92/sep
        FILE    -r--r--r--   18891 bytes  17:00  9 Sep 1992  ImageMagick.V2.0.part.1.gz
        FILE    -r--r--r--   18227 bytes  17:00  9 Sep 1992  ImageMagick.V2.0.part.10.gz
        FILE    -r--r--r--   17890 bytes  17:00  9 Sep 1992  ImageMagick.V2.0.part.11.gz
```

Figure 1.2. *Results of raw Archie search.*

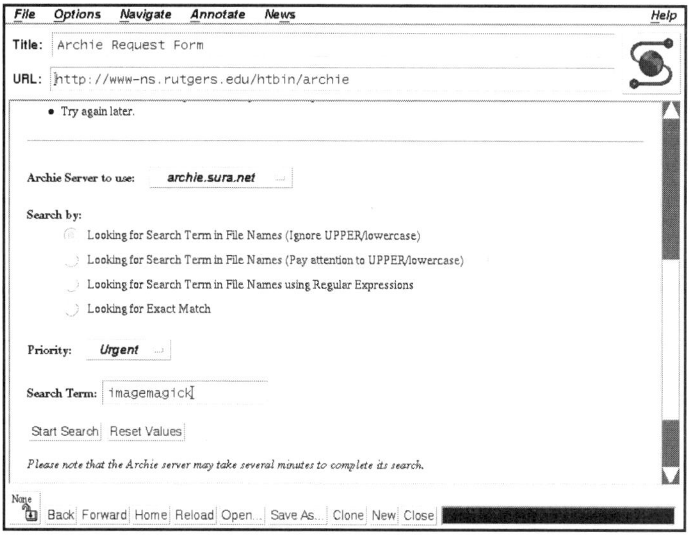

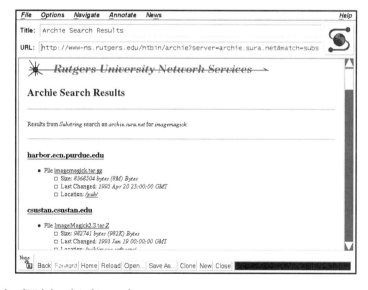

Figure 1.3. *Web-based Archie search.*

Figure 1.4. *Results of Web-based Archie search.*

As you can see, the Web interface is significantly more accessible; the difference literally speaks for itself. Instead of a raw list of anonymous FTP servers and lengthy directory paths, you see a nicely formatted list of locations with the ability to download the located file just by clicking the link. Even if you use the raw approach, you still have to turn around and use FTP, a completely different service with a different user interface, to retrieve the file you want. Even assuming you can find the data you want, which Internet program do you use to access it? And where did you put the obscure set of instructions for this particular program? Actually using the *ante*-Web Internet then was not an easy proposition, particularly for casual computer users.

In 1993, Tim Berners-Lee and other researchers at the European Particle Physics Lab (*Conseil Européen pour la Recherche Nucléaire,* or CERN) in Geneva, Switzerland, developed a means of sharing data among their colleagues using something they called *hypertext.* CERN users could view documents on their computer screens using new *browser* software. Special codes embedded in these electronic documents allowed users to jump from one document to another on screen just by selecting a *hyperlink.* Internet capabilities were built into these browsers. Just as a user could jump from one text document on a computer to another, he could jump from a document on one computer to a document on another remote computer. Moreover, each of the major Internet services listed above was added to the browser software. A researcher could transfer a file from a remote computer to her local system, or log into a remote system just by hitting on a hyperlink, rather than using the clumsy FTP or Telnet mechanisms. CERN's breakthrough work is the basis of today's World Wide Web and its Web server and browser software (now being maintained by the World Wide Web Consortium with the current versions available on the accompanying CD-ROM) were the first of their kind.

Note: CERN has now moved on, or rather back, to its main mission of doing research on particle physics, but its Web-related legacy has been passed on to the World Wide Web Consortium, a group of academic and commercial organizations dedicated to the advancement of the Web. W^3, as it's called, remains active in the development of the Web, and Berners-Lee is still right in the thick of things at W^3. You may want to visit the W^3 Web site at `http://www.w3.org/`.

Unlike today's Web browsers, CERN's Web browser was a *plain-text* package in which cursor keys were used to move around the computer screen and the Enter key to select hyperlinks. While it could access both hypertext documents and *ante*-Web Internet services like FTP, Gopher, and Telnet, it had no graphical capabilities. Marc Andreesen, a graduate student working part time at the University of Illinois National Center for Supercomputer Applications, picked up CERN's work and turned it into what would become today's *NCSA Mosaic,* the first graphical Web browser with point-and-click capabilities. First developed for UNIX computer systems running the X Windows graphical user interface, NCSA Mosaic was quickly ported to Windows and Macintosh PCs. Mosaic rapidly became the proverbial "killer application" for the Internet. Just as Mosaic descended from the work at CERN, all subsequent graphical Web browsers come from this common ancestor.

Along the way, NCSA also developed its own Web server software for UNIX systems. Copies of NCSA Mosaic for PCs and several UNIX systems are on the CD-ROM accompanying this book, as is the NCSA Web server software and source code for both.

Web Browsers

Besides NCSA Mosaic, there are a large number of other Web browsers, including, of course, the widely used Netscape Navigator package, now the leading Web browser in terms of market share. (incidentally, Marc Andreesen left NCSA to co-found Netscape Communications Corporation.)

While this book concentrates on NCSA Mosaic and Netscape Navigator, there are a lot of Web browser software packages to choose from besides these two. Take a quick look at some of the others.

◆ Cello—A free browser from Cornell University that runs under Windows and OS/2.

◆ WinWeb—Shareware developed by Microelectronics and Computer Technology Corporation that runs under Windows and OS/2.

◆ MacWeb—Shareware developed by Microelectronics and Computer Technology Corporation that runs on Macs.

◆ Enhanced Mosaic—The commercial version of Mosaic from SpyGlass, Inc. It's available for PCs and Macs.

◆ Chimera—Freeware from the University of Nevada that runs under UNIX.

◆ MidasWWW—Freeware from Stanford University that runs under UNIX.

◆ WebWorks Mosaic—Formerly called *GWHIS*, this commercial browser from Quadralay, Inc. runs under UNIX.

◆ ViolaWWW—Freeware from the University of California that runs under UNIX.

◆ TKWWW—Freeware from the Massachusetts Institute of Technology that runs under UNIX.

◆ Lynx plain-text browser—Freeware from Kansas University for UNIX systems and low-end PCs (doesn't require Windows).

◆ W³C (formerly CERN)—This line-mode browser is the original Web browser. It's freeware from the W³ Consortium.

How Web Browsers Work

Graphical or not, all Web browsers work in essentially the same way. Look at what happens when you click on a hyperlink.

◆ Your browser reads a document written in HTML and displays it for you, interpreting all the markup codes in the document.

◆ When you click a hyperlink in that document, your browser uses the HyperText Transfer Protocol (HTTP) to send a network request to a Web server to access the new document or service specified by the hyperlink.

◆ Also using the HTTP protocol, the Web server responds to the request with the document or other data you requested.

◆ Your browser software then reads and interprets that information and presents it to you in the correct format.

As you can see a simple click on a hyperlink starts a pretty significant series of events involving not only your Web browser software but also a Web server somewhere on the Internet. Figure 1.5 shows this sequence of events.

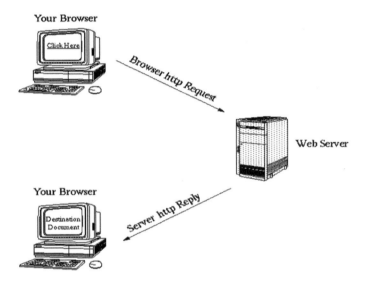

Figure 1.5. Web browser/server communication using HTTP.

Note: For purposes of your Intranet, it's important to note that Web servers always identify the type of data they send in response to browser requests. Most of the time the data returned is text data with HTML markup, but any kind of data can be returned. This bit of information is critical to the potential capabilities of your Intranet: As long as your Web server can identify the data it's sending, your users' Web browsers can be set up to handle almost any kind of data including word processing files, spreadsheets, and the datafiles used by a wide variety of other applications. This simple-but-powerful mechanism explained in detail in Chapter 7 is what you can use to turn your Intranet into an interactive tool for getting your company's everyday work done.

Web Servers

Web browsers like Mosaic or Netscape communicate over a network (including the worldwide Internet) with Web servers, using HTTP. Browsers send network messages to servers asking that specific documents or services be provided by the server. The server returns the document or service if it's available also using the HTTP protocol, and the browser receives and understands it.

There are many network protocols spoken on the Internet, each one for a specific and limited purpose. There are network protocols for electronic mail, file transfers, and other services you may have heard of, including *Gopher*, *Telnet*, and *WAIS*. Each of these protocols works well for its own purpose, and you can use individual programs on your computer that communicate with the protocols to locate and retrieve information on the Net. The HTTP protocol was designed to incorporate these, and other, network protocols into a single protocol. What's important to the World Wide Web user is that Web browsers speak the HTTP protocol, taking care of locating, retrieving, and, most important, interpreting the data, regardless of the actual underlying protocol or service.

Your Intranet will utilize the HTTP protocol and all the other TCP/IP protocols it subsumes to provide point-and-click access to a wide variety of your mission-critical information and services. This is an important point, and we'll come back to it in the final section of this chapter.

World Wide Web Server Software

World Wide Web server software is available for a variety of computer systems in both no-cost and commercial packages. A few are mentioned in this section. Details on setting up and using these packages are in Chapter 3 and Appendix A, "Setting Up a Web Server."

UNIX Software

The HTTP protocol and the Web servers and clients that use it were initially developed at CERN. The W³ Consortium still maintains the CERN HTTPd server software package, now renamed as the W³C HTTPD server. (You may have noticed that *HTTP* has become *HTTPD* in this context. UNIX server programs are frequently referred to as *daemons* (because they run as background processes on the system), hence, HTTPD is used to refer to server software, while HTTP refers to the protocol.) The W³C HTTPD server software runs on UNIX (and VAX/VMS) systems and is on the accompanying CD-ROM. In the United States, the National Center for Supercomputing Applications (NCSA) at the University of Illinois has also developed Web server software for UNIX systems. NCSA's software is also on the CD-ROM. Both source code and binary distributions of the two UNIX packages are included. See Appendix A for details on setting up the CERN and NCSA Web server packages on your UNIX system.

Web Server Software for PCs

You don't have to have a UNIX computer system to set up and run a World Wide Web server. Server software is available for IBM-compatible PCs running Windows 3.1, Windows 95, Windows NT, OS/2, and for Macintosh PCs. In the former category, the NCSA HTTPd server is available in a shareware version for Windows PCs, while a commercial version is available for Windows 95 and NT.

Most desktop PCs and Macs do a less-than-outstanding job of *multitasking* (essential for Web servers that must be able to respond to many HTTP requests in a short time). Current PC and Mac operating systems weren't designed to do true multitasking; they *simulate* multitasking instead. Also, desktop PCs are underpowered for high-traffic Web servers. If you choose a PC or Mac for a server platform, you'll probably want to dedicate a high-end machine to this task, rather than trying to run a server on somebody's desktop PC while it's in use.

A good alternative for IBM-compatible PCs is a PC version of UNIX, such as Solaris, BSDI, Esix, SCO UNIX, or even—if you're up to it—one of the freeware UNIX lookalikes, Linux or FreeBSD. Because UNIX is a true multitasking operating system, potential problems in running and managing a Web server in Windows are avoided. PCs that by today's standards are low-end (such as a 386) can comfortably run a Web server under UNIX.

Chapter 3 goes into more detail to help you select the hardware and software to make up your Intranet.

Commercial Web Server Software Features

As you might guess, demand for HTTPd server software is high, and a number of companies have announced commercial Web server software, most prominently, the Netscape *Netsite* server for UNIX and Windows NT systems available from the same company that developed the Netscape Navigator Web browser. See `http://home.netscape.com/comprod/server_central/` for more information. In addition, O'Reilly and Associates' *WebSite* server (descendant of the above-mentioned NCSA HTTPd shareware package for Windows) runs on Windows NT and Windows 95. Information on *Website* is available at `http://website.ora.com/`. *WebStar* for the Macintosh, named both Best Internet Product and Best Overall Software Product for 1995 by *MacUser* magazine, is available from StarNine Technologies, with information at `http://www.starnine.com`.

These commercially developed server software packages have features above and beyond the freeware server software described. Following is a list of some of these:

♦ *Encryption* of sensitive information (credit card numbers and other personal or business information, for example).

♦ *Authentication* of users accessing the server to ensure confidentiality.

♦ Accurate *tracking* of who accesses the server.

♦ Tracking of *data retrievals,* so software and other data can actually be sold interactively over the Net.

Of course you should also be able to expect commercial-grade support from Web server software vendors. This is a potentially critical matter especially if you don't have in-house expertise in managing the software. Free software packages are invariably not free when you have to provide your own support.

Other TCP/IP Services in Your Intranet

Although we've touched on this subject once or twice earlier, it's worth specific, focused attention for your Intranet. The HTTP protocol spoken by both Web servers and browsers, includes a number of other TCP/IP services, including:

- FTP (file transfer protocol)—usually used for downloading files from one computer to another
- Gopher—a menu-based hierarchical information retrieval system
- USENET news—provides access to the world's largest computer bulletin board system
- Wide Area Information Servers (WAIS)—used for searching indexed data using keywords
- Remote login services (Telnet)—used for terminal emulation when logging in to remote computer systems
- Electronic mail
- Other services such as the previously-mentioned archie service available directly or via fill-in forms using the CGI mechanism (see Chapter 5).

Because these services are built into the HTTP protocol, your Intranet can include any of them. Moreover, you can integrate any of these services without requiring your users to learn the service's native interfaces. Web browsers provide a common, point-and-click front end to all these services. You can, for example, set up an FTP server in your Intranet for distributing software updates or any other computer data. Similarly, you can use USENET news services as a means of collaboration and information sharing within your organization. In either case, your users—the people defined in Chapter 2, "Designing an Intranet," as your Intranet's customers—need to learn only one interface, their Web browser, to access any of the services you're providing on your Intranet.

All this is true regardless of whether your network is connected to the Internet. Because you need TCP/IP networking running in your corporate network in order to set up an Intranet (see Chapter 3), you can turn around and use this infrastructure to extend your Intranet. Doing so enables you to include a wide variety of other TCP/IP network services. Anonymous FTP, for example, need not be limited to the outside world; you can use it within your company just as well. Index internal data with WAIS, then make it available to your users. Provide point-and-click remote login services within your network to mainframe or high-end computers for those who need them. Use e-mail distribution lists within your company and your Web browser to read and send messages.

The upshot of this is that your Intranet need not be limited to the passive retrieval of HTML documents, or to extended use of helper applications described in this book. Because Web browsers understand virtually all TCP/IP network protocols, you're free to extend the capabilities of your Intranet to include any of the TCP/IP services that might be useful to your company's or organization's mission. Further, you can do so without incurring the organizational overhead of teaching people to use each and every different service that might be useful.

Summary

We've introduced the World Wide Web in this chapter, then put a spin on it that's applicable to the use of its technology in a corporate Intranet. We've introduced the following subjects, each of which are covered in detail in other chapters.

- ◆ An overview of the World Wide Web and the Internet
- ◆ World Wide Web client software
- ◆ World Wide Web servers and their software
- ◆ The client/server relationship between Web browsers and Web servers
- ◆ How the Web fits into the worldwide TCP/IP Internet
- ◆ Related TCP/IP networking technologies and how they can be made a part of your Intranet

Chapters 2, 3, 4, and 5 form a cluster, each focusing on a set of tools for building your Intranet.

CHAPTER 2

Designing an Intranet

This chapter is about the process by which you will design your Intranet. Although you will no doubt find your design will change as you actually implement your Web, and the people who use it will want further changes, you should nevertheless go through this process before you begin the nuts-and-bolts work of putting it together. Planning your Intranet now will result in building it more effectively and in less overall time. To this end, we'll assume in this chapter only that you have used a World Wide Web browser (like Mosaic or Netscape) and that you therefore have a general familiarity with the Web as a whole. You'll learn about the tools you can use to implement your server, but let's brainstorm first.

Chapter Objectives

As with the rest of the chapters in this book, let's begin by laying out some chapter objectives. This will help you get oriented to the material to be presented; you may want to refer back to this list as you work your way through the chapter. In this chapter, you'll

◆ Learn what an Intranet is and how it is different from what you've seen on the World Wide Web.

◆ Identify the customers in your company for whom your Intranet is designed.

◆ Determine the kind of information you will make available on your Intranet.

◆ Decide who in your company or organization (or what organizational component) is best as the keeper of your Intranet.

◆ Consider high-level issues about the design and organization of your Intranet server(s).

◆ Identify and target your Intranet's customers and sell them on the idea of an Intranet.

You'll find these subjects are closely interrelated, and that your decisions in one of these areas inevitably affect the others. As a result, the process of designing an Intranet won't turn out to be the straight-line process these bulleted items seem to suggest.

The What and Why of an Intranet?

This book uses the term *Intranet* to refer to organizations' use of World Wide Web and related Internet technology to do their essential work, that of helping to produce the goods or services the organization exists to produce.

In the rush to get on the Web, most organizations think in terms of making information available to people outside the organization. Many companies have installed Web servers and made them accessible on the Internet with the idea of making corporate information available to others or of selling things on the Web. Interestingly, though, the initial objective of the Web pioneers at the European Particle Physics Lab (CERN) in Geneva, was to create a means by which CERN scientists could more easily share information. Thus, the first Web was, in fact, an *Intranet*, designed to distribute information *within* an organization to the organization's own people. Without detracting from the proven business value of World Wide Web services in making information available to those outside organizations and companies, this book focuses on how purely within an organization, Web and related technology may be used to further the purpose for which the organization exists.

Your Customers

Given this premise, the definition of those who will use your Intranet is sharply different than that of those who use a company's public Web. Traditionally, when a company sets up a Web server, the intended audience is one or more of the following: the general public, current and future customers, stockholders, and even competitors. What all these have in common, of course, is that all of them are *outside* the business. Figure 2.1 shows a typical business home page offering public information, news releases, and the like about a major international company.

While many of Conoco's employees may have an interest in this Web site, you can see that its primary focus is on presenting information to *outsiders*. General information about the company is available, as are public news releases about company earnings and activities. There's even a page about the company's people and its community service activities, and another about company environmental activities. Both contain valuable public relations information. Clearly, the potential audience of this Web site is external to that company.

Figure 2.1. *The Conoco home page. Copyright Conoco, Inc., 1995, 1996. All rights reserved.*

By contrast, Figure 2.2 shows the home page for the University of Kansas campus-wide information center. Here the focus is on those people inside or closely associated with the organization: students, faculty, and administrators of the university. You see information about the university's campuses, calendars of events, course listings and schedules, departmental and campus organization information, and information such as the campus phone book.

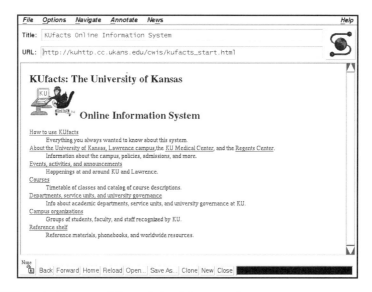

Figure 2.2. *KUFacts, the University of Kansas Online Information System.*

While there's no doubt some of the information available on this Web server would be useful to people outside the university, its primary audience is clearly campus insiders. The campus phone book or the football schedule may be of wider interest. On the other hand, the History department's fall 1995 schedule of classes (see Figure 2.3) showing that History 565, *Imperial Russia and the Soviet Union*, taught by Professor Alexander (a course the author took with the same professor in 1969!), meets on Mondays, Wednesdays, and Fridays at 11:30 in Room 4002, is probably of interest only to a few history students at the university who are trying to fulfill graduation requirements and/or fit a course into their schedule.

Figure 2.3. *KU History department schedule of classes.*

Note: You'll note the decidedly nongraphical approach taken by the university's Web site. KU is the home of *lynx*, a text-only Web browser that is freely available and widely used. Nongraphical browsers are important in situations in which users have dumb terminals or other nongraphical devices that cannot display the images and other graphical features of the Web. Intentionally unable to support graphics, *lynx* and other plain-text browsers provide the ability for users to follow hyperlinks, download files, send e-mail, read and post USENET news articles, and access other Internet services, pretty much just as the more fortunate of us who have access to Netscape or Mosaic. *Lynx* source code for UNIX systems and executables for MS-DOS (not Windows) is on the CD ROM. Figure 2.4 shows the same KU History department class schedule as Figure 2.3, this time viewed in *lynx*. More information about *lynx* is available at http://www.ukans.edu/about_lynx/about_lynx.html.

```
                                                              (p10 of 18)
    HIST 520 THE AGE OF THE RENAISSANCE
    3.00   WH    34532 - ------
               10:30-11:20   M W F   158  ST      CORTEGUERA LUIS

    HIST 529 INTELLECTUAL HISTORY OF 19TH CENTURY EUROPE
    3.00   WH    34540 - ------
                1:00- 2:20   T R    4002 WES     SAX BENJAMIN

     HIST 531 HISTORY OF AMERICAN WOMEN--1870 TO PRESENT
SAME AS AM S 0511.
SAME AS W S 0511.
    3.00   H     34548 - ------
                7:00- 9:50PM T      4002 WES     SCHOFIELD ANN

    HIST 537 FRANCE FROM THE RENAISSANCE TO THE FRENCH REVOLUTION
    3.00   H     34556 - ------
               11:00-12:20   T R    156  ST      BOSSENGA GAIL

    HIST 539 BRITAIN AND IRELAND TO 1200 C.E.
    3.00   H     34564 - ------
               11:00-12:20   T R    4002 WES     BITEL LISA

    HIST 565 IMPERIAL RUSSIA AND THE SOVIET UNION
    3.00   WH    34572 - ------
               11:30-12:20   M W F  4002 WES     ALEXANDER JOHN T
    DISC         WH    34580 - ------
               12:30- 1:20       F   426  SUM     ALEXANDER JOHN T
ABOVE SECTION: VOLUNTARY DISCUSSION, DO NOT ENROLL.

    HIST 570 THE MIDDLE EAST SINCE WORLD WAR II
    3.00   WH NW 34588 - ------
                2:30- 3:50   T R    4012 WES     GREAVES ROSE L

    HIST 575 HISTORY OF MEXICO
    3.00   WH    34596 - ------
-- press space for next page --
   Arrow keys: Up and Down to move. Right to follow a link; Left to go back.
  H)elp O)ptions P)rint G)o M)ain screen Q)uit /=search [delete]=history list
```

Figure 2.4. *KU History department schedule of classes viewed in* lynx.

Your Insiders Are Your Customers

The distinction between the intended audience of the two Web servers you've examined should now be clear. When you begin to consider the design of your Intranet, your first consideration must be a clear definition of your intended audience, your *customers*, if you will. As you've seen, KUFacts' customers are clearly different from Conoco's. The University's primary business is education and research, with its primary customers being students, educators, and researchers, all of whom are members of the organization. KUFacts supports those business objectives by providing information services primarily to those customers. Conoco's primary business is exploration for and production of energy products (oil, natural gas, and the like); its Web site customers are primarily the very same people who consume the company's products, the vast majority of whom are outside the organization.

While your company may already have a World Wide Web server with a constituency like Conoco's, your Intranet will take on the primary characteristics and orientation of KUFacts. Your organization's primary business might be the manufacture of ball bearings, the provision of health insurance services, or the payment of government benefits, but your Intranet's customers are not the same as the customers who buy or receive those products and services. Rather, in this case, your customers are the people inside your organization. Further, your customers are the people who make those products or provide those services.

These are critical distinctions that must be kept in view when conceiving and designing your Intranet. How you design your Intranet and what information it contains must be based on your target audience: your customers on the inside. Later in this chapter, we'll consider further focusing the definition of this audience. Accordingly, this book uses the term *customer* from here on to refer to people inside your organization, company, or agency.

Your Business Is Providing Services to Your Customers

Similarly, there is a business aspect of an Intranet. Your company provides services of one or more kinds for its employees (customers). These services may cover a wide range.

◆ Human Resources (personnel) services.

◆ Materiel and logistical services such as office space, equipment (desks, telephones, computers, machinery, and so on), supplies, and all the physical services involved in operating an organization.

◆ Information systems services.

In fact, most businesses have a formal or informal organization that reflects these services, with Materiel and Logistical, Human Resources, Information Systems, and other similar departments providing services to insiders. Whether your organization is a small shop, multinational corporation, government agency, or other institution, one of its business activities is the provision of these kinds of services. Looking at them is the first major step toward defining the content and layout of your Intranet.

This book takes a frank, strong, customer-is-always-right point of view. Just as your business is all about selling goods or services to your outside customers, your Intranet is all about doing the same with your inside customers.

Information and Services Your Customers Need

We've just cast the people in an organization as customers of some of the organization's goods and services. In addition, we've likened the provision of those goods and services as a business activity. Let's now bring those two ideas together by thinking about the sorts of things that might go into an Intranet. Just what specific things among those goods and services might fit? Consider this question using the major breakdown of business activities listed previously.

Human Resources Services

Whether or not your company has a formal Personnel department, you know there is a great deal of paperwork involved. Much of that paperwork is information your customers need. These are, just to name a few:

◆ Employee manuals, codes of conduct, information about health insurance plans, pay and vacation information, procedures for buying things or getting reimbursed for expenses, and so on

◆ Company bulletin boards papered with government notices about minimum wages and nondiscrimination policies, job announcements, work schedules, training courses, cafeteria menus, softball schedules, used-tires-for-sale notices, and a hundred other pieces of paper

◆ Employee records of time, attendance, vital information (marital status, home address, and so on), performance reviews etc.

◆ Employee newsletters with company announcements and other communications

◆ All the varied substantive and procedural documents a Human Resources department might use to hire, fire, promote, transfer, train, keep records on, and otherwise manage the employment and benefits of employees

Here is a veritable treasure trove of information for an Intranet! Imagine how your Human Resources department might provide these kinds of information in a better, more up to date, and more easily accessible way with a World Wide Web server. You may even already have some of this information in some kind of electronic form (you consider the conversion of existing electronic data for use on your Web server in Chapter 6, "Quick and Dirty Intranet"). Employees then can use their Web browser to retrieve for themselves current copies of the documents you've previously stored in file cabinets, saving both the employee's and your own time and money.

For example, suppose an employee wants to know whether the company health insurance plan covers a particular surgical procedure. If the health plan brochure is available on your Web server, the employee can look it up herself at her own convenience and in a confidential, private way. Again, the employee nearing retirement age may want information about the pension plan, possibly even a benefit computation. Why not make it possible for him to get this information himself? Similarly, how about giving your people the opportunity to file trip reports, including requests for reimbursement of travel expenses, or apply for a job vacancy? How about the company phone book or the old-fashioned suggestion box?

Your Personnel department is a rich source of information for your Intranet.

Materiel and Logistics Services

Every organization, large or small, provides to its customers desks, telephones, computers, office supplies, trash removal and cleaning services, and a whole host of other related services. Fire extinguishers are serviced, parking lots and sidewalks are maintained and cleared of snow, mail is picked up and delivered, equipment and furniture is moved and repaired, and goods and services are purchased. Records are kept of all these things, some of which (Occupational Safety and Health Administration records, for example) are required by government agencies.

Here is another source of information and services your Intranet can provide. Some possible examples:

◆ A Web-searchable listing of excess office furniture, machinery, or computer equipment can save money in a large company, allowing people and excess equipment to be matched.

◆ Nested, clickable image maps (see Appendix B, "HTML and CGI Quick Reference") of building blueprints available to building services staff can bring up increasingly detailed architectural/structural drawings of buildings and their rooms. Ditto for engineering drawings of industrial equipment and all of the underground facilities (water, heat, electricity, network connections) at a large campus.

◆ Similar, but less detailed, image maps can provide a graphical front end to the company telephone book allowing employees to locate each other easily. Clicking on a building on a campus map can bring up the building's phone book; clicking on a room in a building can bring up the names of its occupants.

◆ A wide range of fill-in forms for searching and updating inventories, filling orders, locating and ordering supplies, maintaining required records, and a hundred other tasks.

As you can see, these can range from administrative trivia (locating a used file cabinet) to essential company services. The last idea listed is especially intriguing. You've seen fill-in forms on the Web that allow you to sign electronic guest books and do searches on the Web using Web search services such as Yahoo (http://www.yahoo.com/) or Lycos (http://www.lycos.com/). Because a fill-in form is merely a means of collecting information and passing it off to a computer program for processing using the *Common Gateway Interface*, or CGI (see Appendix B) you can now provide a Web interface to a plethora of services that must be requested. Bureaucracies already have hundreds of forms employees must fill out to get things or to get things done. Figure 2.5 shows a simple Web fill-in form that could be a replacement for the paper purchase order or requisition form.

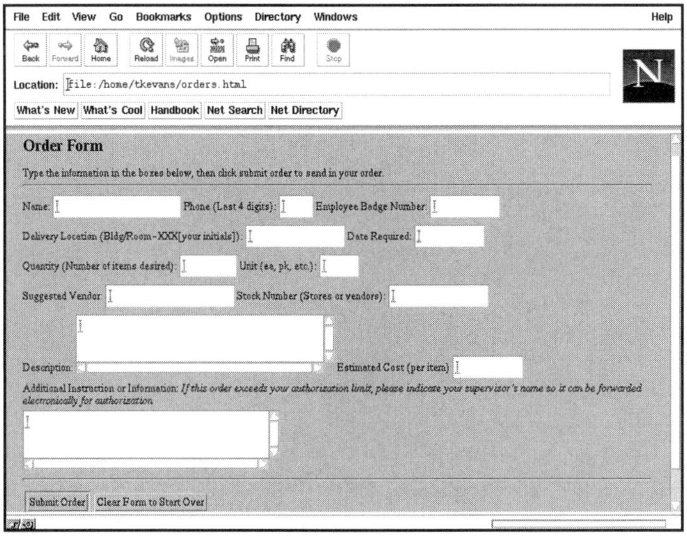

Figure 2.5. *Simple order form.*

This form, generated in a few minutes with just over 40 lines of very simple HTML markup (see Appendix B), when backed up with an equally simple CGI script, can take the information the user enters and e-mail it to data entry personnel in the Purchasing department. With a more elaborate back-end CGI script the very same simple form could be used to enter the order directly into an electronic ordering system, debit the orderer's charge code, update company inventory if the order is for capital equipment, and fire off return e-mail acknowledging the order. In fact, leaving questions of authorization aside, the information in the fill-in form could just as easily be sent via Internet e-mail or fax directly to the supplier, bypassing company purchasing altogether (though, probably, you'd want the program at least to leave a copy for them).

Information Systems Services

Your organization's Information Systems department, if you have one, is already in the business, at least in part, of providing data processing services to customers inside the company. (We use the term Information Systems Services here to mean any information your organization has stored on computers, all the way from the MIS mainframes to your desktop PCs and any services these computer systems provide.) As a result, you'll find crossover between Information Systems Services and the two other broad categories we've drawn in this chapter. Your Personnel department for instance surely uses some data processing services in doing its work whether those services are on the company mainframe or on desktop PCs. In fact, all the potential customers of your Intranet, because they must have computers to access it, are already users of some of these services.

Accordingly, perhaps here is your most fertile source of resources for your Intranet. These services will then form most of the meat of your Intranet. Let's look at some ideas, all of which are covered in detail in later chapters.

◆ If computer use is widespread in your company, you may have a Help Desk staff that answers phone calls from users about hardware, software, and other related matters. People operating Help Desks know there are questions that come up over and over which, not surprisingly, have the same answers. How do I set up my modem so I can dial into the office from my home PC? How do I change my password? How do I print mailing labels with my word processor? These canned answers to common questions can form the heart of an Intranet Help Desk. Using Netscape or Mosaic, your Help Desk staff can use fill-in forms like the ones on Yahoo or Lycos to search for answers (and create new ones). Taken a step further, there's no reason you can't make the Intranet Help Desk available directly to users, allowing them to search for the information they need at their own convenience.

◆ Web-based interfaces to both commercial and homegrown database applications are available. No matter what you may use a database for, it has two major functions: entering or updating information and retrieving information. While your database application may have special screens for users to perform these functions, both of these functions can just as easily be done with Web fill-in forms and back-end CGI scripts that access the database. The advantage? Users see an interface they recognize and with which they're comfortable, because you've implemented it for many purposes in your Intranet.

◆ Existing word processing documents, spreadsheets, and other application datafiles can be shared using Web technology. Proper set up of your Web server and your users' Web browsers can, for example, allow a company executive to click on a hyperlink and open current sales or operational data directly into his spreadsheet program for what-if analysis, then graph the results for inclusion into presentations or word processing documents.

◆ Scientists, engineers, and technicians can share datafiles from their computer applications on your Intranet. Chemists can fire up molecular modeling programs just by clicking on a hyperlink pointing to a datafile and engineers can bring up CAD drawings in the same way.

◆ You can wrap an entire custom computer application program your company uses inside a Web interface with Netscape as its interface and with built-in help for its users.

As you've read this section, you've no doubt thought about existing Information Systems resources in your company that might be made accessible on your Intranet. Just this brief listing of possibilities can lead you to think about legacy information (that is, existing documents and other data) that will be an immediate source of data you'll be able to tap to get your Intranet up and running quickly, as discussed in Chapter 6.

Who Will Do This?

We now move from thoughts about the substantive content of your Intranet to those of organizational responsibility and design. In earlier years, when MIS departments had a monopoly on data and data processing, it would have been easy to assign responsibility for Intranet setup and design: the MIS Department would do it of course. Today, though, the Web is based on distributed computing, and MIS can't control everyone's PC or workstation. This presents a terrific opportunity for the consumers of Information Systems Resources, who presumably know the most about what they need to take an active role in the design and construction of your Intranet. Neither Web server setup (see Appendix A) nor the HyperText Markup Language (see Appendix B) are rocket science. (The author's book, *10 Minute Guide to HTML*, published by sams.net's sister imprint, Que Publishing, ISBN 0-7897-0541-9, starts where Appendix B leaves off.) With freely available Web server and supporting software on the CD-ROM, it's easy for almost anyone with a PC or workstation to create a Web home page and make it available.

Central Control or No Control?

This ease of setup can be both a blessing and, the MIS folks will be quick to remind you, a curse. If anyone can set up a Web server and/or a home page, who will control your Intranet? This question is valid not only from an authoritarian point of view (after all, people are supposed to use their computers to do their jobs) but also from other points of view as well. Here are some issues you may have to deal with:

◆ Will you want your Intranet to have a common organization and look, or is substance all you care about?

◆ Will someone approve each and every piece of information before it goes on your Intranet, or can anyone put up anything they like?

◆ If people are free to put up anything they like, will you be concerned about inappropriate material and/or inappropriate use of your organization's Information Systems and personnel resources?

◆ Will you accept and welcome the inevitable evolution of your Intranet as you and its users figure out new things it might do?

If you've used the World Wide Web to any extent, you've recognized it as the world's largest vanity press; people can, and do, put anything they want on it. This is a sword that cuts both ways. You can find truly amazing (in all senses of the word) things on the Web, many of which may be offensive (again, in all senses of the word). How you feel about this sort of anarchy will inevitably color how you approach assigning responsibility and setting standards for your Intranet. At the same time, the fundamental nature of the Web as a distributed service provides unparalleled opportunities for individual and organizational development, and imposing a rigid, authoritarian structure on your Web might well inhibit the sort of creativity that can bring about breakthroughs in your company's work.

Organizational Models

Based on the philosophical approach you decide to take in assigning responsibility for your Intranet, there are several models you can follow. Here are three:

◆ *Centralized model* with a single Web server administered by a specific organization in your company, and a formal process for developing and installing new services.

◆ *Decentralized model* with anyone free to set up a Web server and place resources of their choice on it.

◆ *Mixed model* with elements of both the centralized and decentralized models.

Centralized Model

In this top-down model all Web services are centralized. Just one computer system in your company runs a Web server. You have a specific individual or group responsible for the setup, design, and administration of the server. All Web pages (documents, forms, and so on) are designed centrally at the request of customers. Thus, if the Personnel department wanted to put employee benefit information on the Web, a formal request would be required, including content and design requests. The Web staff would, in consultation with Personnel, design and refine the employee benefits page and once the process is complete, make the page available on the Web server. Figure 2.6 shows the centralized model of Web administration with all Web-related development funneled through an approval process before any information is placed on the central Web server.

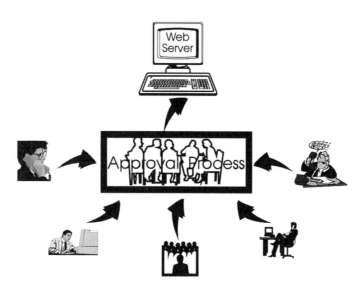

Figure 2.6. *Centralized model of Web administration.*

There are a number of good reasons this approach is sound. First and foremost, by focusing Web server administration, page design, and production in a single person or group, it provides the opportunity for you to develop a consistently designed Intranet. You can develop and use common Web page templates to ensure layout consistency as well as a standard set of substantive and navigational images. Users will see a coherent, well-thought-out Web server with each part consistent with your overall design, layout, and content standards.

Another strong argument in favor of the centralized model is that it simplifies the setup and administration of your Intranet. Only one computer system runs the server. All updates, both Web pages and server software, need only be applied once. Security (see Chapter 9, "Intranet Security") can be focused on the single machine, which can also be physically secured. Backups are easy to do because everything that needs backing up is on the one system.

Unfortunately, there are equally strong reasons this approach is the wrong one to take. From a philosophical point of view, it runs counter to pretty much everything that's happened in data processing over the past two decades. With the rise of the personal computer and workstation, data processing has moved out of the glass-walled MIS data center and onto people's desks. Taking the centralized approach to your Intranet may satisfy the MIS diehards, but it also contradicts everything the Web stands for.

More practically speaking, bureaucratized administration of your Intranet's development can choke it to death before it ever gets off the ground as endless memoranda about "standards" circulate before any real development takes place. Your primary objective in setting up an Intranet is to get information to your customers. Centralized administration can easily get bogged down in organizational and turf matters, cutting off the potential of rapid response to your customers.

> **Tip:** It's useful to note in this connection that because your target audience is inside your company, not outside, the standards you'd apply to the former will probably be very different from those for the latter. The employee looking for help in setting up his PC probably doesn't care whether the help document he finds on your Intranet has the correctly proportioned corporate logo on it. Rather, he's interested in the substance of the document. Your company's outside Web server, aimed at a completely different audience, can—and probably will—be subject to a more rigorous set of standards.

Finally, the centralized model places all your Web eggs in a single basket. If the computer system running your Intranet server goes down, everyone is cut off. This policy requires a decision between potentially expensive downtime and expensive duplicative hardware—another hot, spare computer ready to run in the event the main system goes down. This adds not only the extra cost of the hardware and software for the system but introduces a new aspect of the system's administration, that of making sure all changes to the primary system get mirrored to the backup.

Decentralized Model

At the other end of the spectrum lies the decentralized model. Web server software is widely available both commercially and as freeware or shareware. The software runs on desktop PCs (including both Windows PCs and Macs) and on UNIX systems. This software is relatively easy to set up and run. The HTML language, the markup language used to create Web pages with all their nice formatting and image and hyperlink capabilities, can be picked up by just about anyone in a couple of hours. Using free software or shareware, some of which is included on the accompanying CD-ROM, even a moderately experienced PC user can have a Web server up and running with some HTML documents in an afternoon. Figure 2.7 shows the decentralized model of Web administration with users free to develop their own Web documents and even set up individual Web servers.

As with the centralized model, there are both strong and weak points to this one. The most compelling argument for this model is that the user who sets up her own Web server (and who is also, you should be reminded, one of your Intranet's customers) may be the single best person to do so because she knows precisely the service she wants to provide with it. That is, if an engineer wants to share engineering drawings and technical reports with her colleagues, she and her colleagues are in the best position to decide what is to be shared and how it is best presented. In the centralized model, this customer with information to share has to negotiate the standards process before being able to get the information to her colleagues. Similarly, the Personnel Specialist who has new pension information to make available, or the Office Manager announcing the staff holiday party, is more concerned about getting the information posted than whether it's properly formatted according to some standard or whether the proper colors are used in the corporate logo.

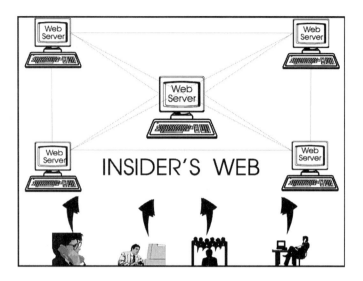

Figure 2.7. *Decentralized model of Web administration.*

In other words, the main advantage of the decentralized model is that it allows those who have information to share to share it quickly and with a minimum of fuss. If you're running a Web server on your PC, for instance, you can put up a new Web page on some subject in your expertise in just a few minutes. This is also the main disadvantage of the model. The fact that it is so easy to set up Web pages lends itself to what may best be termed *anarchy*, with users putting up related or unrelated (who decides which is which?) Web pages all over the company. A casual walk around the World Wide Web shows how this anarchy can and does lead from the sublime to the absurd to the downright obscene.

> **Tip:** It's important also to note that the overall tone of a Web server can lead to increased or decreased support from both its customers and its sponsors. Too much anarchy often turns users off and they just stop using the service. And, of course, there are few things that could be worse for the overall health of your Intranet than to have the president of the company stumbling across a particularly inappropriate or offensive link on some junior researcher's home page.

The nature of your organization will help you evaluate this model. Academic and research institutions may find the intellectual freedom of their researchers outweighs the high noise level of the Web created under this model. Businesses may want a tighter focus on the work at hand, finding this sort of anarchy has too much potential for abuse and/or misdirected time and effort. I have seen numerous examples of otherwise useful, well-focused Web pages with just one clinker of a hyperlink pointing off to some other Web page that's egregiously unrelated to the rest of the page, and inappropriate to any conceivable purpose of the page.

Mixed Model

Somewhere between these two extremes is probably where most organizations will land when setting up Intranets. For example, you may want to establish a broad policy that your Web's primary purpose is to support a specific group of your customers and that anything consistent with that purpose is permitted. In this case, you'd rely on that part of the centralized model that dictates the overall direction and purpose of your Web but use those aspects of the decentralized model that leave most details to your customers. There will inevitably be gray areas or even outright violations of the overall policies, but you can deal with them on a case-by-case basis as *management* issues, just as you do with, say, misuse of company telephones or time-and-leave abuse.

Please don't make firm decisions on a model for administering your Intranet quite yet. You still need to focus on its primary objectives, and doing so will help you focus your decision-making on these administrative issues. In the following sections, you'll look at these questions as well as lay out some of the technical possibilities for implementing the mixed model.

Design and Layout of Your Intranet

Having considered the foregoing administrative matters, let's now turn to more interesting things: the substantive design and content of your Intranet.

What Is the Purpose of Your Intranet?

You probably bought *Building an Intranet* because you had some idea of what you might be able to do with an internal corporate Web server or some idea of what you would like to do with one. So far in this chapter, you've established a framework that should help you bring your ideas into clearer definition. We first brought out the concept of thinking of the potential users of your Intranet as customers, and provided some possibilities based on this concept. Next, we discussed some of the high-level administrative aspects of setting up and running an Intranet. By now you perhaps have a clearer focus on who your potential customers are and some definite ideas on the sorts of information you want to make available.

Statement of Purpose

Putting your ideas together into an Intranet *Statement of Purpose* is your first concrete step toward realizing your ideas. Let's look at a few example Statements of Purpose, based on the possibilities listed under the previous heading *Information and Services Your Customers Need*.

◆ Provide customers with information about their employee benefits.

◆ Give customers access to a searchable database of PC hardware and software technical support information.

♦ Provide customers a Web browser interface to the corporate inventory and ordering database.

♦ Use Web technology to enable customers to share data files from common applications.

As you can see, each of these is both specific and limited. Developing your Statement of Purpose allows you to define the task ahead of you in terms both you and your potential customers can easily grasp. There is, of course, no reason you can't write a larger Statement of Purpose incorporating several of these (or other) purposes, such as "Provide customers with Human Resources, materiels and logistics, and information system services using World Wide Web technology." Such a far-reaching Statement of Purpose is certainly acceptable, provided of course that you're able to clearly define the objectives that fall under it, possibly using lower-level Statements of Purpose for each of the major subdivisions, Human Resources, Materiel and Logistics, and Information Systems. Some people may want to start out with more limited Statements of Purpose like those listed, then expand on them later. The method you choose depends on your own ideas as to what you want your Intranet to accomplish.

Besides giving you a pole star toward which to steer in developing your Intranet, your Statement of Purpose also implies some substantive choices about the work you're cutting out for yourself. For example, it's one thing to take a batch of Microsoft Word documents and put them up on a Web server as a boilerplate library (see Chapter 10, "Your Word Processor and the Web," and Chapter 20, "Intranet Boilerplate Library") for customers to browse and grab. Most computer literate people can put such a library together and generate the HTML code to index it. It's quite another thing, though, to develop the CGI scripts to back up forms-based data entry and retrieval (see Chapter 14, "Web Access to Commercial Database Applications"). The order form example earlier in this chapter is quite simple, but the program that it executes will not be. You'll need competent programmers to write the scripts in whatever programming language you choose on your system.

Implementation Goals

Once you have a Statement of Purpose, particularly if yours is a broad one like the one mentioned, you'll need to develop more concrete *implementation goals*, or specific objectives of the information and services your Intranet will provide to your customers. Following the Employee Benefits Statement of Purpose, you might, then, define a series of goals.

♦ Provide online health benefits information.

♦ Provide online job vacancy announcements, the capability of customers to read both summary and detailed information.

♦ Allow customers to enter change-of-address and/or family status information using fill-in forms.

♦ Allow customers to calculate an estimated pension benefit based on their years of service and projected earnings between now and retirement age using a fill-in form.

Your implementation goals can now be translated into clusters of specific tasks to be performed in order to implement and manage them. For example, if your job vacancy announcements are created using your word processor; they can be quickly saved in plain text form (or converted to HTML by a conversion package) then placed on your Web server. As they expire, old announcements can be removed and replaced by new ones. You'll need to designate someone to be responsible for managing the job announcements and, if necessary, train them in using HTML. Depending on the administrative model you've chosen for managing your Intranet, you may also need to train the individual in the process of actually placing the job announcements on the Web server so they become available.

Purposes and Goals Evolve

As you develop your overall purpose statement and implementation goals, bear in mind that once a Web server starts getting hits (that is, customers start accessing it), you and they will start thinking of new ideas you could implement using Web technology. Accordingly, you shouldn't cast your plans in stone. Rather, you'll want to leave room for evolution. Good ideas often beget other good ideas, so don't lock yourself out with a purpose statement that's too restrictive to allow new goals.

The job vacancy announcement goal example used above is a good illustration of how such a seemingly specific goal might evolve over time. You might start out with simple one-line announcements and find customers wanting more information about the positions. Adding more details to the announcements helps, but sometimes people want to be able to communicate with a real person to ask questions not covered in the announcements, so you add contact information to the announcements. Later, someone asks about using the *mailto* Uniform Resource Locator (see Appendix B) and you realize you can add hyperlinks to the job announcements that allow your customers to send e-mail to the contact person just by clicking on a hyperlink. Still later, customers ask why they can't just go ahead and apply for the job directly using a Web fill-in form. So it goes.

Web Design and Layout

With your Statement of Purpose and implementation goals ready, you can turn to the design and layout of your Intranet. It's useful to break this process down into two related pieces: *logical* and *physical*.

Logical Design of an Intranet

The logical design and layout is the process of arranging the information on your Intranet according to some overall plan. (Later you'll see you can reflect your logical design in your physical design.) Much like you begin the process of writing a book by organizing your material with an outline, with major subjects placed into some sort of logical arrangement, your Intranet design should begin with some organizational layout. The information you're planning on placing on your Intranet often naturally breaks down into logical chunks, so you can reflect these natural divisions in its logical design. In fact, you might do well to start out with a traditional outline of the material. Use the Statement of Purpose developed and generate a brief outline.

Statement of Purpose

Provide Customers with Human Resources, Materiel and Logistics, and Information System Services Using World Wide Web Technology.

Human Resources Information
Employee benefits information
Job announcements
Other HR Information
Materiel and logistics information
Inventory database
Purchase orders
Building and grounds plans
Other M&L information
Information systems services
Computer hardware and software Help Desk
Boilerplate libraries
Spreadsheet data libraries
Other IS Information
Other departments
Engineering
Research
Manufacturing

Looking at this short summary outline (most of the details have been left out for space reasons of course) it's easy to see how you can organize the overall logical structure of your Intranet. Let's collapse this outline to make this clear.

ABC Company Home Page

Statement of Purpose

Provide Customers with Human Resources, Materiel and Logistics, and Information System Services Using World Wide Web Technology.

Major Subdivisions of this Web

Human Resources information
Materiel and Logistics information
Information systems services
Other departments

You've laid out not only the overall design of a Web, but also all but written its home page. Go ahead and look at this as a home page, in Figure 2.8.

Figure 2.8. *Simple home page.*

> **Tip:** Your network capabilities and your customers' hardware capabilities can provide important cues to help you in your Web's logical design. For example, if all your customers have high-speed network connections and graphical Web browsers such as Mosaic or Netscape, you can plan on using graphics heavily in your Intranet. If some of your customers work with dumb terminals and/or some have only modem dial-up connections to your network, you'll want to downplay graphics and make sure your Web pages are accessible to the graphics impaired.

Hierarchies and Hypertext

Within this design, as you no doubt have guessed, each of the ABC Company's major subdivisions also has a home page with the information and services to be offered. This is a simple hierarchical design, and for purposes of the sort of high-level layout you're considering here, it's a good way of beginning your own Intranet design. Within your Intranet, though, you'll want to take advantage of the ability to create *hyperlinks* to other pages so your customers can get around easily and intuitively. Rigid adherence to some purely hierarchical design can limit you in Intranet design. Books are usually designed to be read sequentially, page by page, from front to back, and hierarchical design is apparent in such an arrangement. People who pick up a book expect this arrangement.

On the other hand, the World Wide Web, as you know, has introduced the concept of *hypertext*, a most assuredly nonhierarchical element. Through the use of hyperlinks, users can jump from place to place on the Web with little attention to page hierarchies or other structure. As a result, Web pages (and Web servers themselves) lend themselves to more human design. Users follow hyperlinks based on their own interests, predilections, and the needs of a given moment.

As you design your Intranet, the nice, neat hierarchical design you might lay out at the top level can handcuff you once you get down into the actual meat of your Web. You'll want to therefore be receptive to the use of non-linear design as your Intranet develops. It's probably a good idea, for example, to include hyperlinks on pretty much every page (or every major page, at least) that allow the customer to jump back to the top-level page from anywhere without having to backtrack. Cross-references among documents are also great things to use as hyperlinks. If a document mentions another document, the user may want to see the referred-to document, and a hyperlinked cross reference allows this.

At the same time, your overall design decisions can set limits on where hyperlinks might take your customers. Many people like hypertext because it seems somehow more like how they actually think, but others are more literal in their thinking and prefer a well-organized, hierarchical structure to things. In either case, total reliance on hypertext features without any overall organization can lead to confusion and frustration and to the loss of your Intranet's customers. This is one reason, as we will consider in Chapter 5, "Skill Sets," it's critical for you to involve your customers early in the process of designing your Intranet, as well as keeping them involved in the form of feedback. It's difficult, if not impossible, for you to anticipate what your customers will and will not like about their Intranet, so it's critical you get them involved in issues like design and layout.

Physical Design of a Web

There are a number of ways to lay out the physical aspects of your Intranet. Your decisions on the administrative and logical aspects discussed in this chapter can give you important clues here as well. As suggested earlier, when discussing the centralized model of Web administration, a single computer running Web server software lends itself well to the administrative model selected. If you're using this model, you need not be concerned about the physical layout of a Web in which multiple servers in multiple locations operate; your server is inside a secure room, accessible only by its administrators. All your Web pages, and all the administration and configuration of your server takes place in one location. This vastly simplifies server administration, maintenance, system backups, and, of course, server security.

Paradoxically, the decentralized model of Web administration, where anyone is free to set up and maintain their own Web server as part of an Intranet, is also simpler for you to administer. That is, you don't. Just by making the administrative decision that any user can set up a Web server and place anything on it, you've washed your hands of all these issues of physical layout, design, and server administration. Users are free to set up servers, placing documents on them according to whatever logical design they find applicable, and are responsible for doing so, as well as for maintaining their servers and documents. Any central administration can be limited to maintaining an overall home page for your Intranet with hyperlinks pointing to all the other servers. This administrative (and physical) layout can further suggest hardware and software requirements: if all your central Web server does is serve a home page with links to other servers, you don't need a powerful computer to run it.

As you can probably surmise, the mixed administrative model provides the most flexibility in both the logical and physical layout of your Intranet, while retaining your ability to manage its structure. For example, you might design an Intranet with a main server and several departmental servers. The example Intranet used in this chapter lends itself to this setup. Each of the major subdivisions of your Intranet, corresponding to the major administrative departments of the ABC Company, can be hosted on a separate computer system running Web server software. Thus, the Personnel department would run and manage a Web server devoted to Human Resources, while Materiel and Logistics would run another. Having delegated the administration of those logical pieces of your Web to the departments, you can also, if you choose, delegate the physical ones. As with the decentralized model, this choice can impact your needs for hardware.

Personnel may not really want the responsibility of physically maintaining a computer system, however. The decentralized model can still allow the logical layout of your Web to allow Personnel to maintain its own substantive Intranet content. The HTML language is not difficult to learn, and ABC's departments could share a single computer system running a Web server physically maintained by a dedicated individual or staff but still maintain their own documents on that server. HTML documents can be created and/or edited using almost any editing tool on desktop PCs, then uploaded to your main Web server. You can even use file-sharing mechanisms to make Web server administration completely transparent. Through appropriately secured use of Appleshare, Novell Netware, or UNIX-based Network File Systems (NFS), your Web server's filesystems can be shared so users see them as local volumes or filesystems with HTML documents directly accessible for editing. As far as the user is concerned, he's just creating or editing documents on his own PC, yet the documents are available to everyone else on your Intranet.

As with most three-choice models, your actual implementation of an Intranet is unlikely to be as clear cut as described here. It should seem clear to you that the mixed model described is what we would recommend, but there are is virtually infinite number of variations possible. The nice, neat, logical and/or physical division among ABC's departments probably won't fit your needs. It's more likely Personnel will need one sort of setup, while Engineering might need a completely different one because the two groups have different skill sets and interests. You may find that one department wants their piece of your Intranet rigidly administered with all sorts of preset standards and procedures, while another department wants a completely decentralized model. Fortunately, you can accommodate both. Intranet server design and setup are anything if not flexible and what you start out with may well change as you gain experience.

Selling Your Intranet

In this final section, you'll turn your attention to how you can get your customers to buy into your Intranet. Web technology, or, more properly, the things Web technology makes possible, is very seductive. The ongoing explosion of the Internet has been driven in very large part by the Web. People really like using Mosaic or Netscape to find interesting things on the Web. As many managers are recognizing, there's a seductive, recreational aspect to the World Wide Web, as the widely used terms *Playing Web* and *Surfing the Web* indicate. The Web, in large respect, sells itself. This book is about using this seductive technology on an everyday basis in your company's work.

Defining Your Audience

This might seem a no-brainer. After all, your Intranet is for people within your company. While this is generally true, a closer look reveals the fact that you need to fine tune your definition. First, unless everyone in your company has a computer (or access to one) your audience is immediately defined as the group of users who will have some sort of access to your Intranet. Even this, however, isn't a true audience definition, rather it's a definition of your potential audience. You still need to break this audience down based on common characteristics. The kind of work a group of individuals do can help you define their needs as customers of your Intranet. Members of a clerical pool, for example, constitute an audience for the sort of boilerplate library of documents discussed in Chapter 20. Your scientists and engineers comprise a completely different group who'll have more interest in using your Web in their own work of the sort described in Chapter 15, "Scientific, Mathematical, and Technical Applications on Your Intranet." Both these groups, however, fall into the larger audience of company employees with an interest in the sorts of Human Resources and/or Materiel and Logistics information and services described in this chapter.

Hardware Considerations

Your larger potential audience also breaks down in another way based on the capabilities of the computer hardware they'll use to access your Web. Do they all have graphical Web browser capabilities and high-speed network connections? This question raises further questions that go to both the substantive content of your Intranet and to its physical and logical nature (that is, hardware capabilities and the concomitant limits they may place on the logical design of it). Let's look at how hardware can affect your audience definition and also provide important Intranet design input.

Computer use is widespread, but not nearly universal, in organizations. Millions of people have computers on their desks at work or at home, but millions more don't. This obvious fact acts to define your Intranet's audience. Further, though, even among the group of people who do have computer access, there can be a wide variation in both access and hardware capabilities. While some users have PCs or UNIX workstations with full graphical capabilities, others may be using dumb terminals with little or no graphics. In either case, a number of users may be sharing these seats.

These are important audience characteristics which speak not only to the relative ease by which your customers can access your Intranet but also to what they can see when they do access it. The user with a dumb terminal can't see graphics and can't use clickable image maps (see Appendix B), so your Web design decisions must take this into account. Do you do so by not using graphics at all, dragging that part of your audience with graphical Web capabilities down to the lowest common denominator, or do you attempt to design a Web that everyone can use even with their hardware limits? Similarly, if large numbers of your customers share PCs or terminals—on a factory floor, for example—the timeliness and immediacy of your Intranet's information is affected, because not everyone will have easy, immediate access.

As with each of the other major subjects covered in this chapter—Intranet administration and design/layout—the characteristics of your intended audience can provide valuable help in the overall development of your Intranet.

Web Users, Web Mockups, and Focus Groups

You can help focus your audience definition as well as generate valuable information that can contribute to the design and content of your Intranet by involving potential customers in its development process using *focus groups*. Getting your customers involved early—and keeping them involved—generates an investment on their part in your Intranet. This investment will pay dividends by helping you create the right Intranet, the one your customers want.

Mockups and Demos

Before you get your focus group(s) together, be sure you have something to show them. Getting a group of people together to shoot the bull about getting an Intranet going without first having prepared some sort of presentation, is a poor way of starting out. You may have a few people who have Web experience, and some of them may already have ideas you can use, but as much as two-thirds of your Focus group may never have seen the World Wide Web. If you don't have something to show them, they'll have a great deal of trouble understanding what it is you want from them. To a person with no experience of the Web, even the crude home page shown in Figure 2.6 is a dramatic demonstration, particularly if there are hyperlinks to similar home pages for the major divisions shown on the page and an actual document or two linked into them. Even a simple demonstration can let you use that Web seductiveness we spoke of earlier to spark interest in your Intranet, getting your customers to invest early.

Encourage your demonstration participants to discuss possibilities based on what you've shown them. As we've said repeatedly, even Web novices know the information they want from their organization. Showing them real information as well as the potential capabilities of an Intranet, will surely stimulate ideas on their part. Your focus group(s), also including your organization's information providers, should provide a lively and useful means by which you'll further define your audience and its interests. This, in turn, will help you pin down the actual kinds of information your customers will want, thereby generating audience investment and support in your Intranet.

Users and Focus Groups

You probably already have a good deal of experience with the World Wide Web, and have based your own ideas about your Web on things you've seen. If you have good ideas from your own Web experiences, it's a good bet there are others in your company who have them too, or would have if you asked them to think about it. Experienced Web users who are also your potential customers are in the unique position of both knowing a lot about the capabilities and possibilities of Web technology and of knowing what they, as potential customers of your Web, want to see. Get these customers together, informally or in formal focus groups to talk about your ideas and theirs.

Don't limit your focus groups to those with Web experience, though. The employees of a company or the members of an organization have definite ideas about the information they want. Even if they've never seen a Web browser, they can give you information that's important to your Intranet design. Similarly, don't forget to include people we might call Intranet information *resellers*. We've used the example of employee benefits and other personnel-related information in this chapter as potential Intranet content. The people in your Human Resources department who provide this information now, and who will be providing it on your Intranet, should also be part of your focus groups. They know the information they provide, and probably have a good idea of how often their customers ask for it.

Summary

This chapter, part hardware, part philosophy, dealt with the overall process of designing an Intranet. We covered a number of major, interrelated, topics, including

- What an Intranet is, and how it is different from what you've seen on the World Wide Web.
- Identification of the customers in your company for whom your Intranet is to be designed.
- Determination of the kind of information you will make available on your Intranet.
- Decisions on who in your company or organization (or what organizational component) is best as the keeper of your Intranet.
- Consideration of high-level issues about the design and organization of your Intranet.
- Targeting of your Intranet's customers and selling them on the idea of an Intranet.

For more detailed information on these topics, you may want to check out *The World Wide Web Unleashed*, by John December and Neil Randall, also published by sams.net (ISBN 0-672-30737-5). For information on this and other sams.net books, see the World Wide Web URL http://www.mcp.com, or check your bookstore.

In the next chapter, we'll discuss Intranet infrastructure, the hardware and software tools you'll need to get started building your Intranet.

Tools for Implementing an Intranet Infrastructure

The last chapter was devoted to high-level issues involving the overall design and objectives of your Intranet. In this chapter, the first of three *tools* chapters (the others are on content development and skill sets, respectively), you'll turn from abstract consideration of purpose statements and audience definition to some hardware and software specifics. Here you'll survey the software and hardware tools you need to get set up. Many of the software tools discussed in this chapter are available on the CD-ROM accompanying this book, although some are commercial packages. Mentions of specific commercial software packages are examples only and don't imply any endorsement of them by the author or by Sams.net.

Chapter Objectives

As with the rest of the chapters in this book, let's begin by laying out some chapter objectives. This will help you get oriented to the material to be presented; you may want to refer back to this list as you work your way through the chapter.

In this chapter, we address

◆ TCP/IP (Transmission Control Protocol/Internet Protocol) networking and its essential role in any Web

◆ Computer hardware suitable for running a Web server, ranging from desktop PCs to UNIX systems

◆ World Wide Web server software for a variety of computer systems ranging from desktop PCs to UNIX systems

◆ Software tools for creating documents in the HyperText Markup Language; the language of the Web

◆ World Wide Web browser software for a variety of computer systems ranging from desktop PCs to UNIX systems

◆ Common software packages, called helper applications, that work in conjunction with Web browser software

◆ How to integrate with your Intranet with other office and/or technical applications you may use

◆ Other network services accessible using Web technology and how they might fit into your Intranet

This chapter is an overview. In subsequent chapters and appendixes you will find more detailed information about the tools discussed here. Even so, this book does not get into the internals of TCP/IP networking. While we highlight the setup of World Wide Web server software, particularly as it relates to the main purpose of this book, many of the technical details of Web server software are beyond our scope. Similarly, we'll refer to other Internet standard software you can integrate into your Web, but leave details to other references. Appendix B introduces the HTML markup language but only at a basic level. While we provide a good deal of specific setup information about several Web browser software packages, this book is not a complete reference on those packages. You'll find a variety of book-length treatments of these subjects in your favorite bookstore. For information about other sams.net books relating to the World Wide Web and the Internet, access Macmillan Computer Publishing's Information SuperLibrary at World Wide Web URL `http://www.mcp.com/`.

TCP/IP Networking Required

If you're already using the World Wide Web, you're already using TCP/IP, the fundamental Internet networking protocols. Only the TCP/IP networking protocols, the foundation of the worldwide Internet, support the Web over local area and wide area networks, including both the Internet and your LAN. In order for you to set up an Intranet, you must be running TCP/IP networking on your network. Without TCP/IP there would be no Internet and no World Wide

Web; without it on your LAN, you'll have no Intranet. Designed from the very beginning to operate over different communication media, TCP/IP works on Ethernet and token ring LANs; it even operates over ordinary telephone lines using modems, as you may know if you have a home Internet-access package such as CompuServe's *Internet in a Box* or Apple's *Internet Connection Kit.*

A Brief History of TCP/IP and the Internet

In the 1970s, the United States Department of Defense (DoD) contracted with researchers at the University of California at Berkeley and a company named BBN to develop networking for DoD computers worldwide. The primary objectives of the research project were to develop computer networking that

◆ Worked on a variety of computer hardware

◆ Operated over different communications media to link both individual computers and computer networks

◆ Was robust enough to automatically reconfigure itself in the event of network failures

More than after-the-fact Cold War speculation, the last of the points relates to the then-real possibility of large parts of the DoD network disappearing in a nuclear war and the need for the network to withstand it. In fact, today's Internet does exactly that: if a large portion of the network were to disappear because of some massive hardware failure, the rest of the network would simply find a way around the service interruption and keep on working.

Even though the DoD funded most of the development of what came to be known as TCP/IP networking, the free thinkers at Berkeley managed to get permission to redistribute the network software they developed and the specifics of its protocols written into the contract with DoD. At about the same time, Berkeley was developing its own revised version of the UNIX operating system software, which it had licensed from AT&T (where UNIX was invented) as a research project. In short, TCP/IP networking was dropped right into BSD (Berkeley Software Distribution) UNIX, which was then made available to other academic institutions, also for research purposes, for the mere cost of a computer tape.

The wide distribution of these BSD tapes to other colleges, universities, and research institutions was the beginning of the Internet. TCP/IP networking not only allows individual computers to be linked into a network, but it also allows networks of computers to be linked to other networks with the illusion that all the computers on all the linked networks are on the very same *Internet.* Universities began building local networks, linking them together, then moved toward connecting their local networks with remote networks at other locations or other institutions, laying the foundation for today's Internet explosion. The DoD built its own private Internet, called MILNET, using TCP/IP, and many other U.S. government agencies set up networks as well, some of which eventually became part of the Internet.

TCP/IP Implementations

Because the implementation nuts and bolts of TCP/IP networking (that is, the detailed descriptions of the network protocols themselves) were publicly defined in documents known as Internet *Requests for Comments*, software companies and individuals were free to develop and sell or give away their own TCP/IP software. For example, the first implementation of TCP/IP for the IBM PC was a university master's thesis project and the resulting software was given away; the authors went on to found ftp Software, Inc., makers of one of today's leading TCP/IP software packages, *OnNet* (formerly called PC/TCP), for IBM PCs and compatibles. Dozens of other vendors sell TCP/IP software for PCs, and Microsoft's Windows 95 has it as a standard feature. Most modern UNIX systems have TCP/IP networking built in as a standard feature. Apple and other vendors sell TCP/IP networking software for the Macintosh PC. Even mainframe computers like IBM and DEC machines can and do run TCP/IP software in addition to, or in lieu of, the vendors' proprietary networking products like DECNet or SNA.

Several vendors, including IBM, have announced plans to develop inexpensive computing devices that will have TCP/IP networking built in. Not full-blown PCs, but also not dumb terminals, these *Internet appliances* would include not only TCP/IP, but also graphical capabilities and World Wide Web browser software. These appliances could prove to be a valuable part of your Intranet, because they'd give users access to any Web services you might make available and at substantially lower cost than full-capability PCs or workstations.

Hardware for Your Web Server

You're just about unlimited in selecting a kind of computer system hardware on which to run a Web server. Almost any modern computer system equipped for networking, including TCP/IP network software, can host a Web server. The most widely used systems for Web servers are UNIX machines, such as Sun, IBM, Digital, and Hewlett-Packard workstations or servers. According to a University of Arizona survey (see Figure 3.1, or for details, see the survey's Web page at `http://www.mirai.com/survey/`), more than half of all Web servers are UNIX systems, with the largest share being Sun Microsystems machines. This is no surprise because multitasking, UNIX systems with mature TCP/IP software built in, are particularly well-suited to being Web servers. Surprisingly, perhaps, the second leading platform for Web servers in this survey, with a share of about 17 percent of the market, is the Macintosh. IBM-compatibles came in third in this survey with 15 percent.

The hardware you select for your Intranet server(s) is dependent on a number of factors including your anticipated traffic levels, ease of setup, your in-house technical expertise, and other requirements. Macintosh and Windows server software is quick and easy to set up with a good deal of point-and-click configuration. You can have a Web server running on a Mac or PC in just a few minutes, just as you can with many other PC and Mac software packages. This can be a strong attraction to organizations with lower levels of technical experience or who simply want to stay with PC platforms. Also, if you choose to use the decentralized or mixed models of Web administation described in Chapter 2, individual users can easily take advantage of this software on their own desktop PCs.

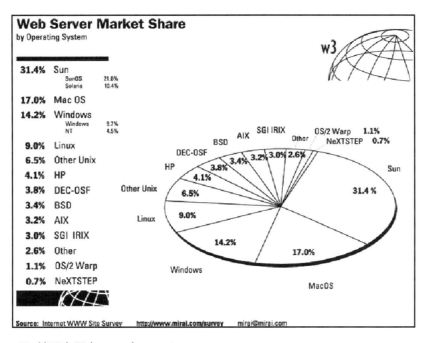

Figure 3.1. World Wide Web servers, by operating system.

If you don't expect your Web server to have high traffic, you may find that dedicating a Mac or PC to it will meet your needs. Except for personal Web servers, you should not, however, plan on running a Web server on a PC that is also somebody's everyday desktop machine. If you expect a high level of traffic, or plan to use common gateway interface scripts heavily, you'll do better to set up camp on a UNIX system.

> **Tip:** As you consider Web server hardware platforms, don't neglect PC-based UNIX systems such as Sun's Solaris for x86, SCO UNIX, Novell's UnixWare, or even Linux, the freeware UNIX clone for Intel-based PCs. UNIX is natively multitasking and, with TCP/IP networking built in, running a PC UNIX without all the overhead of a graphical user interface (for example, Microsoft Windows), you can put an relatively underpowered 386 PC to work as a useful Web server, although you'll want a system with at least 8MB RAM.

Software for Your Web Server

Just two Web server software packages dominate the UNIX share of the market: the *NCSA httpd* (hypertext transfer protocol daemon) and *CERN httpd* servers. The former, from the National Center for Supercomputing Applications (which also developed the NCSA Mosaic Web browser) has, in fact, the largest share of any Web server, with about 39 percent of the market. The CERN package, now maintained by the W³ Consortium, holds about 17 percent. Both of these packages are freely available at no cost and are on the CD-ROM accompanying this book in both source code and binary format for several UNIX systems. The leading commercial Web server for UNIX systems is *Netsite* from Netscape Communications, maker of the Netscape Navigator Web browser. (You should expect these figures to change, especially as Netscape is aggressively marketing its several server packages available for both UNIX and Windows NT/Windows 95 with no-cost 60-day test drive promotions, available at `http://www.netscape.com/comprod/server_central/test_drive.html`.)

If you are concerned about security in your Web server (see Chapter 9, "Intranet Security"), you will probably want to consider the *Netscape Commerce server*, which supports secure, encrypted communications. *MacHTTP*, formerly a shareware package but now commercially marketed by StarNine Technologies under the name *WebStar*, is the leading server package for the Macintosh. MacHTTP/WebStar is available for 30-day demos at URL `http://www.starnine.com/machhttp/machhttpsoft.html`.

Windows httpd leads the Microsoft Windows market. This package is licensed free of charge for personal and non-commercial use and may be used on a trial basis for 30 days in a business or commercial application. Windows httpd is on the *Building an Intranet* CD-ROM; for more information, see the URL `http://www.city.net/win-httpd/`. Author Bob Denny has upgraded his Windows httpd package into an on-the-move commercial package for Windows NT and Windows 95 under the name Website. Evaluation copies of Website are available from O'Reilly & Associates (`http://website.ora.com/`) and are widely available in major bookstores. For more information, see Figure 3.2.

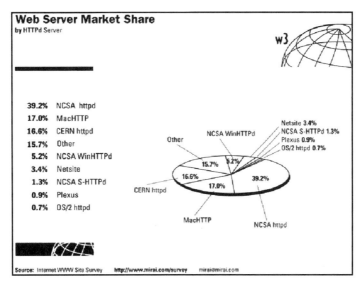

Figure 3.2. *Web server market share by package.*

HTML Editors and Tools

You can create Web pages with the HyperText Markup Language using any text editor you want, including generic UNIX *vi* or *emacs*, an X Window graphical editor such as Sun's *textedit*, Microsoft Windows *NotePad*, MS-DOS *edit*, Macintosh *TeachText*, or your favorite word processor in plain text mode. While HTML documents are plain ASCII text with simple markup codes, you may want to use a specialized HTML editor or conversion tool. There are a wide range of these tools, and they can be broken down into several categories:

◆ Word processor *add-ons* (style sheets, templates, and macros) that allow you to use your own word processor to more easily create documents with HTML markup

◆ Standalone HTML editors, some of which provide *WYSIWYG* (What You See Is What You Get) capabilities, rendering your HTML markup as you go

◆ Tools to convert one sort of legacy document or another into HTML

Chapter 6, "Quick and Dirty Intranet," discusses conversion tools. Meanwhile, you'll find a long listing of all sorts of HTML-related tools at the URL `http://www.w3.org/WWW/Tools`. Figures 3.3 and 3.4 show a couple of examples: the HoTMetaLPro editor from SoftQuad and Microsoft's Internet Assistant for Word, respectively.

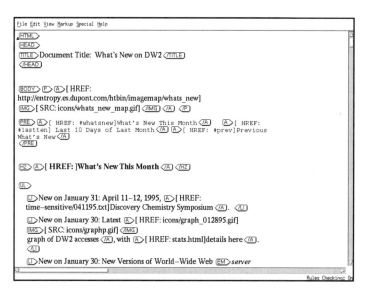

Figure 3.3. *SoftQuad HoTMeTaLPro WYSIWYG editor.*

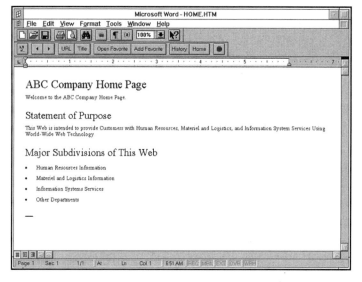

Figure 3.4. *Microsoft Internet Assistant for Word.*

World Wide Web Browsers

NCSA Mosaic and Netscape Navigator are the two most widely used Web browser packages. Both are available for Windows, Macintoshes, and for a wide variety of UNIX systems. Figures 3.5 and 3.6 show Netscape and Mosaic, respectively. NCSA Mosaic is free software. Versions of Mosaic for Windows, the Macintosh, and several UNIX systems are on the *Building an Intranet*

CD-ROM. You can get later releases, if available, over the Internet at URL `ftp://ftp.ncsa.uiuc.edu /Mosaic/` or through anonymous ftp at `ftp.ncsa.uiuc.edu` in the `/Mosaic` directory. Netscape is a commercial package, but you can download a copy from the Netscape home page, `http:// home.netscape.com/`, or via anonymous ftp at `ftp.netscape.com`. Netscape is free for people in educational and nonprofit institutions and for personal use. Commercial users must pay for the package if they use it beyond an evaluation period. For details, see the licensing information that comes with the Netscape software. Due to these licensing restrictions, Netscape is not included on the *Building an Intranet* CD-ROM.

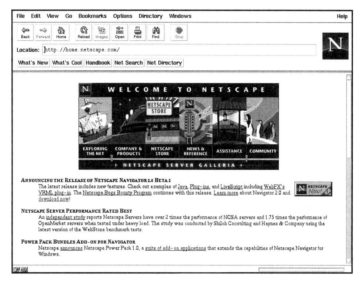

Figure 3.5. *Netscape Navigator 2.0.*

Both Netscape and NCSA Mosaic are highly capable Web browsers, and many users hold near-religious views on which is "best." Netscape tends to be flashier, and its Release 2 version has a number of unique features, including support for the emerging Java technology. Netscape also implements a number of proprietary *extensions* to the HTML language that improve document formatting, but these extensions aren't compatible with other Web browsers. (If you use these extensions in creating Web pages for your Intranet be sure to view the pages with other browsers to ensure they're readable unless your organization standardizes on Netscape for all users.)

Mosaic has been licensed for commercial resale by Spyglass, Inc. This company sells the rights to its enhanced Mosaic (now called *Spyglass Mosaic*, but previously marketed as *Enhanced Mosaic*) to other companies for resale or corporate use. While you cannot buy individual copies of Spyglass Mosaic, several commercial Web browsers are in fact rebranded versions. In addition, a number of large corporations and other organizations have contracted with Spyglass for mass redistribution of Spyglass Mosaic within their company. As a result, if you're interested in standardizing on a commercial-quality Web browser, this is an alternative to Netscape. You can get more information about Spyglass Mosaic, and download an evaluation copy, at URL `http://www.spyglass.com/` (a good example of a poorly laid out Web server, incidentally, as you'll see when you connect).

Spyglass' contractual arrangements with NCSA are unique in that, while Spyglass is a commercial company with a commercial product, enhancements to Mosaic are to be made available back to NCSA for incorporation in the no-cost version of Mosaic.

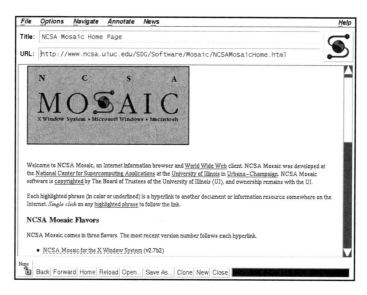

Figure 3.6. NCSA Mosaic version 2.7 beta.

A number of lesser-known Web browsers are also available. You've already seen *Lynx* (see Figure 3.7), the nongraphical browser from the University of Kansas. This package is freely available and runs on UNIX systems. A special version of Lynx, called *doslynx*, is available for IBM PC compatibles; it runs under MS-DOS, not Microsoft Windows, and includes TCP/IP networking built in. This version can be an important addition to your Intranet, because it can give users with very old PCs the ability to access it. For more information on Lynx, see the URL `http://www.ukans.edu`. The *Arena* graphical Web browser (see Figure 3.8) is being developed by the W[3] Consortium as a reference platform for the still-developing HTML version 3 standards. Still in pre-release, Arena runs on UNIX systems and is also freely available; it's included on the *Building an Intranet* CD-ROM. For more information or a later version, see the URL `http://www.w3.org./`

> **Tip:** The W[3] Consortium is an industry cooperative that exists to develop common standards for the evolution of the World Wide Web. Operated jointly by the Massachusetts Institute of Technology's Laboratory for Computer Science and the French National Institute for Research in Computer Science and Control (INRIA), the Consortium is funded by its members, which include a large number of high-tech companies. The Consortium has taken over the work formerly done at CERN, the European Particle Physics Lab, which includes among other things the CERN *httpd* World Wide Web server software (see Appendix A), the CERN *line-mode browser*, a nongraphical Web browser similar to Lynx, and the Arena graphical browser.

Figure 3.7. The Lynx nongraphical browser supports the graphics impaired.

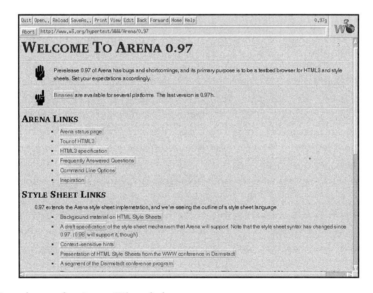

Figure 3.8. The Arena browser functions as W³ test bed.

Selection of a Web Browser

Some of the decisions you make with respect to the design of your Intranet may have implications in Web browser selection, and vice versa. Netscape, for example, supports a significant set of semi-proprietary extensions to HTML standards, including special capabilities for image placement and font selection, along with version 2's Java and Frames support. These extensions may not be supported in other browsers, so you'll need to consider whether to use them in your Web server's HTML documents. This, in turn, affects your choice of a browser. Specifically, if you want to take advantage of Netscape's HTML extensions on your Web, you'll probably want to standardize on Netscape as a browser. To turn this statement on its head, if you like Netscape and decide to standardize on it, this gives you additional capabilities you can implement on your Web. If, at the other extreme, your Web will have large numbers of customers who don't have graphical capabilities, you may want to standardize on the Lynx browser. This choice, too, has implications for your Web design, because you must deal with the inability of many users to view images while still providing more-than-plain-text services to those who do have graphical browsers. The emerging Internet appliances with built-in Web browser software can also be of relevance here.

Whether you choose to standardize on a particular browser also is a function of how you choose to administer and lay out your Intranet. The decentralized and mixed models described in the last chapter inevitably result in a wide range of Web services, some of which may use Netscape HTML extensions, for instance, while others use no special features at all. As a result, you may want to leave the choice of a Web browser to individuals.

Web Browser Helper Applications

Web browser software usually can display graphical images found on the World Wide Web as previous figures show. Other kinds of data, however, require the use of helper applications, also known as *external viewers*. As explained in detail in Chapter 7, "MIME and Helper Applications," Web technology—that is, both Web servers and browsers—uses a common mechanism called MIME (Multi-part Internet Mail Extensions) to match up types of data with helper applications. As a result, for example, although your Web browser may not itself be able to play an audio file you find on the Web, it can pass off that audio file to a sound-playing application on your computer just by clicking on its hyperlink in your Web browser. Figure 3.9 shows use of a video helper application (*xanim*, which is on the *Building an Intranet* CD-ROM) with Netscape on a UNIX system. As you can see from the screenshot, Netscape is still running in the background as xanim is called up. The video data came from clicking a hyperlink on the weather page while in Netscape; the incoming data stream, recognized as video data, was passed off to xanim for display. Once the user is finished viewing the video (with xanim, there are VCR-like controls to play, rewind, fast-forward, and so on), control passes back to Netscape.

Flexibilty of Helper Application Mechanism—a Key to Your Intranet

Based on MIME, the helper application mechanism using MIME is almost infinitely flexible. You're not limited to viewing videos. Imaginative use of this mechanism is one of the central themes of this book. We'll show you how you can use almost any computer program as a helper application, including the standard office applications you use every day, to view and use your own organization's information. In addition, we'll provide examples of more specialized programs you can use as helper applications. Where these examples involve freely available packages as helper applications, we provide copies of the applications on the *Building an Intranet* CD-ROM.

Figure 3.9. *xanim video helper application.*

Common Web Browser Helper Applications

You'll find extensive lists of common Web helper applications downloadable with your Web browser at these URLs:

◆ `http://www.ncsa.uiuc.edu/SDG/Software/XMosaic/faq-software.html` (for UNIX systems)

◆ `http://www.ncsa.uiuc.edu/SDG/Software/WinMosaic/viewers.htm` (for Windows)

◆ `http://www.ncsa.uiuc.edu/SDG/Software/MacMosaic/helpers.html` (for the Macintosh)

We will return to the subject of helper applications and the detailed instructions on how you can set them up in your Intranet in Chapter 7.

Other Office Applications

Integration of everyday office applications into your Intranet is one of the most exciting topics you learn about in this book. We show you how (and how easy it is) to allow your customers to point and click using their Web browser to access live corporate information for use in their daily work. Moreover, they'll be able to do much more with that information than just look at it. Statistical data can be provided in the format your company's favorite spreadsheet package uses, for example.

Managers can use their Web browsers to access this data and bring it directly into their local spreadsheet application for what-if analysis, graphing, or other manipulation of the data. Figure 3.10 shows Microsoft Excel used as a Web helper application in NCSA Mosaic on a PC running Windows.

Figure 3.10. *Microsoft Excel as a helper application.*

All the user had to do to bring up the data in her local copy of Excel was to click on a Web page hyperlink. Mosaic received the data, identified it as Excel spreadsheet data, and handed it off to Excel for display. It's important to note a couple of things about this.

◆ The user is not just passively looking at this data. All the features of the spreadsheet package are available to use on the data; it can be manipulated, changed, recalculated, saved, printed, graphed, whatever.

◆ The data on the Web server, which the user downloaded into Excel, is not changed. The user's copy is a temporary one.

Naturally, the particular applications you use vary and you can't anticipate all of them. Nonetheless, the examples provided should show you how to set up your own applications.

Other Services Accessible via Web Technology

Besides the rich set of possibilities for your Intranet using helper applications, there's a wide variety of TCP/IP-based network services you can integrate into your Intranet. While these services are commonly seen as over-the-Internet services, there's no reason you can't implement and use them locally as part of your Intranet even if your organization is not actually connected to the Internet.

In fact, we consider the ability to use these services a major dividend paid by your investment in the TCP/IP networking that underlies your Intranet. Without TCP/IP networking capabilities, you'd have no capability of using World Wide Web services, but having installed it, you now also have access to a much wider range of services that will extend and enrich your Intranet.

Web browsers know about many Internet services, including, but not limited to

◆ The *file transfer protocol* (FTP) service used for transferring files between computers

◆ The *gopher* service: a search-and-retrieval service based on hierarchical menus

◆ *USENET news*: the mother of all bulletin board systems

◆ Several data indexing facilities, including *WAIS* (Wide Area Information Servers)

◆ Access to *electronic mail* (e-mail) using a Web browser

◆ Remote login and terminal emulation services to enable users to access other computer systems and use them from their own desk

Chapter 8, "Adding Services to Your Intranet Adds Value," discusses these additional, Internet-based services, as well as subsequent chapters, where you focus on using them to provide added value to your customers in an Intranet. Particular software packages that are freely available are included on the CD-ROM.

Summary

This chapter has been a survey of the basic hardware and software infrastructure you'll need to implement an Intranet in your organization. You've learned about

◆ TCP/IP networking and its essential role in any Web

◆ Computer hardware suitable for running a Web server

◆ World Wide Web server software for a variety of computer systems

◆ Software tools for creating documents using the HyperText Markup Language

◆ World Wide Web browser software for a variety of computer systems

◆ Common software packages, called helper applications

◆ How other applications you use can be integrated as helper applications

◆ How other network services that are accessible using Web technology might fit into your Web

Chapter 4, "Content Development Tools," continues the discussion of the tools you need to get your Intranet started, focusing on the tools you can use for the development of the actual content of your Web. This includes conversion of existing (legacy) documents, image manipulation, and programming tools.

Content Development Tools

This is the second of three chapters discussing the tools you'll use to set up your Intranet. Chapter 3, "Tools for Implementing an Intranet Infrastructure," focused on infrastructure—TCP/IP networking, Web server and browsers, HTML editing tools, helper applications, and other Internet services. This chapter discusses some of the software tools you'll use to create and manipulate data for your Web server with particular focus on how you can convert your existing data. Chapter 5, "Skill Sets," turns to the skill sets you'll need.

Chapter Objectives

As with the rest of the chapters in this book, let's begin by laying out some chapter objectives. This will help you get oriented to the material to be presented; you may want to refer back to this list as you work your way through the chapter.

This chapter addresses

- ◆ Tools you can use to convert existing electronic data, called legacy documents, into the HyperText Markup Language (HTML) format quickly and easily
- ◆ Tools for creating, converting, and manipulating image data for use on your Intranet
- ◆ Tools you can use to develop Common Gateway Interface (CGI) scripts to enable two-way communication on your Intranet
- ◆ The developing Java technology, which can vastly extend the helper application model
- ◆ The Virtual Reality Modeling Language (VRML), which can enable you to create and view three-dimensional virtual worlds on your Intranet.

As with the previous chapter, this one is a high-level survey of the technologies mentioned with the aim of providing you with an understanding of what is possible. It doesn't go deeply into the technical details of using these technologies, however. For example, while it introduces Java and describes exemplary uses of it on the Web, this chapter is not a comprehensive reference to the Java programming language, nor is it a complete reference to the programming languages you might use to create CGI scripts on your Web server. Where appropriate, references to other works or World Wide Web URLs with points of interest are included that can get you started with the technical details of these technologies.

Conversion Tools

The biggest source of information for your Intranet are your legacy documents: data you already have in some sort of electronic format that you might want to make available on your Intranet. A large share of these legacy documents are probably documents created by your office word processor. While you want to set up your word processor as a Web browser helper application, a subject covered in detail in Chapter 10, "Your Word Processsor and the Web," you also want to know how to get existing documents out of the proprietary format used by the program and into a form you can immediately use on your Intranet. Two methods are described. You can convert your documents into plain ASCII text. Second, using a two-step process, you can convert them all the way into HTML. Our examples use Microsoft Word and Novell's WordPerfect. If you are using a different word processor, you'll need to check its documentation for details on how to do these steps.

Conversion to Plain Text

The fastest and easiest thing you can do with your word processor documents is convert them to plain ASCII text. All Web browsers can read plain text files, and virtually all word processors have the capability of saving a document as a plain text file. Both Microsoft Word and WordPerfect have Save As options on the File Menu. Just select this option, then using the scroll bar select Text Only With Line Breaks (in Word) or ASCII Text (7 bit) (in WordPerfect), give the file a name, and click

OK. See Figures 4.1 and 4.2 for very similar examples of this process in Word and WordPerfect. Once you've made this conversion, your document is a plain text file you can use directly on your Web server. (Note that your original word processing format document was not changed; you created a completely new file.)

Figure 4.1. Microsoft 6.0 Save As dialog box with Text Only with Line Breaks selected.

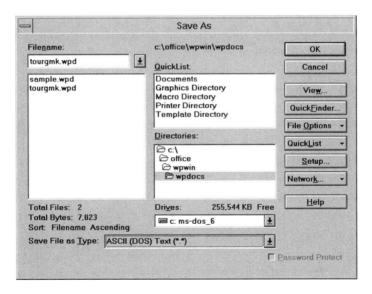

Figure 4.2. WordPerfect 5.1 Save As dialog box with ASCII Text (7 bit) selected.

> **Note:** In WordPerfect, be sure to select ASCII Text (7 bit). Other formats are described as 8 bit, but your objective is to create plain-text files without any binary data. Seven-bit ASCII files are plain text.

Unfortunately, when you save word processing documents as plain text you lose the benefit of the special formatting features in the originals. Text enhancements like boldface, underlining, and font selections all disappear. In addition, if you have tables or other specially formatted portions in a document, they are rearranged into something that may not resemble their original format, if not lost altogether. Graphics disappear too. So while large portions of your original documents survive the transfer intact, you can lose significant portions. Depending on the content of your original documents, the output document may well be usable on your Web, but it also may require more work.

Rich Text

It was the closely related problem of exchanging documents between different word processors that led Microsoft to develop the *Rich Text Format* (RTF) for documents. RTF is an open standard for saving documents to a format that can be read by a different word processor or, as is important here, by another program on your computer. The Rich Text Format is an enhanced, ASCII plain-text format, but which preserves your document-formatting information much like PostScript. Common document-formatting features, such as underlining, boldface, footnotes, and so on, can be preserved as a document is moved from WordPerfect to Word, for example, through the intermediary of RTF. Both packages can save documents in Rich Text and both also read Rich Text documents, including those created by the other. Figures 4.3 and 4.4, respectively, show the Word and WordPerfect Save As dialog boxes, this time showing the document being saved in RTF. Many other word processors and desktop publishing packages, such as FrameMaker, Interleaf, and others, also support saving and reading files in RTF; check your manual.

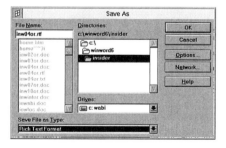

Figure 4.3. *Microsoft Word Save As dialog box with Rich Text Format selected.*

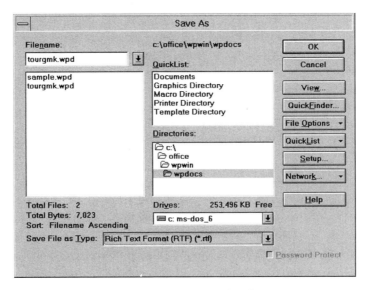

Figure 4.4. *WordPerfect Save As dialog box with Rich Text Format selected.*

You've probably noticed both Word and WordPerfect have options in their Save As dialog to generate the other's datafile format directly, and you may wonder why RTF is needed at all. In fact, if your objective is to transfer documents between these two word processors, there is of course no need to use Rich Text. However, your initial objective was to get your legacy documents out of your word processor format and into HTML; RTF can help you do this.

Rich Text to HTML

Because the Rich Text Format is publicly defined by Microsoft, anyone is free to write programs or modify existing ones to read it. This is what other word processor manufacturers have done to enable RTF compatibility in their own products. Chris Hector, at Cray Research, Inc., maintains a freely available program called rtftohtml, which converts previously saved RTF documents directly into HTML. Binary versions of rtftohtml for SunOS 4.1.x and SunOS 5.x UNIX (aka Solaris 2.x), the Macintosh, and MS-DOS are on the *Building an Intranet* CD-ROM. For other UNIX system users, we provide the rtftohtml source code, which can be compiled on your system. Except for the Macintosh version, which has a graphical user interface, rtftohtml is a *command-line-operated program*; Windows users must access the MS-DOS prompt to run it, or run it by selecting Run from the File Manager's File Menu.

Operation of rtftohtml is simple. You supply it with the name of an RTF file and it converts it to HTML using the same file naming conventions as the original file. For example, you'd type this command at a UNIX shell prompt (the dollar sign represents the UNIX shell prompt):

```
$ rtftohtml myfile.rtf
```

Similarly, at your MS-DOS prompt you'd type the following (note the eight-character limit on the filename results in `rtftohtml` being called `rtftohtm` in DOS):

```
C:>rtftohtm myfile.rtf
```

In either case, the program runs and unless you make a command-line error (for example, specifying a nonexistent input file), it creates the output file `myfile.html` (`myfile.htm` on PCs). `rtftohtml` supports a number of command-line options to modify its default behavior, which you can read about in the online manual for the package at URL `ftp://ftp.cray.com/src/WWWstuff/RTF/rtftohtml_overview.html`. While you're here, check to see if a later version is available. Figure 4.5 shows a portion of the `rtftohtml` user's manual, which describes its capabilities. Note that the package not only deals with standard text formatting, but also preserves tabular material, footnotes, and embedded graphics.

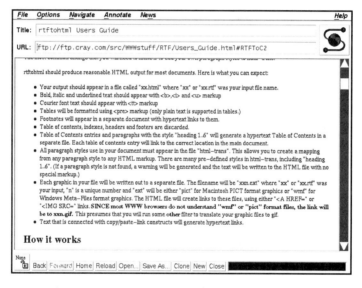

Figure 4.5. `rtftohtml` *capabilities.*

You'll find `rtftohtml` does a superb job of doing basic conversion of your RTF documents to HTML. Because the program is run from the command line, it will be simple for you to mass process a lot of documents in a short time using simple shell loops. For example, on a UNIX system, the following simple Bourne shell command sequence would convert all the RTF files in a directory to HTML in a single loop (the dollar sign represents the shell prompt):

```
$ for file in *.rtf
>do rtftohtml $file
>done
```

DOS users can develop similar looping commands to process a large number of documents at once with DOS batch files. The Macintosh version of `rtftohtml` has a crude graphical front end with pop-ups prompting you for filenames and such, but it works in pretty much the same manner as the UNIX and DOS versions; this is convenient, but it makes it more difficult to convert many files quickly—so much for user friendliness.

Unfortunately, not every conversion is perfect, so you may find you need to do some fiddling with the output files `rtftohtml` generates, particularly if you have tabular material in your documents. Maintaining table column and row alignments is a particular sticking point, as is dealing with embedded graphics, a subject covered in more detail later in the section "Image Conversion and Manipulation."

Summary of RTF and `rtftohtml` Conversions

Conversion of your legacy word processing documents to HTML is a two-step process. First, use your word processor's Save As feature to save your documents in RTF, then use `rtftohtml` to convert the intermediary RTF document to HTML. `rtftohtml` preserves the document's original formatting in large part, with some possible cleanup necessary. You can learn more about RTF by reading the specifications for it at URL `ftp://ftp.primate.wisc/edu/pub/RTF/`. Here, you not only find RTF defined in detail, but also some other filtering tools that convert RTF documents into several other common document formats. As discussed in the following section, `rtftohtml` can handle embedded graphics in your word processing files, but you'll need to do some manipulation of the resulting image files before they're usable in your Web.

Direct Conversion to HTML

Recent Windows versions of Microsoft Word and Novell's WordPerfect allow you, with add-ons available at no cost from the vendors, to save existing documents directly in HTML. WordPerfect version 6.1 users can get Novell's WordPerfect Internet Publisher (IP) at the URL `http://hp.novell.com/elecpub/intpub.htm` or by calling WordPerfect (Internet Publisher on diskette costs $9). For Microsoft Word version 6.0 users, Internet Assistant (IA) is available at URL `http://www.microsoft.com/msoffice/freestuf/msword/download/ia/default.htm`. Internet Assistant is now also available for Word for Windows 95 (`http://www.microsoft.com/MSOffice/MSWord/Internet/IA/default.htm`) but is not yet available for Macintosh Word users. As with your other documents, take care with conversions between Word version 6.0 and the newer one. You'll find conversion tools at Microsoft's Web site, `http://www.microsoft.com/MSOffice/MSWord/fs_wd.htm`.

Both of these packages allow you to use your familiar word processor to create HTML documents and, most importantly in the context of this chapter, to save existing documents in the HTML format. Conversions are as simple as selecting Save As from the File menu, then picking the HTML format from the menu. Figure 4.6 shows the Microsoft Word Save As dialog box; WordPerfect's is similar.

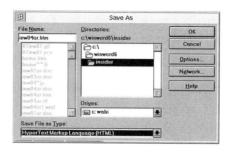

Figure 4.6. *Microsoft Word Save As dialog box with HyperText Markup Language selected.*

> **Tip:** Both Internet Publisher and Internet Assistant allow you to view HTML documents and see their formatting onscreen. Both also include ancillary World Wide Web browsers with which you can access Web servers and/or view HTML documents. Although both contain nonstandard HTML features, primarily to enable creating and viewing of formatting that is unique to the underlying word processor, both can render normal HTML as well. If your documents have special formatting requirements that rely on these unique features, the HTML documents these packages generate may or may not be viewable in standard Web browsers like Mosaic or Netscape. Depending on your needs, you may want to provide your users with copies of the standalone Microsoft Word Viewer or WordPerfect Envoy Viewer. Both of these packages can be used as standalone Web browsers, outside of the word processors, allowing you to view HTML documents created by IA and IP, respectively, which contain these special formatting features. Chapter 10 shows you how to set up these packages as helper applications so your customers aren't forced into giving up their favorite Web browser just to look at a few specially formatted documents generated by IA or IP.

FrameMaker version 5, released in late 1995, now supports direct creation of HTML-formatted documents as well as the conversion of existing frame documents in HTML. Because FrameMaker documents are portable among UNIX, Windows, and Macintosh versions of the package, you'll be able to move around your legacy FrameMaker documents with ease, then convert them as needed. You'll also find other major desktop publishing and word processor packages are adding either direct or indirect support for HTML, though you may be required to upgrade to the current version of your particular package to get this support. See FrameMaker's home page at `http://www.frame.com/`.

Other Document Conversions

There are a wide range of tools generally available for UNIX systems for converting other widely used file formats more or less directly into HTML. TeX and LaTeX are widely used in the scientific and computing communities for sophisticated text layout, including mathematical-equation formatting. The LaTeX2HTML package, maintained by Nikos Drakos in the United Kingdom (available on the accompanying CD-ROM), is one example. LaTeX2HTML is based on perl

(Practical Extraction and Report Language). You'll also find a wide variety of other such filters, including UNIX man page converters, troff (a UNIX typesetting package) converters, e-mail converters, USENET news article converters, and others. As with LaTeX2HTML, most of these have been written in perl; some of them use RTF as an intermediate step in converting documents, so you may need to use `rtftohtml` here as well. You'll find links to a large number of these filters at these two URLs, `http://www.ncsa.uiuc.edu/SDG/Software/Xmosaic/faq-software.html` and `http://www.w3.org/pub/WWW/Tools/Filters.html`.

Image Conversion and Manipulation

Legacy graphics files you may want to include on your Intranet generally fall into two main categories, those that are embedded in word processing documents and those that are standalone image files. Both are discussed here.

rtftohtml and Images

As noted previously, `rtftohtml` conversions of word processing documents with embedded graphics don't quite complete the job. As indicated in Figure 4.5, `rtftohtml` takes your embedded graphics and stores them in separate files with hyperlinks added to the output HTML file pointing to the separate image files. The graphics files created by `rtftohtml`, however, are not immediately usable in Web pages. This is because they are stored as either Windows Metafile (WMF) or Macintosh Pict (PICT) formats (the former in Windows and on UNIX systems, the latter on Macs). The text of the hyperlinks created by `rtftohtml` pointing to the WMF or PICT images, however, specifies GIF image files. That is, even though `rtftohtml` takes your embedded images and turns them into WMF or PICT images (with filenames like `filename.wmf`), the HTML source code it generates contains `<img src=filename.gif>` hyperlinks. As you may recall, most Web browsers support a few types of image formats, including GIFs, but don't support all formats, with WMF and PICT files being among the unsupported ones.

While you can change the HTML source documents to specify `<img src=filename.wmf>`, for example, then set up Web browser helper applications to view WMF files, this is inconvenient because anyone who might want to view your documents must also obtain and set up the correct helper applications. The solution to this problem is to run a conversion on your image files, turning them into GIF images, the most widely supported format in graphical Web browsers. There are a number of packages available to do this sort of conversion, including:

- netpbm (UNIX systems; freeware; source code is on the accompanying CD-ROM)
- HiJaaK Pro (Windows; commercial; available on CompuServe: type **GO INSET**)
- Graphic Workshop (Windows; shareware; on the accompanying CD-ROM)
- Graphics Converter (Macintosh; shareware; on the accompanying CD-ROM)

These packages take WMF or PICT files as input and convert them to the GIF (or other) format.

Other Image Conversion/Manipulation

Outside of your legacy word processor documents, you may also have standalone image data you'd like to use on your Intranet. We discuss helper applications for viewing different kinds of image files (Chapter 8, "Adding Services to Your Intranet Adds Value"), and special image formats such as those generated by CAD packages (Chapter 15, "Scientific, Mathematical, and Technical Applications on Your Intranet"). Here, you concentrate on simple conversions of existing images into formats widely supported in Web browsers. The two most widely supported image formats for Web browsers are the *GIF* (Graphic Interchange Format) and *JPEG* (Joint Photographics Experts Group) format. Both NCSA Mosaic Release 2 (on the *Building an Intranet* CD-ROM) and Netscape support these formats natively, as do most other graphical Web browsers.

Image Conversions on UNIX Systems with ImageMagick

ImageMagick, also on the *Building an Intranet* CD-ROM in source-code and binary executable formats, is a set of several image-manipulation utilities for UNIX systems and the Macintosh. The convert package does just what its name suggests: It converts images in one format to another format. Chapter 6 provides a list of the wide variety of image formats supported by ImageMagick, along with examples for using convert.

> **Note:** While you're primarily concerned at this point with ImageMagick's convert utility, you'll want to look at the rest of the package, which includes utilities for displaying and modifying images, creating montages of images, and creating animations from a series of images, as well. ImageMagick's other utilities can be valuable in the creation of new image data for your Intranet.

> **Tip:** If your legacy images are stored on your PC, you can use your FTP utility to transfer them to a UNIX system over your network, then take advantage of ImageMagick on the UNIX system to do conversions. After all, you're probably going to be using a UNIX system as your Web server and your data must get transferred there sooner or later anyway. See the manuals for your PC TCP/IP software package if you're not familiar with using FTP. Macintosh users may want to use *fetch* (a graphical interface to FTP, also on the *Building an Intranet* CD-ROM) to transfer image and other files to your UNIX system and your Macintoshes.

Image Conversions on PCs and Macs

Earlier in this chapter, several Microsoft Windows and Macintosh image packages were mentioned. According to its promotional literature, HiJaaK Pro (Windows; commercial) converts images to/from over 70 formats. Graphic Workshop (Windows; shareware) includes image-conversion facilities. Graphics Workshop (Macintosh; shareware) converts among a long list of formats. Wherever your images are stored, you should be able to use one of these packages (or ImageMagick's convert) to convert them to a format usable on your Intranet, then place them on your Web server using FTP or other file-transfer methods.

Image Conversions from Other Applications

If you're using computer-aided drafting (CAD) packages, or other application programs that create files containing images, check the package documentation for an *export* feature. Many packages allow you to save datafiles in other formats much like your word processor's Save As feature. The CorelDraw drawing package, for example, has an Export selection on its File menu. Selecting it opens a dialog box (see Figure 4.7 for the UNIX version of CorelDraw) with a range of export formats including familiar image formats like PC PaintBrush (pcx), TIFF (Macintosh), and PostScript. Once you've exported your drawing into one of these formats, you can use one of the image-conversion packages described to move the exported image files into formats directly supported by your Web browser (for example, GIF or JPEG format). As with rtftohtml, this process make take a couple of steps, but it does provide a relatively easy way to move your legacy image data into a format you can use on your Intranet.

Figure 4.7. *CorelDraw Save As dialog box.*

Programming Tools for CGI

The Common Gateway Interface (CGI) is a standardized way of passing data users enter in Web *fill-in forms* (see Appendix B) to back-end programs (usually referred to as *CGI scripts*) you provide on your Web server. While this book is not a technical guide to writing CGI scripts, it can introduce the facility, as well as pointing you to some tools for developing them.

Simplified, there are four main parts to the CGI mechanism.

- ◆ Collection of user input (usually, though not always, through information typed into a Web fill-in form)
- ◆ Passing that information off as variables to the main program lying behind the fill-in form
- ◆ Receiving the results of the back-end program
- ◆ Returning the results to the user in a format that is readable in the user's Web browser

Any program you might write, using almost any programming language, can function as the back-end script provided it can negotiate these four steps. Whether your CGI script does a simple search for a text string in a group of files or does elaborate SQL (structured query language) searches in your corporate database, these four steps apply in pretty much the same fashion. Specifically, your CGI script, running on your Web server, must be able to accept incoming data from another program (usually referred to as *standard input*) and process that incoming data in some way. Further, the results of the processing must be passed back to the CGI mechanism via *standard output,* then formatted so a Web browser can interpret and display it. The latter step usually involves having the script create HTML (HyperText Markup Language) data on the fly.

As noted previously, CGI scripts run on your Web server computer, and any programming language available on the server is available for you to use in creating the CGI scripts. You can write CGI scripts in the C or C++ languages, FORTRAN, UNIX shell scripts, Visual BASIC on PCs, or virtually any other language you want to use. The most widely used language for CGI scripts is perl, several versions of which are available on the CD-ROM. Particularly if your Web server is running on a UNIX system, you'll want to learn about perl and access important archives of no-cost perl CGI scripts available on the Internet. You'll find some sample CGI scripts (both simple UNIX shell scripts and perl scripts) distributed with the NCSA and CERN httpd server packages on the CD-ROM. In addition, the whttpd (Windows) server distribution includes some examples written in old-fashioned MS-DOS batch files and in Visual BASIC 3.0.

For more information about CGI and CGI scripts, check out these URLs. First, access `http://hoohoo.ncsa.uiuc.edu/cgi/`, NCSA's Common Gateway Interface tutorial, a great place to start. Next, try Yahoo's `http://www.yahoo.com/Computers_and_Internet/Internet/World_Wide_Web/CGI__Common_Gateway_Interface/`, a high-level index of CGI resources on the Web. In both places, you'll find not only documentation on using the CGI mechanism, but also archives of CGI scripts (mostly written in perl) people have written and made available to others for unrestricted use.

Because most of the CGI script examples you'll find at these URLs are written in perl, you'll want more information about it as well. Check out the official perl Frequently Asked Questions document, at `ftp://ftp.cis.ufl.edu/pub/perl/faq/FAQ`.

Tools of the Future: Java and VRML

Rapid development continues on the World Wide Web, with next-generation technology that may become an important part of your Intranet. Two important technologies you'll want to explore are Java and VRML.

Java

With a Java-capable Web browser (Sun's HotJava browser is shown in Figure 4.8), users not only can access static Web pages but also dynamically download and run Java application programs just by clicking on hyperlinks. Sun's Java technology is recipient of a November 1995 Award for Technical Excellence in Internet Tools from *PC Magazine*.

Chapters 10 through 12 describe how you can set up common office applications as Web helper applications. This is valuable information, but Java allows the concept of helper applications to be taken an important step further. Rather than requiring each user to pre-configure their Web browser for helper applications, and making sure each user has a copy of the application, Java-capable browsers actually download the application to be run (*applets*, in Java-speak) as users click on hyperlinks. Once downloaded, the applet runs on the user's computer. Java applets can be interactive, so users aren't left sitting looking at a static Web page containing somebody else's idea of what they want to see. More importantly, though, Java applets actually do something. Figure 4.8 shows an interactive electrical transistor circuit simulator. Note the sliders, which allow the user to vary voltage, circuit width, and other factors, which interactively change the graph display.

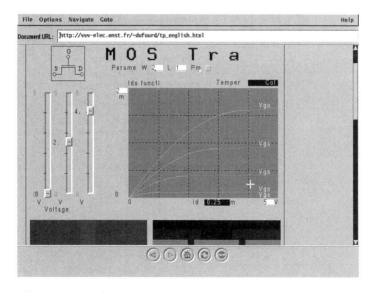

Figure 4.8. *Sun's HotJava browser displaying Java applet.*

Java is already being put to use on corporate Intranets. National Semiconductor, for example, uses Java to enable complex searches of its database of integrated circuits by electronics systems designers building new products. The HotJava browser is not the only Java-capable Web browser. Netscape Version 2 also has Java capabilities. Spyglass, Inc., manufacturers of Spyglass Mosaic, has also signed an agreement with SunSoft for inclusion of Java support in the next release of their product. For Web browsers without Java capabilities, Java applets can be run using Java as a helper application.

VRML

The Virtual Reality Modeling Language is somewhat analogous to HTML, but its markup describes *three-dimensional graphics*, rather than plain Web pages. VRML encodes computer-generated graphics into a compact format for transmission over a network. Using VRML browsers, users can not only look at 3D graphics, but also use them interactively to view, and move around inside *virtual worlds*. Not just for game-playing, VRML can be useful to industrial and other designers, who can examine virtual designs from a near-real perspective. Interior decorators, for example, can design a room in VRML, then use a VRML browser to actually go inside the room and view it in three dimensions.

 VRML markup itself is heavily based on Silicon Graphics' Open Inventor file format but has been adapted to include HTML hyperlink compatibility, making VRML files accessible on the World Wide Web. SGI has made available a VRML browser called *WebSpace*; it's on the *Building an Intranet* CD-ROM in versions for various systems. Figure 4.9 shows the freeware VRML viewer *VRWeb* (also on the CD-ROM in both source-code and Microsoft Windows executable format). As you can see from the screenshot, the 3D image of the office and furniture has been rotated upward and to the left, creating a view from below. Note the instructional legend at the bottom of the window for manipulating the image using your mouse buttons. VRWeb works in both standalone mode and as a Web browser helper application.

If you plan on using VRML in your Intranet, you'll need both VRML browsers and other related tools. A good place to start is *The VRML Repository* at the San Diego Supercomputer Center, URL `http://rosebud.sdsc.edu/vrml/`. Here, you'll find software, including several VRML browsers/viewers, documentation, example VRML source, and fellow VRML travelers who share your interests, as well as plenty of virtual worlds to explore for new ideas.

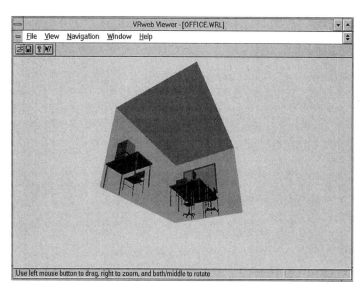

Figure 4.9. VRWeb VRML Viewer.

Summary

You've learned about a number of tools you can use to develop the content on your Intranet in this chapter, especially those that can help you get your existing data on your Web quickly. These tools include:

- ◆ Tools to convert your legacy documents to HTML
- ◆ Tools for converting your existing image data
- ◆ Tools to develop CGI scripts
- ◆ Java technology to extend the helper application model
- ◆ VRML to create and view 3D virtual worlds.

Chapter 5 completes your survey of the tools you need to create your Intranet and discusses the skill sets you'll need.

CHAPTER

Skill Sets

This is the last of three chapters dealing with the tools you'll use to create your Intranet. Chapter 3, "Tools for Implementing an Intranet Infrastructure," and Chapter 4, "Content Development Tools," focused on infrastructure and content development tools, respectively. Here, you turn to the skill sets your people need. Most of these skills are directly related to Web matters—server administration, CGI script programming, and the like—but others are routine, computer system administration skills. As your Intranet develops into a mission-critical system for your organization, both sets of skills become crucial.

Chapter Objectives

As with the rest of the chapters in this book, let's begin by laying out some chapter objectives. This will help you get oriented to the material to be presented; you may want to refer back to this list as you work your way through the chapter.

This chapter addresses

- ◆ The skills required for the setup and administration of your Intranet server(s), including everyday system administration
- ◆ How your organization's people skills interrelate with your choices in assigning administrative and substantive responsibilities in your Intranet
- ◆ Training for both you and your customers
- ◆ Getting and responding to customer feedback, including customer requests for expanded services on your Intranet

Like the two previous chapters, this one is not intended to be a comprehensive technical reference to the subjects it covers. While Appendix A, "Setting Up a Web Server," gives you a good deal of information on Web server setup, you'll eventually want to consult a more detailed reference, such as David Chandler's *Running a Perfect Web Site* (ISBN 0-7897-0210-X), published by Sams.net's sister imprint, Que Publishing. Check with your local bookstore, or access the Macmillan Information SuperLibrary Web server at URL `http://www.mcp.com/` for more information and/or online ordering. In the same context, check out the Macmillan HTML Workshop at `http://www.mcp.com/general/workshop/` for reference books on the HyperText Markup Language. Figure 5.1 shows the HTML Workshop page.

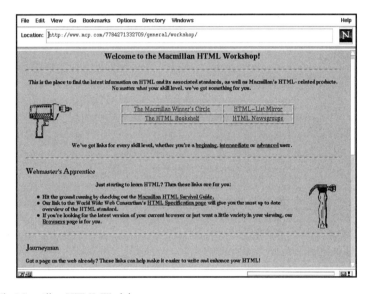

Figure 5.1. *The Macmillan HTML Workshop.*

Web Server Setup and Administration

Obviously, the very first set of people skills you need are those encompassing basic Web server setup and administration. This set of skills is also probably the single most important one to the success of your Intranet.

Your Webmaster

Your choice of a model for the administration of your Intranet (see the discussion of these models in Chapter 2, "Designing an Intranet") has important corollary choices, most importantly with respect to your need for a *Webmaster*—a person with overall responsibility for setting up and maintaining your Web server(s). If you choose the centralized or mixed model, your Webmaster is the most critical part of your Web. (We use this term with no gender connotation, as *Webmistress* somehow seems inappropriate.) While many organizations add Web-server administration to the responsibilities of existing staff, a growing number of companies are creating dedicated positions. In fact, Webmastering skills are in high demand, with salaries to match. A recent survey of Webmasters in Fortune 500 companies by *Web Week* magazine showed a full two-thirds of corporate Webmasters earning more than $45,000, and nearly 40 percent with salaries over $65,000, reflecting the value companies place on their skills.

However you assign responsibilities in this area, it's vital you recognize the value of your Webmaster(s) and ensure he has the skills he needs. This may seem to contradict earlier statements about the relative ease of basic Web server setup and the simplicity of HTML. In fact, while it's true you can set up a simple Web server on a PC using point-and-click methods and have it running in a few minutes, setup and administration of a major Web server on a UNIX system, with fill-in forms, CGI scripts, Java applets, appropriate security, and all the other extras you and your customers will want added is considerably more involved and requires additional skills. Just as you shouldn't skimp on the hardware to run your Web server, don't expect to save money in the long run by throwing an inexperienced staffer into the job of setting up and running a major Web server. Because your Webmaster is such a vital cog in your Intranet, we'll devote a good deal of attention to the skills he or she needs.

If you're unsure where to look for your Webmaster, experienced UNIX system administrators make good choices for Webmasters because they already have many of the needed skills. You may have potential Webmasters in your MIS department. There are few experienced SysAdmins who don't already have these skills and knowledge even if they've never set up a Web server—an increasingly rare situation, with the rapid growth of the Web. It can't be overemphasized that many of the most useful and important details of Web server setup are less than obvious to people who are used to installing software by typing `a:\setup` in the Microsoft Windows Program Manager's Run dialog box. UNIX system administration is part science, part art. The accumulated experience and intuition of a good SysAdmin can keep your Web server in top shape, tuning the performance of the server and ensuring the system is available. If your Intranet becomes mission critical, you'll want a seasoned Webmaster running it.

Look at some of the most critical skills your Webmaster will need. We're assuming here that your main Web server is a UNIX system, although some of the subjects to be covered apply to PC and Mac Web servers as well.

Web Server Setup Details

While the NCSA, CERN, and Netscape Commerce Web servers come with default settings for many operational details, your Webmaster needs a good understanding of what they mean, how they might be changed, and what effects changes may have. For example, does your Web administration model allow for user accounts on the system running your Web server? If so, will you allow these users to create their own HTML documents to be served, or disable the default feature of the server software that allows it? Further, if you allow users to create CGI scripts in their home directory area, it's critical that your Webmaster understand what the scripts do and educate users on the security aspects of CGI. There are a number of other details of Web server setup that need to be understood, most of which require a thorough grounding in UNIX system administration. These include

◆ Selecting the *server mode*, standalone or under the control of the inetd daemon

◆ Setting the server's TCP/IP *port number*

◆ Setting the userid (UID) and groupid (GID) under which the server will run

◆ Maintaining and processing the server's *logfiles*

◆ Understanding and using the server's *identity-checking* feature

◆ Understanding the *MIME* mechanism (see Chapter 7, "MIME and Helper Applications")

◆ The server's real and virtual *filesystem organization*, including file and script *aliasing*

◆ Setting up the server's *directory-indexing* capabilities

◆ Managing and adding default server *icons*

◆ Understanding and using *per-directory access restrictions*, including user passwords and groups and/or TCP/IP network address restrictions to limit access to some or all of your Web server's data

◆ Understanding the *security* and *performance* aspects of these and other choices and how they interrelate

You'll probably want to consult more detailed references on Web server setup and administration. A good place to start is the comments in the sample server configuration files distributed with the server software (see the short descriptions of these sample files in Appendix A). Like much UNIX documentation, these sometimes cryptic comments contain essential information but assume a good deal of system administration experience. Supplement this with NCSA's HTTPd server documentation, online at `http://hoohoo.ncsa.uiuc.edu/docs/Overview.html`. See also NCSA's series of online, server-related (and other) tutorials at `http://www.ncsa.uiuc.edu/SDG/Software/Mosaic/Docs/web-index.html`, including those on access control, CGI, and imagemaps. For additional, detailed Web server setup information, see *Running a Perfect Web Site* referred to previously.

CGI Script Development

Creation of effective and safe (see Chapter 9, "Intranet Security") CGI scripts requires not only programming skills but also a fundamental understanding of UNIX, a complex and powerful operating system, the Web's Hyper Text Transfer Protocol (http), and TCP/IP in general. Recall from Chapter 4, "Content Development Tools," that the CGI mechanism works by taking the information entered in Web fill-in forms and passing it as *standard input* to a *back-end script* or program for processing. When finished, the back-end script returns the results of its run as *standard output*, usually in the form of *HTML markup*, which can be interpreted and displayed by the user's Web browser software.

Simple CGI scripts may use only a couple of pieces of information such as a simple text string for which to search and a list of files in which to search for it. More complex ones, however, may throw around a long list of input data, requiring elaborate variable handling, use of data arrays, and use of underlying operating system calls. Further, you'll want to validate data entered by users before processing it. You'll probably not be able to manage such complex scripts except in a full-feature programming language like C or perl. Experienced UNIX system administrators already have a working knowledge of these languages, and this experience is easily portable to CGI programming. Perl is widely used for CGI scripting because of its power (including access to operating system calls), portability, and relative ease of use.

Whether you use perl, C, or some other programming language for your CGI scripts, you need to be concerned about the security aspects of the scripts. While you're less likely to have efforts to break the security of your Web server if your server is not on the Internet, there are still good reasons to follow good security practices. Programming languages like perl or C include access to underlying operating system resources, including the ability to access, read, and manipulate memory and files. At the very least, you need to make sure your scripts don't inadvertently overwrite important files on your system or create memory buffer overflows when users enter incorrect information in Web fill-in forms. Curious or, in the extreme, malicious users might enter shell metacharacters or even UNIX commands in Web forms; your CGI scripts need to validate the data that's entered to make sure nothing but appropriate data gets passed. Even simple typographical errors are potential problems if data isn't validated. These security considerations, of course, are even more important if your Web server is accessible on the Internet. Chapter 9 discusses general security questions.

For additional information about Perl, see the Web resources listed in Chapter 4. In addition, you may want to get David Till's book, *Teach Yourself Perl in 21 Days* (ISBN 0-672-30586-0), also published by Sams.net, soon available in a second edition. You can learn about this book at the Macmillan Information SuperLibrary, at URL `http://www.mcp.com/`, or in your local bookstore. Macmillan Computer Publishing also has a wide range of reference books on other programming languages such as *Teach Yourself C Programming in 21 Days, Premier Edition*, by Peter Aitken and Brad Jones (ISBN 0-672-30736-7). Scope them out at the SuperLibrary URL.

If you're running your Intranet Web server on Microsoft Windows, or Windows NT, you'll find several choices for your CGI scripting. First, it's possible to use DOS *batch* files called from Windows as CGI scripts, although you have to read and write the information that would usually be passed as standard input/standard output through temporary files (DOS having no support for `stdin`/`stdout`). Visual Basic is a better choice, particularly because the shareware Windows httpd server (on the *Building an Intranet* CD-ROM) and the WebSite commercial server have CGI gateways to Visual Basic. You'll even find DOS and Windows NT versions of perl available on the CD-ROM. Windows, too, suffers from the inability to use `stdin`/`stdout`, so use of temporary files is a must in CGI scripting. See the sample CGI scripts that come with the *whttpd* server, on the CD-ROM. And, of course, if you have access to C, C++, or other high-level language compilers, you can write PC CGI scripts in those languages.

CGI scripting on Macintosh Web servers is usually done with AppleScript. Macintosh perl is available on the CD-ROM. And of course if you have access to C, C++, or other high-level language compilers, you can write Macintosh CGI scripts in those languages.

Java Programming Skills

Java applets are a little harder to identify because they have characteristics in common with CGI scripts, HTML documents, and Web browser helper applications. Like CGI scripts, applets are computer programs that run on the user's computer, not on the Web server. Like HTML documents, Java applets are first downloaded from a Web server just by clicking on a hyperlink. The client machine runs the applet then discards it when done. Helper applications, on the other hand, are programs that already exist on the user's computer that are run when data for the application is downloaded from a Web server.

Java is a completely new programming language something like C++ in that it's object-oriented. As you might guess, it's hardware and operating-system independent; Java applets run on any computer system with a Java viewer or Java-compatible Web browser. Many of the standard features of high-level programming languages have purposely not been implemented in Java for both efficiency and security reasons. For instance, Java can't access or manipulate memory registers. Security experts remain skeptical, as the whole idea of running uninspected, unknown programs downloaded from sources over which they have no control just by clicking on a Web hyperlink is more than a little scary, assurances about Java's built-in security features notwithstanding. While Java applets are considered immune from external virus infection, it's not completely clear why. Java applets are usually network-safe, although reports of insecurities in Java were surfacing as *Building an Intranet* was going to press.

There is much new ground to be explored with Java for both possibilities and risks. You'll need the ability to learn Java programming if you intend to use it on your Intranet. Moreover, you'll want to be intimately familiar with its possible security implications for your customers. For more information about Java, see John December's book, *Presenting Java* (ISBN 1-57521-039-9), also published by Sams.net. For SunSoft's view on Java, along with extensive documentation, copies of the *HotJava* Web browser for Sun Sparc and PC's running Solaris 2.x and demonstration Java applets, access the Java home page (shown in Figure 5.2) at `http://java.sun.com/`. Also, Netscape has Java demos at `http://home.netscape.com/comprod/products/navigator/version2_0/java_applets/index.html`.

Web Server Security Skills

Even if your Intranet is completely isolated from the Internet, and even if you trust all of your customers, it's still a good idea to manage your Web server(s) with routine security. If you do make your Web server(s) accessible on the Internet, doing so is critical. Web server software, like the NCSA or CERN HTTPd packages, has built-in security, but it's pretty much turned off by default. As a result, you need to understand the details of server security, including access control.

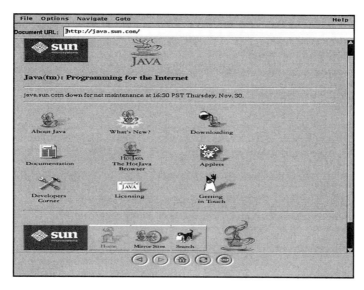

Figure 5.2. *Java home page.*

As noted above, because CGI scripts run on your Web server, it's critical you make sure there are no possibilities for them to compromise the server's security through intentionally inappropriate data being passed to them by malicious users. Just like you should inspect any other software you may retrieve from the Internet or some BBS before running it, make sure any CGI scripts you may download are secure. You can only do this by inspecting and understanding the scripts' code. In practice, this means you must understand perl because it is the language of choice for CGI programming and its relationship to the underlying operating system.

Your customers will demand and use fill-in forms on your Intranet; some of them may even want to write their own CGI scripts and/or obtain them from others. One of your security-related decisions is that of restricting CGI scripts to your server's protected filesystem or allowing users' CGI scripts to run out of their own home directories. Choosing the latter means you need to inspect the user scripts for security implications. This doesn't mean you don't trust your customers who just want to get their work done. It does mean you can't necessarily expect customers to be attuned to the potential for intentional (or unintentional) misuse of CGI scripts and their security aspects. You'll want to inspect customer CGI scripts to make sure they're appropriately secure and counsel users on them.

The security of your Web server is also impacted by the administrative decisions you make with respect to managing your Web. While it's clear in the centralized model that only authorized people can place Web documents and CGI scripts on your server, and you can take the necessary practical and management steps to enforce this policy, this is less clear in the other models.

Finally, your Web server is only as secure as the computer on which it's running. All the security precautions in the world are worth nothing if everyone in the office has the root, or superuser, password to your UNIX system or if you haven't closed well-known security holes in the system.

System and network security are meat and potatoes to experienced UNIX System Administrators, and security considerations alone present a strong argument for your Webmaster to have an extensive background in system administration. These considerations are especially important if your organization is connected to the Internet. The overall security of your network should be secured by a *firewall* system of some kind, and you should carefully configure the access-control features of your Web server(s) to limit access to authorized users.

Note: As the word implies, a firewall system isolates your network from the Internet, limiting access between the two networks. Usually, firewalls are set up to permit certain Internet services, such as e-mail, to enter your network but block other services that might be insecure or subject to abuse. Firewalls can also be used to selectively permit access by users in an organization to outside Internet services, such as FTP or World Wide Web servers. For more information on Internet firewalls, see *Internet Firewalls and Network Security*, by Karanjit Siyan and Chris Hare (ISBN 1-56205-437-6), published by Sams.net's sister imprint New Riders. Many commercial firewall vendors have Web pages, including Raptor Systems (`http://www.raptor.com/`), with its Eagle product line, Trusted Information Systems (`http://www.tis.com/`), with its Gauntlet product line, and others. For general firewall information, including access to the home pages of a long list of firewall and security vendors, see the *Firewall Product Developers Consortium* Web page, maintained by the National Computer Security Association, at `http://www.ncsa.com/fwpdmem1.html`. The NCSA (not to be confused with the National Center for Supercomputing Applications, makers of NCSA Mosaic and the NCSA httpd server) has a home page (see Figure 5.3) with useful security information at `http://www.ncsa.com/`, where it takes pains to note the acronym "NCSA" is its registered trademark.

Figure 5.3. *National Computer Security Association.*

Running a Web server on a PC or Macintosh raises even more security questions. PCs have little or no security. Leaving a PC Web server running unattended in a non-secure area is an invitation to both the malicious and the curious: You might as well forget any security on that server. Implementing the access-control features of the Web server software is especially critical on a PC server because there is no concept of operating system security on a PC.

> **Note:** Viewer security is also a potential problem in another way. While you may implement access control on your Web server, limiting access to all or part of your Web server to specific TCP/IP addresses in your network (see Chapter 9 for more information), an unattended PC, workstation, or terminal that is already viewing protected documents is not, of course, secure. For example, if you hope to restrict access to confidential personnel information to management, you need to counsel management users in these security issues. Leaving one's desk for coffee while viewing such confidential information without starting up a screen lock or taking some other security measure breaks all the Web server access controls.

General System Administration Skills

A final, catch-all, set of Webmaster skills is the overall administration of your Web server system. These skills range from everyday backups of the system to performance tuning to disk-space and user account management. While routine in some respects, the performance of these duties is a critical factor in the care and feeding of your Intranet. Even if you have hardware and software maintenance/support contracts with outside vendors, there's no substitute for the experience and intuition of a System Administrator when problems arise. Provided your System Administrator follows good backup practices, for example, restoring lost or erroneously deleted files can take just a few minutes. Webmasters and System Administrators are also important in the training of your customers in the use of your Web.

Most UNIX system vendors have training programs including intensive system administration training at basic and advanced levels. A beginner needs several weeks of these courses, particularly if programming courses are required. Other alternatives include college courses in programming (the C language is a frequent course offering, even at community colleges). You'll also find frequent one- and two-day seminars on system administration subjects such as perl, usually in conjunction with UNIX conferences and shows, such as the annual UNIX Expo in New York, or the Washington, D.C., SANS (System Administration, Networking, and Security) and USENIX Conferences. (USENIX Conferences are held twice a year in various locations around the United States, usually in warm places in the winter and cool places in the summer.) The single most useful book on UNIX system administration is *UNIX System Administration Handbook* by Nemeth, Snyder, Seabass, and Hein (ISBN 0-13-151051-7). Be sure to get the Second Edition, published in 1995; a bound-in CD-ROM with a wealth of system administration tools is an important bonus. The book has its own Web page at http://www.admin.com/.

If you need to recruit a UNIX System Administrator and aren't sure how to define the job, you may want to look at the sample job descriptions developed by SAGE, the USENIX Association's

System Administrators' Guild. Including recommended skills for novice, intermediate/advanced, and senior system administrators, you'll find this document at the URL `ftp://ftp.sage.usenix.org/pub/sage/jobs/jobs-description.html`.

Management of Web Development

The decisions you make on the management of your Intranet, theoretically discussed in Chapter 2, come back into play when you consider the skill sets your people need. (Of course, this statement is easily stood on its head: The skills your people have can help you choose the administrative model and may lead you to reconsider earlier decisions.) If you choose the decentralized model, you're deciding to leave most, if not all, of the management and development of your Web to its users, or at least to those interested enough to be setting up individual Web servers for their own data. This model also assumes the skills needed to do Web server setup, creation of HTML files, and the like best reside at the user level. Similarly, the need for training will be at the same level, with your customers themselves deciding who needs what in the way of training.

In the centralized model these decisions are reversed, with the delegation of responsibilities and the necessary skills focused in your Webmaster(s). Here, you and your Webmaster(s) can determine where training is required and, as noted previously, what training you can provide to your customers to develop and manage the training process. In the more realistic mixed model, you delegate responsibilities in a more flexible fashion, based on the needs of the components of your organization.

It's also important for you to develop policies about customer contributions to your Web. Besides regular customer feedback (see the following), you should anticipate, if not solicit and welcome, resources for your Intranet that are contributed by your customers. Even if your Intranet follows the centralized model of administration, it's important you recognize that customers often have the best idea of what they want to see on it especially if it's in their area of expertise. Empowering customer input by providing a way for them to contribute resources directly to your Intranet is a fine way of developing both customers and your Intranet and is sure to lead to further contributions.

Training

We've already mentioned general UNIX System Administration training opportunities. You'll also find a wide variety of Web-specific training offerings from commercial vendors as well as short seminars associated with major expositions and conferences. In fact, several Web-specific conferences are already occurring on a regular basis; you'll find advertisements for them in publications devoted to Web subjects, such as *Web Week* (URL `http://pubs.iworld.com/ww-online/`) and *Web Developer* (URL `http://pubs.iworld.com/wd-online/`), and in even more general networking publications like *NetworkWorld* (`http://www.nwfusion.com/`). Here you'll find courses in Web server administration, HTML markup, CGI scripting, perl, Java programming,

VRML, and the like. You'll also, of course, find useful articles on Web-related subjects, including technical features, in these publications. Figure 5.4 shows the *Web Developer* magazine home page. You'll also find a wide variety of Web books, from books on Webmastering to use of specific Web browsers like Mosaic or Netscape, in your local shopping mall bookstore, including those specifically recommended in this book.

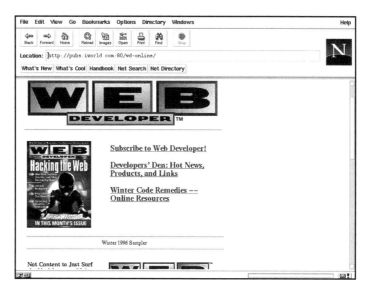

Figure 5.4. Web Developer *magazine.*

If you have a competent Webmaster, there is no reason not to tap her knowledge in running your own training courses on these same subjects. She'll undoubtedly be answering questions from customers on a regular basis, so you might as well formalize this relationship with training courses. Of course, Webmasters cannot only train the people who will use your Intranet, but other Webmasters as well. Don't neglect the value of the wide variety of Web-related books as training tools for users. Books on Web browsers include

◆ The author's *10-Minute Guide to Netscape for X Windows* (ISBN 0-7897-0571-0), published by Que Publishing

◆ *Plug-N-Play Netscape for Windows,* by Angela Gunn and Joe Kraynak (ISBN 0-57521-010-X), published by Sams.net

◆ *Plug-N-Play Mosaic for Windows,* by Angela Gunn, (ISBN 0-672-30627-1), published by Sams.net

◆ *Special Edition Using Netscape 2,* by Mark R. Brown and a cast of thousands, including the author of *Building an Intranet* (ISBN 0-7896-0612-1), also published by Que

You can learn more about these and other Macmillan Computer Publishing books at the Information SuperLibrary, http://www.mcp.com/. Figure 5.5 shows the SuperLibrary Home Page.

Figure 5.5. *Macmillan Information SuperLibrary.*

Customer Feedback

In Chapter 2, we recommended use of customer *focus groups* to help define the purpose and content of your Intranet. You should continue meeting with your focus groups even after your Intranet is up and running; you may find even more valuable feedback from your customers. Also expect customer feedback outside your formal focus group arrangements.

They Inevitably Want More

Once your customers get the idea of using Web technology in their everyday work, as opposed to recreational Web *surfing*, they'll begin bombarding you with suggestions for changes and requests for new information. Listen to these suggestions and requests. As Chapter 2 suggested, your customers know best the kinds of information they want to see and how well your Web presents it. Employees often have useful ideas on how to go about doing their jobs because they are the people most intimately familiar with the jobs. Expect them to have ideas for your Intranet as well for exactly the same reason. For example, if you've ever designed a database application you know this process. Even having gone through a formal process of soliciting user input on your application before you ever started its design, within minutes of the time you sit a user down in front of your prototype, he's asking questions like

◆ If I can do a thus-and-so query, can't I also do a that-and-so one?

◆ Wouldn't this data-entry screen be better if this box's position and that box's were reversed?

◆ This is a great report, but can't you fit it on one page? And while you're at it, how about showing the quarterly figures, too?

In other words, real users using your application—whether it's a corporate database or your Intranet—for real work will quickly have ideas on how it can be made better. Most of their ideas will be good ones, too.

Get Them to Contribute

In your Intranet, customer ideas won't be limited to requests for new information or changes in presentation. Users will quickly recognize the *collaborative* aspects of Web technology. Chapter 24, "Web Groupware: Collaboration on Your Intranet," discusses more about this aspect, but it needs a touch here. Chapter 2, for instance, suggested the idea of engineers and scientists sharing engineering drawings, application datafiles, and/or technical reports with colleagues by placing them on your Web. As a Web designer, you can't possibly identify this sort of specific information, but your engineer and scientist customers surely can and will. Regardless of the administrative model you've selected for your Web, it's important you make it easy for customers to contribute resources for it. This is where the decentralized and mixed models shine: customers using your Web can create and make their own resources available on your Web for sharing with other customers.

Simple HTML markup is easily within the grasp of just about anyone who uses a computer, as are most of the legacy data conversion tools described in Chapter 4. Point-and-click setup of PC and Macintosh Web server software makes it possible for almost anyone to set up a barebones Web server on his desktop to share these specific resources. Just as anyone can thumb tack a notice on a cork bulletin board in the office, on your Intranet they can tack up CAD drawings of circuit boards, building blueprints, or directions to the office holiday party. You may also want to set up a "free for all" fill-in form on your Web that allows customers to add links to their resources. Figure 5.6 shows such a form, part of the Lycos catalog of the Internet, where users can enter their favorite URL for inclusion in the catalog. (For more information on Lycos, see `http://www.lycos.com/`.)

Customer contributions may turn out to be the most important aspect of your Intranet. To this end, make sure your customer training and Web-related communications emphasizes the value and continuing need for their input. It's vitally important that you create a welcoming, inclusive atmosphere. Your Intranet is, after all, for your customers. Involving them in the Intranet design process, then keeping them involved by welcoming their contributions, ensures its value, to them and to your organization. Losing this customer focus, on the other hand, will lead to your Intranet becoming stale and unused; if customers find no value, they'll go elsewhere.

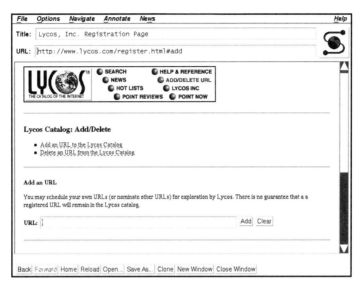

Figure 5.6. *Lycos add/delete URL page.*

Summary

This chapter has focused on the skill sets you'll need in setting up, running, and using your Intranet, completing a set of three tools-related chapters. You've learned about

◆ The skills required for the setup and administration of your Intranet server(s)

◆ How your skill sets interrelate with administrative and substantive responsibilities in your Intranet

◆ Training, for both you and your customers

◆ Getting and responding to customer feedback

Chapter 6, "Quick and Dirty Intranet," takes these tools and uses them to do a quick and dirty setup of a Web server using your legacy data. This allows you to get a server running with real information resources for your customers. Later chapters show you how to add new features to your Intranet.

CHAPTER

Quick and Dirty Intranet

In the first five chapters of this book, you've worked through the Intranet design process, decided how to manage your Intranet, and looked at the infrastructure, content development, and skill sets you need to get started. Now it's time to move away from the theoretical material and begin some real Intranet development. In this chapter, you'll take your existing corporate or organizational information and get it up and running on your Intranet. Your Intranet will not be complete by any means when you finish this chapter, but you'll have made a good start.

Chapter Objectives

Let's begin by laying out some objectives to accomplish in this chapter. You may want to refer to this list as you work your way through. In this chapter, you will

- ◆ Survey the information that your organization is already providing to its customers.
- ◆ Determine how much of that information is already in some sort of electronic format.
- ◆ Convert your legacy data into formats that can be used on your Intranet. This may involve a variety of software and hardware tools, including last-resort devices like document scanners and screen snapshot software.
- ◆ Learn about common Web browser helper applications that you can put to use quickly in your Intranet.

We'll assume for purposes of this chapter that you already have a World Wide Web (httpd) server up and running in your organization. If you don't have a server running, you'll want to consult Appendixes A and B for essential information on Web server setup and HTML, respectively. General Web server setup is beyond the scope of this book, so you may need to supplement the information in the appendixes with other references. Additional information on setting up a Web server can be found in *The World Wide Web Unleashed 1996*, by John December and Neil Randall (ISBN 1-57521-040-1), and the author's book, *10 Minute Guide to HTML* (ISBN 0-7897-0541-9). Information about both books, as well as others published by Sams.net, Que, and other Macmillan Computer Publishing imprints, is available on the World Wide Web at the Macmillan Information SuperLibrary `http://www.mcp.com/`.

As you go through this chapter, you'll see real examples of how to jump-start an Intranet using various tools and techniques.

Using What You Already Have

The main source of information for your quick and dirty Intranet is the body of documents and data you already have available. This data, particularly if it's already in electronic format, will form your Intranet's foundation.

Taking Inventory

If yours is a typical organization, you probably have a lot of potential Intranet information lying around in file cabinets and on bookshelves and computer disks. Before you dive into the exciting waters of Sections II, III, and IV of this book, you'll want to dig up all this existing information, and determine how much of it you can make available on your Intranet without too much time and effort.

Begin this process by taking inventory of the information already available in your company. Here are some of the items to look for

- ◆ Manuals of operational procedures
- ◆ The company phone book
- ◆ Catalog and inventory lists
- ◆ Employee benefits information
- ◆ Other informational material for employees, such as bulletin boards, job postings, and in-house newsletters or publications
- ◆ Stored letters, memoranda, and other word processing documents, from active disk drives or on backup tapes or diskettes

◆ Anything else you might find around the office, in a file cabinet, in a drawer, on a bookshelf, or even tacked on a wall or bulletin board

It is important that you cast a wide net here. Think of your Intranet as a big bank of filing cabinets containing every piece of paper and scrap of data your company owns. You save information in filing cabinets for a reason—because someone might need to look up the information in the future. The same goes for the information you'll put into your Intranet—anything that someone might need in the future is a candidate for inclusion.

After identifying the total pool of available data, the next question is which of that information can you easily make available on your Intranet? Not all of your data can be included with equal ease, so you'll need to evaluate which information is worth the time and effort necessary to make it usable on your Intranet.

The Easy Part First

Obviously, material that's already in electronic format is your prime and most accessible source of Intranet data. Within this category, you'll likely find old word processing documents to be the single best source of information, particularly if your organization uses formal electronic filing procedures of some kind. Even if you have no document-management apparatus, you'll probably find important recent documents still sitting on your hard drive or on backup tapes, just waiting to be put on your Intranet.

Your word processor's Save As feature is one of the most powerful tools for putting your word processing documents on your Intranet. All modern word processors have a Save As feature, which enables you to convert quickly the word processor's documents to plain text files, also called ASCII text files. Plain text files are directly usable in your Intranet. You can place them on your Web server as-is, with no further conversion. From there, your customers can view them with their Web browsers.

Figures 6.1 and 6.2 show the Save As dialog boxes for Microsoft Word and WordPerfect, respectively. Check your own word processor's documentation for a Save As feature. As you can see from the figures below, both Word and WordPerfect have scrollable lists of file formats in which they can save documents; both support saving as plain ASCII text. The default filename for converted documents in both Word and WordPerfect uses the extension .txt. You should accept this default extension, because the plain text MIME data type/sub-type is directly supported by all Web servers and browsers, using the .txt extension. (Refer to Chapter 7, "MIME and Helper Applications," for information about MIME data types/sub-types.)

> **Note:** When you use the Save As feature, your original word processing document is not changed; you create a completely new file.

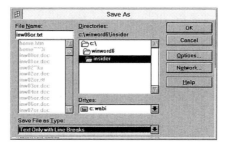

Figure 6.1. *The Microsoft Word 6.0 Save As dialog box, set to save the file as Text Only with Line Breaks, Word's way of saying "ASCII Text."*

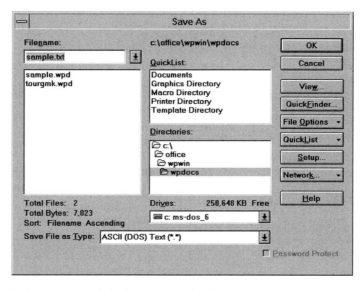

Figure 6.2. *The WordPerfect 6.1 Save As dialog box, set to save the file as ASCII (DOS) Text.*

This simple Save As feature can make it possible for you to create a large library of documents for your Intranet in a very short time. Just load the document, select Save As, give your document a new name, and click OK. It's even possible to use your word processor's macro command facility to partially automate this process.

Of course, if you're part of a large operation, with a formal document-management system for your word processing documents, it's an equally simple matter for your staff to spend a morning or afternoon mass-converting documents for your Intranet. After all, you're already organized to manage your word processing data.

Either way, once you've saved your files in ASCII format, you can create an HTML document containing a list of the converted documents as hyperlinks—and get your Intranet off the ground with almost no difficult work.

Figure 6.3 shows a first cut at a dummy *Building an Intranet* Web server home page. You can see links to several chapters which have been converted from Microsoft Word to plain ASCII text using the Save As feature of Word. The entire process of converting the documents and creating the home page itself took less than half an hour.

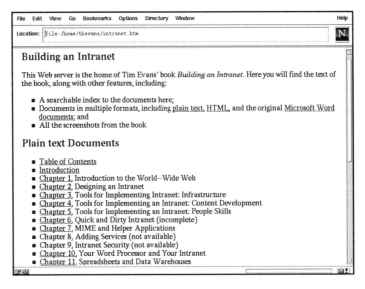

Figure 6.3. *The* Building an Intranet *dummy home page, shown in plain text format.*

The HTML markup to create this page is quite simple, using just a few features of the language to create a bulleted list of the book's table of contents. As you can see from Figure 6.3, several of the chapters are hyperlinks, although the page is not yet complete.

Let's take a look at the HTML source for this page.

```
<HTML><HEAD><TITLE>Building an Intranet</TITLE></HEAD>
<BODY>
<H1>Building an Intranet</H1>

This Web server is the home of Tim Evans' book <EM>Building an Intranet</EM>. Here
you will find the text of the book, along with other features, including:
<UL><LI>A searchable index to the documents here;</LI>
<LI>Documents in multiple formats, including <A HREF="#plain">
plain text</A>, <A HREF="#HTML">HTML</A>, and
the original <A HREF="#word">Microsoft Word documents</A>; and</LI>
<LI>All the screenshots from the book</LI></UL>
<H2><A NAME=plain>Plain text Documents</H2>
<UL><LI> <A HREF="inwtoc.txt">Table of Contents</A></LI>
<LI><A HREF="inw00or.txt">Introduction</A></LI>
<LI><A HREF="inw01or.txt">Chapter 1</A>, Introduction to the
World-Wide Web</LI>
<LI><A HREF="inw02or.txt">Chapter 2</A>, Designing an Intranet</LI>
<LI><A HREF="inw03or.txt">Chapter 3</A>, Tools for Implementing
Intranet: Infrastructure</LI>
<LI><A HREF="inw04or.txt">Chapter 4</A>, Tools for Implementing
```

```
an Intranet: Content Development</LI>
<LI><A HREF="inw05or.txt">Chapter 5</A>, Tools for Implementing
an Intranet: People Skills</LI>
<LI><A HREF="inw06or.txt">Chapter 6</A>, Quick and Dirty
Intranet (incomplete)</LI>
<LI><A HREF="inw07or.txt">Chapter 7</A>, MIME and Helper Applications</LI>
<LI>Chapter 8, Adding Services (not available)</LI>
<LI>Chapter 9, Intranet Security (not available)</LI>
<LI><A HREF="inw10or.txt">Chapter 10</A>, Your Word Processor
and Your Intranet</LI>
<LI><A HREF="inw11or.txt">Chapter 11</A>, Spreadsheets and Data Warehouses</LI>
<LI><A HREF="inw12or.txt">Chapter 12</A>, Other Common Office Applications</LI>
<LI>Chapter 13, Indexing and Searching Your Data (not available)</LI>
<LI>Chapter 14, Access to Commercial Database Applications (not available)</LI>
<LI>Chapter 15, Homegrown Database Applications (not available)</LI>
<LI>Chapter 16, Scientific and Technical Applications (not available)</LI>
<LI>Chapter 17, Help Desk (not available)</LI>
<LI>Chapter 18, Company Practices/Procedures Manuals (not available)</LI>
<LI>Chapter 19, Numbers for Number Crunchers (not available)</LI>
<LI>Chapter 20, Ordering and Inventory (not available)</LI>
<LI>Chapter 21, Boilerplate Library (not available)</LI>
<LI>Chapter 22, Computer-Based Training/Presentations (not available)</LI>
<LI>Chapter 23, Newsgroups for Group Discussions (not available)</LI>
<LI>Chapter 24, Intranet Front End for Custom Applications (not available)</LI>
<LI>Chapter 25, Java and VRML (not available)</LI>
<LI>Chapter 26, Intranet Collaboration (not available)</LI>
<LI>Appendix A, Setting up a Web Server (not available)</LI>
<LI>Appendix B, HTML and CGI Quick Review (not available)</LI>
<LI>Appendix C, The Intranet CD-ROM (not available)</LI>
</UL>
<H2><A NAME=html>HTML Documents, with Screenshots</H2>
<H2><A NAME=word>Original Microsoft Word Documents</H2>
</BODY>
</HTML>
```

Later in the chapter, this HTML source will be extended to add the same set of documents in HTML format. Even without them, however, a working Intranet could be in place with this simple HTML markup, containing a dozen or so documents. The documents converted from Word using Save As could now be sitting on a Web server, accessible to anyone on the Intranet using his Web browser. It doesn't matter that the user might not have access to Microsoft Word, because the documents appear in plain text format. Figures 6.4 and 6.5 show a couple of the actual documents, viewed from Netscape.

Even though the pictures in Figures 6.4 and 6.5 are reduced in size from the original screens, you can still see that these are perfectly readable plain text documents. While they don't show any fancy formatting, the text of the originals is there and is readable. Your customers can save, print, or do anything they like with these documents. You're on your way to getting your Intranet going already.

Figure 6.4. *A Netscape view of a plain text table of contents.*

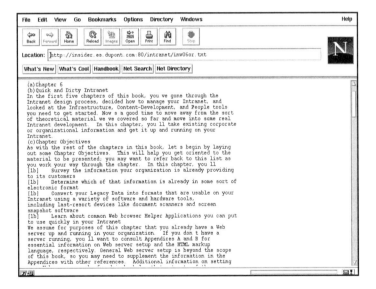

Figure 6.5. *A Netscape view of a plain text chapter.*

Retaining Document Formatting

Unfortunately, when you save word processing documents as plain text, you lose the benefit of some of the package's special formatting features. Text enhancements like **boldface**, <u>underlining</u>, *italics*, and font selections all disappear. What's left are perfectly readable lines of plain text, but you'd probably like to have some of the original document's formatting back.

Besides losing formatting, you may also lose some actual content from a document when you convert it to ASCII format. Tables suffer especially in saving a document as plain text—they seldom resemble their original form when converted. Graphics usually disappear altogether. As a result, even though you've made rapid strides in creating your Intranet, you'll want to take some additional steps with at least some of your documents, to preserve the documents' integrity.

We introduced the Rich Text Format (RTF) in Chapter 4, "Content Development Tools." As you'll recall, Microsoft developed RTF as a means of enabling portability of documents among different applications, including different word processing packages. The specifications for RTF were made public and most of Microsoft's competitors in the word processor market have added support for RTF to their products. Using this feature and the `rtftohtml` program provided on the CD-ROM included with this book, you can convert your existing word processing documents first into RTF, and then into HTML. As Figure 6.6 shows, Word supports RTF as one of the document formats available through the same Save As dialog box; WordPerfect's similar RTF conversion is shown in Figure 6.7.

Figure 6.6. *The Microsoft Word Save As dialog box, saving the document in Rich Text Format.*

> **Note:** Chapter 4 also mentions Microsoft's Word add-on, *Internet Assistant*, which, when installed, adds HTML as an option to the Word Save As menu of file formats. Unfortunately, the author found the HTML documents created by Internet Assistant unsatisfactory, with typeface/fonts done poorly. Saving in HTML format with Save As is also extremely slow, taking several minutes to convert moderately long documents. While Microsoft may well have upgraded Internet Assistant to resolve these problems by the time you read this, Save As RTF is a more reliable way of exporting Word documents for eventual conversion to HTML using `rtftohtm`.

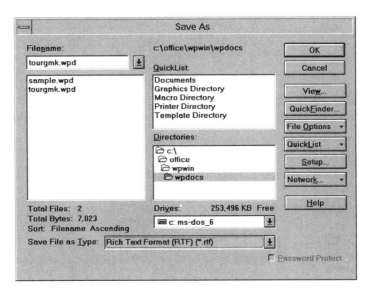

Figure 6.7. *The WordPerfect Save As dialog box, saving the document in Rich Text Format.*

In Chapter 4, you learned a short UNIX command sequence that converted a batch of RTF files into HTML using rtftohtml. Here's a comparable MS-DOS command that you can run from a DOS prompt:

```
c:> for %f in (*.rtf) do rtftohtm %f
```

This command expands the list of files matching the wildcard (all files in the current directory ending in .rtf), and then runs rtftohtm on each one in turn until all are converted to HTML. (Note that if you put this kind of command into a DOS batch file, you'll need to use double percent symbols in both places; see your MS-DOS documentation for details.)

Before we try to view the converted RTF files, let's modify the dummy *Building an Intranet* home page to add the new HTML files. Most of the previous version has been omitted here since it didn't change. The boldfaced lines in the listing below show what's been added:

```
<LI>Appendix B, HTML and CGI Quick Review (not available)</LI>
<LI>Appendix C, The Intranet CD-ROM (not available)</LI>
</UL>
<H2><A NAME=html>HTML Documents, with Screenshots</H2>
<ul><LI> <A HREF="inwtoc.htm">Table of Contents</A></LI>
<LI><A HREF="inw00or.htm">Introduction</A></LI>
<LI><A HREF="inw01or.htm">Chapter 1</A>, Introduction to the World-Wide
Web</LI>
<LI><A HREF="inw02or.htm">Chapter 2</A>, Designing an Intranet</LI>
<LI><A HREF="inw03or.htm">Chapter 3</A>, Tools for Implementing an
Intranet: Infrastructure</LI>
<LI><A HREF="inw04or.htm">Chapter 4</A>, Tools for Implementing an
Intranet: Content Development</LI>
<LI><A HREF="inw05or.htm">Chapter 5</A>, Tools for Implementing an
Intranet: People Skills</LI>
```

```
<LI><A HREF="inw06or.htm">Chapter 6</A>, Quick and Dirty Intranet
(incomplete)</LI>
<LI><A HREF="inw07or.htm">Chapter 7</A>, MIME and Helper Applications</LI>
<LI>Chapter 8, Adding Services (not available)</LI>
<LI>Chapter 9, Intranet Security (not available)</LI>
<LI><A HREF="inw10or.htm">Chapter 10</A>, Your Word Processor and
Your Intranet</LI>
<LI><A HREF="inw11or.htm">Chapter 11</A>, Spreadsheets and Data Warehouses</LI>
<LI><A HREF="inw12or.htm">Chapter 12</A>, Other Common Office Applications</LI>
<LI>Chapter 13, Indexing and Searching Your Data (not available)</LI>
<LI>Chapter 14, Access to Commercial Database Applications (not available)</LI>
<LI>Chapter 15, Homegrown Database Applications (not available)</LI>
<LI>Chapter 16, Scientific and Technical Applications (not available)</LI>
<LI>Chapter 17, Help Desk (not available)</LI>
<LI>Chapter 18, Company Practices/Procedures Manuals (not available)</LI>
<LI>Chapter 19, Numbers for Number Crunchers (not available)</LI>
<LI>Chapter 20, Ordering and Inventory (not available)</LI>
<LI>Chapter 21, Boilerplate Library (not available)</LI>
<LI>Chapter 22, Computer-Based Training/Presentations (not available)</LI>
<LI>Chapter 23, Newsgroups for Group Discussions (not available)</LI>
<LI>Chapter 24, Intranet Front End for Custom Applications (not available)</LI>
<LI>Chapter 25, Java and VRML (not available)</LI>
<LI>Chapter 26, Intranet Collaboration (not available)</LI>
<LI>Appendix A, Setting up a Web Server (not available)</LI>
<LI>Appendix B, HTML and CGI Quick Review (not available)</LI>
<LI>Appendix C, The Intranet CD-ROM (not available)</LI></UL>
<H2><A NAME=word>Original Microsoft Word Documents</H2>
</BODY>
</HTML>
```

As you can see by comparing the two HTML listings, chunks of the original listing have been copied-and-pasted, then all the .txt filename extensions changed to .htm.

In just a few minutes' time, a batch of Word documents were converted into HTML, using Word's Save As feature to create intermediate .rtf files. The intermediate files were then converted to HTML using the freeware rtftohtm package. Finally, a simple copy-and-paste was used to extend the HTML document containing links to the new files. The *Building an Intranet* Web has been quickly and easily extended using existing word processing documents and simple, available conversion tools.

Your Intranet can be populated with useful documents just as quickly. Figures 6.8 and 6.9 show the modified *Building an Intranet* dummy home page and one of the book's chapters, respectively. Note in particular how Figure 6.9 shows that rtftohtm has retained the boldface side headings as well as the italicized book titles (in the last paragraph of the text).

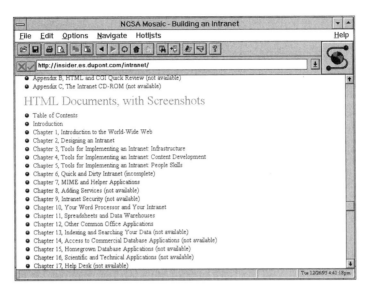

Figure 6.8. *The* Building an Intranet *home page, HTML section.*

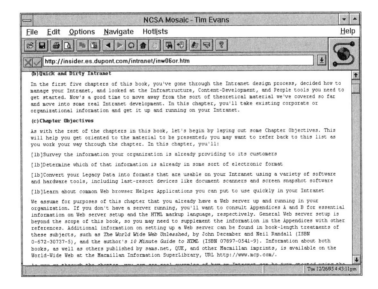

Figure 6.9. *Portion of Chapter 6 of* Building an Intranet *in HTML format.*

Adding the Screenshots

Let's finish constructing this part of your Intranet by inserting image files. Let's continue with the dummy *Building an Intranet* Web server by adding some of the screenshots you see in the book.

Macmillan Computer Publishing requires all screenshots to be submitted in PC Paintbrush (.pcx) format. Unfortunately, most Web browsers don't support direct viewing of .pcx files without a helper application. While helper application setup is quite simple in most browsers, and viewers for PCX files are widely available, there's little reason to require all your customers to change their browser setup. It's a better idea to convert the existing .pcx images into a format all Web browsers can read directly, such as .gif (Graphic Interchange Format) or .jpeg (Joint Photographic Experts Group).

In Chapter 4, you'll find a list of graphics conversion packages for PCs and UNIX systems. Because this book strongly recommends using a UNIX system for your Intranet's main Web server, let's focus on ImageMagick's convert utility, available on the *Building an Intranet* CD-ROM. See the introduction to Cristy's ImageMagick in Chapter 4 for more information about it. convert supports a long list of image formats and will take an image file in any one of them and convert it to one in any other one.

Table 6.1. The list of image formats supported by convert, with the customary filename extensions.

Filename Ext	File Type
AVS	AVS X image file.
BMP	Microsoft Windows bitmap image file.
CMYK	Raw cyan, magenta, yellow, and black bytes.
EPS	Adobe Encapsulated PostScript file.
EPSF	Adobe Encapsulated PostScript file.
EPSI	Adobe Encapsulated PostScript Interchange format.
FAX	Group 3 Facsimile.
FITS	Flexible Image Transport System.
GIF	CompuServe Graphics image file.
GIF87	CompuServe Graphics image file (version 87a).
GRAY	Raw gray bytes.
HDF	Hierarchical Data Format.
HISTOGRAM	Image color historgram.
HTML	HyperText Markup Language.
JBIG	Joint Bi-level Image experts Group format.
JPEG	Joint Photographic Experts Group format.
MAP	Colormap intensities and indices.

Filename Ext	File Type
MATTE	Raw matte bytes.
MIFF	Magick image file format.
MPEG	Motion Picture Experts Group file interchange format.
MTV	Ray-Tracing format.
NULL	NULL image.
PCD	Photo CD.
PCX	ZSoft IBM PC Paintbrush file.
PDF	Portable Document Format.
PICT	Apple Macintosh QuickDraw/PICT file.
PNG	Portable Network Graphics.
PNM	Portable bitmap.
PS	Adobe PostScript file.
PS2	Adobe Level II PostScript file.
RAD	Radiance image file.
RGB	Raw red, green, and blue bytes.
RGBA	Raw red, green, blue, and matte bytes.
RLE	Utah Run length encoded image file; read-only.
SGI	Irix RGB image file.
SUN	SUN Rasterfile.
TEXT	Raw text file; read only.
TGA	Truevision Targa image file.
TIFF	Tagged Image File Format.
UYVY	16bit/pixel interleaved YUV.
TILE	Tile image with a texture.
VICAR	Read only.
VID	Visual Image Directory.
VIFF	Khoros Visualization image file.
X	Select image from X server screen.
XC	Constant image of X server color.
XBM	X11 bitmap file.
XPM	X11 pixmap file.
XWD	X Window System window dump image file.
YUV	CCIR 601 1:1:1 file.
YUV3	CCIR 601 2:1:1 files.

Using `convert` is quite simple. Simply give it an input filename and an output filename (use your desired output filetype's extension, from Table 6.1), right on the UNIX command line. This example converts the existing PC Paintbrush image file `06inw02.pcx` to a Graphics Interchange Format (GIF) file, `06inw02.gif`. As with other UNIX examples in this book, the dollar sign represents the shell prompt.

```
$ convert 06inw02.pcx 06inw02.gif
```

As you might guess from the filenames used here, this graphic file is the screenshot for Figure 6.2 in this chapter you're reading now. Figure 6.10 shows a portion of Chapter 6 from the dummy *Building an Intranet* Web server. Near the middle of the page, a new hyperlink points to Figure 6.2. Here's the bit of HTML code that creates this link:

```
<a href="06inw02.gif">Figure 6.2</a><em>WordPerfect 6.1 Save As
```

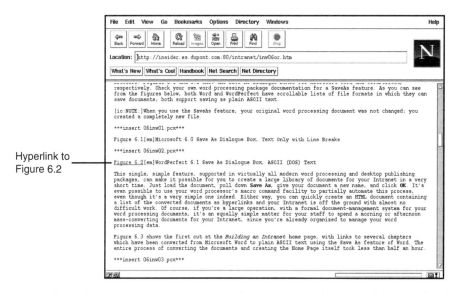

Figure 6.10. *The dummy* Building an Intranet *Web server showing Chapter 6 with an image hyperlink.*

Clicking on that link loads the converted .pcx file (now a .gif), as shown in Figure 6.11.

While this sequence is a bit circular—a screenshot showing another screenshot from this book—the lessons should be clear:

◆ Converting legacy word processing documents from their initial format to HTML is a simple, two-step process using `rtftohtm`.

◆ Adding legacy images in a format not normally supported by Web browsers is equally simple, using simple HTML markup and `convert`.

Figure 6.11. *An image from Chapter 6 displayed in Netscape.*

> **Tip:** convert also can do on-the-fly manipulations of images, including resizing them, annotating them, changing their orientation, and more. For details, see the convert manual page, the HTML pages contained in the ImageMagick distribution on the CD-ROM, or the ImageMagick home page on the Web at `http://www.wizards.dupont.com/cristy/ImageMagick.html`.

Let's take our image-conversion example one step further and add a thumbnail copy of our image to the Chapter 6 HTML document on the dummy *Building an Intranet* Web server. Here, we'll use the ability of convert to resize an image, then insert it directly into the HTML document. First, the image conversion:

```
$ convert -geometry 72x52 06inw02.gif 06inw02t.gif
```

The original image size is 800 by 600 pixels; in this example, it's reduced to thumbnail size, 72 by 52. convert attempts to maintain the aspect ratio when it resizes images, so as to avoid distorting them, so your resulting image may not be exactly the size you specify. Figure 6.12 shows the modified page from Chapter 6 with the thumbnail image embedded.

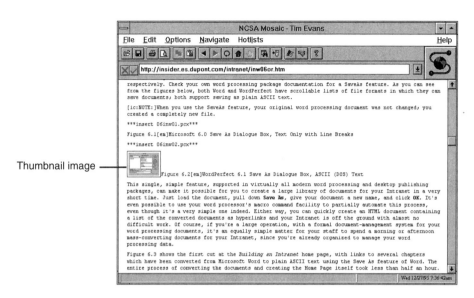

Thumbnail image —

Figure 6.12. *Web page with clickable image.*

> **Note:** The thumbnail image is outlined, indicating that it's part of the hyperlink. The larger image can be loaded by clicking either on the text hyperlink Figure 6.2 or on the image itself.
>
> ```
> <a href="06inw02.gif"><img src="06inw02t.gif">Figure 6.2</a><em>WordPerfect 6.1
> Save As
> ```
>
> As you can see, the code for including the thumbnail image (`<img src="06inw02t.gif">`) was added right into the hyperlink. See Appendix B, "HTML and CGI Quick Reference," for more information on using images in the HyperText Markup Language.

Interactive Image Resizing With Convert

You can resize images interactively with another of ImageMagick's utilities, `display`. Use `display` to show your image from the UNIX shell command line. Adding the ampersand puts the command "in the background," returning your shell prompt for additional commands while that one's running.

```
$ display 06inw02.pcx &
```

When the image appears, click left to bring up the ImageMagick menu. Then click on View, then on Resize from the submenu that appears. A dialog box appears, as shown in Figure 6.13.

You can resize either by absolute horizontal and vertical pixel size or by percentage. For example, you can reduce the image to 50 percent of its original size, or specify a pixel size, such as "800x600."

As with `convert`, unless you specify otherwise, `display` will maintain aspect ratio (that is, the relationship between height and width) for an image. An exclamation point after a size can be used to override the aspect ratio. For instance, 640x480! will resize the image to exactly 640 pixels wide and 480 pixels high, even if the image must be distorted in order to do it.

You can continue to resize your image interactively with `display` until you're satisfied with it. Once you're done, click left again and then click on File, and then Save.

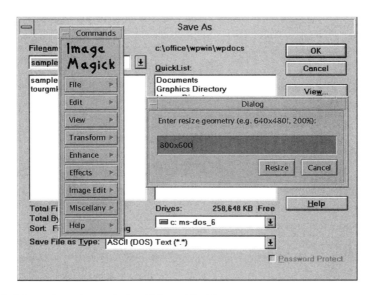

Figure 6.13. *Resizing an image interactively with ImageMagick* `display`.

As you can see from `display`'s menu, there are many other features to this program. These include the capability to manipulate your images in several ways, including rotating them, reversing them, enhancing them, and adding special effects like embossing. You'll want to explore these options as you convert your legacy image data for inclusion in your Intranet. Note in particular there's a shortcut menu, click right to bring up the shortcut menu, where you'll find `display`'s most commonly used functions.

Automating this Whole Process

In this process of converting from the original word processor document format and image format, most of the work can be at least partially automated.

◆ Word processor macro commands can make quick work of saving documents in plain text or RTF format.

◆ UNIX or MS-DOS batch processing can finish the conversion from RTF to HTML format with `rtftohtm`.

◆ Similar use of `convert` in shell loops can mass-convert your legacy images.

As to running `convert` in shell loops, you can do something like this in the UNIX shell to convert a batch of images in one operation:

```
$ for IMAGE in *.pcx
> do convert $IMAGE $IMAGE.gif
> done
```

Here, each file in the current directory with the extension .pcx is converted to a .gif image, and the converted file's name is the same as the original but with .gif tacked onto the end.

The only time-consuming part of this whole process of converting your legacy documents is adding the hyperlinks for your images or links which point to other documents. You need not add these hyperlinks immediately, because your main objective is to get your Intranet up and running quickly. It's easy to come back later to insert hyperlinks. Right now, you have an Intranet that has been populated with an initial set of documents, possibly a very large set of them, with very little work on your part.

WordPerfect Conversions

While you can use the just-described procedures to save your WordPerfect documents in plain text or in RTF for use on your Intranet, you'll also want to know about direct conversions from WordPerfect to HTML. WordPerfect has an HTML utility called Internet Publisher, which is described in Chapter 4. Like Word's Internet Assistant, it enables you to convert documents to HTML, but it is considerably less capable than Internet Assistant. It is quite good at creating new HTML documents, with a whole set of HTML-related items on a re-engineered toolbar, but using it to convert an existing WordPerfect document to HTML is quite clumsy, and, on the whole, unsatisfactory unless your documents are very simple ones. Internet Publisher supports only WordPerfect 6.1.

Novell (the owner of WordPerfect) has chosen not to add a Save As HTML function in Internet Publisher, comparable to Word's Save As function. Instead, you must use a somewhat lengthy procedure to convert a WordPerfect document to HTML:

1. Create a new, empty document, selecting HTML as the format;
2. Open your existing WordPerfect format document in a separate window;
3. Copy and paste from the original document into the HTML document;
4. Save the new document as a WordPerfect format file; and
5. Export the new document as an HTML file by clicking on an HTML item on the toolbar.

Even after all those steps, you lose all your WordPerfect formatting except for your paragraph breaks. Special character attributes like **boldface**, *italics*, and underline are gone. You're left with a pretty much raw HTML document, which you then must reformat using the Internet Publisher HTML toolbar. The HTML toolbar contains controls for creating headlines, typeface selections (for example, boldface), and the like.

Figure 6.14 shows a raw HTML document in Internet Publisher after conversion from WordPerfect format. As you can see, there is no formatting of any kind, except for preservation of paragraph breaks. To format a headline, for instance, highlight the target text, then click the H button on the toolbar. The Select a Heading Type dialog box shown in Figure 6.15 appears. Select the heading type you want, then click OK. Figure 6.16 shows the result, choosing Major Heading (H2) (the name WordPerfect uses for the Level-2 headline in HTML) for a headline. You can add the rest of the HTML markup using pretty much the same procedure of selecting and highlighting text, then clicking one of the toolbar buttons to make the change.

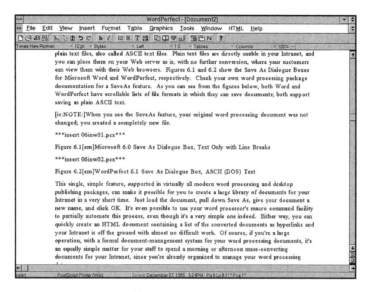

Figure 6.14. *A raw HTML document produced by Internet Publisher.*

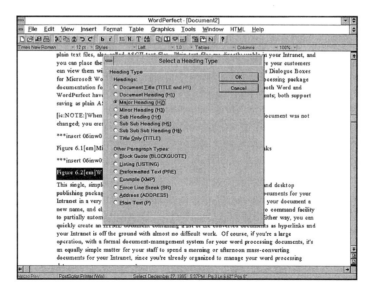

Figure 6.15. *Internet Publisher's Select a Heading Type dialog box.*

Figure 6.16. *Headline formatted with Internet Publisher.*

As noted, Internet Publisher works fine when you're creating new HTML documents, because you have to do all the formatting anyway. But if you have an existing WordPerfect document that's already formatted, you may want to consider a different route to conversion, because virtually all the formatting is lost in converting to HTML.

As with Microsoft Word's Save As feature, you'll probably find that saving the original WordPerfect document to RTF and converting it with `rtftohtm` is both easier and more effective at preserving WordPerfect formatting.

> **Note:** You may be able to run Internet Publisher under SunSoft's Wabi (Windows Application Binary Interface). This program emulates Microsoft Windows on IBM RISC System 6000 and Hewlett-Packard UNIX systems, and on Sun Sparc and x86 systems running Solaris 2.x. Check with your system salesperson or with SunSoft for information on Wabi. Insignia Solutions' product SoftWindows is an alternative to Wabi. This product also allows Windows applications like WordPerfect and Internet Publisher to run on UNIX systems from Digital, HP, IBM, Motorola, Silicon Graphics, and Sun.

You'll find the C-language source code for an alternative WordPerfect conversion tool, `wp2x`, on the *Building an Intranet* CD-ROM. `wp2x` can convert WordPerfect 5.1 files to HTML, as well as into a short list of other formats, including TeX, LaTeX, troff, and others. You'll need a C compiler to build `wp2x`, but it may be your only alternative to `rtftohtml` on UNIX systems with WordPerfect Version 5.1, since Internet Publisher is not available for UNIX systems (except those using Wabi or SoftWindows). You can find more information about `wp2x` at its home page on the Web, `http://www.milkyway.com/People/Michael_Richardson/wp2x.html`. The version of `wp2x` provided on the

CD does not support WordPerfect Version 4.2, but an earlier version of wp2x may still be available; send e-mail to Raymond Chen, rjc@math.princeton.edu.

Other Legacy Data Conversions

Besides your word processing documents, you no doubt have other kinds of information stored in electronic format. Let's look at how some of this legacy data can be converted for your Intranet, focusing on spreadsheet datafiles first.

Spreadsheet Data Files

You'll learn in Chapter 11 how to create a data warehouse on your Intranet with live spreadsheet data files. Since you're in a hurry to get your Intranet off the ground, though, let's get some static information from your legacy spreadsheet files up and accessible. As with your word processor, your spreadsheet probably has a Save As command that enables you to save data in plain text format.

Both Microsoft Excel and Lotus 1-2-3 have such features, as shown in Figures 6.17 and 6.18, respectively. Both use the default filename extension .txt for converted files. As with the word processing files, you should accept this default, since the text/plain MIME data type/sub-type is directly supported by all Web servers and browsers. (Refer to Chapter 7 for information about MIME data types/sub-types.) If you're using another spreadsheet package, check its documentation for a plain text save feature. Such files are directly usable in your Intranet, so any tabular data you have in your legacy spreadsheet files can be made available on your Intranet as quickly and easily as your word processing files.

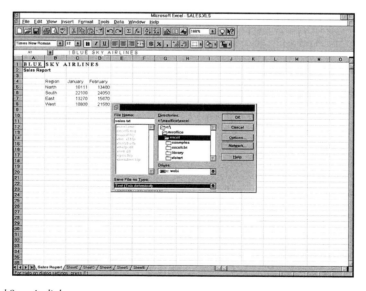

Figure 6.17. *Excel Save As dialog.*

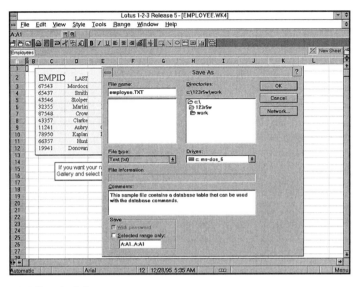

Figure 6.18. *Lotus 1-2-3 Save As dialog.*

Miscellaneous Legacy Data Conversions

Most relational database packages have one means or another of saving tables of data to text files you can use on your Intranet. For example, Microsoft Access has an Output To function, as shown in Figure 6.19, which can save database tables not only to plain text but also to RTF. The latter capability is interesting in that you can run the resulting RTF file through rtftohtm to convert your data to HTML. Other database packages have the same or a similar feature, although you may need to design a simple database report and direct its output to a plain text file to get what you want. As a result, you can export data from almost any database application for viewing in your Intranet, again with relatively minimal effort.

If you have legacy data in other formats, you'll want to check out some of the filters and converters listed by the W³ Consortium at http://www.w3.org/pub/WWW/Tools/. Several of these are included on the *Building an Intranet* CD-ROM, including

◆ **TeX2HTML** and **LaTeX2HTML**, for converting TeX and LaTeX data files. These are typesetting languages used primarily by mathematicians and scientists who need strong formatting capabilities for complex equations and figures. LaTeX2HTML turns equations, for example, into small GIF images and inserts markup code in output documents to embed them in the right place.

◆ **infothtml**, for converting TeXInfo files. TeXInfo is used by the Free Software Foundation's GNU Project for all its documentation. If you use *gcc, emacs,* or any of the other GNU packages, or have written your own documentation in TeXInfo, you'll find this worthwhile.

◆ **mma2html** converts Mathematica Notebooks to HTML. (Mathematica is an expensive commercial mathematics software package, though, as with TeX, some think of it as a religion.)

◆ **Frame2html** and **MifMucker**, for converting FrameMaker desktop publishing documents to HTML. (FrameMaker has plain text and PostScript Save As features built-in, and the recently released Version 5 of the package supports HTML creation/conversion directly.)

◆ **troff2html**, **ms2html**, and **me2html**, all based on the UNIX roff family of typesetting markup languages, convert their respective formats to HTML. If you've written traditional UNIX man pages or other documents using nroff or troff markup, you can convert them with these.

Check out `http://www.w3.org/pub/WWW/Tools/` for a much longer list of available filters and converters that you can use to turn almost any existing data file into HTML.

Figure 6.19. *The Microsoft Access Output To dialog box.*

PostScript and Adobe Portable Document Format (PDF) Legacy Data

Although it's likely you'll prefer to retain the special formatting of PostScript and Adobe PDF documents and use helper applications to view them on your Intranet, it's still possible to convert these documents to plain text using ghostscript. This package, on the *Building an Intranet* CD-ROM, is usually used for *viewing* such documents, but it also includes scripts to convert PostScript to plain ASCII text. In addition, the ImageMagick `convert` package (discussed above in connection with image conversions) supports both PostScript <-> PDF and PostScript/PDF <->

graphical image conversions, using ghostscript as a back end. Here's a short UNIX shell program using ghostscript (author unknown) which converts a PostScript document directly to plain text:

```
#!/bin/sh -f
# Extract ASCII text from a PostScript file.  Usage:
# ps2ascii [infile.ps [outfile.txt]]
# If outfile is omitted, output goes to stdout.
# If both infile and outfile are omitted, ps2ascii acts as a filter,
# reading from stdin and writing on stdout.
if ( test $# -eq 0 ) then
    gs -q -dNODISPLAY -dNOBIND -dWRITESYSTEMDICT -dSIMPLE gs_2asc.ps - quit.ps
elif ( test $# -eq 1 ) then
    gs -q -dNODISPLAY -dNOBIND -dWRITESYSTEMDICT -dSIMPLE gs_2asc.ps $1 quit.ps
else
    gs -q -dNODISPLAY -dNOBIND -dWRITESYSTEMDICT -dSIMPLE gs_2asc.ps $1 quit.ps >$2
fi
```

While you may or may not have a lot of PostScript files lying around that you want to convert, don't dismiss this section as irrelevant to your Intranet. In most applications, you can direct the output of graphical data to PostScript disk files. For example, Figure 6.20 shows how the simple graphing package xgraph enables you to output the graph it generates to a PostScript file.

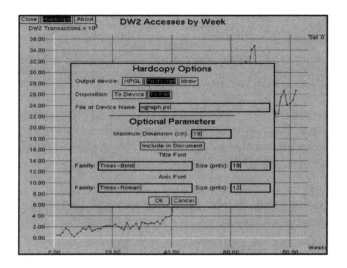

Figure 6.20. *xgraph outputs to a PostScript disk file.*

You can then use convert to create .gif or .jpeg image files from the PostScript, like this:

```
$ convert -geometry 800x600 xgraph.ps xgraph.gif
```

Here, you've taken your PostScript file and turned it into a .gif, with a size of 800x600 pixels.

Screen Snapshots and Scanning

Even if you can't save graphical onscreen data to PostScript disk files, you can take screen snapshots and use them on your Intranet. For example, the ImageMagick package contains import, a program that takes screenshots. Using `import`, you can reduce the above `xgraph` sequence to just two steps. Just call up `xgraph` to display your data points, then use `import` to take a picture of the display:

```
$ xgraph xgraph.dat &
$ import -geometry 800x600 xgraph.gif
```

After you enter the `import` command, your mouse cursor turns into a cross. Just move the cursor/ cross anywhere in the image and click left. `Import` beeps once, then twice; when your shell prompt returns, your screenshot is complete, ready to pop onto your Intranet for viewing by your customers.

Many of the screenshots in this book were taken with `import` on a UNIX system, while others were taken on a PC with a commercial package, Collage Complete. In many cases, the Collage screenshots were manipulated with ImageMagick's `convert`, primarily to resize them. You can also take screen snapshots on Sun systems with Snapshot Tool, a graphical package. Figure 6.21 shows the main Snapshot Tool window on a Solaris 2.4 system. Snapshot Tool is limited, however, in that it can only save in Sun raster format (although it can load and display GIF images). If you use Snapshot Tool, you'll no doubt want to supplement it with ImageMagick `convert` so you can get your raster format screenshots into a format usable on your Intranet.

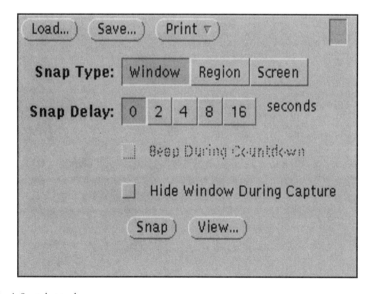

Figure 6.21. *Sun's Snapshot tool.*

`convert` also understands the newer Adobe Portable Document Format (.pdf). Although you'd normally use Adobe Acrobat as a Web browser helper application to view PDF files directly, your objective in this chapter is to get your Intranet up and running quickly. If you have PDF files, ImageMagick can quickly convert them into .gif images.

Scanning

As a final resort, you can use a scanner to make your legacy data available on your Intranet. For the most part, anything you can take a photocopy of can be fed into a scanner and turned into an image you can use on your Intranet. Figure 6.22 shows Apunix's OpenScan software running on a Sun Solaris 2.5 system, with an ordinary magazine cover scanned in. Other scanner software is available for PCs and Macintosh computers, as well as for UNIX systems. Most of them allow you to manipulate the item to be scanned—for instance, crop, rotate, or magnify it.

Be sure to note the file formats supported by your scanner software. Many scanner packages, for instance, support the .tiff image format, which generates extremely large data files. You'll want to save your scanned information in .gif or .jpeg image format if possible, since these formats are directly supported in most Web browsers. Otherwise, you'll need to use ImageMagick convert, some other image-conversion package (see the list of these in Chapter 4), or an alternative image viewer as a Web browser helper application.

Figure 6.22. OpenScan Scanner Software.

Helper Applications for Your Customers

You may remember helper applications from Chapter 3, "Tools for Implementing an Intranet Infrastructure." They're computer programs to which your Web browser can pass data that it cannot display directly by itself. This sort of data typically includes audio or video, but, as you'll learn in Chapter 7, "MIME and Helper Applications," almost anything can be supported by the correct helper application.

Because it's possible that you may have legacy data in video or audio format, or in image formats not directly supported by Web browsers, you'll want to provide your users with some basic helper applications. (We'll tell you in Chapter 8 how to set up a means of distributing helper applications and other software/data on your Intranet.) Check the list of Web URLs in Chapter 3 for common helper applications. Here's the minimum you'll want to obtain for your customers:

◆ For your PC/Windows users—the Adobe Acrobat Reader, Ghostscript, Lview Pro, Mpegplay, QuickTime, and Wplany.

◆ For your Macintosh users—the Adobe Acrobat Reader, Fast Player for QuickTime movies, Sound Machine audio player, and Sparkle movie player.

◆ For your UNIX users—the Adobe Acrobat Reader, X Play Gizmo, mpegplay, and ghostscript/ghostview. ImageMagick's `display` utility can also be used as a helper application.

Except for the Acrobat Reader, all these package are either freeware or shareware, and are on the *Building an Intranet* CD-ROM.

Adobe Acrobat Reader is a free, read-only application which can display PDF documents; you can't use it to create documents. You can retrieve the Acrobat Reader directly from Adobe's Web site at `http://www.adobe.com/Software/Acrobat`, where versions are available for Windows PCs, for the Macintosh, and for Sun Sparc (SunOS 4.1.x and Solaris 2.x), Hewlett-Packard, and Silicon Graphics UNIX systems. You'll also find a version for MS-DOS, which may be useful for users running the low-end doslynx Web browser package. See Chapter 3 for information about doslynx.

> **Note:** If you have full-capability Adobe Acrobat software, you'll want to look at Adobe's free Acrobat Plug-Ins, available at `http://www.adobe.com/Software/Acrobat`. Here you'll find, among several others, WebLink, which allows Acrobat Exchange users to insert live World Wide Web hyperlinks in PDF documents. When viewing or editing these PDF files, clicking on an inserted hyperlink will fire up Netscape or NCSA Mosaic to retrieve the link. WebLink is available only for Windows PCs and the Macintosh.

Helper application setup is a subject to be covered in a great deal of detail in Chapter 7 and others. Nonetheless, let's take a quick look at it here, using both Netscape and NCSA Mosaic on a Windows PC as examples. We'll set up the mpegplay package for viewing MPEG video files. These quick instructions assume you've already installed mpegplay on your PC.

Netscape is already partially set up for MPEG videos. Open the Options Menu, select Preferences, and then click the Helpers tab (as shown in Figure 6.23). You can fill yours in by copying the information from Figure 6.23.

1. Use the scroll bar in the main window to locate the entry for video/mpeg. (It's shown highlighted in the Figure 6.23.)

2. Click the Launch the Application option button.

3. Click the Browse button and locate the mpegplay program on your disk.

4. Click OK to save the change.

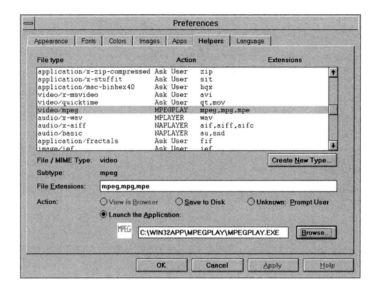

Figure 6.23. *The Netscape Helpers Preferences dialog box.*

You're now set up so that Netscape will call mpegplay as a helper application whenever it encounters a file with the .mpeg extension. (Netscape will assume from the filename extension that it's video data in the MPEG format; it's therefore important to use correct filenaming.) Setting up NCSA Mosaic to use mpegplay is much the same, although there's one extra step.

In Mosaic, open the Options menu, select Preferences, then click the Viewers tab. This brings up the Preferences dialog box shown in Figure 6.24. Click on the down arrow to open a scrollable list; you'll see there's no pre-set entry for .mpeg videos, so you'll need to add one. Here's how:

1. Click Add. This brings up a new dialog box, shown in Figure 6.25.

2. Fill in the boxes on your screen using the information shown in Figure 6.25. Be sure to include the filename extensions in the third box.

3. Click Browse to locate the mpegplay application program on your system.

4. Click Add, which returns you to the screen shown in Figure 6.24, and then click OK to commit the change.

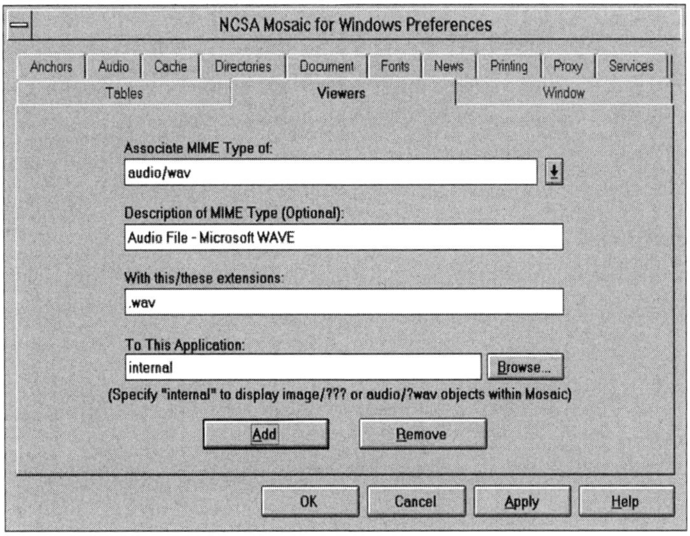

Figure 6.24. The NCSA Mosaic Viewers tab in the Preferences dialog box.

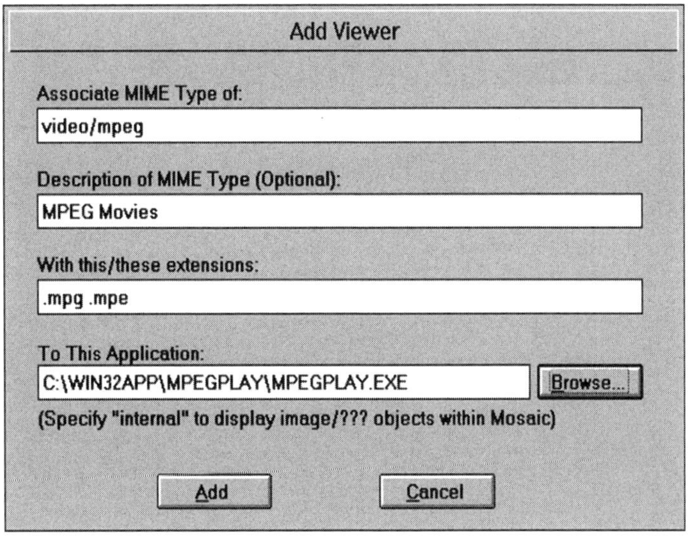

Figure 6.25. The NCSA Mosaic Add Viewer dialog box.

You're now set up so that Mosaic will call mpegplay as a helper application whenever it encounters a file with the .mpeg extension (Mosaic will assume from the filename extension that it's video data in the MPEG format; it's therefore important to use correct filenaming). You'll learn a good deal more about helper applications and their setup in later chapters.

Summary

This chapter has focused on helping you get your Intranet up and running using legacy data you already have on hand. The main benefit of this approach, which will be extended in later chapters, is to get your Intranet online as quickly as possible. As you've seen from this relatively short chapter, it's easily done using just a few tools off the *Building an Intranet* CD-ROM and your existing data of many types. We've covered how you can:

◆ Evaluate the information your organization is already providing for possible inclusion on your Intranet.

◆ Focus on that information which is in electronic format.

◆ Convert your legacy data so it can be immediately usable on your Intranet.

◆ Configure common Web browser helper applications for viewing your data.

Chapter 7, "MIME and Helper Applications," delves quite deeply into important details you will need to add value to your Intranet, including some basic information about how helper applications work. This information will help you extend the helper application paradigm in new directions for your Intranet's customers.

II
PART

Getting Set Up

CHAPTER

7

♦

MIME and Helper Applications

In the first six chapters of *Building an Intranet*, you've developed the plan for your Intranet, organized its structure, assigned responsibility for its development and maintenance, reviewed the hardware and software you need to implement it, and gotten your customers involved in its planning. In Chapter 6, "Quick and Dirty Intranet," you did a rudimentary setup of your Intranet using existing company information and some quick-and-dirty document conversion tools.

This chapter assumes you already have a Web server up and running, at least in the minimal sense described in Appendix A, "Setting Up a Web Server." If this is not the case, you'll probably want to get your server up, so you can see and manipulate the sample Web server and browser configuration files provided here for yourself.

We'll now turn to some fundamentals for your Intranet. There's some tedious information in this chapter and you'll probably wonder what some of it has to do with your Intranet. In subsequent chapters, you'll use these building blocks to help your customers access specific information in their everyday work.

The information on configuring a Web server that comes with the server software, and which is summarized in Appendix A, is fairly cryptic. The documentation discusses several configuration files, but it doesn't pay much attention to the one which is most important to the purpose of this book: the mime.types file. This file—its contents, its meaning in Web technology, and how you can use it to set up your Intranet—is central to this book. As a result, a full chapter is devoted to it here.

Chapter Objectives

In this chapter, which forms the very heart of this book, you will learn

- ◆ What Web helper applications are.
- ◆ What MIME (Multi-Purpose Internet Mail Extensions) is, and where it came from.
- ◆ How the developers of the World Wide Web adopted MIME as a critical part of Web technology.
- ◆ How Web servers and browsers use MIME information to identify and process data.
- ◆ The relationship between MIME and Web browser helper applications.
- ◆ How MIME and the CGI mechanism work together.

Web Helper Applications

Web browsers like Netscape and Mosaic are amazing packages. They not only enable you to search the World Wide Web for interesting and useful information, documents, images, and other data, but they also provide a friendly interface for older Internet services such as ftp and Gopher. These browsers can display not only plain text and HTML text (and HTML hyperlinks), but also several common types of image files, even without any helper applications.

But even these amazing programs have their limits. People use a mind-boggling array of different formats to store their data on computers, and new formats are being invented all the time. Your Web browser can't possibly handle all the existing kinds of data, let alone the new formats just being invented. That's where helper applications come in.

The pioneering developers of Web technology, scientists at CERN, the European Particle Physics Lab, were concerned with developing some means of integrating various kinds of data into a single, user-friendly interface. Fortunately, the folks at CERN made a critical choice toward this end early in their work—to allow for a Web browser to call other computer programs to handle data that it can't handle itself. You probably know these other programs as *helper applications*, though some people call them *external viewers*. Whatever they're called (the term helper application is used in this book), the decision to enable Web browsers to hand off data to a different, outside program was sheer genius.

You've probably already set up your browser to use helper applications for viewing Web video or listening to Web sounds. What you may not realize is that the mechanism for handing off data to helper applications is a standardized one, and you can use it for almost anything you can imagine. Helper applications aren't just for viewing video clips. Here are a few examples:

- ◆ Your everyday word processor can function as a helper application, enabling you to distribute boilerplate documents with your Web server.

- ◆ Your spreadsheet program can be set up as well, enabling your customers to download live data and then manipulate it.

- ◆ You can use a your presentation graphics package as a helper application, opening up computer-based training possibilities for your customers.

We'll come back to the specifics of setting up helper applications later in this chapter. First, though, you need to understand this mechanism by which Web browsers pass off data they can't handle internally to external programs. This may seem a lengthy digression from your Intranet, but understanding it is critical to your success. As a first step, you'll need to become acquainted with MIME.

Multi-Purpose Internet Mail Extensions (MIME)

The original Web developers at CERN decided on a single interface for a variety of data types. Rather than re-inventing the wheel toward this end, the developers implemented this decision by adopting an existing mechanism called Multi-Purpose Internet Mail Extensions, or MIME.

As the name implies, MIME hails from the world of Internet electronic mail, or data file. E-mail is one of the oldest Internet services, predating the World Wide Web by many years. E-mail is still one of the most popular Internet services and, next to the Web, is often given as the reason organizations and people want Internet access. Despite its popularity, though, Internet e-mail has been limited by the requirement that only plain ASCII text can be used in messages. This means that non-text files, such as applications, data files that include formatting (like word processor files), and other binary files can't be e-mailed as-is. It also means that even simple non-ASCII characters, such as non-English characters used in many languages around the world, won't pass e-mail muster.

As is often the case with computers and the Internet, there are means by which you can work around this limitation to get a binary data file from one place to another intact. For example, the file transfer protocol (ftp) can be used to transfer any kind of file from one computer to another over the Internet. Also, if you've used Internet e-mail to send data files very much, particularly on UNIX systems, you may know about the uuencode and uudecode programs. uuencode converts a binary file into a specially encoded ASCII text file so it can be send via e-mail. Its companion utility, uudecode, converts the encoded file back into its original format on the recipient's end.

> **Note:** The UNIX uuencode and uudecode utilities are relatively easy to use. Encoding a data file and mailing it is a two-step process. These examples are UNIX commands, issued from your shell prompt (signified by the dollar sign).
>
> ```
> $ uuencode mydatafile mydatafile > tmpfile
> $ mail username@system.name < tmpfile
> ```

In this example, the file `mydatafile` is uuencoded, with its filename included in the encoded file (hence the double use of the filename in the first command), and output into the temporary file `tmpfile`. The second command data e-mails the contents of the temporary (encoded) file to the recipient.

The recipient must reverse the process, first saving the incoming message to a temporary file, and then decoding it with this command:

```
$ uudecode tmpfile
```

`uudecode` restores the file to its original data format, naming it, in this case, `mydatafile`. Some mail programs allow shortcut of this save-and-decode process by allowing you to pass off messages to system commands. For example, the widely-used freeware UNIX mailer `elm` has a "pipe-to" feature which enables you to uudecode an encoded message without exiting from elm.

Neither of these workarounds is really convenient, though. Both require not only extra steps, but also a certain amount of skill and knowledge on the part of both the sender and receiver of the message—skill and knowledge that the casual e-mail user may not have. Sophisticated, user-friendly e-mail tools have developed in the past few years, and most have point-and-click features for attaching any kind of data file to a message. These tools are easy to use, and work well for exchanging non-text data, provided both sender and recipient are using the very same package.

Unfortunately, users of different proprietary-format e-mail programs—a cc:Mail user and a Microsoft Mail user, for instance—can't easily exchange data files via e-mail. Both cc:Mail and Microsoft Mail use a proprietary message format. Although there are gateway packages for both, they are expensive and don't always work well. Graphical e-mail tools for UNIX users, such as Sun's `mailtool`, also use a proprietary mechanism. `mailtool` users can easily attach data files to e-mail messages, and things work great as long as the addressee of the message is also using `mailtool`; if not, the recipient may be able to read the message only with great difficulty—if at all.

While Lotus (manufacturer of cc:Mail) and Microsoft would have you believe that the solution to these incompatibility problems lies in your buying *their* package for every user, or buying an expensive piece of e-mail gateway software and dedicating hardware on which to run it, these solutions are inadequate in the context of the Internet. These vendors may wish they could sell their packages to every one of the millions of Internet e-mail users, but this is unlikely. If you need to send Internet e-mail, sooner or later, you'll find that your fancy mailer's file attachment feature breaks down, most likely, just when you need it most.

Enter MIME

In 1991, Nathaniel S. Borenstein of Bellcore proposed major extensions to Internet electronic mail standards. Called Multi-Purpose Internet Mail Extensions, or MIME, Borenstein's proposal extended the existing Simple Mail Transport Protocol (SMTP) standards to offer a "standardized way to represent and encode a wide variety of media types, including textual data in non-ASCII character sets, for transmission via Internet mail."

The MIME proposal, which was issued as Internet Requests for Comments (RFC) 1522 and 1523, amended earlier RFCs which defined the Simple Mail Transport Protocol (primarily RFC 822), to allow the attachment of virtually any kind of data file to an Internet e-mail message using a simple mechanism.

Note: The Internet has a long history of development-through-consensus. The TCP/IP networking protocols, developed at first with U.S. Government (Department of Defense) support, were worked out through give-and-take revolving around publicly-proposed standards called Internet Requests for Comments. Developers issued proposed standards for the nuts-and-bolts of the Internet, calling for comment from the then-small Internet community. Coordinated by the Internet Engineering Task Force (IETF), a process for building consensus for developing standards grew up, with feedback on RFCs eventually incorporated into the final standards the IETF issued. To date, more than 2,000 Internet RFCs have been issued. Many of them have made their way into final standards, guaranteeing that different vendors' TCP/IP networking applications can interoperate. (The complete set of Internet RFCs can be found at `http://www.internic.net/ds/dspg0intdoc.html`.)

Thus, RFC 822 defined the Simple Mail Transport Protocol. Anyone who wants to develop an Internet e-mail program to sell or give away can follow the requirements of RFC 822 to ensure the package works with all other RFC 822-compliant data file packages.

Under the terms of RFC 822, an Internet data file message has two parts:

◆ A header, often likened to the envelope in which you mail a letter at the post office, which contains addressing and postmark information.

◆ A body, like the information inside the envelope, which contains the actual text of the message.

Figure 7.1 is a typical data file message, with the two parts marked.

```
From tkevans Wed Aug 16 15:20:50 1996
Subject: Test Message
To: ben@foo.com
Date: Wed, 16 Aug 1995 15:20:50 -0400 (EDT)
Phone: (302) 234-9151; (302) 695-9353
Reply-To: tkevans@dupont.com
X-Mailer: ELM [version 2.5 PL0a6]
MIME-Version: 1.0
Content-Type: text/plain; charset=US-ASCII
Content-Transfer-Encoding: 7bit
Content-Length: 68

This is a test message. Please try to reply. Thanks.
```

Figure 7.1. A typical data file message with headers.

As you can see, this one-line message consists of two separate (and unequal) parts: (1) the header information and, separated by a simple blank line, (2) the body of the message, in this case just the single line beginning This is a test.... RFC 822 dictates this basic form for all Internet e-mail—a simple division of the message into two parts, separated by a blank line. (This is a gross oversimplification of the requirements; RFC 822 itself goes on for 47 pages with details about headers.)

This division of e-mail messages into a header section and a body section is critical to MIME and, as you will see later in this chapter, it is also important in World Wide Web services. Consequently, this will be important to you in setting up your Intranet. Take a look at the headers in the example message above. Note first they all have the same general format:

◆ A header name (From, To, Date, etc.), followed by a colon and a single blank space. (Multiword header names, such as Reply-To, are hyphenated.)

◆ The header content, such as the addressee's e-mail address, time, and sender's e-mail address.

Some of the headers shown are required by RFC 822, while others are optional. The important point is that all follow the same format, with the colon and one (only) blank space separating the header name and contents. You will see additional headers on your own e-mail messages, including what might be termed postmarks of all the Internet hosts which handled your message on its way to you. Even so, all follow this simple format, and the headers section of all e-mail messages, regardless of how many headers there are, is separated from the body by a single blank line.

If you're interested in looking at the headers on your own e-mail messages, many mail programs have a setup command to let you choose whether or not you want to see all the headers on a message. Also, you can view the full content of your mailbox to see all this. On a UNIX system, use the more or pg command to view your mailbox file, usually named /var/spool/mail/yourlogin (or /var/mail/yourlogin). You'll see that each message contains header and body parts.

How MIME Works

As noted, the broad division of Internet data file messages into the header and body sections is always present, with the simple header format just described. Borenstein's MIME proposal, also grossly simplified here, was to extend this basic division by

◆ Adding a new header type, specifying whether a message is a multipart message, with some or no normal text and zero or more attachments, in a specified format.

◆ Enabling the data to be encoded into a special ASCII text format, then attached to the message body, with separating/identifying information.

You can read the details of MIME in two RFCs, numbers 1522 and 1523. In essence, the new header type allows one or more of a set of message content types to be identified and attached to messages. The content types include image, audio, video, application data, and, of course, text. In addition, a special content type allows multiple attachments of differing data types to the same message.

Figure 7.2 shows a short, MIME-compliant data file message.

```
Date: Tue, 31 Oct 1996 12:30:51 -0500
Message-Id: <9510311730.AA03398@enterprise.taratec.com>
X-Sender: gturnbul@enterprise.taratec.com
X-Mailer: Windows Eudora Version 1.4.3
Mime-Version: 1.0
To: tkevans@taratec.com
From: GTurnbull@taratec.com (Geoff Turnbull)
Subject: Christmas Party
Content-Type: text/plain; charset="us-ascii"
Content-Length: 94


Tim,
Saturday December 14, 1996 is the date. Official notice will be given soon.
Geoff
```

Figure 7.2. *A MIME-compliant e-mail message.*

You'll note several MIME headers, including *Mime-Version*, *Content-Type*, and *Content-Length*. You can read about these in detail in the MIME RFCs. The important part to note is that these are just additional headers, following the standard Internet e-mail message format.

MIME-capable mail user agents parse incoming messages for the MIME-extended headers. Based on the content type of the message, and a set of user-configurable rules associating particular content types with application programs (or viewers), the MIME mailer passes attachments off to other application programs on the system which are capable of dealing with them. For example, an incoming MIME-formatted e-mail message may have an audio file attached. The recipient's MIME-compliant mail tool recognizes the sound file attachment from the extended headers in the message and fires off an audio player to play the sound. This is much the same as a Web browser helper application: your Web browser passes off data it cannot handle directly to other application programs on your system which can handle the data.

As you'll see later in this chapter, this mechanism is a part of World Wide Web server and browser technology and is one of the real conceptual centers of this book.

> **Note:** Internet e-mail handling programs are usually divided into two categories. First, users creating, sending, and reading e-mail messages use Mail User Agents (MUAs). Examples of MUAs include not only the traditional character-based program (called `mail` on most UNIX systems) but also freeware mail tools like `elm` and `mh` (mail handler) and graphical packages like Sun's `mailtool`.
>
> Usually, however, a separate program does the work of routing and delivering e-mail. These separate programs are usually referred to as Mail Transport Agents (MTAs). UNIX `sendmail` is the primary MTA used on the Internet. PC MUAs, like Eudora, however, generally have some MTA features built in—at least enough so that the mail you create gets handed off immediately to a mail server for delivery.

Similarly, MIME-compliant MUAs create MIME-formatted messages automatically. Attaching a file is simple for the user—it's usually a point-and-click operation in graphical MUAs, with the encoding handled internally by the program.

Probably the most widely used MIME-compliant MUA is the PC and Macintosh package called Eudora. It's a basic Internet e-mail package with most of the standard MUA features, but it's also MIME-compliant. Both shareware and commercial versions of Eudora are available; the former is on the *Building an Intranet* CD-ROM. On UNIX systems and PCs, the commercial package Z-Mail is MIME-compliant. (Z-Mail is included as a standard part of Silicon Graphics IRIX operating system on SGI machines.)

A group of UNIX vendors is collaborating on the Common Desktop Environment (CDE), which will provide a uniform graphical environment on their systems. CDE provides a graphical, MIME-compliant mail tool. IBM's AIX version 4.1.x and Sun's Solaris 2.5 includes CDE, and TriTeal Corporation sells an enhanced CDE package for several UNIX systems. Nathaniel Borenstein maintains a freely available, command-line oriented package called `metamail` for UNIX systems. The compilable source code for `metamail`, along with a PC executable, is included on the *Building an Intranet* CD ROM.

MIME and the World Wide Web

Let's tie up this discussion of MIME by relating it to the World Wide Web, and to the purpose of this book. You know from using your WWW browser that you can deal with many kinds of data and Internet services. Your Web browser can display images, access Gopher and ftp services, and, when properly equipped with helper applications, play movies or audio that you find on the Web. Since you've set up a Web server of your own, you also know you can make these and other data types available on your server, and you know how to write the HTML to include them in your Web pages. You may not know, however, that it's the very same MIME mechanism just described that makes this all possible.

To see how this works, let's delve more deeply into the details of MIME as it relates to Web servers, browsers, and helper applications in this section. You'll learn:

◆ How Web servers use MIME to distinguish among the types of data they're serving.

◆ How Web servers use MIME to tell Web browser clients what sort of data is being sent in every single transaction.

In the next section, you'll see how Web browsers like Netscape and Mosaic make use of this MIME information.

MIME and Web Servers

Web servers understand MIME information and provide it to Web browsers in every httpd transaction. Let's look at how this works.

MIME Types

As described earlier in this chapter, MIME is able to identify a number of data types (called content types in the MIME discussion earlier) and subtypes. Web server software uses an extensive database of MIME content type information. This database is usually contained in a file named mime.types, although PC Web servers like whttpd are constrained by DOS file-naming conventions, so the file will probably be named mime.typ. Listing 7.1 shows that standard mime.types file distributed with the NCSA httpd server.

Listing 7.1. NCSA-Distributed mime.types file.

```
# This is a comment. I love comments.
application/activemessage
application/andrew-inset
application/applefile
application/atomicmail
application/dca-rft
application/dec-dx
application/mac-binhex40
application/macwriteii
application/msword              doc
application/news-message-id
application/news-transmission
application/octet-stream        bin
application/oda                 oda
application/pdf                 pdf
application/postscript          ai eps ps
application/remote-printing
application/rtf                 rtf
application/slate
application/x-mif               mif
application/wita
application/wordperfect5.1
application/x-csh               csh
application/x-dvi               dvi
application/x-hdf               hdf
application/x-latex             latex
application/x-netcdf            nc cdf
application/x-sh                sh
application/x-tcl               tcl
application/x-tex               tex
application/x-texinfo           texinfo texi
application/x-troff             t tr roff
application/x-troff-man         man
application/x-troff-me          me
application/x-troff-ms          ms
application/x-wais-source       src
application/zip                 zip
application/x-bcpio             bcpio
application/x-cpio              cpio
application/x-gtar              gtar
application/x-shar              shar
application/x-sv4cpio           sv4cpio
application/x-sv4crc            sv4crc
```

continues

Listing 7.1. continued

```
application/x-tar             tar
application/x-ustar           ustar
audio/basic                   au snd
audio/x-aiff                  aif aiff aifc
audio/x-wav                   wav
image/gif                     gif
image/ief                     ief
image/jpeg                    jpeg jpg jpe
image/tiff                    tiff tif
image/x-cmu-raster            ras
image/x-portable-anymap       pnm
image/x-portable-bitmap       pbm
image/x-portable-graymap      pgm
image/x-portable-pixmap       ppm
image/x-rgb                   rgb
image/x-xbitmap               xbm
image/x-xpixmap               xpm
image/x-xwindowdump           xwd
message/external-body
message/news
message/partial
message/rfc822
multipart/alternative
multipart/appledouble
multipart/digest
multipart/mixed
multipart/parallel
text/html                     html htm
text/x-sgml                   sgml sgm
text/plain                    txt
text/richtext       rtx
text/tab-separated-values     tsv
text/x-setext                 etx
video/mpeg                    mpeg mpg mpe
video/quicktime               qt mov
video/x-msvideo               avi
video/x-sgi-movie             movie
```

Anatomy of the `mime.types` File

Let's take a look at the format and syntax of the `mime.types` file. To help you make your way through this, several lines in the example in Listing 7.1 have been **boldfaced**.

The file is a plain, ASCII text file; you can edit it with any text editor on your system, such as `vi` or `emacs`, or with a graphical text editor like Sun's `textedit`. As the first line of the file indicates, you can include comments in the file, using the familiar pound sign (#) notation; anything to the right of a pound sign on a line is ignored by the Web server reading this file. It's pretty obvious the `mime.types` file is laid out in two columns, separated by white space (either spaces or tabs will do).

With that quick view in mind, let's look at the file's format in detail.

Left Column of `mime.types` File

The `mime.types` file's left column is further subdivided into two parts by the forward slash. Let's consider the text to the left of the slash first. You'll recall from the discussion of MIME earlier in the chapter that the proposed MIME standards include a set of data types (content types) that can be attached to e-mail messages. The entries in the left column of the `mime.types` file are, in fact, these very same data types. Looking at just the part of the left column before the slash, you can see seven data types:

◆ application

◆ audio

◆ video

◆ image

◆ message

◆ multipart

◆ text

These seven types are the very same content types proposed in Nathaniel Borenstein's MIME RFCs, and the same types supported by the MIME-compliant e-mail packages listed earlier. Thus, this short list of MIME data types is incorporated into your Web server.

Of course, there are different kinds of data that can fall into these broad categories, so the MIME data types are subdivided into MIME data sub-types. You're no doubt familiar with several kinds of images, for example, including .gif, .jpeg, .xbm, and others. The matter to the right of the slash in the `mime.types` file's left column signifies subtypes of the seven major MIME data types. Thus, you'll see a number of entries for the image data type, one each for the major image subtypes, such as `image/jpeg`. Similarly, you'll see a couple of different video and audio subtypes, including `video/mpeg`.

You're starting to get to the good part now. Perhaps the largest number of subtypes are those of the application data type. As you can see from the `mime.types` file in Listing 7.1, there are a large number of well-known application programs listed. These range from everyday office word processors (like `application/msword`), to standard UNIX utilities like `tar` and `cpio`, to special purpose packages like `TeX` (a specialized text formatting system used for complex scientific and mathematical manuscripts) and `FrameMaker` (a commercial desktop publishing system. MIME provides support for all of these application programs and the mechanism to use them. If you use these, or any of the other applications listed in the `mime.types` file, your Web server knows about them, and, using the information in this book, you'll be able to put them to work as a part of your Intranet.

Right Column of `mime.types`

Now let's look at the right column of the file. Notice first not every entry has something in the right column. That's okay; nothing is required until you need to use a particular application type, at which point you can customize your `mime.types` file as needed. You'll learn how later.

The MIME mechanism associates filename extensions (in other words, the part of a filename which follows the last period in the filename) with data types/sub-types. (UNIX systems—and now Windows 95—allow filenames to contain more than one period.) The right column of `mime.types` contains filename extensions, to be associated with the MIME data type/sub-type in the left column. For example, the `mime.types` entry for `image/gif` uses the filename extension `gif`, while the `application/postscript` uses several filename extensions, `ai`, `ps`, and `eps`. (Just as you can have zero filename extensions on the right side of `mime.types`, you can have more than one.)

To put this another way, the `mime.types` file helps Web browsers tie filename extensions to specific computer programs. Your Web server knows, from the `mime.types` file, a .doc file is a data file for Microsoft Word, a .ps file is a PostScript document, and an .mpeg file is an MPEG (Motion Picture Experts Group) video movie. This is an important piece of information for your Intranet, because now your Web server can tell your clients (that is, Netscape, Mosaic, or another Web browser) what sort of data is coming when your customers click on a hyperlink.

Clients and Servers and MIME Types

Just as Web servers know about MIME types and include the information in every piece of data they send to Web browsers, the Web browsers, too, understand MIME.

Web Servers Say What They're Sending

Web servers always precede anything they send in response to a client request (for example, when you click on a hyperlink) with some preliminary header information. Since we've already discussed MIME headers in the e-mail context, you can probably guess these headers contain MIME data type/subtype information. Specifically, when a Web server responds to a request from a Web browser for a document or other piece of data, the server announces to the browser in one or more headers the type of data it is sending, using the associations in the `mime.types` file. Thus, when you click on a hyperlink pointing to a video file (`volcano.mpeg`, for example) the first bit of information sent back to your browser about the link is its MIME type/subtype, `video/mpeg`. Your browser, then, knows what sort of data is coming in even before it arrives.

Web Browsers Understand MIME Types Too

Your Web browser, whether it's Mosaic, Netscape, Lynx, or some other one, understands MIME and its data types/subtypes. Your browser reads the incoming MIME type header information from the Web server, and decides what to do with the incoming data based on its type. Thus, your

Web browser knows what to do with data of the MIME type text/html (regular Web pages in HTML) or image/gif (a .gif image). It has a built-in ability to properly handle these and other common types of data. That's how you're able to read most documents you find on the Web, and see most images as well.

Your Browser, Helper Applications, and MIME

So far, this is nothing earthshaking. As noted at the beginning of this chapter, though, Web browsers can't possibly handle all kinds of data. You already know about common helper applications. What you might not know is that the MIME information we've been considering is intimately involved here. This is where your helper applications come in. Web browsers use the MIME type header information they get from Web servers—using the very same set of data type/subtype and filename extension —to pass off the data to helper applications. This is how you play Web movies or sound files. And this is how, as you'll learn in later chapters, you can use MIME information to create your own associations between data and your own helper applications for your Intranet.

Here's an imaginary dialog between a Web browser and Web server, written in plain English instead of in the Hypertext Transfer Protocol (HTTP), with its MIME headers, which illustrates what happens:

Browser says (to the server): Click. Send me the data this link points to.

Server says: OK, but first you should know that it is of this MIME data type/subtype. Now, here it comes.

Browser says (to itself): Ohhhh, it's *that* kind of MIME data type/subtype. Let's see, that means I can't display it myself, so I have to send it to a helper application which understands that data type. Let me look at my list. Which one does this MIME data type/subtype? Oh, yeah, this one. I can do that.

Browser says (to the selected helper application): Here, deal with this data.

Using MIME to Set Up Web Helper Applications

This section outlines the process of setting up a Web server and browsers to use helper applications. Let's focus on the general principles used here, and use an imaginary helper application called PluPerStat. We don't really care what this program does or anything about the data it produces/uses, but let's assume a couple of things about it:

◆ PluPerStat has some kind of proprietary data format.

◆ PluPerStat stores its files with the filename extension .plu.

Edit the `mime.types` File on Your Web Server

Your first step in setting up PluPerStat as a helper application for your Intranet is to edit the `mime.types` file on your Web server to add an entry for it. This file, which may be named `mime.typ` on a PC server, usually resides in a subdirectory named `conf` in your main server software directory. (See your server documentation to make sure of the name and location of this file.)

Use any text editor to edit the file. (You'll need super-user, or root, access to your UNIX system.) We'll use the `application` data type, the `x-pluperstat` data subtype, and the `.plu` filename extension, like this (following the `mime.types` convention of preceding nonstandard application data type/subtypes with `x-`, for experimental, since the default `mime.types` file doesn't define it):

```
application/x-pluperstat      plu
```

Just add this line anywhere in the `mime.types` file. You might also want to add a comment describing it, so your entry might look like this:

```
# Support for PluPerStat added 11/2/96; tkevans
application/x-pluperstat      plu
```

Save and close the edited file. Next, restart your Web server software, so it rereads the edited file. On a UNIX system, use the `kill -HUP` command to send a hang-up signal to the httpd process; otherwise, restart the server in whatever way is appropriate for your system.

Set Up the New Helper Application on Your Browser(s)

Before you can use PluPerStat as a helper application, you need to tell your Web browser about it and its MIME data type/sub-type. Different browsers have different mechanisms for adding helper applications. Let's cover NCSA Mosaic and Netscape here, for PCs, Macs, and UNIX systems. If you're using another browser, check your documentation.

Mosaic on PCs and Macs

Here are the steps for setting up NCSA Mosaic Version 2 to use PluPerStat. First, though, a clarification: Mosaic uses the term *external viewer* (sometimes, just *viewer*) rather than *helper application*; both mean the same.

1. Open the Options menu and select Preferences.
2. Click the Viewers Tab. (The Preferences screen looks like a file cabinet drawer, with tabs representing the various Preferences dialog boxes that are available.)
3. Click Add.

There are several boxes to be filled in here, shown in Figure 7.3. Let's take them one at a time.

1. First, in the box labeled Associate MIME Type of, enter the same information you put in your server's `mime.types` file just a moment ago, `application/x-pluperstat`. Don't forget the forward slash between the MIME data type and subtype.

2. The next box is labeled Description of MIME type (Optional). Enter any text here you want, or nothing at all. Nothing is required, but if your application is an obscure one, or one you don't use frequently, you may want to put in a description of PluPerStat here.

3. With this/these extensions is for the filename extension(s) you've associated with PluPerStat, back in the `mime.types` file. In this case, enter `plu` (the leading period isn't required, but will be accepted).

4. Finally, the last box, To This Application, needs the complete folder/directory path to the PluPerStat program on your system, such as `c:\pluper\pluper`. If you don't know exactly where the package is installed, click the Browse button to look for it; once you've located it, select it.

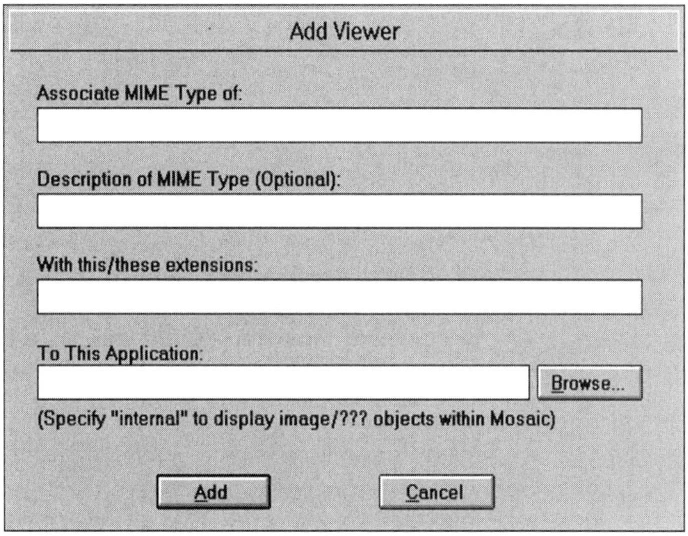

Figure 7.3. *NCSA Mosaic Add Viewer dialog box.*

When you've finished, click Apply, then OK to save the new viewer information and exit the Viewers dialog box. (This last step causes Mosaic to reread the entire Viewer setup, so you're ready to use the change immediately.)

Your PC/Mac Mosaic is now configured to use PluPerStat as a helper application whenever it encounters the MIME type/sub-type `application/x-pluperstat` or the filename extension `.plu`. Figure 7.4 shows the filled-in Viewers tab of the Mosaic Preferences dialog box.

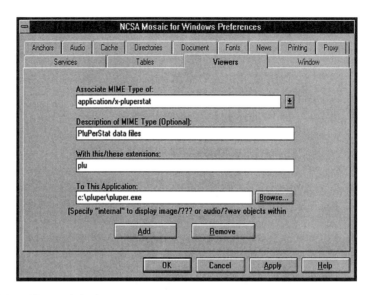

Figure 7.4. The Mosaic Viewers dialog box.

Why Both MIME Type and Filename Extension?

Careful readers will notice the first sentence in the preceding paragraph says "whenever it encounters the MIME type/subtype application/x-pluperstat *or* the filename extension .plu." You may wonder why it's necessary to include both the MIME type/subtype and filename extension. After all, you've learned the Web server includes this information in the MIME data type/subtype headers, so why does Mosaic (or any other Web browser) have to be configured to specify both pieces of information?

While this is indeed redundant information when communicating with a Web server, Web browsers also communicate with other kinds of Internet information servers, such as ftp and Gopher servers. These Internet services predate both the World Wide Web and MIME; they don't know anything about MIME types. Moreover, since they send back only one kind of data, not one of many kinds of data like a Web server, they have no reason to precede the data they send with any identifying header information at all. Since an ftp server, for example, has no way of telling a Web browser what sort of data is coming, Web browsers use a workaround, keying off the filename extension to a MIME data type/subtype. You've no doubt seen your browser display a set of canned icons, representing different file types, when you connect to an ftp or Gopher server. This is your browser's MIME mechanism at work, using the filename extensions it finds and a built-in list of MIME data types/subtypes.

Thus, if you're connected to an ftp server with your Mosaic browser and you click on a link pointing to a file with the .plu extension, Mosaic can make the assumption the file is in fact a PluPerStat data file, because you've configured a helper to do so. There's no guarantee, though, that the .plu file is really a PluPerStat data file. After all, people are free to name files anything they want.

The `mime.types` file contains a semi-official list of MIME types and filename extensions, and Web browsers are built to rely on that list. While you added a new one—`application/x-pluperstat`—to your `mime.types` file, there's no guarantee that other Web or Internet servers won't have used the same filename extension for some other kind of data file. Still, the key point is Web browsers have a built-in list of filename extension/MIME type associations on which to fall back in the absence of any MIME header information coming from the server.

Ftp, Gopher, and other Internet services will be covered in Chapter 8, with detail on how the MIME mechanism works with these services to enable Web browsers to deal with them rationally.

Mosaic on UNIX Systems

Unfortunately, NCSA Mosaic for X Window on UNIX systems doesn't yet have the nice point-and-click Preferences dialog boxes that the PC and Mac versions have, although it's promised in future releases. But you can still set up helper applications, and if you're an experienced UNIX user you can undoubtedly do so in less time than it takes to fill in the blanks on that PC or Mac screen. Here's how.

Helper applications for UNIX Web browsers, including Mosaic, are set up using very simple, plain text files on your system. There are two of them you can create and edit using any text editor. First, in your home directory, you can create your own `mime.types` file, naming it `.mime.types` (note the leading period). Add the same line shown earlier to it, like this:

```
application/x-pluperstat     plu
```

If Mosaic finds a `.mime.types` file (note the leading dot in the filename) in a user's home directory, it'll use that information to determine the MIME data type/subtype of incoming data, ignoring what the server tells it in the MIME headers. Thus, users can use personal `.mime.types` files to override the information in a Web server's own `mime.types` file. You may want to make a copy of the master `mime.types` file from your own Web server, and place it in your home directory under the name `.mime.types`. Doing so gives you all the standard MIME data type/subtypes, but also allows you to override them where necessary. After all, you can't control what headers might come from a Web server somebody else controls, even if it's part of your Intranet. It's probably best, however, for all the Webmasters in your Intranet to use the same master `mime.types` file.

The second of the two files you need to deal with to set up a helper application for UNIX Mosaic is `.mailcap` (again, note the leading period in the filename), also in your home directory. Add the following line to enable PluPerStat as a helper application:

```
application/x-pluperstat;     /path/to/pluperstat %s
```

There are several critical differences between the `.mailcap` and `.mime.types` files:

◆ There is a semicolon at the end of the left column of the `.mailcap` file.

◆ The name of the PluPerStat executable program must be specified. (Unless the executable in your normal search path, you should use the full directory path, as shown.)

◆ There's a third column to the file, with the characters `%s` representing the incoming PluPerStat data file. This is a sort of placeholder for the command, indicating that the temporary filename under which the PluPerStat data file is stored when received by Mosaic will be passed to the PluPerStat executable as a command-line argument. This will be interpreted just the same as if you had typed the command `pluperstat filename.plu` on the command line.

That's it. Save your `.mailcap` file and exit your editor. Your Mosaic is all set up to use PluPerStat as a helper application. If you already had Mosaic running, you need to tell it to reread its setup files. Do so by opening the Options menu and selecting Reload Config Files, as shown in Figure 7.5. Otherwise, the changes you've made will not take effect until you exit Mosaic and start it again.

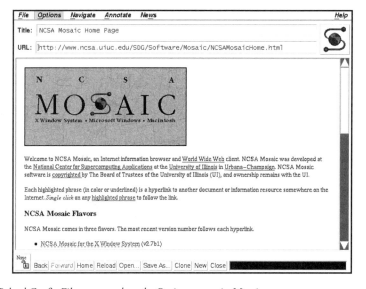

Figure 7.5. The Reload Config Files command on the Options menu in Mosaic.

Tip: A System Administrator can save everyone the time and trouble of creating personal `.mime.types` and `.mailcap` files by creating system-wide versions everyone can use. Like a lot of UNIX programs, Mosaic looks first for system-wide setup files, then looks for versions in user home directories, and resolves any differences in favor of the latter. By default, Mosaic will first look in the directory `/usr/local/lib/mosaic` for files named `mime.types` and `mailcap`. Just copy the `mime.types` file that came with your Web server software distribution to `/usr/local/lib/mosaic/mime.types`.

A semi-official master `mailcap` file, with common MIME data type/subtype application pairs, comes with metamail package, mentioned earlier. Although metamail and its companion programs expect the `mailcap` file to be in the `/etc` directory on your system, you can copy it, or symbolically link it, to the `/usr/local/lib/mosaic/mailcap` file.

While users' own `.mime.types` and `.mailcap` filestake precedence over the system-wide files, users who wish to make changes need not copy the whole system-wide files to their home directory before modifying them. Only those items they want to change need to be put in their own files. Suppose, for example, your System Administrator is on vacation and has not added the PluPerStat entries to the system-wide `mime.types` and `mailcap` files, but you need them immediately for a critical project. Users can create the `.mime.types` and `.mailcap` files in your home directory, with just the single entry in each to support PluPerStat, as the examples above show. Mosaic will now read the system-wide files, and then read your own files and merge the two.

Netscape for PCs and Macs

Netscape on PCs and Macs has a Preferences dialog box, much like the one in Mosaic. Here are the steps:

1. Open the Options menu and select Preferences.

2. Click the Helper Apps tab, and then click Create New Type. The Create New Mime Type dialog box opens, as shown in Figure 7.6.

Figure 7.6. *Mosaic's Configure New Mime Type dialog box.*

3. Enter `application` in the Mime Type box and `pluperstat` in the Mime SubType box, then click OK.

4. The main Helper Applications dialog box reappears. Locate the File Extensions box and enter `plu`.

5. In the lower part of the screen, click the button labeled Launch the Application, then enter the full folder/pathname to the PluPerStat executable program, such as `c:\utils\pluper`. As with Mosaic, you can click Browse to search for the program if you don't know its path.

6. Finally, click OK to finish the setup and have Netscape reread your configuration.

Figure 7.7 shows the finished Netscape Helper Applications dialog box.

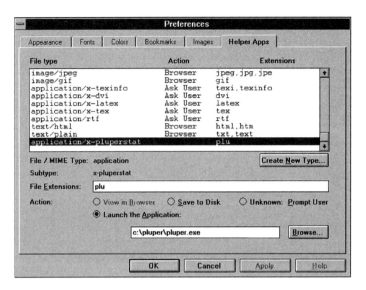

Figure 7.7. *The Netscape Helper Applications dialog box.*

Netscape on UNIX Systems

Netscape for UNIX systems has a Helper Applications Preferences dialog box, but don't get too excited about it—it's mostly an information-only box. It's accessed in the same way as in Windows or Mac Netscape: open the Options menu, then select General Preferences and click the Helpers tab. Figure 7.8 shows the Helpers tab for Netscape Version 2 on an IBM RS/6000 system running AIX 4.1.4.

Figure 7.8 is a somewhat confusing screen, which is made more so by the poor terminology Netscape uses. Netscape distinguishes two pairs of MIME configuration files: Global and Personal, corresponding to the generic system-wide files (mime.types and mailcap in the /usr/local/lib/netscape directory) and user home directory files mentioned earlier, respectively. Within each set is the now-familiar mime.types (Netscape calls it just "Types") and Mailcap (Netscape capitalizes it in this dialog box) files. As you can see, defaults are set (the matter in *italics* will need to be changed to specify your Home Directory):

Global Types:	/usr/local/lib/netscape/mime.types
Personal Types:	*home*/*directory*/.mime.types
Global Mailcap:	/usr/local/lib/netscape/mailcap
Personal Mailcap:	*home*/*directory*/.mailcap

Of course, these are the very same setup files Mosaic uses, which were described earlier. The only difference is the location of the Global (system-wide) files, which are located in /usr/local/lib/netscape instead of /usr/local/lib/mosaic.

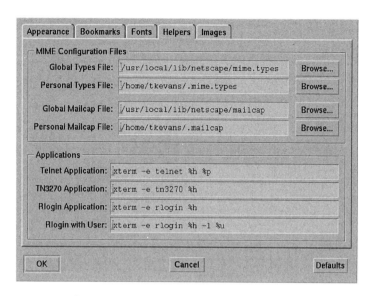

Figure 7.8. *The UNIX Netscape Helper Applications dialog box.*

The Helper Applications dialog box enables users to change the *names* of the Global and/or Personal setup files, but doesn't allow you to make changes to the files themselves. There is little reason to change the names of the Personal files, although users certainly can if they want. The files have to be hand-edited to make changes, just as described earlier for Mosaic. If users on your system use both Mosaic and Netscape, you may want to have them configure Netscape to look for the `mime.types` and `mailcap` file in `/usr/local/lib/mosaic` instead, enabling you to provide just one set of these files for both applications, while not worrying about keeping two sets of files in synch. An even better alternative, which doesn't require users to change anything here, is to use a UNIX symbolic link between `/usr/local/lib/mosaic` and `/usr/local/lib/netscape`. This enables you to maintain a single copy of `mime.types` and `mailcap`, available to users of both Mosaic and Netscape.

Incidentally, the Netscape Helper Applications dialog box has a Browse button, but it doesn't work like the similar button in the PC and Mac version. All this Browse button does in the UNIX version is to let your browse around the file system looking at directory and file names; you cannot change your Netscape setup using this button. Whatever you find with the Browse feature, you'll have to jot it down for later manual editing.

Now that you've identified Netscape's setup filenames, the procedure for adding PluPerStat as a helper application is exactly the same as that described above for Mosaic. You must hand-edit:

◆ The system-wide (Global, in Netscape-spcak) `mime.types` and `mailcap` files and/or

◆ Your Personal (home directory) `.mime.types` and `.mailcap` files.

Enter exactly the same lines to these two files as shown above for Mosaic. For `mime.types/`
`.mime.types`:

```
# Support for PluPerStat added 11/2/96; tkevans
application/x-pluperstat     plu
```

For `mailcap/.mailcap`:

```
application/x-pluperstat;     /path/to/pluperstat %s
```

Last, you must tell Netscape to reread the setup files to register your changes. Do this by opening the Options menu and selecting Save Options. Your Netscape is now set up to use PluPerStat as a helper application. Clicking on a hyperlink to a PluPerStat data file will result in Netscape handing off the data to PluPerStat, starting up that program on a copy of the data sent by the Web server.

MIME and CGI

By now, you should have a good feel for the relationships between the MIME standard, with its three-way association of data types/subtypes with filename extensions and applications programs, and Web browser helper application setup. It's easy to configure Web browsers to use almost any application program, and this configuration is the key to the examples later in this book. You're well on your way to getting your Intranet in shape, with the helper applications your customers need.

From here, it's but a short step to the final subject of this chapter: MIME and CGI. The Common Gateway Interface is a standard way of passing information from the Web fill-in forms you've seen to back-end CGI scripts or other CGI programs which deal with the data. CGI is briefly described in Appendix B, but if you're interested in its details and implementation, as well as in setting up your own CGI scripts, you may want to obtain the book *HTML and CGI Unleashed* by John December and Neil Randall from sams.net (ISBN 0-672-30737-5). Check your local bookstore, or access the Macmillan Computer Publishing Web site at URL `http://www.mcp.com`, where you can get information about (and order) books published by sams.net and the other Macmillan imprints. You can also visit December's Web page for this book at `http://www.rpi.edu/~decemj/works/wdg.html`.

CGI is MIME-aware, which accounts for much of its power. CGI scripts on your Intranet can return data from your Web server in response to browser requests, in much the same way as when you click on a hyperlink. While most people think of the data being returned from a Web server as being from static files on the server—Web pages written in HTML, images, and so on—CGI scripts and programs can actually generate data on the fly in response to user requests. Such requests can be, for example, based on a fill-in form. The user enters information in the form, then clicks a Submit button, at which point the CGI script processes the information entered, generates a new stream of data based on the user input, and returns it to the client. Thus, a fill-in form can solicit input from a user such as search criteria in a database application, construct a query using the user data, run the query against the database, and return the results to the user's Web browser as an HTML document.

The mechanics of this CGI on-the-fly data generation use the MIME mechanism. Just as your Intranet server, sending back data in response to a mouse click on a hyperlink, precedes that data with header information containing the MIME data type/subtype of the data to be sent, your CGI scripts must return the same sort of information about the data stream they're about to send. Thus, any perl CGI script's very first output statements might be something like this:

```
print "Content-Type: text/html\n";
print "\n";
```

In other words

◆ generate the string of characters Content-Type: text/html followed by a newline, and

◆ print a blank line.

You've seen Content-Type before, just a few pages back, as well as the necessary blank line. Recall the discussion of the fundamental RFC-822 e-mail requirement: messages must be separated into a header area and a body area with a blank line between them. What you have here is exactly the same: the CGI script generates a MIME data type/subtype header (in this case Content-Type: text/html), followed by a blank line, as the very first bit of data to be returned to the Web browser. In this example, as required in all CGI scripts that are to return data to the user's Web browser, the program informs the browser that the forthcoming data is of the MIME type text and subtype html. The rest of the data generated by the script is, in fact, text data with HTML markup codes.

Tip: Perl, Larry Wall's freely available Practical Extraction and Report Language, or *perl*, is widely used for CGI scripts on the Web. Source code for perl, which you can compile on virtually any UNIX system, is included on the CD-ROM, as are DOS and Macintosh executables. The use of perl in CGI scripting is presented in a good deal of detail the book *HTML and CGI Unleashed*, described earlier.

Such data can include any and all HTML markup, including URLs pointing to other Web documents, images, or even other CGI scripts. Use of variable substitution in CGI scripts, for example, can enable you to generate documents, forms, or anything else than can be flagged in HTML, all with the simple use of one MIME type/subtype header preceding the data.

This simple-but-powerful example uses the text/html MIME type/subtype, but there is no reason your CGI scripts can't return any other valid MIME type/subtype. Provided you've set up your Web server's mime.types file and your users' Web browsers have corresponding helper application setup, there's almost no limit to what you can return from your CGI scripts. For example, the perl print statements above could just as well be:

```
print "Content-Type: application/x-pluperstat\n";
print "\n";
```

Your script would then select and return a PluPerStat data file, based on information the user enters into a fill-in form on your Intranet. This way, you can make a library of PluPerStat data available on your Web server, enable your customers to grab pieces of it using their Web browsers, and then then interact with the data using the PluPerStat program itself. You've just made your Intranet something more than just a look-at-pictures-and-read-pictures-and-read-text-files server: your customers can actually use it for their real work. This is, after all, why you bought this book. In later chapters, we'll talk about your own application programs, applying the generic information you've learned in this chapter to real programs that do real work.

Summary

This chapter is the very heart of this book. In it you've learned

- ◆ What Web helper applications are.
- ◆ What MIME is and where it came from.
- ◆ How the developers of the World Wide Web adopted MIME as a major part of Web technology.
- ◆ How Web servers and browsers use MIME to identify and process data.
- ◆ The relationship between MIME and Web browser helper applications.
- ◆ The basics of helper application setup in Mosaic and Netscape.
- ◆ How MIME and the CGI mechanism work together.

In the next chapter, we'll cover important security aspects of your Intranet, so you can make sure the data you make available is accessible only to the customers who need it. We'll also talk about potential exposure of your data if your Intranet is accessible on the Internet.

CHAPTER 8

Adding Services to Your Intranet Adds Value

In this chapter, you'll learn how to integrate several traditional TCP/IP network services that pre-date the World Wide Web, but which can nonetheless be important to your customers. As noted earlier, the developers of Web technology took care to build support for a number of older network services into the HTTP protocol, integrating these services into Web browsers and servers. Because you've established a TCP/IP networking infrastructure for your Intranet, you can use these older services easily in it, mostly using free software.

This book began by arguing that problems of differing—and difficult-to-master—user interfaces to older networking services were prime movers in the development of the Web. Of course, this doesn't mean those older services no longer have value. E-mail, FTP, remote login, Gopher, Archie, WAIS, and other such services remain at the heart of the Internet. Earlier, you saw how a Web-based front end to the Archie file-locator service vastly simplified a difficult interface, making it accessible to nontechnical users. You'll learn in this chapter how you can use these other services in your Intranet and provide Web-based front ends to them for your customers. In doing so, you'll substantially expand the range of services available on your Intranet without requiring additional customer training.

Chapter Objectives

As with the rest of the chapters in this book, let's begin by laying out some chapter objectives. This will help you get oriented to the material to be presented. You may want to refer back to this list as you work your way through the chapter. In this chapter, you will

◆ Review the MIME information you learned in Chapter 7, "MIME and Helper Applications," from the perspective of adding services to your Intranet.

◆ Learn how the ftp service can be used in your Intranet for the distribution of software and other data and how to install/configure it.

◆ Learn how the USENET news service can be used in your Intranet to facilitate customer collaboration and online discussion and how to install/configure it.

◆ Learn how the Wide Area Information Service (WAIS) can be adapted for your Intranet to provide searchable indexes of your data that are accessible using Web browsers and how to install/configure it.

◆ Learn how the Gopher service (a nongraphical, menu-based Internet browser) can be used to provide simple search-and-retrieval on your Intranet using Web browsers and learn how to install/configure it.

◆ Learn how you can use your Web browser's e-mail features to access e-mail distribution lists.

◆ Learn how you can use your Web browser's e-mail features to execute file/document retrievals.

◆ Learn how to install/configure several such e-mail–based services.

Support for each of these services is built into both the Web network protocol and your customers' Web browsers. Integrating them into the "quick-and-dirty" Intranet you built in Chapter 6, "Quick and Dirty Intranet," will provide new and powerful services to your customers, making your Intranet even more valuable.

MIME and Other Intranet Services

You learned in Chapter 7 how Web servers and browsers use the MIME mechanism to identify data by MIME data types/subtypes. Also, you learned Web servers include this identifying information in MIME data type/subtype headers when sending data back to a Web browser. You may have wondered, then, why Web browsers also have to be configured with MIME information because they receive it from the server.

This is a good question, and the answer is fundamental to the information in this chapter. While MIME data type/subtype information coming from a Web server may indeed be redundant to the properly setup browser, Web browsers also communicate with other kinds of Internet information services, such as ftp and Gopher. These Internet services pre-date both the World Wide Web and MIME, so they don't know anything about MIME types. Moreover, since they send back only one kind of data, not one of many kinds of data like a Web server, they have no reason to provide any identifying information. An ftp server simply sends and receives data using the ftp protocol and no other; the same goes for Gopher servers. These servers simply respond to clients by sending out data; it's up to the clients to know what to do with the data. Standalone ftp and Gopher client software, of course, know what sort of data to expect.

Fortunately, Web browsers deal with it, too—and they can use the MIME mechanism to enhance their handling of the data, even in the absence of any incoming identifying information.

Let's take these two points in order. First, as mentioned before, the HyperText transfer protocol (HTTP), which is the Web protocol, has support for a list of older Internet services built in. This support includes both ftp and Gopher, as well as several others. Your Web browser automatically senses when it's speaking with an ftp or Gopher server and acts accordingly. As far as you're concerned, though, you're just pointing and clicking, just as you would when dealing with a Web server. If you want to retrieve a file, just click on its hyperlink. Your browser identifies the incoming data and handles it properly.

Second, you've no doubt noticed that your Web browser often dresses up the display of ftp and Gopher server listings with identifying icons. Figure 8.1 shows a typical display in NCSA Mosaic while connected to an ftp server. File folder icons represent directories, while other icons identify plain text and binary files; occasionally, you'll see some other icon types too. You may not have thought of this, but normally, ftp servers are completely text-based, with no graphical displays. Since an ftp server, for example, has no way of telling a Web browser what sort of data is coming, Web browsers use a workaround, keying off the filename extension to a MIME data type/subtype. The set of canned icons representing different file types that you see when you connect to an ftp or Gopher server does not come from the server. Rather, this is your browser's MIME mechanism at work, using the filename extensions and a built-in list of MIME data types/subtypes. (See the semi-official list of MIME type/subtypes in Chapter 7; it's distributed with the NCSA httpd server software.)

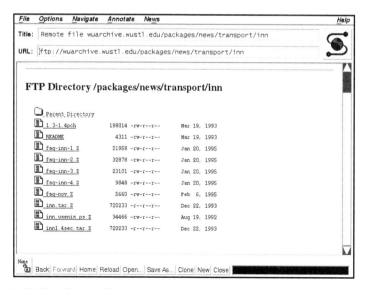

Figure 8.1. *Mosaic's MIME mechanism displays graphical icons in an FTP session.*

As does Mosaic, Netscape supports a long list of standard MIME types/subtypes in communicating with non-httpd services, such as gopher or FTP servers, and provides a built-in set of generic icons to represent them. Table 8.1 shows MIME types and subtypes from Netscape:

Table 8.1. MIME types/subtypes.

Content Type	Extensions	Description
text/plain	txt text	Plain Text
text/html	html htm	Hypertext Markup Language
application/rtf	rtf	Rich Text Format
application/x-tex	tex	TeX Document
application/x-latex	latex	LaTeX Document
application/x-dvi	dvi	TeX DVI Data
application/x-texinfo texi	texinfo	GNU TeXinfo Document
image/gif	gif	Compuserve Image Format
image/jpeg	jpeg jpg jpe	JPEG Image
image/tiff	tiff tif	TIFF Image
image/x-cmu-raster	ras	CMU Raster Image
image/x-xbitmap	xbm	X Bitmap
image/x-xpixmap	xpm	X Pixmap
image/x-xwindowdump	xwd	X Window Dump Image
image/x-portable-anymap	pnm	PBM Image
image/x-portable-bitmap	pbm	PBM Image
image/x-portable-graymap	pgm	PGM Image
image/x-portable-pixmap	ppm	PPM Image
image/x-rgb	rgb	RGB Image
application/fractals	fif	Fractal Image Format
audio/basic	au snd	ULAW Audio Data
audio/x-aiff	aif aiff aifc	AIFF Audio
audio/x-wav	wav	WAV Audio
video/mpeg	mpeg mpg mpe	MPEG Video
video/quicktime	qt mov	Quicktime Video
video/x-msvideo	avi	Microsoft Video

Content Type	Extensions	Description
video/x-sgi-movie	movie	SGI Video
application/mac-binhex40	hqx	Macintosh BinHex Archive
application/x-stuffit	sit	Macintosh Archive
application/x-zip-compressed	zip	Zip Compressed Data
application/x-shar	shar	Unix Shell Archive
application/x-tar	tar	Unix Tape Archive
application/x-gtar	gtar	GNU Tape Archive
application/x-cpio	cpio	Unix CPIO Archive
application/octet-stream	exe bin	Binary Executable
application/postscript	ai eps ps	Postscript Program
application/x-csh	csh	C Shell Program
application/x-sh	sh	Bourne Shell Program
application/x-tcl	tcl	TCL Program
application/x-troff	t tr roff	TROFF Document
application/x-troff-me	me	TROFF Document
application/x-troff-ms	ms	TROFF Document
application/x-troff-man	man	Unix Manual Page
encoding/x-compress	Z	Compressed Data
encoding/x-gzip	gz	GNU Zip Compressed Data

You can use Netscape to view this list, together with the associated icons, at `http://www.netscape.com/assist/helper_apps/mimedefault.html`. A portion of the list is shown on screen in Figure 8.2. Note the icons used for the various MIME types/subtypes, including the film strip icon for video files, the image icon for images, and the loudspeaker icon for audio files.

> **Note:** Web browsers' built-in lists of supported MIME types/subtypes rely solely on filename extensions when dealing with Internet services such as ftp that don't provide MIME header information. Since people are free to name files anything they want, you may encounter files on the World Wide Web that are misidentified by your browser because they've been given an extension that conflicts with your browser's built-in list. You'll want to make sure you use consistent file-naming conventions in your Intranet, following your browsers' built-in lists, to ensure that your customers don't encounter files that their browsers can't identify.

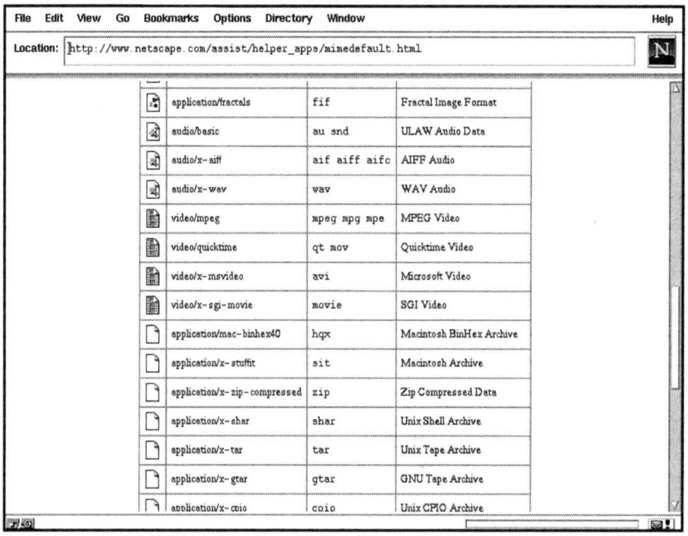

Figure 8.2. The Netscape page of default MIME types.

Adding FTP to Your Intranet for Software and Data Distribution

The TCP/IP file transfer protocol (ftp) is one of the Internet's mainstays. You probably used ftp to download your first Web browser software. The process probably looked something like Figure 8.3. FTP is a text-based application, and is not particularly user-friendly for the uninitiated. Figure 8.3 shows a couple of directory changes (the cd commands) and directory listings (the dir commands). Finally, binary transfer mode was turned on (the bin command) and the file MOS21B1.EXE was downloaded with the ftp get command. Contrast this with the very same transaction in NCSA Mosaic, shown in Figure 8.4. All that's needed to download the file in Mosaic is a simple mouse click. (Note Mosaic's use of the generic binary file icon and the generic file folder icon, representing a directory.)

You may have software or other data that you'd like to make widely available to your customers. Setting up an ftp server on your Intranet makes this easy. If your Web server is running on a UNIX system, or if you have UNIX systems in your Intranet, you already have ftp server software you can use. Setting it up is fairly simple. You can even set up an ftp server on a PC or Macintosh. Most of your customers will access your ftp server using their Web browsers, so they won't need to learn about ftp, or even know that they're accessing an ftp server, in order to download files.

```
226 Transfer complete.
ftp> cd Beta
250-Please read the file README.TXT
250-  it was last modified on Sun Dec 17 23:03:52 1995 - 13 days ago
250 CWD command successful.
ftp> dir
200 PORT command successful.
150 Opening ASCII mode data connection for /bin/ls.
total 22
drwxrwxr-x   5 12984     10           2048 Dec 17 23:03 .
drwxr-xr-x   7 12873     wheel        2048 Dec 17 22:52 ..
-rw-rw-r--   1 12984     10            906 Dec 17 23:03 README.TXT
drwxrwxr-x   2 12984     10           2048 Dec 17 22:54 Win31x
drwxrwxr-x   2 12984     10           2048 Dec 17 22:54 Win95
drwxrwxr-x   4 12984     10           2048 Dec 17 22:55 WinNT
226 Transfer complete.
ftp> cd Win31x
250 CWD command successful.
ftp> dir
200 PORT command successful.
150 Opening ASCII mode data connection for /bin/ls.
total 4608
drwxrwxr-x   2 12984     10           2048 Dec 17 22:54 .
drwxrwxr-x   5 12984     10           2048 Dec 17 23:03 ..
-rw-r-----   1 12984     10        2354206 Dec 17 22:54 MOS21B1.EXE
226 Transfer complete.
ftp> pwd
257 "/Web/Mosaic/Windows/Beta/Win31x" is current directory.
ftp> bin
200 Type set to I.
ftp> get MOS21B1.EXE
200 PORT command successful.
150 Opening BINARY mode data connection for MOS21B1.EXE (2354206 bytes).
226 Transfer complete.
2354206 bytes received in 163.4 seconds (14.07 Kbytes/s)
local: MOS21B1.EXE remote: MOS21B1.EXE
ftp> bye
221 Goodbye.
fallst:/home/tkevans $
```

Figure 8.3. *A command-line ftp download.*

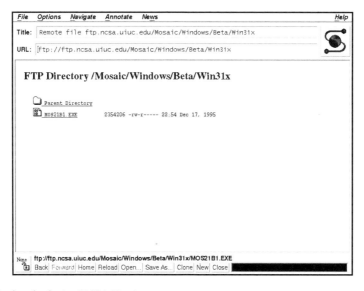

Figure 8.4. *An ftp download using NCSA Mosaic.*

How Can You Use FTP on Your Intranet?

Probably the best way to use your Intranet's FTP server is as a distribution point for Web-related software, including both browser and server software. Not only can you make it easier and faster for your customers to get the latest copy of NCSA Mosaic (or Netscape, if you've licensed it), but you'll also take a major load off your company's Internet connection by downloading the software from the outside once, then having local copies of the software available on the Intranet. Your network administrators will thank you for reducing the load on their Internet link, and your customers will thank you for faster service.

You'll also do a good deed for the online community by relieving the load on the ftp server where the original software resides. Whenever a new release becomes available, you can grab a copy and make it instantly available for your customers. Major anonymous ftp servers like `ftp.ncsa.uiuc.edu`, home of NCSA Mosaic, are invariably very busy in the days immediately following a new release of Mosaic. Accesses are often denied when the system is too busy to handle all the requests for copies of the new software release.

Similarly, you can redistribute Web server software for those of your customers who may want to set up another server and make it part of your Intranet. Your ftp server is a good place to store libraries of image files for use in HTML markup, for much the same reason. Be sure, however, that you read and follow licensing restrictions on the redistribution of copyrighted software, including shareware.

How To Set Up FTP on a UNIX System

All network-aware UNIX systems include both ftp client and server software. Usually named `ftpd` or `in.ftpd`, the ftp daemon (server) software is documented on the UNIX man page for that command. Access it like this:

```
$ man ftpd
```

As you'll read in the ftpd man page, the server software runs under the control of the system's Internet services daemon, inetd, which also has a man page. Most systems are shipped with the ftpd daemon enabled. You can find out if yours is by examining inetd's configuration file, `/etc/inetd.conf`. You'll probably find an entry like this:

```
ftp    stream   tcp   nowait   root   /usr/sbin/in.ftpd   iIn.ftpd
```

Your entry may differ slightly, depending on what sort of UNIX system you're running. For one thing, the exact command path to the ftpd executable program (the sixth field of this entry) may differ; this one is for a Sun Solaris 2.x system. For another, the entry may have a comment sign or pound sign (the # character) at the beginning of this line; this indicates the ftpd server has been disabled on the system. Re-enable it by deleting the hash mark, then telling the inetd process to reread the file. Identify the process ID (pid) of the inetd process, then send it a Hangup signal, like this:

```
# ps -ef ¦ grep inetd
root    177      1 80   Dec 17 ?         0:01 /usr/sbin/inetd -s
tkevans  6947   394 11 13:30:31 pts/3   0:00 grep inetd
# kill -HUP 177
```

Here the pid 177 was identified for inetd, then the `kill` command was used to send the signal. (You must be logged in as the UNIX superuser, or root, to issue this command.)

For the purposes of your Intranet, you'll want to set up your ftp server to use *anonymous ftp*, which allows unrestricted access to the data you've made available on your ftp server. All Web browsers negotiate the process of logging into an anonymous ftp server completely transparently. (We'll discuss non-anonymous ftp in a later chapter.)

Anonymous ftp setup creates a special, restricted account on your system, which is bottled up in a secure area of the computer's file system. Within this limited file system, anyone can access the system and download files using anonymous ftp or their Web browser. You'll find detailed instructions for setting up anonymous ftp in the ftpd man page. Be sure to follow them very carefully, since anonymous ftp can be a security problem if not set up correctly. (See Chapter 9, "Intranet Security," for more information on security.)

On some systems, you'll find a shell script that'll do the anonymous ftp setup for you. IBM's AIX version 3.2.x, for example, provides the script /usr/lpp/tcpip/samples/anon.ftp; in AIX version 4.1.x, this script has moved to /usr/samples/tcpip/anon.ftp.

Sun provides a sample script in the ftpd man page for Solaris 2.x (though not for SunOS 4.1.x), but you'll have to extract it from the man page before you can use it. Look for the script, which starts out like this:

```
#!/bin/sh
# script to setup SunOS 5.x anonymous ftp area
```

You can extract the script from the man page in a couple of ways. First, using two OpenWindows xterms, display the man page in one, then use your mouse to copy the script from the man page into a vi or other editor session running in the other xterm. (Use your left mouse button to highlight the script, then your middle button to copy it into the other window.) The other way is to redirect the output of the man command to a file, using a command like this:

```
$ man ftpd > ftp.script.sh
```

Next, edit the new file to delete those parts of the man page that aren't part of the script, save it, and make it executable using the chmod command.

Internet Security Systems in Norcross, GA maintains a Frequently Asked Questions (FAQ) document about anonymous ftp setup, a copy of which you'll want to grab. Do so using your Web browser at http://iss.net, or via anonymous ftp to host iss.net in the /pub directory (ftp://iss.net/pub/). This valuable document includes not only general information about setting up anonymous ftp, but also specific instructions for several different versions of UNIX. You should supplement your local man pages with the instructions in this document. The FAQ also provides a checklist of things you can do to ensure your anonymous ftp server is properly set up and secure.

Note: In case you want to make your anonymous ftp server available on the Internet, the anonymous ftp FAQ also tells you how to register it with the Archie service.

Populating Your Intranet's Anonymous FTP Server

Since setting up anonymous ftp creates a walled-off file system, dedicated to your ftp server, you'll want to set up a directory/subdirectory structure that corresponds with the data you're distributing. Use the server's /pub directory as the top of your file tree, with additional directories created within it based on your Intranet's needs. Be sure to follow the instructions in the ftpd man page or the Anonymous ftp FAQ in setting ownership and permissions in this file tree.

> **Tip:** Some people use the same file tree for their anonymous ftp and Web servers, putting the anonymous ftp file tree within the httpd DocumentRoot file tree. (See Appendix A, "Setting Up a Web Server," on how to set up the DocumentRoot for your Web server.) This can make maintenance of both your Web server and your anonymous ftp server more convenient. You need to watch your directory/file permissions, though, to ensure you don't disable with one server the security you may have set up with the other. This is particularly relevant if you set up password-protected portions of your Web server tree, a subject covered in some detail in Chapter 9.

Logging Accesses of Your FTP Server

You'll probably want to have some idea of who's using your anonymous ftp server. By default, ftpd doesn't do much of any logging unless you tell it to do so. Check out the ftpd man page, where you'll see there are two optional command-line flags, -d and -l. To enable ftpd logging, you'll need to edit the /etc/inetd.conf file once again and add one or both of these. To enable bare bones logging, modify the inetd.conf entry to add the -l flag; once changed, it'll read as follows:

```
ftp  stream  tcp  nowait  root  /usr/sbin/in.ftpd  in.ftpd -l
```

As when you edited the inetd.conf file, you'll need to send a Hangup signal to the inetd process. Refer back to the earlier discussion for the specifics on doing this.

Next, edit the /etc/syslog.conf file to modify the configuration of the syslogd daemon to provide for the additional logging. Syslogd is an all-purpose logging daemon. It's documented in its own man page and also on the man page for the configuration file, syslog.conf. The syslogd program operates using a set of facilities, each of which can be set for one of several levels of logging. On Sun systems, you'll find the following line in the syslog.conf file, which you can modify to add ftpd logging, using the daemon facility.

```
mail.debug    ifdef('LOGHOST', /var/log/syslog, @loghost)
```

This entry logs debug-level information about the electronic mail facility on your system and puts the information in the file /var/log/syslog. The period in the line separates the syslogd facility and level. The entry can be easily modified to add ftpd logging, though you need to pay careful attention to the use of the accent grave and single quote marks surrounding 'LOGHOST', as shown:

```
mail.debug;daemon.debug      ifdef('LOGHOST', /var/log/syslog, @loghost)
```

The ftpd daemon is associated for syslogd purposes with the daemon facility. Here, we've simply added the new `daemon.debug` facility and level to the previous entry for `mail`. Note the semicolon is used as a separator. As with the inetd daemon, when you modify the `syslog.conf` file, you'll need to send the syslogd process a Hangup signal to have it reread the file and pick up your changes.

Once you've made these changes, you'll start seeing entries like the following in your `/var/log/syslog` file.

```
Dec 31 17:21:50 osprey.wizards.raptor.com ftpd[7977]: FTPD: connection from
saturn.wizards.dupont.com at Sun Dec 31 17:21:50 1995
```

Entries like this are fairly easy to read. From left to right, you see:

◆ The date and time of the entry.

◆ The hostname of the ftp server.

◆ The name and process id of the ftpd daemon. (Recall that the ftpd program is started by the Internet services daemon, inetd. Each ftp connection will show a different process id, since a new instance of ftpd is spawned with each connection.)

◆ A syslogd label indicating the name of the program being logged, in this case `ftpd`.

◆ The connection entry itself, showing the hostname of the remote computer and the date/time.

This is relatively little logging, and you may want to know more. To get more logging information out of standard ftpd, you'll need to modify both your `inetd.conf` and `syslog.conf` entries. Here are the revised entries for the two files, respectively:

```
ftp  stream  tcp  nowait  root  /usr/sbin/in.ftpd  in.ftpd -d -l
daemon.info;daemon.debug      ifdef('LOGHOST', /var/log/syslog, @loghost)
```

Here, we've added the `-d` (debug) flag to the `ftpd` entry in the `inetd.conf` file, and called for both the info and debug levels of the daemon facility in `syslog.conf`. After having sent Hangup signals to both inetd and syslogd, you'll see a great deal more detail in your `/var/log/syslog` file for ftp connections. Here is a detailed sample, in which you see the anonymous user login/password sequence, a change directory command, and a directory listing command, followed by the closing of the connection:

Listing 8.1. Syslog trace of FTP an session.

```
Dec 31 17:52:57 osprey.wizards.raptor.com ftpd[8182]: FTPD: connection from
saturn.wizards.dupont.com at Sun Dec 31 17:52:57 1995
Dec 31 17:52:58 osprey.wizards.raptor.com ftpd[8182]: <-- 220
Dec 31 17:52:58 osprey.wizards.raptor.com ftpd[8182]: osprey.wizards.raptor.com FTP
server (UNIX(r) System V Release 4.0) ready.
Dec 31 17:53:01 osprey.wizards.raptor.com ftpd[8182]: FTPD: command: USER anonymous
Dec 31 17:53:01 osprey.wizards.raptor.com ftpd[8182]: <-- 331
```

continues

Listing 8.1. continued

```
Dec 31 17:53:01 osprey.wizards.raptor.com ftpd[8182]: Guest login ok, send ident as
password.
Dec 31 17:53:03 osprey.wizards.raptor.com ftpd[8182]: FTPD: command: PASS <passwd>
Dec 31 17:53:03 osprey.wizards.raptor.com ftpd[8182]: <-- 230
Dec 31 17:53:03 osprey.wizards.raptor.com ftpd[8182]: Guest login ok, access restric-
tions apply.
Dec 31 17:53:25 osprey.wizards.raptor.com ftpd[8182]: FTPD: command: PORT
205,128,123,9,13,0
Dec 31 17:53:25 osprey.wizards.raptor.com ftpd[8182]: <-- 200
Dec 31 17:53:25 osprey.wizards.raptor.com ftpd[8182]: PORT command successful.
Dec 31 17:53:25 osprey.wizards.raptor.com ftpd[8182]: FTPD: command: LIST
Dec 31 17:53:26 osprey.wizards.raptor.com ftpd[8182]: <-- 150
Dec 31 17:53:26 osprey.wizards.raptor.com ftpd[8182]: ASCII data connection for /bin/
ls (205.128.123.9,3328) (0 bytes).
Dec 31 17:53:26 osprey.wizards.raptor.com ftpd[8182]: <-- 226
Dec 31 17:53:26 osprey.wizards.raptor.com ftpd[8182]: ASCII Transfer complete.
Dec 31 17:53:31 osprey.wizards.raptor.com ftpd[8182]: FTPD: command: CWD pub
Dec 31 17:53:31 osprey.wizards.raptor.com ftpd[8182]: <-- 250
Dec 31 17:53:31 osprey.wizards.raptor.com ftpd[8182]: CWD command successful.
Dec 31 17:53:33 osprey.wizards.raptor.com ftpd[8182]: FTPD: command: PORT
205,128,123,9,13,1
Dec 31 17:53:33 osprey.wizards.raptor.com ftpd[8182]: <-- 200
Dec 31 17:53:33 osprey.wizards.raptor.com ftpd[8182]: PORT command successful.
Dec 31 17:53:33 osprey.wizards.raptor.com ftpd[8182]: FTPD: command: LIST
Dec 31 17:53:34 osprey.wizards.raptor.com ftpd[8182]: <-- 150
Dec 31 17:53:34 osprey.wizards.raptor.com ftpd[8182]: ASCII data connection for /bin/
ls (205.128.123.9,3329) (0 bytes).
Dec 31 17:53:34 osprey.wizards.raptor.com ftpd[8182]: <-- 226
Dec 31 17:53:34 osprey.wizards.raptor.com ftpd[8182]: ASCII Transfer complete.
Dec 31 17:53:55 osprey.wizards.raptor.com ftpd[8182]: FTPD: command: QUIT
Dec 31 17:53:55 osprey.wizards.raptor.com ftpd[8182]: <-- 221
Dec 31 17:53:55 osprey.wizards.raptor.com ftpd[8182]: Goodbye.
```

You'll note the process id [8182] in each line of the listing is the same, indicating all of the above comes from a single, very brief ftp session, lasting only a little more than 50 seconds and consisting only of a single directory-change and one directory-list commands. There wasn't even a single file transferred. It therefore follows that, on a busy ftp server, you're going to get vast amounts of data in your logfiles if you turn on both logging and debugging output at this level. If you do, you'll need to develop automated scripts to analyze this voluminous output.

Unfortunately, most stock ftpd programs in UNIX systems don't allow you to dial back this amount of logging to something manageable, while still getting something more meaningful than the bare bones logging shown earlier (in which only the initial connection is logged). In the next section, you'll learn about a replacement ftpd package that has better logging facilities as just one of many advantages.

Replacing Your Stock ftpd with wuftpd

System Administrators at Washington University in St. Louis, Missouri, who maintain one of the Internet's busiest anonymous ftp archives (wuarchive.wustl.edu), have developed a replacement for the standard UNIX ftpd daemon. This package, the source code for which is on the *Building*

an Intranet CD-ROM, has many outstanding features. You'll want to consider installing it on your Intranet's anonymous ftp system for a number of reasons:

◆ It's substantially easier to secure than vendors' stock ftpd packages.

◆ Its security is finer-grained, so you can provide different privileges to different groups of users based not only on username but also on the host from which they're accessing your server. You can even deny access altogether based on hostname or domain name.

◆ If your company is a large organization, or the computer on which you're running your ftp server is underpowered, you can limit the number of concurrent accesses and even use time-of-day access limits. (This enables you to, for instance, use the same computer as a Web server and as an ftp server, while ensuring that ftp accesses don't interfere with the Web server during busy periods.)

◆ You can set up subdirectory aliases, to make getting around your archive easier and enable users to change directories using short alias names rather than long pathnames.

◆ Its logging facilities can be fine-tuned so you get just the amount of logging you want.

Installing wuftpd

The wuftpd package comes in C-Language source code that you must compile on your system. Because there is some minimal localization required, the *Building an Intranet* CD-ROM does not contain prebuilt binaries for common systems. You'll find installation instructions in a file called INSTALL contained within the distribution.

There are three major steps in building/installing wuftpd. Your first step is to edit the file pathnames.h in the src subdirectory. This file sets basic directory and pathnames for use in your server. You won't need to change many of the items in this file, and you may end up changing none at all. Take a look at the file anyway, to see if the default directory and filenames fit in on your system. Changes you might want to make include the location of the wuftpd man pages or logfiles. If you don't need to change anything, that's fine.

Next, you compile the source code. wuftpd comes with a shell script called build which is set up to compile the package on a number of common UNIX systems. These include IBM's AIX, standard BSD UNIX systems, Hewlett-Packard's HP-UX, Sun's Solaris 2.x and SunOS 4.1.x, and Digital's Ultrix. (You'll find instructions inside the package for setting up wuftpd on other systems using a generic configuration file as a skeleton.) To do the compile on your system, simply type build systemname at your shell prompt, using the correct system name from the following table.

System Type	System Name
IBM AIX	ibm
BSD	bsd
HP-UX	hpx
Solaris 2.x	sol
SunOS 4.1.x	s41
Ultrix	ult

For example, on an HP-UX system you'd compile wuftpd by typing this command at your shell prompt:

```
# build hpx
```

You shouldn't get any compilation errors on these supported systems, so if you do, you may have made a typo in the pathnames.h file. Check there first. Assuming no errors, you can simply type build install to install the package, including the main ftpd executable, man pages, and some utility programs.

Once you've made the installation, you'll need to edit your /etc/inetd.conf file to reflect the new installation. Two changes are necessary:

◆ Changing the pathname to the new ftpd executable.

◆ Adding any command-line arguments.

Here's the standard ftpd entry from /etc/inetd.conf, which you've seen earlier.

```
ftp  stream  tcp  nowait  root  /usr/sbin/in.ftpd  in.ftpd -l
```

By default, wuftpd's replacement ftpd daemon executable is installed in the /usr/local/etc directory, though you may have changed this when you edited the pathnames.h file. You'll probably want to comment out the above entry and use a new one for wuftpd. Just place a hash mark, or #, at the beginning of the existing line. Copy the line, minus the comment mark, and change the pathname to the wuftpd executable, like this:

```
ftp  stream  tcp  nowait  root  /usr/local/bin/ftpd  ftpd -l
```

Be sure you change the actual name of the executable in both the sixth and seventh fields.

Two of wuftpd's major advantages are its superior logging facilities and fine-grained access control. To implement them, the package's authors have added several new command-line options for the new ftpd executable. Besides the standard options you already know about from the stock ftpd man page (-l, -d, and others), wuftpd adds (not a complete list):

◆ -a and -A, for enabling and disabling use of the access-control file, usually named ftpaccess, respectively; and

◆ -i and -o, for enabling logging of every file upload and download, respectively.

See the wuftpd man page for detailed explanations of these options, as well as a couple of others. Add any of these command-line options you want to the /etc/inetd.conf entry. Note that the -a option (use the ftpaccess file) is the default, so you need not enter it except as a visual reminder to yourself. If, for example, you'd like to use the ftpaccess file to control access to your system and log all outgoing file transfers (downloads), use this entry:

```
ftp  stream  tcp  nowait  root  /usr/local/bin/ftpd  ftpd -o
```

To log both downloads and uploads, and also get ftpd's debug output in your syslog file, use this:

```
ftp  stream  tcp  nowait  root  /usr/local/bin/ftpd  ftpd -o -i -d
```

As you can see, you can simply string out all the command-line options you need on the same line. Once you've finished your changes to the /etc/inetd.conf file, have the inetd daemon reread the file by sending the process a Hangup signal.

wuftpd Activity Logs

The wuftpd package allows you to log ftp activity on your system to either or both of two places: the standard syslogd facility (as described earlier) and its own logfile. The latter is usually the file /var/adm/xferstats, although you could have changed this before doing the wuftpd build by editing the pathnames.h file. In either case, you must run the new ftpd daemon in its default mode, using the ftpaccess file. (Using the -A option in the command disables use of this file, but you would almost never want to disable it.) The ftpaccess file is used to set up many of wuftpd's enhanced features, so you'll want to read about it in detail. Here, you'll focus on logging of ftp activity on your server.

You can have wuftpd log either or both user commands and file transfers. Let's consider the former. The package enables you to use syslogd to log every single user command, making possible even more extensive logging than that shown in the last logging example. You can cut down the amount of logged information by using wuftpd's capability of breaking up users into groups, and then logging only the activity of the groups you want. For example, while you might not care to see every single directory change made by anonymous users, you might want to see the commands issued by ordinary users using their own accounts. To enable command logging, add these keywords to the ftpaccess file:

```
log commands usertype
```

The wuftpd package provides for three usertypes, *real* (signifying normal login users on your system, such as root and others), *anonymous*, and *guest*. (Guest users have real login names and passwords, but limited access, though less limited than *anonymous* users). To enable command logging through an ftpaccess file entry like this, you must specify at least one usertype. If you share administration of your ftp server, you'll want to use this feature to keep everyone aware of what's being uploaded to your server by the administrators. Here's a sample ftpaccess entry for command logging, followed by excerpts from the /var/log/syslog file:

```
log commands real

Dec 30 12:28:09 molson ftpd[1149]: STOR MOS21B1.EXE
Dec 31 15:30:24 molson ftpd[1397]: STOR ImageMagick-3.7.1.zip
Dec 31 23:47:21 molson ftpd[1449]: STOR ImageMagick-3.7.1.tar.gz
```

In the syslogd output, you see that three files have been uploaded to the ftp server named molson. (STOR signifies an upload.)

As noted earlier, wutfpd also can log all uploads and downloads in its own logfile, /var/adm/xferstats. You'll need to add another set of keywords to the ftpaccess file to enable this kind of logging. Here's an example, which logs both uploads and downloads by both anonymous and real users:

```
log transfers anonymous,real inbound,outbound
```

This entry generates logging not in the syslog file, but in the xferstats file. It looks like this:

```
Sun Dec 31 12:02:36 1995 32 somehost.something.com 2354206 /pub/mosaic/MOS21B1.EXE b
_ o a anonymous@somehost.something.com ftp 0 *
```

Although the information logged in this file is too extensive to explain in detail, if you squint, you can see a user on the host named somehost.something.com used anonymous ftp to retrieve the 2MB file MOS21B.EXE from the /pub/mosaic directory using the password anonymous@somehost.something.com.

Fortunately, you don't have to try to analyze this file by yourself. It was built to be parsed by a computer program, and the wutfpd package includes a utility script (written in perl) named xferstats. The script parses the xferstats file for you and generates a nice report that looks like this.

Listing 8.2. Report of wuftpd activity from xferstats script.

```
TOTALS FOR SUMMARY PERIOD Mon Dec 11 1995 TO Sat Dec 30 1995
Files Transmitted During Summary Period          276
Bytes Transmitted During Summary Period     120104903
Systems Using Archives                             0
Average Files Transmitted Daily                   20
Average Bytes Transmitted Daily              8578922
Daily Transmission Statistics
                 Number Of    Number of    Average     Percent Of   Percent Of
      Date       Files Sent  Bytes  Sent  Xmit  Rate  Files Sent   Bytes Sent
---------------  ----------  ----------   ----------   ----------   ----------
Mon Dec 11 1995       9        4389615    13.8 KB/s       3.26         3.65
Tue Dec 12 1995      28       13741446    16.2 KB/s      10.14        11.44
Wed Dec 13 1995      49       13071776    13.3 KB/s      17.75        10.88
Thu Dec 14 1995      38       14825622    14.6 KB/s      13.77        12.34
Fri Dec 15 1995      22        7971626    12.4 KB/s       7.97         6.64
Mon Dec 18 1995       8        3595222    17.6 KB/s       2.90         2.99
Tue Dec 19 1995      35       13376188     5.3 KB/s      12.68        11.14
Wed Dec 20 1995      18        4778815    20.8 KB/s       6.52         3.98
Thu Dec 21 1995      13       13452811    20.9 KB/s       4.71        11.20
Fri Dec 22 1995       8        8892917     6.8 KB/s       2.90         7.40
Wed Dec 27 1995       8        5274156    16.0 KB/s       2.90         4.39
Thu Dec 28 1995      16       11470216    15.7 KB/s       5.80         9.55
Fri Dec 29 1995      23        5244834    15.8 KB/s       8.33         4.37
Sat Dec 30 1995       1          19659    19.7 KB/s       0.36         0.02
Total Transfers from each Archive Section (By bytes)
                                              ---- Percent  Of ----
      Archive Section      Files Sent Bytes Sent  Files Sent Bytes Sent
---------------------      ---------- ----------  ---------- ----------
/pub/mosaic                    66      62996010     23.91       52.45
/pub/dos                       30      16195529     10.87       13.48
/pub/mosaic/readers            10      12852248      3.62       10.70
/pub/mosaic/cern                8       5521252      2.90        4.60
/pub/mosaic/winnt               1       3849659      0.36        3.21
/pub/mosaic/win95               2       3665744      0.72        3.05
/pub/mosaic/arena               2       3170608      0.72        2.64
/pub/macintosh                  5       2878125      1.81        2.40
```

```
/pub/liberation              11    1352759    3.99    1.13
/pub/dos/gif                 19    1317833    6.88    1.10
/pub/unix/aix_bin             1     966524    0.36    0.80
/pub/mclean                   9     843220    3.26    0.70
/pub/unix/ImageMagick         1     709384    0.36    0.59
/pub/unix/solaris_bin         2     675744    0.72    0.56
/pub/mosaic/vms       ,       1     561589    0.36    0.47
/pub/cd/pc                   20     491222    7.25    0.41
/pub/unix                     1     404466    0.36    0.34
/pub/jones                    4     366856    1.45    0.31
/pub/unix/sunos_bin           2     337035    0.72    0.28
/pub/unix/solx86_bin          1     278708    0.36    0.23
/pub/mosaic/line-mode_bro    20     164688    7.25    0.14
/pub/clipart/corel           11     159252    3.99    0.13
/pub/dos/images              12      86871    4.35    0.07
/pub                         11      70763    3.99    0.06
/pub/dos/elvis                1      67192    0.36    0.06
/pub/clipart/1mileup          1      53487    0.36    0.04
/bin                          1      24576    0.36    0.02
/pub/vms/ImageMagick          2      15600    0.72    0.01
/pub/mosaic/icons            17      10172    6.16    0.01
/pub/dos/zip                  1       6932    0.36    0.01
/pub/vms/imtools              1       6023    0.36    0.01
/pub/clipart/micromap         1       4793    0.36    0.00
/etc                          1         39    0.36    0.00
```

This is just a part of the standard report produced by the xferstats script. As you can see, in addition to a brief summary of the period's activity and a daily summary of activity, the report shows the number of files and bytes downloaded from each subdirectory in the /pub filetree. It also does some arithmetic on the downloads for you to show how the ftp activity breaks down by area. The standard report also does an hourly breakdown of downloads, allowing you to get an idea of the hours your server is being used; this part of the report is not shown.

What Does This Information Tell Me?

You can probably guess from looking at this report that this ftp server is used as a software distribution machine for World Wide Web software and related data, with 128 of the 276 downloaded files coming from the /pub/mosaic directory or its subdirectories. This demonstrates the value of using an anonymous ftp server on your Intranet, as suggested above, as a software-distribution facility for Web software.

USENET News for Collaboration and Discussion

Besides electronic mail, USENET news was probably the first groupware package. It's still a great means of online collaboration and discussion. Netnews might be called the Mother of All Computer BBSs, so great is its reach and breadth. The idea was first developed in the 1970s, when computer researchers at a couple of universities in North Carolina wanted an open means of discussing and sharing ideas. The basic idea of USENET, which is still pretty much what it's all about, is that people can post articles for others to see. *Articles* is a formal word, but you shouldn't think of netnews articles in any way like magazine or newspaper articles. Rather, an article can be anything anyone considers worthy of posting in an electronic forum. Netnews articles range from treatises on TCP/IP networking to recipes to comparative reviews of 4×4 truck tires. Once posted, a netnews article is available to anyone on the local computer system who might want to look at it. Article readers can also post follow-up articles in response to other articles, possibly starting a dialog or group discussion. The follow-up articles are also available to everyone on the system to read and, of course, respond to with further follow-ups.

Netnews articles may also be sent out from the local system to remote systems, where remote users can read/respond to them. Using a flooding algorithm, news articles that aren't purely local are distributed all over the Internet very quickly to thousands of systems with hundreds of thousands (possibly millions) of people who can read and respond to them. USENET is almost-infinitely divided, with more than 10,000 newsgroups in seven major categories:

◆ Computers (comp)

◆ Science (sci)

◆ Recreation (rec)

◆ Social Topics (soc)

◆ Talk (talk)

◆ USENET News itself (news)

◆ Alternative Groups (alt)

Each newsgroup category is the tip of a vast iceberg of related newsgroups, subdivided into thousands of very specialized topics. Besides the major groups,you'll find biz (business), bionet (biology), misc (miscellaneous), and local groups. Major Web browser software, including both NCSA Mosaic and Netscape, includes the ability to post, read, and respond to USENET news articles. Figures 8.5 and 8.6 show the NCSA Mosaic netnews interface in Windows. (The UNIX interface is a little different.) In Figure 8.5, a list of articles in the newsgroup comp.infosystems.www.browsers.ms-windows appears. Figure 8.6 shows one of the articles selected.

Netscape's netnews interface is substantially different from Mosaic's, and has gone through a number of recent changes; you may see something different by the time you read this book. In any event, Figure 8.7 shows the same newsgroup listing as that in Figure 8.5 except in UNIX Netscape, while Figure 8.8 shows the same news article as Figure 8.6, also in UNIX Netscape.

An interesting feature of Netscape USENET news interface is its ability to resize any of the three panes of the netnews window. Figure 8.7 shows the newsgroup and article listing panes (the two upper ones) having been resized to fill the full screen. In Figure 8.8, these panes have been resized smaller to show the news article itself. You can also drag the newsgroup listing pane to the right to enlarge it.

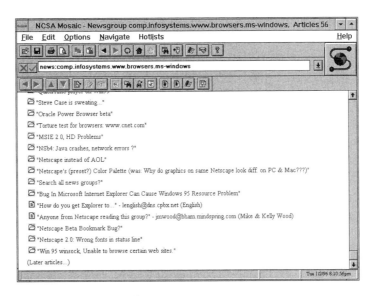

Figure 8.5. *A newsgroup listing viewed through NCSA Mosaic.*

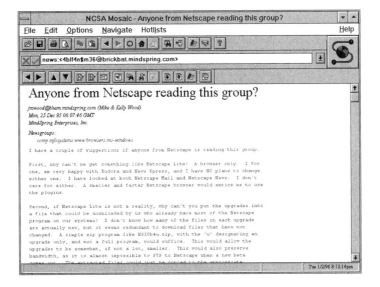

Figure 8.6. *A netnews article being read in NCSA Mosaic.*

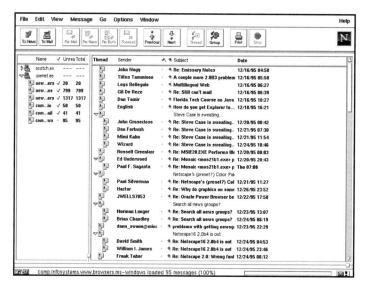

Figure 8.7. *A newsgroup listing in Netscape Version 2.*

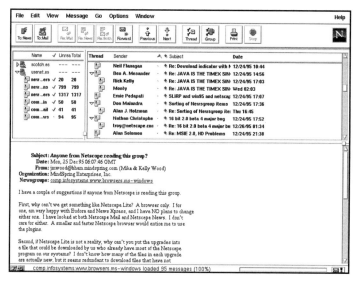

Figure 8.8. *A newsgroup article displayed in Netscape Version 2.*

How You Can Use Netnews in Your Intranet

It's important to note that the USENET news server software provides for the creation of *local* newsgroups. You need not be a part of the Internet's USENET system to run a news server. On the contrary, your netnews server can be entirely local, with your news articles not being sent anywhere outside your organization. All your customers can have access to your local USENET news, and can use their Web browsers to read and respond to local news articles.

If you've spent any time reading USENET news, you know how discussions often seem to pick up a life of their own. They often last for weeks as multiple readers post follow-up articles, then respond to the follow-ups of others. Although they frequently degenerate into personal insults, USENET news threads (articles in a single discussion thread) can often be an important means of collaboration as consensus is hammered out in public discussion. You can use the same process to enable collaboration on your Intranet, with your customers using their Web browsers as news readers.

> **Note:** In Chapter 3, "Tools for Implementing an Intranet Infrastructure," you learned about Internet Requests for Comments (RFCs) as part of the development of today's TCP/IP networking standards. The consensus-building that led (and still leads) to Internet RFCs is a good example of netnews collaboration through discussion.

Installing USENET News on Your Intranet

USENET news can provide an important discussion forum for your customers on your Intranet. The *Building an Intranet* CD-ROM contains source code for INN, Internet News, server software for UNIX systems. Building INN is a relatively complex process, but the process is eased by good documentation and a terrific set of FAQs that are accessible on the Web. Your first reading assignment is the file `Install.ms`, at the top level of the INN software distribution. The file is in UNIX nroff format, so, unless you enjoy reading between the nroff markup, you'll want to format it, like this:

```
$ nroff -ms Install.ms > Install.txt
```

This creates the formatted file, `Install.txt`, which you can read onscreen or print.

Before you go any further, it's a good idea for you to grab the multipart INN Frequently Asked Questions document as additional reference material. Rich Salz's INN documentation is slanted toward the technically oriented, and you'll want the FAQ's amplification if this is your first foray into USENET server software. You'll find the INN FAQ on the Web at `ftp://rtfm.mit.edu/pub/usenet-by-group/news.software.nntp`. It's broken into five pieces; you'll want to read the overview in Part 1 and the Installation Guide in Part 4 before you even begin to do the INN install. The other parts of the FAQ tell you how to configure INN once you've compiled the software.

HyperNews: USENET, This Is the Web; Web, This Is USENET

NCSA's Daniel LaLiberte is developing a kind of merger between USENET and the World Wide Web called HyperNews, which he hopes will eventually replace USENET altogether. The application is worth looking at for your Intranet because it enables another means of Web collaboration.

HyperNews uses the USENET post-and-follow-up model, but it is more closely focused on the idea of conferencing using the Web. The idea is fairly simple: someone posts an initial base article and invites others to comment. Others comment, and the responses are integrated into the HyperNews archive. New readers can use their Web browsers to point-and-click their way through the discussion and add responses of their own to be integrated into the discussion.

As suggested by Figure 8.9, HyperNews has some useful features. First, the base article and all the responses are shown as hyperlinks, accessible via point-and-click from your Web browser. What's more, both base articles and responses can contain more than just plain text. As Figure 8.9 shows, articles can contain HTML markup as well. This enables users to create articles and responses containing images and even other hyperlinks pointing to other Web resources on remote systems. If you're discussing the HTML markup language, for example, you can add a hyperlink to a Web site with HTML resources right into your HyperNews posting. Readers can point and click to access that site.

You can find more information about HyperNews, and download the current beta release of the software, on the Web at `http://union.ncsa.uiuc.edu/HyperNews/get/hypernews.html`. (Source code for HyperNews is not included on the *Building an Intranet* CD-ROM because it's changing quite rapidly and any version included would be obsolete by the time you read this.)

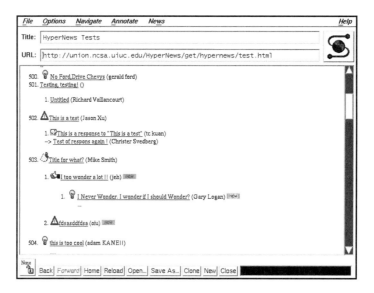

Figure 8.9. *HyperNews Demonstration page.*

As with anonymous ftp, USENET news can be an important addition to your Intranet. This is true even if you're not connected to the Internet, or even if don't want to deal with USENET except for your local newsgroups.

Wide Area Information Server (WAIS)

WAIS is a system for indexing large amounts of data and making it searchable over a TCP/IP network. It's misnamed, though, because it works just as well on a local network as it does over the Internet. WAIS server software indexes data and responds to requests from WAIS clients to search the indexes and return a list of documents that match the search. Based on an ANSI standard for indexing library materials in computer systems (Z39.50), WAIS can form an important part of your Intranet.

WAIS supports not only simple keyword searches, but also Boolean queries (for example, *thiskeyword* AND *thatkeyword*) and even plain English searches. In addition, WAIS can do relevance searching—you can select part or all of a document that your WAIS search has found, and ask for a new search based on the selection. In other words, WAIS will find more documents like the one it found.

WAIS was originally developed as free software at Thinking Machines, Inc., then the software was commercialized by WAIS, Inc. (WAIS, Inc., incidentally, is now owned by America Online; the Internet buying frenzy continues.) At the time *Building an Intranet* was being written, AOL hadn't yet announced plans for WAIS, Inc. and its technology. Fortunately, the original WAIS software was made available at no cost and a couple of major currents of free WAIS development still run.

For some time, CNIDR, the Clearing House for Networked Information and Discovery, oversaw development of the freeWAIS package, successor to the original Thinking Machines package. Version 5 of freeWAIS, dated in early May 1995, appears to be the latest release. The original CNIDR freeWAIS package has been extended to introduce text, date, and numeric field structures within a document, which allows a document to be indexed using potentially overlapping fields. The package now also supports complex Boolean searches, word stemming, and sounds-like (soundex) searches.

More recent development in the WAIS area is focused around the freeWAIS-sf package, with work going on at the University of Dortmund, Germany. The -sf suffix on the package name stands for structured fields, meaning the package allows documents with a structure (such as e-mail messages) to be indexed by their fields. freeWAIS-sf also has an easier installation than freeWAIS and numerous bug fixes. Source code for the freeWAIS-sf package is on the *Building an Intranet* CD-ROM.

How WAIS Can Be Used in Your Intranet

freeWAIS-sf knows about a large number of document types (see Table 8.2) and can build indexes from any of them, then search them using your Web browser.

Table 8.2. File formats supported by freeWAIS-sf.

Text	Simple Text Files
bibtexB	ibTeX / LaTeX format
bio	Biology abstract format
cmapp	CM applications from Hypercard
dash	Entries separated by a row of dashes
dvi	dvi format
emacsinfo	The GNU documentation system
essence	CU-Boulder Essence Summaries
first_line	First line of file is headline
filename	Uses only the filename part of the pathname for the title
ftp	Special type for ftp files. First line of file is headline
gif	gif files, indexes only the filename
irg	Internet resource guide
jargon	Jargon File 2.9.8 format
mail_digest	Standard Internet mail digest format
mail_or_rmail	mail or rmail or both
medline	medline format
mh_bboard	MH bulletin board format
netnews	netnews format
nhyp	HyperText format, Polytechnic of Central London
one_line	Each line is a document
para	Paragraphs separated by blank lines
pict	Pict files, indexes only the filename
ps	Postscript format
refer	refer format
irlist	irlist mail or rmail or both
formfeed	Entries separated by a formfeed
bibdb	Steve file entries separated by a formfeed
bibinf	bibinf entries separated by an empty line
rn	Netnews saved by the rn newsreader

Text	Simple Text Files
server	Server structures for the dir of servers
tiff	tiff files, indexes only the filename
URL what-to-trim what-to-add	URL
oneline_phonix	Phonebooks PHONIX
oneline_soundex	Phonebooks SOUNDEX
listserv_digest	Standard Internet mail digest format
fields	Document format given in <database>.fmt

As you can see from this table, you can index almost anything with freeWAIS-sf. For example, you can index your Web server's filetree, or your anonymous ftp server's files. You can index plain text files, so virtually any text file you have on your Intranet can be indexed. (Many of the formats are highly specialized ones, common on some UNIX systems and/or used by specialized application programs.) You can even specify new kinds of files to be indexed by creating format description files.

Of course, freeWAIS-sf indexes can also be searched. NCSA Mosaic already has built-in support for WAIS searches, although you may want to recompile it using the freeWAIS-sf libraries to add support for the extended search capabilities of freeWAIS-sf.

Although NCSA Mosaic has built-in WAIS support, Netscape doesn't. As a result, you'll need to run a WAIS gateway on your Intranet to support Netscape users. Fortunately, the freeWAIS-sf developers have built one, called SFgate. It's available on the *Building an Intranet* CD-ROM. SFgate is a Web server CGI script, written in perl, which interfaces with both freeWAIS and freeWAIS-sf servers. You can use HTML fill-in forms as front ends for SFgate searches and the script will pass the form data off to the freeWAIS server for handling. SFgate returns the results of searches in HTML format, with matched documents as clickable hyperlinks.

In fact, this support for fill-in forms as a front end may lead you to use SFgate for *all* freeWAIS searches on your Intranet through both Netscape and Mosaic, even though Mosaic has direct WAIS support. Figures 8.10 and 8.11 show a demonstration SFgate search of a freeWAIS-sf database of bibliographic information using Netscape. Figure 8.10 shows part of the fill-in form used to make the search. Figure 8.11 shows the results of the search, all nicely formatted in HTML, with hyperlinks to each of the located documents. Notice in particular the fetch documents button and the check boxes next to each document. (Those next to items 2 and 5 have been checked and appear shaded.) Once you have selected one or more documents using the check boxes, you can click on the fetch documents button to retrieve all of the selected documents for display.

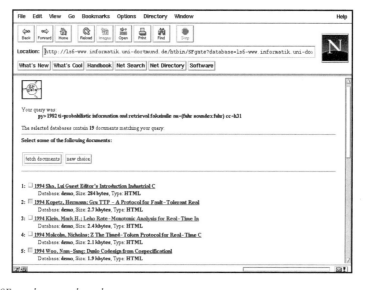

Figure 8.10. *The SFgate demo fill-in form.*

Figure 8.11. *The SFgate demo search results.*

Installing freeWAIS-sf

Like a growing number of software packages, freeWAIS-sf uses the GNU Project's autoconf to self-configure. Once you've unzipped and untarred the source code, change to the top-level directory and run the shell script Configure. This script asks you a few questions, but it mostly figures out for itself what sort of system you're running and builds all the necessary Makefiles to compile the system.

You may run into a few quirks. In running the Configure script on a Solaris 2.4 system, the author learned the package doesn't like the standard SunPro C compiler, preferring GNU's gcc instead. Also, Configure needed to be told to link with Sun's networking libraries, libnsl, libresolv, and libsocket. After the correct answers to the libraries question were supplied, the freeWAIS-sf package promptly built with no errors, except for failing its German-language test.

Creating freeWAIS-sf Indexes

freeWAIS-sf indices are created using the waisindex program generated when you compiled the package. This program takes a number of command-line options, including:

- ◆ The name of the index to be created (-d index-filename)
- ◆ The -a option, to append to an existing index
- ◆ The -r option, to recursively index a directory's subdirectories
- ◆ The -export flag, to make the index searchable over the network
- ◆ The type of files (-t type) to be indexed, from Table 8.2.

A sample command-line invocation might go something like this:

```
# waisindex -d intranet -export -t text *.txt
```

This command indexes all files with the filename extension .txt, which are plain text files, into the index named intranet and makes the index searchable across the network.

> **Tip:** One of freeWAIS-sf's supported formats is netnews (USENET news articles). If you're using netnews as a means of discussion or collaboration on your Intranet, you can archive and index your discussions and make them searchable with freeWAIS-sf.

More Information About freeWAIS-sf

As with most Internet things, there's a FAQ for freeWAIS-sf; you'll find a copy in the doc subdirectory of the source code distribution, but you may want to look for a more recent version. You'll find the latest FAQ at ftp://ls6-www.informatik.uni-dortmund.de/pub/wais/. There's a mirror site in the United States at ftp://ftp.maxwell.syr.edu/infosystems/wais/FreeWAIS-sf/.

Other WAIS-like Packages

We've already discussed freeWAIS-sf's predecessor package, freeWAIS, which you can find at ftp://ftp.cnidr.org/pub/NIDR.tools/freewais/. (It's not included on the *Building an Intranet*

CD-ROM because development work on the package seems to have stopped.) A less-powerful but still useful package called SWISH (Simple Web Indexing System for Humans) is also available, and you may find it easier to use. As the title implies, SWISH was written (by Kevin Hughes) especially to index World Wide Web sites. You can read about SWISH at `http://www.eit.com/software/swish/swish.html`. SWISH source code is on the *Building an Intranet* CD-ROM.

SWISH uses a simple configuration file that's easy to set up and customize for your Intranet. Once you've compiled it and customized the configuration file, you can create an index of your Web server's filetree, and then test the index by running the program from the UNIX command line. Once you're satisfied with your configuration and your index, you'll want to make your index searchable on your Intranet by your customers using their Web browsers. Hughes has provided a CGI-bin gateway program called wwwwais, which works via a fill-in form. Also on the *Building an Intranet* CD-ROM, you'll find the latest documentation for wwwwais at `http://www.eit.com/software/wwwwais/wwwwais.html`.

wwwwais generates a very simple fill-in form (shown in Figure 8.12), but this simplicity shouldn't be taken to mean the program isn't capable. For one thing, it'll search not only SWISH-generated indices but also freeWAIS ones as well. This means you can use it as a front end to either kind of index. And, like SFgate, wwwwais outputs the results of its searches in HTML, with hyperlinks to each located document. This enables your customers to select documents with point-and-click and then refine their searches, all using their Web browsers. Because wwwwais is a CGI-bin gateway script, it doesn't matter which Web browser is used, or if that browser has built-in WAIS capabilities.

In Chapter 13, we'll discuss WAIS and other indexing packages in some depth.

Figure 8.12. *The wwwwais search form.*

Tunneling Your Intranet with Gopher

Before the World Wide Web burst onto the Internet stage in 1993, the sexiest Internet technology was something called Gopher. Developed at the University of Minnesota (whose athletic teams take the nickname Golden Gophers), Gopher was the first successful attempt to join several existing TCP/IP networking technologies into a single, easy-to-use interface.

The main Gopher interface is a plain text menu of choices, like that shown in Figure 8.13. You start out at such a top-level menu and work your way down a hierarchy of nested menus until you find the subject you're after. Once you find your subject, you're able to view text files on the subject onscreen, and in some cases transfer files across the Internet to your own computer. Selecting a Gopher menu item can do one of several things:

◆ Take you to another menu of choices

◆ Display a document onscreen

◆ Jump you to another Gopher server in some other location

◆ Connect you to an altogether different Internet service, such as a remote login using telnet or ftp for file transfer

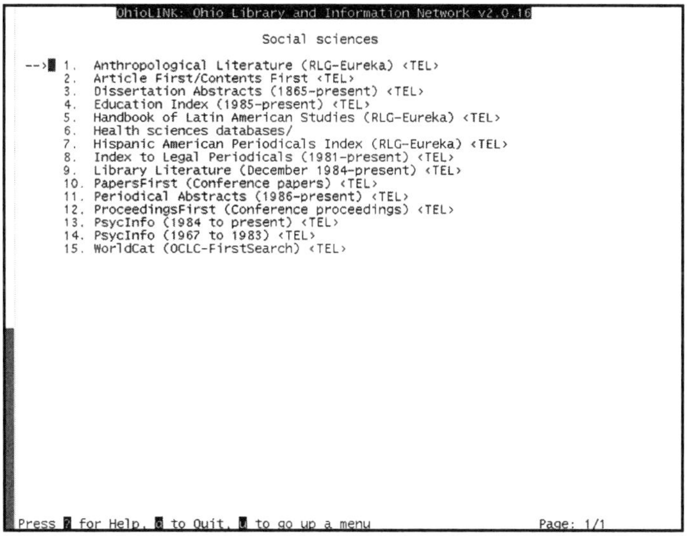

```
OhioLINK: Ohio Library and Information Network v2.0.16

                         Social sciences
-->  1.  Anthropological Literature (RLG-Eureka) <TEL>
     2.  Article First/Contents First <TEL>
     3.  Dissertation Abstracts (1865-present) <TEL>
     4.  Education Index (1985-present) <TEL>
     5.  Handbook of Latin American Studies (RLG-Eureka) <TEL>
     6.  Health sciences databases/
     7.  Hispanic American Periodicals Index (RLG-Eureka) <TEL>
     8.  Index to Legal Periodicals (1981-present) <TEL>
     9.  Library Literature (December 1984-present) <TEL>
    10.  PapersFirst (Conference papers) <TEL>
    11.  Periodical Abstracts (1986-present) <TEL>
    12.  ProceedingsFirst (Conference proceedings) <TEL>
    13.  PsycInfo (1984 to present) <TEL>
    14.  PsycInfo (1967 to 1983) <TEL>
    15.  WorldCat (OCLC-FirstSearch) <TEL>



Press ? for Help, q to Quit, u to go up a menu          Page: 1/1
```

Figure 8.13. The OhioLink Gopher menu.

The last two items are key to Gopher's success. By simply selecting a menu item, you can move transparently from one Gopher server to another one. You don't have to know anything about how to get there, the second server's Internet address, or anything else. Even more importantly, Gopher folds in pre-existing Internet services such as telnet and ftp. As a result, you can access a remote computer for login and terminal emulation, or transfer a file using ftp, just by selecting a Gopher menu item. Figure 8.14 shows another Gopher screen, this time that of an anonymous ftp server. Notice the <Bin> notations on many of the menu items, indicating that those entries are downloadable files. (Other entries are followed by forward slashes, indicating subdirectories.)

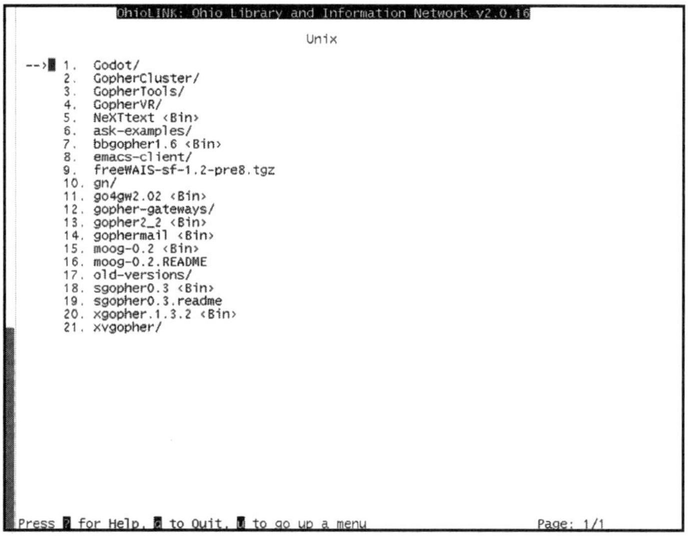

```
       OhioLINK: Ohio Library and Information Network v2.0.16
                              Unix
  -->█ 1.  Godot/
      2.  GopherCluster/
      3.  GopherTools/
      4.  GopherVR/
      5.  NeXTtext <Bin>
      6.  ask-examples/
      7.  bbgopher1.6 <Bin>
      8.  emacs-client/
      9.  freeWAIS-sf-1.2-pre8.tgz
     10.  gn/
     11.  go4gw2.02 <Bin>
     12.  gopher-gateways/
     13.  gopher2_2 <Bin>
     14.  gophermail <Bin>
     15.  moog-0.2 <Bin>
     16.  moog-0.2.README
     17.  old-versions/
     18.  sgopher0.3 <Bin>
     19.  sgopher0.3.readme
     20.  xgopher.1.3.2 <Bin>
     21.  xvgopher/




 Press █ for Help, █ to Quit, █ to go up a menu        Page: 1/1
```

Figure 8.14. A Gopher display of an anonymous ftp directory.

If you're thinking that Gopher is beginning to sound a lot like the World Wide Web, you're right on target. You can do many of the same things with Gopher that you can do on the Web, such as jumping transparently from one computer system to another, accessing other Internet services, and even searching Gopherspace (see Figure 8.15). Gopher, then, can be seen as a the Web's most immediate ancestor, with many of the same capabilities in a nongraphical interface.

In fact, the Web's httpd protocol reflects this ancestry: Gopher is one of the Internet services that are built into the World Wide Web. You can use your Web browser to access Gopher services, as Figures 8.16 through 8.18 show with NCSA Mosaic. (These are the very same Gopher resources shown in Figures 8.13 through 8.15, respectively.) Any Gopher server, file, ftp server, or searchable Gopher index is accessible using a Web browser.

> **Note:** The graphical icons shown in the Gopher listings in Figures 8.16 through 8.18 don't come from the Gopher servers. Rather, your Web browser, using the MIME mechanism and its built-in list of filename extensions/MIME type/subtype associations, generates them to dress up the display.
>
> Besides the MIME mechanism, Mosaic also uses a telnet icon (shown in Figure 8.16) based on the data received from the Gopher server. Notice the <TEL> tags on the menu items in Figure 8.13, the plain text Gopher menu. Netscape, incidentally, uses a different icon for Gopher telnet menu selections: it looks like a colorful little computer terminal.

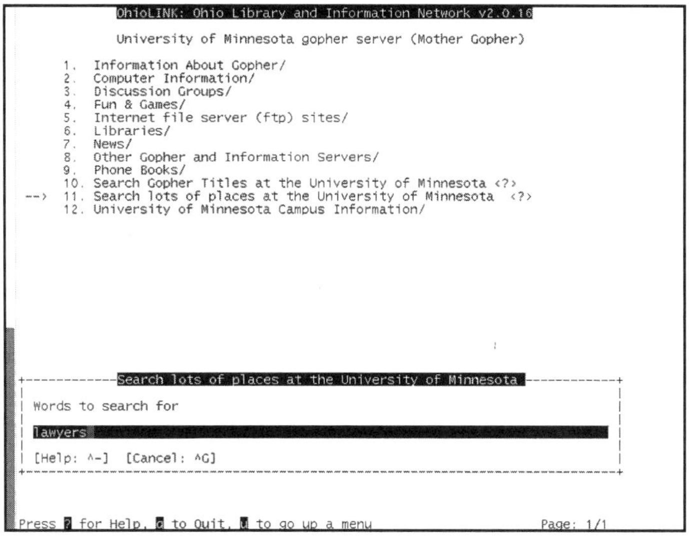

Figure 8.15. *Gopher search.*

Figure 8.16. *The same OhioLink Gopher menu as in Figure 8.13, but accessed with Mosaic.*

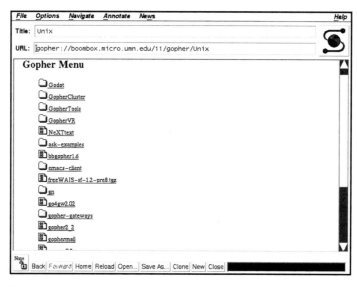

Figure 8.17. *The Gopher display of anonymous ftp directory from Figure 8.14, accessed with Mosaic.*

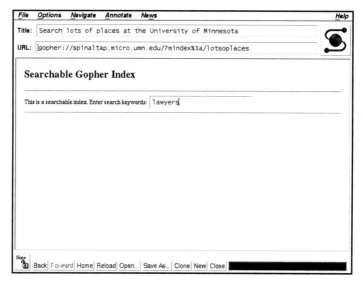

Figure 8.18. *The Gopher search from Figure 8.15, accessed with Mosaic.*

Why Should I Use Gopher, Then?

If you can do everything with your Web browser that you can do with a Gopher client, you may well wonder why you would want to bother with it on your Intranet. Gopher services have limitations not present in the Web. Most notably, you can't include graphics and hyperlinks within Gopher documents and can't, therefore, jump directly from one document to another, though you can jump using Gopher menus. Nonetheless, there are some strong reasons for you to consider setting up Gopher services as part of your Intranet.

The primary reason is that Gopher's strongest suit is plain text files. You don't have to learn HTML, and setting up a Gopher server is substantially easier than setting up a Web server. In fact, Gopher is a favorite with many U.S. government agencies for just these reasons. The government generates vast quantities of plain text documents, and it's quite easy to throw them up on a Gopher server. With plain text files, indexing them (with WAIS or other indexing tools) is easy, and Gopher can search the indices that these tools create. If a lot of the data you plan to make available on your Intranet is plain text data, Gopher is for you. You may not even need a Web server and all the time and trouble of converting documents described in Chapter 6. There is little reason for you to learn HTML and how to convert image data if your data is plain text and you have no images to use.

Installing and Configuring a Gopher Server on Your Intranet

Source code to the latest available Gopher server software for UNIX systems is on the *Building an Intranet* CD-ROM. Once you've unpacked the source code, you'll need to edit two files, Makefile.config and conf.h. Most of the configuration items in these have to do with how the server is to be set up, and there are liberal comments in these files to point you in the right direction. There are, however, some operating-system-specific items in Makefile.config. For example, you'll have to change the RANLIB definition on a System V, Release 4 machine such as Solaris 2.x, and select the appropriate libraries for your system. The conf.h file contains configuration options for both the server and for the included Gopher client software. Note the special instructions in the doc/INSTALL file if you plan to build WAIS support into your Gopher server. (There is support for freeWAIS-sf in Gopher release 2.)

Once the server and client software have been compiled, you'll need to edit the server's runtime configuration file, gopherd.conf. This file controls the behavior of your Gopher server when it responds to connections from Gopher clients. Details include the server's name, levels of access, and some global attributes such as the server administrator e-mail address, the name of your organization, and so on.

Next, you'll create the Gopher server's data filetree. gopherd uses the UNIX chroot facility to limit access to a specified portion of your computer's file system for security purposes. The gopherd daemon can be started out of one of your system's rc files (such as /etc/rc.local on a SunOS 4.1.x system or a separate script in /etc/rc2.d on a System V UNIX machine). Alternatively, you can run gopherd out of the Internet server daemon, inetd. Your choice is based on how busy your machine is, or how busy you expect it to be. On a busy machine, the rc-file route is best.

Your next-to-last job in getting your Gopher server running is to populate its data filetree with documents for your Intranet's customers. gopherd will automatically create menus for you based on the files and directories you place in the data directory. You may, however, want to exercise some control over the naming and presentation of data entries on your menus. You'll find information on doing so in the doc subdirectory of the Gopher software distribution. The server.doc file is the place to start, but, as this file indicates, the latest information is included in the Gopherd manual page, gopherd.8. This file is in traditional UNIX man page format, so you'll want to format it for readability:

```
$ nroff -man gopherd.8 > gopherd.txt
```

You can then view the output file, gopherd.txt, onscreen or print it for reference.

Your Gopher server is almost ready for your customers. The final step in getting it ready is to create gopher links. Links are the items you place on Gopher menus which enable the user to jump from one place to another. That is, a link can point to

- Another Gopher menu
- Another Gopher server
- A telnet session on a remote host
- A special telephone directory database known as a CSO Phone book server
- An ftp server
- A WAIS index
- A computer program script that generates data on-the-fly when selected from a Gopher menu

Gopher links are created by editing files named .Links in each directory of your Gopher server's data directory tree. A simple .Links file, with just one item in it, looks like this:

```
Name=OhioLink
Type=1
Path=1/
Host=gopher.ohiolink.edu
Port=70
```

This .Links file, in fact, points to the top level of the OhioLink Gopher server shown in Figures 8.13 and 8.16.

> **Note:** Actually, Gopher's links files need not specifically be named .Links. Any filename beginning with a period will do, though .Links is commonly used.

More Important Information About Gopher

You'll find the inevitable FAQ document about Gopher at gopher://mudhoney.micro.umn.edu/00/Gopher.FAQ. Be sure also to read the University of Minnesota's licensing policy on the Gopher server software. The software is freely distributable, but commercial use of it, including use on an internal corporate Intranet, requires payment of a licensing fee to the University of Minnesota. Gopher licensing fees are negotiated on a case-by-case basis for commercial users. Academic and nonprofit use of the Gopher server software is free. You can read the details of this licensing policy at ftp://boombox.micro.umn.edu/pub/gopher/gopher-software-licensing-policy. Contact Shih

Pau Yen at the University of Minnesota (e-mail: `yen@boombox.micro.umn.edu`) for more information.

Electronic Mail Distribution Lists and List Servers on Your Intranet

If you've used e-mail, you probably know that you can create distribution lists of your associates' and friends' e-mail addresses and then send messages to the lists just as if they were individual addressees. You probably also know there are thousands of special-interest Internet e-mail distribution lists, ranging from those discussing Internet Firewalls (see Chapter 9) to those discussing feminism and/or men's rights. These lists are used for communication, discussion, and collaboration among like-minded people.

Besides these distribution lists, there are automated list servers on the Internet that will do something for you if you send e-mail to them. Some list servers will automatically add your e-mail address to an e-mail distribution list (or take it off). Others will respond to specially worded e-mail messages to retrieve information for you and deliver it to you via e-mail. Special FTPMail servers will actually perform an anonymous ftp file retrieval for you while you sleep, and then deliver the file with the rest of your e-mail.

As with all the other TCP/IP network services covered in this chapter, there's no reason you can't put these e-mail-based services to work in your Intranet. Web browsers are adding support for sending and reading e-mail (see Figures 8.19 and 8.20). You can piggyback this built-in e-mail support onto both simple e-mail distribution lists and list servers, thereby providing your customers with value-added services on your Intranet.

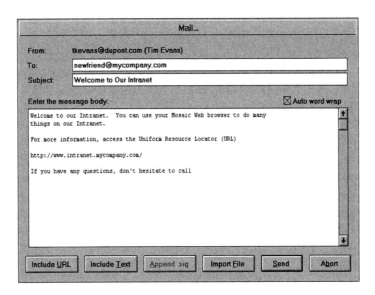

Figure 8.19. *Sending an e-mail message in NCSA Mosaic for Windows.*

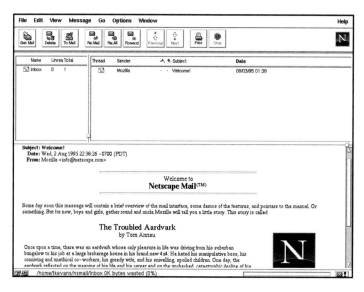

Figure 8.20. *Reading an e-mail message in Netscape.*

Simple E-Mail Distribution Lists

Experienced UNIX System Administrators know that creating an e-mail distribution list is as simple as editing the `/etc/aliases` file on the system's main e-mail machine. You can create a group e-mail alias (that is, a distribution list) by adding an entry to this file like this one:

```
# this is a comment
# mailing list for Intranet users
intranet:user1,user2,user3,user4
```

Once this entry is added, any user on your system can address e-mail using their Web browser (or standard e-mail program) to the alias `intranet`, and it'll get delivered to all the users in the distribution list. This distribution list may also come in handy to your Intranet administrator: she can use it to send important notices to your Intranet's customers.

> **Tip:** If you're running the Network Information Services (NIS, formerly called Yellow Pages) on your UNIX systems and have the aliases map under its control, don't forget to push any changes to the aliases map using the NIS Makefile, usually in `/var/yp`.

There's another useful format to the `/etc/aliases` file which is good for maintaining distribution lists. Here's an example:

```
# expand list from the contents of a file
# intranet::include /myhome/intranet.alias
```

Because super-user authority is required to change the /etc/aliases file, you may want to take the include-file approach shown here, keeping the file containing the list of users in your own home directory. The format of the include file is very simple, one name to a line, like this:

```
user1
user2
user3
user4
```

From then on, whenever you need to change your distribution list, you just edit the include file; you never have to touch the actual /etc/aliases file or deal with NIS.

Majordomo for Automated E-Mail List Services

Majordomo is a set of scripts, written in perl, for administering one or more e-mail distribution lists. (The package, originally written by Brent Chapman, now maintained by John Rouillard, is on the *Building an Intranet* CD-ROM.) The package's scripts help automate much of the work of creating, running, and managing a distribution list. People send e-mail messages to the list-administration address, and Majordomo adds and deletes users. It also sends help and other messages back to the senders. Majordomo can also retrieve files and, if configured to do so, send information about the membership of the distribution list. For example, users can subscribe to a Majordomo-managed distribution list by sending it a simple message containing text like this:

```
subscribe name-of-list
```

Unsubscribing is equally simple. In addition, users can send a message containing just the single word help. Majordomo will respond with an e-mail message containing instructions for using Majordomo and all its commands. Users can ask for lists of documents available to Majordomo, and then ask for certain of them to be e-mailed to them, all with e-mail messages containing simple commands. Majordomo will also archive all the traffic on your distribution lists. Later, you can index the archived e-mail, using WAIS or another indexing package, and make it searchable on your Intranet using a CGI-bin gateway script. Distribution lists managed by Majordomo can be moderated, with all messages sent to the list being sent first to a moderator for approval before being sent on the distribution list itself.

Installing Majordomo

Even though most of Majordomo is written in perl, and therefore doesn't need to be compiled, there's still some preparatory configuration needed to install it. You'll find a Makefile, in which a number of configuration items is set before you run a make. The Makefile will install the package from your temporary working directory into its final destination, set permissions, and compile a security wrapper program, which enables the package to run with correct authorities for creating and writing to files and directories. There's also a main majordomo.cf script that you'll need to customize for your Intranet. Finally, set up your distribution lists themselves and configure Majordomo to handle them. You'll want to read the Majordomo FAQ, available on the Web at URL `http://www.greatcircle.com/majordomo/`.

Automated File Retrievals with FTPMail

If your Intranet involves a wide-area network (WAN) with slow links between the remote sites, your customers may tire of waiting for Web-browser-initiated ftp transfers to finish. FTPMail offers a possible solution to this problem, although its interface is a throwback to command-line ftp, and you'll want to make a workaround. Some Intranets' only connection to the outside world is via e-mail, for security or other reasons. In these situations, FTPMail may be the only way you and your customers can retrieve files from anonymous ftp servers in the outside world.

As with Majordomo, users send e-mail containing commands to an FTPMail address. The program (actually another set of perl scripts, written by Lee McLoughlin) responds to those commands by sending back e-mail containing the command results, including files. The commands sent to FTPMail are normal ftp commands, just as a user would type them on the old fashioned text-based ftp command line. As a result, users who don't know how to use this interface will have a learning curve to climb. An example FTPMail message might look like this:

```
cd /packages/ftpmail
ls
bin
mime
get ftpmail-1.23.tar.gz
bye
```

Here, we've issued a series of commands in the e-mail message, including ftp directory-change, directory-listing and binary-transfer commands. We've told FTPMail to return files in MIME-encoded format, requested a specific file, and, finally, ended the ftp session. (The requested file is, of course, the source distribution of FTPMail itself.)

If you've used a standalone ftp client package, you may recognize most of these commands as just what you'd enter on your screen, and you might be discouraged by this apparent return to the not-so-user-friendly days of yesteryear. You're a WebMaster, though, so don't give up. You can make all of this easier for your Intranet's customers by creating Web-based fill-in forms and CGI-bin gateway scripts. Users can order files via FTPMail from your Intranet's ftp server just by filling in a Web form, checking off boxes, or selecting the file(s) to be retrieved from a list. The gateway script can bundle up the user information into correct FTPMail syntax and ship off the request via e-mail.

In a WAN situation, FTPMail may turn out to be very useful, particularly if you have distributed e-mail servers. One of the primary reasons is that, like all other e-mail transactions, FTPMail transactions take place asynchronously. Users aren't twiddling their thumbs, sitting and watching the transfer take place, so they can go on to other work in the meantime. Second, you can control the priorities of FTPMail by having it, say, respond to requests for files based on size of file. Small files can be transferred immediately, while larger ones can be postponed. FTPMail can be configured to take time of day into account as it does its work, delaying transfer until off hours when WAN bandwidth is not so precious.

Using Distribution Lists, Majordomo, and FTPMail in Your Intranet

E-mail distribution lists can become major workhorses in your Intranet. Here are just a few uses; note how they can interrelate in potentially valuable ways.

◆ Users can communicate/collaborate by using their Web browsers to send and read e-mail messages using your Intranet's distribution lists.

◆ E-mail sent to distribution lists can be archived and then indexed for subsequent search and retrieval using a CGI-bin gateway to the indices.

◆ File transfers over slow WAN links can be queued to run asynchronously using CGI-bin gateway scripts, using limited WAN bandwidth more efficiently.

Summary

This chapter has covered a number of related TCP/IP networking services that can add value to your Intranet. All these services can be accessed by your customers using their World Wide Web browsers, and they can extend your Intranet to make it more useful to your company or organization. Although each of them is a standalone network service, and some have archaic user interfaces, putting a Web-based front end on them can make them easy to use. In this chapter, you have

◆ Reviewed MIME from the perspective of adding services to your Intranet.

◆ Learned how the ftp service can be used in your Intranet.

◆ Learned how the USENET news service can be used in your Intranet.

◆ Learned how WAIS can be adapted for your Intranet.

◆ Learned how the Gopher service can be used on your Intranet.

◆ Learned how you can use several e-mail services on your Intranet.

Each of these services can add value to your Intranet and can be accessed by your customers using their Web browsers. Don't think of them in isolation, however. As we've suggested throughout the chapter, you can combine these services in imaginative ways to create truly unique and valuable additions to your Intranet, examples include using WAIS to index e-mail distribution lists archives for subsequent search and retrieval using Web fill-in forms and CGI-bin gateway scripts. These potential combinations of service, provided using Web browser front ends, constitute more than the simple sums of their parts; they create new, powerful applications for your Intranet.

In Chapter 9, we'll turn to issues of Intranet security. While your objective in setting up an Intranet is to make information available to your customers, you'll want to pay attention to its security, particularly if any part of your Intranet is accessible to the Internet. In addition, implementation of some Intranet security features can enhance the value of your Intranet's services.

CHAPTER 9

Intranet Security

You might think that there is little reason to be concerned about security in an Intranet. After all, by definition an Intranet is *internal* to your organization; outsiders can't access it. Also, because one of your objectives in setting up your Intranet is to provide your customers with access to a wide variety of *public* documents there might seem little need to secure access to them. These are strong arguments for the position that an Intranet should be completely open to its customers, with little or no security. You may not have considered your Intranet in any other light.

On the other hand, implementing some simple, built-in security measures in your Intranet can allow you to provide resources you may not have considered possible in such a context. For example, you can give access to some Web pages to some people without making them available to your entire customer base, with several kinds of authentication. In this chapter, you'll learn how simple security measures can be used to widen the scope of your Intranet.

Chapter Objectives

As with the rest of the chapters in this book, let's begin by laying out some chapter objectives. This will help you get oriented to the material to be presented; you may want to refer back to this list as you work your way through the chapter. In this chapter, you'll

◆ Consider the overall security aspects of your Intranet

◆ Learn how implementing security on your Intranet can actually broaden the ways in which it can be useful in your organization

◆ Learn how to set up username/password authentication to limit access to resources on your Intranet

- ◆ Learn how to provide secure access to Intranet resources to groups of customers
- ◆ Learn how to restrict access to sensitive resources based on customers' computer hostnames or network addresses
- ◆ Learn about the security aspects of CGI-bin scripting
- ◆ Learn about using encrypted data transmission on your Intranet to protect critical information
- ◆ Learn important information about securing access to your Intranet when your corporate network is attached to the Internet
- ◆ Learn how to provide—and limit—secure access to your Intranet from outside your immediate local network

Intranet security is, then, a multifaceted issue, with both opportunities and dangers, especially if your network is part of the Internet. We'll walk through the major ones, with detailed information on using built-in Intranet security features, in this chapter.

> **Warning:** Except in the sections of this chapter that are specifically devoted to Internet security issues, it's assumed your Intranet is *not* accessible from outside your organization. If you are on the Internet, the Intranet security measures discussed in this chapter may not be sufficient to secure your system. If you want to make the services and resources of your Intranet accessible from the outside, you'll need to take significant additional steps to prevent abuse and/or unauthorized access. Some of these steps are described at the end of this chapter in the section "Your Intranet and the Internet."

Why Security?

Many people view computer and network security in a negative light, thinking of it only in terms of restricting access to services. One major view of network security is "that which is not expressly permitted is denied." While this view is a good way of thinking about how to connect your organization to the Internet, you can, and possibly should, view Intranet security from a more positive angle. Properly set up, Intranet security can be an *enabler*, enriching your Intranet with services and resources you would not be able to otherwise provide. Such an overall security policy might be described as "that which is not expressly denied is permitted."

This chapter takes the latter approach, presenting Intranet security in terms of its opportunities for adding value to your Intranet. For example, some of your customers might have information they'd like to make available, provided access to it can be limited to a specified group—for example, confidential management or financial information. Without the ability to ensure that only those who have the right to see such information will have access, the custodians of such data will not be willing to put it on your Intranet. Providing security increases your organization's ability to use the important collaborative aspects of an Intranet.

The more defensive approach, preventing abuse of your Intranet, is also given play, however. Organizations' needs for security in an Intranet can vary widely. Businesses in which confidentiality and discretion is the norm in handling proprietary information and corporate intellectual property have different needs than a college or university, for example. Academic institutions generally tilt toward making the free exchange of ideas a primary interest. At the same time, though, the curiosity (to use a polite word) of undergraduates imposes strong needs for security. Keeping prying sophomores out of university administration computing resources is a high priority, for example; students have been known to try to access grade records (their own or those of others) for various reasons. Even simple adolescent high jinks take on new dimensions on a computer network.

What Are the Security Features of an Intranet?

Before going into great detail about how you can use security to enhance your Intranet, let's take a high-level look at what security features are available to you. These break down into three main categories. First, you can take steps on your Web server to set up security. Second, you can take steps with the other TCP/IP network services you've set up on your Intranet to enhance their security. Third, you can secure customers' Web browsers themselves to limit what they can do with them.

Web Server Security

There is a wide range of very flexible security features you can implement on your Web server(s). Here's a summary:

◆ Access to Web servers, individual Web pages, and entire directories containing Web pages can be set to require a username and password.

◆ Access to Web servers, individual Web pages, and entire directories containing Web pages can be limited to customers on specific computer systems. (In other words, access will be denied unless the user is at his or her usual computer or workstation.)

◆ You can organize individuals into groups and grant access to individual Web servers, Web pages, and entire directories containing Web pages based on group membership.

◆ You can organize computers into groups, and grant access to individual Web servers, Web pages, and entire directories containing Web pages based on group membership.

◆ CGI-bin scripts on your Web server(s) can use any of the above access restrictions, though you must take care in writing them to ensure you don't make security-related mistakes.

◆ Some httpd server software is capable of communicating with compatible Web browsers in a verifiably secure, encrypted fashion, defeating even network-level sniffers and ensuring confidential data transmission across your Intranet.

You can combine these features in a number of ways, such as requiring a password and limiting access to a group of users who must access your Web server from a specific group of computer systems. You'll see a good deal of detail about Web server security setup in this chapter.

Security in Your Other Intranet Applications

In addition to the access controls you can set up on your Web servers, you can implement security in some of the other network services that you learned about in Chapter 8. Here are some of the steps you can take:

◆ Access to your anonymous ftp server can be limited in several important ways, much like with your httpd server, while still enabling authorized customers to upload files to it.

◆ Access to your USENET news server can be limited in much the same way.

◆ Access to searchable Intranet indexes and databases (see Chapters 13 and 14) can be controlled through password-protected Web interfaces.

◆ Access to Gopher services can be controlled based on TCP/IP network address, and separate browse, read, and search permissions can be set on a per-directory basis.

This chapter, already quite long, doesn't provide any additional information about these services. You'll want to refer to the documentation for these network packages to learn about how to handle access-control and other security features in them.

Securing Customers' Web Browsers

Some Web browsers can be set up in *kiosk* mode, which limits the features of the package that users can access. Available primarily in NCSA Windows Mosaic and Mosaic-based browsers, kiosk mode runs the browser with a limited set of features. Users cannot save, print, or view the Web pages' HTML source, and hotlist/bookmark editing is not allowed. The user cannot even exit from the browser and restart it in normal mode without exiting from Windows altogether. Even the overall Mosaic window cannot be minimized or maximized, and the normal pull-down control-menu box for Windows is missing.

Figure 9.1 shows NCSA Mosaic for Windows in kiosk mode, while Figure 9.2 shows the same page in standard Mosaic for your comparison. As you can see, many of the usual toolbar buttons are missing, as is the Options menu. The remaining pull-down menus are also limited in the available features. Kiosk mode is primarily for use in library or trade-show environments, where users need to be limited in what they can do, but you may find a use for it in your Intranet if you need to limit what some customers can do with the package. The Netscape Navigator browser does not have a kiosk mode.

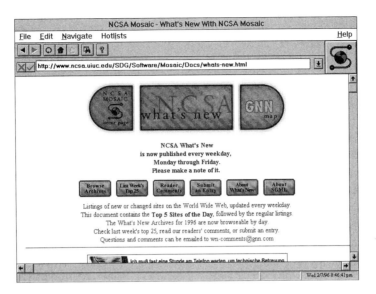

Figure 9.1. *NCSA Mosaic for Windows in kiosk mode.*

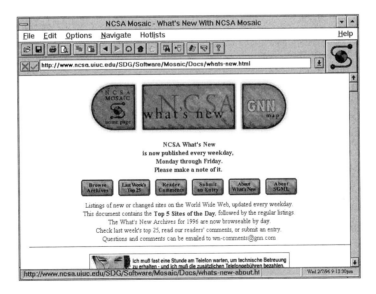

Figure 9.2. *NCSA Mosaic for Windows in Normal mode.*

Tip: Resourceful users will quickly figure out they can manually edit their PC's `autoexec.bat` file or Web browser `.ini` file to override kiosk mode, undoing the limitations you've placed on them. If you're concerned about such things, you'll need to place user startup and Windows and browser setup files on a file server to which users have read permission only.

You'll also need to limit access to the Mosaic startup command itself, or else users would simply use the Windows Program Manager's Run command to start another Mosaic session. As a result, kiosk mode may not be worth your trouble except in limited situations, such as at a trade show.

It's Your Call

It's your responsibility to determine the level of security you need on your Intranet, and, of course, to implement it. Putting most of the security measures mentioned into place, as you'll learn in the following sections, is not difficult. Your primary concern will be explaining to customers how Intranet security works, not so much as a limiting factor but as an opportunity for increased use and collaboration using your Intranet. Assuring decision-makers that they can make information available on your Intranet in a secure fashion can go a long way toward making your Intranet a success. At the same time, it's important to make sure both information providers and their customers understand a number of critical aspects of Intranet security, so they don't inadvertently defeat the purpose of it.

There are network security commonplaces, unrelated to Intranet security specifically, that need your attention. All the security precautions in the world can't protect your Intranet from overall poor security practices. Poor user choices on passwords always lead the list of computer and network security risks. If Bob uses his own name as his password, or his significant other's or pet's name, password-guessing is simple for anyone who knows him. Some people write their passwords down and tape them to their keyboards or monitors—so much for the security of those passwords. You can limit access to a sensitive Web resource based on the TCP/IP network address of the boss's PC, but if the boss walks away and leaves his PC unattended without an active screenlock, anyone who walks into the empty office can access the protected resources.

In other words, the same good security practices that should be followed in any networked computing environment should also be made to apply to your Intranet. Not doing so negates all the possible security steps you can take and reduces the value of your Intranet. Even in the absence of malice, the failure to maintain any security on your Intranet will inevitably result in an Intranet with little real utility and value to its customers.

Security on Your Web Server(s)

It's useful to break the overall subject of World Wide Web server security down into three pieces and discuss them separately. We'll do so in this section, covering user and password authentication, network address access limitations, and transaction encryption. Bear in mind throughout the discussion of these separate pieces that you can combine them in various ways to create flexible and fine-grained access control. In fact, combining two, or even all three, of these methods provides the best overall security.

Controlling Access Globally and Locally

Before we turn to the individual methods, let's cover some high-level information about Web server security setup.

Whichever individual security mechanism(s) you implement on your Web server(s), the first thing you need to know is that you can implement them at either or both of two levels. First, you can specify high-level access control in a Global Access Configuration File (GACF), specifying overall access rules for your server. In the NCSA httpd server, and those which are derived from it, such as the Windows httpd and Apache servers, the GACF is called access.conf. The CERN/W³ server doesn't have a separate GACF; rather, all access control information is in the main server configuration file, httpd.conf. The Netscape servers have a graphical interface (actually, Netscape Navigator itself) for overall server administration, including setting up access control. If you feel more comfortable editing configuration files, the Netscape server does allow them, calling them Dynamic Configuration Files. While you can do both global and local configuration using the graphical tool, a top-level Netscape Dynamic Configuration File can be created and hand-edited to function as a GACF.

Second, you can set up per-directory access control using local ACFs (LACFs) for each directory or subdirectory tree. Usually named .htaccess or .www_acl (note the leading periods in the filenames), LACFs lay out access control for an individual directory and its subdirectories, although subdirectories can also have their own LACFs. The CERN/W³ server can even extend protection to the individual file level using LACFs. In the Netscape server, lower-level Dynamic Configuration Files serve as LACFs. You can change the names of LACFs in both the NCSA and Netscape servers, but you're stuck with .www_acl in CERN/W³.

With a few important exceptions, you can do everything with an LACF you can do with a GACF. Although you can control access to every directory in your Web server document tree from the GACF, you'll probably not want to do so, especially if your needs for access control are complex. It's easy to make mistakes in a lengthy configuration file like the GACF, and you'll get unexpected, unintended results when you do. These may be hard to track down, and may not even show up without extensive testing. Overall, it's better to use your GACF to establish high-level security policy, and then set up lower-level, simpler controls using LACFs.

> **Note:** The CERN/W³ server's LACF files have a completely different format than its GACF. Most of the examples in this chapter apply only to the GACF format.

What's the GACF for, then? Most Webmasters use the GACF to establish a general access policy for their Web server. For example, if your Web server is accessible to the Internet at large and you're not using a Firewall system (see below) to limit access to your network from the outside, you may want to establish a policy in your GACF that only computers with TCP/IP network addresses that are inside your network can access your Web server's document tree. Similarly, you can use the GACF to segregate public and private areas on your Web server according to some criteria, and require usernames and passwords for access to the private area(s).

Once you've established your overall policies, you can implement LACFs to fine-tune your setup. In doing so, you can selectively apply different access controls to the directory or directories controlled by the LACF.

Earlier, exceptions to the statement that you can do everything with an LACF you can do with a GACF were mentioned. Here is a quick, incomplete list; you'll want to consult detailed server documentation for comprehensive explanations of these and others. The first one applies to all httpd servers, while the last three refer only to UNIX servers.

◆ If you want to control all access on your Web server with your GACF, you can use it to prohibit the use of LACFs altogether.

◆ You can deny use of a potentially dangerous and CPU-hogging feature called *server-side includes*, which actually cause the server to execute outside commands each time a page containing them is accessed, in user Web pages.

◆ You can limit access to CGI-bin scripts in the server's main CGI-bin directory, preventing users from creating potentially dangerous ones in their own Web directories.

◆ You can prevent potential security problems that can come from following UNIX symbolic links.

With respect to symbolic links, confidential files on the system that are completely outside of your Web server tree could be compromised by a naive or malicious user. For example, if a user created a symbolic link in her home directory pointing to the UNIX /etc/passwd file, which contains usernames and encrypted passwords, outside users could obtain a copy of that file using their Web browser, and then run a password-cracker on it offline. Of course, a malicious user can grab /etc/passwd himself and run the cracker directly, or e-mail the file to someone else for the same reason, but that's no reason to make it easy to do so via your Intranet. (The UNIX System V /etc/shadow file is not readable by non-root users, nor is the IBM AIX /etc/security/passwd file.) See "The Common Gateway Interface (CGI) and Intranet Security" later in this chapter for discussion of CGI-bin and server-side include security issues.

These generalities out of the way, let's turn our attention to the three major elements of Web server security.

Username/Password Authentication

The first major element of Web server security is username/password authentication. All the sample Web servers discussed in this book provide this basic kind of security. Let's kick off this discussion by looking at what the Web browser user sees when he encounters a Web page that requires username/password authentication for access. Figure 9.3 (part of NCSA's excellent access-control tutorial, at http://hoohoo.ncsa.uiuc.edu/docs/tutorials/) shows a Prompt dialog box asking for a username. Once the username is entered, a new dialog box asks for a password, as shown in Figure 9.4.

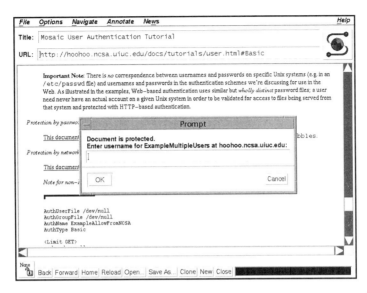

Figure 9.3. *The user is prompted to enter a username on a protected Web page.*

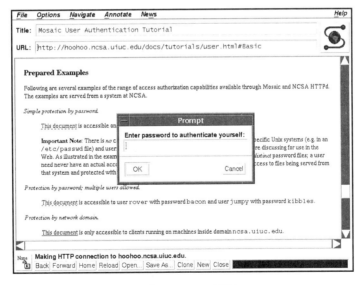

Figure 9.4. *The user is also prompted for a password on a protected Web page.*

As you can infer from Figures 9.3 and 9.4, there are three aspects of username/password authentication: the *username*, the *password* that applies to that username, and what is permitted to that user when a correct username and password are supplied. Usernames and passwords are meaningless unless you specify a directory, directory tree, or filename to which your username/password access restrictions apply.

To make this more understandable, let's look at an example. Suppose your httpd server's DocumentRoot directory contains three main subdirectories, named public, management, and personnel. Using your GACF, you can specify that access to the management and personnel subdirectory trees requires username/password authentication, while public is left wide open for anyone to access without being prompted for username and password. You can also set up LACFs within the protected subdirectories to further limit access to particularly sensitive documents by using usernames/passwords.

Setting Up Username/Password Authentication in a Netscape Server

Of the servers covered in this book, setting up username/password authentication is simplest in the Netscape servers. The Netscape servers actually use the Netscape browser itself as a graphical interface for administering the server, providing a set of private Web pages and configuration scripts to do so. Using the Server Manager page, you can easily enter new users and their passwords into what Netscape calls the user database. (Your empty user database must first be created before you can add any users and passwords to it.) Figure 9.5 shows the User Database Management screen. Notice there's an Administrative password which must be given, as well as the Username and Password for the user being added to the database. Once you've entered this information, click on Make These Changes.

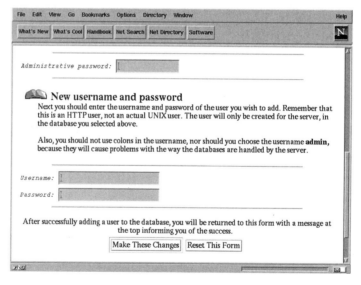

Figure 9.5. *The Netscape Communications Server add-user form.*

Once you've set up one or more users, you can continue to use the Server Manager to apply access-control rules to users. You can associate groups of users together for purposes of authentication, and define access-control rules that apply to groups as well as to individuals. With group access controls, users must still provide their own usernames and passwords, but access to a specified area of the server filetree (Netscape calls this a *realm*) can be controlled by requiring that a user be a member of a group for access. Even if a user provides the correct username and password, he may be denied access based on group access-control rules if he is not a member of that realm's group.

Setting Up Username/Password Authentication in the CERN/W[3] httpd Server

The CERN/W[3] httpd server uses a UNIX-like password file (but with only three colon-separated fields) containing usernames, encrypted passwords, and users' real names. The password file is controlled using the htadm program that comes with the httpd server software. This program enables you to create and delete user accounts, as well as change and verify existing passwords. Although you can provide all the information htadm needs on the command line, it's easier to let the program prompt you for it. For example, to add a new username and password:

```
# path/to/htadm /path/to/passwordfile
```

You must specify the name of the password file on the command line, but htadm will prompt you for the function you want to perform and the actual username, password, and user's real name, as appropriate. (You can use multiple words in the realname field to include a full name and/or other information.) If you're in a hurry, or have a long list of users to add or delete, you can take advantage of specifying all the htadm command-line arguments at once, like one of these examples:

```
# htadm -adduser passwordfile joeuser joespassword Joe User
# htadm -deluser passwordfile baduser
```

The first example creates the user joeuser with the password joespassword, while the second deletes the user baduser. This enables you to do mass account deletion using shell looping and/ or to take username, password, and realname input from a file. You'll need something like the expect package (described in Chapter 14, "Web Access to Commercial Database Applications") to do automated mass account creation. There are also -passwd and -check command-line arguments to htadm which enable you to change and verify passwords, respectively.

As with the Netscape server, the CERN/W[3] httpd server also enables you to associate individual users with groups. You can set up group authentication rules in LACFs that control access to portions of your Web server document tree. CERN/W[3] uses a group file, the format of which is based on the standard UNIX /etc/group format, but it has an added feature for defining access-control rules and for recursive inclusion of groups into meta-groups. A simple group file, which we'll use for examples in this chapter, might be something like this:

```
management: tom, mary, joan
personnel: anne, joe, jerry
staff: management, personnel
public: All, Anybody
```

Here, four groups are defined. The first two each contain a list of several individual usernames, but the last two are groups of groups. (Two special groups, *All*, meaning all authenticated users, and *Anybody* meaning anyone, authenticated or not, are predefined by the CERN/W[3] httpd server software, and refer to anyone who might access the server; see the server documentation for details on the distinction between All and Anybody.)

After setting up your password and group files, you can add access-control protection to your server. As noted above, high-level rules go in `httpd.conf`, the GACF. Access-control rules in `httpd.conf` use the Protect directive and associated protection rulesets. Here's a simple Protect directive, based on the group file shown above. It implements the example division of your Web server's document tree into public, management, and personnel sub-trees:

```
Protect /personnel/* Personnel
```

This example indicates that all subdirectories and files in the `personnel` sub-tree of your Web server `DocumentRoot` are to subject to the rules in the protection ruleset named `Personnel`. (You can name protection rulesets with any name you want, but it makes sense to use meaningful names.) According to this Protect directive, the ruleset itself also appears in the GACF, under the label `Personnel`, and might look like this:

```
Protection Personnel {
     AuthType      Basic
     Passwordfile /usr/local/etc/httpd/passwd
     GroupFile    /usr/local/etc/httpd/group
     GetMask      personnel
}
```

> **Note:** Your Protect directive can specify the protection ruleset be read from a file, rather than from another part of the GACF. In this case, the directive would look like this:
>
> ```
> Protect /personnel/* /usr/local/etc/httpd/acls/Personnel
> ```
>
> Here, the absolute pathname to the file named `Personnel` (not relative to the server `DocumentRoot`) is specified. This example assumes you've created a special subdirectory (`/usr/local/etc/httpd/acls`) in which to store all your access-control information. If you use individual files like this to define your protection rulesets, you need not enter the curly braces that are required in the GACF.

This simple example applies username/password authentication access control to all files and subdirectories in the `personnel` directory, using the following criteria, all of which must be met before access is granted:

- ◆ Users must enter a username and password.
- ◆ Usernames and passwords are validated against the file `/usr/local/etc/httpd/passwd`.
- ◆ Authenticated usernames are checked for membership in the group named `personnel` in the groups file `/usr/local/etc/httpd/group`.

Going back to our sample group file above, you can see only users Anne, Joe, and Jerry will be granted access to files in this directory tree. Even if Tom provides his correct password, he will not be given access.

This has been a very cursory look at user authentication in the CERN/W³ httpd server. Your Protect directives and protection rulesets can be quite detailed, including other features not described here. In addition, you can set up both a default protection ruleset and progressively more limited protection rulesets according to your own criteria, adding access control all the way down to the individual file level. For details, see the documentation which comes with the CERN/W³ httpd server software (on the *Building an Intranet* CD-ROM). Alternatively, check out the World Wide Web Consortium's online CERN/W³ httpd documentation at `http://www.w3.org/pub/WWW/Daemon/User/Admin.html`.

Setting Up Username/Password Authentication in the NCSA httpd Server

The NCSA httpd server, along with those derived from it (WinHttpd for Windows and the Apache package for UNIX systems), provides similar username/password authentication mechanisms. Except where there are differences among these packages, we'll discuss them as a group.

While these packages use authentication methods that are similar to the methods used in the CERN/W³ httpd package, there are differences. Let's first focus on the similarities. Most importantly, the NCSA packages support both GACFs and LACFs, enabling you to set high-level policy at the server level and then fine-tune it at the directory and subdirectory levels. In addition, both individual-user and group authentication are provided for. Finally, some configuration commands affecting critical items listed earlier, such as AllowOverride, may only appear in a GACF. You can also preclude the server-side includes use and symbolic link following, for example, as described earlier.

The GACF in the NCSA packages is the file named `access.conf` (`access.cnf` in WinHttpd), and is located in the `conf` subdirectory of your Web server's file tree. On UNIX systems, the server is usually installed in `/usr/local/etc/httpd`, while on Windows systems, the server is in `c:\httpd`. In both cases, there exists a `conf` subdirectory in the top-level httpd directory. The layout and syntax of the access.conf file is significantly different from the GACF in the CERN/W³ httpd server, however.

The NCSA file is divided into sections, one for each directory to be controlled. Each directory section in `access.conf` looks something like this:

```
<Directory /absolute/directory/path>
[ Various configuration commands ]
</Directory>
```

Like HTML markup, each `Directory` (the literal word `Directory` must appear) section is marked off by the `access.conf` tags `<Directory>` and `</Directory>`, surrounded as shown with angle brackets. Case is not significant in the word `Directory`, though it may be significant in the actual directory name.

It's important to note the directory path here is an absolute pathname, and is not relative to either the Web server's `ServerRoot` or `DocumentRoot` directories. If you mean `/usr/local/etc/htdocs/`, for example, you must specify it in full, and not just simply use `/htdocs`. Within each `Directory` section of the file, you specify one or more options, or configuration commands, which will be applied by the server to the specified directory. There are a number of different options, but we're concerned here with username/password authentication.

Of course, before you can apply a username/password access control, you need to have established users and passwords on your server. Usernames and (encrypted) passwords are stored in a special httpd password file. NCSA provides a utility program, htpasswd, for creating this file; you'll find it in the support subdirectory of your NCSA httpd server file tree, and you may need to compile it. The syntax of the htpasswd command is substantially simpler than that of the CERN/W³ htadm command, as are its capabilities. To add a user to your password file, or change his password, use this syntax:

```
# htpasswd /path/to/passwordfile username
```

If you don't already have a password file, you need to modify this command a bit:

```
# htpasswd -c /path/to/passwordfile username
```

The -c argument creates a new password file, so you use it only once. If you use it again, you'll erase your current password file. You can name your password file anything you like.

You can't remove a user from your password file with the htpasswd command. Instead, you'll have to hand edit the password file with a text editor and delete the user's entry. The format of the file is quite simple, with just two fields in each record, separated by a colon:

```
tkevans:TyWhfX9/zYd7Y
```

Obviously, the first field is the username. The second field is the encrypted password. Permissions on the password file must be set so as to be readable by the system user under whose userid the httpd server runs (usually, the no-privileges user nobody), so passwords are not stored in clear text.

Besides the httpd password file, the NCSA servers also respect a group file, in which you can define groups of users. Groups can be treated like individual users with respect to access control, so the group file can both add capabilities and save data-entry time. For the most part, syntax of the NCSA httpd group file is exactly the same as that shown earlier in this chapter for the CERN/W³ group file.

There is one significant difference in what the two group files may contain, however. As noted above, the CERN/W³ group file can include group entries which consist of other groups. The NCSA group file can include only individual users as members of groups. Thus, the recursive staff group consisting of all the members of the personnel and management groups is not possible in NCSA. To create such a group, you'd need to re-enter each user's name in the group entry for staff.

Now that you've set up your password and group files, you're ready to add username/password authentication in your GACF or LACFs. Let's first look at an example, then take it apart:

```
# Anybody in the personnel group can get to the top level
# of the personnel filetree
<Directory /usr/local/web-docs/personnel>
```

```
AuthType Basic
AuthName Personnel Only
AuthUserFile /usr/local/etc/httpd/userpw
AuthGroupFile /usr/local/etc/httpd/ourgroup
<Limit GET>
Require group personnel
</Limit>
</Directory>
```

Here, in the GACF file, we've limited access to the top level of the personnel tree of our Web server. Only members of the predefined group personnel (defined in the ourgroup file) are allowed to GET (access) files in the directory tree, and they must provide a valid username and password, verifiable against the encrypted password in the userpw file.

Most of the lines in the example are clear, but a couple need a little more explanation. AuthName is just an arbitrary label for your rule; you should put something there that'll make sense when you read the rule a year from now, and you can use a phrase here. The <Limit GET> subsection of the file is, of course, the critical section, in which you actually specify who has access. Note that you can also include comments in the file, as indicated by the first two lines, where the # symbol is used.

As we've noted, you can use LACFs to refine the access rules in your GACF. Here's an example of an NCSA httpd LACF: a file named .htacces in the personnel/executive subdirectory. See if you can translate its meaning:

```
AuthType Basic
AuthName Anne Only
AuthUserFile /usr/local/etc/httpd/userpw
AuthGroupFile /usr/local/etc/httpd/ourgroup
<Limit GET>
Require user anne
</Limit>
```

You're right—this rule limits access to the executive subdirectory to a single user: anne. The heart of this rule is, of course, the matter between the <Limit> and </Limit> tags near the end of the file. Other users, including the other members of the personnel group, are denied access, even if they give a correct password for themselves. A dialog box will demand Anne's username and password. Notice that this LACF file, which controls access to a single directory (personnel/executive), does not require the opening and closing <Directory> and </Directory> tags required in the server's GACF since there are no subdirectories in this directory.

Important Warnings About Username/Password Authentication

Unless the access rules change (that is, new LACFs are encountered) as a user moves around on your Intranet Web pages (as with the personnel/executive subdirectory in the example above), he will be prompted only once in his browser session for a username and password. As long as he continues his browser session, he can access all of the files and directories available to him under the most recent access rule, without being prompted again for his password. This is for convenience—customers shouldn't have to repeatedly provide their usernames and passwords at each step of the way when the access rule hasn't changed.

However, this situation has important ramifications if you follow it out logically. Suppose Anne, having authenticated herself to access the `executive` subdirectory, leaves her Netscape or Mosaic session running, as most of us do. Her privileged access remains open to all the files protected by that one-time, possibly days-old, authentication. If she leaves her workstation, PC, or terminal unattended when she goes to lunch or goes home for the day, without any sort of active screen or office door lock, anyone can sit down and browse the files and directories that are supposed to be limited to Anne's eyes only. This is a potential security breach, and one which you as Webmaster can do little about. This is really no different from a user who leaves his workstation unattended without logging off. While you can try to educate your customers about such everyday security matters, even though they have very little to do with your Intranet, you'll agree a security breach like this can be potentially harmful to all your work.

As a further technical note, user passwords are transmitted over your network by most Web browsers in a relatively insecure fashion. It is not terribly difficult for a user with a network snooper running to pick out the httpd network packets containing user passwords. While the passwords are not transmitted in clear text, the encoding/encryption method is a very old and widely-used one. Every UNIX system, for example, has a program (`uudecode`) which can decode the encrypted password in a captured httpd packet. If you believe this may be a problem on your Intranet, you'll want to consider the secure Web servers and browsers which encrypt user-transmitted data, as discussed in the section, "Secure/Encrypted Transactions," later in this chapter.

Authentication Based on Network Hostname or Address

All the Web servers we've discussed in this chapter provide an additional authentication method, using the TCP/IP hostname or numerical network address of customer workstations or PCs as access criteria. As you'll learn in later chapters, in the context of CGI-bin programming, every Web browser request for a document or other Intranet resource contains the numerical IP address of the requesting computer. Servers look up hostnames using these addresses and the Domain Name Service. You can set up rules in your GACFs and LACFs based on either of these, making a considerable amount of fine-tuning possible. Let's look at the three main servers we've been considering.

Hostname/Address Authentication in the NCSA Servers

Because the format of the NCSA `access.conf` file is still fresh in your mind from the last section, let's look at this one first in the context of hostname/network address authentication. As you'll accurately presume, you'll place your rules for this sort of authentication within the `<Limit>` and `</Limit>` tags of the server's GACFs or LACFs `<Directory>` sections. Do this with several new access-control directives, including

- `Order`, which specifies the order in which the other directives in the file are to be evaluated
- `Allow`, which permits access based on a hostname or IP address
- `Deny`, which denies access based on a hostname or IP address

Here's a simple example limiting access to the `personnel` subtree of your Web server. (The opening and closing `<Directory>` tags have been left off so as to cut right to the chase.) For purposes of this example, we'll assume your company's TCP/IP network domain is subdivided along operational lines, and that there is a `personnel` subdomain, in which all of the computers have IP addresses beginning with 123.45.67.

```
<Limit GET>
order deny,allow
deny from all
allow from personnel.mycompany.com
allow from 123.45.67
</Limit>
```

In plain English, this example rule says "access is denied to all hostnames and IP addresses *except* those in the subdomain `personnel.mycompany.com` and those in the numerical IP address family `123.45.67`. Notice that both the subdomain name and IP address family are wildcards that may match many computers; you can also use individual hostnames or addresses for even finer-grained control.

As you can see, we've used each of the three directives listed, and you might wonder why both `allow` and `deny` statements are used. The World Wide Web was built with openness in mind, not security. The server therefore assumes, without instructions to the contrary, all directories are accessible to all hostnames/addresses. (This is the same as the username/password authentication about which you learned earlier. In the absence of a username/password requirement, all directories and files are accessible to all users.) Without a `deny` directive, the rule might just as well not exist. The server assumes, in the absence of a `deny` directive, all hostnames/addresses are allowed access. Why have any rule at all, then, since all are allowed access? In other words, it makes no sense to have rules with `allow` directives without `deny` directives.

Because you must have both `deny` and `allow` directives in order to have meaningful access rules, the order in which the rules are evaluated is important. One way to do this is to follow the actual order in which the directives appear in the file, but it's easy to make mistakes with this approach. Instead, NCSA httpd uses the `order` directive so you can explicitly instruct that your directives be processed in the order you want. The example uses `order deny,allow`, indicating all incoming requests are to be tested against the `deny` directive(s) first, then tested against the `allow` directives. In the example, you set up a general `deny` rule, then make exceptions to it. The `order` directive can also be turned around, with `allow` rules processed first. Using this sequence, you can make your server generally available, then add selective denials. For example:

```
<Limit GET>
order allow,deny
allow from all
deny from .mycompetitor.com
</Limit>
```

Here, you're granting access to your server to everyone *except* your competitor. For more information about hostname/IP address authentication, see the NCSA httpd server documentation on the *Building an Intranet* CD-ROM, or the authentication tutorial at NCSA's Web site, `http://hoohoo.ncsa.uiuc.edu/docs/tutorials/`.

Hostname/Address Authentication in the CERN/W³ Server

You can also impose hostname/IP address access control with the CERN/W³ httpd server. Although you can accomplish the same ends as with the NCSA server, the method of doing so is different, and the access-control file formats are different. As you'll recall from the earlier username/password authentication, the CERN/W³ httpd server uses protection rulesets in the GACF or LACF. Let's modify the earlier example, in which we limited access to the personnel portion of your Web server by groupname, to illustrate hostname/IP address authentication. For purposes of this example, let's assume your company's TCP/IP network domain is subdivided along operational lines, and that there is a personnel subdomain, all of the computers in which have IP addresses beginning with 123.45.67.

```
Protection Personnel {
     AuthType    Basic
     Passwordfile /usr/local/etc/httpd/passwd
     GroupFile   /usr/local/etc/httpd/group
     GetMask     @*.personnel.mycompany.com,@123.45.67.*
}
```

As you can see, the only thing changed about this ruleset is the GetMask line. In the earlier example, we used GetMask to limit access based on membership in a defined group of usernames, personnel. Here, we've done access-control limitation in two ways. First, we specified an Internet Domain Name Server (DNS) subdomain name (personnel.mycompany.com). Second, the rule contains a numerical IP address family. In both cases, we've used a special wildcard syntax; note the use of both the @ symbol and the asterisk (*). You can think of the string @*.personnel.mycompany.com as meaning any user at any computer in the personnel subdomain. Similarly, @123.45.67.* refers to any user at any computer with an IP address beginning with 123.45.67.

You may be wondering why, because all computers in the personnel subdomain have IP addresses in the 123.45.67 family, we've included both rules. This is done for a couple of reasons. The first reason, obviously, is to show that you can use either symbolic host/domain/subdomain names or numerical IP addresses.

The second reason is a more technical one. In some cases, your httpd server won't be able to resolve the hostname of a computer making a request for a document from the numerical IP address it receives in the browser request. The reasons for this inability vary, but they usually involve out-of-date or inaccurate DNS information. In growing networks, newly networked computers may not get added to the database promptly. Errors in DNS configuration, such as misspelled hostnames, can also result in unresolvable hostnames. To be safe, placing both symbolic host/domain name and numerical IP address information in your GetMask is a good idea; there's nothing like having the boss's brand-new PowerMac being denied access to your Intranet's Web server on his very first try because its DNS entry hasn't been made by the network operations staff yet.

Hostname/Address Authentication in the Netscape Server

As with most aspects of Netscape Communications Server administration, you can set up hostname/IP address access control using a graphical interface. Start up the Administration Manager, and select Restrict Access From Certain Addresses. This opens a document with extensive instructions for setting up access restrictions. You'll find fill-in boxes in this document for hostname/IP address restrictions. Figures 9.6, 9.7, and 9.8 show the essential parts of this form. You have all the same choices here for restricting access that you saw in the NCSA and CERN/W³ httpd servers.

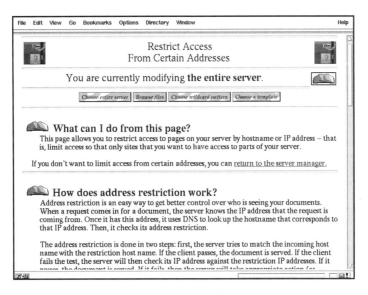

Figure 9.6. *The Netscape Communications Server host restriction (Part 1).*

Your first step is to select what Netscape calls a *resource* to which you'll apply hostname/IP address restriction. For this purpose, a resource can be the entire Web server tree, a particular part of it, or one or more individual files. Clickable buttons (as shown at the top of Figure 9.6) enable you to select the resource you want. In our example, your resource would be the `/usr/local/web-docs/personnel` subdirectory of your httpd server tree. Once you've selected your resource, scroll down the form to the headline `What To Protect` (see Figure 9.7). Here, you'll two important choices.

If you like, you can simply accept the default of protecting everything in the selected resource. Or, if you prefer, you can specify a wildcard filename pattern to match the files you want to protect. Notice the hyperlink labeled `wildcard pattern`, which takes you to a detailed document describing how wildcard pattern-matching works in the Netscape servers. (Essentially, it's standard UNIX shell filename expansion, but has some additional features.)

For the purposes of our example, you need not enter anything, since we're going to accept the default restriction to all files and directories in the `personnel` resource. However, you could have entered the wildcard pattern for the files to which you wanted to apply your hostname/IP address restrictions in the boxed labeled Pattern of files to protect. The Addresses to allow section, which starts in Figure 9.7 and ends in Figure 9.8, tells you how to enter hostnames and IP addresses.

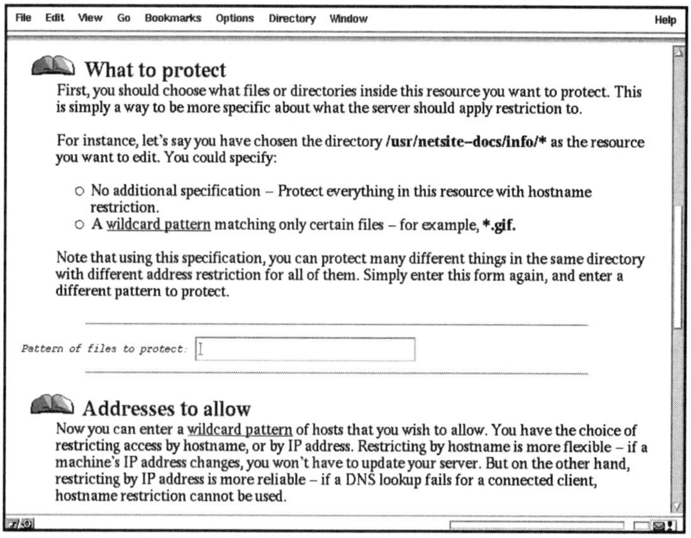

Figure 9.7. *Netscape Communications Server host restriction (Part 2).*

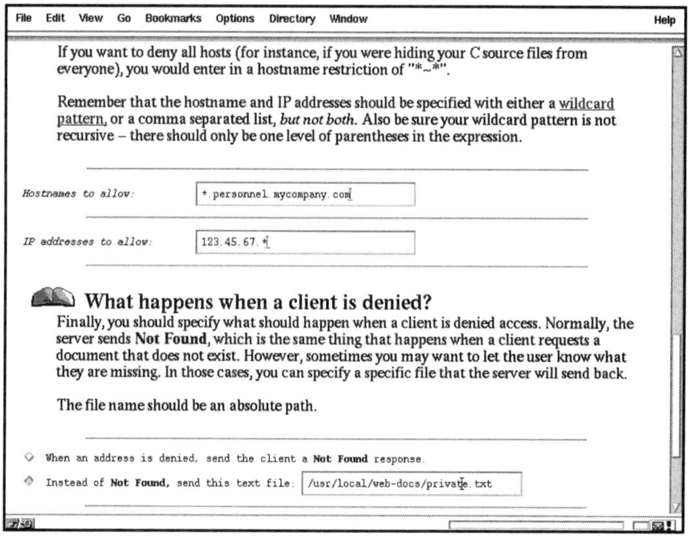

Figure 9.8. *Netscape Communications Server host restriction (Part 3).*

As with filenames, you can enter either specific individual hostnames or IP addresses, or wildcard patterns that match multiple hosts. The hostnames to allow and IP addresses to allow boxes are shown in Figure 9.8 with our `personnel` example filled in.

The bottom of Figure 9.8 shows how you can set up a custom message to users who try to access restricted resources, giving them a reason for the denial of their request. You need not use this, but it can be friendlier than the generic `Not Found` message most httpd servers return. Here, we've set things up so the contents of the file /usr/local/web-docs/private.txt will be returned. This file could explain politely, for example, that access to personnel resources on the Web server is limited to the Personnel Department. Once you're finished with the form, scroll all the way to the bottom (not shown in Figure 9.8) and click Make These Changes to apply your restrictions.

An Important Warning About Hostname/IP Address Authentication

All of the Web server software we've described in this chapter of *Building an Intranet* trustingly accepts the word of a requesting computer when it sends its IP address. There is no verification possible of this information. It's relatively easy for a user to change the hostname/IP address of a UNIX system, and laughably easy to change that of a PC or Mac. A curious, mischievous, and/ or malicious person can reconfigure his computer to impersonate someone else's simply by changing the IP address of his own. While this is an overall network security issue, not specifically one for your Intranet, it's important you know about it because it can affect the security of your access-controlled documents. Security-minded network administrators can use special hardware and software to prevent this sort of IP spoofing, but for your Intranet's purposes, you'll probably want to combine hostname/IP address authentication with username/password authentication, as outlined in the following section.

Combined Authentication

Now that you understand how username/password and hostname/IP address authentication work separately, let's consider how you can combine the two to beef up your access control. Let's begin with the Netscape Communications server.

Combined Authentication in the Netscape Server

Netscape's scanty $40 documentation for the Communications server doesn't address this subject directly, but you can infer from it how to implement combined username/password and hostname/IP address authentication. As you learned earlier, the Netscape server uses one or more user databases to store usernames and passwords, and you can apply access-control limits based on both individual usernames and on group membership. Also, the Netscape server can restrict access by hostname/IP address, as described in the previous section. While the Netscape Communications Server manual, and its essentially-identical online help, describe these two methods as an either-or choice, it would appear that applying both kinds of access control to a single resource would result in both methods being applied. In other words, you can:

◆ Define a set of users, such as the example personnel group we've used, in the Netscape user database.

◆ Apply username/password authentication, such as to the personnel resource, limiting access to the members of the personnel group in the user database.

◆ Apply hostname/IP address restrictions, such as to the same personnel *resource*, limiting access to those computers in the personnel subdomain (or even to the individual computers of the members of the personnel group).

Because the documentation doesn't say what happens in such a situation, including whether there is an order of precedence in the testing of the access-control rules, you should very carefully check how things work when you set up intersecting access-control rules of this sort. For example, it isn't clear if the username/password authentication rule would be applied first, prompting the customer for a username and password, only to have the hostname/IP address rule kick in to deny access even to an authenticated user, or whether the latter rule would be applied first, which should be the case.

Fortunately for those who want to have their access-control rules perform exactly as they want them to, Netscape provides another means of access control, using Dynamic Configuration Files (DCFs). You can think of Netscape's DCFs as what we've called LACFs in this chapter—access-control files which apply to a single directory or subdirectory on your Web server. Usually named .nsconfig (note the leading period in the filename), DCFs are organized into discrete sections with HTML-like markup. Each section is marked off by the tags `<Files>` and `</Files>`, between which are access-control and other rules which apply to the files specified. You can do many things with Netscape DCFs; here's an example which replicates the combined username/password and hostname/IP address access control to the personnel section of the example Web server.

```
<Files *>
RequireAuth dbm=webusers userpat="anne¦joe¦jerry" userlist="anne,joe,jerry"
RestrictAccess method=HTTP method-type=allow ip=123.45.67.*
dns=*.personnel.mycompany.com
</Files>
```

This DCF, which goes in the top level of the /usr/local/web-docs/personnel directory, applies to all files and subdirectories in that directory tree. It requires username/password authentication, limiting access to users anne, joe, and jerry listed in the Netscape user database named webusers. It further limits access by both numerical IP address and symbolic hostname, both using wildcards. Notice that it's not necessary to specify both allow and deny rules; Netscape's server takes a more conservative approach to access restrictions than do NCSA and CERN/W[3].

> **Tip:** Netscape DCFs in lower-level directories take precedence over the rules in a DCF in a higher-level directory. Thus, by creating a .nsconfig file in the personnel/executive subdirectory, you can limit access to files in that directory to the user anne, as you did earlier in this chapter. Such a DCF might look like this:
>
> ```
> <Files *>
> RequireAuth dbm=webusers userpat=anne userlist=anne
> RestrictAccess method=HTTP method-type=allow ip=123.45.67.89
> dns=annspc.personnel.mycompany.com
> </Files>
> ```

You can enable Netscape DCFs using fill-in forms similar to those shown earlier for setting up hostname/IP address access control. For example, you can enable a DCF for a given server resource, and the graphical interface will create a skeleton .nsconfig file. However, you'll need to use a text editor to add your own detailed access-control and other directives.

Combined Authentication in the NCSA Servers

Combining username/password and hostname/IP address authentication in the NCSA httpd servers is fairly simple. You'll extend the rules in the <Limit> section(s) of either the GACF or LACF. Here's our now-familiar personnel example, modified to combine the two access-control methods.

```
AuthType Basic
AuthName Personnel Only
AuthUserFile /usr/local/etc/httpd/userpw
AuthGroupFile /usr/local/etc/httpd/ourgroup
<Limit GET>
order deny,allow
deny from all
allow from personnel.mycompany.com
allow from 123.45.67
Require group personnel
</Limit>
```

As you can see, all that was needed was to pull in both of the two sample methods shown in the earlier NCSA examples. Notice that order counts in the <Limit> section. Here, the hostname/IP address access control rules are applied first (using the deny and then allow sequence). Once those rules are satisfied, the user is prompted for a password as the username/password authentication is applied. Based on this example, it's easy to modify this rule for a LACF in the personnel/ executive subdirectory, simply by replacing Require group personnel with Require user anne.

Combined Authentication in the CERN/W³ Server

The CERN/W³ Server is similarly capable of combining username/password and hostname/IP address authentication. Here, you'll modify the GetMask directive in your GACF. Again, here is our modified personnel example, this time limiting access using both methods.

```
Protection Personnel {
    AuthType      Basic
    Passwordfile  /usr/local/etc/httpd/passwd
    GroupFile     /usr/local/etc/httpd/group
    GetMask       @*.personnel.mycompany.com, @123.45.67.*,
                  personnel
}
```

As with the NCSA example above, this one applies hostname/IP address access-control first (because it appears on the GetMask line first), and then username/password authentication. Both rules must be satisfied before access is permitted. To further restrict access, you'll need to develop LACFs for individual directories and subdirectories. As noted earlier, the CERN/W³ LACF format is completely different from that of the server's GACF. Here's one (note the file must be named .www_acl) that can be placed in the personnel/executive directory to limit access to the subdirectory to user anne, and only from a specific hostname/IP address:

```
 *  :  GET  : anne@annspc.personell.mycompany.com,
ann@123.45.67.89
```

This simple file has just one rule. (The rule is usually a single line, with colon-separated records, but it can be wrapped, as shown above, after a comma.) No one other than the user anne (who must give a password under the rule in the previous example) can access any files in the personnel/executive directory. Moreover, anne must be accessing the files from her normal PC to be granted access, even if she gives the correct password. For more information on CERN/W³ LACFs, check out the online documentation at http://www.w3.org/pub/WWW/Daemon/User/Admin.html.

Secure/Encrypted Transactions

You can further enhance security on your Intranet by encrypting Web transactions. When you use an encryption facility, information submitted by customers using Web fill-in forms—including usernames, passwords, and other confidential information—can be transmitted securely to and from the Web server.

There is a wide range of proposed and/or partially implemented encryption solutions for the Web, but most are not ready for prime time. Of the several proposed methods, only two have emerged in anything like full-blown form. Let's look at the Secure HTTP (S-HTTP) and Secure Socket Layer (SSL) protocols in this chapter. Unfortunately, the two are not compatible with each other, though compatibility is possible. Worse, Web browsers and servers which support one method don't support the other, so you can reliably use one or the other only if you carefully match your Web server and customers' browsers.

S-HTTP

Secure HTTP was developed by Enterprise Integration Technologies and RSA Data Security, and the public S-HTTP standards are now managed by CommerceNet, a not-for-profit consortium that is conducting the first large-scale market trial of technologies and business processes to support electronic commerce over the Internet. (For general information on CommerceNet, see http://www.commerce.net/.) S-HTTP is a modified version of the current httpd protocol. It supports:

◆ User and Web server authentication using Digital Signatures and Signature Keys using both the RSA and MD5 algorithms.

◆ Privacy of transactions, using several different key-based encryption methods.

◆ Generation of key certificates for server authentication.

EIT has developed modified versions of the NCSA httpd server and NCSA Mosaic (for both UNIX systems and Microsoft Windows) which support S-HTTP transactions. While the licensing terms allow for NCSA to fold EIT's work into its free httpd server and Mosaic browsers, there's been no public indication of NCSA's plans to do so. Meanwhile, the CommerceNet secure NCSA httpd server and Mosaic browser are available only to members of CommerceNet. You'll find information about both packages, including full-text user manuals, at the CommerceNet home page http://www.commerce.net/.

SSL

S-HTTP seems to have been engulfed in the 1995 Netscape tidal wave. Unwilling to wait for widely-accepted httpd security standards to evolve (as it was with HTML as well), Netscape Communications Corporation developed its own Secure Sockets Layer encryption mechanism. SSL occupies a spot on the ISO seven-layer network reference below that of the httpd protocol, which operates at the application layer. Rather than developing a completely new protocol to replace httpd, SSL sits between httpd and the underlying TCP/IP network protocols and can intervene to create secure transactions. Netscape makes the technical details of SSL publicly available. In addition, C-language source code for a reference implementation of SSL is freely available for noncommercial use.

The Netscape Navigator Web browser has built-in SSL support, as does the Netscape Commerce server; the Netscape Communications server does not support SSL. Given Netscape's share of the Web browser market, it's hard to see how S-HTTP has much of a chance at becoming widely available. With the exception of NCSA Mosaic, most other Web browsers have—or have promised—SSL support. Some of them are Spry's Internet in a Box, that company's newer product, Mosaic in a Box for Windows 95, and Release 2 of Microsoft's Internet Explorer for Windows 95 and the Macintosh. By the time you read *Building an Intranet*, all of these packages may have completed their SSL implementations.

> **Note:** Even though a browser might support secure transactions using SSL or S-HTTP, no transactions are actually secure except those between the browser and a compatible Web server. Thus, using Netscape, for example, won't provide any security unless you're also using the Netscape Commerce server. It's also important to note that most mechanisms for passing Web services through network Firewalls (that is, proxying) don't support secure transactions unless *both* the proxy server and the destination server do.

As noted in the preceding section, the Netscape Commerce server supports the company's SSL security mechanism. Other packages that support SSL include the Secure WebServer package from Open Market, Inc. (http://www.openmarket.com/), which also supports S-HTTP, and IBM's Internet Connection Secure Server, which runs under IBM's UNIX, AIX Version 4, and OS/2 Warp. (Evaluation copies of Secure WebServer for several UNIX systems are available at the Open Market Web site.)

Both Secure WebServer and Internet Connection Secure Server are based on Terisa Systems, Inc.'s SecureWeb Client and Server Toolkit. This package provides source code for developers building secure Web servers and browsers. The Terisa Toolkit supports both SSL and S-HTTP. For more information about the package, visit Terisa's Web site at http://www.terisa.com/. Open Market's promotional announcements about Secure WebServer state that the package supports secure transactions through Internet Firewalls, but no details on just how this works are provided.

The Common Gateway Interface (CGI) and Intranet Security

CGI is the mechanism that stands behind all the wonderful interactive fill-in forms you'll want to put on your Intranet. Your customers demand these kinds of Intranet resources, and *Building an Intranet* provides a number of technical tips on creating CGI-bin scripts. You need to be aware, though, CGI-bin scripting is susceptible to security problems, and take a good deal of care to do your scripting to avoid them.

You can minimize much of your risk for security breaches in CGI-bin scripting by focusing in one particular area: include in your scripts explicit code for dealing with unexpected user input. The reason for this is simple: you should never trust any information a user enters in a fill-in form. Just because, for instance, a fill-in form asks for a user's name or e-mail address, there is no guarantee that the user filling in the form won't put in incorrect information. Customers make typographical errors, but probing crackers, even those inside your organization, may *intentionally* enter unexpected data, in an attempt to break the script. Such efforts can include UNIX shell metacharacters and other shell constructs (for example, the asterisk, the pipe, the back tick, the dollar sign, the semicolon, and others) in an effort to get the script to somehow give the user shell access. Others intentionally try to overflow fixed program text buffers to see if the program can be coaxed into overwriting the program's stack. To be secure, your CGI-bin scripts have to anticipate and deal safely with unexpected input.

Other problems inherent with CGI-bin scripts include:

- ◆ Calling outside programs, opening up potential security holes in the external program. The UNIX sendmail program is a favorite cracker target.
- ◆ Using server-side includes in scripts which dynamically generate HTML code. Make sure user input doesn't include literal HTML markup that could call a server-side include when your script runs.
- ◆ Using SUID scripts are almost always dangerous, whether in a CGI-bin context or not.

Paul Phillips maintains a short but powerful list of CGI-bin security resources on the Web. Check out `http://www.cerf.net/~paulp/cgi-security`, where you'll find a number of documents spelling out these and other risks of CGI-bin scripting. For an extensive list of general CGI-related resources, go to Yahoo's CGI page, at `http://www.yahoo.com/Computers_and_Internet/Internet/World_Wide_Web/CGI___Common_Gateway_Interface/index.html`.

Your Intranet and the Internet

Is your Intranet accessible from the Internet? If so, all of the security problems of the Internet are now your Intranet's problems, too. Throughout this book, an implicit assumption has been made that your Intranet is private to your organization. You can, however, connect safely to the Internet, and still protect your Intranet. You can even use the Internet as a means of letting remote sites in your company access your Intranet.

First, let's look at some Internet security basics.

Firewalls

It's a fact of Internet life there are people out their who want to break into other people's networks via the Internet. Reasons vary from innocent curiosity to malicious cracking to business and international espionage. At the same time, the value of the Internet to organizations and businesses is so great that vendors are rushing to fill the need for Internet security with Internet Firewalls. An Internet Firewall is a device which sits between your internal network and the outside Internet. Its purpose is to limit access into and out of your network based on your organization's access policy.

A Firewall can be anything from a set of filtering rules set up on the router between you and the Internet to an elaborate application gateway consisting of one or more specially-configured computers which control access. Firewalls permit desired services coming from the outside, such as Internet e-mail, to pass. In addition, most Firewalls now allow access to the World Wide Web from inside the protected networks. The idea is to allow some services to pass but to deny others. For example, you may be able to use the telnet utility to log into systems out on the Internet, but users on remote systems cannot use it to log into your local system because of the Firewall.

Here are a couple of good general Web resources about Internet Firewalls:

- ◆ Marcus Ranum's Internet Firewalls Frequently Asked Questions document at `http://www.greatcircle.com/firewalls/info/FAQ.html`
- ◆ Kathy Fulmer's annotated list of commercial and freeware Firewall packages (with many hyperlinks to Firewall vendor Web pages) at `http://www.greatcircle.com/firewalls/vendors.html`.

If your company is also connected to the Internet, you'll want to know how to make sure your Intranet isn't generally accessible to the outside world. While you learned earlier in this chapter about denying access to your Web server using hostname and IP address authentication, the fact that IP addresses can be easily spoofed makes it essential that you not rely on this mechanism as your only protection. You'll still want to rely on an Internet Firewall to protect your Intranet, as well as all your other network assets. Moreover, in all likelihood, unless your corporate network is not connected to the outside world at all, you'll want to ensure the security of your other Intranet services, including not only your Web servers, but also your ftp, Gopher, USENET news, WAIS, and other TCP/IP network services.

Virtual Intranet

More and more companies with widely distributed offices, manufacturing sites, and other facilities are turning to use of the Internet to replace private corporate networks connecting the sites. Such a situation involves multiple connections to the Internet by the company, with the use of the Internet itself as the backbone network for the company. While such an approach is fraught with security risks, many organizations are using it for nonsensitive information exchange within the company. Using a properly set up Firewall, companies can provide access to services inside one site's network to users at another site. Still, however, the data which flows across the Internet backbones between the corporate sites is mostly unencrypted, plain text data which Internet snoopers can easily read. Standard Firewalls don't help with this situation.

A number of Firewall companies have recently developed Virtual Private Network (VPN) capabilities. Essentially, VPN is an extension of standard Firewall capabilities to permit authenticated, encrypted communications between sites over the Internet. That is, using a VPN, users at a remote site can access sensitive data at another site in a secure fashion over the Internet. All the data that flows on the public Internet backbones is encrypted before it leaves the local network, then decrypted when it arrives at the other end of the connection.

The most mature VPN product comes from Raptor Systems (http://www.raptor.com/), part of the company's Eagle family of products, while others are available from Checkpoint (http://www.checkpoint.com/) and Telecommerce (http://www.telecommerce.com/).

Figure 9.9 shows a schematic drawing of a VPN, re-printed with the permission of Raptor Systems, Inc. The cloud represents the Internet, and the Firewall system, local network, and remote site are shown as workstations. The broad line connecting the workstation at the remote site to the local workstation illustrates the VPN. Such products make it possible for you to extend the availability of your Intranet to remote company sites without having to set up a private network.

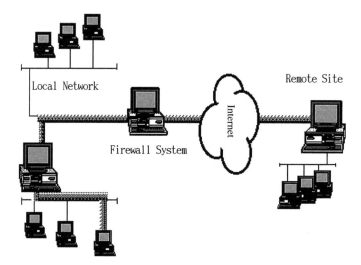

Figure 9.9. Virtual Private Network.

Summary

This chapter has dealt with implementing security on your Intranet. Although an Intranet is, by definition, internal to an organization, security is important not so much because it prevents things, but because it enables them. Judicious use of built-in security features of Web servers and other Intranet resources can add value to your Intranet by making new things possible. In this chapter, you have:

◆ Considered the overall security aspects of your Intranet.

◆ Learned how implementing security can actually broaden the ways in which your Intranet can be useful in your organization.

◆ Learned how to use username/password authentication to limit access to resources on your Intranet.

◆ Learned how to provide secure access to Intranet resources to groups of customers.

◆ Learned how to restrict access to sensitive resources based on customers' computer hostnames or network addresses.

◆ Learned about the security aspects of CGI-bin scripting.

◆ Learned about encrypted data transmission on your Intranet to protect critical information.

◆ Learned important information about securing access to your Intranet in the case where your corporate network is attached to the Internet.

◆ Learned how to provide—and limit—secure access to your Intranet from outside your immediate local network.

In the next section of *Building an Intranet*, we'll turn to the setup and use of everyday office applications as Intranet tools.

PART

Setting Up Common Office Applications

CHAPTER

10

Your Word Processor and the Web

Your word processing software is probably one of the most frequently used packages in your organization. People use it for everything from quick notes to complex, book-length documents. In this chapter, you'll learn how to set up your Intranet so that your customers can retrieve documents using their Web browser and automatically bring them up in their favorite word processor for revision, document assembly, and other purposes.

Chapter Objectives

As with the rest of the chapters in this book, let's begin by laying out some chapter objectives. This will help you get oriented to the material to be presented; you may want to refer back to this list as you work your way through the chapter. In this chapter, you'll

◆ Learn why it's important to be able to retrieve documents directly into your word processor using a Web browser.

◆ Learn how to configure your Web server software to understand your word processor's document files.

◆ Learn how to configure your Web browser software to handle your word processor documents.

◆ Learn about special read-only viewers for word processing files that work with your Web browser. These enable you to view files created in other word processors to which you may not have access.

◆ Understand some potential uses of the foregoing capabilities.

The chapter is organized in standalone sections, each devoted to a particular major word processing package, including Microsoft Word, WordPerfect, FrameMaker, and others, including the standard Windows package, Write. You need not read the entire chapter to learn how to set up your particular package, as each section contains all the instructions you need to set up your Web browsers. If your organization uses multiple packages for word processing, you'll be able to use the separate sections independently, without having to page back and forth.

In each section, examples are shown using both NCSA Mosaic and Netscape, the two most widely used Web browsers. Each section contains lots of screenshots, showing you step-by-step how to set up your word processor as a Web browser helper application. But before we begin looking at the individual word processors, let's take a moment to consider why we want to set one up in the first place.

Why Integrate Your Word Processor in Your Intranet?

Like most people who use computers for general office work, you probably use your word processing package more than any other application. Graphical user interfaces like Microsoft Windows integrate your word processor into your everyday desktop, along with all your other commonly used applications, allowing you to start it up with a simple mouse click.

Integrating your word processor (and other applications, as you'll learn in the next few chapters) in your Web is, in a sense, creating a whole new graphical interface for your users based on your Web browser. In fact, some people have predicted an overall graphical user interface based on Netscape or Mosaic may eventually replace Microsoft Windows or the Macintosh desktop. While this may seem a bit farfetched, it is nonetheless both possible and simple to broaden the scope of your Web browser to tie in links to your everyday tools like your word processor, giving them a new interface with a common look and feel.

More important, you can use your Web server, HTML, and other tools to put together shareable libraries of word processing documents. Such libraries can be complete with searchable indexes and point-and-click access via your Web browser. Locating and opening a document no longer involves finding a file and then starting up your word processor to read or edit it. Rather, using Mosaic, Netscape, or other Web browser, your customer can merely click on a Web hyperlink for the document and have the word processor fire up with a copy of the desired document loaded, all in one simple process.

Helper Applications

In earlier chapters, we talked about helper applications (a.k.a. external viewers), which are computer programs your Web browser uses when it can't directly display the data represented by a hyperlink. For example, neither Netscape nor Mosaic can play audio or video files you might run across on the Web, but both can be set up to pass incoming audio or video data off to an audio- or video-playing helper application. When you click on a hyperlink pointing to a sound or video file, your Web browser receives it from a Web server, recognizes it as a sound or video file, and hands it off to the audio or video helper application you've set up.

In this chapter, your word processor is treated as a helper application, just like a sound or video player. There's very little difference between the setup of one of these common helper applications and the setup of Word or WordPerfect, but there's a major difference in the implications of doing so. Playing video and audio on your computer may be remarkable and enjoyable, but unless you are in the video or audio business, it accomplishes little of your substantive, everyday work. Your word processor, on the other hand—along with the other common office applications we'll discuss in the next several chapters—is the workhorse of many days. Integrating it into your Intranet, then, can be a potentially major productivity enhancement, fundamentally changing the way your customers—and therefore your company—do their work.

Web Server Setup

Regardless of which word processor you use, your first steps in setting it up as a helper application involve configuring your Web server to know about your word processor's documents. With small differences, which will be explained as we go, the instructions in this section apply to any word processor.

As you learned in Chapter 7, "MIME and Helper Applications," Web servers use the MIME mechanism to identify documents according to their MIME data type/subtype. Recall that the MIME mechanism divides data into a relatively small handful of data types, with each type further subdivided into subtypes. Word processing documents fall into the application data type. You also learned in Chapter 7 how Web servers use filename extensions to map data files on the server to a MIME data type/subtype. This association of filename extensions with MIME type/subtype is done in the Web server's configuration file `mime.types` (`mime.typ` on a PC server).

Editing the `mime.types` File

As you'll recall from Chapter 7, the `mime.types` file is a plain text file, containing a simple, two-column listing of MIME types/subtypes and associated filename extensions. Here's a short excerpt from the standard `mime.types` file distributed with the NCSA httpd server software; for a full listing, refer back to Chapter 7.

```
application/mac-binhex40
application/macwriteii
application/news-message-id
application/news-transmission
application/octet-stream      bin
application/oda              oda
application/pdf              pdf
application/postscript       ai eps ps
```

Here you can see the association between the pdf filename extension and the MIME type/subtype application/pdf, representing the Adobe Portable Document Format. Similarly, PostScript documents are represented by the application/postscript data type/subtype. In that case, as you can see on the last line of the above listing, there are three filename extensions associated: ai, eps, and ps. Several of the entries have no filename extensions listed; these can be added as required.

> **Note:** The Netscape Communications server uses a different format for the mime.types file. The format is more complex, but potentially easier to understand, because the two columns of each entry have labels. Here's an excerpt:
>
> ```
> type=application/oda      exts=oda
> type=application/pdf      exts=pdf
> type=image/jpeg           exts=jpeg,jpg,jpe
> ```
>
> As you can see, Netscape has added labels to the two columns of the mime.types file, with the left column containing not only the MIME data type/subtype (image/jpeg, for example), but also the identifying label type, separated by an equal sign (=). Similarly, the right column includes the label exts, along with the actual filename extensions. The Netscape mime.types file also includes an optional third column, not found in other servers' files, specifying an icon to be associated with the MIME data type/subtype. The Netscape server also provides for a secondary mime.types file, with your localizations, specified in the magnus.conf file. For more information about this file and overall Netscape Communications Server configuration, see Appendix A, "Setting up a Web Server," or the Netscape Communications server documentation.

To set up your Web server for your word processor, you'll need to make changes in the mime.types file. You can edit the file with any text editor, such as vi or emacs (on a UNIX system), NotePad in Windows, edit in MS-DOS, TeachText on the Macintosh, or even your favorite word processor in plain text mode.

> **Note:** If your Web server runs on a UNIX system, you'll need root (or superuser) access to edit the mime.types file.

You'll find there are already entries in mime.types for Microsoft Word and WordPerfect documents. They look like this, respectively:

```
application/msword
application/wordperfect5.1
```

As you can see, these are missing the filename extensions that you need in order to have your Web server associate their data files with the particular application program. Normally, Word uses the filename extension doc, although you can use anything you like. Early versions of WordPerfect had no default filename extension, but the latest releases use .wpd. You may need to use both .wpd and one or more of your own choosing. Here are the above two `mime.type` entries, revised to show some possibilities.

```
application/msword          doc wrd
application/wordperfect5.1  wp wpf wpd
```

As with the PostScript entry shown earlier, you've associated multiple filename extensions with each of the two MIME data type/subtypes.

Warning: Double-check your filename extensions to make sure they don't duplicate any of the standard `mime.types` entries. Otherwise, you may get unexpected results.

Note: The distributed `mime.types` file's entry for WordPerfect specifies Release 5.1 of that package. Unless you're sure everyone in your company uses Release 6, you should leave this as is. The reason for this is that, while Release 6 can handle documents created under Release 5.1, the reverse may not be true.

There are no ready-made entries for the other word processors we're covering in this chapter, FrameMaker and Windows Write, so you'll need to add a `mime.types` entry for the one(s) you use. Here are sample entries for these two packages.

```
application/framemaker      fm mak
application/write           wri
```

Here we've associated the filename extensions .fm and .mak with FrameMaker, which has no default extension, and the customary .wri with Write. If you're using a different word processor than any of these, you'll need to add an entry to `mime.types` for it. If it uses a default filename extension for its data files, use it in `mime.types`. Otherwise, you're free to use whatever you want, provided it doesn't conflict with other entries in the `mime.types` file.

When you're finished editing the `mime.types` file, save it and exit your editor.

Implementing Changes in `mime.types`

Since you've changed the configuration of your Web server by editing one of its setup files, you now need to make the server aware of your changes. If your server isn't already running, it will read the changes as part of its normal startup. If the server is already running, you can have it reread its configuration files in any of several ways.

On a Macintosh or Windows server, just stop the server and restart it. For example, in the whttpd server, open the Control menu and select Exit, and then restart the server by double-clicking on its icon or by using the Program Manager's Run command.

UNIX servers provide a more convenient way of having the setup files reread. They enable you to do so without actually shutting down the server and interrupting access to it. It's done by what's called *sending a hang-up signal* to the server process. All processes running on UNIX systems have a unique process id, or pid. You can find your server's pid using the UNIX process status command, ps. Here's an example, using the grep command to filter out all but the processes in which we're interested:

```
# ps -ax ¦ grep httpd
   250 ?         S  0:06 /usr/local/etc/httpd/httpd
   255 ?         S  0:06 /usr/local/etc/httpd/httpd
   258 ?         S  0:06 /usr/local/etc/httpd/httpd
   686 ?         S  0:05 /usr/local/etc/httpd/httpd
  6383 ?         S  0:02 /usr/local/etc/httpd/httpd
  7096 ?         S  0:01 /usr/local/etc/httpd/httpd
 19304 pts/6     S  0:00 grep httpd
```

> **Note:** In this example, the BSD UNIX -ax arguments to the ps command have been used, as on a SunOS 4.1.x system. If your machine is a System V UNIX, such as SunOS 5.x, SGI IRIX 5.x, or other system, you'll need to use this command:
>
> ```
> # ps -ef ¦ grep httpd
> ```
>
> The output of the System V ps command is a bit different, but will give the same information (along with additional information).
>
> ```
>    root    250      1 80   Nov 13 ?          0:06 /usr/local/etc/httpd/httpd
>  nobody    255    250 80   Nov 13 ?          0:07 /usr/local/etc/httpd/httpd
>  nobody    686    250 80   Nov 14 ?          0:06 /usr/local/etc/httpd/httpd
>  nobody   7096    250 80   Nov 24 ?          0:02 /usr/local/etc/httpd/httpd
>  nobody    258    250 80   Nov 13 ?          0:06 /usr/local/etc/httpd/httpd
>  nobody   6383    250 80   Nov 22 ?          0:03 /usr/local/etc/httpd/httpd
> tkevans  19310    384 12   06:02:45 pts/6    0:00 grep httpd
> ```

In the output of the first example of the ps command, process ids are shown in the first column, with the main server pid being 250. As indicated in Appendix A, the most recent releases of the NCSA httpd server generate a parent httpd process and several child processes; the lowest numbered pid is the parent process. This distinction is more clear with the System V ps command, with the pids shown in the second column and the pid of the process which started each shown in the third column.

As you can see, the parent process id (ppid) of the main httpd server process is 1, indicating the process was started at boot time by the UNIX init daemon. Each of the child httpd processes shows the main httpd process (pid 250) as its parent.

Having identified the pid of the main httpd server process, you can send it a hang-up signal like this:

```
# kill -HUP 250
```

This command, run by the superuser, tells the httpd process that something has changed in its configuration, and that it must reread the setup files without exiting. Afterward, the server is still running, but using the revised setup.

The NCSA and CERN httpd servers provide a shortcut to this whole process, which doesn't require you to find out the server's pid. When the server starts up, it stores its pid in a file in the top level of the server software tree; the file is named httpd.pid. The shortcut to having the server reread its configuration files is this command:

```
# kill -HUP 'cat /usr/local/etc/httpd/httpd.pid'
```

This command uses the special UNIX feature under which the command surrounded by the backward single quotes (also called *accent grave*) is run first, with its output substituted in the main command. Since the content of the httpd.pid file is merely the pid of the main server process (in our example, 250), the actual command that's run here is the same as the example above. What's different is that you didn't have to look up the pid yourself by running the ps command.

Note: The Netscape Communications Server has a graphical interface, called the Server Manager, which allows you to restart the server. This soft restart causes the server to reread its configuration files without interrupting the ongoing operation of the server.

Adding Word Processing Documents to Your Web Server

If you followed along in the preceding sections of this chapter, you've finished setting up your Web server to properly identify and serve your word processor's documents. Your next step is to populate your server with some documents.

You can transfer your documents to your Web server using your network file transfer utilities (such as ftp, in binary mode) or via floppy diskette or tape. Whichever method you use, it's probably a good idea to put them in a dedicated directory for word processing documents. If you use more than one word processor, you'll want to create a separate directory for each. Once you've done so, you'll need to create some sort of HTML listing of them. This can be as simple or as complex as you like, because including hyperlinks to word processing documents is exactly the same as setting up links to other kinds of documents. A simple HTML listing might be something like this, using Microsoft Word as an example.

```
<HTML><HEAD><TITLE>Word Documents</TITLE></HEAD>
<BODY>
<H1>Microsoft Word Documents</H1>

This directory contains a set of Word Documents. Just click on one to open it up in
Word.

<UL><LI><A HREF="health.doc">Document 1</A>, Memo about Health Insurance</LI>
<LI><A HREF="holiday.doc">Document 2</A>, 1996 Holiday Schedule</LI>
```

```
<LI><A HREF="usedfurn.doc">Document 3</A>, Used Office Furniture Inventory</LI></UL>
```

```
If you haven't already done so, you must set up your Web browser to understand Word
documents. <A HREF="word_setup.html">Here are instructions.</A>
```

```
</BODY></HTML>
```

This code can be modified easily to use another word processor's documents. Figure 10.1 shows this HTML code, rendered in NCSA Mosaic. As you can see, it looks like just any other Web page. Users with properly set up Web browsers can click on the hyperlinks to run Word (or whatever word processor you've set up) on a copy of the selected document. Before you can use this page to load the hyperlinked Word documents, however, your Web browser must be set up to use your specific word processor as a helper application.

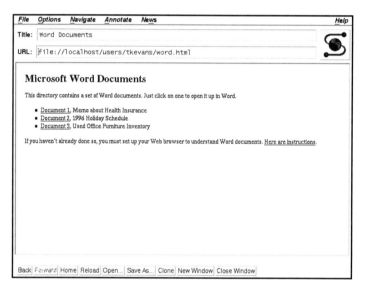

Figure 10.1. The HTML page we've been creating for Word documents, as it will appear in Mosaic.

Setting Up Microsoft Word as a Helper Application

Now that you have set up your Web server to know about Word documents, and populated it with some actual data files from the package, your next step is to set up Word as a helper application. The concept of setting up helper applications for Web browsers is a general one, but the steps for actually doing it differ among browsers. We'll go through the steps for NCSA Mosaic and Netscape. If you're using another browser, you'll need to take a look at its documentation to find out how to do it.

NCSA Mosaic and Word on Windows PCs

NCSA Mosaic in Windows provides a graphical interface for setting up helper applications, although Mosaic uses the term *external viewer* rather than helper application. In Mosaic, open the Options menu, then select Preferences. The Preferences dialog box opens. Click on the Viewers tab.

As you can see in Figure 10.2, there are four fill-in boxes and several buttons which enable you to control the external viewers used. Figure 10.2 shows the dialog box already filled in for the Microsoft WAVE audio player.

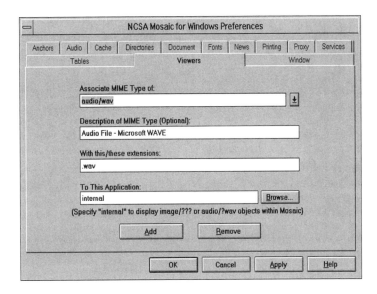

Figure 10.2. *The Mosaic Preferences dialog box with the Viewers tab selected.*

Let's take a look at the labels on the fill-in boxes before going any further. We'll take them slightly out of order. You'll recognize some familiar items here. First, the top box, Associate MIME Type of, contains a MIME data type/subtype pair—in this case audio/wav. This item is, of course, right out of the mime.types file. The third fill-in box, With this/these extensions, is also familiar. It contains the same info as the filename-extension column in your mime.types file, with the extension .wav entered.

The second fill-in box is an optional description of a kind of data file—in our example, it's Audio File - Microsoft WAVE. The last fill-in box, To This Application, is where you specify which program will function as your helper application. In Figure 10.2, the special keyword internal is used there, indicating Mosaic can handle this MIME type/subtype by itself, without a helper application. Before we go on, note the Browse button next to this box, because we'll be using it to set up Word as your helper application.

Now that your tour of the Viewers tab is complete, let's configure Microsoft Word as your helper application. Click the Add button to open the Add Viewer dialog box shown in Figure 10.3. This box has the same four fill-in boxes as Figure 10.2, but they're blank, for you to enter your own information.

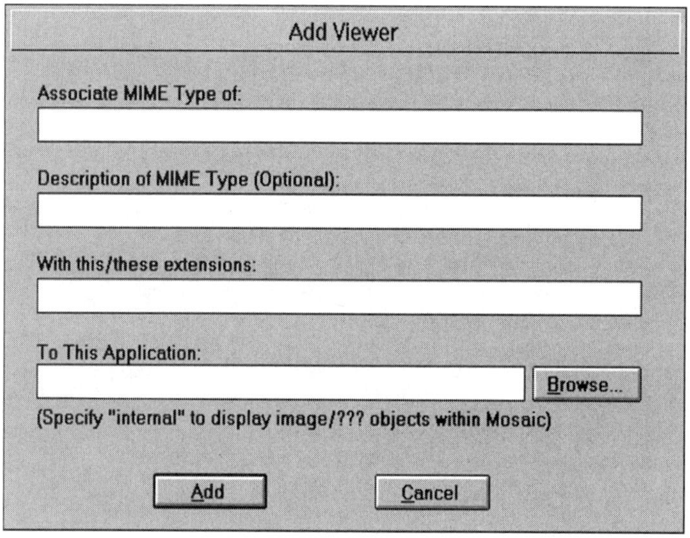

Add Viewer

Associate MIME Type of:

Description of MIME Type (Optional):

With this/these extensions:

To This Application:

Browse...

(Specify "internal" to display image/??? objects within Mosaic)

Add   Cancel

Figure 10.3. *The NCSA Mosaic Add Viewer dialog box.*

Using the information you added to your `mime.types` file earlier, you can quickly fill in these blanks.

- In the Associate MIME Type of box, enter `application/msword`.

- In the Description of MIME Type (Optional) box, enter something like `Microsoft Word Document`. Note that you're not required to enter anything in this box, although it's a good idea if you do so for future reference.

- In the With this/these extensions box, enter `doc wrd`. (As you'll recall, we entered both these filename extensions into the `mime.types` file earlier.)

- Finally, in the To This Application box, enter the full drive and pathname to the Microsoft Word executable program. If you're not sure about this, click the Browse button, which works like most Windows Browse buttons, enabling you to locate the executable you want. Once you've found it, select it.

Figure 10.4 shows the filled-in Add Viewer dialog box. (Your drive and path to the Word executable may be different than the one shown, so make sure you locate yours, rather than just copying what's shown in the figure.) Once you're set, click Add to save your changes.

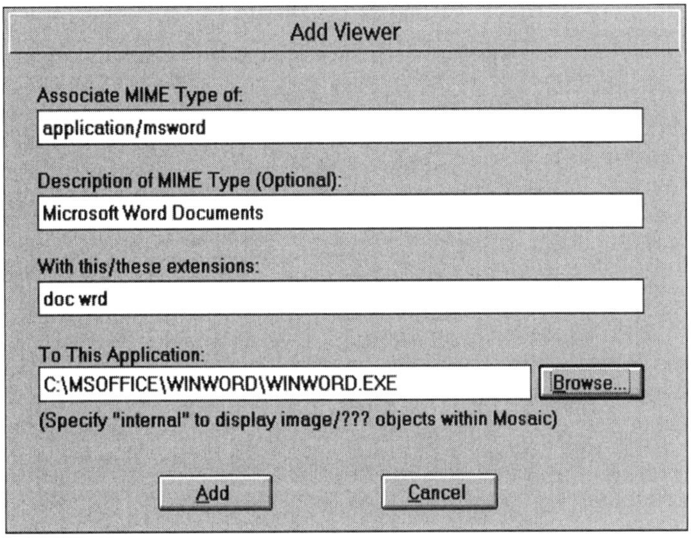

Figure 10.4. *The NCSA Mosaic Add Viewer dialog box, filled in for Microsoft Word.*

That's it. You're now ready to try out your new setup. Close the Preferences dialog box by clicking OK, and then select Open Document from the Mosaic File menu. Enter the URL of a Word document on your Web server. Mosaic contacts the Web server and asks for the document. As described in detail in Chapter 7, the server sends back header information identifying the document as the MIME type/subtype application/msword. Mosaic reads this information, and then passes the incoming document off to Word for viewing, dynamically starting up Word with a copy of the document.

Figure 10.5 shows Mosaic with Word tiled on top. At this point, you have all the features and power of Word available to you to edit, save, and print the document.

> **Note:** It's important to note that you're working with a temporary copy of the document, not the original, which is still safe on your Web server. As a result, you're free to make any changes to the document you need to make.

> **Note:** If you get errors about Word being unable to load your document, and you're sure that you've specified the correct URL on your Web server and the permissions on the file are correct, you may be experiencing a memory problem. Close down other open applications and/or turn off some of Word's features to conserve memory. You may also need to use a memory manager like QEMM or the Microsoft memmaker.

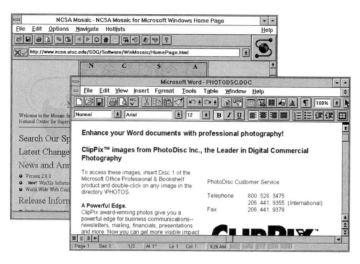

Figure 10.5. *Mosaic with Microsoft Word as a helper application.*

Netscape and Word on Windows PCs

Netscape in Windows provides a graphical interface for setting up helper applications. Open the Options menu, and then select General Preferences. The Preferences dialog box appears. Click on the Helpers tab (shown in Figure 10.6).

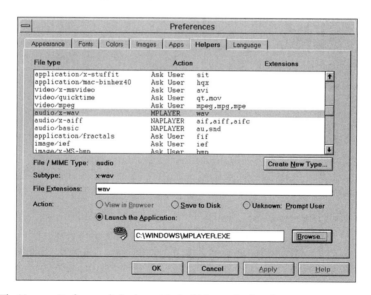

Figure 10.6. *The Netscape Preferences dialog box with the Helpers tab selected.*

As you can see in Figure 10.6, there is a scrollable File type list that contains preset helper applications; clicking on one of them brings up some details of the setup. In Figure 10.6, the audio/ x-wav file type has been selected. Below the File type window, you'll see File / MIME Type, with Subtype on the next line. Below that, there's a fill-in File Extensions box, several option buttons, and another fill-in box.

Figure 10.6 shows the dialog box already filled in for the Microsoft WAVE audio player, mplayer. Let's take a look at this figure before going any further. You'll recognize some familiar items here. First, the File type window should remind you of the contents of the mime.types file on your Web server, with its columns specifying MIME data types/subtypes (on the left) and filename extensions (on the right). Below that box, you'll find the File / MIME Type item filled in as audio and the subtype filled in as x-wav. The File Extensions box contains wav.

At the bottom, there are several option buttons which enable you to choose what to do with incoming data of the MIME type/subtype application/x-wav. In Figure 10.6, Launch the Application is selected. The bottommost box is where you enter the name and path of the program that you want to function as your helper application. In Figure 10.6, the drive and path to the Microsoft Windows Media Player application, mplayer is filled in. Notice Netscape has picked up the Windows icon for mplayer, displaying it just to the left of the box. Before we go on, note the Create New Type and Browse buttons, as we'll be using them to set up Word as a helper application.

Your tour of the Helpers tab completed, let's configure Microsoft Word as your helper application. Click the Create New Type button to open the Configure New Mime Type dialog box shown in Figure 10.7. This box has two fill-in boxes for your information about the new MIME type/sub-type. In Figure 10.7, the information for Word has been filled in, right out of the mime.types file.

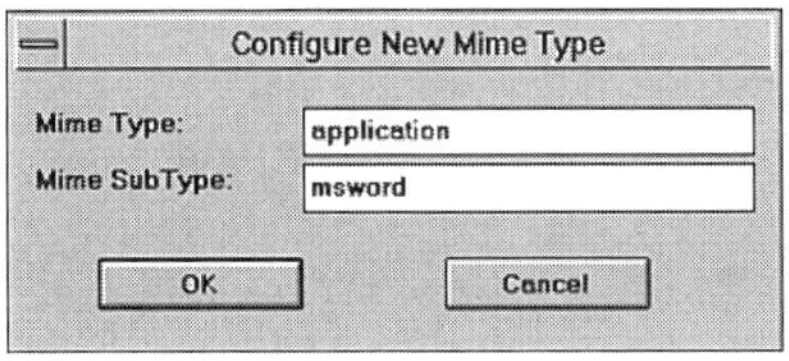

Figure 10.7. Netscape Configure New Mime Type dialog box.

Fill yours in, and then click OK. This returns you to the previous dialog box, with the MIME type information you just entered filled in. You now need to enter doc and wrd in the File Extensions box. (As you'll recall, we entered both these filename extensions into the mime.types file earlier.) Finally, click the Launch the Application option button and fill in the full drive and pathname to the Microsoft Word executable program. If you're not sure about this, click the Browse button, which works like most Windows browse buttons, enabling you to locate the executable you want. Once you've found it, select it. Notice that in Figure 10.8, Netscape has located and displayed the Word icon.

Figure 10.8 shows the Helpers tab filled in with Microsoft Word information. (Your drive and path to the Word executable may be different than the one shown, so make sure you locate yours, rather than just copying what's shown in the figure.) Once you're set, click OK to save your changes.

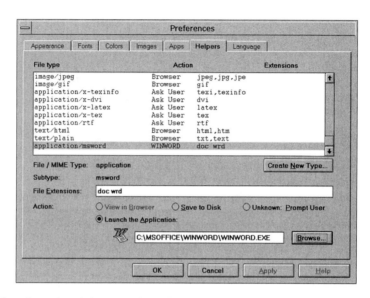

Figure 10.8. *The Helpers tab with the Microsoft Word information entered.*

That's it. You're now ready to try out your new setup. Close the Preferences windows by clicking OK, and then click the Open button on Netscape's toolbar. Enter the URL of a Word document on your Web server. Netscape contacts the Web server and asks for the document. As described in detail in Chapter 7, the server sends back header information identifying the document as the MIME type/subtype application/msword. Netscape reads this information, and then passes off the incoming document to Word for viewing, dynamically starting up Word with a copy of the document. Figure 10.9 shows Netscape with Word tiled on top. At this point, you have all the features and power of Word available to you to edit, save, and print this document.

> **Note:** It's important to note that you're working with a temporary copy of the document, not the original, which is still safe on your Web server. As a result, you're free to make any changes to the document you need to make.

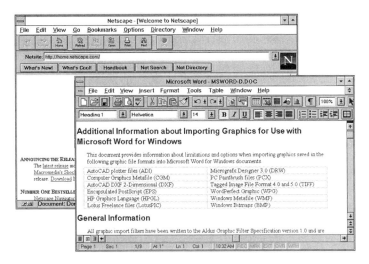

Figure 10.9. *Netscape with Microsoft Word as a helper application.*

Note: If you get errors about Word being unable to load your document, and you're sure you've specified the correct URL on your Web server and permissions on the file are set correctly, you may be experiencing a memory problem. Close down other open applications and/or turn off some of Word's features to conserve memory. You may also need to use a memory manager like QEMM or the Microsoft memmaker.

Mosaic, Netscape, and Word on the Macintosh

Macintosh users will find the process of setting up Word as a viewer/helper application virtually identical to that for Windows. The only difference is in specifying the folder and executable names for Word. You can use the Browse process, just as in Windows, with the browser displaying Mac folder names in place of PC directory names.

Setting Up WordPerfect as a Helper Application

After you have set up your Web server to know about WordPerfect documents, and populated it with some actual data files from the package, your next step is to set up WordPerfect as a helper application. The concept of setting up helper applications for Web browsers is a general one, but the steps for actually going about it differ depending on the Web browser you're using. We'll go through the steps for NCSA Mosaic and Netscape. If you're using another browser, you'll need to take a look at its documentation to see how to accomplish this.

NCSA Mosaic and WordPerfect on Windows PCs

NCSA Mosaic in Windows provides a graphical interface for setting up helper applications, although Mosaic uses the term *external viewer* rather than helper application. In Mosaic, open the Options menu, and then select Preferences and click on the Viewers tab. The Preferences dialog box opens. Click on the Viewers tab (see Figure 10.10).

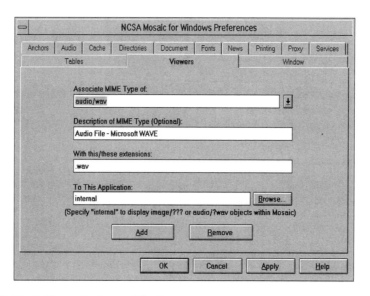

Figure 10.10. *Mosaic Viewers Preferences dialog box.*

As you can see in Figure 10.10, there are four fill-in boxes and several buttons that enable you to control the external viewers used. Figure 10.10 shows the dialog box already filled in for the Microsoft WAVE audio player.

Let's take a look at the labels on the fill-in boxes before going any further. We'll take them slightly out of order. You'll recognize some familiar items here. First, the top box, Associate MIME Type of, contains a MIME data type/subtype pair—in this case audio/wav. This item is, of course, right out of the mime.types file. The third fill-in box, With this/these extensions, is also familiar. It contains the same info as the filename-extension column in your mime.types file, with the extension .wav entered.

The second fill-in box is an optional description of kind of data file—in our example, it's Audio File - Microsoft WAVE. The last fill-in box, To This Application, is where you specify which program will function as your helper application. In Figure 10.10, the special keyword internal is used there, indicating Mosaic can handle this MIME type/subtype by itself, without a helper application. Before we go on, note the Browse button next to this box, because we'll be using it to set up WordPerfect as your helper application.

Now that your tour of the Viewers tab is complete, let's configure WordPerfect as your helper application. Click the Add button to open the Add Viewer dialog box show in Figure 10.11. This box has the same four fill-in boxes as Figure 10.10, but they're blank, for you to enter your own information.

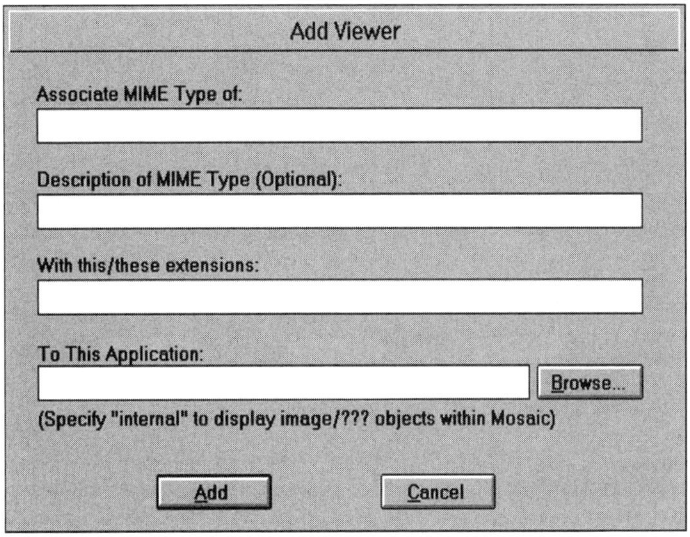

Figure 10.11. *NCSA Mosaic Add Viewer dialog box.*

Using the information you added to your `mime.types` file earlier, you can quickly fill in these blanks.

◆ In the Associate MIME Type of box, enter `application/wordperfect5.1`.

◆ In the Description of MIME Type (Optional) box, enter something like `WordPerfect Document`. Note that you're not required to enter anything in this box, although it's a good idea to do so for future reference.

◆ In the With this/these extensions box, enter `wp wpf wpd`. (As you'll recall, we entered these filename extensions to the `mime.types` file earlier.)

◆ Finally, in the To This Application box, enter the full drive and pathname to the WordPerfect executable program. If you're not sure about this, click the Browse button, which works like most Windows browse buttons, enabling you to locate the executable you want. Once you've found it, select it.

Figure 10.12 shows the filled-in Add Viewer dialog box. (Your drive and path to the WordPerfect executable may be different than the one shown, so make sure you locate yours, rather than just copying what's shown in the figure.) Once you're set, click Add to save your changes.

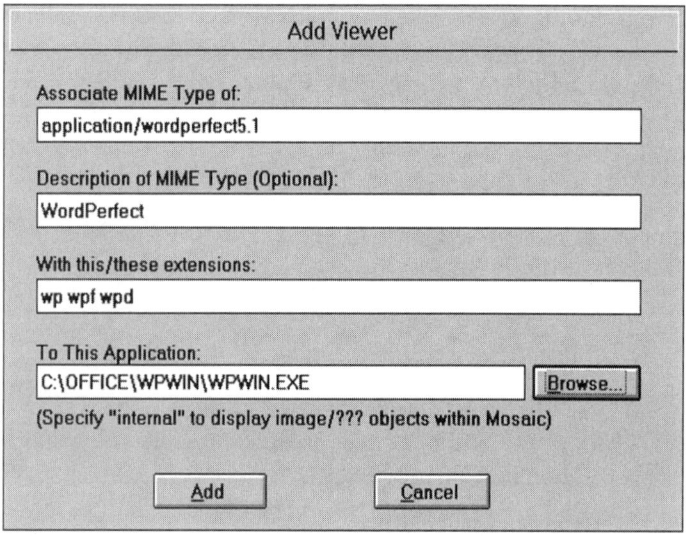

Figure 10.12. NCSA Mosaic Add Viewer dialog box (filled in).

That's it. You're now ready to try out your new setup. Close the Preferences dialog box by clicking OK, and then select Open Document from the Mosaic File menu. Enter the URL of a WordPerfect document on your Web server. Mosaic contacts the Web server and asks for the document. As described in detail in Chapter 7, the server sends back header information identifying the document as the MIME type/subtype `application/wordperfect5.1`. Mosaic reads this information, and then passes the incoming document off to WordPerfect for viewing, dynamically starting up WordPerfect with a copy of the document.

Figure 10.13 shows Mosaic with WordPerfect tiled on top. At this point, you have all the features and power of WordPerfect available to you to edit, save, and print this document.

> **Note:** It's important to note that you're working with a temporary copy of the document, not the original, which is still safe on your Web server. As a result, you're free to make any changes to the document you need to make.

> **Note:** If you get errors about WordPerfect being unable to load your document, and you're sure that you've specified the correct URL on your Web server and the permissions on the file are correct, you may be experiencing a memory problem. Close down other open applications and/or turn off some of WordPerfect's features to conserve memory. You may also need to use a memory manager like QEMM or the Microsoft memmaker.

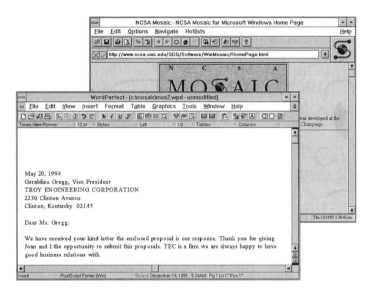

Figure 10.13. *Mosaic with WordPerfect as a helper application.*

Netscape and WordPerfect on Windows PCs

Netscape in Windows provides a graphical interface for setting up helper applications. Open the Options menu, and then select General Preferences. The Preferences dialog box appears. Click on the Helpers tab (shown in Figure 10.14).

As you can see in Figure 10.14, there is a scrollable File type list that contains preset helper applications; clicking on one of them brings up some details of the setup. In Figure 10.14, the audio/x-wav file type has been selected. Below the File type window, you'll see File / MIME Type, with Subtype on the next line. Below that, there's a fill-in File Extensions box, several option buttons, and another fill-in box.

Figure 10.14 shows the dialog box already filled in for the Microsoft WAVE audio player, `mplayer`. Let's take a look at this figure before going any further. You'll recognize some familiar items here. First, the File type window should remind you of the contents of the `mime.types` file on your Web server, with its columns specifying MIME data types/subtypes (on the left) and filename extensions (on the right). Below that box, you'll find the File / MIME Type item filled in as `audio` and the subtype filled in as `x-wav`. The File Extensions box contains `wav`.

At the bottom, there are several option buttons that enable you to choose what to do with incoming data of the MIME type/subtype `application/x-wav`. In Figure 10.14, Launch the Application is shown selected. The bottommost box is where you enter the name and path of the program that you want to function as your helper application. In Figure 10.14, the drive and path to the

Microsoft Windows Media Player application, mplayer, has been filled in. Notice that Netscape has picked up the Windows icon for mplayer, displaying it just to the left of the box. Before we go on, note the Create New Type and Browse buttons, as we'll be using them to set up WordPerfect as a helper application.

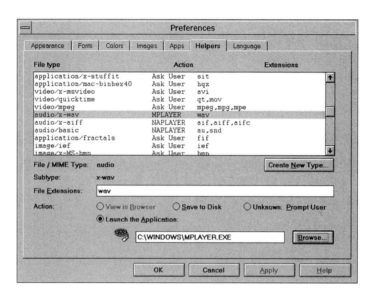

Figure 10.14. *The Netscape Preferences dialog box with the Helpers tab selected.*

With your tour of the Helpers tab completed, let's configure WordPerfect as your Netscape helper application. Click the Create New Type button, to open up the Configure New Mime Type dialog box shown in Figure 10.15. This box has two fill-in boxes for your information about the new MIME type/sub type. In Figure 10.15, the information for Word has been filled in, right out of the mime.types file.

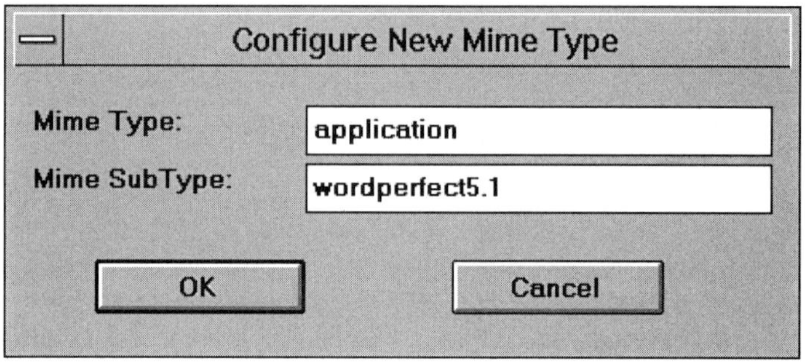

Figure 10.15. *Netscape Configure New Mime Type dialog box.*

Fill yours in, and then click OK. This returns you to the previous dialog box, with the MIME type information that you just entered filled in. You now need to enter wp, wpf, and wpd in the File Extensions box. (As you'll recall, we entered these filename extensions into the mime.types file earlier.) Finally, click the Launch the Application option button and fill in the full drive and pathname to the WordPerfect executable program. If you're not sure about this, click the Browse button, which works like most Windows browse buttons, enabling you to locate the executable you want. Once you've found it, select it.

Figure 10.16 shows the Helpers tab filled in with WordPerfect information. (Your drive and path to the WordPerfect executable may be different than the one shown, so make sure you locate yours, rather than just copying what's shown in the figure.) Once you're set, click OK to save your changes.

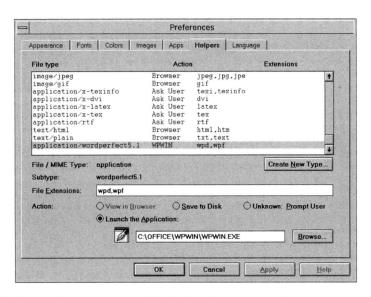

Figure 10.16. *The Netscape Helpers tab with the WordPerfect information entered.*

That's it. You're now ready to try out your new setup. Close the Preferences windows by clicking OK, and then click the Open button on Netscape's toolbar. Enter the URL of a WordPerfect document on your Web server. Netscape contacts the Web server and asks for the document. As described in detail in Chapter 7, the server sends back header information identifying the document as the MIME type/subtype application/wordperfect5.1. Netscape reads this information, and then passes the incoming document off to WordPerfect for viewing, dynamically starting up WordPerfect with a copy of the document.

Figure 10.17 shows Netscape with WordPerfect tiled on top. At this point, you have all the features and power of WordPerfect available to you to edit, save, print this document.

Note: It's important to note you're working with a temporary copy of the document, not the original, which is still safe on your Web server. As a result, you're free to make any changes to the document you need to make.

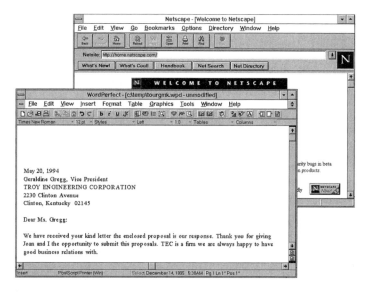

Figure 10.17. *Netscape with WordPerfect as a helper application.*

Note: If you get errors about WordPerfect being unable to load your document, and you're sure you've specified the correct URL on your Web server and the permissions on the file are set correctly, you may be experiencing a memory problem. Close down other open applications and/or turn off some of WordPerfect's features to conserve memory. You may also need to use a memory manager like QEMM or the Microsoft memmaker.

Mosaic/Netscape and WordPerfect on the Macintosh

Macintosh users will find the process of setting up WordPerfect as a viewer/helper application virtually identical to that for Windows. The only difference is in specifying the folder and executable names for WordPerfect. You can use the Browse process, just as in Windows, with the browser displaying Mac folder names in place of PC directory names.

Mosaic/Netscape and WordPerfect on UNIX Systems

WordPerfect is widely available on UNIX systems. There is, however, no graphical interface to setting up helper applications in UNIX Mosaic, and only minimal graphical help in Netscape.

Instead, you configure helper applications in both Mosaic and Netscape by editing some plain text files on your system.

In Mosaic, by default, you specify Mosaic helper applications in the file /usr/local/lib/mosaic/ mailcap on your system. (You must be the superuser to create or edit this file.) The file has a relatively simple format. Here is a sample:

```
image/*;                 /usr/local/bin/display %s
audio/*;                 /usr/openwin/bin/audiotool %s
application/postscript;   /usr/openwin/bin/imagetool %s
video/*;                 /usr/local/bin/xanim %s
```

Some of this will be familiar to you after having edited your Web server's mime.types file to support WordPerfect as a helper application. You will recognize the matter in the first column of this file as MIME data type/subtypes. This part of the file has a different syntax than you've seen before, however. While application/postscript looks like entries from the mime.types file, the others look a little strange. The explanation is simple. This file uses the asterisks you see to represent all of the MIME subtypes of the particular MIME type. (You'll recall from Chapter 7 the number of MIME types is quite small, but each has subtypes.) Thus, image/* refers to all kinds of images, normally spelled out in the server's mime.types file as image/gif, image/jpeg, etc.

On the right side of the file, you see the complete pathname to an executable program. These are the helper applications that are set up for image, audio, PostScript, and video files. Here, display (an all-purpose image display program from the ImageMagick package, on the *Building an Intranet* CD-ROM) is configured as the helper application to display all image data the Web browser encounters. Similarly, xanim is configured to play all video data.

> **Note:** There are a couple of other important nits to mailcap file's format. First, note that the two columns of the file are separated by a semicolon and some white space. Second, on the right side, you'll note each entry ends with the characters %s. These characters are a placeholder, representing the name of the file Mosaic receives from the Web server. Each entry in the mailcap file must have the two columns, separated by the semicolon and white space; the right side must end with the %s characters.

Now that we've covered the format of the mailcap file, let's enable WordPerfect as a UNIX Mosaic helper application by adding a new line to the file. Here's the line:

```
application/wordperfect5.1;     /usr/wp/wpbin/xwp %s
```

Here, the WordPerfect executable xwp is located in the directory /usr/wp/wpbin. Having added this line to the mailcap file, you're now ready to use WordPerfect as a helper application. Check your local WordPerfect installation for the actual path to the package on your system, which may not be the same as the location shown in this example.

> **Note:** The `/usr/local/lib/mosaic/mailcap` file is read by all users on a UNIX system. It contains system-wide configuration. Individual users, however, may want to override part of all of the `mailcap` file by creating a file called `.mailcap` in their home directory. (Note that the filename begins with a period, or dot.) The formats of the `mailcap` and `.mailcap` files are identical, but anything in the individual user's `.mailcap` file that conflicts with the system-wide `mailcap` file takes precedence for that user. Although it is unlikely that different versions of WordPerfect will be installed on a system, this feature enables a great deal of flexibility for users in setting up other helper applications.

UNIX Netscape provides a bit of graphical help in setting up helper applications, which you can use in setting up WordPerfect. Figure 10.18 shows the Netscape: General Preferences dialog box, with the Helpers tab displayed. The Helpers tab shows the package's MIME configuration files, as seen in Figure 10.18. This dialog box doesn't do anything to help you set up your helper applications, but does let you look around the system with the Browse button for files to use.

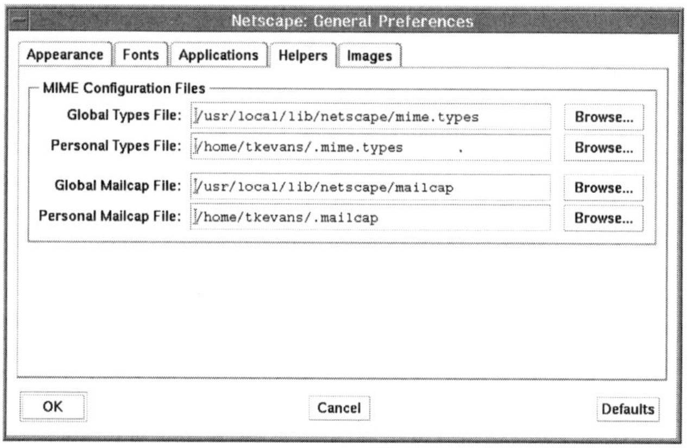

Figure 10.18. *The Netscape: General Preferences dialog box in UNIX with the Helpers tab selected.*

In Figure 10.18, we're concerned with the lower of the two sets of files, the Global Mailcap File and Personal Mailcap File. Although the Global Mailcap File is by default in a different location for Netscape than for Mosaic (it's in `/usr/local/lib/netscape/mailcap`), the files for both Mosaic and Netscape are identical in format and syntax, and, of course, are both named `mailcap`. In fact, you can use the same file for both by copying it from one location to the other or by using a file link.

The instructions for editing the mailcap file to specify helper applications in Mosaic are exactly the same for Netscape. The relationship between the global and personal mailcap files is also the same as with Mosaic, and, of course, the personal mailcap file has the same filename and location, `.mailcap` in the user's home directory.

Setting Up FrameMaker as a Helper Application

After you have set up your Web server to know about FrameMaker documents, and populated it with some actual data files from the package, your next set is to set up FrameMaker as a helper application. The concept of setting up helper applications for Web browsers is a general one, but the steps for actually going about it differ depending on the Web browser you're using. We'll go through the steps for NCSA Mosaic and Netscape. If you're using another browser, you'll need to take a look at its documentation to see how to accomplish this.

NCSA Mosaic and FrameMaker on Windows PCs

NCSA Mosaic in Windows provides a graphical interface for setting up helper applications, although Mosaic uses the term *external viewer* rather than helper application. In Mosaic, open the Options menu, and then select Preferences and click on the Viewers tab. The Preferences dialog box opens. Click on the Viewers tab (see Figure 10.19).

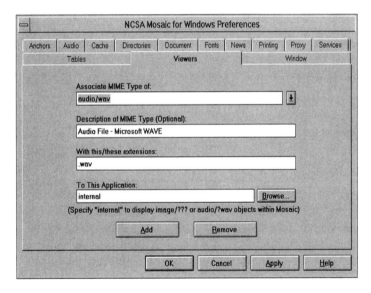

Figure 10.19. *The Mosaic Preferences dialog box with the Viewers tab displayed.*

As you can see in Figure 10.19, there are four fill-in boxes and several buttons which enable you to control the external viewers used. Figure 10.19 shows the dialog box already filled in for the Microsoft WAVE audio player.

Let's take a look at the labels on the fill-in boxes before going any further. We'll take them slightly out of order. You'll recognize some familiar items here. First, the top box, Associate MIME Type of, contains a MIME data type/subtype pair—in this case audio/wav. This item is, of course, right out of the `mime.types` file. The third fill-in box, With this/these extensions, is also familiar. It contains the same info as the filename-extension column in your `mime.types` file, with the extension *wav* entered.

The second fill-in box is an optional description of kind of data file—in our example, it's `Audio File - Microsoft WAVE`. The last fill-in box, To This Application, is where you specify which program will function as your helper application. In Figure 10.19, the special keyword `internal` is used there, indicating Mosaic can handle this MIME type/subtype by itself, without a helper application. Before we go on, note the Browse button next to this box, as we'll be using it to set up FrameMaker as your helper application.

Now that your tour of the Viewers tab is complete, let's configure FrameMaker as your helper application. Click the Add button, to open the Add Viewer dialog box, shown in Figure 10.20. This box has the same four fill-in boxes as Figure 10.19, but they're blank, for you to enter your own information.

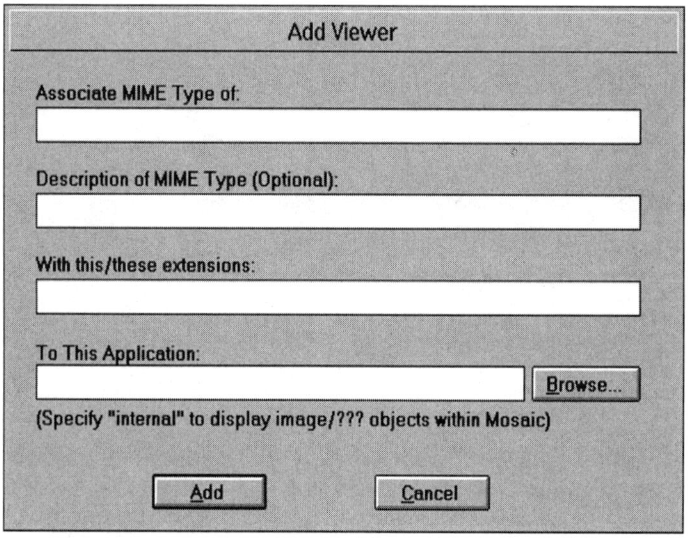

Figure 10.20. NCSA Mosaic Add Viewer dialog box.

Using the information you added to your `mime.types` file earlier, you can quickly fill in these blanks.

- ◆ In the Associate MIME Type of box, enter `application/framemaker`.

- ◆ In the Description of MIME Type (Optional) box, enter something like `FrameMaker Document`. Note that you're not required to enter anything in this box, although it's a good idea to do so for future reference.

- ◆ In the With this/these extensions box, enter `fm` and `mak`. (As you'll recall, we entered both these filename extensions to the `mime.types` file earlier.)

◆ Finally, in the To This Application box, enter the full drive and pathname to the FrameMaker executable program. If you're not sure about this, click the Browse button, which works like most Windows browse buttons, enabling you to locate the executable you want. Once you've found it, select it.

Figure 10.21 shows the filled-in Add Viewer dialog box. (Your drive and path to the FrameMaker executable may be different than the one shown, so make sure you locate yours, rather than just copying what's shown in the figure.) Once you're set, click Add to save your changes.

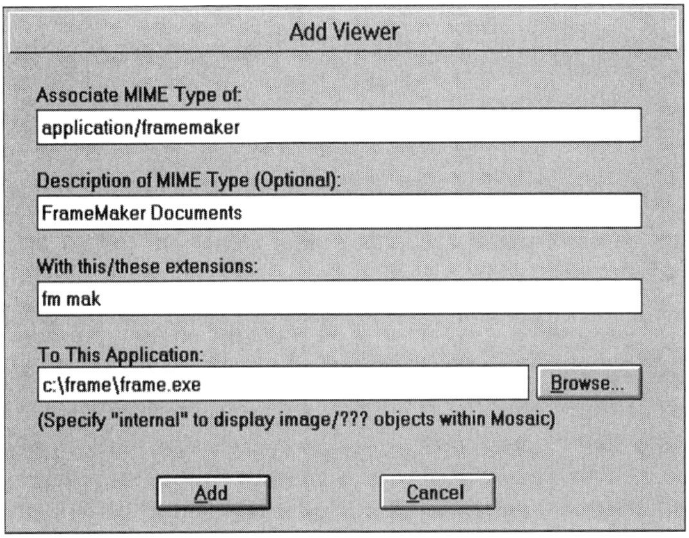

Add Viewer

Associate MIME Type of:

`application/framemaker`

Description of MIME Type (Optional):

`FrameMaker Documents`

With this/these extensions:

`fm mak`

To This Application:

`c:\frame\frame.exe`   Browse...

(Specify "internal" to display image/??? objects within Mosaic)

Add   Cancel

Figure 10.21. The NCSA Mosaic Add Viewer dialog box, with FrameMaker information entered.

That's it. You're now ready to try out your new setup. Close the Preferences windows by clicking OK, and then select Open Document from the Mosaic File menu. Enter the URL of a FrameMaker document on your Web server. Mosaic contacts the Web server and asks for the document. As described in detail in Chapter 7, the server sends back header information identifying the document as the MIME type/subtype `application/framemaker`. Mosaic reads this information, and then passes the incoming document off to FrameMaker for viewing, dynamically starting up FrameMaker with a copy of the document.

Figure 10.22 shows Mosaic with FrameMaker tiled on top. At this point, you have all the features and power of FrameMaker available to you to edit, save, and print this document.

> **Note:** It's important to note that you're working with a temporary copy of the document, not the original, which is still safe on your Web server. As a result, you're free to make any changes to the document you need to make.

Figure 10.22. *Mosaic with FrameMaker as a helper application.*

> **Note:** If you get errors about FrameMaker being unable to load your document, and you're sure that you've specified the correct URL on your Web server and the permissions on the file are set correctly, you may be experiencing a memory problem. Close down other open applications and/or turn off some of FrameMaker's features to conserve memory. You may also need to use a memory manager like QEMM or the Microsoft memmaker.

Netscape and FrameMaker on Windows PCs

Netscape in Windows provides a graphical interface for setting up helper applications. Open the Options menu, and then select General Preferences. The Preferences dialog box appears. Click on the Helpers tab (shown in Figure 10.23).

As you can see in Figure 10.23, there is a scrollable File type list that contains preset helper applications; clicking on one of them brings up some details of the setup. In Figure 10.23, the audio/x-wav File type has been selected. Below the File type window, you'll see File / MIME Type, with Subtype on the next line. Below that, there's a fill-in File Extensions box, several option buttons, and another fill-in box.

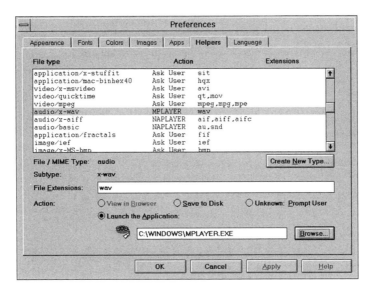

Figure 10.23. *Netscape Preferences dialog box with the Helpers tab selected.*

Figure 10.23 shows the dialog box already filled in for the Microsoft WAVE audio player, mplayer. Let's take a look at this figure before going any further. You'll recognize some familiar items here. First, the File type window should remind you of the contents of the mime.types file on your Web server, with its columns specifying MIME data types/subtypes (on the left) and filename extensions (on the right). Below that box, you'll find the File / MIME Type item filled in as audio and the subtype filled in as x-wav. The File Extensions box contains wav.

At the bottom, there are several option buttons that enable you to choose what to do with incoming data of the MIME type/subtype application/x-wav. In Figure 10.23, Launch the Application is shown selected. The bottommost box is where you enter the name and path of the program that you want to function as your helper application. In Figure 10.23, the drive and path to the Microsoft Windows Media Player application, mplayer has been filled in. Notice Netscape has picked up the Windows icon for mplayer, displaying it just to the left of the box. Before we go on, note the Create New Type and Browse buttons, as we'll be using them to set up FrameMaker as a helper application.

Your tour of the Helpers tab completed, let's configure FrameMaker as your helper application. Click the Create New Type button, to open the Configure New Mime Type dialog box shown in Figure 10.24. This box has two fill-in boxes for your information about the new MIME type/ sub type. In Figure 10.24, I've filled in the information for FrameMaker, right out of the mime.types file.

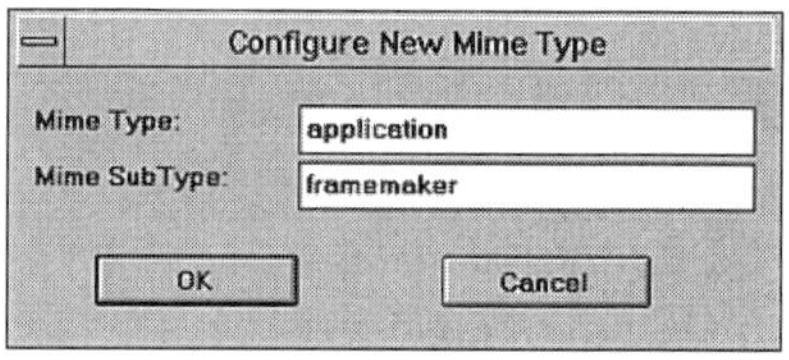

Figure 10.24. Netscape Configure New Mime Type dialog box.

Fill yours in, then click OK. This returns you to the previous dialog box with the MIME type information you just entered filled in. You now need to enter fm mak in the File Extensions box. (As you'll recall, we entered both these filename extensions to the mime.types file earlier.) Finally, click the Launch the Application option button and fill in the full drive and pathname to the FrameMaker executable program. If you're not sure about this, click the Browse button, which works like most Windows browse buttons, allowing you to locate the executable you want. Once you've found it, select it.

Figure 10.25 shows the Helpers tab filled in with FrameMaker information. (Your drive and path to the FrameMaker executable may be different than the one shown, so make sure you locate yours, rather than just copying what's shown in the figure.) Once you're set, click OK to save your changes.

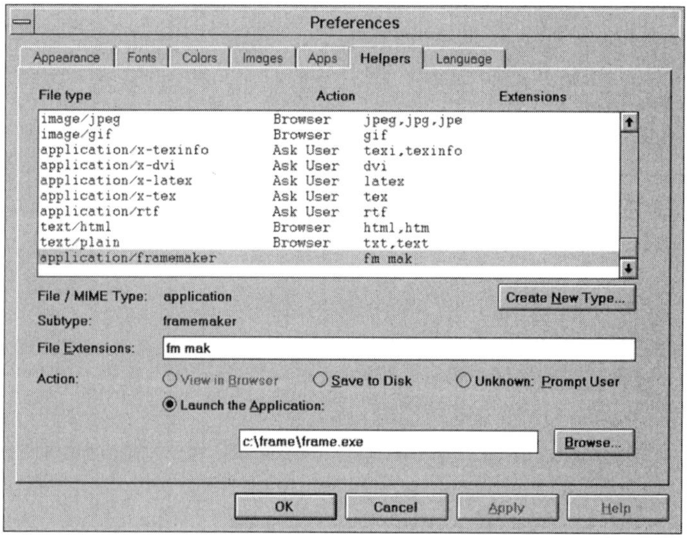

Figure 10.25. Netscape Helper tab with the FrameMaker information entered.

That's it. You're now ready to try out your new setup. Close the Preferences windows by clicking OK, and then click the Open button on Netscape's toolbar. Enter the URL of a FrameMaker document on your Web server. Netscape contacts the Web server and asks for the document. As described in detail in Chapter 7, the server sends back header information identifying the document as the MIME type/subtype `application/framemaker`. Netscape reads this information, and then passes the incoming document off to FrameMaker for viewing, dynamically starting up FrameMaker with a copy of the document.

Figure 10.26 shows Netscape with FrameMaker tiled on top. At this point, you have all the features and power of FrameMaker available to you to edit, save, and print this document.

> **Note:** It's important to note you're working with a temporary copy of the document, not the original, which is still safe on your Web server. As a result, you're free to make any changes to the document you need to make.

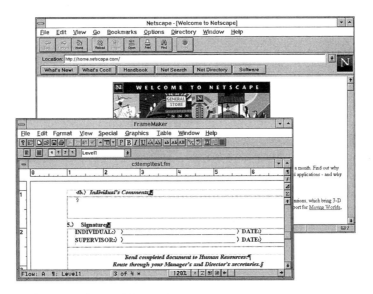

Figure 10.26. *Netscape with FrameMaker as a helper application.*

> **Note:** If you get errors about FrameMaker being unable to load your document, and you're sure you've specified the correct URL on your Web server and the permissions on the file are set correctly, you may be experiencing a memory problem. Close down other open applications and/or turn off some of FrameMaker's features to conserve memory. You may also need to use a memory manager like QEMM or the Microsoft memmaker.

Mosaic/Netscape and FrameMaker on the Macintosh

Macintosh users will find the process of setting up FrameMaker as a viewer/helper application virtually identical to that for Windows. The only difference is in specifying the folder and executable names for FrameMaker. You can use the Browse process, just as in Windows, with the browser displaying Mac folder names in place of PC directory names.

Mosaic/Netscape and FrameMaker on UNIX Systems

FrameMaker is widely available on UNIX systems. There is, however, no graphical interface to setting up helper applications in UNIX Mosaic and only minimal graphical help in Netscape. Instead, you configure helper applications in both Mosaic and Netscape by editing some plain text files on your system.

By default, in Mosaic you specify Mosaic helper applications in the file `/usr/local/lib/mosaic/mailcap` on your system. (You must be the superuser to create or edit this file.) The file has a relatively simple format. Here is a sample:

```
image/*;               /usr/local/bin/display %s
audio/*;               /usr/openwin/bin/audiotool %s
application/postscript; /usr/openwin/bin/imagetool %s
video/*;               /usr/local/bin/xanim %s
```

Some of this will be familiar to you after having edited your Web server's `mime.types` file to support FrameMaker as a helper application. You will recognize the matter in the first column of this file as MIME data type/subtypes. This part of the file has a different syntax than you've seen before, however. While `application/postscript` looks like entries from the `mime.types` file, the others look a little strange. The explanation is simple. This file uses the asterisks you see to represent all of the MIME subtypes of the particular MIME type. (You'll recall from Chapter 7 the number of MIME types is quite small, but each has subtypes.) Thus, `image/*` refers to all kinds of images, usually spelled out in the server's `mime.types` file as *image/gif, image/jpeg*, etc.

On the right side of the file, you see the complete pathname to an executable program. These are the helper applications that are set up for image, audio, PostScript, and video files. Here, `display` (an all-purpose image display program from the ImageMagick package, on the *Building an Intranet* CD-ROM) is configured as the helper application to display all image data the Web browser encounters. Similarly, `xanim` is configured to play all video data.

> **Note:** There are a couple of other important nits to mailcap file's format. First, note that the two columns of the file are separated by a semicolon and some white space. Second, on the right side, you'll note each entry ends with the characters `%s`. These characters are a placeholder, representing the name of the file Mosaic receives from the Web server. Each entry in the `mailcap` file must have the two columns, separated by the semicolon and white space; the right side must end with the `%s` characters.

Now that we've covered the format of the mailcap file, let's enable FrameMaker as a helper application by adding a new line to the file. Here's the line:

```
application/framemaker; /usr/local/bin/maker.sh %s
```

This is a bit tricky, involving the use of a short shell script to start FrameMaker, but it's been worked out with Frame Technical Support. UNIX FrameMaker is more complex than the PC versions, and often runs under the control of a network license manager; the script negotiates all this. Here is the content of the maker.sh script:

```
#!/bin/sh
# script to start up Maker as Web browser helper application
# on UNIX systems
FM_PROGNAME="maker +viewerIsServer"      # suppress dialog box
FMHOME=path/to/frame/home/directory
FRAMEUSERSD_HOST=licensehost
FM_FLS_HOST=licensehost
PATH=$FMHOME/bin:$PATH
export FM_PROGNAME FMHOME PATH FRAMEUSERSD_HOST FM_FLS_HOST
$FMHOME/bin/fmclient -f $1
# delay while file downloaded
wait
sleep 15
exit
```

The script sets a couple of environment variables, pointing to your FrameMaker filetree and your network license host, and then starts the master FrameMaker script fmclient on the downloaded file. Figure 10.27 shows a full UNIX desktop with a FrameMaker document loaded from within Mosaic.

> **Note:** The /usr/local/lib/mosaic/mailcap file is read by all users on a UNIX system. It contains system-wide configuration. Individual users, however, may want to override part of all of the mailcap file by creating a file called .mailcap in their home directory. (Note the filename begins with a period, or dot.) The formats of the mailcap and .mailcap files are identical, but anything in the individual user's .mailcap file that conflicts with the system-wide mailcap file takes precedence for that user. Although it is unlikely that different versions of FrameMaker will be installed on a system, this feature enables a great deal of flexibility for users in setting up other helper applications.

UNIX Netscape provides a bit of graphical help in setting up helper applications, which you can use in setting up FrameMaker. Figure 10.28 shows the Netscape: General Preferences dialog box, with the Helpers tab displayed. The Helpers tab shows the package's MIME configuration files, as seen in Figure 10.28. This dialog box doesn't do anything to help you set up your helper applications, but it does let you look around the system with the Browse button for files to use.

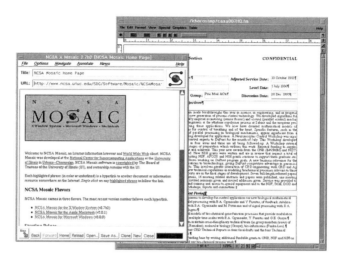

Figure 10.27. *FrameMaker working as a Mosaic helper application.*

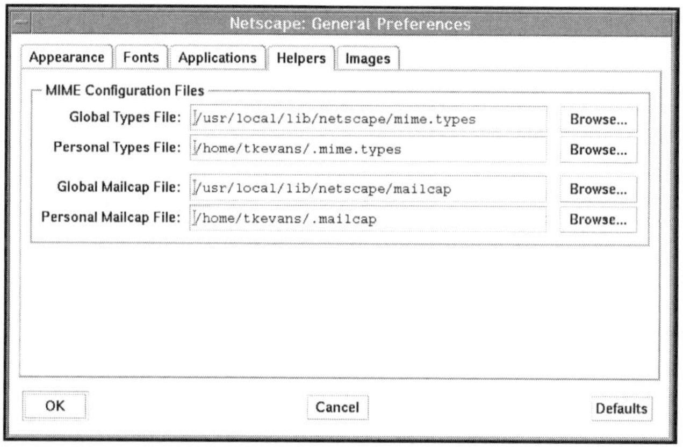

Figure 10.28. *Netscape: General Preferences Dialog Box in UNIX with the Helpers tab selected.*

In Figure 10.28, we're concerned with the lower of the two sets of files, the Global Mailcap File and Personal Mailcap File. Although the Global Mailcap File is by default in a different location for Netscape than for Mosaic (it's in `/usr/local/lib/netscape/mailcap`), the files for both Mosaic and Netscape are identical in format and syntax, and, of course, are both named `mailcap`. In fact, you can use the same file for both by copying it from one location to the other or by using a file link.

The instructions for editing the mailcap file to specify helper applications in Mosaic are exactly the same for Netscape. The relationship between the global and personal mailcap files is also the same as with Mosaic, and, of course, the personal mailcap file has the same filename and location, .mailcap in the user's home directory.

Setting Up Write as a Helper Application

After you have set up your Web server to know about Write documents, and populated it with some actual data files from the package, your next set is to set up Write as a helper application. The concept of setting up helper applications for Web browsers is a general one, but the steps for actually going about it differ depending on the Web browser you're using. We'll go through the steps for NCSA Mosaic and Netscape. If you're using another browser, you'll need to take a look at its documentation to see how to accomplish this.

NCSA Mosaic and Write

NCSA Mosaic in Windows provides a graphical interface for setting up helper applications, although Mosaic uses the term *external viewer* rather than helper application. In Mosaic, open the Options menu, and then select Preferences and click on the Viewers tab. The Preferences dialog box opens. Click on the Viewers tab (see Figure 10.29).

As you can see in Figure 10.19, there are four fill-in boxes and several buttons that enable you to control the external viewers used. Figure 10.29 shows the dialog box already filled in for the Microsoft WAVE audio player.

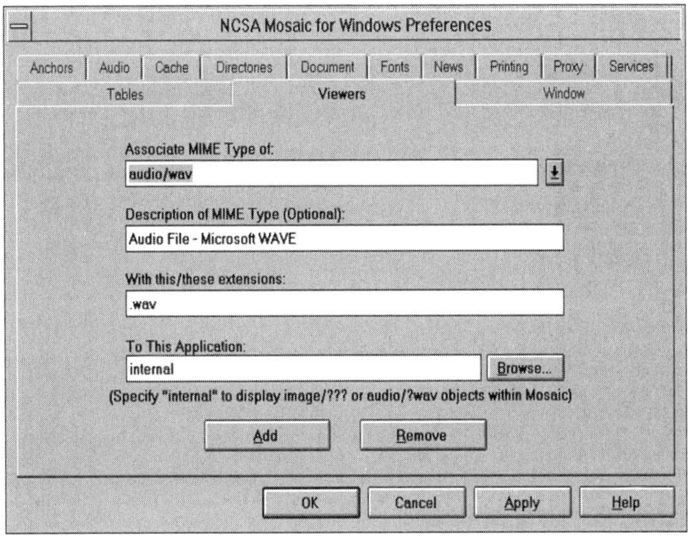

Figure 10.29. *The Mosaic Preferences dialog box with the Viewers tab displayed.*

Let's take a look at the labels on the fill-in boxes before going any further. We'll take them slightly out of order. You'll recognize some familiar items here. First, the top box, Associate MIME Type of, contains a MIME data type/subtype pair—in this case audio/wav. This item is, of course, right out of the mime.types file. The third fill-in box, With this/these extensions, is also familiar. It contains the same info as the filename-extension column in your mime.types file, with the extension .wav entered.

The second fill-in box is an optional description of kind of data file—in our example, it's Audio File - Microsoft WAVE. The last fill-in box, To This Application, is where you specify which program will function as your helper application. In Figure 10.29, the special keyword internal is used there, indicating Mosaic can handle this MIME type/subtype by itself, without a helper application. Before we go on, note the Browse button next to this box, as we'll be using it to set up Write as your helper application.

Now that your tour of the Viewers tab is complete, let's configure Write as your helper application. Click the Add button, to open up the Add Viewer dialog box, show in Figure 10.30. This box has the same four fill-in boxes as Figure 10.29, but they're blank, for you to enter your own information.

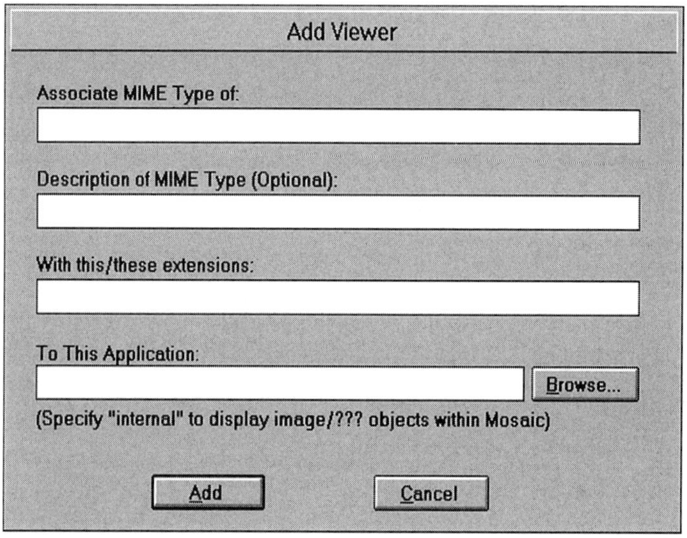

Figure 10.30. *NCSA Mosaic Add Viewer dialog box.*

Using the information you added to your mime.types file earlier, you can quickly fill in these blanks.

◆ In the Associate MIME Type of box, enter **application/write**.

◆ In the Description of MIME Type (Optional) box, enter something like Write Document. Note that you're not required to enter anything in this box, although for future reference it's a good idea to do so.

◆ In the With this/these extensions box, enter `wri wrt` (As you'll recall, we entered both these filename extensions to the `mime.types` file earlier.)

◆ Finally, in the To This Application box, enter the full drive and pathname to the Write executable program. If you're not sure about this, click the Browse button, which works like most Windows browse buttons, enabling you to locate the executable you want. Once you've found it, select it.

Figure 10.31 shows the filled-in Add Viewer dialog box. (Your drive and path to the Write executable may be different than the one shown, so make sure you locate yours, rather than just copying what's shown in the figure.) Once you're set, click Add to save your changes.

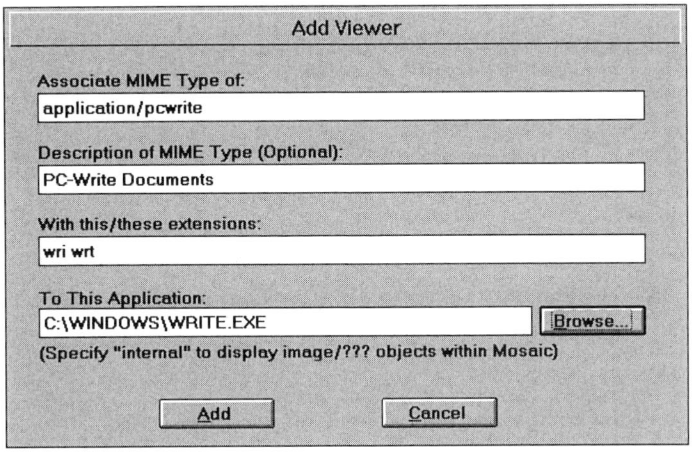

Figure 10.31. The NCSA Mosaic Add Viewer dialog box, with Write information entered.

That's it. You're now ready to try out your new setup. Close the Preferences windows by clicking OK, and then select Open Document from the Mosaic File menu. Enter the URL of a Write document on your Web server. Mosaic contacts the Web server and asks for the document. As described in detail in Chapter 7, the server sends back header information identifying the document as the MIME type/subtype `application/write`. Mosaic reads this information, and then passes the incoming document off to Write for viewing, dynamically starting Write with a copy of the document.

Figure 10.32 Mosaic with Write tiled on top. At this point, you have all the features and power of Write available to you to edit, save, and print this document.

> **Note:** It's important to note that you're working with a temporary copy of the document, not the original, which is still safe on your Web server. As a result, you're free to make any changes to the document you need to make.

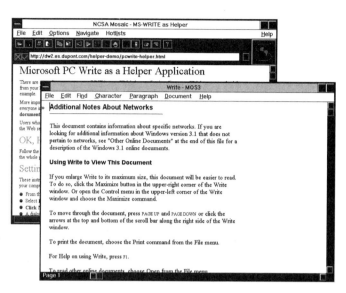

Figure 10.32. *Mosaic with Write as a helper application.*

Netscape and Write on Windows PCs

Netscape in Windows provides a graphical interface for setting up helper applications. Open the Options menu, and then select General Preferences. The Preferences dialog box appears. Click on the Helpers tab (shown in Figure 10.33).

As you can see in Figure 10.33, there is a scrollable File type list that contains preset helper applications; clicking on one of them brings up some details of the setup. In Figure 10.33, the audio/x-wav File type has been selected. Below the File type window, you'll see File / MIME Type, with Subtype on the next line. Below that, there's a fill-in File Extensions box, several option buttons, and another fill-in box.

Figure 10.33 shows the dialog box already filled in for the Microsoft WAVE audio player, mplayer. Let's take a look at this figure before going any further. You'll recognize some familiar items here. First, the File type window should remind you of the contents of the mime.types file on your Web server, with its columns specifying MIME data types/subtypes (on the left) and filename extensions (on the right). Below that box, you'll find the File / MIME Type item filled in as audio and the subtype filled in as x-wav. The File Extensions box contains wav.

At the bottom, there are several option buttons which enable you to choose what to do with incoming data of the MIME type/subtype application/x-wav. In Figure 10.23, Launch the Application is shown selected. The bottommost box is where you enter the name and path of the program that you want to function as your helper application. In Figure 10.33, the drive and path to the Microsoft Windows Media Player application, mplayer, has been filled in. Notice that Netscape has picked up the Windows icon for mplayer, displaying it just to the left of the box.

Before we go on, note the Create New Type and Browse buttons, as we'll be using them to set up Write as a helper application.

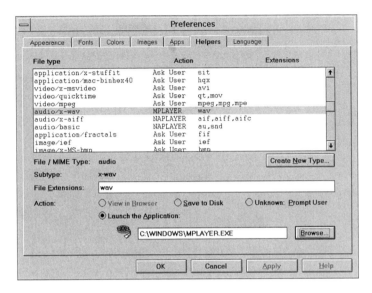

Figure 10.33. Netscape Preferences dialog box with the Helpers tab selected.

Your tour of the Helpers tab completed, let's configure Write as your helper application. Click the Create New Type button, to open the Configure New Mime Type dialog box shown in Figure 10.34. This box has two fill-in boxes for your information about the new MIME type/subtype. In Figure 10.34, the information for Write has been filled in, right out of the mime.types file.

Fill yours in, then click OK. This returns you to the previous dialog box, with the MIME type information you just entered filled in. You now need to enter wri wrt in the File Extensions box. (As you'll recall, we entered both these filename extensions to the mime.types file earlier.) Finally, click the Launch the Application option button and fill in the full drive and pathname to the Write executable program. If you're not sure about this, click the Browse button, which works like most Windows browse buttons, allowing you to locate the executable you want. Once you've found it, select it.

Figure 10.35 shows the Helpers tab filled in with Write information. (Your drive and path to the Write executable may be different than the one shown, so make sure you locate yours, rather than just copying what's shown in the figure.) Note that Netscape picks up the Write icon and places it in the Helpers window. Once you're set, click OK to save your changes.

That's it. You're now ready to try out your new setup. Close the Preferences windows by clicking OK, and then click the Open button on Netscape's toolbar. Enter the URL of a Write document on your Web server. Netscape contacts the Web server and asks for the document. As described in detail in Chapter 7, the server sends back header information identifying the document as the MIME type/subtype application/pcwrite. Netscape reads this information, then passes the incoming document off to Write for viewing, dynamically starting PC-Write with a copy of the document.

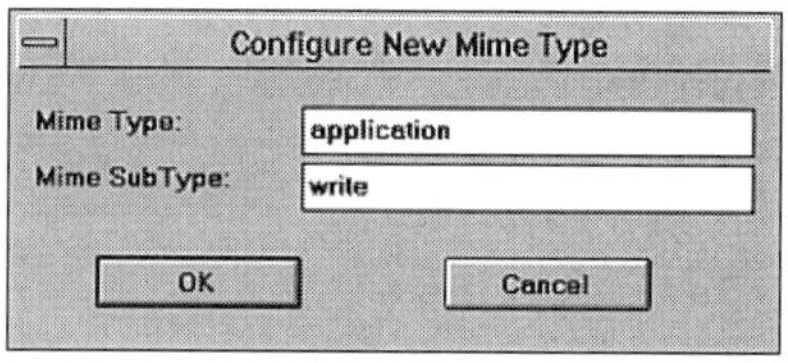

Figure 10.34. Netscape Configure New Mime Type dialog box.

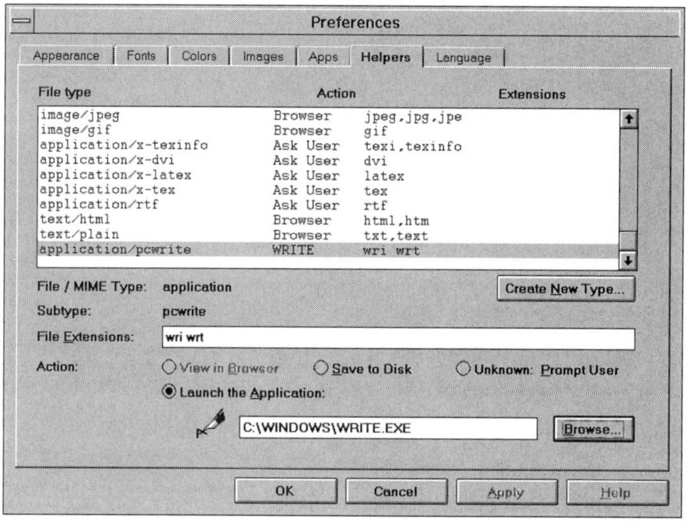

Figure 10.35. Netscape Helper tab with the Write information entered.

Figure 10.36 shows Netscape with Write tiled on top. At this point, you have all the features and power of Write available to you to edit, save, and print this document.

> **Note:** It's important to note that you're working with a temporary copy of the document, not the original, which is still safe on your Web server. As a result, you're free to make any changes to the document you need to make.

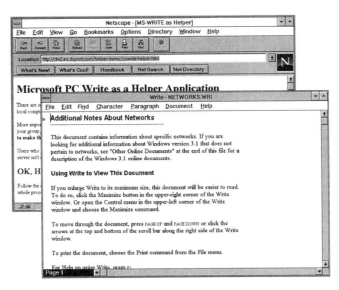

Figure 10.36. *Netscape with Write as a helper application.*

Other Word Processors

You should be able to use the general principles described in this chapter to set up other word processing packages as helper applications. As each of the foregoing sections has shown, the major steps in doing so are 1) add entries to the `mime.types` file on your Web server for your word processor's data files; 2) set up some word processor documents on your Web server; and 3) configure your word processor as a helper application for your Web browser using the fill-in screens shown in this chapter.

Read-Only Viewers

While we discussed in Chapter 4 that some word processors can read documents created in others, and that many use Rich-Text Format as a means of converting documents from one format to another, the problem of dealing with foreign word processor documents (that is, documents created by word processing packages other than your own) is a perennial one. Each of the three major word processor manufacturers whose products we've covered in this chapter—Microsoft,

WordPerfect, and Adobe's Frame Technologies—have made available free *read-only viewers* for their documents. These include:

◆ Microsoft's Word Viewer, available at URL `http://www.microsoft.com/msoffice/freestuf/msword/download/viewers/default.htm` (for Windows 3.1 and Windows 95 only).

◆ Envoy, available at URL `http://wp.novell.com/busapps/win/tocen10w.htm` (for Windows only).

◆ Frame Reader, available at URL `ftp://ftp.frame.com/pub/techsup/product_updates`, where you'll find UNIX, Windows, and Macintosh subdirectories.

Each of these packages will read and display documents created by their associated word processor. You need not own the particular word processor with which these viewers are associated to use them. Although you cannot edit the documents, you can save or print them.

While these packages work in standalone mode for viewing documents, you can also set them up as Web browser helper applications. In other words, you can set up your Intranet web server to know about each of the formats, and then provide the read-only viewers to your customers instead of the full applications. That way, customers can view all the available documents, whether or not they have the correct word processor. Helper application setup for the viewers is exactly the same as described in this chapter. Just substitute the read-only viewer as the executable program to be launched based on the MIME type/subtype of the documents. Figure 10.37 shows the WordPerfect Envoy product, set up as a Mosaic helper application.

Figure 10.37. *The Envoy read-only viewer can substitute for the full WordPerfect product if your customers need to read but not edit WordPerfect documents.*

Summary

Chapter 10 has focused on setting up your Intranet to use common office word processors as Web helper applications. Using the information in this chapter, you can set up libraries of documents in your own word processor file format and make them available on your Web. Your customers can use their Web browsers to locate documents in the library, then start up their word processors simply by clicking on a Web hyperlink. Specifically, this chapter has covered, in standalone sections for each of several major word processors:

◆ The importance of being able to retrieve documents directly into your word processor using a Web browser.

◆ Configuration of your World Wide Web server software to understand your word processor's document files.

◆ Configuration of your World Wide Web browser software to handle word processor documents, including viewing foreign word processor documents.

◆ Potential uses of these capabilities.

Chapter 11, "Spreadsheets and Data Warehouses," will cover office spreadsheet package, showing you how to set up Microsoft Excel, Lotus 1-2-3, and the UNIX spreadsheet package Xess to function as Web browser helper applications.

CHAPTER 11

◆

Spreadsheets and Data Warehouses

In Chapter 10, you learned how to set up your word processor as a Web browser helper application. In this chapter, you'll learn how to set up your Intranet so that customers can retrieve spreadsheet data files using their Web browser and automatically open the files in their favorite spreadsheet software for revision, what-if analysis, recalculation, graphing, and more.

Chapter Objectives

As with the rest of the chapters in this book, let's begin by laying out some chapter objectives. This will help you get oriented to the material to be presented; you may want to refer back to this list as you work your way through the chapter. In this chapter, you will:

◆ Learn why it's important to be able to retrieve spreadsheet data files directly into your spreadsheet package using a Web browser.

◆ Learn how to configure your World Wide Web server software to understand your spreadsheet's document files.

◆ Learn how to configure your World Wide Web browser software to handle your spreadsheet data files.

◆ Learn about supporting multiple spreadsheet data formats.

◆ Learn about other ways of making your spreadsheet data portable.

◆ Understand some potential uses of these capabilities.

The chapter is organized in standalone sections, each devoted to a particular spreadsheet package. The sections cover Microsoft Excel, Lotus 1-2-3, the UNIX spreadsheet package Xess (made by Advanced Information Systems), and others. You need not read the entire chapter to learn how to set up your particular package, because each section is complete in itself, containing all the instructions you need to set up your Web server and your Web browsers.

If your organization uses multiple spreadsheet packages, you'll be able to use the separate sections of this chapter independently, without having to page back and forth. Examples are provided using both NCSA Mosaic and Netscape in each section, as well as a lot of screenshots showing you step-by-step how to set up your spreadsheet as a Web browser helper application. We'll also cover portability of spreadsheet datafiles from one package to another.

Why Integrate Your Spreadsheet in Your Intranet?

Modern operating environments like Microsoft Windows integrate application software like spreadsheets into the desktop environment, enabling the user to start up any spreadsheet with a simple mouse click.

Integrating your spreadsheet in your Web is, in a sense, creating a whole new graphical interface for users, based on your Web browser. In fact, some people have predicted an overall graphical user interface based on Netscape or Mosaic may eventually replace the Microsoft Windows or the Macintosh desktop. While this may seem a bit farfetched, it is nonetheless both possible and simple to broaden the scope of your Web browser. Doing so allows you to tie in links to your everyday tools, like your spreadsheet, giving a new interface with a common look and feel that's both easy and fun to use.

More importantly, you can use your Web server, HTML, your spreadsheet package, and other tools to put together shareable data warehouses of spreadsheet data files. Such libraries can be complete with searchable indices and point-and-click access via your Web browser. Locating and bringing up a spreadsheet data file is no longer a process of finding a file, and then starting up your spreadsheet to read or use it. Rather, using Mosaic, Netscape, or another Web browser, your customer can merely click on a Web hyperlink and have the spreadsheet fire up with a copy of the data file loaded, all in one simple process. Once the spreadsheet program has loaded the file, your customers have all the capabilities of their spreadsheet package at their disposal—they can change the data, recalculate it, graph it, print it, save it, or whatever.

As with commercial groupware packages like Lotus Notes (see Chapter 24, "Web Groupware: Collaboration on Your Intranet," expensive data warehouse software packages are available, but you can easily replicate many of their features in your Intranet. Moreover, you can do so at a substantially lower cost, and without requiring users to learn to use yet another new software package. Because they'll be using their familiar Web browser as the interface to your homegrown data warehouse and their everyday spreadsheet package to examine and manipulate the stored data, you need not purchase such a package.

You can store company sales or production data, for example, on your Web server in spreadsheet format, complete with formulae and macro commands. Properly set up, your Web server can serve those data files when users select hyperlinks pointing to them. Web browsers can then take the data and hand it off to your customers' spreadsheet package, which they can use to play with the numbers for forecasting or preparing presentation graphics.

Even if you use your Intranet exclusively to serve spreadsheet data files, you may well spend less money on hardware and software to do so than you would spend in buying a commercial data warehouse package. If your Web is already serving other purposes, a few minutes' work can set it up to function as an essentially free data warehouse. While there are features of these commercial packages that you won't be able to replicate in your Intranet, the price of implementing those features you can replicate is certainly right—and you may find that you're able to replicate enough of these features to make it unnecessary to buy that data warehouse package.

You'll recall from earlier chapters the term *helper application* (a.k.a. *external viewer*) to refer to computer programs that your Web browser uses when it can't directly display the data represented by a hyperlink. In this chapter, your spreadsheet package is treated like a helper application, just like a sound or video player. There's very little difference between the setup of one of these common helper applications and the setup of Excel or Lotus 1-2-3, but there's a major difference in the implications of doing so. Playing video and audio on your computer may be remarkable and enjoyable, but, unless you are in the video or audio business, it gets little of your substantive, everyday work done. Your spreadsheet package, on the other hand (along with the other common office applications discussed in this book), is the workhorse of many days. Integrating your spreadsheet package into your Intranet, then, can be a potentially major productivity enhancement, fundamentally changing the way your customers—and therefore your company—do their work.

Web Server Setup

Regardless of which spreadsheet package you use, your first step in setting up your spreadsheet as a helper application is to configure your Web server to know about your spreadsheet's data files. With small differences, as are noted in context, the instructions in this section apply to any spreadsheet.

As you learned in Chapter 7, "MIME and Helper Applications," Web servers use the MIME mechanism to identify documents according to their MIME data type/subtype. Recall the MIME mechanism divides data into a relatively small handful of data types, with each type further subdivided into subtypes. Spreadsheet data files fall into the application data type. You also learned in Chapter 7 how Web servers use filename extensions to map data files on the server to a MIME data type/subtype. You associate the filename extensions with MIME types/subtypes in the Web server's configuration file `mime.types` (`mime.typ` on a PC server).

Editing the `mime.types` File

As you'll recall from Chapter 7, the `mime.types` file is a plain text file containing a simple, two-column listing of MIME types/sub-types and associated filename extensions. Here's a short excerpt from the standard `mime.types` file distributed with the NCSA httpd server software; for a full listing, refer to Chapter 7.

```
application/mac-binhex40
application/macwriteii
application/news-message-id
application/news-transmission
application/octet-stream      bin
application/oda               oda
application/pdf               pdf
application/postscript        ai eps ps
```

Here you can see the association, for example, between the pdf filename extension and the MIME type/sub-type `application/pdf`, representing the Adobe Portable Document Format. Similarly, PostScript documents are represented by the `application/postscript` data type/sub-type; in this case, there are three filename extensions associated. Also note that several of the entries have no filename extensions listed; you can add these as required.

Note: The Netscape Communications server uses a different format for the `mime.types` file. The format is more complex, but potentially easier to understand, since the two columns of each entry are labeled. Here's an excerpt:

```
type=application/oda      exts=oda
type=application/pdf      exts=pdf
type=image/jpeg           exts=jpeg,jpg,jpe
```

As you can see, Netscape has added labels to the two columns of the `mime.types` file, with the left column containing not only the MIME data type/sub-type (image/jpeg, for example), but also the identifying label type, separated by an equal (=) sign. Similarly, the right column includes the label exts, along with the actual filename extensions. The Netscape `mime.types` file also includes an optional third column, not found in other servers' files, specifying an icon to be associated with the MIME data type/sub-type. The Netscape server also provides for a secondary `mime.types` file, with your localizations, specified in the `magnus.conf` file. For more information about this file and overall Netscape Communications Server configuration, see Appendix A, "Setting up a Web Server," or the Netscape Communications server documentation.

To set up your Web server for your spreadsheet, you'll need to make changes in the `mime.types` file. You can edit the file with any text editor, such as vi or emacs (on a UNIX system), the Windows Notepad or DOS edit, Macintosh TeachText, or even your word processor in plain text mode.

> **Note:** If your Web server runs on a UNIX system, you'll need root, or superuser, access to edit the `mime.types` file.

The `mime.types` file distributed with the NCSA httpd server doesn't contain any entries for spreadsheet packages, but it's easy to add them, using the existing entries in the file as models. As noted above, the MIME type for all spreadsheet packages is application, so you can start out with entries for your spreadsheet, possibly using one of the example packages we're using in this chapter. They'll look like this:

```
application/msexcel
application/lotus
application/xess
```

As you've realized, these are missing the filename extensions you need in order to have your Web server associate their data files with the particular application program. Normally, Microsoft Excel uses the filename extension `.xls`. Lotus 1-2-3 uses some variation (depending on the release level) of `.wk` or `.wks`. Xess Version 3 uses `.xs3`. You're not required to use these filename extensions, although it's a good idea to standardize on one or two. Here are the above three `mime.types` entries, revised to show some possibilities.

```
application/msexcel     xls xcl
application/lotus        wks wk4 lotus
application/xess         xs3 xess
```

As with the PostScript entries earlier in this section, you've associated two or more filename extensions with each of the three MIME data type/subtypes for spreadsheet data files.

> **Note:** UNIX systems have different and much more lenient rules about file naming than DOS/Windows systems. Because Xess is a UNIX package and 1-2-3 is available for UNIX systems as well, we've used filename extensions longer than three characters here just to illustrate what is permitted on UNIX systems. If your Web server is a PC, however, you'll need to stick with three-character filename extensions.

> **Warning:** Double check your spreadsheet filename extensions you're entering to make sure they don't duplicate any of the standard `mime.types` entries. You may have unexpected results otherwise.

If you're using a different spreadsheet, you'll need to add an entry to `mime.types` for it. If it uses a default filename extension for its data files, use it in `mime.types`. Otherwise, you're free to use whatever you want, provided it doesn't conflict with other entries in the `mime.types` file.

You're done editing the `mime.types` file, so you can save it and exit your editor.

Implementing Changes in `mime.types`

Because you've changed the configuration of your Web server by editing one of its setup files, you need to make the server aware of your changes in its setup. If your server isn't already running, it will read the changes when you start it. If the server is already running, you can have it reread its configuration files in one of a couple of ways. On a Macintosh or Windows server, just stop the server and restart it. For example, in the httpd server, open the Control menu and select Exit, and then restart the server by double-clicking on its icon or by using the Program Manager's Run command.

UNIX servers provide a more convenient way of having the setup files reread, enabling you to do so without actually shutting down the server and interrupting access to it. It's called sending a hang-up signal to the server process. All processes running on UNIX systems have a unique process id, or pid. You can find your server's pid using the UNIX process status command, ps. Here's an example, using the grep command to filter out all but the processes in which we're interested:

```
# ps -ax | grep httpd
    250 ?         S  0:06 /usr/local/etc/httpd/httpd
    255 ?         S  0:06 /usr/local/etc/httpd/httpd
    258 ?         S  0:06 /usr/local/etc/httpd/httpd
    686 ?         S  0:05 /usr/local/etc/httpd/httpd
   6383 ?         S  0:02 /usr/local/etc/httpd/httpd
   7096 ?         S  0:01 /usr/local/etc/httpd/httpd
  19304 pts/6     S  0:00 grep httpd
```

> **Note:** The BSD UNIX `-ax` arguments to the ps command are used here, as on a SunOS 4.1.x system. If your machine is a System V UNIX, such as SunOS 5.x, SGI IRIX 5.x, or other system, you'll need to use this command:
>
> ```
> # ps -ef | grep httpd
> ```
>
> The output of the System V ps command is a bit different, but gives the same information (along with additional information).
>
> ```
>     root    250     1 80     Nov 13 ?           0:06 /usr/local/etc/httpd/httpd
>   nobody    255   250 80     Nov 13 ?           0:07 /usr/local/etc/httpd/httpd
>   nobody    686   250 80     Nov 14 ?           0:06 /usr/local/etc/httpd/httpd
>   nobody   7096   250 80     Nov 24 ?           0:02 /usr/local/etc/httpd/httpd
>   nobody    258   250 80     Nov 13 ?           0:06 /usr/local/etc/httpd/httpd
>   nobody   6383   250 80     Nov 22 ?           0:03 /usr/local/etc/httpd/httpd
>  tkevans  19310   384 12 06:02:45 pts/6         0:00 grep httpd
> ```

In the output of the first example of the ps command, process ids appear in the first column, with the main server pid being 250. As indicated in Appendix A, the most recent releases of the NCSA httpd server generate a parent httpd process and several child processes; the lowest number pid is the parent process. This distinction is more clear with the System V ps command, with the pids shown in the second column and the pid of the process that started each one shown in the third column. As you can see, the parent process id (ppid) of the main httpd server process is 1, indicating that the process was started at boot time by the UNIX init daemon. Each of the child httpd processes shows the main httpd process (pid 250) as itsppid.

After you identify the pid of the main httpd server process, you can send it a hang-up signal like this:

```
# kill -HUP 250
```

This command, run by the superuser, tells the httpd process something has changed in its configuration and that it must reread the setup files without exiting. Afterwards, the server is still running, but using the revised setup.

The NCSA and CERN httpd servers provide a shortcut to this whole process that doesn't require you to find out the server's pid. When the server starts up, it stores its pid in a file named httpd.pid in the top level of the server software tree. This command is the shortcut to having the server reread its configuration files:

```
# kill -HUP 'cat /usr/local/etc/httpd/httpd.pid'
```

This command uses the special UNIX feature under which the command surrounded by the backward single quote (the "`" character, also called *accent grave*) is run first, with its output substituted in the main command. Because the content of the httpd.pid file is merely the pid of the main server process (in our example, 250), the actual command that's run here is the same as the example above. What's different is that you didn't have to look up the pid yourself by running the ps command.

> **Note:** The Netscape Communications Server has a graphical interface, called the Server Manager, which allows you to restart the server. This soft restart causes the server to reread its configuration files without interrupting the ongoing operation of the server.

Adding Spreadsheet Data Files to Your Web Server

Now that you've completed the setup of your Web server, to properly identify and serve your spreadsheet data files your next step is to populate your server with some data files for your package. You can transfer your data files to your Web server using your network file transfer utilities (such as ftp, in binary mode) or via floppy diskette or tape. Whatever method you use, it's probably a good idea to put the files in a dedicated directory for your particular spreadsheets.

Next, you'll need to create some sort of HTML listing of them. This can be as simple or as complex as you like, because including hyperlinks to spreadsheet data files is exactly the same as setting up links to other kinds of documents. A simple HTML listing, using Microsoft Excel as an example, might be something like this.

```
<HTML><HEAD><TITLE>Excel Spreadsheets</TITLE></HEAD>
<BODY>
<H1>Microsoft Excel Spreadsheets</H1>
```

This directory contains a set of Excel spreadsheets. Just click on one to open it up in Excel.

```
<UL><LI><A HREF="qrtrly_sales.xls">Spreadsheet 1</A>, Last Quarter's Sales</LI>
<LI><A HREF="qrtrly_prod.xls">Spreadsheet 2</A>, Last Quarter's Production</LI>
<LI><A HREF="cpi_forecast.xls">Spreadsheet 3</A>, Consumer Price Index Forecasts</
LI></UL>
```

If you haven't already done so, you must set up your Web browser to understand Excel spreadsheet data files.

```
<A HREF="excel_setup.html">Here are instructions.</A>
</BODY></HTML>
```

Figure 11.1 shows this HTML code, rendered in NCSA Mosaic. As you can see, it looks like just any other Web page. Users with properly set up Web browsers can just click on the hyperlinks to open a copy of the selected spreadsheet in Excel. Before you can use this page to load the hyperlinked Excel spreadsheets, however, you must set up your Web browser to use Excel as a helper application, as described in the following section.

Figure 11.1. *Web browser rendering of Microsoft Excel spreadsheet page.*

Setting Up Microsoft Excel as a Helper Application

Now that you have set up your Web server to know about spreadsheet data files, and populated it with some actual data files from the package, your next step is to set up Excel as a helper application. The concept of setting up helper applications for Web browsers is a general one, but the steps for actually going about it differ, depending on the Web browser you're using. Let's go through the steps for NCSA Mosaic and Netscape in this chapter. If you're using another browser, you'll need to take a look at its documentation to find out how to accomplish this.

NCSA Mosaic and Excel on Windows PCs

NCSA Mosaic in Windows provides a graphical interface for setting up helper applications, although Mosaic uses the term *external viewer* rather than *helper application.* In Mosaic, open the Options menu and select Preferences. The Preferences dialog box appears. Click on the Viewers tab to see the options shown in Figure 11.2.

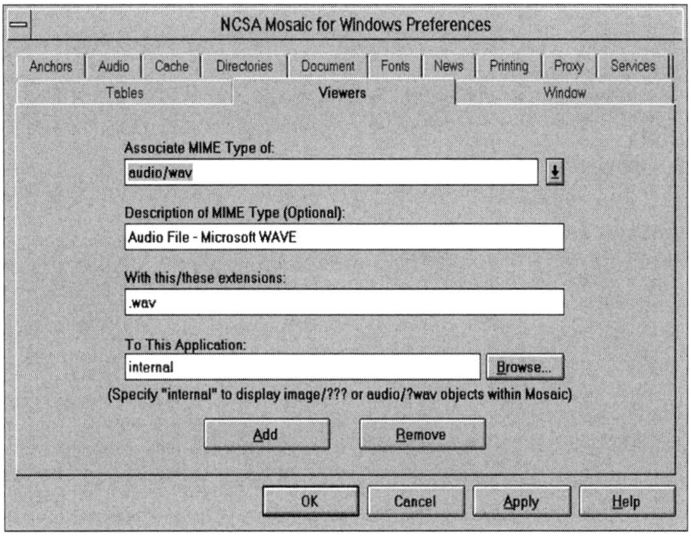

Figure 11.2. *The Mosaic Preferences dialog box with the Viewers tab selected.*

As you can see, there are four fill-in boxes and several buttons that enable you to control the external viewers used. Figure 11.2 shows the dialog box already filled in for the Microsoft WAVE audio player.

Let's take a look at the labels on the fill-in boxes before going any further. We'll take then slightly out of order. You'll recognize some familiar items here. First, the top box, Associate MIME Type of, contains a MIME data type/subtype pair—in this case audio/wav. This item is, of course, right out of the mime.types file. The third fill-in box, With this/these extensions, is also familiar. It contains the same info as the filename-extension column in your mime.types file, with the extension wav entered.

The second fill-in box is an optional description of the kind of data file—in our example, it's Audio File - Microsoft WAVE. The last fill-in box, To this application, is where you specify which program will function as your helper application. In Figure 11.2, the special keyword internal is used there, indicating Mosaic can handle this MIME type/subtype by itself, without a helper application. Before we go on, note the Browse button next to this box, as we'll be using it to set up Excel as your helper application.

Now that your tour of the Viewers tab is complete, let's configure Microsoft Excel as your helper application. Click the Add button to open the Add Viewer dialog box, shown in Figure 11.3. This box has the same four fill-in boxes as Figure 11.2, but they're blank for you to enter your own information.

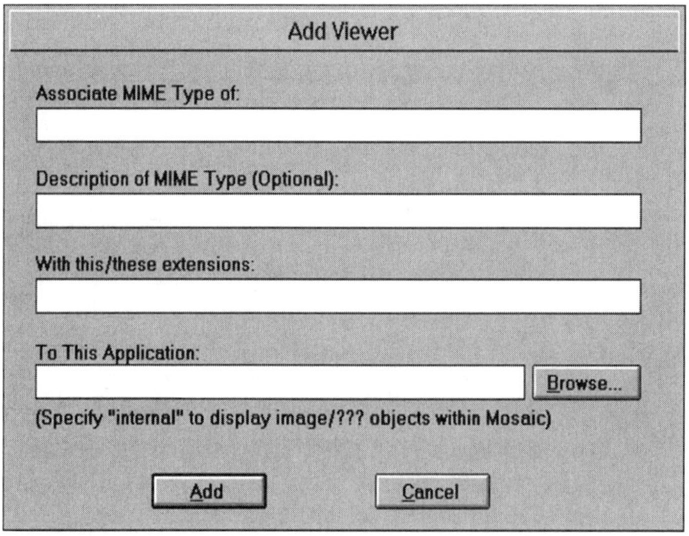

Figure 11.3. *The NCSA Mosaic Add Viewer dialog box.*

Using the information you added to your `mime.types` file earlier, you can quickly fill in these blanks.

- ◆ In the Associate MIME Type of box, enter `application/msexcel`.
- ◆ In the Description of MIME Type (Optional) Box, enter something like `Microsoft Excel Spreadsheet`. Note that you're not required to enter anything in this box, although it's a good idea to do so for future reference.
- ◆ In the With this/these extensions box, enter `xls xcl`. (As you'll recall, we entered both these filename extensions into the `mime.types` file earlier.)
- ◆ Finally, in the To This Application box, enter the full drive and pathname to the Microsoft Excel executable program. If you're not sure about this, click the Browse button, which works like most Windows browse buttons, enabling you to locate the executable you want. Once you've found it, select it.

Figure 11.4 shows the filled-in Add Viewer dialog box. (Your drive and path to the Excel executable may be different than the one shown, so make sure you locate yours, rather than just copying what's shown in the figure.) Once you're set, click Add to save your changes.

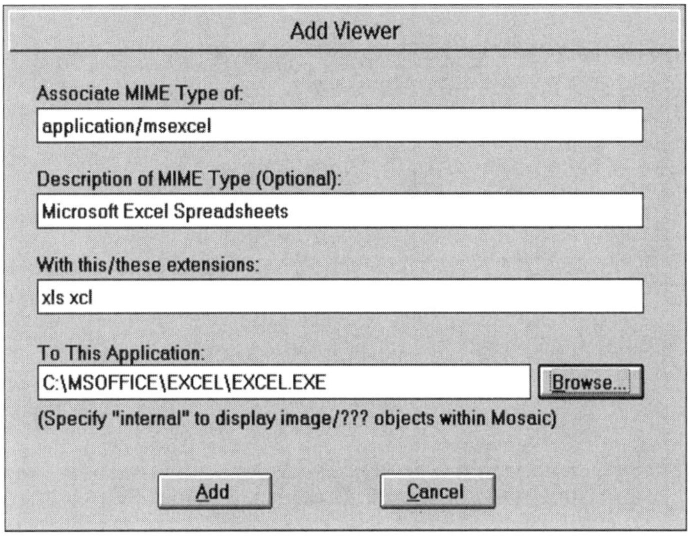

Figure 11.4. The NCSA Mosaic Add Viewer dialog box, filled in for Microsoft Excel.

That's it. You're now ready to try out your new setup. Close the Preferences windows by clicking OK, and then select Open Document from the Mosaic File menu. Enter the URL of an Excel spreadsheet on your Web server, or click on one in an HTML document listing them. Mosaic contacts the Web server and asks for the document. As described in detail in Chapter 7, the server sends back header information identifying the document as the MIME type/subtype `application/msexcel`. Mosaic reads this information, and then passes the incoming document off to Excel for viewing, dynamically starting up Excel with a copy of the spreadsheet.

Figure 11.5 shows Mosaic with Excel tiled on top. At this point, you have all the features and power of Excel available to you to edit, recalculate, graph, save, and print this spreadsheet.

> **Note:** It's important to note you're working with a temporary copy of the spreadsheet, not the original, which is still safe on your Web server. As a result, you're free to make any changes to the spreadsheet you need to make.

> **Note:** If you get errors about Excel being unable to load your document, and you're sure that you've specified the correct URL on your Web server and the permissions on the file are correct, you may be experiencing a memory problem. Close down other open applications and/or turn off some of Excel's features to conserve memory. You may also need to use a memory manager/optimizer like QEMM or the Microsoft memmaker.

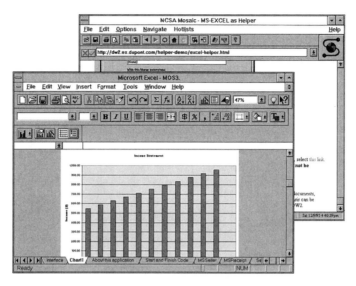

Figure 11.5. *Mosaic with Microsoft Excel as a helper application.*

Netscape and Excel on Windows PCs

Netscape in Windows provides a graphical interface for setting up helper applications. Open the Options menu, then select General Preferences. The Preferences dialog box appears. Click on the Helpers tab (shown in Figure 11.6).

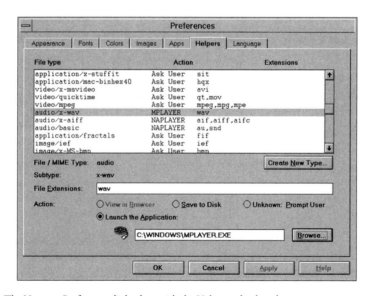

Figure 11.6. *The Netscape Preferences dialog box with the Helpers tab selected.*

As you can see, there is a scrollable File type list that contains preset helper applications; clicking on one of them brings up some details of the setup. In Figure 11.6, the audio/x-wav file type has been selected. Below the File type window, you'll see File / MIME Type, with Subtype on the next line. Below that, there's a fill-in File Extensions box, several option buttons, and another fill-in box.

Figure 11.6 shows the dialog box already filled in for the Microsoft WAVE audio player, mplayer. Let's take a look at this figure before going any further. You'll recognize some familiar items here. First, the File type window should remind you of the contents of the mime.types file on your Web server, with its columns specifying MIME data types/subtypes (on the left) and filename extensions (on the right). Below that box, you'll find the File / MIME Type item filled in as audio and the subtype filled in as x-wav. The File Extensions box contains wav.

At the bottom, there are several option buttons that enable you to choose what to do with incoming data of the MIME type/subtype application/x-wav. In Figure 11.6, Launch the Application is shown selected. The bottommost box is where you enter the name and path of the program you want to function as your helper application. In Figure 11.6, the drive and path to the Microsoft Windows Media Player application, mplayer, has been filled in. Notice Netscape has picked up the Windows icon for mplayer, displaying it just to the left of the box. Before we go on, note the Create New Type and Browse buttons, as we'll be using them to set up Excel as a helper application.

Your tour of the Helpers dialog box complete, let's configure Microsoft Excel as your Netscape helper application. Click the Create New Type button to open the Configure New Mime Type dialog box shown in Figure 11.7. This box has two fill-in boxes for your information about the new MIME type/subtype. Here, we've filled in the information for Excel, right out of the mime.types file.

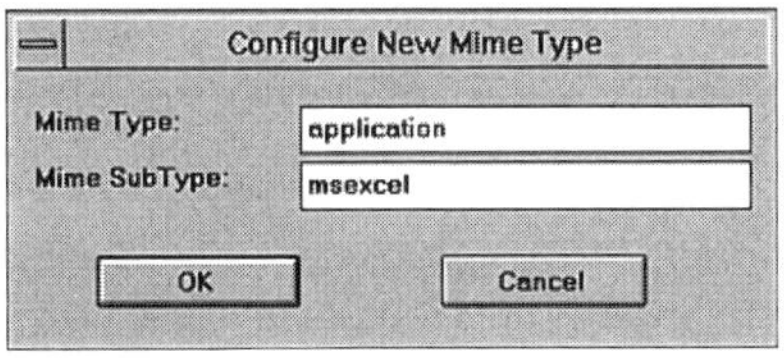

Figure 11.7. *Netscape Configure New Mime Type dialog box.*

Fill yours in, and then click OK. This returns you to the previous dialog box, with the MIME type information you just entered filled in. You now need to enter xls and xcl in the File Extensions box. (As you'll recall, we entered both of these filename extensions to the mime.types file earlier.) Finally, click on Launch the Application and fill in the full drive and pathname to the Microsoft Excel executable program. If you're not sure about this, click the Browse button, which works like most Windows browse buttons, allowing you to locate the executable you want. Once you've found it, select it. As with mplayer, Netscape has located and displayed the Excel icon.

Figure 11.8 shows the Helpers tab filled in with Microsoft Excel information. (Your drive and path to the Excel executable may be different than the one shown, so make sure you locate yours, rather than just copying what's shown in the figure.) Once you're set, click OK to save your changes.

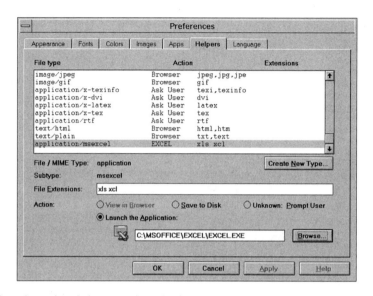

Figure 11.8. The Helpers tab with the Microsoft Excel information entered.

That's it. You're now ready to try out your new setup. Close the Preferences windows by clicking OK, and then click the Open button on Netscape's toolbar. Enter the URL of an Excel spreadsheet on your Web server, or click on a hyperlink pointing to one. Netscape contacts the Web server and asks for the file. As described in detail in Chapter 7, the server sends back header information identifying the document as the MIME type/sub-type `application/msexcel`. Netscape reads this information, and then passes the incoming document off to Excel for viewing, dynamically starting up Excel with a copy of the spreadsheet. Figure 11.9 shows Netscape with Excel tiled on top.

At this point, you have all the features and power of Excel available to you to edit, recalculate, graph, save, and print this spreadsheet.

> **Note:** It's important to note you're working with a temporary copy of the spreadsheet, not the original, which is still safe on your Web server. As a result, you're free to make any changes to the spreadsheet you need to make.

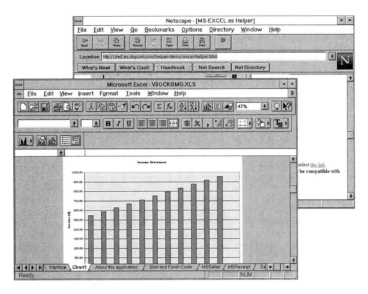

Figure 11.9. *Netscape with Microsoft Excel as a helper application.*

Note: If you get errors about Excel being unable to load your document, and you're sure you've specified the correct URL on your Web server and permissions on the file are set correctly, you may be experiencing a memory problem. Close down other open applications and/or turn off some of Excel's features to conserve memory. You may also need to use a memory manager/optimizer like QEMM or the Microsoft memmaker.

Mosaic/Netscape and Excel on the Macintosh

Macintosh users will find the process of setting up Excel as a viewer/helper application virtually identical to that for Windows. The only difference is in specifying the folder and executable names for Excel. You can use the Browse process, just as in Windows, with the browser displaying Mac folder names in place of PC directory names.

Setting Up Lotus 1-2-3 as a Helper Application

Now that you have set up your Web server to know about spreadsheet data files and populated it with some actual data files from the package, your next step is setting up Lotus as a helper application. The concept of setting up helper applications for Web browsers is a general one, but the steps for actually going about it differ, depending on the Web browser you're using. We'll go through the steps for NCSA Mosaic and Netscape. If you're using another browser, you'll need to take a look at its documentation for how to accomplish this.

NCSA Mosaic and Lotus 1-2-3 on Windows PCs

NCSA Mosaic in Windows provides a graphical interface for setting up helper applications, although Mosaic uses the term *external viewer* rather than *helper application.* In Mosaic, open the Options menu and select Preferences. The Preferences dialog box appears. Click on the Viewers tab to see the options shown in Figure 11.10.

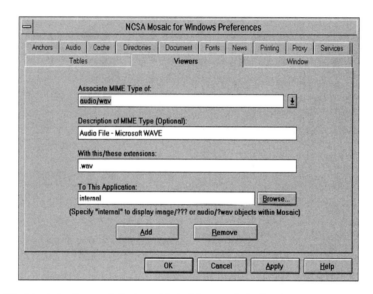

Figure 11.10. The Mosaic Preferences dialog box with the Viewers tab displayed.

As you can see, there are four fill-in boxes and several buttons that enable you to control the external viewers used. Figure 11.2 shows the dialog box already filled in for the Microsoft WAVE audio player.

Let's take a look at the labels on the fill-in boxes before going any further. We'll take then slightly out of order. You'll recognize some familiar items here. First, the top box, Associate MIME Type of, contains a MIME data type/sub-type pair—in this case, audio/wav. This item is, of course, right out of the mime.types file. The third fill-in box, With this/these extensions, is also familiar. It contains the same info as the filename-extension column in your `mime.types` file, with the extension `.wav` entered.

The second fill-in box is an optional description of the kind of data file—in our example, it's `Audio File - Microsoft WAVE`. The last fill-in box, To this application, is where you specify which program will function as your helper application. In Figure 11.10, the special keyword `internal` is used there, indicating that Mosaic can handle this MIME type/subtype by itself, without a helper application. Before we go on, note the Browse button next to this box, as we'll be using it to set up 1-2-3 as your helper application.

Now that your tour of the Viewers tab is complete, let's configure Lotus 1-2-3 as your helper application. Click the Add button to open up the Add Viewer dialog box, shown in Figure 11.11. This box has the same four fill-in boxes as Figure 11.10, but they're blank, for you to enter your own information.

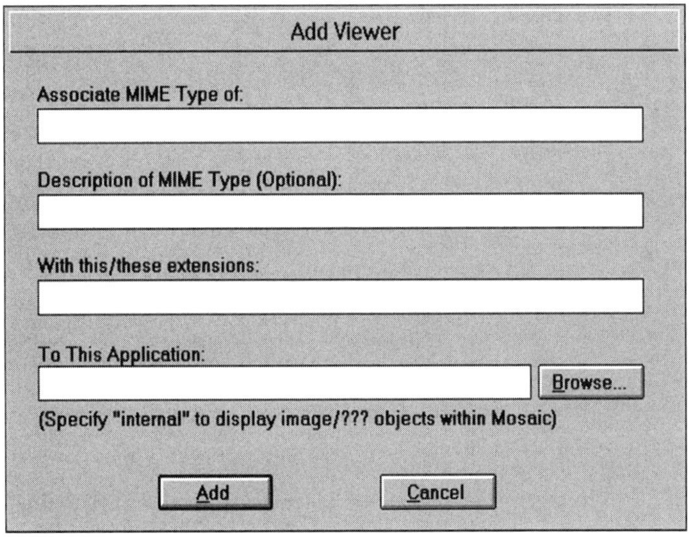

Figure 11.11. The NCSA Mosaic Add Viewer dialog box.

Using the information you added to your `mime.types` file earlier, you can quickly fill in these blanks.

◆ In the Associate MIME Type of box, enter `application/lotus`.

◆ In the Description of MIME Type (Optional) Box, enter something like `Lotus 1-2-3 Spreadsheet`. Note that you're not required to enter anything in this box, although it's a good idea to do so for future reference.

♦ In the With this/these extensions box, enter .wks lotus. (As you'll recall, we entered both these filename extensions to the mime.types file earlier.)

♦ Finally, in the To This Application box, enter the full drive and pathname to the Lotus 1-2-3 executable program. If you're not sure about this, click the Browse button, which works like most Windows browse buttons, enabling you to locate the executable you want. Once you've found it, select it.

Figure 11.12 shows the filled-in Add Viewer dialog box. (Your drive and path to the 1-2-3 executable may be different than the one shown, so make sure you locate yours, rather than just copying what's shown in the figure.) Once you're set, click Add to save your changes.

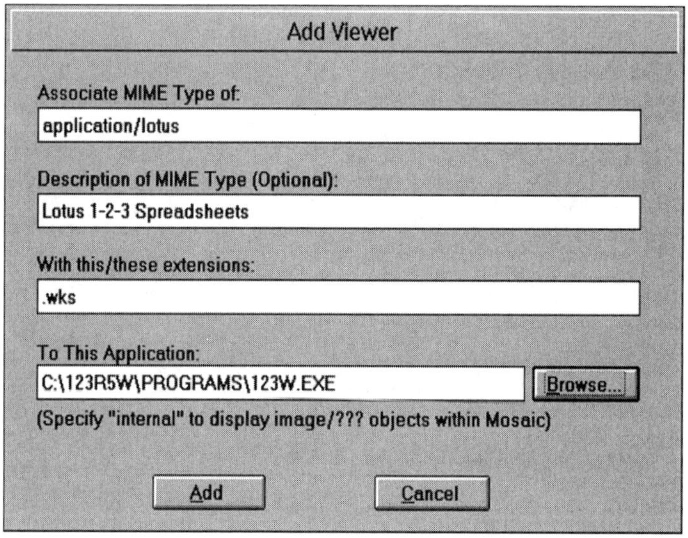

Figure 11.12. The NCSA Mosaic Add Viewer dialog box, filled in for Lotus 1-2-3.

That's it. You're now ready to try out your new setup. Close the Preferences windows by clicking OK, and then select Open Document from the Mosaic File menu. Enter the URL of a 1-2-3 spreadsheet on your Web server. Mosaic contacts the Web server and asks for the document. As described in detail in Chapter 7, the server sends back header information identifying the document as the MIME type/sub-type application/lotus. Mosaic reads this information, and then passes the incoming document off to 1-2-3 for viewing, dynamically starting up 1-2-3 with a copy of the spreadsheet.

Figure 11.13 shows Mosaic with Lotus 1-2-3 tiled on top. At this point, you have all the features and power of Lotus 1-2-3 available to you to edit, recalculate, graph, save, and print this document.

Note: It's important to note that you're working with a temporary copy of the spreadsheet, not the original, which is still safe on your Web server. As a result, you're free to make any changes to the spreadsheet you need to make.

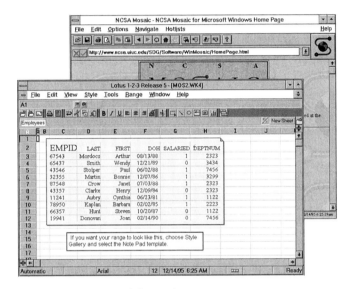

Figure 11.13. Mosaic with Lotus 1-2-3 as a helper application.

Note: If you get errors about 1-2-3 being unable to load your document, and you're sure you've specified the correct URL on your Web server and the permissions on the file are correct, you may be experiencing a memory problem. Close down other open applications and/or turn off some of 1-2-3's features to conserve memory. You may also need to use a memory manager/optimizer like QEMM or the Microsoft memmaker.

Netscape and Lotus 1-2-3 on Windows PCs

Netscape in Windows provides a graphical interface for setting up helper applications. Open the Options menu, then select General Preferences. The Preferences dialog box appears. Click on the Helpers tab (shown in Figure 11.14).

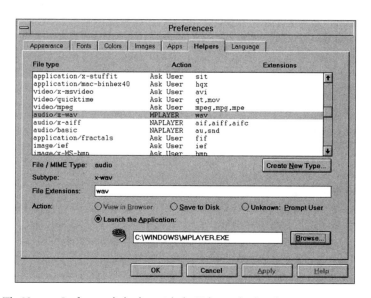

Figure 11.14. *The Netscape Preferences dialog box with the Helpers tab selected.*

As you can see, there is a scrollable File type list that contains preset helper applications; clicking on one of them brings up some details of the setup. In Figure 11.14, The audio/x-wav file type has been selected. Below the File type window, you'll see File / MIME Type, with Subtype on the next line. Below that, there's a fill-in File Extensions box, several option buttons, and another fill-in box.

Figure 11.14 shows the dialog box already filled in for the Microsoft WAVE audio player, mplayer. Let's take a look at this figure before going any further. You'll recognize some familiar items here. First, the File type window should remind you of the contents of the mime.types file on your Web server, with its columns specifying MIME data types/subtypes (on the left) and filename extensions (on the right). Below that box, you'll find the File / MIME Type item filled in as audio and the subtype filled in as x-wav. The File Extensions box contains wav.

At the bottom, there are several option buttons that enable you to choose what to do with incoming data of the MIME type/subtype application/x-wav. In Figure 11.14, Launch the Application is shown selected. The bottommost box is where you enter the name and path of the program that you want to function as your helper application. In Figure 11.14, the drive and path to the Microsoft Windows Media Player application, `mplayer`, has been filled in. Notice Netscape has picked up the Windows icon for `mplayer`, displaying it just to the left of the box. Before we go on, note the Create New Type and Browse buttons, as we'll be using them to set up 1-2-3 as a helper application.

Your tour of the Helpers dialog box complete, let's configure 1-2-3 as your Netscape helper application. Click the Create New Type button, to open up the Configure New Mime Type dialog box shown in Figure 11.15. This box has two fill-in boxes for your information about the new MIME type/subtype. Here, we've filled in the information for 1-2-3, right out of the `mime.types` file.

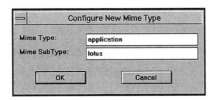

Figure 11.15. Netscape Configure New Mime Type dialog box.

Fill yours in, and then click OK. This returns you to the previous dialog box, with the MIME type information you just entered filled in. You now need to enter `wks` and `lotus` in the File Extensions box. (As you'll recall, we entered both these filename extensions to the `mime.types` file earlier.) Finally, click on Launch the Application and fill in the full drive and pathname to the Lotus 1-2-3 executable program. If you're not sure about this, click the Browse button, which works like most Windows browse buttons, allowing you to locate the executable you want. Once you've found it, select it. As with mplayer, Netscape has located and displayed the Lotus 1-2-3 icon.

Figure 11.16 shows the Helpers tab filled in with Lotus 1-2-3 information. (Your drive and path to the Lotus 1-2-3 executable may be different than the one shown, so make sure you locate yours, rather than just copying what's shown in the figure.) Once you're set, click OK to save your changes.

That's it. You're now ready to try out your new setup. Close the Preferences windows by clicking OK, and then click the Open button on Netscape's toolbar. Enter the URL of a 1-2-3 spreadsheet on your Web server. Netscape contacts the Web server and asks for the file. As described in detail in Chapter 7, the server sends back header information identifying the document as the MIME type/subtype `application/lotus`. Netscape reads this information, and then passes the incoming document off to 1-2-3 for viewing, dynamically starting up 1-2-3 with a copy of the spreadsheet. Figure 11.17 shows Netscape with 1-2-3 tiled on top.

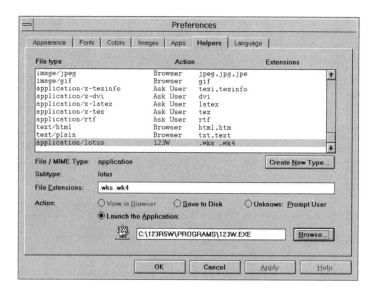

Figure 11.16. *The Helpers tab with the Lotus 1-2-3 information entered.*

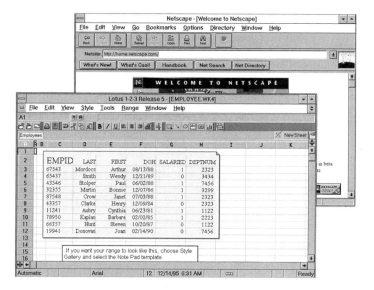

Figure 11.17. *Netscape with Lotus 1-2-3 as a helper application.*

At this point, you have all the features and power of 1-2-3 available to you to edit, recalculate, graph, save, and print this spreadsheet.

> **Note:** It's important to note you're working with a temporary copy of the spreadsheet, not the original, which is still safe on your Web server. As a result, you're free to make any changes to the spreadsheet you need to make.

> **Note:** If you get errors about Lotus 1-2-3 being unable to load your document, and you're sure you've specified the correct URL on your Web server and permissions on the file are set correctly, you may be experiencing a memory problem. Close down other open applications and/or turn off some of Lotus 1-2-3's features to conserve memory. You may also need to use a memory manager/optimizer like QEMM or the Microsoft memmaker.

Mosaic/Netscape and Lotus on the Macintosh

Macintosh users will find the process of setting up Lotus 1-2-3 as a viewer/helper application virtually identical to that for PCs. The only difference is in specifying the folder and executable names for Lotus 1-2-3. You can use the Browse process, just as in Windows, with the browser displaying Mac folder names in place of PC directory names.

Mosaic/Netscape and Lotus 1-2-3 on UNIX Systems

Lotus 1-2-3 was formerly available on UNIX systems, though it has been withdrawn and is no longer sold. Some of you may nonetheless be using it, and you may be interested in setting it up as a helper application in your Intranet. You should be able to configure it using the following generic instructions. There is no graphical interface for setting up helper applications in UNIX Mosaic, and only minimal graphical help in Netscape. Instead, you configure helper applications in both Mosaic and Netscape by editing some plain text files on your system.

In Mosaic, by default, you specify helper applications in the file `/usr/local/lib/mosaic/mailcap` on your system. (You must be logged in as the superuser to create or edit this file.) The file has a relatively simple format. Here is a sample:

```
image/*;                  /usr/local/bin/display %s
audio/*;                  /usr/openwin/bin/audiotool %s
application/postscript;   /usr/openwin/bin/imagetool %s
video/*;                  /usr/local/bin/xanim %s
```

Some of this will be familiar to you, since you have edited your Web server's `mime.types` file to support Lotus 1-2-3 as a helper application. You will recognize the matter in the first column of this file as MIME data type/subtypes. This part of the file has a different syntax than what you have seen before, however. While `application/postscript` looks like entries from the `mime.types` file, the others look a little strange. The explanation is simple. This file uses asterisks to represent all of the MIME subtypes of an overall MIME type. (You'll recall from Chapter 7 the number of MIME types is quite small, but each has subtypes.) Thus, `image/*` refers to all kinds of images, normally spelled out in the server's `mime.types` file as `image/gif`, `image/jpeg`, etc.

 On the right side of the file, you see the complete pathname to an executable program. These are the helper applications that are set up for image, audio, PostScript, and video files. Here, `display` (an all-purpose image display program from the ImageMagick package, on the *Building an Intranet* CD-ROM) is configured as the helper application to display all image data the Web browser encounters. Similarly, `xanim` is configured to play all video data.

> **Note:** There are a couple of other important nits to the `mailcap` file's format. First, note that the two columns of the file are separated by a semicolon and some white space. Second, on the right side, you'll note each entry ends with the characters `%s`. These characters are a placeholder, representing the name of the file Mosaic receives from the Web server. Each entry in the `mailcap` file must have the two columns, separated by the semicolon and white space; the right side must end with the `%s` characters.

Now that you understand the format of the `mailcap` file, let's enable Lotus 1-2-3 as a helper application by adding a new line to the file. Here's the line:

```
application/lotus; /path/to/lotus/executable %s
```

(You'll, of course, need to substitute the actual UNIX filesystem path to the Lotus executable program on your system in the `mime.types` entry.)

> **Note:** The `/usr/local/lib/mosaic/mailcap` file is read by all users on a UNIX system. It contains system-wide configuration. Individual users, however, may want to override part of all of the `mailcap` file. They can do so by creating in their home directory a file called `.mailcap` (note the filename begins with a period, or dot). The format of the `mailcap` and `.mailcap` files is identical, but anything in the individual user's `.mailcap` file that conflicts with the system-wide `mailcap` file takes precedence for that user only. Although it is unlikely different versions of Lotus 1-2-3 will be installed on a system, this feature allows for a great deal of flexibility for users in setting up other helper applications.

UNIX Netscape provides a bit of graphical help in setting up helper applications, which you can use in setting up Lotus 1-2-3. Figure 11.18 shows the Netscape General Preferences dialog box, with the Helpers tab selected to show the package's MIME Configuration Files information. This dialog box doesn't do much of anything, but it does allow you to look around the system for files to use with the Browse button.

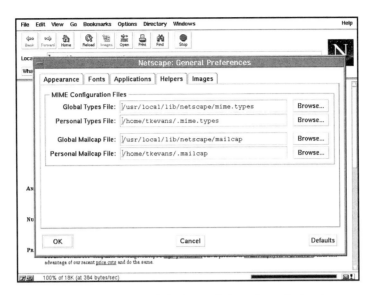

Figure 11.18. *The Netscape General Preferences dialog box, with the Helpers tab selected.*

In Figure 11.18, we're concerned with the lower of the two sets of files, the Global Mailcap File and Personal Mailcap File. Although the Global Mailcap file is by default in a different location for Netscape than for Mosaic (it's in `/usr/local/lib/netscape/mailcap`), the files for both Mosaic and Netscape are identical in format and syntax and have the same name (`mailcap`). In fact, you can use the same file for both by copying it from one location to the other or by using a file link.

The instructions for editing the `mailcap` file to specify helper applications in Netscape are exactly the same for Mosaic. The relationship between the global and personal `mailcap` files is also the same as with Mosaic, and, of course, the personal `mailcap` file has the same filename and location, `.mailcap` in the user's homedirectory.

Mosaic/Netscape and Xess Spreadsheet on UNIX Systems

There is no graphical interface to setting up helper applications in UNIX Mosaic and only minimal graphical help in Netscape. Instead, you configure helper applications in both Mosaic and Netscape by editing some plain text files on your system.

In Mosaic, by default, you specify Mosaic helper applications in the file `/usr/local/lib/mosaic/mailcap` on your system. (You must be the superuser to create or edit this file.) The file has a relatively simple format. Here is a sample:

```
image/*;              /usr/local/bin/display %s
audio/*;              /usr/openwin/bin/audiotool %s
```

```
application/postscript; /usr/openwin/bin/imagetool %s
video/*;                /usr/local/bin/xanim %s
```

Some of this will be familiar to you after having edited your Web server's `mime.types` file to support Lotus as a helper application. You will recognize the matter in the first column of this file as MIME data type/subtypes. This part of the file has a different syntax than you have seen before, however. While `application/postscript` looks like entries from the `mime.types` file, the others look a little strange. The explanation is simple. This file uses the asterisks you see to represent all of the MIME subtypes of a given MIME type. (You'll recall from Chapter 7 the number of MIME types is quite small, but each has subtypes.) Thus, `image/*` refers to all kinds of images, normally spelled out in the server's `mime.types` file as `image/gif`, `image/jpeg`, etc.

On the right side of the file, you see the complete pathname to an executable program. These are the helper applications that are set up for image, audio, PostScript, and video files. Here, `display` (an all-purpose image display program from the ImageMagick package, on the *Building an Intranet* CD-ROM) is configured as the helper application to display all image data the Web browser encounters. Similarly, `xanim` is configured to play all video data.

> **Note:** There are a couple of other important nits to the `mailcap` file's format. First, note the two columns of the file are separated by a semicolon and some white space. Second, on the right side, you'll note each entry ends with the characters `%s`. These characters are a placeholder, representing the name of the file Mosaic receives from the Web server. Each entry in the `mailcap` file must have the two columns, separated by the semicolon and white space; the right side must end with the `%s` characters.

Now that we've covered the format of the `mailcap` file, let's enable Xess as a helper application by adding a new line to the file. Here's the line:

```
application/xess3; /usr/local/xess.sh %s
```

As with UNIX FrameMaker (see Chapter 10, "Your Word Processor and the Web"), we've used a short shell script to start up Xess. Here's the script:

```
#!/bin/sh
# xess startup script
XESS_LICENSE_FILE=/usr/local/lib/xess/xess_license.dat
export XESS_LICENSE_FILE
/usr/local/bin/xess3 "$*"
```

This very short script does just a couple of things. First, because Xess is controlled by a license manager on multi-user systems, the script sets a UNIX environmental variable to point to the Xess license file. The script checks for a valid license and, if one is available, it gets "checked out" to the user running the script. Second, the script starts the actual Xess executable program (in this case, `/usr/local/bin/xess3`) with zero or more command-line arguments, represented by the matter inside the double quotes (which are required). Usually, the command-line arguments include the name of the Xess spreadsheet data file to load with the program. For purposes of this section, the

`$*` used here and the `%s` used above in the `mailcap` file are equivalent, both functioning as placeholders for the data filename.

> **Note:** The `/usr/local/lib/mosaic/mailcap` file is read by all users on a UNIX system. It contains system-wide configuration. Individual users, however, may want to override part of all of the `mailcap` file by creating in their home directory a file called `.mailcap`. (Note that the filename begins with a period, or dot.) The format of the `mailcap` and `.mailcap` files is identical, but anything in the individual user's `.mailcap` file that conflicts with the system-wide `mailcap` file takes precedence for that user. Although it is unlikely different versions of Xess will be installed on a system, this feature enables a great deal of flexibility for users in setting up other helper applications.

UNIX Netscape provides a bit of graphical help in setting up helper applications, which you can use in setting up Xess. Figure 11.19 shows the Netscape: General Preferences dialog box with the Helpers tab displayed. The Helpers tab shows the package's MIME configuration files. This dialog box doesn't do much of anything, but it does enable you to look around the system for files to use with the Browse button.

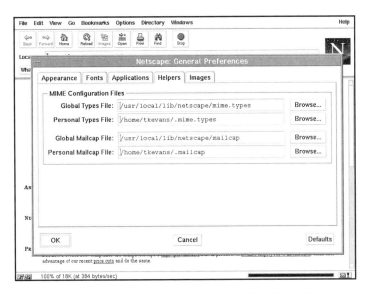

Figure 11.19. *Netscape: General Preferences dialog box in UNIX with the Helpers tab selected.*

Here, we're concerned with the lower of the two sets of files: the Global Mailcap File and Personal Mailcap File. Although the Global Mailcap file is by default in a different location for Netscape than for Mosaic (it's in `/usr/local/lib/netscape/mailcap`), the files for both Mosaic and Netscape are identical in format and syntax, and have the same name (`mailcap`). In fact, you can use the same file for both by copying it from one location to the other or by using a file link.

The instructions for editing the mailcap file to specify helper applications in Netscape are exactly the same for Mosaic. The relationship between the global and personal mailcap files is also the same as with Mosaic, and, of course, the personal mailcap file has the same filename and location, .mailcap in the user's home directory.

Figure 11.20 shows the X Windows desktop running Netscape with Xess tiled on top of it. Xess was loaded by clicking on a hyperlink in the document shown in the Netscape window. The spreadsheet shown is an example file provided with Xess Version 3, a loan-calculation spreadsheet application. Having loaded the application by clicking on the Web hyperlink, the user is free to enter loan amounts and repayment terms, then have the spreadsheet recalculate monthly payments, total interest payments, and the like, then save and/or print the results. From this example, you can see how either live data or spreadsheets with formulae in their cells can be shared on your Intranet.

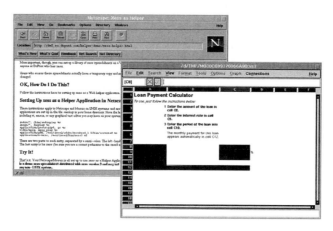

Figure 11.20. *Xess is being used as Netscape helper application.*

Other Spreadsheet Packages

You should be able to use the general principles described in this chapter to set up other spreadsheet packages as helper applications. As each of the preceding sections has shown, the major steps in doing so are: 1) add entries to the `mime.types` file on your Web server for your spreadsheet's data files; 2) set up some data files on your Web server; and 3) configure your spreadsheet as a helper application for your Web browser using the fill-in screens shown in this chapter.

Spreadsheet Data File Portability

Because your organization may use multiple spreadsheet packages, you'll want to anticipate your customers' needs for data file portability. In this section, we'll discuss two options:

◆ Supporting multiple spreadsheet formats

◆ Converting spreadsheet data to other formats

Supporting Multiple Spreadsheet Data File Formats

Your organization may use more than just a single spreadsheet program, and, if so, you're probably wondering how you make the various data files portable. Like many word processors, many spreadsheet packages can read data files in other spreadsheet programs' native formats. Excel and Xess, for example, can directly read 1-2-3 files, and 1-2-3 can read Excel's. As a result, if your company uses multiple spreadsheet packages, you can share your data among them using their abilities to read each others' data file formats.

Warning: Be careful not to use duplicate entries in your Web server's `mime.types` file. For example, *don't* do this:

```
application/msexcel     xls xcl wks
application/lotus       wks xls xcl
application/xess3       xs3 wks
```

Web servers read the `mime.types` file linearly, from top to bottom, until they find a match of filename extensions. With entries like those above, your Web server's MIME type/sub-type header information for `.wks` files will always be read as `application/msexcel`. This may not be what you want if you have Lotus or Xess customers.

Because of this, each spreadsheet customer in your Web will need to configure his browser based on the spreadsheet he uses. Web browsers will override the MIME type/subtype header information they receive if you have configured them to do so.

As you configured your Web helper applications, you may have wondered why both the Web server (in the `mime.types` file) and the Web browser need to have filename-extension information. At first glance, it would seem that as long as one side of the server-client conversation knows the association between a filename extension and a MIME type/subtype, things should work properly. You learned in Chapter 7, in fact, that Web browsers have a built-in list of supported MIME type/subtypes for dealing with older Internet services, such as ftp and Gopher servers, which don't send MIME type/subtype header information. In these situations, Web browsers consult their internal list of MIME type/subtypes and associated filename extensions and attempt to guess the correct MIME type/subtype.

Any new MIME type/subtype information you've added in your helper application setup in your Web browser is added to the browser's internal list. If you've set up your browser to use 1-2-3 as a helper application when it encounters the filename extension .wks, it will use 1-2-3 on any file with that extension, even if:

◆ The server provides no MIME type/subtype information at all, as is the case with an ftp or Gopher server; or

◆ The server does provide MIME type/subtype information, but that information is for a different spreadsheet package.

In other words, your local helper application setup can both fill in missing MIME type/subtype information and override what it gets from the Web server. For example, suppose you've set up your Web server's mime.types file to have entries like the following:

```
application/msexcel     xls xcl
application/lotus       wks lotus
```

Further suppose that a particular customer has only the 1-2-3 spreadsheet package on her PC. Since you know Excel can directly read 1-2-3 data files, you can extend the Excel helper application setup above by adding a 1-2-3 filename extension, as shown in Figure 11.21. Here, you see Mosaic set up to use Excel not only for files with the .xls and .xcl extensions, but also for those with .wks. (Note that the Description of MIME Type field has been modified to include a reminder of this change.)

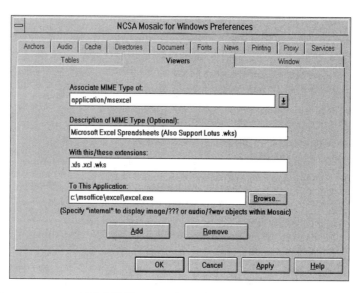

Figure 11.21. You can support multiple MIME types with Excel.

On UNIX systems, there's no graphical interface to making this sort of change. Instead, you'll need to edit (or create, if it doesn't exist) the file named .mime.types (note the leading dot in the name)

in your home directory. Refer to Figure 11.19, where the Global and Personal MIME Configuration Files on a UNIX system with Netscape are listed. The format of the Personal MIME Configuration File (i.e., `.mime.types`) is exactly the same as the one you edited on your Web server. Anything you put in your personal file, however, overrides both MIME header information sent by a Web server and anything in the Global MIME configuration file (i.e., `/usr/local/lib/netscape/mime.types`), if it exists. You need not copy the entire `mime.types` file to your home directory just to make this one change in it. Instead, just add a single line, like one of these:

```
application/xess     xs3 xess wks
application/lotus    wks xls xcl
```

Everything else in the global `mime.types` file, if it exists, will apply, except for this one MIME type/subtype. Similarly, any MIME header information a Web server sends will be followed, except for this one MIME type/subtype. In either case, when you click on a hyperlink pointing to a file with the extension `.wks` (or `.xls`), Xess (or 1-2-3, as the case may be) will fire up as your helper application.

There's another means of making spreadsheet data files more portable in your Intranet. In addition to some spreadsheets being able to directly read the data files created by others, most have a Save As feature that allows you to save a native data file in some other spreadsheet package's format. Excel, for example, supports saving data files in several variations of Lotus 1-2-3's .wks format, as well as several others. Lotus has a similar feature, enabling you to save data files in Excel's .xls format.

Further, there's a semi-universal spreadsheet data file format many packages support, the Symbolic Link Format, often using a filename extension .slk. This format is much like the Rich-Text Format used in making word processing documents portable. All three of the example spreadsheet packages discussed in this chapter support the Symbolic Link Format. You can use these facilities to make multiple copies of spreadsheet data files on your Web server, with versions for each spreadsheet package your customers use. Alternatively, because all three packages support the Symbolic Link Format, you may just want to use that format for all your data files. If you do so, be sure your Web server's `mime.types` file and your customers' browser setup correspond.

Converting Spreadsheet Data to Other Formats

Both Excel and 1-2-3 have Save As functions that enable you to not only save spreadsheet data files in other spreadsheet formats, but also to save a spreadsheet in plain text format. Xess has the same capability, along with the ability to save in PostScript format. Although recalculation and other capabilities are lost, of course, when a spreadsheet is saved in plain text or PostScript, the tabular layout and data is preserved. You can view these plain text files in your Web browser, just like any other text file. PostScript files can be viewed with an appropriate PostScript viewer helper application.

Jordan Evans (no relation to the author), of the U.S. National Aeronautics and Space Administration, has written XL2HTML, a Visual Basic macro for Excel 5.0 that converts an Excel spreadsheet into an HTML table. Written for Excel 5.0 for Windows, the package also works on both Macintosh Excel 5.0 and the Windows 95 version, Excel 7.0 (according to its author). A copy is on the *Building an Intranet* CD-ROM. You can specify a range of cells to be converted, and XL2HTML outputs HTML Table markup, retaining character formatting, such as boldface, underlining, etc., from the original spreadsheet. (See Appendix B, "HTML and CGI Quick Review," for information on HTML table markup.)

You can learn more about XL2HTML at `http://www710.gsfc.nasa.gov/704/dgd/xl2html.html`; instructions are included. Figure 11.22 shows an example table provided by the author of XL2HTML. As with spreadsheet files saved in plain text, customer interactivity (the ability to change and recalculate the spreadsheet) is lost in XL2HTML, while it would not be when using the spreadsheet program itself as a helper application. Nonetheless, you may find situations in which XL2HTML is useful for your Web.

File Edit View Go Bookmarks Options Directory Windows						Help

Eclipse Time for 2 Sun Synch. Orbits

This table is the eclipse time for Sun Synchronous, Low Earth Circular Orbits of 700km and 900km Radii.

ECLIPSE.XLS

Orbital Altitude	700	km	Orbital Altitude	900	km
Inclination	98.19	deg	Inclination	99.03	deg
Mean Radius – Earth	6378.145	km	Mean Radius – Earth	6378.145	km
Ecliptic	23.5	deg	Ecliptic	23.5	deg
Period	98.77	min	Period	102.99	min

Beta	Te (% of orbit)	Time (min.)	Beta	Te (% of orbit)	Time (min.)
74.69	0	0	74.69	0	0
76.69	0	0	76.69	0	0
78.69	0	0	78.69	0	0
80.69	0	0	80.69	0	0
82.69	0	0	82.69	0	0
84.69	0	0	84.69	0	0
86.69	0	0	86.69	0	0
88.69	0	0	88.69	0	0
90.69	0	0	90.69	0	0
92.69	0	0	92.69	0	0
94.69	0	0	94.69	0	0
96.69	0	0	96.69	0	0
98.69	0	0	98.69	0	0
100.69	0	0	100.69	0	0
102.69	0	0	102.69	0	0

Figure 11.22. *An HTML table created by XL2HTML.*

Microsoft now has available for free download from its Web site (`http://www.microsoft.com`) a version of its Internet Assistant (IA) for Excel. Like the companion IA products for Microsoft Word and PowerPoint, this package allows saving Office datafiles (in this case, Excel spreadsheets) directly to HTML format for use on your Intranet. IA supports version 5.0 of Excel in both Windows 3.1 and NT and Macs and version 7.0 on Windows 95.

Tip: While you're visiting the Microsoft Web site, you may also want to download a copy of a read-only Excel Viewer for Windows 95. Just as you set up Excel itself as a Web browser helper application, you can set up the Excel Viewer as one for customers who don't have their own copy of Excel.

Summary

This chapter has shown you how to use your spreadsheet package as a Web browser helper application to create low-cost data warehouses containing live spreadsheet data. Using this information, you'll be able to replicate many features of expensive commercial software packages at very little cost. The data files you make available to your customers on your Intranet will make it possible for them to point and click to load interactive spreadsheet data into their favorite spreadsheet package, and then manipulate the data as needed. The material we've covered in this chapter has included:

◆ Why it's important to retrieve spreadsheet data files directly into your spreadsheet package using a Web browser.

◆ Configuring your World Wide Web server to understand your spreadsheet's document files.

◆ Configuring your World Wide Web browser software to handle your spreadsheet data files.

◆ Supporting multiple spreadsheet data formats.

◆ Other ways of making your spreadsheet data usable on your Web.

◆ Some potential uses of these capabilities.

In Chapter 12, "Other Common Office Applications," we'll cover the use of other common office applications as helper applications, focusing on the rest of the packages in the Microsoft Office suite, as well as some common Windows applications.

CHAPTER

Other Common Office Applications

Setting up your word processor and spreadsheet packages has been the subject of the last two chapters, respectively. This chapter turns to several other everyday office applications you can use in your Intranet. We'll cover a variety of simple and complex packages, ranging from the Microsoft Windows Cardfile, to a couple of UNIX Rolodex programs, to two other Microsoft Office applications we haven't covered yet: Access and PowerPoint.

Chapter Objectives

As with the rest of the chapters in this book, let's begin by laying out some chapter objectives. This will help you get oriented to the material to be presented; you may want to refer back to this list as you work your way through the chapter. In this chapter, you will

- ◆ Learn how you can use a wide variety of common office application programs as Web browser helper applications
- ◆ Learn how to configure your World Wide Web server software to understand a variety of common office applications' data files
- ◆ Learn how to configure your World Wide Web browser software to handle the data files from a wide variety of common office applications
- ◆ Understand some potential uses of these capabilities

Even if you don't use Microsoft Office, there are comparable commercial and free/shareware applications to those in this integrated suite of programs. Office has, in addition to Word and Excel, which we've already covered in Chapters 10 and 11, respectively, several other programs many people use frequently. Competitive "office suite" packages like Novell's Perfect Office and Lotus's SmartSuite have similar applications. Microsoft Office covers such a wide range you should read this chapter in its entirety, even if you're not an Office user. You'll undoubtedly pick up ideas on how you can use your own applications from the examples in this chapter.

Why Set Up These Applications on Your Intranet?

Your primary objective in setting up your Intranet is to make it easy for your customers to retrieve and share information using World Wide Web technology. You can do this with data files generated by virtually any application your customers use. As with word processing documents and spreadsheet data files, there are other ways of sharing them, ranging from NetWare and other kinds of fileservers to passing floppy disks around the office. What's different with your Intranet is your customers have access to the data you're sharing using their favorite World Wide Web browser, a single, easy-to-use front end virtually everyone already knows how to use—and likes. Using the sample applications in this chapter on your Intranet will enable you to make important corporate information available to your customers with just a click of their mouse. Here are some simple examples:

◆ Use the Microsoft Windows Cardfile, or one of the UNIX Rolodex programs described, to distribute an always-up-to-date group or corporate telephone book via your Web.

◆ Use Microsoft Access to enable access to corporate Access databases, directly from your customers' World Wide Web browser.

◆ Use Microsoft PowerPoint to distribute presentation graphics to your customers, or to conduct corporate training via your Intranet.

You'll come up with more ideas of your own as you go through the examples in this chapter, but first we need to go through some setup preliminaries.

You'll recall from earlier chapters the use of the term *helper application* (or *external viewer*) to refer to computer programs that your Web browser uses when it can't directly display the data represented by a hyperlink. For example, neither Netscape nor Mosaic can play audio or video files you might run across on the Web, but both can be set up to pass off incoming audio or video data to audio- or video-playing helper applications. When you click on a hyperlink pointing to a sound or video file, your Web browser receives it from a Web server, recognizes it as a sound or video file, and hands it off to the audio or video helper application you've set up.

In this chapter, you'll learn to treat a number of common office applications like helper applications, just like a sound or video player. There's very little difference between the setup of one of these common helper applications and the setup of PowerPoint or Access, but there's a major difference in the implications of doing so. Playing video and audio on your computer may be remarkable and enjoyable, but, unless you are in the video or audio business, it gets little of your substantive, everyday work done. Accessing an online phone book, preparing and using presentation graphics, and accessing corporate databases, on the other hand, are frequent (if not daily) activities for many of your customers. Integrating these applications into your Intranet, then, can be a potentially major productivity enhancement, fundamentally changing the way your customers—and therefore your company—do their work.

Web Server Setup

Regardless of the application to be set up, your first steps in setting up your package as a helper application involve configuring your Web server to know about the application's data files. As you learned in Chapter 7, "MIME and Helper Applications," Web servers use the MIME mechanism to identify documents according to their MIME data type/subtype. Recall the MIME mechanism divides data into a relatively small handful of data types, with each type further subdivided into subtypes. All of the data files to be discussed in this chapter fall into the application data type.

We also described in Chapter 7 how Web servers use filename extensions to map data files on the server to a MIME data type/subtype. This association of filename extensions with MIME type/subtype is done in the Web server's configuration file `mime.types` (`mime.typ` on a PC server).

Editing the `mime.types` File

As you'll recall from Chapter 7, the `mime.types` file is a plain text file, containing a simple, two-column listing of MIME types/subtypes and associated filename extensions. Here's a short excerpt from the standard `mime.types` file distributed with the NCSA httpd server software; for a full listing, refer back to Chapter 7.

```
application/mac-binhex40
application/macwriteii
application/news-message-id
application/news-transmission
application/octet-stream        bin
application/oda                 oda
application/pdf                 pdf
application/postscript          ai eps ps
```

Here you can see the association, for example, between the pdf filename extension and the MIME type/subtype `application/pdf`, representing the Adobe Portable Document Format. Similarly, PostScript documents are represented by the `application/postscript` MIME data type/subtype; in this case, there are three filename extensions associated. Also note several of the entries have no filename extensions listed; you can add these as required.

> **Note:** The Netscape Communications server uses a different format for the mime.types file. The format is more complex, but potentially easier to understand, because the two columns of each entry are labeled. Here's an excerpt:
>
> ```
> type=application/oda      exts=oda
> type=application/pdf      exts=pdf
> type=image/jpeg           exts=jpeg,jpg,jpe
> ```
>
> As you can see, Netscape has added labels to the two columns of the mime.types file, with the left column containing not only the MIME data type/subtype (image/jpeg, for example), but also the identifying label type, separated by an equals sign. Similarly, the right column includes the label exts, along with the actual filename extensions. The Netscape mime.types file also includes an optional third column, not found in other servers' files, specifying an icon to be associated with the MIME data type/subtype. The Netscape server also provides for a secondary mime.types file with your localizations, specified in the magnus.conf file. For more information about this file and overall Netscape Communications Server configuration, see Appendix A, "Setting Up a Web Server," or see the Netscape Communications server documentation.

To set up your Web server for your spreadsheet, you'll need to make changes in the mime.types file. You can edit the file with any text editor, such as vi or emacs (on a UNIX system), the Windows Notepad or MS-DOS edit, Macintosh TeachText, or even your word processor in plain text mode.

> **Note:** If your Web server runs on a UNIX system, you'll need root, or superuser access to edit the mime.types file.

The mime.types file distributed with the NCSA httpd server doesn't contain entries for any of the packages we're to discuss in this chapter, but it's easy to add them, using the existing entries in the file as models. As noted above, the MIME type for all our packages is application, so you can start out with entries for your particular package, possibly using one of the example packages we're using in this chapter. They'll look like this:

```
application/mscardfile
application/rolo
application/msaccess
application/mspowerpoint
```

As you've probably realized, these are missing the filename extensions that you need in order to have your Web server associate their data files with the particular application program. The four applications listed use the following default filename extensions:

- ◆ Windows Cardfile   .crd
- ◆ mrolo and xrolo   .rolo (both read the same file format)
- ◆ Microsoft Access   .mdb
- ◆ Microsoft PowerPoint   .ppt

Based on this list and the application(s) you want to set up on your Intranet, you can add one of more of the following entries to your `mime.types` file.

```
application/mscardfile      crd
application/rolo            rolo
application/msaccess        mdb
application/mspowerpoint    ppt
```

You can use any filename extensions you want for these applications, in addition to or instead of these. If you use nonstandard ones, you'll want to make sure you use them consistently, so your customers can set up their Web browsers to access the data you're providing using the right filename extensions.

> **Note:** UNIX systems have different, much more lenient rules about file naming than DOS/Windows systems. Since a couple of UNIX packages are discussed in this chapter, a filename extension (rolo) longer than three characters is shown just to illustrate what is permitted on UNIX systems. If your Web server is a PC, however, you'll need to stick with three-character filename extensions.

> **Warning:** Double check your filename extensions to make sure they don't duplicate any of the standard `mime.types` entries. Otherwise, your customers will see incorrect or inconsistent results.

For other applications, you'll need to add entries to `mime.types` for them. If an application uses a default filename extension for its data files, use it in `mime.types`. Otherwise, you're free to use whatever you want, provided it doesn't conflict with other entries in the `mime.types` file.

You're done editing the `mime.types` file, so you can save it and exit your editor.

Implementing Changes in `mime.types`

Because you've changed the configuration of your Web server by editing one of its setup files, you need to make the server aware of your changes in its setup. If your server isn't already running, it will read the changes as part of its normal startup. If the server is already running, you can have it reread its configuration files in one of two ways. On a Macintosh or Windows server, just stop the server and restart it. For example, in the whttpd server, open the Control menu and select Exit, and then restart the server by double-clicking on its icon or by using the Program Manager's Run command.

UNIX servers provide a more convenient way of having the setup files reread, enabling you to do so without actually shutting down the server and interrupting access to it. It's called sending a hang-up signal to the server process. All processes running on UNIX systems have a unique process id, or pid. You can find your server's pid using the UNIX process status command, ps. Here's an example, using the grep command to filter out all but the processes in which we're interested:

```
# ps -ax | grep httpd
   250 ?       S   0:06 /usr/local/etc/httpd/httpd
   255 ?       S   0:06 /usr/local/etc/httpd/httpd
   258 ?       S   0:06 /usr/local/etc/httpd/httpd
   686 ?       S   0:05 /usr/local/etc/httpd/httpd
  6383 ?       S   0:02 /usr/local/etc/httpd/httpd
  7096 ?       S   0:01 /usr/local/etc/httpd/httpd
 19304 pts/6   S   0:00 grep httpd
```

> **Note:** The BSD UNIX -ax arguments to the ps command here, as on a SunOS 4.1.x system. If your machine is a System V UNIX, such as SunOS 5.x, SGI IRIX 5.x, or other system, you'll need to use this command:
>
> ```
> # ps -ef | grep httpd
> ```
>
> The output of the UNIX System V ps command is a bit different, but will give the same information (along with some additional information).
>
> ```
>    root    250     1 80   Nov 13 ?           0:06 /usr/local/etc/httpd/httpd
>  nobody    255   250 80   Nov 13 ?           0:07 /usr/local/etc/httpd/httpd
>  nobody    686   250 80   Nov 14 ?           0:06 /usr/local/etc/httpd/httpd
>  nobody   7096   250 80   Nov 24 ?           0:02 /usr/local/etc/httpd/httpd
>  nobody    258   250 80   Nov 13 ?           0:06 /usr/local/etc/httpd/httpd
>  nobody   6383   250 80   Nov 22 ?           0:03 /usr/local/etc/httpd/httpd
> tkevans  19310   384 12 06:02:45 pts/6       0:00 grep httpd
> ```

In the output of the first example of the ps command, process ids appear in the first column, with the main server pid being 250. As indicated in Appendix A, the most recent releases of the NCSA httpd server generate a parent httpd process and several child processes; the lowest number pid is the parent process. This distinction is more clear with the System V ps command, with the pids shown in the second column and the pid of the process that started each shown in the third column. As you can see the parent process id (ppid) of the main httpd server process is 1, indicating the process was started at boot time by the UNIX init daemon. Each of the child httpd processes shows the main httpd process (pid 250) as its parent.

Having identified the pid of the main httpd server process, you can send it a hang-up signal like this:

```
# kill -HUP 250
```

This command, run by the superuser, tells the httpd process that something has changed in its configuration and that it must reread the setup files, but without exiting. Afterward, the server is still running, but using the revised setup. The NCSA and CERN httpd servers provide a shortcut to this whole process that doesn't require you to find out the server's pid. When the server starts up, it stores its pid in a file named httpd.pid in the top level of the server software tree. The shortcut to having the server reread its configuration files is this command:

```
# kill -HUP `cat /usr/local/etc/httpd/httpd.pid`
```

This command uses the special UNIX feature under which the command surrounded by single back quotes (also called *accent grave* or back ticks) runs first, with its output substituted in the main command. Since the content of the `httpd.pid` file is merely the pid of the main server process (in our example, 250), the actual command that's run here is the same as the example above. What's different is you didn't have to look up the pid yourself by running the `ps` command.

> **Note:** The Netscape Communications Server has a graphical interface called the Server Manager that enables you to restart the server. This soft restart causes the server to reread its configuration files without interrupting the ongoing operation of the server.

Adding Application Data Files to Your Web Server

You've completed the setup of your Web server to properly identify and serve your applications' data files. Next, you'll need to populate your server with some data files for your package. You can transfer your data files to your Web server using your network file transfer utilities (such as ftp, in binary mode) or via floppy diskette. Whichever method you use, put them in a dedicated directory for each particular application.

Once you've done so, you'll need to create some sort of HTML listing of them. This can be as simple or as complex as you like, since including hyperlinks to application data files is exactly the same as setting up links to other kinds of documents. A simple HTML listing, using Microsoft PowerPoint slides as an example, might be something like this.

```
<HTML><HEAD><TITLE>PowerPoint Slides</TITLE></HEAD>
<BODY>
<H1>PowerPoint Slides</H1>
```

This directory contains a set of Microsoft PowerPoint slides. Just click on one to open it in PowerPoint.

```
<UL><LI><A HREF="qrtrly_sales.ppt">Slide 1</A>, Last Quarter's Sales</LI>
<LI><A HREF="qrtrly_prod.ppt">Slide 2</A>, Last Quarter's Production</LI>
<LI><A HREF="cpi_forecast.ppt">Slide 3</A>, Consumer Price Index Forecasts</LI></UL>
```

If you haven't already done so, you must set up your Web browser to understand PowerPoint slide data files.

```
<A HREF="ppt_setup.html">Here are instructions.</A>
</BODY></HTML>
```

Figure 12.1 shows this HTML code, rendered in NCSA Mosaic. As you can see, it looks like just any other Web page. Users with properly set up Web browsers can just click on the hyperlinks to run PowerPoint on a copy of the selected slide. Before you can use this page to load the hyperlinked data files, however, your Web browser must be set up to use the correct program as a helper application.

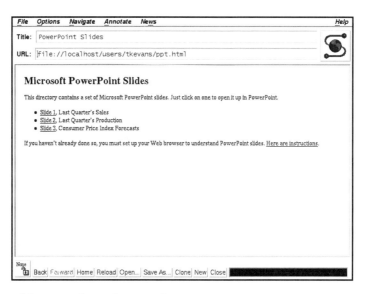

Figure 12.1. *A Web browser rendering of a Microsoft PowerPoint page.*

Cardfiles and Rolodexes

There are a number of applications that enable you to store and retrieve information. Some are relatively elaborate Personal Information Managers (PIMs), while others arc simple computer cardfiles and/or Rolodexes. You can set these up to work as Web browser helper applications on your Intranet. We'll look at three of them here: the Microsoft Windows Cardfile (a standard part of Windows 3.1) and two similar Rolodex programs for UNIX systems, xrolo and mrolo. You can set up any of the three to enable your customers to access a group or company telephone book using their Web browser. Cardfile comes with Windows 3.x and the two UNIX Rolodexes are free (the source code for them is on the *Building an Intranet* CD-ROM). Very large organizations will probably prefer to use a true telephone-book database application, as we'll describe in Chapter 13, "Indexing and Searching your Data." These simple, familiar applications can go a long way toward sharing information about people on your Intranet.

Windows Cardfile as a Helper Application

Now that you have set up your Web server to know about Windows Cardfile data files and populated it with some actual data files from the package, your next step is to set up Cardfile as a helper application. The concept of setting up helper applications for Web browsers is a general one, but the steps for actually going about it differ, depending on the Web browser you're using. We'll go through the steps for NCSA Mosaic and Netscape. If you're using another browser, you'll need to take a look at its documentation to learn how to accomplish this.

NCSA Mosaic and the Windows Cardfile

NCSA Mosaic in Windows provides a graphical interface for setting up helper applications, although Mosaic uses the term *external viewer* rather than *helper application.* In Mosaic, open the Options menu and select Preferences. The Preferences dialog box appears. Click on the Viewers tab (shown in Figure 12.2).

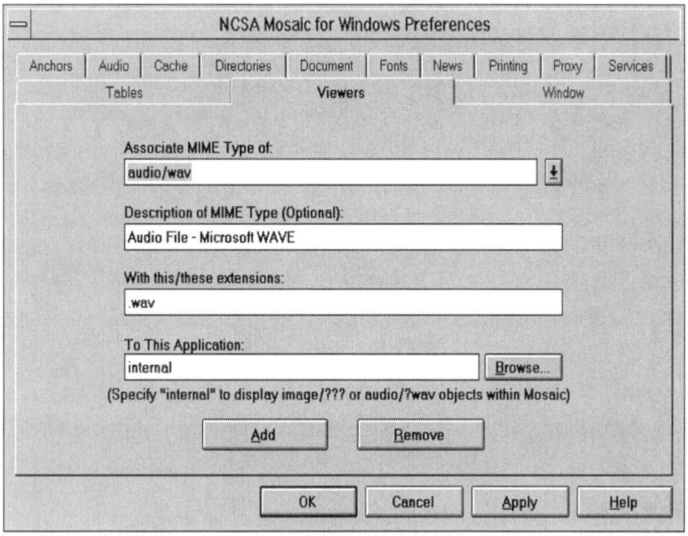

Figure 12.2. *The Mosaic Preferences dialog box with the Viewers tab displayed.*

As you can see, there are four fill-in boxes and several buttons that enable you to control the external viewers used. Figure 12.2 shows the dialog box already filled in for the Microsoft WAVE audio player.

Let's take a look at the labels on the fill-in boxes before going any further. We'll take them slightly out of order. You'll recognize some familiar items here. First, the top box, Associate MIME Type of, contains a MIME data type/subtype pair, in this case audio/wav. This item is, of course, right out of the `mime.types` file. The third fill-in box, With this/these extensions, is also familiar. It contains the same info as the filename-extension column in your `mime.types` file, with the extension `.wav` entered.

The second fill-in box is an optional description of the kind of data file—in our example, it's `Audio File - Microsoft WAVE`. The last fill-in box, To This Application, is where you specify which program will function as your helper application. In Figure 12.2, the special keyword `internal` is used there, indicating Mosaic can handle this MIME type/subtype by itself, without a helper application. Before we go on, note the Browse button next to this box, as we'll be using it to set up Cardfile as your helper application.

Now that your tour of the Viewers tab is complete, let's configure Cardfile as your helper application. Click the Add button to open up the Add Viewer dialog box, shown in Figure 12.3. This box has the same four fill-in boxes as Figure 12.2, but they're blank, for you to enter your own information.

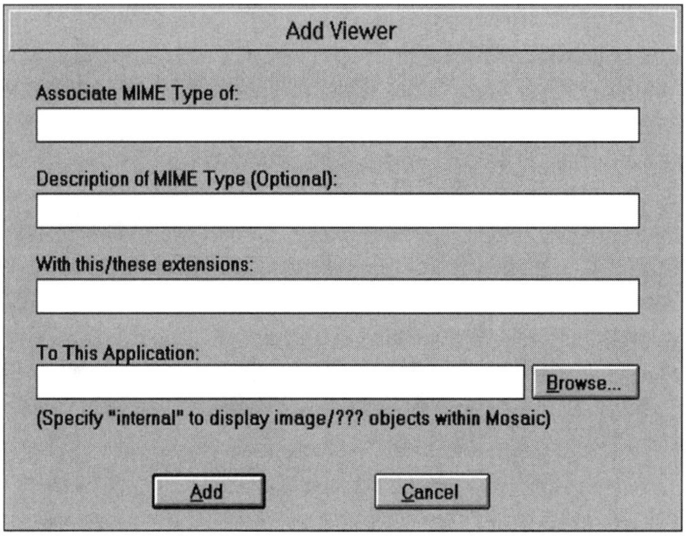

Figure 12.3. *The NCSA Mosaic Add Viewer dialog box.*

Using the information you added to your `mime.types` file earlier, you can quickly fill in these blanks.

◆ In the Associate MIME Type of box, enter `application/mscardfile`.

◆ In the Description of MIME Type (Optional) box, enter something like `Windows Cardfile Index`. Note that you aren't required to enter anything in this box, although it's a good idea to do so for future reference.

◆ In the With this/these extensions box, enter `crd`. (As you'll recall, we entered this filename extension to the `mime.types` file earlier.)

◆ Finally, in the To This Application box, enter the full drive and pathname to the Windows Cardfile executable program. If you're not sure about this, click the Browse button, which works like most Windows browse buttons, allowing you to locate the Cardfile executable. Once you've found it, select it.

Figure 12.4 shows the filled-in Viewers dialog box. (Your drive and path to the Cardfile executable may be different than the one shown, so make sure you locate yours, rather than just copying what's shown in the figure.) Once you're set, click Add to save your changes.

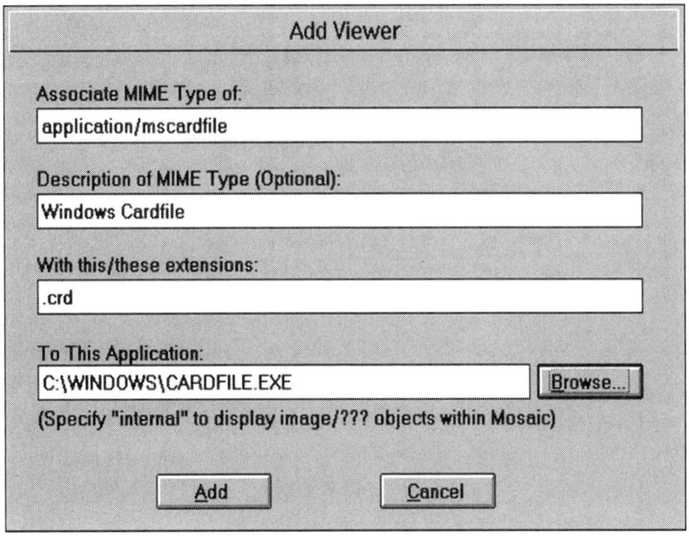

Figure 12.4. The NCSA Mosaic Add Viewer dialog box, filled in for Cardfile.

That's it. You're now ready to try out your new setup. Close the Preferences window by clicking OK, and then select Open Document from the Mosaic File menu. Enter the URL of a Cardfile index on your Web server, or click on a hyperlink pointing to one. Mosaic contacts the Web server and asks for the document. As described in detail in Chapter 7, the server sends back header information identifying the document as the MIME type/sub-type `application/mscardfile`. Mosaic reads this information, and then passes the incoming document off to Cardfile for viewing, dynamically starting up Cardfile with a copy of the index.

Figure 12.5 shows Mosaic with Cardfile tiled on top. At this point, you have all the features and power of Cardfile available to you to search, edit, save, and print this index, including the Cardfile's telephone dialer.

> **Note:** It's important to note you're working with a temporary copy of the index, not the original, which is still safe on your Web server. As a result, you're free to make any changes to the cardfile you need to make. This may cause a bit of confusion, as customers may be used to thinking of their Cardfile index as their own, rather than as a corporate phone list.

Figure 12.5. *Mosaic with Windows Cardfile as a helper application.*

Netscape and the Windows Cardfile

Netscape in Windows provides a graphical interface to setting up helper applications. Open the Options menu, and then select General Preferences. The Preferences dialog box appears. Click on the Helpers tab (shown in Figure 12.6).

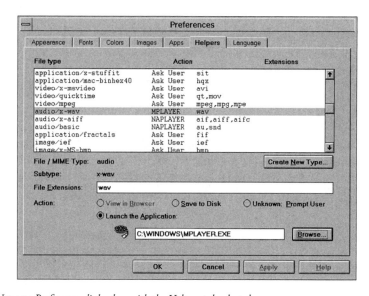

Figure 12.6. *Netscape Preferences dialog box with the Helpers tab selected.*

As you can see, there is a scrollable File type list that contains preset helper applications; clicking on one of them brings up some details of the setup. In Figure 12.6, the audio/x-wav file type, has been selected. Below the File type window, you'll see File / MIME Type, with Subtype on the next line. Below that, there's a fill-in File Extensions box, several option buttons, and another fill-in box.

Figure 12.6 shows the dialog box already filled in for the Microsoft WAVE audio player, `mplayer`. Let's take a look at this figure before going any further. You'll recognize some familiar items here. First, the File type window should remind you of the contents of the `mime.types` file on your Web server, with its columns specifying MIME data types/subtypes (on the left) and filename extensions (on the right). Below that box, you'll find the File / MIME Type item filled in as `audio` and the subtype filled in as `x-wav`. The File Extensions box contains `wav`.

At the bottom, there are several option buttons that enable you to choose what to do with incoming data of the MIME type/subtype `application/x-wav`. In Figure 12.6, Launch the Application is shown selected. The bottommost box is where you enter the name and path of the program that you want to function as your helper application. In Figure 12.6, the drive and path to the Microsoft Windows Media Player application, `mplayer`, has been filled in. Notice Netscape has picked up the Windows icon for `mplayer`, displaying it just to the left of the box. Before we go on, note the Create New Type and Browse buttons, as we'll be using them to set up Cardfile as a helper application.

Your tour of the Helpers dialog box complete, let's configure the Windows Cardfile as your helper application. Click the Create New Type button, to open up the Configure New Mime Type dialog box shown in Figure 12.7. This box has two fill-in boxes for your information about the new MIME type/subtype. Here, we've filled in the information for Cardfile, right out of the `mime.types` file.

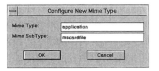

Figure 12.7. Netscape Configure New Mime Type dialog box.

Fill yours in, and then click OK. This returns you to the previous dialog box, with the MIME type information you just entered filled in. You now need to enter `crd` in the File Extensions box. (As you'll recall, we entered this filename extension in the `mime.types` file earlier.) Finally, click on Launch the Application and fill in the full drive and pathname to the Windows Cardfile executable program. If you're not sure about this, click the Browse button, which works like most Windows browse buttons, enabling you to locate the Cardfile executable. Once you've found it, select it. As with mplayer, Netscape has located and displayed the Cardfile icon.

Figure 12.8 shows the Helpers tab filled in with Cardfile information. (Your drive and path to the Cardfile executable may be different from the one shown, so make sure you locate yours, rather than just copying what's shown in the figure.) Once you're set, click OK to save your changes.

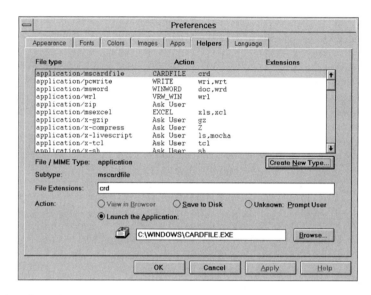

Figure 12.8. *The Helpers tab with the Cardfile information entered.*

That's it. You're now ready to try out your new setup. Close the Preferences windows by clicking OK, and then click the Open button on Netscape's toolbar. Enter the URL of a Cardfile index on your Web server. Netscape contacts the Web server and asks for the file. As described in detail in Chapter 7, the server sends back header information identifying the document as the MIME type/subtype application/mscardfile. Netscape reads this information, and then passes off the incoming document to Cardfile for viewing, dynamically starting up Cardfile with a copy of the document.

Figure 12.9 shows Netscape with Cardfile tiled on top. At this point, you have all the features and powers of Cardfile available to you to search, edit, save, and print this index, including the Cardfile's telephone dialer.

> **Note:** It's important to note you're working with a temporary copy of the index, not the original, which is still safe on your Web server. As a result, you're free to make any changes to the cardfile that you need to make. This may cause a bit of confusion, as customers may be used to thinking of their Cardfile index as their own, rather than as a corporate phone list.

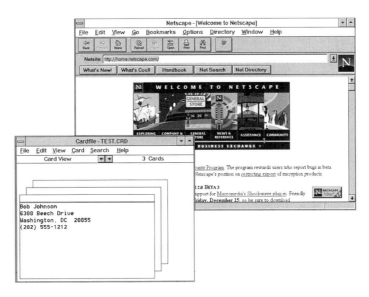

Figure 12.9. *Netscape with Windows Cardfile as a helper application.*

Two UNIX Rolodexes

Many UNIX users rely on one of two freeware Rolodex packages, xrolo or mrolo. These are quite similar; the former is a Sun OpenWindows application and the latter has a Motif interface. The two packages even use the same file format and default filename for the Rolodex data file.

> **Note:** OpenWindows is based on the soon-to-be obsolete OpenLook X Windows interface. Several UNIX vendors, including Sun, have banded together to produce a new X Windows graphical environment called the Common Desktop Environment (CDE), which is based on the Motif interface. Motif's look and feel is quite similar to that of Microsoft Windows. Long a holdout for OpenWindows, Sun has now conceded the X desktop to Motif and has become one of the cooperating vendors in CDE. The latest release of Sun's UNIX, SunOS 5.5 (part of its Solaris 2.5 environment) includes both OpenWindows and CDE. All the UNIX screenshots in this book were done in the CDE environment. The full-screen images show the overall CDE desktop, with its trademark dashboard (adapted from Hewlett-Packard's VUE—Visual User Environment—graphical interface on HP-UX UNIX systems).

xrolo was written by Ron Hutchins and Luis Soltero, and mrolo was written by Gregg Hanna. Both use the same data file format, so we'll cover them together. Source code for both is on the *Building an Intranet* CD-ROM.

Mosaic/Netscape and xrolo/mrolo

There is no graphical interface for setting up helper applications in UNIX Mosaic, and only minimal graphical help in Netscape. Instead, you configure helper applications like xrolo and mrolo in both Mosaic and Netscape by editing some plain text files on your system.

In Mosaic, by default, you specify Mosaic helper applications in the file /usr/local/lib/mosaic/ mailcap on your system. (You must be the superuser to create or edit this file.) The file has a relatively simple format. Here is a sample:

```
image/*;               /usr/local/bin/display %s
audio/*;               /usr/openwin/bin/audiotool %s
application/postscript; /usr/openwin/bin/imagetool %s
video/*;               /usr/local/bin/xanim %s
```

Some of this will be familiar to you, since you have already edited your Web server's mime.types file to support these Rolodex applications as helper applications. You will recognize the matter in the first column of this file as MIME data type/subtypes. This part of the file has a different syntax, however, than you have seen before. While application/postscript looks like the entries from the mime.types file, the others look a little strange. The explanation is simple. This file uses asterisks to represent all of the MIME subtypes of the overall MIME type. (You'll recall from Chapter 7 the number of MIME types is quite small, but each has subtypes.) Thus, image/* refers to all kinds of images, normally spelled out in the server's mime.types file as image/gif, image/jpeg, etc.

On the right side of the file, you see the complete pathnames to executable programs. These are the helper applications that are set up for image, audio, PostScript, and video files. Here, display (an all-purpose image display program from the ImageMagick package, on the *Building an Intranet* CD-ROM) is configured as the helper application to display all image data the Web browser encounters. Similarly, xanim is configured to play all video data.

> **Note:** There are a couple of other important nits to this file's format. First, note that the two columns of the file are separated by a semicolon and some white space. Second, on the right side, you'll note each entry ends with the characters %s. These characters are a placeholder, representing the name of the file Mosaic receives from the Web server. Each entry in the mailcap file must have the two columns, separated by the semicolon and white space; the right side must end with the %s characters.

How that you understand the format of the mailcap file, let's enable xrolo/mrolo as helper applications by adding a new line to the file for the one you use. Here are entries for each package:

```
application/rolo; /usr/local/bin/xrolo -f %s
application/rolo; /usr/local/bin/mrolo -f %s
```

(Of course, you'll need to substitute the actual UNIX file system path to the executable Rolodex program on your system in the entry. The `/usr/local file system` is a common place for applications that aren't part of your UNIX vendor's standard distribution.)

Both xrolo and mrolo use the command-line option `-f` to tell the program to load the file specified in the next command-line argument (in this case, the `%s`). Be sure your `mailcap` file command line includes both the `-f` and the `%s`. Otherwise, the package will look for a file named *.rolo* in the customer's home directory.

Note: The `/usr/local/lib/mosaic/mailcap` file is read by all users on a UNIX system. It contains system-wide configuration. Individual users, however, may want to override part or all of the `mailcap` file. They can do so by creating in their home directory a file called `.mailcap`. (Note that the filename begins with a period, or dot.) The formats of the `mailcap` and `.mailcap` files are identical, but anything in the individual user's `.mailcap` file that conflicts with the system-wide `mailcap` file takes precedence (for that user only). This feature gives users a great deal of flexibility in setting up helper applications and provides users a means of choosing either xrolo or mrolo, assuming both are installed on your system.

UNIX Netscape provides a bit of graphical help in setting up helper applications. Figure 12.10 shows the Helpers tab of the Netscape: General Preferences dialog box, which shows the package's MIME Configuration Files. This dialog box doesn't do much of anything, but it does enable you to look around the system for files to use with the Browse button.

In Figure 12.10, we're concerned with the lower of the two sets of files: Global Mailcap File and Personal Mailcap Files. Although the Global Mailcap file is by default in a different location for Netscape than for Mosaic (it's in `/usr/local/lib/netscape/mailcap`), the files for both Mosaic and Netscape are identical in format and syntax, and have the same name (`mailcap`). In fact, you can use the same file for both by copying it from one location to the other or by using a file link.

The instructions for editing the `mailcap` file to specify helper applications in Netscape are exactly the same as those for Mosaic. The relationship between the Global and Personal Mailcap files is also the same as with Mosaic, and, of course, the Personal Mailcap file has the same filename and location (`.mailcap` in the user's home directory).

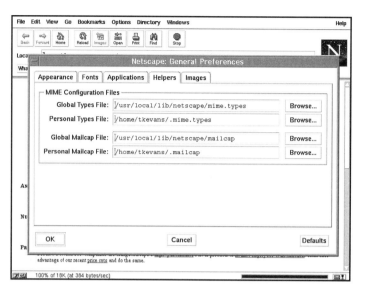

Figure 12.10. *The Netscape: General Preferences dialog box, with the Helpers tab displayed.*

Figures 12.11 and 12.12 each show a full X Windows desktop with one of the Rolodex programs dynamically loaded by clicking on a hyperlink pointing to the Rolodex data file. The first figure (12.11) shows Netscape and the mrolo application, while Figure 12.12 show NCSA Mosaic with xrolo. Both show the same Rolodex card, or entry. mrolo requires an additional mouse click on the line item to open the full card. (You can also see how the two packages use differing visual metaphors.)

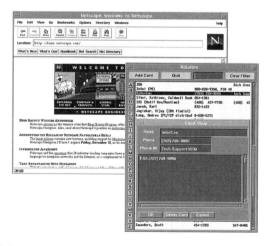

Figure 12.11. *mrolo Rolodex as a Netscape helper application.*

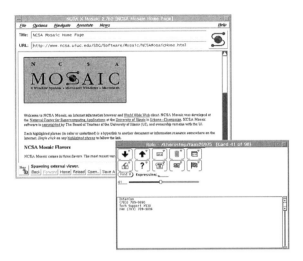

Figure 12.12. *xrolo Rolodex as a Mosaic helper application.*

Both Rolodex packages have search features, and, like the Windows Cardfile, xrolo (but not mrolo) has the ability to dial a telephone number from a Rolodex card (note the telephone icon) using a modem attached to your system.

> **Tip:** Although your primary use for these Rolodex packages is probably to distribute a phone directory on your Intranet, users can save and edit personal copies with both. With xrolo, simply clicking the Save icon (which looks like a card being inserted into file drawer) creates a file named .rolo in the user's home directory, with all the entries from the data file down-loaded from our Web server. The filename begins with a period.
>
> Saving a copy of the whole Rolodex file with mrolo is a little tricky. Both Mosaic and Netscape (as well as other Web browsers) store downloaded files in some temporary location on your system. Depending on the Web browser your customers use, the temporary directory may be /tmp, /var/tmp, or the directory pointed to by the user's TMPDIR environment variable, if set. For example, in the exercise from which Figure 12.11 was shot, Netscape stored a copy of the Rolodex file in the file /tmp/M030D2DF380350C8A.rolo. This is a dynamically-generated filename that will change with each Netscape download, but it does have the .rolo filename extension.
>
> Any edits the user may make—card additions, deletions, or changes—are applied to the temporary copy of the Rolodex file. To save the temporary copy of the Rolodex file for later use, users will need to move this temporary file into their home directory and name it .rolo, and then use the standalone mrolo program to view it. That is, once the user has edited and saved the Rolodex data file, it must be accessed outside of a Web browser. As set up with the instructions in this Chapter, the Web browser would always bring up the master copy from your Web server, not the personal copy.

Microsoft Access

Now that you have set up your Web server to know about Access files data files and populated it with some actual data files from the package, your next step is setting up Access as a helper application. The concept of setting up helper applications for Web browsers is a general one, but the steps for actually going about it differ, depending on the Web browser you're using. We'll go through the steps for NCSA Mosaic and Netscape. If you're using another browser, you'll need to take a look at its documentation for how to accomplish this.

NCSA Mosaic and Microsoft Access

NCSA Mosaic in Windows provides a graphical interface for setting up helper applications, although Mosaic uses the term *external viewer* rather than *helper application*. In Mosaic, open the Options menu and select Preferences. The Preferences dialog box appears. Click on the Viewers tab to see the options shown in Figure 12.13.

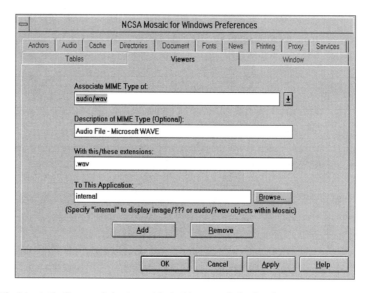

Figure 12.13. *The Mosaic Preferences dialog box with the Viewers tab displayed.*

As you can see, there are four fill-in boxes and several buttons that enable you to control the external viewers used. Figure 12.13 shows the dialog box already filled in for the Microsoft WAVE audio player.

Let's take a look at the labels on the fill-in boxes before going any further. We'll take them slightly out of order. You'll recognize some familiar items here. First, the top box, Associate MIME Type of, contains a MIME data type/subtype pair—in this case audio/wav. This item is, of course, right out of the `mime.types` file. The third fill-in box, With this/these extensions, is also familiar. It contains the same info as the filename-extension column in your `mime.types` file, with the extension `wav` entered.

The second fill-in box is an optional description of the kind of data file—in our example, it's `Audio File - Microsoft WAVE`. The last fill-in box, To This Application, is where you specify which program will function as your helper application. In Figure 12.13, the special keyword `internal` is used there, indicating that Mosaic can handle this MIME type/subtype by itself, without a helper application. Before we go on, note the Browse button next to this box, as we'll be using it to set up Access as your helper application.

Now that your tour of the Viewers tab is complete, let's configure Access as your helper application. Click the Add button to open up the Add Viewer dialog box, shown in 12.14. This box has the same four fill-in boxes as Figure 12.13, but they're blank, for you to enter your own information.

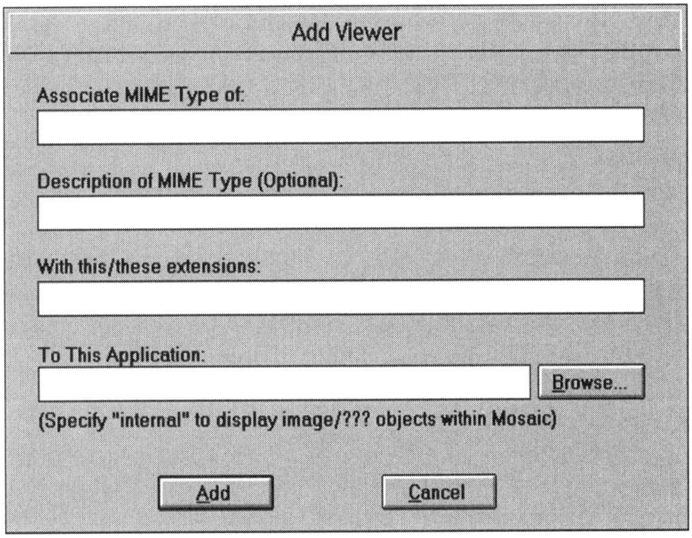

Figure 12.14. The NCSA Mosaic Add Viewer dialog box.

Using the information you added to your `mime.types` file earlier, you can quickly fill in these blanks.

◆ In the Associate MIME Type of box, enter `application/msaccess`.

◆ In the Description of MIME Type (Optional) box, enter something like `Microsoft Access Database`. Note that you aren't required to enter anything in this box, although it's a good idea to do so for future reference.

♦ In the With this/these extensions box, enter `mdb`. (As you'll recall, we entered this filename extension to the `mime.types` file earlier.)

♦ Finally, in the To This Application box, enter the full drive and pathname to the Microsoft Access executable program. If you're not sure about this, click the Browse button, which works like most Windows browse buttons, enabling you to locate the Microsoft Access executable. Once you've found it, select it.

Figure 12.15 shows the filled-in Viewers dialog box. (Your drive and path to the Access executable may be different from the one shown, so make sure you locate yours, rather than just copying what's shown in the figure.) Once you're set, click Add to save your changes.

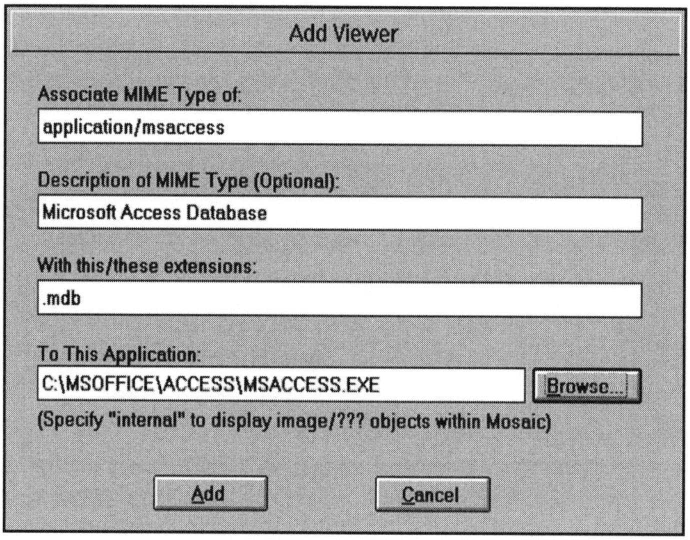

Add Viewer

Associate MIME Type of:

application/msaccess

Description of MIME Type (Optional):

Microsoft Access Database

With this/these extensions:

.mdb

To This Application:

C:\MSOFFICE\ACCESS\MSACCESS.EXE   Browse...

(Specify "internal" to display image/??? objects within Mosaic)

Add   Cancel

Figure 12.15. NCSA Mosaic Add Viewer dialog box, filled in for Microsoft Access.

That's it. You're now ready to try out your new setup. Close the Preferences windows by clicking OK, and then select Open Document from the Mosaic file menu. Enter the URL of an Access database file on your Web server, or click on a hyperlink pointing to one. Mosaic contacts the Web server and asks for the document. As described in detail in Chapter 7, the server sends back header information identifying the document as the MIME type/subtype `application/msaccess`. Mosaic reads this information, and then passes the incoming document off to Access for viewing, dynamically starting up Access with a copy of the database.

Figure 12.16 shows Mosaic with Access tiled on top. At this point, you have all the features and powers of Access available to you to search, edit, save, and print the data.

Note: It's important to note you're working with a temporary copy of the index, not the original, which is still safe on your Web server. As a result, you're free to make any changes to the database you need to make, save them, export the data for access within one of the other Microsoft Office packages, etc.

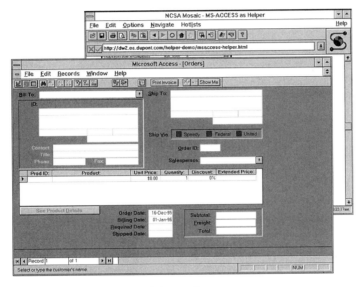

Figure 12.16. *Mosaic with Microsoft Access as a helper application.*

Netscape and Microsoft Access

Netscape on PCs running Microsoft Windows provides a graphical interface to setting up helper applications. Open the Options menu and select General Preferences. The Preferences dialog box appears. Click on the Helpers tab (shown in Figure 12.17).

As you can see, there is a scrollable File type list that contains preset helper applications; clicking on one of them brings up some details of the setup. In Figure 12.17, the audio/x-wav file type, has been selected. Below the File type window, you'll see File / MIME Type, with Subtype on the next line. Below that, there's a fill-in File Extensions box, several option buttons, and another fill-in box.

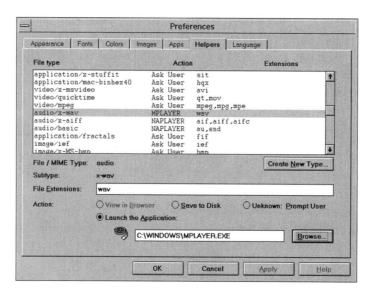

Figure 12.17. *The Netscape Preferences dialog box with the Helpers tab selected.*

Figure 12.17 shows the dialog box already filled in for the Microsoft WAVE audio player, mplayer. Let's take a look at this figure before going any further. You'll recognize some familiar items here. First, the File type window should remind you of the contents of the mime.types file on your Web server, with its columns specifying MIME data types/subtypes (on the left) and filename extensions (on the right). Below that box, you'll find the File / MIME Type item filled in as audio and the subtype filled in as x-wav. The File Extensions box contains wav.

At the bottom, there are several option buttons that enable you to choose what to do with incoming data of the MIME type/subtype application/x-wav. In Figure 12.17, Launch the Application is shown selected. The bottommost box is where you enter the name and path of the program that you want to function as your helper application. In Figure 12.17, the drive and path to the Microsoft Windows Media Player application, mplayer, has been filled in. Notice Netscape has picked up the Windows icon for mplayer, displaying it just to the left of the box. Before we go on, note the Create New Type and Browse buttons, as we'll be using them to set up Access as a helper application.

Your tour of the Helpers dialog box complete, let's configure Access as your helper application. Click the Create New Type button, to open up the Configure New Mime Type dialog box shown in Figure 12.18. This box has two fill-in boxes for your information about the new MIME type/subtype. Here, we've filled in the information for Access, right out of the mime.types file.

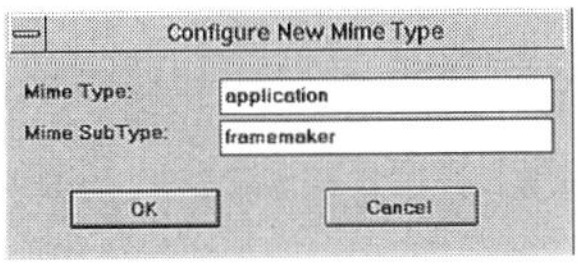

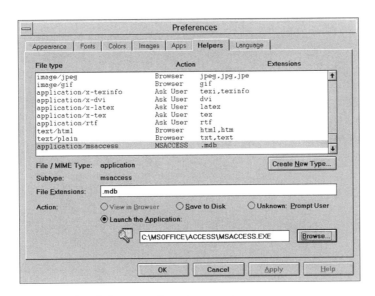

Figure 12.18. *The Netscape Configure New Mime Type dialog box.*

Fill yours in, then click OK. This returns you to the previous dialog box, with the MIME type information you just entered filled in. You now need to enter mdb in the File Extensions box. (As you'll recall, we entered this filename extension in the mime.types file earlier.) Finally, click on Launch the Application and fill in the full drive and pathname to the Microsoft Access executable program. If you're not sure about this, click the Browse button, which works like most Windows browse buttons, allowing you to locate the Access executable. Once you've found it, select it. As with mplayer, Netscape has located and displayed the Access icon.

Figure 12.19 shows the filled-in Helpers dialog box. (Your drive and path to the Access executable may be different from the one shown, so make sure you locate yours, rather than just copying what's shown in the figure.) Once you're set, click OK to save your changes.

That's it. You're now ready to try out your new setup. Close the Preferences windows by clicking OK, and then click the Open button on Netscape's toolbar. Enter the URL of an Access database file on your Web server, or click on a hyperlink pointing to one. Netscape contacts the Web server and asks for the document. As described in detail in Chapter 7, the server sends back header information identifying the document as the MIME type/subtype application/msaccess. Netscape reads this information, and then passes the incoming document off to Access for viewing, dynamically starting up Access on a copy of the database. Figure 12.20 shows Netscape with Access tiled on top.

Figure 12.19. *The Helpers tab with the Access information entered.*

At this point, you have all the features and powers of Access available to you to search, edit, save, and print this database file.

> **Note:** It's important to note you're working with a temporary copy of the index, not the original, which is still safe on your Web server. As a result, you're free to make any changes to the database you need to make, save them, export the data for access within one of the other Microsoft Office packages, whatever.

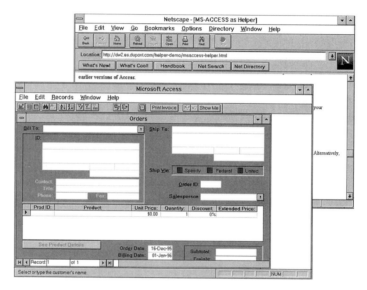

Figure 12.20. *Netscape with Microsoft Access as a helper application.*

As you can see from Figure 12.20, which displays a sample Access database application that comes with Microsoft Office, this is part of an order-taking and sales application. In Chapter 19, "Ordering and Inventory," you'll learn how you can create such order-taking applications on your Intranet using Web fill-in forms and CGI-bin scripts that access your database, including Microsoft Access databases, as a back end.

Access Read-Only Viewer

Microsoft has available for free download from its Web site (http://www.microsoft.com/) Access Ready-to-Run, a read-only viewer for Access database applications. This package enables users who don't have a full copy of Access to read and run queries against Access databases. Access Ready-to-Run supports Windows 95 only, but can read older Access databases.

Microsoft PowerPoint

Now that you have set up your Web server to know about Microsoft PowerPoint data files and populated it with some actual data files from the package, your next step is to set up PowerPoint as a helper application. The concept of setting up helper applications for Web browsers is a general one, but the steps for actually going about it differ, depending on the Web browser you're using. We'll go through the steps for NCSA Mosaic and Netscape. If you're using another browser, you'll need to take a look at its documentation to learn how to accomplish this.

NCSA Mosaic and Microsoft PowerPoint

NCSA Mosaic on Microsoft Windows PCs provides a graphical interface for setting up helper applications, although Mosaic uses the term *external viewer* rather than *helper application.* In Mosaic, open the Options menu and select Preferences. The Preferences dialog box appears. Click on the Viewers tab to see the options shown in Figure 12.21.

As you can see, there are four fill-in boxes and several buttons that enable you to control the external viewers used. Figure 12.21 shows the dialog box already filled in for the Microsoft WAVE audio player.

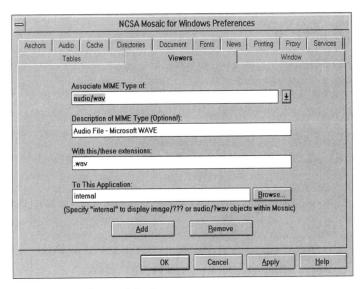

Figure 12.21. *Mosaic Viewers Preferences dialog box.*

Let's take a look at the labels on the fill-in boxes before going any further. We'll take then slightly out of order. You'll recognize some familiar items here. First, the top box, Associate MIME Type of, contains a MIME data type/subtype pair—in this case audio/wav. This item is, of course, right out of the `mime.types` file. The third fill-in box, With this/these extensions, is also familiar. It contains the same info as the filename-extension column in your `mime.types` file, with the extension `wav` entered.

The second fill-in box is an optional description of the kind of data file—in our example, it's `Audio File - Microsoft WAVE`. The last fill-in box, To This Application, is where you specify which program will function as your helper application. In Figure 12.21, the special keyword `internal` is used there, indicating that Mosaic can handle this MIME type/subtype by itself, without a helper application. Before we go on, note the Browse button next to this box, as we'll be using it to set up PowerPoint as your helper application.

Now that your tour of the Viewers dialog box is complete, let's configure Microsoft PowerPoint as your helper application. Click the Add button, to open up the Add Viewer dialog box, shown in Figure 12.22. This box has the same four fill-in boxes as Figure 12.21, but they're blank, for you to enter your own information.

Using the information you added to your `mime.types` file earlier, you can quickly fill in these blanks.

- ◆ In the Associate MIME Type of box, enter `application/mspowerpoint`.
- ◆ In the Description of MIME Type (Optional) box, enter something like `Microsoft PowerPoint Slides`. Note that you're not required to enter anything in this box, although it's a good idea to do so for future reference.
- ◆ In the With this/these extensions box, enter `ppt`. (As you'll recall, we entered this filename extension to the `mime.types` file earlier.)
- ◆ Finally, in the To This Application box, enter the full drive and pathname to the Microsoft PowerPoint executable program. If you're not sure about this, click the Browse button, which works like most Windows browse buttons, allowing you to locate the PowerPoint executable. Once you've found it, select it.

Figure 12.23 shows the filled-in Viewers dialog box. (Your drive and path to the Access executable may be different from the one shown, so make sure you locate yours, rather than just copying what's shown in the figure.) Once you're set, click Add to save your changes.

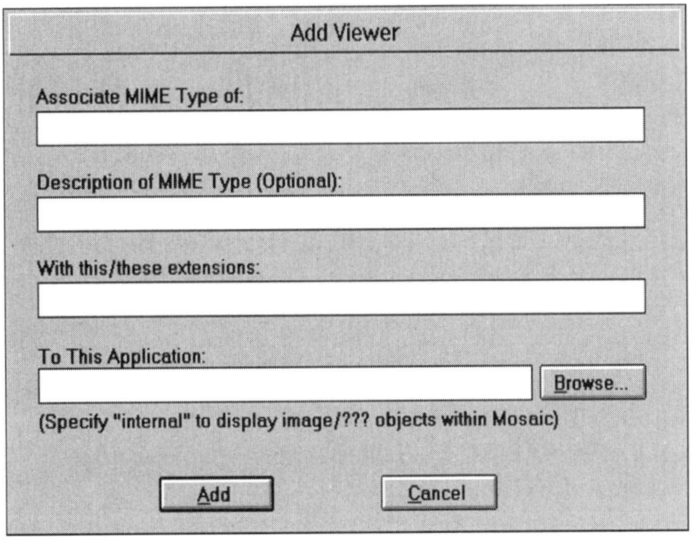

Figure 12.22. *The NCSA Mosaic Add Viewer dialog box.*

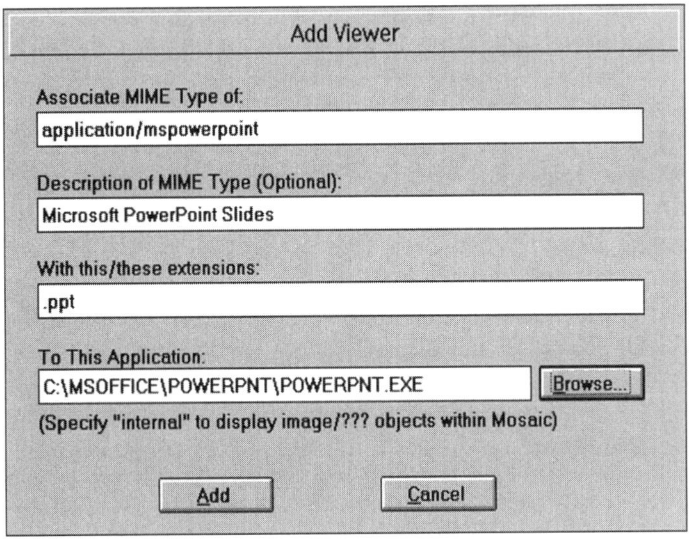

Figure 12.23. *The NCSA Mosaic Add Viewer dialog box, filled in for PowerPoint.*

That's it. You're now ready to try out your new setup. Close the Preferences windows by clicking OK, and then select Open Document from the Mosaic File menu. Enter the URL of a PowerPoint file on your Web server, or click on a hyperlink pointing to one. Mosaic contacts the Web server and asks for the document. As described in detail in Chapter 7, the server sends back header information identifying the document as the MIME type/subtype `application/mspowerpoint`. Mosaic reads this information, and then passes the incoming document off to PowerPoint for viewing, dynamically starting up PowerPoint with a copy of the slide. Figure 12.24 shows Mosaic with PowerPoint tiled on top.

At this point, you have all the features and powers of PowerPoint available to you to search, edit, save, and print the slide. You can also, of course, run the PowerPoint slide show if the hyperlink you've loaded contains more than one slide.

Note: It's important to note you're working with a temporary copy of the slide(s), not the original, which is still safe on your Web server. As a result, you're free to make any changes to the slide(s) you need to make, save them, export the data for access within one of the other Microsoft Office packages, and so on.

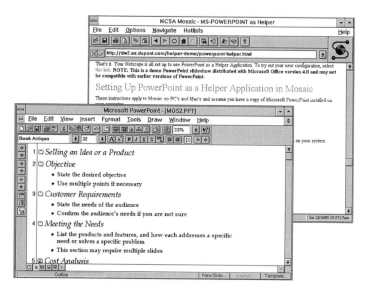

Figure 12.24. *Mosaic with Microsoft PowerPoint as a helper application.*

Netscape and Microsoft PowerPoint

Netscape in Windows provides a graphical interface for setting up helper applications. Open the Options menu, then select General Preferences. The Preferences dialog box appears. Click on the Helpers tab (shown in Figure 12.25).

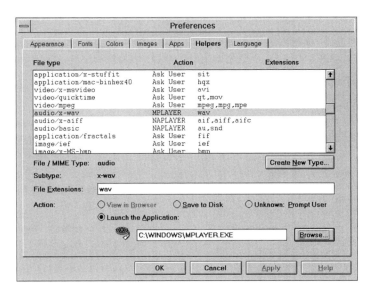

Figure 12.25. *The Netscape Preferences dialog box with the Helpers tab selected.*

As you can see, there is a scrollable File type list that contains preset helper applications; clicking on one of them brings up some details of the setup. In Figure 12.25, the audio/x-wav file type has been selected. Below the File type window, you'll see File / MIME Type, with Subtype on the next line. Below that, there's a fill-in File Extensions box, several option buttons, and another fill-in box.

Figure 12.25 shows the dialog box already filled in for the Microsoft WAVE audio player, mplayer. Let's take a look at this figure before going any further. You'll recognize some familiar items here. First, the File type window should remind you of the contents of the mime.types file on your Web server, with its columns specifying MIME data types/subtypes (on the left) and filename extensions (on the right). Below that box, you'll find the File / MIME Type item filled in as audio and the subtype filled in as x-wav. The File Extensions box contains wav.

At the bottom, there are several option buttons that enable you to choose what to do with incoming data of the MIME type/sub-type application/x-wav. In Figure 12.25, Launch the Application is shown selected. The bottommost box is where you enter the name and path of the program that you want to function as your helper application. In Figure 12.25, the drive and path to the Microsoft Windows Media Player application, mplayer, has been filled in. Notice Netscape has picked up the Windows icon for mplayer, displaying it just to the left of the box. Before we go on, note the Create New Type and Browse buttons, as we'll be using them to set up PowerPoint as a helper application.

Your tour of the Helpers dialog box complete, let's configure PowerPoint as your helper application. Click the Create New Type button to open up the Configure New Mime Type dialog box shown in Figure 12.26. This box has two fill-in boxes for your information about the new MIME type/subtype. Here, we've filled in the information for PowerPoint, right out of the mime.types file.

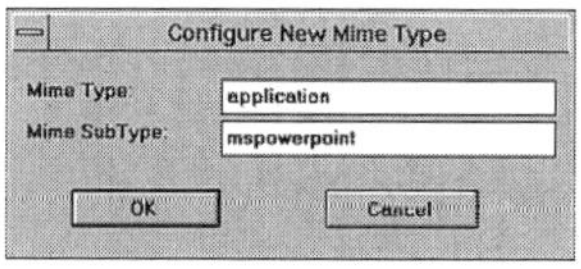

Figure 12.26. *The Netscape Configure New Mime Type dialog box.*

Fill yours in, and then click OK. This returns you to the previous dialog box, with the MIME type information you just entered filled in. You now need to enter ppt in the File Extensions box. (As you'll recall, we entered this filename extension to the mime.types file earlier.) Finally, click on Launch the Application and fill in the full drive and pathname to the Microsoft PowerPoint executable program. If you're not sure about this, click the Browse button, which works like most Windows browse buttons, enabling you to locate the PowerPoint executable. Once you've found it, select it. As with mplayer, Netscape has located and displayed the PowerPoint icon.

Figure 12.27 shows the filled-in Helpers tab. (Your drive and path to the PowerPoint executable may be different from the one shown, so make sure you locate yours, rather than just copying what's shown in the figure.) Once you're set, click OK to save your changes.

That's it. You're now ready to try out your new setup. Close the Preferences windows by clicking OK, and then click the Open button on Netscape's toolbar. Enter the URL of a PowerPoint slide data file on your Web server, or click on a hyperlink pointing to one. Netscape contacts the Web server and asks for the document. As described in detail in Chapter 7, the server sends back header information identifying the document as the MIME type/subtype application/mspowerpoint. Netscape reads this information, and then passes the incoming document off to PowerPoint for viewing, dynamically starting up PowerPoint on a copy of theslide datafile. Figure 12.28 shows Netscape with PowerPoint tiled on top.

At this point, you have all the features and powers of PowerPoint available to you to search, edit, save, and print this slide. You can also, of course, run the PowerPoint slide show if the hyperlink you've loaded contains more than one slide.

> **Note:** It's important to note you're working with a temporary copy of the slide(s), not the original, which is still safe on your Web server. As a result, you're free to make any changes to the slide(s) you need to make, save them, export the data for access within one of the other Microsoft Office packages, whatever.

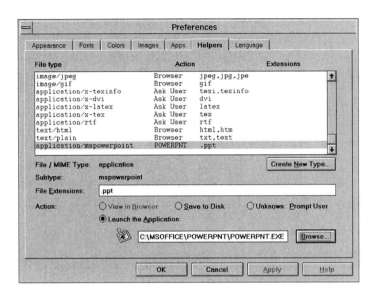

Figure 12.27. *The Helpers tab filled in with PowerPoint information.*

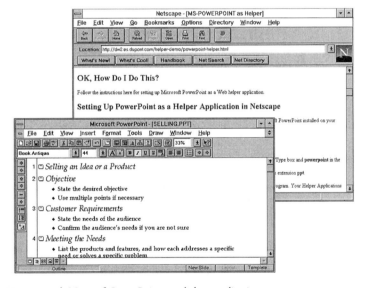

Figure 12.28. *Netscape with Microsoft PowerPoint as a helper application.*

Converting PowerPoint Slides to HTML

Microsoft now has available for free download from its Web site (http://www.microsoft.com) a version of its Internet Assistant (IA) for PowerPoint. Like the companion IA products for Microsoft Word and Excel, this package enables saving Microsoft Office datafiles (in this case, PowerPoint slides) directly to HTML format for use on your Intranet. Exported HTML slides include hyperlinks to all the slides in a multi-slide presentation. IA for PowerPoint supports Windows 95 only.

> **Tip:** While you're visiting Microsoft's Web site, you may also want to download a copy of PowerPoint for Windows 95 32-bit Viewer, a read-only viewer for PowerPoint presentations. Just as you set up PowerPoint itself as a Web browser helper application, you can set up the PowerPoint Viewer as one for customers who don't have their own copy of PowerPoint.

Summary

This has been the last of a group of three chapters devoted to using everyday office applications as Web browser helper applications in your Intranet. In this one, you've learned about a range of useful productivity applications including personal information managers like Windows Cardfile and two UNIX Rolodex programs; the Microsoft Access database package; and Microsoft PowerPoint, a presentation slide maker. Using these packages as examples, you've learned:

◆ How you can use a wide variety of common office application programs as Web browser helper applications.

◆ How to configure your World Wide Web server software for common office applications' data files.

◆ How to configure Web browser software to handle these data files.

◆ Some potential uses of these capabilities.

By now, you have a basic understanding of the helper application mechanism, including how to use MIME data type/subtype information to integrate almost any application your customers might use on your Intranet. You should have an inkling of the virtually unlimited possibilities for your organization represented by these capabilities. Subsequent chapters will build on these fundamentals to help you bring more advanced, specific capabilities into play on your Web.

IV

PART

Advanced Applications for Your Intranet

CHAPTER

Indexing and Searching Your Data

By now, you've gotten a good deal of data up and available on your Intranet—or at least you have some ideas on what you want to put up. In all likelihood, your data is going to add up to a substantial quantity. The obvious next question is "How are your customers going to be able to find anything among all your data?" The equally obvious answer is for you to provide searchable indexes on your Intranet. You'll learn in this chapter how to enable your customers to both search your indexes and retrieve documents (or other data files) using their Web browsers.

Chapter Objectives

As with the rest of the chapters in this book, let's begin by laying out some chapter objectives. This will help you get oriented to the material to be presented; you may want to refer back to this list as you work your way through the chapter. In this chapter, you'll

- ◆ Learn more about WAIS, the Wide-Area Information Service that I introduced in Chapter 8, "Adding Services to Your Intranet Adds Value," for creating custom, searchable indexes.

- ◆ Learn about glimpse, another data indexing tool, and its companion package glimpseHTTP, for incorporating glimpse indexes into a Web server.

◆ Learn about Harvest, a tool for gathering information about indexed data on World Wide Web servers, including data indexed by both WAIS and glimpse.

◆ Learn about ph, a specialized network database for corporate telephone books, and how it can be integrated into your Intranet.

◆ Survey several commercial index-and-retrieve packages for Intranets.

The discussion of WAIS in this chapter is based on the freeWAIS-sf package, available on the *Building an Intranet* CD-ROM. Installing this package was described in Chapter 8; if you haven't already installed it, you may want to do so now. Also on the CD-ROM, you'll find the glimpse and ph packages. This chapter includes information on installing these packages.

WAIS and Your Intranet

You'll recall from Chapter 8 that WAIS is a means of creating and searching indexes across TCP/IP networks. WAIS can work locally (on a single computer or across your Intranet) or remotely (across the Internet).

WAIS server software, running on a computer system in your Intranet, responds to requests from networked WAIS clients for keyword searches. You can do such searches using stand-alone WAIS client software (included with the freeWAIS-sf distribution), as well as with some Web browsers, such as NCSA Mosaic. In addition, if you use a CGI-bin gateway program such as SFgate (also described in Chapter 8), your customers can use Web fill-in forms to do custom searches with their Web browsers, and then can retrieve the documents that match their query for viewing. Figures 13.1 and 13.2 show sample SFgate WAIS searches—the former showing a filled-in query form and the latter the search results.

WAIS search results include relative weighting of the found documents based on a number of useful criteria, such as word frequency within the individual documents and the index as a whole. With multiword and Boolean searches, the weighting takes all of the search words into account, so a document containing all of your search words would get more weight than one that contained multiple instances of just one of them, for example.

In this chapter, you'll learn how to use freeWAIS-sf to create indexes of several kinds of data on your Intranet. You'll also learn more about the SFgate WAIS gateway script in this chapter, including how to use fill-in forms to initiate searches. Later, in Chapter 22, "Newsgroups for Group Discussions and Collaboration," you'll learn even more about WAIS, as you index your local USENET newsgroups.

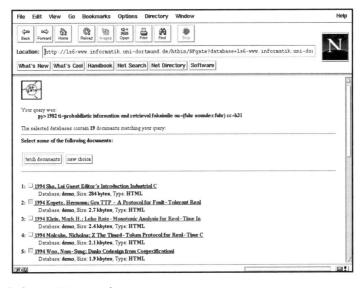

Figure 13.1. *An SFgate example search form.*

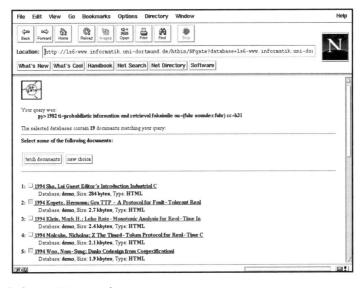

Figure 13.2. *Results from an SFgate search.*

If your Intranet is like most others, much of the data you'll want to index is in (or can be put into) plain text files of one kind or another. As described in Chapter 8, freeWAIS-sf understands a wide variety of text formats. In addition, freeWAIS-sf also knows about several kinds of image formats, and can be coaxed into indexing them (or at least their filenames). In addition, the package has special features that make it easy to integrate your data indexing into your Intranet, with a focus on Web-related capabilities. One major source of data that you may want to index is the data on your Web server itself. Finally, as if these capabilities weren't enough, you can teach freeWAIS-sf to recognize and index new data formats. We'll discuss indexing other kinds of data in Chapter 14, "Web Access to Commercial Database Applications."

Let's begin our look at WAIS by looking at the freeWAIS-sf indexer, `waisindex`. Before you can do any WAIS searches, you need to create your WAIS databases with `waisindex`. In Chapter 8, you saw a very simple example of a `waisindex` command:

```
# waisindex -d intranet -export -t text *.txt
```

This command indexes all the plain text files ending in the filename extension `.txt` in the current directory into the WAIS database named `intranet` and makes it available for network access. Since `waisindex` is a complex program, let's look more closely at its command-line options. Here's a list, annotated to indicate which are required and which are optional. After this list, you'll find a bit more detail about each option that isn't self-explanatory.

Table 13.1. Waisindex command-line options.

Option	Description
`-a`	Adds to existing WAIS index. Optional.
`-d database`	Specifies database name for WAIS index (creates new database without -a). Required.
`-stem`	Uses word stemming. Optional.
`-r`	Recursively indexes subdirectories. Optional.
`-mem mbytes`	Amount of memory, in megabytes, to use in creating the database. Optional.
`-register`	Sends e-mail registering the database with the master Internet directory of servers. Optional.
`-export`	Makes database network accessible. Optional.
`-e filename`	Log errors in `filename`. Optional.
`-l number`	Sets log level (0 through 10). Optional.
`-v`	Prints the version of the software. Optional.
`-stdin`	Reads filenames to be indexed from UNIX standard input. Optional.
`-pos or -nopos`	Include (or don't include) word position information. Optional. Not currently supported in freeWAIS-sf.
`-nopairs or -pairs`	Don't include (or do include) word pairs. Optional. Currently disabled in freeWAIS-sf.

Option	Description
-nocat	Don't create catalog file. Optional.
-contents	Indexes the contents, even if the document type is not normally subject to such indexing. Optional.
-nocontents	Indexes only the filename, not the contents, even if the contents are normally indexable. Optional.
-stop *stopfile*	Overrides default stoplist and uses contents of *stopfile* instead. Optional.
-keywords *string*	Uses *string* as keyword(s) in indexing. Optional.
-keyword_file *filename*	Takes indexing keyword from filename. Optional.
-T *type*	Announces "TYPE" of the document. Optional.
-M *type,type*	Multitype documents. Optional.
-t *type*	Actual type of the files. Optional.

The first two options (-a and -d) control whether a new database is created or an existing one is appended to. The -d option is, of course, required in all `waisindex` commands.

The stemming (`-stem`) feature, a feature in older versions of freeWAIS, has been enhanced in freeWAIS-sf. Before indexing or searching, it reduces words to their most basic word stem. For example, the word stem *comput* is the basis for many words. In freeWAIS-sf, the words *computer*, *computers*, *compute*, and *computing* are all treated the same in both creation of freeWAIS-sf index databases and keyword searches of the database.

By default, `waisindex` will index only the files you specify. If you use the `-r` switch, it will index all specified recursively.

You can speed up `waisindex` by giving it a large `-mem` parameter. Expressed in megabytes, this is the amount of your system's virtual memory (not physical RAM) to be used in creating index databases. Using too high a number here might interfere with the computer's other tasks, so be careful if your system is busy. Running your indexing jobs in off hours, when the system is less busy, can enable you to use more memory. If the default memory utilization (that is, with no `-mem` specification at all on the `waisindex` command line) slows your system down, you'll want to use this argument to limit the amount of memory used, rather than to increase it.

The two related options `-register` and `-export` might seem similar, but they do entirely different things. Let's take them in reverse order. In order for you to make your WAIS index database fully searchable over your Intranet, you must use the `-export` option. This modifies the `database.src` file, making it possible for standalone WAIS clients to access the database over a network. Web browsers or CGI-bin gateway scripts like SFgate don't need this information, but it's useful to add it anyway.

Using the `-export` option does not advertise your index database to the Internet. This is what `-register` does. The `-register` option actually creates and sends an e-mail message to two main WAIS index registries on the Internet. This is, in effect, a public Internet announcement that your index is available to be searched from anywhere. If you don't want to make your index universally available, don't use this option. Also, if your network is not connected to the Internet, or is behind a network security Firewall (see Chapter 9, "Intranet Security"), the -register option is unlikely to be of any use.

Two options, -e and -1, enable you to control whether your WAIS server will create logfiles of its transactions (that is, all the searches that are done) on your index. In addition, you can control how much logging takes place. The first option (-e logfile) tells the server that you want a log kept in the file *logfile*.

By default, if you have logging enabled, the most verbose logging is done. To reduce the amount of information that's logged, use the -1 option with a number between 0 and 9. (Level-10 logging is the default if -e is used alone.) The lower the number, the less verbose the logging. If you use default logging, watch the size of your logfiles to ensure they don't fill up your file system.

Rather than typing in a list of filenames on the waisindex command line, you may want to use other UNIX utilities to prepare a list of files for you based on some criteria. You can then feed that list to waisindex using the -stdin option. For example, you could use the following command pipeline:

```
$ find /some_directory -depth -name "*.txt" -print ¦ waisindex -d mycompany -stdin -
some_other_options
```

Later on in this chapter, you'll learn how to automate the maintenance of your WAIS index databases using -stdin and the UNIX cron daemon to run update scripts in the wee hours of the night.

In some searches, the fact that two or more keywords appear in close proximity to one another in a document can be significant. You can compile the freeWAIS-sf software with proximity searching enabled, but in the current release, doing so disables literal string search. If you enable proximity searching, special query syntax is required, such as acid w/5 rain, signifying the two words "acid" and "rain" appearing within five words of each other in the documents. Proximity searching is superior to the older -pairs option, which is now disabled in freeWAIS-sf. You can easily modify the freeWAIS-sf source code to re-enable -pairs and its partner -nopairs, but freeWAIS-sf's author recommends against doing so.

One of the files created by waisindex is known as the *catalog file*. This file contains the headline of every document in a WAIS index database. If your database is large, this file can get quite large. It's really nothing more than a long list of the files in your database, annotated with a descriptive headline. Failed searches may result in the headline file being returned to your customer, and a long list of headlines may or may not be helpful. The catalog file is not required for the WAIS server to function, or for your customers to do searches, so you can dispense with it if you're short on disk space by running waisindex with the -nocat option.

Ordinarily, waisindex knows there are some kinds of files whose contents can't usefully be indexed. Examples include image files and other kinds of binary data. Based on the -t option, for example, `waisindex` will index the contents of several kinds of text files about which it knows. If, on the other hand, you'd like to inhibit content indexing of ordinarily indexable files, use `-nocontents`.

Word frequencies being what they are, you'll not want your WAIS index databases to be full of pointers to words like *the, a, and, if,* and the like. freeWAIS-sf has a list of several hundred such *stop words* built in. If you'd like to create you own stop file and use it instead of the standard list, use the `-stop filename` option. (You may find it easier, though, to modify the default stop list contained in the freeWAIS-sf source code.)

With respect to your stop words, it's useful to know that `waisindex` will generate new stop words based on the actual frequency of word occurrence in your indexed documents. These new words are added to a special stop file for the index and appended to the default list. If your business is a U.S. government agency, for instance, `waisindex` may well decide the word Federal occurs so frequently in your documents that it adds it to the stop file.

If you want to make sure that your WAIS index database contains specific keywords, even if some or all of the documents don't actually contain them, use `-keywords string` and specify them on the command line, or use `-keyword_file filename` and specify them in a file. Your extra keywords will be added to the normal indexing. This feature is useful when indexing image filenames and other binary data.

The two options `-T` and `-t` are confusing ones, since they both appear to specify a document type. The difference is subtle but important. You can think of the two as specifying a document format and a document type, respectively.

Let's take `-t` first. In Chapter 8, you saw a long list of the document types recognized by `waisindex`. (You can get this list by entering the `waisindex` command with no options at all on your command line.) For the most part, these are types of plain text files whose internal file format `waisindex` understands and can interpret. Examples include USENET news articles and e-mail messages. The program expects such files to conform to the standard format of those kinds of files, with a certain layout and structure. For example, as you learned in Chapter 7, "MIME and Helper Applications," all Internet e-mail messages have a specified format, with headers and a body. Thus, the `-t` option deals with the format of documents—how they're laid out, what divides records, and the like.

As you'll also recall from Chapter 7, as well as from various other chapters, Web servers and browsers know about a list of MIME data type/subtypes. This is where the `-T` option to `waisindex` comes in. Since freeWAIS-sf is built to integrate into a Web, it has MIME hooks built in. When you index data with `waisindex`, you can use the `-T` command-line option to specify a MIME type that'll be announced when your index is searched by a Web browser or cgi-bin script. When a Web browser or CGI-bin gateway script retrieves the document, the MIME type is returned and your Web browser deals with it appropriately. Thus, if you index JPEG image files using `-T JPEG` on the `waisindex` command line, your customers' Web browsers will know what to do with the files they retrieve from your WAIS server—open them as JPEG images.

> **Note:** In some instances, the -T and -t options appear to have the same file type specified. For example, since waisindex knows about GIF images, you might specify -T gif and -t gif on the same command line when indexing GIF files. Since the two options mean different things, their use isn't redundant.

> **Tip:** When using both the -t and -T options with waisindex, always put the -t option first on your command line. In some cases, -t may imply a -T, as the overall default for -T is TEXT, so you may not need both options.

There's another, special reason to use the -T option in freeWAIS-sf. Because the package allows you to define your own new document types using custom format files, it's important to be able to tell waisindex about the new format(s) you've invented. Incidentally, you may want to update your Web server's mime.types file to add support for the new WAIS file types you've created.

In connection with MIME types, the -M option to waisindex allows you to specify multiple file types in a single WAIS index database. Suppose, for example, you maintain copies of common word processing documents in several formats, including Microsoft Word, WordPerfect, Rich Text, and plain text (as described in Chapter 20, "Intranet Boilerplate Library"). Using the -M option, you can index all these documents at once using a waisindex command line something like this:

```
$ waisindex -d mywords -M MSWORD,WORDPERFECT5.1,RTF,TEXT -export -other_options files
```

Here, the multiple file types correspond to some of the additions we have made to the mime.types file on your Web server over the course of the last several chapters. Note that you must specify them on the waisindex command line in UPPERCASE.

Using WAIS on Your Intranet

You can use WAIS in many ways on your Intranet. We'll look at a couple in this chapter; in Chapter 22, you'll learn about yet another. How you choose to use WAIS must, of course, be based on your own data and your Intranet's needs. The examples in this chapter will show you some of the subtleties of WAIS.

General Indexing with WAIS

You can use WAIS to create index databases of just about any collection of data. In this and other examples in this chapter, the text of several of this book's chapters has been used as test data. (The original Microsoft Word documents were converted to plain text using Word's Save As command.) Let's begin by looking at the files to be indexed.

```
$ ls -l
-rw-r--r--  1 tkevans  staff    14381 Jan 11 19:26 inw00or.txt
-rw-r--r--  1 tkevans  staff    24303 Jan 11 19:27 inw01or.txt
-rw-r--r--  1 tkevans  staff    61797 Jan 11 19:27 inw02or.txt
-rw-r--r--  1 tkevans  staff    29402 Jan 11 19:28 inw03or.txt
-rw-r--r--  1 tkevans  staff    30373 Jan 11 19:28 inw04or.txt
-rw-r--r--  1 tkevans  staff    34407 Jan 11 19:29 inw05or.txt
-rw-r--r--  1 tkevans  staff    49763 Jan 11 19:29 inw06or.txt
-rw-r--r--  1 tkevans  staff    60392 Jan 11 19:30 inw07or.txt
-rw-r--r--  1 tkevans  staff    84821 Jan 11 19:31 inw08or.txt
-rw-r--r--  1 tkevans  staff    76512 Jan 11 19:31 inw10or.txt
-rw-r--r--  1 tkevans  staff    64659 Jan 11 19:32 inw11or.txt
-rw-r--r--  1 tkevans  staff    60000 Jan 11 19:32 inw12or.txt
-rw-r--r--  1 tkevans  staff    65005 Jan 11 19:33 inw23or.txt
$
```

As you can see, there are 13 documents, ranging in size from around 14K bytes to 85K bytes. All are plain text files, having been converted from Microsoft Word. Since they're plain text files, it's pretty simple to create a WAIS index database with waisindex, using just a couple of the command-line options described earlier.

```
$ waisindex -d intranet -export inw*.txt
```

This command generates a good deal of onscreen output as each file is indexed and waisindex creates the several files that make up a WAIS index database named intranet. One of the final messages gives you a summary of the operation:

```
21924: 18: Jan 11 21:41:12 1996: 100: Total word count for dictionary is: 59372
```

Besides some housekeeping information (date, process id, and the like), this message tells you the total word count for the WAIS dictionary. With a larger collection of documents, you'll also see reference to a stop file being created containing words waisindex finds so frequently in the data that it tosses them out of the indexing process. When the command completes, you'll see the database files waisindex has created:

```
$ ls -l intranet*
-rw-r--r--  1 tkevans  staff      1615 Jan 11 21:41 intranet.cat
-rw-r--r--  1 tkevans  staff    174178 Jan 11 21:41 intranet.dct
-rw-r--r--  1 tkevans  staff       352 Jan 11 21:41 intranet.doc
-rw-r--r--  1 tkevans  staff       602 Jan 11 21:41 intranet.fn
-rw-r--r--  1 tkevans  staff       524 Jan 11 21:41 intranet.hl
-rw-r--r--  1 tkevans  staff    452633 Jan 11 21:41 intranet.inv
-rw-r--r--  1 tkevans  staff      1674 Jan 11 21:41 intranet.src
$
```

You'll notice the files picked up the WAIS database index name (intranet) used on the waisindex command line. Most of these files are binary in content, but several, including the .src and .hl files, are plain text. You can look at them if you're curious.

Now that you have created your intranet index, you can manually test it out with waissearch, the stand-alone WAIS client that comes with the freeWAIS-sf distribution. While you probably won't expect your Intranet's customers to use command-line WAIS searches, it's useful for you to know something about how they work, so you have a quick test mechanism at your disposal. Here's an example:

```
$ waissearch -d intranet waisindex usenet
```

Here, we've asked for a search on the intranet WAIS index database created earlier for the two words waisindex and usenet. (Note we've not done a Boolean "and" search here; just a search for the two words.) Let's take a look at the results of this simple search:

```
Search Response:
  NumberOfRecordsReturned: 6
   1: Score:    93, lines:1075 'inw23or.txt    /users/web-docs/intranet/'
   2: Score:    66, lines:1488 'inw08or.txt    /users/web-docs/intranet/'
   3: Score:    30, lines: 409 'inw01or.txt    /users/web-docs/intranet/'
   4: Score:    27, lines: 498 'inw04or.txt    /users/web-docs/intranet/'
   5: Score:    27, lines: 482 'inw03or.txt    /users/web-docs/intranet/'
   6: Score:    21, lines:1148 'inw02or.txt    /users/web-docs/intranet/'
View document number [type 0 or q to quit]:
```

At this point, you know your WAIS server and index are working. Before we go any further, though, let's take a look at this output. First, as you can see, six documents contained either the word waisindex or the word usenet (or both words). It ranks the hits in descending order using numerical scores. Your WAIS search not only has returned the hits on the keyword search, but has also ranked them based on frequency of occurrence, proximity, and the like, as described earlier. If you'll flip back to the *Building an Intranet* Table of Contents, it shouldn't surprise you Chapter 22 had the highest score, since it specifically focuses on WAIS and USENET news. The output of your search also gives you other information about the documents found, and thus gives you the opportunity to retrieve and view any of them.

Before leaving this, let's use a more refined search:

```
$ waissearch -d intranet waisindex and usenet
Search Response:
  NumberOfRecordsReturned: 2
   1: Score:    35, lines:1075 'inw23or.txt    /users/web-docs/intranet/'
   2: Score:    22, lines:1488 'inw08or.txt    /users/web-docs/intranet/'
View document number [type 0 or q to quit]:
```

Here, the search specified those documents containing both waisindex and usenet. The word *and* on the command line indicates a Boolean search. Because *and* is a standard WAIS stop word (that is, it's not indexed because of its natural frequency of occurrence), you can use it as a Boolean search delimiter. Had you used another Boolean search, asking for waisindex or usenet, your search results would have been the same as the initial search.

Let's look at the same search from the likely view of your customers—the view from behind their Web browser. Figure 13.3 shows a Web fill-in form that uses the SFgate CGI-bin script to search the same intranet WAIS index database using the same two keywords, waisindex and usenet. This is exactly the same search done with waissearch in the first example, and as Figure 13.4 shows, the results are the same as well. The difference between the searches is obvious. In Figure 13.4, the list of document hits appears with each a hyperlink. Clicking on one brings it up in your Web browser, as shown in Figure 13.5. To locate your search term in the retrieved document, use your Web browser's Find feature.

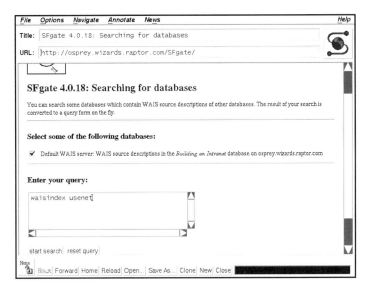

Figure 13.3. *SFGate's fill-in form for a WAIS index search.*

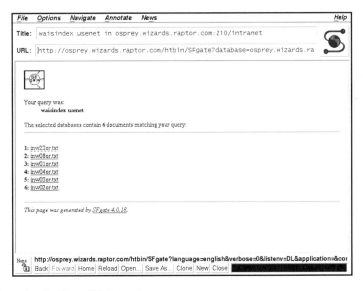

Figure 13.4. *The results of a SFgate WAIS search.*

Figure 13.5. *A document retrieved from a WAIS server.*

Indexing Your Web Server with WAIS

Besides doing general-purpose indexing, you may want to enhance your Intranet's Web server by creating a WAIS index database of the files on it. All of your httpd server's HTML files, with their embedded hyperlinks, can be indexed, as can all of the other data you have on your Web server, such as images and other multimedia files. The index can be searched, just as you searched the WAIS index of plain text files above, using a stand-alone WAIS client, a Web browser, or an SFgate or other WAIS gateway CGI-bin script.

> **Note:** FreeWAIS-sf's author, Ulrich Pfiefer, recommends that the package be compiled with proximity searches enabled for full capability in indexing Web server documents. The Configure script, which you run before you compile the package, presents this option (see Chapter 8).

Let's start out by indexing the same set of files we indexed earlier, but treating the files as if they were part of a Web server, rather than just some set of no-name files to be indexed. Our objective here is not only to create the index of the Web server files, but to have the index return World Wide Web URLs rather than just filenames. This will enable your customers to retrieve the documents from your Web server using their Web browsers. Additionally, if the retrieved documents themselves have Web hyperlinks in them, your customer can follow them. For this purpose, we'll use a special file type that waisindex knows about: URL.

Because we have removed the existing `intranet` WAIS index database we created earlier, let's create a new one. Here's a sample command, which is explained below.

```
$ waisindex -d intranet -export -t URL /users/web-docs/intranet http://
osprey.wizards.raptor.com/intranet /users/web-docs/intranet/inw*.txt
```

This is a fairly complex command, so let's look at it in pieces. First, you're already familiar with several parts of it, including

◆ Designation of the name of the database to be created, with `-d intranet`

◆ Use of the `-export` option, to make the index network-accessible

◆ Specification of the files to be indexed: `/users/web-docs/intranet/inw*.txt`

The rest of the command, still seemingly complex, is the key to your work here. Here's that part of the command on which to focus:

```
-t URL /users/web-docs/intranet http://osprey.wizards.raptor.com/intranet
```

Let's break it down even further. First, we've specified `-t URL`. `waisindex` treats the URL file type specially. The command line calls for a rewrite of part of the filenames being indexed. Specifically, it asks `waisindex` to replace the literal directory path `/users/web-docs/intranet` with a full Web URL. For each file indexed, `waisindex` substitutes the string `http://osprey.wizards.raptor.com/intranet` for the literal directory path. You'll recognize this as pointing to files in the `intranet` subdirectory of Web server `osprey.wizards.raptor.com`. In other words, the `intranet` subdirectory is a first-level directory in the Web server's `DocumentRoot` directory. (See Appendix A, "Setting Up a Web Server," if you're unclear on the meaning of *DocumentRoot*.) Thus, the file `/users/web-docs/intranet/inw06or.txt` gets indexed as `http://osprey.wizards.raptor.com/intranet/inw06or.txt`.

Let's now return to the SFgate search screen shown in Figure 13.3 and rerun our search. Figure 13.6 shows the results. As you can see, the documents found are the same as those found with our earlier WAIS search, but are displayed using Web URLs in this search result rather than the full directory path and filename. Clicking on any one of them brings up the actual document. Instead of retrieving the document from your WAIS server, however, it retrieves the document from your Web server.

This may seem a subtle difference, but it's important for a couple of reasons:

◆ The retrieved documents can be full HTML documents, with hyperlinks and images in them, so your customer gets not just plain text, but all the bells and whistles of his Web browser. Clicking on an embedded hyperlink in the retrieved document enables the customer to jump off to other documents, even to those on other Web servers.

◆ You can spread the load of indexing and retrieving documents out among different computer systems on your Intranet. For example, you can run WAIS and httpd servers on different computers, while still providing access to the services of both through your customers' Web browsers.

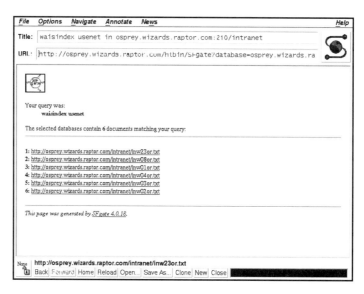

Figure 13.6. The results of the SFgate WAIS search showing URLs.

Images: Extending the Index of Your Web Server

So far, our examples of using WAIS to index documents have used just a small set of plain text documents. You may be wondering why there are two different ways of using waisindex, since both would seem to work equally well for this sort of document.

Most Web servers have more than just plain text documents on them. In particular, Web servers have HTML documents, images, and other multimedia files on them. So let's extend our WAIS index database to add these important files. Let's assume that the example Web server we've used includes a directory tree containing not only the text files you've already indexed, but also one or more subdirectories containing HTML files. Let's first prepare a list of those files, and then feed the list to waisindex.

```
$ find /users/web-docs/intranet -type f -name "*.html" -print > /tmp/filelist
```

Here, we've asked the system to find all regular files in the directory tree beginning at /users/web-docs/intranet that have the filename extension .html and put the list of them in the file /tmp/filelist.

> **Tip:** In Chapter 22, you'll learn how to automate the maintenance of your WAIS index databases using the UNIX cron daemon for while-you-sleep updates.

Next, you can use what you've just learned about `waisindex` to pump up your existing `intranet` index database.

```
$ waisindex -a -d intranet -stdin -t URL /users/web-docs/intranet http://
osprey.wizards.raptor.com/intranet < /tmp/filelist
```

Comparing this command line to the last one you used, you'll notice several differences:

◆ The `-a` option tells `waisindex` to append to the existing `intranet` database.

◆ The `-export` option has been dropped, since the database was exported at the time it was created and need not be exported again.

◆ The `-stdin` option tells `waisindex` to take its list of to-be-indexed files from the UNIX standard input.

◆ The `< /tmp/filelist` item tells `waisindex` to use the list of files you created earlier using the `find` command.

Your WAIS index database now includes all of your Web server's HTML files, as well as the original list of plain text ones.

You may have additional files of various kinds on your Web server that you'd like to add. This can be done as well. For example, you might want to add all of your GIF or JPEG images. The process is much the same as the one you just completed, though it differs in some details. Image files are binary files, and there's little in them you can actually index. In fact, WAIS won't index the contents of binary files like images at all, though it can add references to the files themselves to your index. Let's add all your GIF images to your intranet WAIS index database. First, let's prepare a list of them, much as you did before:

```
$ find /users/web-docs/intranet -type f -name "*.gif" -print > /tmp/giflist
```

Now, run the list through `waisindex`:

```
$ waisindex -a -d intranet -stdin -nocontents -t URL /users/web-docs/intranet http://
osprey.wizards.raptor.com/intranet < /tmp/giflist
```

> **Tip:** Power UNIX users will recognize that these two commands can be combined into a single command pipeline, to update your index in one pass, like this:
>
> ```
> $ find /users/web-docs/intranet -type f -name "*.gif" -print ¦ waisindex -a -d
> intranet -stdin -nocontents -t URL /users/web-docs/intranet http://
> osprey.wizards.raptor.com/intranet
> ```
>
> Having used the `-t URL` option, your SFgate searches (see below) will recognize the URL type and construct an on-the-fly hyperlink for fetching the image from your Web server.

As with the previous `waisindex` command, this one is much the same, but with a couple of differences. Specifically, the `-nocontents` option is used. Remember, GIF images can't be indexed, so just their filenames go into the index (along with any keywords you include using the `waisindex`

-keywords option). If you have additional image files, such as JPEG images, you can repeat this process to add them to your index as well. Be sure to include the -a option to waisindex to avoid wiping out your existing index database.

> **Note:** waisindex will not try to index the contents of image files if you specify their type on the command line (-t gif, for instance), but since this example uses the file type URL (-t URL), it's necessary to add -nocontents to suppress indexing.

If the contents of your images aren't indexed, you may wonder what this operation has added to your WAIS index database, and what you've gained by it. All the filenames of the GIF images in your Web server's file tree are indexed (along with any associated keywords you've added with the -keywords option), so that now you and your Intranet's customers can search for image files the same way you do keyword searches.

As you create more and more HTML documents, you'll collect more and images; waisindexing them enables you to manage them. CGI-bin gateway programs like SFgate can help you and your Intranet's customers search for image files, just as they can help you look for text files. If you have multiple WebMasters, including customers setting up Web servers of their own for your Intranet, having a searchable, retrievable collection of images can be a boon. Everyone can share the same set of images, preventing duplicate work and giving your Intranet a common look.

Other Data

As you've probably guessed, the technique of indexing filenames without indexing their contents, which you just used for images, can be used for almost any kind of data on your Web server. In Chapters 10, "Your Word Processor and the Web," 11, "Spreadsheets and Data Warehouses," and 12, "Other Common Office Applications," you learned how to make word processor documents, spreadsheets, and other applications' data files available on your Intranet. Now you can index them for easy search and retrieval, saving you the time and trouble of maintaining Tables of Contents as documents change. Using exactly the same techniques used in the last section, you can add your other data files to your WAIS index database.

> **Tip:** When using waisindex to index word processor, spreadsheet, or other data files, be sure to use the -keywords option to add key search words to your index. These documents' contents may not get fully indexed, so you'll want to use this important feature.

Your customers can do searches for, say, word processing or spreadsheet files using a fill-in form like that shown in Figure 13.1, and then pull the files directly into their word processors or spreadsheet packages, just by clicking on the ones they want.

> **Tip:** With respect to your Intranet word processing and/or spreadsheet libraries, using a UNIX system as your Web server has distinct advantages. Since most modern UNIX systems allow filenames to be virtually unlimited in length, you can use filenames for documents that clearly indicate their content. You can use filenames like `widget_773_shipping_instruct.doc` or `third_quarter_95_sales.xls`.
>
> In the absence of the ability to fully index data file contents with WAIS, indexing filenames like this creates meaningful headlines in your WAIS index database. Your doing so eases your customers' job in identifying just which spreadsheet or document file they want. Of course, Macintosh, Windows NT, and Windows 95 also allow long filenames, but freeWAIS-sf doesn't run on these platforms.

Now your Intranet's customers' searches of your WAIS-indexed Web server tree can turn up hits like those shown in Figure 13.7. This is the same WAIS index database used in the earlier example, but the database has been extended to include the original Microsoft Word source documents. Using the same search form shown in Figure 13.3 (where the keywords `waisindex` and `usenet` were used), you can now pull up not only the plain text versions of each file found, but also the original `.doc` file. Since your customers' Web browsers are already configured to use Word as a helper application (see Chapter 10), they can simply click on the document they want and load it directly into Word.

Figure 13.7. *SFgate search results with URLs.*

Inventing New File Types with freeWAIS-sf

Earlier in our discussion of WAIS, freeWAIS-sf's ability to invent new file types for indexing was briefly mentioned. Let's turn some brief attention to that feature now.

As mentioned earlier, the *sf* in freeWAIS-sf stands for Structured Fields. That means you can define new kinds of plain text documents for freeWAIS-sf to index based on a file-structure specification, and then index them using the new definition. This enables you to create custom documents, using almost any format you want, and then index and search them with freeWAIS-sf on your Intranet. Here's how this works.

> You define a structure for your document, using blank lines, white space, or other characters to separate records and fields of the document.
>
> You formally describe this document structure in a WAIS index database format file.
>
> You run waisindex with the -t fields file type, which reads your database format file and then indexes your documents based on the field structure you've specified.

WAIS searches, including those done with the SFgate CGI-bin Web gateway script, can include specifications related to the indexed fields of the data files. Searches, then, need not apply only to entire documents, but also (or instead) to specific fields of identically structured documents. The SFgate search illustrated in Figures 13.1 and 13.2 shows such a structured-fields search. As you can see from the form back in Figure 13.1, each fill-in box has a label. Since this is a bibliographic database, these labels refer to such things as Author, Title, Publication Year, and the like. Each of these refers to one of the predefined fields of the underlying database.

FreeWAIS-sf database format descriptions are plain text files organized into well-defined sections. The files are stored in the same location as your intended WAIS index databases, and must be named with the same filename stem as the other index files. Using the example from earlier in this chapter, if you have a WAIS index database named intranet, the freeWAIS-sf database format file must be named intranet.fmt. Each database format file has a record-sep (record separator) and a layout section. The former specifies what is used as the record separator within the data file; the formfeed character, or CTRL-L, is commonly used. Within the layout section, headline keywords specify regions of the document.

FreeWAIS-sf database format documents rely quite heavily on UNIX regular expressions. To-be-indexed documents are read line-by-line, with attempts to match the regular expressions specified in the format file. If you're not an experienced UNIX user, these format files will look like a foreign language to you. *Regular expressions* is a text-string, pattern-matching tool that's widely used by programs like the ed editor and its descendants ex, vi, and sed, the grep file-searching utility, perl, and other UNIX programs. You'll find terse definitions of regular expressions on the ed(1) man page on your system, but you'll probably want to consult something a little more user-friendly if you're not a UNIX guru. If you have printed system manuals, you may have the original AT&T Line Editor (ed) Tutorial lying around the office somewhere. Alternatively, look for a comprehensive book about UNIX, such as SAMS Publishing's *UNIX Unleashed* (ISBN 0-672-30402-3). For more information on this and other UNIX books, access the Macmillan Information SuperLibrary at `http://www.mcp.com/`.

The freeWAIS-sf FAQ document (included in the `doc/SF` subdirectory of the freeWAIS-sf distribution) gives a simple and potentially useful format description for HTML documents, the documents you use on your Web server. Here it is. (The # sign indicates a comment that extends from there to the end of the line.)

```
record-sep: /\n\n/ # never matches
     layout:
     headline: /<[Tt][Ii][Tt][Ll][Ee]>/ /<\/[Tt][Ii][Tt][Ll][Ee]>/ 80
        /<[Tt][Ii][Tt][Ll][Ee]> *./
     end:
     region: /<[Hh][Tt][Mm][Ll]>/
     stemming TEXT GLOBAL
     end: /<.[Bb][Oo][Dd][Yy]>/
```

If you squint, you can make out some of the basic HTML tags: <TITLE>, </TITLE>, <HTML>, <BODY>, and </BODY>. Basically, this format description file uses standard HTML tags to define the structure of an HTML document. Using `waisindex` with this format definition and the URL file type, your index headlines will always contain the URL of the document and, depending on how you configured freeWAIS-sf at compile time, may also include the title of the document, extracted from between the HTML tags <TITLE> and </TITLE>.

The authors of freeWAIS-sf have a sample Web pages index, based on this format description, at URL `http://ls6-www.informatik.uni-dortmund.de/SFgate/www-pages/`. This Web page, shown in two parts in Figures 13.8 and 13.9, clearly illustrates an SFgate fill-in form based on a custom database format description. As you can see, you can search separately on all the major standard parts of an HTML document (title, headlines, etc.), as well as free-form text search in the body of the documents.

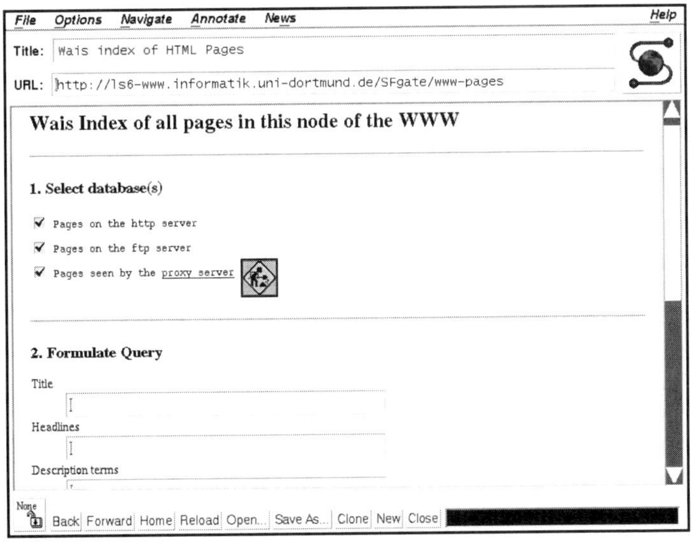

Figure 13.8. A sample SFgate web site search form (Part 1).

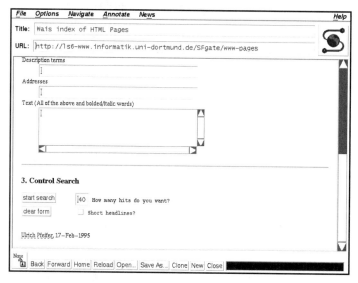

Figure 13.9. *A sample SFgate web site search form (Part 2).*

> **Note:** You may need to do URL indexing for your custom-formatted documents that would ordinarily be indexed using the -t fields option. In this special situation, you can use the -t option twice on the waisindex command line. Order is important, so -t URL should precede -t fields.

FreeWAIS-sf Shortcuts

Although, as shown in Chapter 22, you can build UNIX shell scripts to maintain your WAIS database indexes, you'll want to look at a recently added feature of freeWAIS-sf as an alternative. Version 2 (and later) of freeWAIS-sf include a utility called makedb, which you can use to create, maintain, update, and delete indexes created by waisindex. This feature was so new as *Building an Intranet* was in production that it wasn't yet featured in the freeWAIS-sf user manual, so you may need to look for it in the distribution.

Written in perl, makedb is a front end for waisindex, and it relies on a special configuration file for one or more WAIS indexes. The configuration file, usually named makedb.conf, contains permanent information about the structure of your WAIS database indexes. This includes such things as file lists (including wild-card matching patterns) and search paths, database names, waisindex command-line options, and other housekeeping information about your WAIS indexes. Once you've set up your makedb.conf file, you can update your WAIS indexes quickly and easily, either manually or via cron-run scripts. Here's a sample makedb.conf, taken from the package's man page:

```
# makedb.conf -- makdb configuration file
# Global options
dbdir     = /home/robots/wais/wais-sources
waisindex = /usr/local/ls6/wais/bin/waisindex
wais_opt  = -nocat                  # don't create catalog files
limit     = 10                      # 10 dead files maximum
# User defined variables
docdir    = /home/robots/wais/wais-docs
# the databases
database  = bibdb-html
files     = $docdir/bibdb.html
limit     = 0
options   = -T HTML -t  fields
database  = journals
files     = $docdir/journals/*
limit     = 3
options   = -t  fields
database  = www-pages
wwwroot   = /home/robots/www/pages # new global variable
files     = 'find $wwwroot -name \*.html -print'
options   = -t URL $wwwroot http:
database  = test
dbdir     = /home/crew/pfeifer/tmp/wittenberg
files     = $dbdir/ma*
files    += $dbdir/te*              # append
options   = -t text
```

As you can see, there are three main sections to the makedb.conf file: global options, user-defined variables, and a section defining one or more databases. (This one contains four databases.) Within each section are WAIS index database setup options specific to that database.

> **Tip:** SFgate's author, Ulrich Pfeifer, has also buried an interesting proxy mechanism in that package. (It, too, isn't well documented.) If you run SFgate in proxy mode, it'll scan all incoming HTTP transactions on a system and pass the URLs of HTML documents off to freeWAIS-sf for indexing. This generates a WAIS-searchable index of URLs for later retrieval and/or record keeping. Norbert Govert now maintains Sfgate, while Kai Grobjohann maintains the SFproxy mechanism.

Combining Your Intranet's WAIS Resources

We've talked about using WAIS both as a general indexing tool and as a means of indexing your Web server's document tree. These need not be separate operations, as you've probably guessed from the examples in this chapter.

The computer system used to generate these examples is running both a WAIS server and a Web server, using the same directory tree for both. This illustrates one model you can use in your Intranet: combining the two functions on the same system. Alternatively, you can run your WAIS and Web servers on different systems. This gives you the ability to keep the processing loads of the two separate. In addition, if you want to, you can keep the data completely separate as well. This may make your system maintenance easier to manage.

Don't forget, though, because you're running your Intranet on a TCP/IP network, you have all the facilities of such a network available to use. One feature you can use with your WAIS index databases is the Network File System (NFS), now a standard part of most vendors' TCP/IP networking. NFS allows you to treat a file system on a different computer on your network as if it were local to your computer, as well as to make a file system on your computer available for mounting by other systems on your network. While there are many possible combinations of WAIS and Web services using NFS, one simple example is to run your WAIS server on one computer system and allow that server to NFS-mount your (separate) Web server's file tree for indexing and searching.

glimpse, Another Indexing Tool for Your Intranet

If you've found WAIS to be inappropriate for your Intranet, for whatever reason, you may want to look at the Global Implicit Search tool, glimpse. From programmers Udi Manber and Burra Gopal (University of Arizona) and Sun Wu (National Chung-Cheng University of Taiwan), glimpse is an indexing and query system for searching through files quickly. Glimpse supports searching for misspelled words, as well as Boolean searches, and even searches using UNIX Regular Expressions. It has other advantages over WAIS as well. Unlike standard UNIX word-search utilities like grep, glimpse allows searching without your having to specify which files to search. It simply indexes all the files you tell it to index, and then enables you to issue broad search commands like:

```
$ glimpse keyword
```

glimpse can not only search local file systems, but can also contact a glimpse server running on a remote system to run searches on that remote system's indexed files. Command-line options enable you to tailor your glimpse searches. Reviewers of the glimpse package (see `http://www.scu.edu.au/ausweb95/papers/indexing/morton/`) have stated that, aside from ANSI Z39.50 compatibility issues, glimpse is superior to WAIS, particularly with repect to user functionality. We'll describe the standard glimpse package first, and then move on to a set of tools for putting a Web front end on glimpse searches. The latter will make searches easy for your Intranet's customers, as they can initiate them using fill-in forms on their Web browsers.

Installing glimpse

You'll find both source code and installable binaries for glimpse version 3.0 on the *Building an Intranet* CD-ROM. Binaries are available for Sun Sparc (Solaris 2.x and SunOS 4.1.x), Digital UNIX, Linux, IBM AIX, SGI, HP-UX, freeBSD, and NeXTStep systems; the *Building an Intranet* author also built the package on Solaris 2.4 for x86 using the supplied Solaris Makefile with no modifications. There's also a configure script distributed with the source code. You may be able to use this script to build glimpse on your system if a binary isn't available.

The binary distributions are compressed tar archives. Unpack them with a command pipeline like this one, substituting your system type for *system*:

```
$ zcat glimpse-3.0.bin.system.tar.Z ¦ tar xfv -
```

This will create a new directory named `glimpse-3.0.bin.system` in which you'll find the glimpse binaries and man pages. There's no install script or `Makefile`, so you'll have to manually move the executables and man pages into an appropriate location on your system.

> **Tip:** You'll probably want to check for a later version of glimpse at the glimpse home page, `http://glimpse.cs.arizona.edu:1994/`.

Once compiled, the glimpse package includes several tools:

◆ `glimpseindex`, for creating and maintaining glimpse indexes

◆ `glimpse` and `agrep`, for searching your indexes

◆ `glimpseserver`, for responding to network queries for index searches

Creating a glimpse Index

Building an ordinary glimpse index is quite simple. The basic command is:

```
$ glimpseindex directory_name
```

glimpse will churn away for a few minutes. (The exact time depends on how large your file system is.) Here's a sample run:

```
$ glimpseindex /users/tkevans
This is glimpseindex version 3.0, 1995.
Indexing "/users/tkevans" ...
Size of files being indexed = 27310481 B, Total #of files = 3030
Index-directory: "/users/tkevans"
Glimpse-files created here:
-rw------- 1 staff    137925 Jan 13 11:44 .glimpse_filenames
-rw------- 1 staff     12120 Jan 13 11:44 .glimpse_filenames_index
-rw------- 1 staff   1206716 Jan 13 11:44 .glimpse_index
-rw------- 1 staff      7288 Jan 13 11:44 .glimpse_messages
-rw------- 1 staff       840 Jan 13 11:44 .glimpse_partitions
-rw------- 1 staff     12100 Jan 13 11:44 .glimpse_statistics
```

As you can see, more than 3000 files occupying 273MB of data were indexed. The process took 7 minutes on a 486-66DX2 PC running Solaris 2.4 for x86, while the system was otherwise fairly busy; your mileage will vary depending on what sort of system you're running. The main index file, `.glimpse_index`, is about 1.2MB in size, equivalent to about 4 percent of the total data indexed.

By default, `glimpseindex` skips non-text files in its indexing, although you can force it to index files that have been compressed with `compress`, `gzip`, `binhex`, and `pkzip` utilities, as well as UNIX tar archives. You can have the package build indexes that support faster searching than those built by default, although these indexes will be larger. glimpse's authors recommend using the -o (optimize) option unless you're very tight on available disk space. In addition, you can maintain and add to existing glimpse indexes. For specifics on glimpseindex's many command-line options, see the main glimpseindex Help page on the Web at `http://glimpse.cs.arizona.edu:1994/` `glimpseindexhelp.html`.

glimpse Searches

You can do a simple glimpse search from the command line to test your new index. Here's a sample search, with (edited) output:

```
$ glimpse lynx
/users/tkevans/Mail/akirby: text-only browser 'lynx' instead.)
<option value=\"lynx\">\n" \
/users/tkevans/.newsrc: alt.games.lynx! 1
/users/tkevans/satan-1.1.1/reconfig: @all_www= ("netscape", "Mosaic", "xmosaic",
"lynx");
/users/tkevans/gopher2_2/doc/client.changes:  * text/html viewer support for lynx 2.1
& CERN's www-linemode client
/users/tkevans/gopher2_2/gopher/gopher.rc: map: text/html,lynx -force_html %s,lynx -
force_html -dump %s ¦ lpr
/users/tkevans/gopher2_2/conf.h:  * text/html viewer support for lynx 2.1 &  CERN's
www-linemode client
/users/tkevans/gopher2_2/conf.h: /* #define HTML_COMMAND "lynx -force_html %s" /*
lynx 2.2 or greater */
```

As you can see, the search turned up a number of hits, some in unlikely places. (The search term `lynx` is, of course, the plain text Web browser from the University of Kansas, about which you learned in Chapter 3, "Tools for Implementing an Intranet Infrastructure.") The first hit is in a copy of an old outgoing e-mail message. The next is the `.newsrc` file (a USENET news housekeeping file), and then there are hits in the configuration file for the SATAN Internet scanner, and in several files in the Gopher source code.

The above listing also shows one of glimpse's main advantages over WAIS index searches. As you can see, the hits glimpse brings back are displayed in context, with the full line of the file where it occurs. Glimpse searches, which can be more refined than WAIS searches (see the next paragraph), don't, however, provide the weighted ranking WAIS searches do.

You'll want to check out the main glimpse Help page on the Web at `http://` `glimpse.cs.arizona.edu:1994/glimpsehelp.html` for details, but let's take a quick look at some of the ways you can customize your searches. First, glimpse searches allow an adjustable fudge factor in the spelling of the search words. You can use:

```
$ glimpse -1 'hmtl;thtpd'
```

The -1 (the number 1, not the letter l) option indicates that one spelling error is allowed in each of the two (purposely misspelled) search terms, separated by a semicolon in the example. Further, you can specify you want case-insensitive matches with -i, specify complete words with -w, and restrict your searches to filenames matching a specified pattern with -F. You can also specify with -J that glimpse is to contact a remote computer running the glimpeserver software and do its search there.

The glimpseserver Software

If you expect demand for glimpse searches to be high on your Intranet, or, more likely, if you want to centralize your index, you'll want to install the glimpseserver software on one of your systems. This software can respond to network requests for glimpse searches from other computers on your Intranet. You'll definitely want to do this if you plan to use glimpseHTTP, about which you'll learn later in this chapter.

Besides centralizing your glimpse services, glimpseserver will generally provide faster server for your customers. This is because glimpseserver runs as a UNIX daemon on your server machine. It reads your index at startup time and is therefore faster to respond to search requests than if it had to read the index files at request time.

> **Warning:** glimpseserver has almost no security built in, so you won't want to make any non-public or otherwise confidential indexes available, especially if you're connected to the Internet.

Searching glimpse Indexes with glimpseHTTP

You can write CGI-bin scripts to enable your customers to run glimpse index searches via a Web fill-in form. Relatively simple perl scripts can construct glimpse commands from form data, and then return the results in HTML. You won't want to bother to do this, however, because the glimpse folks at the University of Arizona have already done it for you.

glimpseHTTP is a glimpse search engine-HTTP gateway. Its main advantage is that your searches become a combination of Web browsing and searching. By creating different indexes with glimpse, your customers can browse areas of your Web server, for example, and then initiate searches only after zeroing in on a subject area.

Figures 13.10 and 13.11 show a couple of glimpseHTTP search pages—one apparently quite plain, and the other with jazzy graphics. In both cases, you're allowed to specify your search in considerable detail, using the features of glimpse you learned about earlier. Figure 13.10 is particularly interesting since it uses a variety of HTML form markup to help you specify your search, belying its plain black-and-white appearance. Note the scrollable regions, allowing selection of The Bard's plays and poetry by individual work, by category, or by both. You'll find a long and growing list of Web sites that have implemented glimpseHTTP searches on the glimpseHTTP home page, `http://glimpse.cs.arizona.edu:1994/ghttp/`.

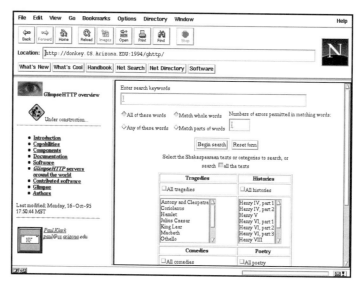

Figure 13.10. *A glimpseHTTP search of Shakespeare's works.*

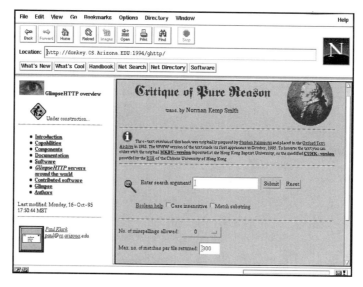

Figure 13.11. *A glimpseHTTP search of Kant's Critique of Pure Reason.*

Harvesting Your Indexed Data

Regardless of the choices you make in indexing your data, you would probably like some sort of high-level tool that gives you and your customers a larger view of your indexed information. In other words, you would like some sort of meta-indexing tool that your Intranet's customers can use to find out what sort of data indexes might be available, and then provide search capabilities to the data itself. Of course, you can hand-edit HTML documents listing all your available indexes, but the ideal solution to this problem is to have your Intranet's computer systems do this for you automatically.

Researchers at the University of Colorado, University of Arizona, University of Southern California, and the Transarc Corporation have developed a system called Harvest for just this purpose. According to the Harvest Home page (`http://harvest.cs.colorado.edu/`), the package is an integrated set of tools to gather, extract, organize, search, cache, and replicate relevant information across the Internet.

This meta-description is not only quite a mouthful, but it also isn't very good as an introduction to the package. Let's try and break it down, describing each of the four main parts of Harvest to make the package's purpose more clear:

- The first major piece of the Harvest system is called Gatherer. Gatherer accesses and catalogs data of many different kinds on the Internet (or your Intranet).

- Harvest Broker retrieves the information cataloged by one or more Gatherers, then indexes it. Broker retrieves information not only from a local system, but also from remote systems on the network where Gatherer may be running. Once Broker has located one or more Gatherer(s), the Gatherer information is re-indexed efficiently. Finally, Broker produces high-level access to the information that it has indexed through HTML fill-in forms for users and their Web browsers.

- Harvest Replicator distributes the information indexed by Broker(s) across the network to other Replicators. Thus, networked Replicators merge all of the indexed information from all known Gatherer/Broker systems, and then make that information searchable from anywhere on the network. Replicator can (optionally) communicate with other Replicators on the Internet at large, including the Harvest Server Registry maintained at the University of Colorado, with information about all known Harvest systems accessible on the Internet.

- The Harvest Object Cache temporarily stores data that has been retrieved from Web, Gopher, and ftp servers on the local network. (See Chapter 8 for information on Gopher and ftp.) When a Web browser calls for the same information again, the information is retrieved from the local cache rather than from across the network. Through a special feature of the Object Cache, you can set up an httpd accelerator to speed up access to Web server data.

Figure 13.12 shows a schematic diagram of the Harvest System, from the Harvest User Manual, reprinted by permission.

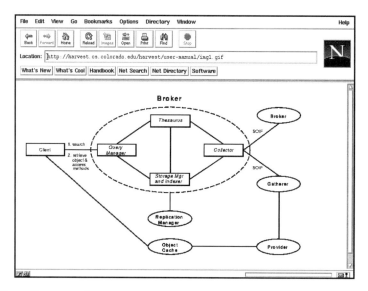

Figure 13.12. *Harvest System overview.*

> **Tip:** Besides the main Harvest system, there are some optional components you may want to look into. These include support for reading and indexing WordPerfect 5.1, MIF (FrameMaker's Maker Interchange Format), and RTF (Rich Text Format) files. Look for these in the `components` subdirectory of the Harvest distribution sites.

Harvest is supported on UNIX systems from Digital Equipment Corporation (OSF/1 2.0 and 3.0, now called Digital UNIX) and Sun Microsystems (SunOS 4.1.x and 5.x). Because the package is still under development, it's not included on the *Building an Intranet* CD-ROM. Binaries for the supported systems, along with source code for the package and unsupported binaries for several other systems, including IBM's AIX, Hewlett-Packard's HP-UX, SGI's IRIX, and Linux, are at the Harvest software-distribution (anonymous ftp) sites. You'll find a list of these sites at `http:/ /harvest.cs.colorado.edu/harvest/gettingsoftware.html`.

Installing Harvest

Binary Harvest distributions (GNU gzipped tar archives) should be unpacked into an empty directory, from which they can be run directly. If you're compiling the Harvest source, run the configure script first, and then enter:

```
# make all install
```

If you need to change any of the Harvest configuration defaults, run `configure`, and then edit the Makefile or `source/common/include/config.h`. Next run these two commands:

```
# make reconfigure
# make all install
```

Harvest is a large package, requiring about 25M of free disk space to build. It'll take you half an hour or longer to do the compile. If you'd rather just build parts of the system, you can build the individual Harvest components (that is, Gatherer, Broker, and so on) separately. Just change to the `src` directory, run `configure`, then:

```
# make component-name install-component-name
```

Configuring Your Web Server for Harvest

Before you can run the Harvest system or its components, you'll need to do some reconfiguration of your Web server to accommodate it. Edit your `srm.conf` file (NCSA httpd) or add `Exec` and `Pass` entries to the CERN httpd's `httpd.conf` file. For the Netscape server, there are several steps:

Select URL mapping, and then map an URL to a local directory and enter the path to the Harvest directory.

Select CGI and Server Parsed HTML, and then Activate CGI as a file type, and finally Browse Files. Select the Harvest directory, and then click I'd like to activate CGI as a file type.

If you've installed the Harvest Broker, you'll need to make a couple of changes to its configuration files to enable the Web interface. Edit both `HarvestGather.cgi` and `BrokerQuery.pl.cgi` to include the path to the main Harvest directory. In the former file, include the path to the GNU `gzip` program. In the latter file, you may need to change the very first line (the path to your perl executable).

Finally, start up the Harvest system by running the script `RunHarvest` in the main Harvest directory. You'll be prompted with a series of questions about your to-be-indexed data.

Should You Use Harvest?

Even this brief description of the Harvest system indicates that the package is a complex one. You're probably wondering whether setting up the system is worth it for your Intranet. Several demonstrations of Harvest-related Web sites can tell you this for sure. Figure 13.13 shows a Harvest broker specializing in free PC software. This simple fill-in form allows you to search six major Internet-accessible archives for software, with WAIS weighted ranking of your hits. (The underlying index is, as this suggests, a WAIS index.) In Figure 13.14, you can see the partial results of a search on the word genealogy. Each hit appears as a clickable hyperlink, accompanied by brief descriptions of the software packages shown, extracted from a WAIS index database. By clicking on the hyperlink, you can download the software package. Here, the Harvest system is used to integrate indexing information on a particular topic—free software for PCs—from a number of different distribution sites around the Internet.

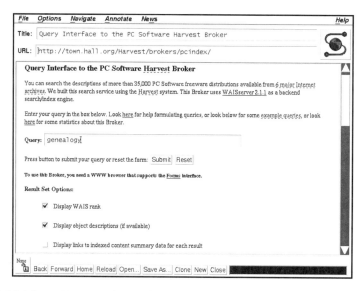

Figure 13.13. *A PC Software Harvest Broker search form.*

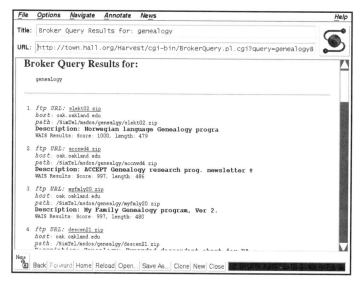

Figure 13.14. *The results of a search in PC Software Harvest Broker.*

As you'd expect, the folks at the University of Colorado, where Harvest originated, have set up a worthwhile demonstration of the package's capabilities. Based on indexes created with glimpseindex, this one, shown in overlapping screen shots in Figure 13.15 and 13.16, is quite complex. Let's look at its features.

◆ Indexed data comes from several sources, including World Wide Web, anonymous ftp, and USENET newsgroups. (See Search by server in the middle of Figure 13.15.) The user can select one or more of them.

◆ Searches can be limited by document type. (See Search only in at the bottom of Figure 13.15.)

◆ Searches can be specified for an individual's documents, or for a particular group's documents using a pull down menu (as shown at the top of Figure 13.16).

◆ You can request that all documents be searched. (See Search all sources in Figure 13.16.)

◆ Several Query Options (shown in the middle of Figure 13.16) are available, including case sensitivity, whole-word search, and allowed misspellings.

◆ At the bottom of Figure 13.16, you can specify Result Set Options—how you want the output of your search to be displayed—including displaying the context of your hits, object descriptions, and any indexed summary information.

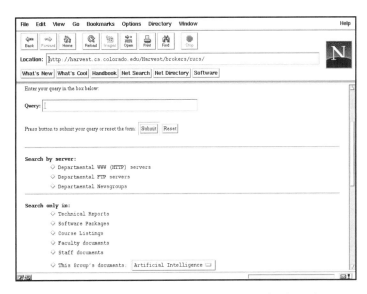

Figure 13.15. *The University of Colorado Computer Science Department Broker (Part 1).*

You may have made several observations about these two Harvest Brokers. First, the underlying indexing that the two use are different. The PC Software broker, as noted earlier, uses a WAIS index. The Colorado Broker uses glimpse, since it features the ability to incorporate misspellings in your searches. This is an important feature of the Harvest system. You can use WAIS, glimpse, or both, as your indexing infrastructure. Harvest's own internal indexing is different from either, but can include both.

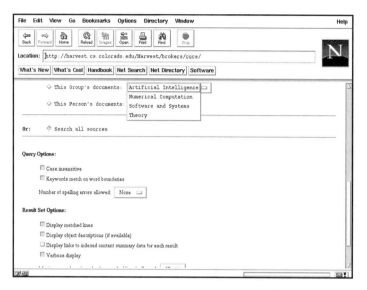

Figure 13.16. *The University of Colorado Computer Science Department Broker (Part 2).*

> **Note:** Harvest also supports use of the Nebula File System, being developed at Pennsylvania State University. NebulaFS, according to its developers, "combines the functionality of a file system with information management operations similar to those provided by an object-oriented database system." For more information on NebulaFS, see `http://www.sys.cse.psu.edu/NEBFS/nebula.html`.

Harvest's developers argue strongly for your including it in your Intranet. Here's what they say:

"Our measurements indicate that Harvest can reduce server load by a factor of over 6,000, network traffic by a factor of 60, and index space requirements by a factor of over 40 when building indexes compared with other systems, such as Archie, WAIS, and the World Wide Web Worm."

> **Note:** The Harvest developers are working on one or more commercial implementations of the package.

Your Corporate Phone Book and Your Intranet

Most books about World Wide Web server setup and administration provide a sample CGI-bin script for searching simple telephone book lists. See, for example, the script demonstrated in David M. Chandler's *Running a Perfect Web Site*, published by Sams.net's sister imprint Que Publishing, ISBN 0-7897-0210-X. (Information on this and other Macmillan Computer Publishing books is available at `http://www.mcp.com/`.)

These scripts are usually very simple perl or UNIX shell scripts that use an HTML fill-in form to collect the user's input, and then pass it off to the UNIX grep command to look up the name in a plain text file containing names and phone numbers. While this sort of thing may be a perfectly adequate Web-based phonebook for your Intranet, if you're part of a large organization you'll want to look at a service called ph. This is a true network database package, specifically developed at the University of Illinois' Computing and Communications Services Office for campus phonebook information. Often referred to as CSO Phonebook, the source code for the ph package is on the *Building an Intranet* CD-ROM. The NCSA httpd server software you may have installed (also on the CD-ROM) includes source code for a front end for ph database queries. This front end generates the fill-in form shown in part in Figure 13.17.

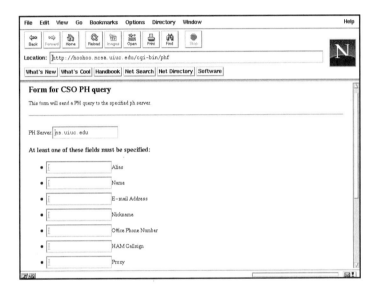

Figure 13.17. *NCSA front end form to a ph phonebook.*

Note: There are stand-alone ph clients available which work independently of Web browsers. You'll find ph clients for several different computer systems, including UNIX systems, Windows, and the Macintosh, at ftp://ftp.cso.uiuc.edu/pub/packages/ph.

Installing ph on Your Intranet

The CSO Phonebook server program itself is called qi, which is short for query interpreter. The distribution is preconfigured for the University of Illinois' own purposes, and there's a good deal of local customization you'll need to do for your own installation. You'll do your local configuration in the configs/defaults file, where you'll find a great deal of UIUC-specific configuration, including local UIUC e-mail addresses, network names and numerical IP addresses, and many other things. You will need to change all of these to reflect your own Intranet.

A couple additional things you can do are to restrict access to your phonebook database by IP address and to add Kerberos authentication. You'll find details on these and other configuration items in the doc subdirectory of the qi distribution. One important thing to note about the configs/defaults file is the specification of a C compiler. The default is cc, but you may need to change this to whatever ANSI-compatible compiler you normally use, such as gcc or Sun's unbundled acc compiler. (The SunOS 4.1.x bundled cc compiler won't work.)

Second, the distribution comes with a Configure script, but it needs a bit of a kick-start to make it properly identify your system. You need to tell Configure the sort of system on which you're building the package. Take a look at the contents of the configs directory, where you'll find configuration files for a large number of UNIX systems. Pick yours and run Configure with it as a command-line argument. For example, to configure qi for an IBM AIX system, use this command:

```
# Configure aix
```

This will dynamically create customized Makefiles in each of the system's subdirectories with AIX-specific setup. You can then build the package with make or, if you're lucky, make install. Since the package is a network package, you'll also need to modify your server's /etc/services and /etc/inetd.conf files to add support. See the qi documentation for details.

Building Your Phonebook Database

Your next step in setting up the qi server is to create your phonebook database itself. You specify your database's format and content in a configuration file you'll build. The default filename extension for this file is .cnf, and you'll find a sample named product.cnf in the sample subdirectory. These files are based on a set of fields that are hard-coded into the qi server source code. UIUC recommends that you not change the source, but rather tailor your .cnf file to the existing fields, making changes as necessary in that file. The field names are just arbitrary labels, so you can use them for your own purposes.

Next, create an input file based on your .cnf file's setup. The input file is simply a plain text file containing the information about each person whose name and information is to go into the database. Each record is a single line, with the appropriate field number and actual data included. The format is simple:

```
field-number:data <TAB> field-number:data <TAB> etc
```

Not all fields are required to be present, and every entry need not have every field filled in. <TAB> represents the TAB character.

Once you're done, you can feed your input file to the indexer to create your index. The qi distribution includes several utilities that make this easy. These include:

◆ sizedb, for figuring out the size of your database based on your .cnf file and your input file.

◆ credb, which creates an empty database of the size you just determined with sizedb.

◆ maked, which actually creates your database, taking its input from your plain text data file.

◆ makei, which creates an index for your database.

◆ build, which completes the database.

Testing Your Phonebook Server

The qi distribution comes with a command-line UNIX client, named ph, with which you can test your database. Here's a sample command line:

```
$ ph -m -s servername name=somename
```

Here's part of the output of a query to the UIUC server using ns.uiuc.edu (the main UIUC qi server) as servername and the last name of NCSA httpd pioneer Rob McCool:

```
-----------------------------------------
          name: mccool robert martin
         phone: (217) 398-5031
       address: 515 bash ct 7
              : champaign, il  61820
office_location: 24 OCB
              : 508 Sixth Street
              : Champaign, IL 61820
     left_uiuc: 10/1995
      email to: r-mccool@uiuc.edu (r-mccool@students.uiuc.edu)
-----------------------------------------
```

Using ph on Your Intranet

Assuming your test went well, you're ready to make your ph server accessible on your Intranet. Let's take a look at how it'll work. Earlier, Figure 13.17 showed a Web front end to the ph service. See Figure 13.18 for the output of the same query from the Netscape browser. As you can see, the output is the same, but the fill-in form interface is a good deal easier to use than the command line version.

As you can see from Figure 13.17, the default ph form provided with the NCSA httpd server software has the UIUC qi server's name hard-coded. Although the onscreen form enables the user to enter a different server name, you'll want to change the UIUC default for your Intranet's own server name. Do this by editing the cgi-src/phf.c file on your Web server, and then recompiling the source using the Makefile. Of course, there's no reason you can't build a custom form and CGI-bin script of your own for your ph server, using the NCSA source as a model and customizing it to your organization.

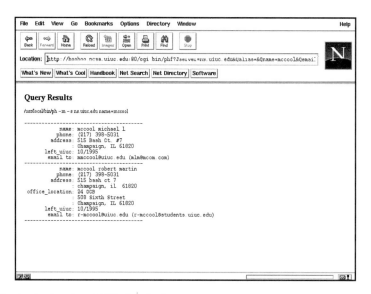

Figure 13.18. *Results of a form-based CSO phonebook query.*

> **Tip:** The ph FAQ document, a copy of which is included in the doc subdirectory of the qi distribution, includes a shell script you can use to update and maintain your CSO phonebook database. This should ease the task of adding, deleting, and changing names in the database. In fact, you can set this script up to run via the cron daemon, and then turn over the basic data entry to your staff. Once a day, or however frequently you choose, your script will automatically fire up and update your database.

Commercial Index-and-Retrieve Packages

A growing number of companies are coming out with commercial software packages for creating Web-searchable index databases for Intranets. As noted in Chapter 8, for example, there's at least one commercial implementation of WAIS, by America Online's new subsidiary WAIS, Inc. Because the main concepts underlying WAIS have been well explored in this chapter, we'll skip over the commercial implementation. Check out the package at http://www.wais.com/. Meanwhile, let's sample several of the other commercial packages.

OpenText and Latitude

OpenText is an indexing search engine from Open Text, Inc. It reads HTML documents on an Intranet (or on the Internet) and indexes them, including following all the hyperlinks in the documents and any subsequently encountered documents and their hyperlinks. Some of OpenText's features include word and phrase search with Boolean operators. In addition, OpenText enables you to assign weights to your search words/phrases and limit your searches to specified parts of HTML documents, such as the document titles or the URLs themselves.

You can retrieve search results as full Web documents, or you can just look at the context in which your search words/phrases were found. As with WAIS, you can use the results of one search to frame another by asking OpenText to "Find similar pages." Although it's a commercial product, you can do demo OpenText searches at http://www.opentext.com/. Figure 13.19 shows an OpenText Power Search form with two search terms, corporate and intranet, filled in; note the specification that the words must be near each other.

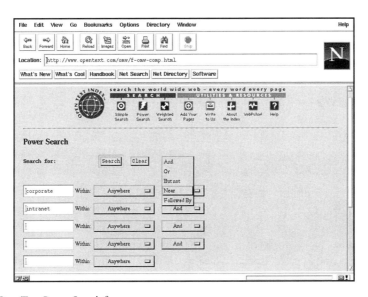

Figure 13.19. *OpenText Power Search form.*

The result of Figure 13.19's OpenText search appears in Figure 13.20. It found four documents. Notice that, in addition to retrieving the entire documents, you can specify See matches on the page and Find similar pages.

Open Text Inc.'s high-end product is called Latitude. Based on the OpenText search engine, this product understands and indexes not only HTML documents, but also a wide variety of other document formats, including, according to the company, over 40 different word processor formats. Based on the published descriptions of this product, the package includes a variety of tools that work as Web helper applications to display located documents in their proper format. The Latitude product suite also includes a Web server. Open Text and Netscape Communications Corporation have announced a joint product incorporating the Netscape Commerce and Communications Web servers into the Latitude suite, apparently replacing the Latitude server.

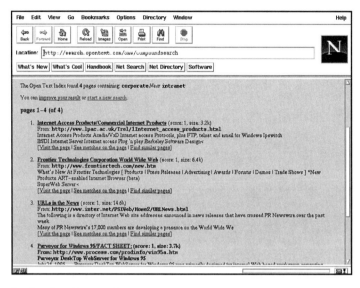

Figure 13.20. *Results of an OpenText search.*

Fulcrum Surfboard

A long-time maker of full-text search technologies, Fulcrum, Inc. now has a Web-based product called Surfboard. As with OpenText, Surfboard can search both local and network indexes, and can search multiple indexes in a single pass. You can use natural language, multiword phrases, fielded searches, wildcard word matching (such as comput* to match computers, computing, computation, and the like), and Boolean constructs. It also supports relevance searching. In addition, you can specify the kind of output you'd like from your search, with choices including listing or tabular arrangement, HTML, plain text, or document native format, and you have several choices for sorting. Figure 13.21 shows a Surfboard search form with multiple database indexes, including remote ones. You'll find more information about Surfboard at `http://www.fulcrum.com/Demo/demoope.htm`.

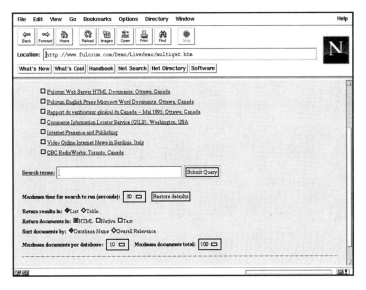

Figure 13.21. *A Fulcrum Surfboard search.*

Verity Topic

Topic is another product suite, consisting of eight products, including both an Enterprise and an Internet indexing/search engine. The former supports major office applications' data file formats, while the latter adds support for HTML documents on a Web. Both search engines support so-called fuzzy-logic searches, as well as concept, weighted, and Boolean searches. Following the overall structure of the Topic system, the Topic client is not a Web browser, but a stand-alone application, and is available for several UNIX systems, Windows NT, OS/2, and the Macintosh. A demo of Topic searches is available at http://www.verity.com/demo/d/Toppic_Demos/tisdemo.html, where you'll find several databases to search, including a newswire database.

Figure 13.22 shows a Topic search on this current events database. Search terms relate to the conflict between New Hampshire and Delaware over the states' 1996 Presidential Primary Elections, while Figure 13.23 shows the results of the search. Retrieved documents display your search terms in boldface.

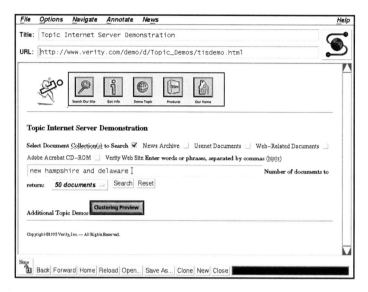

Figure 13.22. *A Topic search form.*

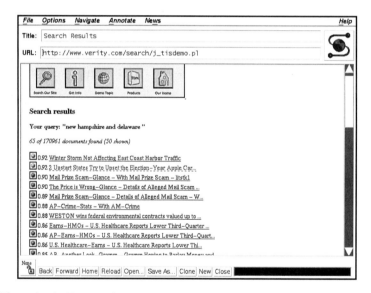

Figure 13.23. *The results of a Topic search.*

Architext Excite

Like Topic and Surfboard, Excite enables users to search multiple database indexes, and includes both concept and keyword search. Queries can be natural language, with search results sorted by what Excite calls Confidence (similar to other weighted relevance searching). Its fill-in search form is quite similar to the others shown in this chapter. Excite indexes only plain text and HTML documents.

Excite's primary distinction is that it's available for no-cost download. You can retrieve it from `http://www00.excite.com/navigate/`. Excite is available for several UNIX systems. The licensing document that comes with the downloadable package indicates that Excite can be used internally without any charge, although you are supposed to register the package. (You must give your e-mail address to download it.) No support comes with the free package, but support contracts, which include the right to future upgrades, are available for purchase. Expect the text- and HTML-only limits to be removed in future versions, since competing products don't have them.

> **Note:** Another UNIX-based index-and-retrieval package, Personal Library Software's PLWeb, is available for no-cost 45-day evaluations to registered users. See `http://www.pls.com` for details of the offer. A demonstration is online there, but you may want to look at what some of PLS' customers are doing with the package. See, for example, AT&T's searchable Toll-Free 800 Directory at `http://www.att.net/`.

Summary

Focusing on indexing and retrieving data on your Intranet, this chapter has covered general-purpose indexing packages that can be accessed using a Web browser. You've learned how to index your data, and how to provide Web-browser interfaces to enable your customers to search and retrieve data from them. In addition, you've learned about a specialized database package that you can use to maintain an online corporate telephone directory for your customers. Finally, you surveyed the commercial index-and-retrieve market. Specifically, you have:

◆ Set up the Wide-Area Information Service on your Intranet, for creating custom, searchable indexes.

◆ Set up Glimpse and its companion package GlimpseHTTP for incorporating Glimpse indexes into your Intranet.

◆ Set up Harvest, a set of tools for gathering and distributing information about indexed data on Web servers and other networked servers, and enabled your customers to access this indexed data using their Web browsers.

◆ Set up the CSO ph package, a specialized network database for corporate telephone books, and integrated it into your Intranet, with your customers able to do phonebook lookups using their Web browsers.

◆ Learned about several commercial packages that you can use to create Web-searchable indexes on your Intranet.

In Chapter 14, "Web Access to Commercial Database Applications," you'll learn about the growing number of Web interfaces to commercial and other database packages, including the major relational database packages that are widely used. You'll also see how you can create your own database applications using other Web tools.

CHAPTER 14

◆

Web Access to Commercial Database Applications

As with so many other computer applications' vendors, commercial database vendors are racing to provide Web-accessible front ends to their packages. If you've struggled to build useful, user-friendly database applications using the tools your database vendor has provided, or using custom programming, you'll no doubt welcome the idea of using a Web browser and fill-in forms as an alternative to building user interfaces from scratch or with vendors' application-building tools.

In this chapter, you'll learn about a number of commercial database vendors' Web front ends, third-party database interfaces that are Web-enabled, and several no-cost Web/database interfaces. You'll also learn about creating custom CGI-bin scripts for accessing your database applications.

Chapter Objectives

As with the rest of the chapters in this book, let's begin by laying out some chapter objectives. This will help you get oriented to the material to be presented; you may want to refer back to this list as you work your way through the chapter. In this chapter, you'll

◆ Review important information about the Web's Common Gateway Interface (CGI), to get a bird's-eye view of how Web access to UNIX databases works.

◆ Learn about no-cost and commercial gateways to UNIX database packages from Oracle, Informix/Illustra, and Sybase, as well as those from third-party vendors.

◆ Learn about developing your own Web front ends to these and other UNIX database packages.

◆ Learn about accessing PC database applications using a Web browser front end.

This chapter does not touch on designing and developing the database applications themselves. You will want to consult your database package's documentation for that information. In this chapter, it's assumed you're already running some database package, and that you have an application you'd like to access using your Web browsers. Of course, you may find once you start accessing your database with your Web browsers, you'll want to change the database's design. This is no different from the traditional database application-development process, in which you use the application for awhile to see how you want to change it.

Accessing Large Commercial Database Packages— The Big Picture

Whatever UNIX database package you use on your Intranet—and whatever bells and whistles it provides for developing database applications, entering queries, and generating reports—database access boils down to two broad processes:

◆ Formulating and submitting structured query language (SQL) queries or data-entry statements to the database engine

◆ Receiving and processing the results of the query

These two processes are, of course, traditional database processes: query and report, and data entry. Whether the user hand-edits SQL queries or fills in an onscreen query or data-entry form, the objective is the same: to pass the query or new data to the database back end. Similarly, when the database spits out the results of a query or data entry, an application has to receive it and generate human-readable output (on screen or on paper) or machine-readable output in some specific format.

Web access to these databases involves exactly the same two processes, with important differences:

◆ Your customers perform queries and data entry using fill-in Web forms (created with HTML), in which they enter query keywords or other search criteria through menu selections, click buttons, free-form text blocks, or fill-in-the-blanks.

◆ CGI-bin scripts take the information entered in the form and bundle it up into valid SQL queries or data-entry updates. They then pass it off to the database back end.

◆ The same CGI-bin scripts receive the results back from the database engine after processing. They format the report in HTML and pass it back to the customer's Web browser for display.

To Thine Ownself Be True—An Example

HTML fill-in forms take the place of the database vendor's graphical interface, your laboriously painted custom graphical interface, or your text-based input forms. Similarly, CGI-bin scripts take the place of the custom programming you've done using the database vendor's development tools, a standalone programming language such as the C language, or other custom tools.

Let's focus on a near-hypothetical SQL query to help you get oriented. Figure 14.1, a slightly different view of a screen you saw in Chapter 13, shows what might be a Web-based interface to a database application. Although this form is actually a front end to the glimpse search engine (described in the last chapter), let's assume for the sake of this example it's an interface to an Oracle, Informix, or other commercial database application. Accordingly, let's take a detailed look at it.

> **Note:** Because this is such a terrific HTML form, you may want to look at the source for it with your Web browser (at http://the-tech.mit.edu/Shakespeare/search.html). In Netscape, open the View menu and select Document Source; in Mosaic, open File menu and select View Source. Or save and print the source for reference if you'd like.

First, notice how the page's author has used several features of standard HTML forms markup to create this striking and quite complex form. At the same time, the form is easy to grasp at a glance. You see small and large fill-in boxes, along with radio buttons and form-housekeeping buttons (such as Begin Search and Reset Form).

More importantly, occupying most of the center of the form are four independent menu selectors, three of which have scroll bars for viewing choices. You can select any or all of them to create an almost infinite number of quite complex queries. Let's create one now. Take a look at Figure 14.2, where a famous line (*To thine ownself be true*) has been entered in the keywords box. Also, several possible works are selected. Among the possible sources selected for the line are two of the Tragedies, one History, and all the Sonnets. This quotation, which is one of Shakespeare's most famous lines, is not (the widespread 1970s Me-First belief to the contrary) one of the Ten Commandments; nor is it from anywhere else in the Bible.

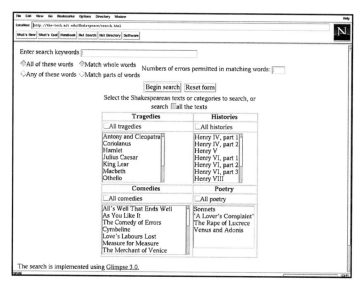

Figure 14.1. *A Shakespeare Web search form.*

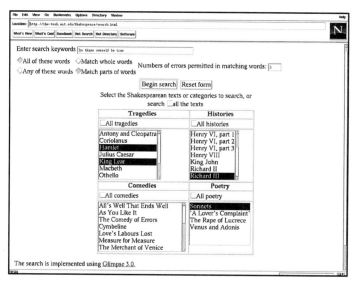

Figure 14.2. *A complex search on a Shakespeare Web form.*

Of course, it would have been possible to have just taken the defaults and had the search hit all the works, but let's stick with the program for just a little longer. Look at the form, and then consider the SQL statement that you would need to produce the same query in a traditional relational database application. Something along the lines of the following might do it:

```
select speaker, title, act, scene from (( tragedies where (title = "King Lear" or
title = "Hamlet")) or ( histories where title = "Richard III" ) or verse from (poetry
where title = "sonnets")) and line = "to thine ownself be true"
```

Now, the above may be illegal, even doggerel, SQL that would be rejected by any self-respecting database application's query parser, even if it does have the right number of opening and closing parentheses. Nevertheless, you get the idea. For even the most computer-macho of your customers, the simple, intuitive fill-in form shown above beats hand-crafting such an SQL query every time. Your first job, as a Web CGI-bin scripter, then, is to build scripts that will take the user input from these fill-in forms, convert them into truly legal SQL syntax, and then pass them off to the database engine.

But wait. You've only done half your job. What do you do with the results that come back from the query? Our not-too-terribly-complex Shakespearean sample query has a simple, four-word answer. Your customer's Web browser, however, is powerless to read it unless your script both passes it back to the browser and does so in a format the browser can recognize.

Just as you have had to negotiate your database's Report Writer to format the output of queries into something meaningful and attractive, you'll need to do the same with the data your CGI-bin scripts pull from the database. The happy news is that you get to use HTML in formatting this output, something you've already learned in building your Intranet. As a result, you're all set to use something like the following perl code in your CGI-bin script to return the answer to your customer in HTML. (The matter after the # signs is commentary.)

```
print "Content-type text/html\n\n"; # send a MIME data type/sub-type header and a
➥blank line
print "<HTML><HEAD><TITLE>Query Response</TITLE></HEAD>"; # send necessary beginning
➥HTML markup and a document title
print "<BODY><H1>Results of Your Query</H1>"; # more HTML markup; print a Level-1
➥HTML headline
print "In Shakespeare's <EM>$play</EM>, Act $act, Scene $scene, Speaker $speaker said
➥\"$line\"\n"; # send back the data, with variable substitution
print "</BODY></HTML> # close up the HTML document with concluding markup
```

This fragment is pretty self-explanatory, but it's your second major key to providing your Intranet's customers access to your database application via their Web browsers. Here, you're dynamically creating a complete HTML document line by line, using perl's print command. (HTML markup appears in uppercase.) The script uses variables that it assigned earlier when it received the data your customer entered into the fill-in form. The data, in the form of variables, was passed off to the database engine. Data coming back is assigned to your variables, and then hot-plugged into the HTML output for viewing in your customer's Web browser. Figure 14.3 shows what such an output would look like.

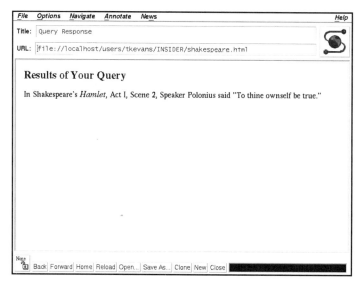

Figure 14.3. *The HTML results of the Shakespeare query.*

Polonius' Point

It doesn't matter that the Shakespeare database we've actually searched in this example is a Glimpse index, not an Oracle database. What *does* matter is you're taking and processing user input using a standard, ready-to-use, interchangeable set of tools, almost custom-made for your Intranet:

◆ The Form subset of the HyperText Markup Language.

◆ The Web's Common Gateway Interface, with its standard methods of receiving data from a form, passing it off to an external program, and getting the results back, using environment variables.

◆ The use of HTML to dynamically format and return the results of the customer's query to his Web browser for viewing.

You could take the Shakespeare search form, and its underlying CGI-bin perl script, and have the hardest half of the work of interfacing your database with your Intranet already done. (As with other things you find on the Web, be sure you don't violate copyrights when you steal them.) Although you can't get to this script, you can get to the SFgate script you saw in Chapter 13; it, too, is a CGI-bin script written in perl. Nearly every freeware and commercial database gateway package uses the same basic, CGI-bin approach; scripts may or may not be in perl (although most are), but the basic ideas behind them are just what you've been learning. Read on for specifics.

Important CGI Basics

Let's leave *Hamlet* behind and take a quick look at some CGI basics. All are relevant to Web database application interfaces, and you'll want to bear them in mind as you work your way through the rest of this chapter.

◆ Each piece of data your customer enters into an HTML fill-in form (query keywords or new data entry) is available to be passed, as UNIX standard input, directly to your database engine by your CGI-bin script.

◆ You can include additional data in form output using the INPUT TYPE=hidden HTML markup (see Appendix B, "HTML and CGI Quick Reference"). You can hard-code this information into your forms or you can dynamically set it based on user behavior—or other factors that the customer doesn't see but that your CGI-bin script might need for processing.

◆ CGI-bin scripts carry with them a good deal of standard information in the form of environment variables. The variables include not only the customer's Web browser type, but also the TCP/IP address and hostname of the user's computer, his userid and access authentication (if the server is configured to provide it), and the MIME data type/sub-types supported by the browser.

Let's talk just a bit about the second and third items above, involving CGI-bin scripts and environment variables. If you're using the NCSA httpd server, you'll find a useful CGI-bin test script comes with the software, which you can run with your browser to get a feel for this. The script should be in the cgi-bin subdirectory of your Web server software tree, under the name test-cgi. You may also find test-cgi.tcl, an alternative version. Figure 14.4 shows part of the output of the latter, run from the NCSA Mosaic X Window (UNIX) browser.

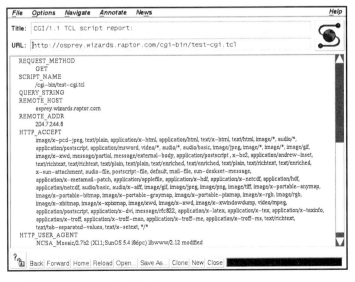

Figure 14.4. The output of the NCSA test-cgi.tcl *script.*

The `test-cgi.tcl` script is not written in perl, but rather in John Ousterhout's *Tool command language* (Tcl). Tcl is an embeddable scripting language, and it comes with a companion graphical user interface builder toolkit called Tk. Tcl/Tk is not as widely used for CGI-bin scripting as perl, but it has a growing and fanatical user base, and it's being used for both CGI-bin scripting and general use.

The latest-available release of Tcl/Tk is on the *Building an Intranet* CD-ROM, but its development continues at Sun Microsystems Labs, with frequent updates, so you'll want to check the Tcl/Tk home page at `http://www.sunlabs.com/research/tcl`. Ousterhout has also written a book about the package, *Tcl and the Tk Toolkit*. Its home page is at `http://www.aw.com/cp/Oust.html`. If you're interested in pursuing Tcl/Tk for your CGI-bin scripts, you'll want a copy, as well as a copy of the NCSA library of Tcl/Tk routines from `ftp://ftp.ncsa.uiuc.edu/Web/httpd/Unix/ncsa-httpd/cgi/tcl-proc-args.tar.Z`. You can find further Web-related Tcl/Tk resources at `http://www.sco.com/Technology/tcl/Tcl.html#Tcl-NetandWeb`.

To continue this digression just a bit further, Don Libes' package, expect, (also on the *Building an Intranet* CD-ROM) is an important Tcl/Tk application for automating ordinarily interactive procedures. While you probably won't use it for CGI-bin scripting, you may find it an otherwise useful tool in maintaining your Intranet. Libes' book *Exploring Expect*, which has a compact introduction to Tcl/Tk, is on the Web at `http://www.ora.com/gnn/ora/item/expect.html`.

CGI-Bin Environment Variables

To get back to the screenshot, although you can't read the fine print, you can see a partial listing of the standard set of CGI-bin environment variables. This is CGI-bin Solid Gold. You're free to use and manipulate all this ready-rolled information with your scripts to supplement the customer's query or data-entry data, which the script also, naturally, passes.

CGI-bin scripts often generate fill-in forms on the fly, based on such things as the initiating user's Web browser type (for example, Netscape, Mosaic, or Lynx). You can tailor your input screens based on the customer's browser type. For example, you might use Netscape's proprietary HTML extensions where appropriate, but not for browsers that don't handle them correctly. (Tables and font changes are two important examples.) You can set and use hidden variables in these scripts for many reasons, not the least important of which is to track the customer's complete session with the database package. (This maintenance-of-state is how the ubiquitous shopping cart CGI-bin scripts you may have used for shopping on the Web work, incidentally.) With perl (and with Tcl/Tk) these environment variables can be read into programming arrays for fast and efficient handling.

CGI-Bin Interaction with Your Database Engine

All this information—both the customer-entered data or query information and the CGI-bin standard environment variables—can be processed as needed, and then handed off to your database engine. Data coming back from the engine is also subject to the same sort of manipulation by your scripts. In this context, it's critical that you have an intimate understanding of your database package's operation, as well as the table and record-and-field structure of your databases themselves. Most importantly, you must know precisely how your database engine accepts and processes UNIX standard input. You need to know how queries have to be formatted, what to do with long lines, whether there are confirmation dialog boxes that have to be negotiated, and the like.

This knowledge can help you craft your CGI-bin scripts so they output SQL queries or data-entry commands that are compatible with both your database package and the database itself. Just as important, you must have a complete understanding of the raw data your database may spit out in response to queries or data entry passed via standard input. CGI-bin scripts must be able to properly parse your database package's output. Thus, if your database returns, say, a stream of line-oriented records, with colons separating the fields of each record, your CGI-bin script will need to separate the records and fields, associate them with the input variables initially generated based on the customer's Web form input, and then reformat and return everything to the customer's Web browser in HTML. Keep all this in mind as you read about the capabilities of the software packages described later in this chapter.

If you're an experienced DBA (database administrator), all this sounds quite familiar to you. Your CGI-bin scripts replace the standard vendor interfaces to database applications. Instead of separate data-entry, query, and reporting mechanisms, you use the HTML fill-in forms and the CGI mechanism to send and receive data to the database application and process its output for the customer. Bearing this in mind, let's look at some actual Web-based interfaces to commercial database applications.

Gateways to Oracle Database Applications

The Oracle Corporation has aggressively embraced Web technology with a complete suite of Web/Oracle products. Oracle has WebSystem, a comprehensive package that includes the Oracle 7 database server, an enhanced httpd server, a Web browser, a custom development package called WebAgent, and a connectivity (*middleware*) package called the Web Listener. You can also add Web services to an existing Oracle 7 database server, using Oracle's add-on product Web Server Option.

Tip: The httpd server and Web browser that Oracle provides appear to be enhanced versions of the NCSA server and browser packages from Spyglass, Inc. Free, fully functional copies of the Spyglass Server for several UNIX systems are available at `http://www.spyglass.com/`.

In addition, via Oracle's Web Listener package, you can integrate existing httpd servers with your Oracle 7 database server. Integrated with this suite are tools for creating/editing HTML documents and creating clickable imagemaps. The Oracle WebSystem package has enhanced security and file handling, including the ability to cache frequently accessed documents for faster response to customer queries. Also, the server has read-ahead caching, in which the server tries to make intelligent guesses at documents about to be retrieved based on those already retrieved and/or in the cache. Finally, Oracle's WebSystem supports automatic national-language and httpd file-type negotiations. For example, if your Web browser isn't capable of displaying a particular kind of image, WebServer will detect this and send you an image you can display.

Oracle's products are, the company says, completely compatible with CGI-bin standards, and the WebAgent package enables you to use your existing stored Oracle PL/SQL procedures. Although WebAgent is implemented using CGI, you don't have to directly create CGI-bin scripts. Instead, you can develop applications using PL/SQL (with which you may already be familiar), and WebAgent will take care of making them work via CGI. As a result, the company indicates, your development work can access not only the Oracle WebServer, but any CGI-compliant Web server. Your WebAgent-developed applications become standard Oracle 7 database objects, with portability across your Intranet. From the user's point of view, she simply clicks on hyperlinks using her Web browser, and your Oracle procedures run.

WebAgent supports extensible HTML encapsulation procedures, run on your Oracle 7 server, which can dynamically create HTML documents in response to Web browser requests. Such procedures can even output different HTML formatting in response to the capabilities of the Web browser making the incoming request.

There's an online demonstration of WebSystem that you can access at `http://support.us.oracle.com:8000/tr/owa/tr.splash`. This page is a travel game in which you're given a set amount of play money and try to get the most miles out of it by traveling among a list of available destinations. Figure 14.5 shows its startup page. Although it's not particularly instructive, you'll note the login and password boxes on the fill-in form, indicating that database security is a major feature.

> **Note:** In early 1995, Oracle made a free Web Interface Kit available on its Web site. This package is apparently no longer available, with WebServer and related products now for sale. You can, however, order a CD-ROM containing WebServer for a 90-day evaluation. See `http://www.oracle.com/products/websystem/html/webSystemOverview.html` for specifics. This page also has links to a good deal of detailed documentation on the Oracle packages.

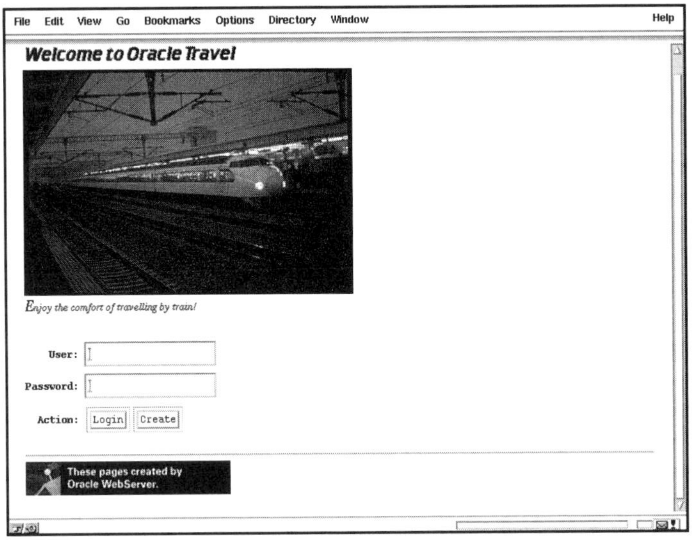

Figure 14.5. *The Oracle WebSystem Demo startup screen.*

> **Note:** As *Building an Intranet* went into production, Oracle had just announced its Universal Server, calling it "the World's first all-purpose server." Universal Server features an underlying Oracle database engine, Web server, text management, messaging, and multimedia support. Details can be found at `http://www.oracle.com/products/oracle7/ Oracle_Universal_Server`.

Oracle's PowerBrowser for PCs

Before leaving Oracle's products, let's take a look at what the company calls its "PowerBrowser browser and application development environment for personal computers." This is a suite of integrated packages, including a Web browser that's programmable (using old-fashioned BASIC, not Visual Basic), an HTML editor with drag-and-drop features, a personal PC httpd server, and a personal database manager called Blaze. Users can build small Web applications with these packages and share them over the network with others, as well as being able to access standard Oracle databases and WebServer. To read more about the PowerBrowser product, see `http://www.oracle.com/products/websystem/powerbrowser/html/index.html`.

GSQL, a Free Gateway to Oracle Databases

As you no doubt realize from a close reading of the preceding discussion of Oracle's Web-related products, particularly the emphasis on CGI standards, you can build your own CGI-bin interfaces to Oracle databases. Moreover, you can do so without having to buy any new products. Your own grounding in CGI-bin scripting, using perl, Tcl/Tk, or other languages, will enable you to access your databases directly. In fact, one of the very first CGI-bin gateways to relational databases can be used with Oracle databases. Early in the period of CGI development at NCSA, NCSA programmer, Jason Ng, developed the NCSA GSQL Toolkit, generic C language tools for database access. (You'll find the source code for the package on the *Building an Intranet* CD-ROM.) GSQL works by reading special configuration files you create called proc files. Proc files contain:

♦ References to the structure (tables and fields) of your database application.

♦ HTML setup information for specifying how forms and retrieved data are to be formatted.

♦ User-authentication information.

The GSQL program first creates an on-the-fly Web fill-in form based on the proc file's HTML setup information. A sample GSQL-generated form appears in Figure 14.6, a trouble ticket database system. Users accessing the database application fill in the form with database query keywords. GSQL then takes the user-entered data and the proc file's information about the database application's structure and creates a formal SQL query. The reformulated query is shipped off to another of the package's programs, sqlmain, for the actual query submission to the database engine. Returned data from the database engine once again passes through GSQL, which uses the proc file for HTML-formatting information, and then returns to the user's Web browser in HTML for viewing.

Figure 14.6. *A GSQL-generated database search form.*

You'll find basic information about GSQL, along with links to several demonstration databases that use it, at `http://www.ncsa.uiuc.edu/SDG/People/jason/pub/gsql/starthere.html`. These demonstrations include Sybase, Interbase, Illustra/Informix, and Windows NT MS-SQL databases, but don't include an Oracle demo. The GSQL source code, however, includes Oracle-specific code and examples, as well as pointers to Oracle-related GSQL work done at Georgia Tech University in the U.S. (`ftp://cc.gatech.edu/pub/gvu/www/pitkow/gsql-oracle`) and at IGD Darmstadt in Germany (`ftp://ftp.igd.fhg.de/pub/packages/oracle`).

Gateways to Sybase Database Applications

At the time *Building an Intranet* went into production, Sybase did not have formal Web-related products, although it was beta-testing a package called web.sql. You can download the beta at `http://www.sybase.com/`. Sybase has taken a different approach than Oracle to enabling Web access to its databases, through proprietary extensions to HTML. web.sql enables Web pages to include hyperlinks to special Sybase HyperText Sybase (HTS) format files, stored directly in Sybase databases.

HTS documents can contain standard HTML markup, and are rendered by Web browsers normally. The format, however, allows Sybase-specific markup. HTS documents can contain literal Sybase Transact-SQL statements or perl code. These blocks of code are executed when the user's Web browser loads the document by passing it through the web.sql middleware package. If your Web server is a standard httpd server (such as the NCSA or CERN servers), the perl code is executed using web.sql CGI-bin scripts. If you're running the Netscape Communications or Commerce servers, however, the Transact-SQL code gets passed directly to the web.sql executable using the Netscape Application Programming Interface (NSAPI), rather than using CGI-bin scripts. In either case, the results of the included code runs are sent back to the user's Web browser (in HTML, of course).

> **Note:** Sybase claims dramatically better performance with web.sql and the Netscape servers through use of the NSAPI. HTS queries go directly to the Netscape server, which has direct access to web.sql, rather than being passed through perl scripts first.

What's Special About web.sql?

The web.sql package is not being marketed as an overall set of Web tools for Sybase databases, but rather as a means of customizing and dynamically updating customer interface to databases. Accordingly, you can build customer profiles that create individualized views into the database application. In addition, you can track customer activity and update the custom profiles dynamically based on the activity. Sybase's web.sql home page (`http://www.newmedia.sybase.com/interact/web_spec.html`) uses one of the company's customers to illustrate these features. Virtual Vineyards (Los Altos, CA) is an Internet wine shop, specializing in small vintner's wines. You can order wines using your Web browser. (The Virtual Vineyards home page is at `http://www.virtualvin.com/`.)

Figure 14.7 shows part of Virtual Vineyards' Personal Account creation form. The form goes on for several screens, and is not particularly remarkable as far as forms go. What's unique about setting up personal accounts at the Virtual Vineyards Web site is the use of Sybase's web.sql to maintain information about your account. Each time you order wine, your customer profile is updated, including the history of your purchases. In addition, you can annotate your account with your own wine taste preferences, using an online Virtual Vineyards Tasting Chart. Later, when you access the Web page again, you'll see startup pages and special offers based on your purchase history and your expressed wine tastes and preferences.

It's the use of these customization techniques that can be of value to your Intranet, not the potential ability to order wine, of course. As customers interact with your databases via CGI-bin scripts, you'll be able to provide custom views of the database based on their habits, which Web browser they're using, and other identifiable data your scripts can pull out of the transactions. As a result, every customer, or group of customers, will have a different view of your database application, customized to their every use of the application, their Web browser, and their work habits.

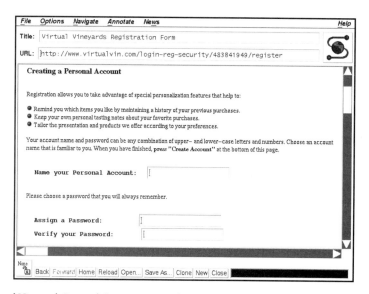

Figure 14.7. *Virtual Vineyards Personal Account creation form.*

Other Sybase Database Web Interfaces

Besides its own work with web.sql, Sybase tracks the activity of others in building Sybase Web gateways. You'll find a list of them at http://www.sybase.com/WWW/. You've already read about the NCSA GSQL Toolkit, which supports several database packages including Sybase. Let's take a look at a couple of the others here.

Sybperl

Michael Peppler of the Swiss firm ITF Management SA has developed Sybase-specific extensions to perl called sybperl. Release 2.0 of the package appears on the *Building an Intranet* CD-ROM. Sybperl adds Sybase's db_library API calls to the perl language. Peppler indicates that the combination of perl with the Sybase API creates an "extremely powerful scripting tool for Sybase DBAs and programmers." As with perl itself, sybperl is useful for those situations when interacting with Sybase's isql in the UNIX shell is too limited, but when writing C programs is the proverbial sledge hammer in search of a fly.

WDB

WDB, a Web-to-database interface, is based on Sybperl. The Sybperl package, then, can be used as a tool in the construction of a higher level Sybase databases. WDB, a copy of which is on the *Building an Intranet* CD-ROM, was developed by programmers at the European Southern Observatory (ESO), an astronomical consortium that operates observatories in South America.

As a perl CGI-bin script, WDB enables dynamic creation of HTML fill-in forms for database access. Perhaps more importantly, WDB enables the data retrieved from Sybase databases to be converted to clickable Web hyperlinks, allowing data to be retrieved by customers' Web browsers using point-and-click. To turn this statement on its head, the WDB FAQ states "The entire database system can be turned into a huge hypertext system." Further yet, Sybase databases can include hyperlinks to outside World Wide Web resources and/or to resources in other databases. Figure 14.8 shows a WDB fill-in form for an ESO telescope schedule database.

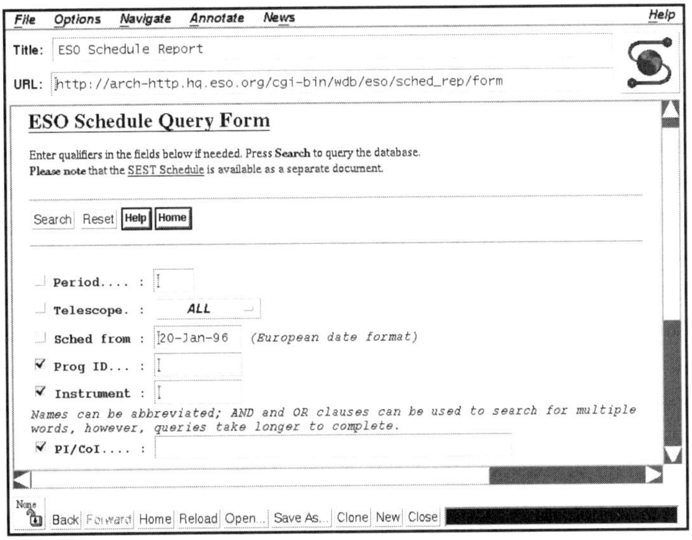

Figure 14.8. *WDB query form.*

Like GSQL (described previously), WDB uses a high-level form definition file to create views into a database. With the package comes a utility for querying a database application for its table structure and using the results to build template form definition files.

> **Note:** Besides Sybase databases, WDB also supports Microsoft mSQL and Informix databases.

Web/Genera

Stan Letovsky's Web/Genera is a set of tools for integrating Sybase databases with the World Wide Web. The package is based on a high-level schema file you'll write, describing both the Sybase database application table-and-field structure and the HTML format to be created when queries are run. Web/Genera was created for scientific purposes in the U.S.–government-financed Human Genome Database (GDB) project. GDB, centered at the Johns Hopkins University in Baltimore, MD, supports biomedical research, clinical practice, and scientific education by providing human gene-mapping information. Web/Genera databases can be queried directly using Web URLs, with the extracted data formatted into HTML on the fly for display in your Web browser. You can do queries not involving SQL via fill-in forms. Figure 14.9 shows part of a quite lengthy Web/Genera query form that accesses an agricultural science database at the University of Missouri.

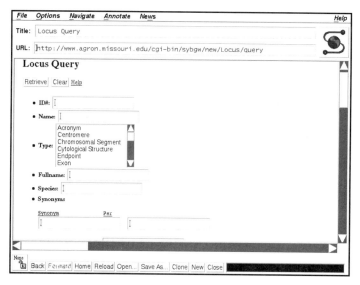

Figure 14.9. *A Web/Genera query form (partial).*

Finally, you can use Web/Genera to dump the contents of Sybase databases to flat text files, based on the same schema files used for Web gateway interfaces. These text files can, in turn, be indexed using indexing utilities like WAIS and Glimpse (see Chapter 13) to provide additional means of Web-based search-and-retrieval. Web/Genera is included on the *Building an Intranet* CD-ROM.

Informix and Illustra

Long-time UNIX relational database leader Informix acquired Illustra Information Technologies, Inc. in late 1995. Both companies previously produced Web-based interfaces to their database applications, so you'll see the two companies' products separately in this section. By the time you read this, though, the products may have merged in some way. It's not clear if the Illustra product will disappear into Informix, or if it will have a continued separate life, but you can expect at least some of its features to turn up in Informix sooner or later.

Informix

Informix has two free Web interface kits available for its Informix-ESQL/C and Informix-4GL products. Of course, you must already own the underlying Informix database application. Both kits are squarely based on the CGI standard.

The Informix-ESQL/C CGI Interface Kit is a ready-to-compile library for simple Web access from applications developed in ESQL/C. It reads and decodes HTML forms, and displays both text and Informix BLOBs (binary large objects) to Web browsers. The Informix-4GL CGI Interface Kit performs the same functions for Informix-4GL database applications. The Informix kits have been certified on Sun, SGI, HP, and IBM UNIX systems, and the company is confident that the packages will build on most other modern UNIX systems. You can download both kits at `http://www.informix.com/informix/dbweb/grail/freeware.htm`. The distributions include sample source code for database access. Documentation, however, is quite sparse.

> **Note:** In February 1996, Informix announced its own Universal Server package, also calling it the first such package. Based on the combined resources of Informix and its recently acquired Illustra package (see the next section), the product is called a "fully extensible relational database management system" that supports numbers, images, maps, sound, video, Web pages, and user-defined rich data types. The package, or parts of it, may be available by the time you read this.

If you have Informix database applications in place, but would prefer to use other means of Web interface, Informix tracks several freeware gateway packages, providing links to them at the URL listed above (though with a lot of negative commentary). First, as noted above, the WDB package supports Informix databases.

Informix-Online database users may be interested in the isqlperl subroutine library written by Bill Hails. A set of reusable Version-4.036 perl subroutines, isqlperl is due to be folded into a successor package, DBperl, which is currently under development and which will support several vendors' database packages, including Informix. (Information on both isqlperl and DBperl is at `ftp://ftp.demon.co.uk/oub/perl/db/`.) Informix-CISAM users may want to check out CISAMperl, available at `http://www.singnet.com.sg/~mathias/software/`. This package implements an interface to the Informix C-ISAM library for indexed sequential access methods search. Also based on perl 4.036, this package, like isqlperl, is quite old and may no longer be maintained.

Another commercial interface to Informix databases comes from SQLweb Technologies, Inc. The company's product, SQLweb, provides "an intelligent, adaptive, and dynamic connection" between Web servers and Informix (and several other) relational database products. It supports all database functions (queries, data entry, and canned procedures). Like the Sybase product, SQLweb features customized user interfaces that can be based on users' past activity in the application.

SQLweb is based on standard CGI principles, but the company claims no perl or other scripting is required. Rather, the product adds proprietary extensions to the HTML markup language. Special database entities called SQLweb pages support HTML and the company's CURSOR, IF, and INCLUDE extended markup tags to accommodate its features. SQLweb pages, when accessed with a Web browser, trigger database queries, updates, and the like. Figure 14.10 shows a schematic diagram of how SQLweb works.

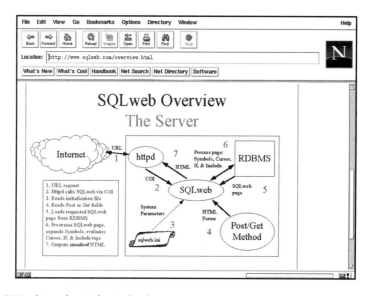

Figure 14.10. *SQLweb interfaces Informix databases.*

SQLweb has one additional feature that sounds interesting, although current company literature does a poor job of explaining it. The SQLweb Toolkit enables reverse engineering of existing HTML documents, presumably enabling conversion of standard HTML to SQLweb pages with extended markup. You'll find more information about SQLweb at `http://www.sqlweb.com/`.

Note: Besides supporting Informix databases, SQLweb also supports Oracle, Sybase, and Microsoft OBDC database products. In addition, the company indicates that the product will support any relational database package that has what they company calls an "adequate" C-language API.

Illustra

The Illustra database server, which the Illustra company calls "The Database for Cyberspace," is an object relational database management system. It handles alphanumeric, character, text, video, image, and document data types in a single database repository.

The company describes the package as the first relational database with object-oriented extensions. In any event, the above-quoted slogan suggests strongly that Illustra databases are meant to be Web accessible. Illustra's home page (`http://www.illustra.com/`) contains a link to a page of Illustra demo applications. Figure 14.11 shows one of these demos: an imaginary, searchable catalog of Sun-logo non-computer products (mugs, T-shirts, and the like). In Figure 14.11, a search on the keywords `purple` and `sun` has been done using a fill-in form. As you can see, the search comes back with several clickable buttons. Clicking on one would bring up details about the selected product.

Figure 14.11. *The Illustra demo database search results.*

A particularly interesting thing about this demo is you can ask to see the SQL statement that your query used. Notice the SQL Statement button near the top of the screen. Clicking on it generates Figure 14.12.

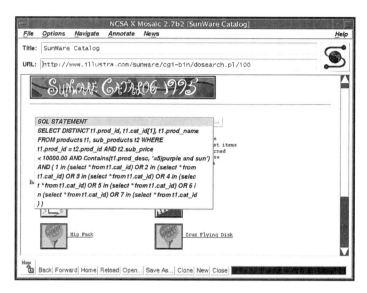

Figure 14.12. *The Illustra SQL statement the query in Figure 14.11 used.*

Illustra does not support standard CGI-bin scripting, sniffing at it as something somehow old-fashioned. Instead, it implements its Web interface using an add-in module (called a DataBlade) to the main database server.

The module works something like that described above with respect to the Sybase HTS product. You can embed literal SQL code in special HTML documents stored directly in the database. These pages, called application pages, directly execute queries, data entry, or stored procedures when loaded with a Web browser. (If you run the search shown in Figure 14.10 and 14.11 yourself, and then use your Web browser's View Source capability, you'll see the SQL code in the source document.) Illustra has provided for yet more proprietary extensions to HTML markup. The extensions go further, adding conditional capabilities that enable you dynamically turn on and off support for different browser capabilities, such as HTML Version-3 tables and other browser-specific features, such as Netscape Frames and image support.

> **Note:** See the earlier note about Informix/Illustra's new Universal Server announcements.

Other Commercial Products

New products for accessing corporate databases using Web technologies are rolling out of third-party software shops all over the Internet. We can't possibly survey them all, but here are brief descriptions of a few of them.

Spider

Supporting Oracle, Informix, and Sybase database products, the Spider Technologies product is a two-part package. First, a visually oriented development tool enables you to build HTML forms to interface with a database application using point-and-click. The interface enables you to view your database structures, selecting tables and relationships, and then build HTML forms and underlying SQL queries dynamically.

Spider 1.5's graphical form-building tool is shown in Figure 14.13. Note the access both to HTML markup tags and to the underlying database application's structure through click buttons, pull-down menus, and the like. You would think this form could be more Web-like in its appearence and operation.

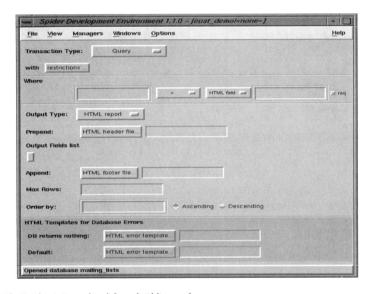

Figure 14.13. *The Spider 1.5 graphical form-building tool.*

The second part of the package is a middleware program that interacts with the database application to run queries, enter data, etc. As middleware, Spider's back end

1. Receives queries from both CGI-bin scripts and from Web browsers through the httpd server.
2. Reads special database application files.
3. Queries the underlying database.
4. Relays the results back to the user's Web browser, in HTML, for viewing.

Figure 14.14 shows this process displayed graphically. You can get more information about Spider at `http://www.w3spider.com/`. While you're there, you can pick up a 30-day evaluation copy of the package at no charge.

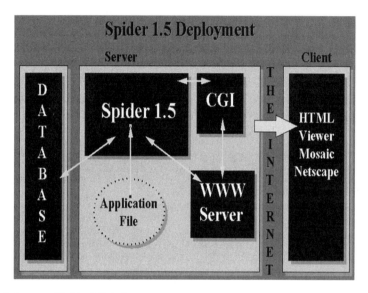

Figure 14.14. *A diagram of Spider 1.5 deployment.*

Sapphire/Web

Informix, Oracle, and Sybase users may also want to check out Bluestone's Sapphire/Web database interface. Sapphire/Web's claim to uniqueness is its ability to automatically produce CGI-bin scripts based on a combination of existing HTML documents and fill-in form templates. Like several of the other packages reviewed in this chapter, this one has a graphical front end (shown in Figure 14.15), which is also decidely un-Web-like. Called the Bind Editor, this tool enables you to drag-and-drop objects from the underlying database and the HTML documents/templates to create CGI-bin code (in C or C++), which can access database contents, including stored procedures. Press reports quote Bluestone as hoping Sapphire/Web will become the "PowerBuilder for the Web," referring to the successful Windows product from Powersoft.

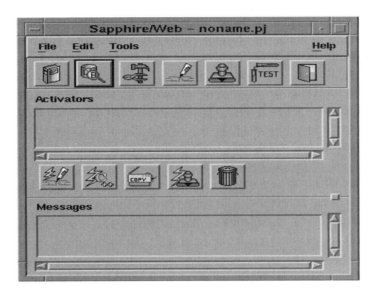

Figure 14.15. *The Sapphire/Web graphical bind editor.*

Sapphire/Web is based on Bluestone's existing graphical database interface builder, db-UIM/X. As a result, code built with the former works directly with your database applications, rather than via any sort of middleware. If you're already using db-UIM/X, you can use your legacy code with Sapphire/Web. No-cost evaluation copies of Sapphire/Web are available at `http:// www.bluestone.com/products/sapphire`.

VisualWave

Described by Parcplace-Digitalk as the "first object-oriented application development environment (ADE) for building live applications," VisualWave supports Sybase, Oracle, and DB2, as well as object-oriented databases, with add-on products. The package's Web Delivery System promises to automate coding of interactive, adaptive Web Applications with graphical drag-and-drop tools.

VisualWave's GUI interface, shown in Figure 14.16, produces both HTML documents and CGI-bin scripts. The package is written in the SmallTalk programming language. Interactive Web Applications built with the package retain state between transactions (HTTP is a stateless protocol, with each transaction completely separate from every other one), unlike many standard CGI-bin scripts. Intelligent program flow is thereby possible based on user input, Web browser capabilities, and the like. (In this connection, VisualWave features an image-conversion feature that creates GIF files, supported in all graphical Web browsers.)

Developers will like the package's features for testing and debugging Web Applications, as well as its Reusable Application Framework and built-in personal Web server for quick and easy application testing. Parcplace-Digitalk promises Java support, along with OLE support, in later versions. For more information about VisualWave, see http://www.parcplace.com/. At the time *Building an Intranet* went into production, evaluation copies of VisualWave were not available on the company's Web site, and the site's promised online demos were not yet active.

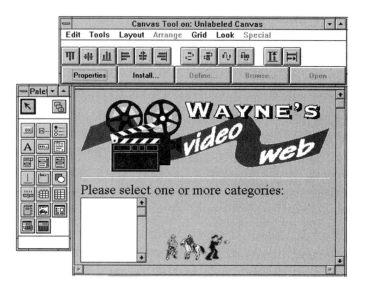

Figure 14.16. *VisualWave Interface Painter.*

Generic UNIX Database Gateways

Besides the several more-or-less generic database gateway packages noted in the preceding sections, (GSQL, WDB, and isqlperl), you may want to look at a number of additional packages. All of them are based on CGI standards, and all are either perl scripts or perl extensions.

Oraperl and Oraywww

Arthur Yasinski, formerly of the Canada Department of Natural Resources' Forest Service, has developed two perl interfaces to Oracle databases, oraperl and oraywww. The former is much like other perl scripts you've seen in this chapter, building a fill-in form dynamically and then taking user input and passing it off to the Oracle back end. Oraywww enables non-programmers to access Oracle databases and interactively build query and data entry forms, as well as to access prebuilt forms. Since the release of oraywww, Yasinski has taken a position with Oracle; presumably his work is reflected in the Oracle Web products described earlier, and his oraperl and oraywww packages are no longer being developed or maintained. You can read about oraperl and oraywww at `http://www.nofc.forestry.ca/features/features.html`.

Other perl Scripts/Extensions

You'll find a collection of perl scripts/extensions at `http://sunsite.doc.ic.ac.uk/packages/dbperl/perl4`. Among the database packages for which you'll find scripts (of varying degrees of currency and utility) are Ingres, Interbase, Postgres, and Unify. You'll find some of these to be quite old, predating the Web. As a result, they are more suitable for standalone operation than as CGI-bin scripts, and would need substantial overhaul to turn them into CGI-bin scripts. You may be able to modify them, or use chunks of them on your Intranet, but they're more likely to be useful as building blocks than as ready-made scripts.

Tim Bunce is working on a standard perl DBI (database interface), and has plans to include support for Oracle, Ingres, mSQL, Informix, Interbase, and DB2. You'll find more information about the ongoing DBI project at `http://sunsite.doc.ic.ac.uk/packages/dbperl/`. You may also wish to check out the University of Florida's perl archive at `http://www.cis.ufl.edu`, where you'll find a wide variety of perl-related resources. You can also check out the Comprehensive Perl Archive Network (CPAN), a very busy FTP archive of perl resources at `ftp://ftp.cis.ufl.edu/pub/perl/`.

WebLib

Tobin Anthony (of the U.S. National Aeronautics and Space Administration) and Erik Dorfman, Jim Gass, and Pradip Sitaram (all of Hughes STX Corporation) are developing WebLib, a package which, if brought to fruition, will provide access to distributed relational database systems in a network. The package can also access WAIS and other document-based indexes. Simple configuration files define the structure of databases that WebLib can access, including the creation and passing of SQL queries to database back ends and the HTML formatting and return of results to Web browsers. Figure 14.17 shows the results of a query on a demo WebLib database. You'll find a copy of WebLib on the *Building an Intranet* CD-ROM, but you'll want to check for a later release, as well as updated documentation on the WebLib home page, at `http://selsvr.stx.com/~weblib/`.

Figure 14.17. WebLib online demo search.

Access to PC Databases

In Chapter 12, you learned how to access Microsoft Access database applications through the Web helper application mechanism. You'll want to refer back to that chapter for details. You can configure your Web server to serve complete Access databases, just as it serves any other file on the server. Your customers' Web browsers can then use their own copies of Access as a Web browser helper application to load them for data search and retrieval and/or export to other Microsoft applications. Figure 14.18 shows an Access database loaded using this approach.

It's important to note that such helper application access to a database application should be considered read-only, since the Web browser downloads a temporary copy of the database to the local system. All queries made by your customer are based on the temporary copy, and any changes that he might attempt to make will not be reflected in the master copy on your Web server. Similarly, updates made to the master server won't get propagated to any client unless the client reloads the database from the Web server. Thus, you'll want to limit the capabilities of such an arrangement to running queries, generating reports, and exporting data from the application.

This limitation is more than offset by other capabilities, however. For example, if your company uses other Microsoft products, such as Microsoft Office or its individual components, you'll be able to use their capabilities to move data from one application to another. You can import information in Access databases, for example, into Word or Excel (and vice versa).

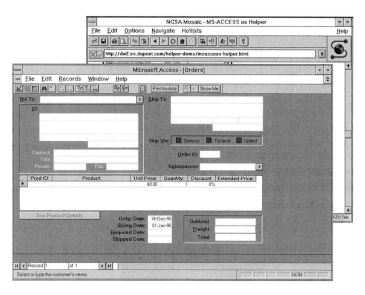

Figure 14.18. *Microsoft Access as a helper application.*

Windows CGI Scripting

You'll also want to develop your own CGI-bin scripts for Windows access to databases. While you can use PC versions of perl, or custom programming in C or C++, you'll probably want to do your scripting in Visual Basic (VB). The Professional Edition of Visual Basic has built-in hooks for native access to database applications in Access, dBASE, Paradox, FoxPro, and Btrieve. Beside this direct access, VB supports the ODBC (Open Database Connectivity) and SQL standards. Databases that are accessible via ODBC and/or SQL include several of the above, plus Lotus Approach. Finally, VB's crossover access via Microsoft's DDE and OLE enables access to those databases that support these standards, as well as to other applications that do so.

CGI-bin scripting in Windows (and in DOS) is problematic, though. This is mainly because there's no easy way to throw all the environment variables CGI scripts use and need around as easily as you can on UNIX systems. Most Windows CGI-bin approaches, such as the examples provided with the Whttpd Web server (on the *Building an Intranet* CD-ROM), write environment information out to temporary files, and then read them back when the information is needed for formatting output and such. This is clearly inefficient, and tends to argue for the retention of major CGI-bin functions on true multitasking systems, such as UNIX or NT systems.

FoxWeb for FoxBase Access

FoxPro users will want to look at a new product from the Aegis Group called FoxWeb. This is a software tool to interface Windows Web servers with FoxPro data and programs. FoxWeb overcomes the limitations of other Windows CGI-bin approaches, which read and write temporary files to pass environment variables between processes. It works by running multiple, backgrounded Visual FoxPro instances simultaneously, each one of which can handle CGI interactions. CGI environment variables are placed into FoxPro arrays and objects for manipulation. All programming is done in FoxPro, rather than in an external scripting language like perl, so your investment in FoxPro programming can be both preserved and leveraged. You can even store reusable HTML code directly in FoxPro databases for easy retrieval, with intelligent branching capabilities.

Aegis claims substantially faster database access compared to ODBC database transactions, although ODBC database applications can access FoxPro databases, as noted earlier. FoxWeb requires Visual FoxPro, Version 3.0. FoxWeb includes login/password security features. Figure 14.19 shows a FoxWeb fill-in form, with access to a job-search FoxPro database at the University of California. For more information about FoxWeb, including a no-cost, 30-day evaluation copy of the package, see `http://www.intermedia.net/aegis/`.

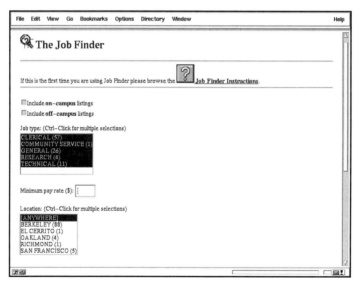

***Figure 14.19.** A sample FoxWeb application.*

WebBase

ExperTelligence, Inc. offers WebBase for all Microsoft Windows platforms. This package is a 32-bit httpd server with built-in hooks for accessing databases, without the use of CGI scripting. As a Web server, WebBase can serve conventional HTML documents in response to Web browser requests. Besides this function, however, the package supports embedded SQL code in special HTML documents, which when accessed, can contact database applications directly to run queries or data-entry commands. WebBase HTML extensions also include a macro language featuring intelligent decision-making constructs like if-then and case branching, as well as forRow and forIndex looping. A number of other useful functions are also provided, such as string-comparison/matching, math, date-handling, and other logic. These features enable customized responses to Web browser requests based on username, IP address, browser type, and the like.

WebBase enables session state to be maintained throughout a user's session, and has login/password security built in. Databases supported include ODBC platforms like Microsoft Access, Excel, and SQL Server, FoxPro, dBASE III and IV, Paradox, and Btrieve, as well as UNIX database servers running Sybase and Oracle. The package can also search fielded text files as a database. Figure 14.20 shows a WebBase application that provides access to the Dallas-Ft. Worth, TX, Realtors' Multiple List Service. Although WebBase can function as an httpd server, you can also run a traditional Web server for better standard httpd service, on the same computer or a different one, because WebBase doesn't provide all the functions of full-featured Web servers. WebBase runs on all Intel Windows platforms. For more information about WebBase, including information about no-cost evaluation copies, see `http://www.webbase.com/`.

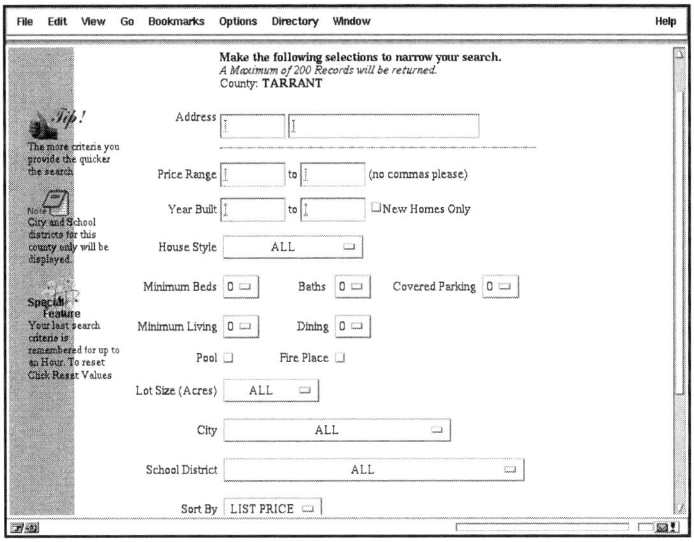

Figure 14.20. A sample WebBase query form.

Summary

While Chapter 13 dealt with Web-accessible, general-purpose indexing databases, this chapter has focused on Web interfaces to relational database packages. You've learned about the widespread support of the CGI standards and the frenetic activities of database vendors and database-access vendors as they scramble to bring products to this important market. We have not mentioned all such vendors, but have surveyed a fairly representative sample, some of them in detail, to give you a firm idea of what's possible in this rapidly growing field. Here's a thumbnail summary of what you've covered in this chapter.

◆ Important information about the Web's Common Gateway Interface, widely used in database access.

◆ No-cost and commercial gateways to UNIX database packages from a number of sources.

◆ Developing your own Web front ends to these and other UNIX database packages.

◆ Accessing PC database applications using a Web browser front end.

In Chapter 15, "Scientific, Mathematical, and Technical Applications on Your Intranet," we'll consider a wide range of Web-accessible scientific and technical applications. Some of these will build on the material you've learned in the last couple of chapters, or elsewhere in *Building an Intranet*. Other material will be new.

15

Scientific, Mathematical, and Technical Applications on Your Intranet

As you've read the last few chapters, you've built Web interfaces to some of your everyday office applications, your searchable document indexes, and your relational database applications for your Intranet. You can also build such interfaces to a wide range of scientific, mathematical, and technical applications the technically oriented members of your organization might use, or already be using. You already have most of the knowledge and tools infrastructure for doing so in place, based on the information you've learned in earlier chapters of *Building an Intranet*.

In this chapter, you'll build on this infrastructure, using a variety of scientific and technical application programs to create new Intranet resources. You may already be using some of these programs, in which case it'll be as easy to add them to your Intranet as was adding your word processor or spreadsheet. Others involve new software applications, some of which you'll find on the *Building an Intranet* CD-ROM. Whatever the case, you'll be able to extend your Intranet in new ways for your organization's scientists, engineers, and other technical professionals, giving them new ways to do their work.

Chapter Objectives

As with the rest of the chapters in this book, let's begin by laying out some chapter objectives. This will help you get oriented to the material to be presented; you may want to refer back to this list as you work your way through the chapter. In this chapter, you'll

- Learn about dynamic graphing and data modeling and apply both to a wide range of uses.

- Learn about the intensive Web-related activity in the field of chemistry.

- Learn about Web-based image processing.

- Learn how to use the Web for graphical visualization of complex relationships among numbers and other objects.

- Learn about using the Web for viewing and exchanging computer-aided drafting (CAD) drawings.

- Learn about existing and planned Web support for standardized scientific data formats.

Many of the application packages referenced in these chapters are UNIX-specific, though some are available for other platforms. Although this affects how you may use them in your Intranet, it doesn't mean you won't be able to make these capabilities available to your Intranet's PC users. As you'll learn, you can integrate these UNIX applications into your CGI-bin scripts or use PC-based X Windows server software to enable all your customers to use them.

Previously in *Building an Intranet* (Introduction and Chapter 8, "Adding Services to Your Intranet Adds Value") we briefly suggested several possibilities for scientific, technical, and engineering collaboration. In this chapter, you'll focus on some actual scientific and technical applications for your Intranet, then, in the next chapter, focus on Intranet collaboration of all kinds.

Graph Data on Your Intranet

Numerical datasets often need graphing to make them meaningful to humans, and the ability to provide such graphing on your Intranet can be useful. There are several ways you can provide graphics displays of numbers on your Intranet.

- Prepare graphs of your datasets ahead of time, using whatever graphing tools you have available to you, such as your spreadsheet, the X Windows xgraph package or the gnuplot or PGplot packages (all discussed subsequently) for viewing in customers' Web browsers or helper applications.

◆ Use Web browser helper applications available to your customers, such as xgraph or a spreadsheet to generate graphed data on demand.

◆ Use custom CGI-bin scripts that convert numerical datasets into images on the fly and then return the images to customers' Web browsers.

Each of these approaches has both advantages and disadvantages, and you'll find uses for each of them on your Intranet. Let's take a look at some of the pros and cons of using each.

> **Note:** We use the terms *graph* and *graphing* in this chapter to refer to the creation of line or bar graphs, pie charts, and the like from numerical datasets. You may be more familiar with the terms *chart* and *charting* in this context, especially if you're accustomed to using a spreadsheet to generate these kinds of charts. Some spreadsheets, Excel and Lotus 1-2-3, for example, actually refer to this practice as *charting* and use the term *graphics* to refer to line-drawing and other similar capabilities you can use to include lines, boxes, circles, and other graphical characters in your spreadsheets. In this chapter, the terms *graph* and *graphing* mean the graphical representation of numerical data.

Advance Preparation of Data Graphs

Datasets that rarely change can be turned into graphs, placed on your Intranet, and made available to your Intranet customers. We'll take a look at several ways to prepare your graphs in this section, beginning with a venerable UNIX package, xgraph.

Quick UNIX Graphing with Xgraph

The now-quite-old X windows xgraph command (which is a graphical front end to the even-older command-line graph command) can take simple, two-column datasets and turn them into on-screen bar or X-Y axis line graphs. (UNIX source code for xgraph is included in the *Building an Intranet* CD-ROM, though the package is no longer being maintained by its author; you'll need the X11R5 libraries, available from ftp://ftp.x.org, to build it.) Capabilities are quite impressive, as shown in Figure 15.1; the dataset used to create this graph contained more than 5,700 X-Y pairs.

As you can see from the screenshot, xgraph has a clickable Hardcopy button, in the upper left, which opens a dialog box for printing the file (see Figure 15.2). Here, you have the option of directing the output of the print job to a PostScript file, rather than to a real printer or plotter. Having saved the output to a PostScript file, you're now set to make the graph available on your Intranet, just as you would any other PostSript file. Users with PostScript viewers (such as GNU ghostscript) set up as Web browser helper applications will be able to view the graphs, just by clicking on Web page hyperlinks.

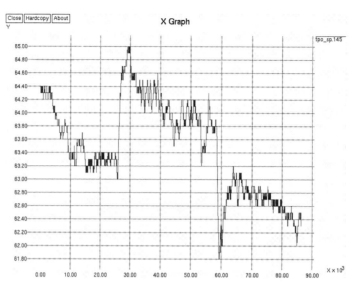

Figure 15.1. *Xgraph.*

Note: Unfortunately, xgraph works only interactively, and has no command-line interface for printing the graphs it generates, either to a printer or a print file such as a PostScript file. As a result, you'll have to use it interactively, generating and saving one image at a time.

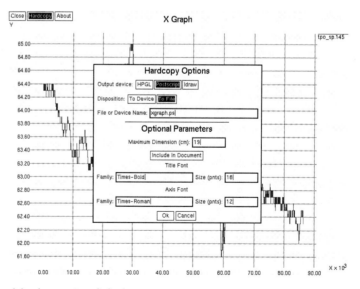

Figure 15.2. *Xgraph hardcopy options dialog box.*

Although there are a number of programs you can use as Web browser helper applications to view PostScript files (such as Sun's imagetool, GNU ghostscript, and others), you'll want to turn these and other single-screen PostScript files into images Web browsers can handle directly. To do this, you'll want to use an all-purpose image-conversion tool like ImageMagick's convert. (The overall ImageMagick image-processing package is on the *Building an Intranet* CD-ROM.) Fortunately, convert does have a command-line interface, so you can mass-convert files in batch mode. The basic syntax of convert is simple:

```
$ convert image.ps image.gif
```

Check out the ImageMagick man pages, or its home page on the Web at http://www.wizards.dupont.com/cristy/ImageMagick.html for details on the package. With respect to convert, you'll want to know it supports resizing image files and can accept standard input. The latter feature enables you to build it into shell scripts for mass-converting files, and, as you'll learn later in this chapter, into your CGI-bin scripts for on-the-fly image conversions.

Quick Graphing with Gnuplot

Another package for graphing numerical datasets is gnuplot, free software written originally by Thomas Williams and Colin Kelley, but with major contributions from many others. Gnuplot is on the *Building an Intranet* CD-ROM (with UNIX source code and binaries for Windows and the Macintosh) and has a number of major advantages over xgraph.

Plotting of two-dimensional functions and data points in many different styles (points, lines, error bars)

Plotting of three-dimensional data points and surfaces in many different styles (contour plot, mesh)

Support for complex arithmetic

Self-defined functions

Support for a large number of operating systems, graphics file formats and devices

Extensive online help

Labels for title, axes, data points

Command line editing and history on most platforms

You can read more about gnuplot in the CD-ROM distribution, the HTML manual at http://arachnid.cs.cf.ac.uk/Latex/Gnuplot/gnuplot.html, or by accessing the gnuplot FAQ at http://www.uni-karlsruhe.de/~ig25/gnuplot-faq/. Figure 15.3 shows a sample gnuplot rendering of one of the demo files included with the package source code.

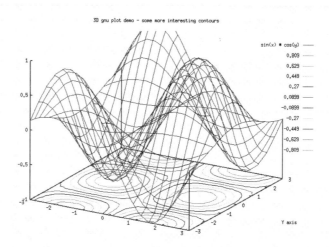

Figure 15.3. *gnuplot.*

> **Note:** The gnuplot package is not part of the Free Software Foundation's GNU project. The names are similar (note that gnuplot is written with lowercase letters) only by a quite involved and lengthy coincidence. Even so, the Free Software Foundation generally includes gnuplot with its overall software distributions.

We're less concerned here about the gnuplot package's overall capabilities than with the ability to quickly generate graphs out of your datasets. Unlike xgraph, gnuplot can be run noninteractively, using script or macro files containing gnuplot commands. Although gnuplot doesn't directly write its output in GIF or JPEG format (formats directly readable by Web browsers), it does support PostScript and Portable Bitmap (PBM) formats. This being the case, it's easy to use the UNIX piping mechanism to send PBM or PostScript output directly to ImageMagick convert for output to GIF or JPEG format. Thus a simple gnuplot macro can automatically convert a numerical dataset into a GIF image file directly usable on your Intranet. Here's the example macro file:

```
set term pbm
set output "¦/usr/local/bin/convert - output.gif"
plot "datafile"
```

You need to read the gnuplot documentation for details on how to write macro files, but this one is short enough—and its value to your Intranet high enough—that it needs to be explained. Gnuplot has an extended concept of terminal types, so the set term command is used here to specify the PBM image format mentioned previously. We also know ImageMagick convert understands PBM-formatted files, and that it can accept image data via standard input. The second line of the macro file uses gnuplot's capability of sending its standard output to another UNIX command. In this case, the output is piped (note the pipe symbol as the first character of the output destination, and that the whole string is quoted) to convert. Convert, taking its input directly from gnuplot, accepts the incoming PBM image data and writes it out in GIF format to the file output.gif. Finally, having set up the gnuplot terminal type and output destination, the last line of the macro file calls the plot command to read the file containing the dataset (note the quotes are required) and plot its contents, right out through the pipe to the GIF image file. Run gnuplot with its macro filename as a command-line argument, like this:

```
$ gnuplot macrofile
```

Gnuplot starts, reading the contents of the macro file, and runs each command in sequence. Before you know it, your GIF image is created and ready for viewing by your Intranet's customers using their Web browsers. It should be readily apparent that you can use gnuplot in this fashion within your shell or perl scripts to mass-generate image files from your numerical datasets. Hold onto this thought, as we'll return to it later, when we discuss CGI-bin scripting.

Quick Graphing with Your Spreadsheet

Your spreadsheet package is a great tool for graphing existing numerical data, including both native spreadsheet data and text files containing columnar data you import into the spreadsheet. Use the ordinary graphing facilities of your spreadsheet and then just leave the graphics output in a spreadsheet datafile. You'll recall from Chapter 11, "Spreadsheets and Data Warehouses," using your favorite spreadsheet package on your Intranet as a Web browser helper application. Having pre-created your spreadsheet charts, you can leverage this capability for your customers, who can view the charts by clicking hyperlinks pointing to the spreadsheet datafiles containing them. Selecting such hyperlinks loads the customer's own copy of the spreadsheet application for viewing the graphed data. Later on in this chapter, we'll extend use of your spreadsheet helper applications to generate charts dynamically.

UNIX spreadsheet packages usually have features beyond those of PC packages and can take advantage of features of the UNIX operating system, such as use of standard input, standard output, and pipes. AIS's spreadsheet package xess (to which some attention was devoted in Chapter 11) is one of these. With its own Application Programming Interface (API), xess can be run noninteractively (that is, from the UNIX shell or from a script) to import numerical datasets and graph them, and then write the output of the graphing back out to usable spreadsheet datafiles. If you're using xess, you'll want to check out the API programming manual to see how you can use these capabilities in your Intranet. Note also xess reads and writes Lotus datafile formats, so you can use this capability to make your spreadsheet data more portable and available to more of your customers.

Graphing Data on Demand

Although pregraphed numerical datasets may be useful in many situations, it's more likely the data you want to visualize in gnuplot's graphics format is data that changes regularly. You may have process-control instruments accumulating data on a regular basis or new data coming in from other applications. In these and similar situations, you'll want to be able to view the very latest data graphically, and last night's, or even last hour's; graphing of the data may not be sufficient. You're in luck, because all three of the approaches described can be used to dynamically generate graphics representations of your datasets. Let's begin discussing on-the-fly graphing with xgraph.

Graph Data with Xgraph

For your UNIX users, xgraph can dynamically generate a line or bar chart of any dataset, including those being updated by automated applications or instruments. Of course, xgraph can be run standalone from the UNIX command line, but that's not what *Building an Intranet* is about; you want your customers to see your graphed data from their Web browsers. Well, xgraph will do that trick, but first you need to

>   Do some Web server configuration
>   Do some customer Web browser helper application setup

Let's consider the Web server setup first. As you'll recall from Chapter 7, "MIME and Helper Applications," Web servers need to be configured to know about nonstandard datafiles, such as your numerical datasets. This is done through changes to the server's mime.types file to specify a new MIME data type/sub-type for your datasets. Xgraph datasets are simple plain-text files, containing two columns of data, with some possible setup information (see the xgraph man page on your system for details). You need to distinguish these files from other plain-text files, and you'll recall the MIME mechanism uses filename extensions for this purpose. Let's use the filename extension xg for your xgraph files in this example. Your first step is to add an entry to the server's mime.types file for your new xgraph MIME data type/sub-type, such as this one:

```
application/x-xgraph    xg
```

Here the custom of prepending x- to nonstandard MIME data type/sub-types has been followed. Once you've edited the mime.types file, your next step is instructing your Web server to reread its setup files to pick up your changes. (If you're unclear about the mime.types file, its use, and how to have your httpd server reread it for changes, you'll want to review Chapter 7, "MIME and Helper Applications.")

Let's now turn from httpd server setup to customer Web browser setup for the xgraph datafiles. You'll recall UNIX Web browsers such as X Mosaic and Netscape use a system-wide mailcap file which associates applications with the MIME data type/sub-type and filename-extension information sent by Web servers. You need to modify the mailcap file to add support for xgraph as a helper application. Here's what you need to add (don't miss the semicolon):

```
application/x-xgraph;    /usr/local/bin/xgraph %s
```

Substitute your own system's path to the xgraph executable, if it's different than the one shown. You'll also recall UNIX users may have a personal mailcap file, usually named `.mailcap` in their home directory; they may prefer to add this line to that file. In either case, your UNIX Intranet customers are now set up to view xgraph data files. (Already-running Web browsers need to be told to reread the setup files to know about changes. In X Mosaic, pull down the Options Menu and select Reread Config Files. In Netscape, select Options, then Preferences, and just click on the OK button.)

Your final step is making the xgraph datafiles available on your Web server. This is done with ordinary HTML markup, just like you use for any other files on your server, so there's nothing unusual here. Once you've added hyperlinks to xgraph documents, users are ready to try them out. Figure 15.4 shows xgraph as an NCSA Mosaic helper application. The schematic diagram shown in the Mosaic window is a clickable imagemap (see Appendix B, "HTML & CGI Quick Reference,") with the process sensors in the diagram being hot links to numerical datasets in xgraph-readable format. Clicking one of the sensors in the diagram fires up xgraph on the datafile. Note xgraph's clickable command buttons, including one for creating hardcopy, are available on the data, so customers have the ability to print the graphed data (including printing it to a file on their computer's disk).

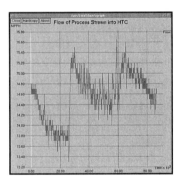

Figure 15.4. *Xgraph as a helper application.*

The discussion of xgraph in the previous section was quite negative, focusing on the limitations of the package in precreating viewable image files for your customers, mainly because of its insistence on being operated interactively. As you can see from this section, however, its value is substantially greater in the context of dynamically creating graphics representations of live data. If you have significant numbers of UNIX customers on your Intranet, you'll want to try it as a helper application. Unfortunately, xgraph is a UNIX-only program, and it won't be available to your PC users except under very special circumstances, described later in the discussion of CGI-bin scripting.

Graph Data on Demand with Gnuplot

Because gnuplot is more portable than xgraph, running on PCs and Macs as well as UNIX systems, you would expect it to be useful as a Web browser helper application for on-demand graphing of data. As Figure 15.5 shows, gnuplot can indeed function in this way. Unfortunately, it can do so only under limited circumstances. Let's cover the helper application setup first and then discuss the limits of the package in using it as a helper.

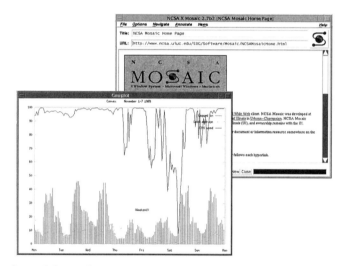

Figure 15.5. *Gnuplot as a helper application.*

As you'll recall from Chapter 7, Web servers need to be configured to know about nonstandard datafiles, like your numerical datasets. This is done through changes to the server's mime.types file. Gnuplot datasets are simple plain-text files, containing two or more columns of data. As you learned previously, you can run gnuplot in noninteractive mode through the use of macro files, containing commands that you'd ordinarily type at the gnuplot interactive prompt. The trick with using gnuplot as a helper application is that you need to set up your Web server to know about the macro files, rather than the datafiles themselves. Here's a sample macro file:

```
set term x11
plot "/path/to/real/gnuplot/datafile"
```

In this macro file, the gnuplot terminal type is set to x11 (X Windows); you would use set term windows on a PC.

Because gnuplot macro files are plain-text files, you need to distinguish them from other plain-text files, and you need to recall the MIME mechanism uses filename extensions for this purpose. Let's use the filename extension gpt for your gnuplot macro files in this example. Your first step is to add an entry to the server's mime.types file for your new gnuplot macro MIME data type/sub-type, like this one:

```
application/x-gnuplot    gpt
```

Here the custom of prepending x- to nonstandard MIME data type/sub-types has been followed. Once you've edited mime.types, your next step is instructing your Web server to reread its setup file to pick up the changes. (If you're unclear about the mime.types file, its use, and how to have the httpd server reread its setup files, you'll want to review Chapter 7.)

Let's now turn from server setup to customer Web browser setup for gnuplot. You'll recall UNIX Web browsers, such as X Mosaic and Netscape, use a system-wide mailcap file that associates applications with the MIME data type/subtype and filename-extension information sent by Web servers. You need to modify the mailcap file to add support for xgraph as a helper application. Here's what you need to add (don't miss the semicolon):

```
application/x-gnuplot;    /usr/local/bin/gnuplot %s
```

Substitute your own system's path to the gnuplot executable, if it's different than the one shown. You'll also recall UNIX users may have a personal mailcap file, usually named .mailcap in their home directory; they may prefer to add this line to that file. In either case, your customers are set up to view gnuplot data files. (Already-running Web browsers need to be told to reread the setup files to know about changes. In X Mosaic, pull down the Options Menu and select Reread Config Files. In Netscape, select Options, then Preferences, and just click the OK button.)

PC Web browsers use a different method of setting up helper applications, as you'll recall from earlier chapters. For example, in Netscape, select Options, then General Preferences, then Helpers to access the Helpers dialog box. Fill in the box with the MIME data type/sub-type, filename extension, and the path to the gnuplot executable program. Figure 15.6 will refresh your memory on this process. Mosaic has a similar Preferences dialog.

Your final step is making the gnuplot datafiles available on your Web server. This is done with ordinary HTML markup, just like you use for any other files on your server, so there's nothing unusual here. Once you've added hyperlinks to gnuplot documents, users are ready to try them.

Gnuplot's noninteractive mode, via the use of macro files containing gnuplot commands (including the command to plot a specified datafile), has some limitations when you use it as a helper application. First, both the gnuplot macro and the datafile have to be available to the Web browser. Web servers, however, won't serve two different files at the same time, so the datafile needs to be directly available to the customers' own computers on a PC network drive or a mounted UNIX NFS filesystem. This isn't a major problem in small organizations, where UNIX systems can use the NFS (network filesystem) automounter to access the Web server's document tree. Most PC TCP/IP networking packages also include an NFS client, though it doesn't have automounter capabilities; you'll need to permanently mount the server's filesystem as a network drive on the PC.

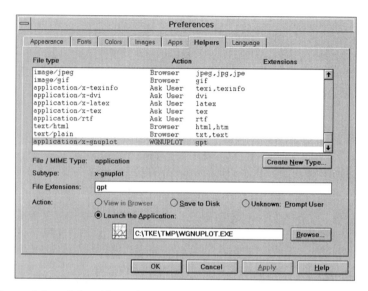

Figure 15.6. *Netscape helpers dialog with gnuplot.*

A second limitation with using gnuplot as a helper application has to do with getting it to remain live with your plotted datafile displayed onscreen. You need to modify your macro file to prevent the package from displaying your plotted data and immediately exiting, taking the plot with it before you get a good look at it. Here's the previous macro revised:

```
set term x11
plot "/path/to/real/gnuplot/datafile"
pause 60
```

The last line tells gnuplot to remain alive for 60 seconds with your plotted data on-screen. You may want to up this pause time substantially, so the plot remains onscreen until customers explicitly close its window. (Your X Windows server may complain about a broken pipe when they do so; this message can be ignored safely.)

Finally, using gnuplot as a helper application in a heterogeneous Intranet where you have different computer types requires separate macro files for each platform. Since gnuplot needs to have a terminal type defined (see the previous macro), you need to create separate files for UNIX, PC, and Macintosh customers, setting the appropriate terminal type.

On the whole, these limitations reduce the value of gnuplot as a helper application, although as noted, you can work around most of them fairly easily. Later on, you'll see gnuplot's strongest suit for purposes of your Intranet lies in its capability to be used in UNIX pipelines in your CGI-bin scripts to create graphics displays of data dynamically.

Graph Data with Your Spreadsheet

Numerical datasets stored in spreadsheet datafiles can be graphed on demand through the use of the spreadsheet package's macro command facilities. Most spreadsheets have the capability to set up a special start-up macro that runs first thing when the spreadsheet datafile containing it loads. Lotus 1-2-3, for example, refers to these as autoexecute macros. You can have your spreadsheet automatically load a dataset and then graph it immediately by setting up a special spreadsheet datafile containing only the autoexecute macro. Here's what you would do (with some Lotus-specific comments in parentheses) to set up one to load and dynamically graph a dataset stored in a plain-text file accessible on your Intranet:

1. Open an empty spreadsheet.
2. Turn on the spreadsheet's macro record facility (in Lotus, pull down the Tools menu and select Macro Record).
3. Import the text file containing the dataset (in Lotus, select File and then Open).
4. Select the cell range to be graphed and create your graph (from the Lotus Tools pull-down menu, select Chart to access the Lotus Chart Assistant).
5. Follow the spreadsheet's prompts to create your graph.
6. Turn off the spreadsheet's macro record (in Lotus, cut and paste the contents of the Transcript window into a cell in the spreadsheet) and save it.
7. Give the macro an appropriate name (in Lotus, you must use \0, that is, backslash-zero as the name for an autoexecute macro).
8. Delete everything in the spreadsheet except for the cell containing your autoexecute macro (that is, delete the data).
9. Save the spreadsheet and exit.

The next time you load the spreadsheet, your autoexecute macro will graph the dataset (which probably has changed, the whole idea being to get the very latest dataset). Your Intranet customers who click hyperlinks pointing to the spreadsheet file will get the same results.

UNIX xess spreadsheet users can accomplish much the same purpose using the xess API. Because xess can monitor datafiles in real time, you can create programs that use the API to read, graph, and output data in xess or Lotus spreadsheet datafiles. Using the UNIX cron daemon, you can monitor the status of your datasets and then fire off xess in background mode to read updated files and create new spreadsheet datafiles with the current data. This way, the most recent date will always be available to your customers, who need not wait for a spreadsheet macro to execute when they click the link to the current datafile. The Lotus Realtime spreadsheet product for UNIX is similarly able to monitor changing data, and you'll be able to use its facilities to update graphs when necessary.

On-the-Fly Data Graphing with CGI-Bin Scripts

The third major way of providing graphical representations of numerical data on your Intranet is the development of CGI-bin scripts, which use some of the tools we've been describing to generate dynamically graphs viewable in users' Web browsers. You've already seen xgraph isn't capable of being run noninteractively, so let's skip it and move directly to your spreadsheet.

Use Your Spreadsheet

Only the UNIX spreadsheets such as xess, which can be run noninteractively, can be used in your CGI-bin scripts, and you'll need to understand their input/output mechanisms, such as the Xess API. PC spreadsheets like Excel or Lotus are limited to the autoexecute macro procedures described previously, though, as you've seen, xess can generate datafiles in Lotus format. Xess's API seems well-suited for use in CGI-bin scripts. Earlier, you learned how xess can be run via the UNIX cron daemon to wake up periodically and look for new data and then graph it and send its output to a loadable spreadsheet datafile. The same general procedure can be used in your CGI-bin scripts to automate the process completely, ensuring the latest dataset is graphed at the time the customer requests it. Rather than using the xess API to output static spreadsheet datafiles containing your graphics, you have it send standard output back to your perl or other CGI-bin script. Your script, in turn, returns an appropriate MIME data type/sub-type header to the customer's Web browser, followed by the spreadsheet data stream. User's Web browsers then call the local copy of the spreadsheet as a helper application to load and display the dynamically generated data.

Although you may think this procedure inappropriate unless all your customers have access to UNIX systems running xess, this isn't the case. As noted previously, xess can generate output in standard Lotus WKS format. Your CGI-bin scripts using the xess API should write their output in WKS format then. Because most other spreadsheet packages can load WKS-format datafiles, your customers' spreadsheets will be able to read the incoming data properly, provided you've set up a spreadsheet helper application that knows about the MIME data type/sub-type the server sends. For those of your PC users who have X Windows server software running on their PCs, xess can display directly to their screens.

Use Gnuplot

Earlier in this section, you learned about several awkward workarounds to limitations in using the gnuplot package as a helper application. Here, you'll learn how this package really shines when it comes to generating graphs via CGI-bin scripts. All the problems described previously with respect to using gnuplot noninteractively disappear when you build it into your scripts. The key to using gnuplot in your CGI-bin scripts is the ability to set its output to be standard output and then pass it to other programs for on-the-fly manipulation. Then you can use ordinary UNIX pipelines to pass the data through other programs for processing. Here's how.

As you'll recall, gnuplot doesn't support creation of the GIF and/or JPEG images Web browsers need for easy image display. It does, however, support creation of PostScript, PBM, and several other image formats that are understood by graphics converters like ImageMagick convert. As a result, you can have gnuplot generate its plots in one of these formats, with output piped directly to convert. Here's a gnuplot macro file fragment which sets this up:

```
Set term pbm color
Set output "¦/usr/local/bin/convert gif:- -"
Plot datafile
```

Having set this up, your CGI-bin script runs gnuplot with the macro filename as its command-line argument. The output of gnuplot, in PBM format, is sent directly to the convert utility via standard input. Convert turns the datastream from PBM to GIF format on the fly and passes it back to your CGI-bin script. The script has meanwhile generated the image/gif MIME type/sub-type header information. When the conversion's done, your script returns the header and the GIF image data stream to your customer's Web browser. The browser displays the image for the customer. The next time the customer runs the CGI-bin script, the datafile (which has changed by now, being dynamically updated by whatever instrument or other data-collection process that's running) is reread by gnuplot with the image being created once again and returned to the Web browser.

Another Graphing Possibility for Scientists

With the continued heavy use of FORTRAN programming among scientists and engineers, you may want to install the PGplot graphics subroutine library (on the *Building an Intranet* CD-ROM). Your FORTRAN programs can link to the PGplot library for device-independent graphics for making simple scientific graphs. An example PGplot graph is shown in Figure 15.7.

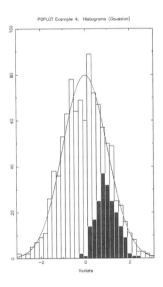
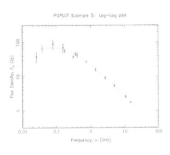

Figure 15.7. Sample graph using PGplot.

> **Note:** PGplot is not a standalone program you can install and run on your computer. Rather, you'll build your own executables, from source code written in FORTRAN, and linked to the PGplot library using your FORTRAN compiler. Your own programs actually load and display your datasets.

For more information about PGplot, see the documentation included with the CD-ROM distribution or at the PGplot home page on the Web, `http://astro.caltech.edu/~tjp/pgplot`. The CD-ROM distribution includes a couple of PC-DOS ports of the package, and you'll find links to several in-progress Windows/Windows NT ports on the PGplot home page. You can get John Salmento's unsupported Macintosh port at `http://www.lehigh.edu/~js0p/js0p.html`.

Molecules and Your Intranet

Professors Henry Rzepa and Benjamin Whitaker of the School of Chemistry, Leeds University, in the United Kingdom, have aggressively led development of chemistry-related tools for the World Wide Web. Although you may not have specific use for chemistry-related information on your Intranet, this work is a wonderful example of how the MIME mechanism and the Web browser helper application facility have been adapted to specialized applications on the Web. To this extent, the Rzepa/Whitaker work is instructive, even for nonchemists.

MIME Types for Chemistry

Many chemists use computer molecular modeling applications for viewing and manipulating images of molecules onscreen. A couple of common file formats have developed that several of these applications support, including the PDB (Protein Database) and XYZ formats. These file formats represent the structure of molecules in a well-defined, plain-text format and the applications render the text description into three-dimensional on-screen models. Rzepa and Whitaker proposed new MIME data type/sub-types for several of these molecular modeling formats. Their objective was to enable the modeling applications to run as Web browser helper applications. As it currently stands, a completely new primary MIME data type has been proposed, chemistry. You'll recall from Chapter 7 there are currently only seven official primary MIME data types: application, audio, video, image, message, multipart, and text. The proposed new chemistry MIME type has two sub-types, pdb and xyz, corresponding, of course, to the two primary molecular modeling file formats mentioned previously.

To implement the new MIME data type/sub-type, you'd add the following lines to your Web server's `mime.types` file, using the standard two-column file format with application/sub-type on the left and the filename extension(s) to be associated on the right.

```
chemistry/pdb    pdb
chemistry/xyz    xyz
```

Next, you need the actual molecular modeling applications to use as helper applications. For UNIX systems, the `xmol` and `rasmol` packages work; both are on the *Building an Intranet* CD-ROM. (As discussed subsequently, rasmol is also available for Windows PCs and the Macintosh.) Add one (not both) of these pairs of lines to your UNIX system-wide mailcap file to support these two applications; comment lines identify the pairs:

```
# xmol
chemical/x-pdb;        xmol -readFormat pdb %s
chemical/x-pdb;        xmol -readFormat xyx %s
# rasmol
chemical/x-pdb;        xterm -e rasmol -pdb %s
chemical/x-pdb;        xterm -e rasmol -xyz %s
```

Figure 15.8 shows NCSA Mosaic for X Windows on a UNIX system with xmol as a helper application. The molecule can be rotated using your mouse, and pull-down menus allow change of perspective, zoom in, and other manipulations.

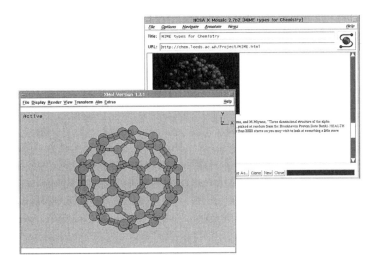

Figure 15.8. *Xmol with NCSA X Mosaic.*

As noted previously the rasmol package is also available for Windows PCs (as raswin) and the Macintosh (as RasMac); both are on the *Building an Intranet* CD-ROM. Configuring helper applications on PC and Macintosh Web browsers is done via the browser's graphical interface, after you've installed the raswin executable on your hard disk. In NCSA Mosaic for Windows, for example, pull down the Options Menu, select Preferences, and then click the Viewers tab. Fill in the blanks as shown in Figure 15.9, specifying the MIME data type/sub-type, filename extension and the path to the raswin executable on your system. As you'll recall, Netscape helper applications are configured similarly, selecting General Preferences from the Options menu and then selecting Helpers. Fill in the blanks with the appropriate information to set up raswin. You'll want to add a descriptive comment to the Description of MIME Type (Optional) box.

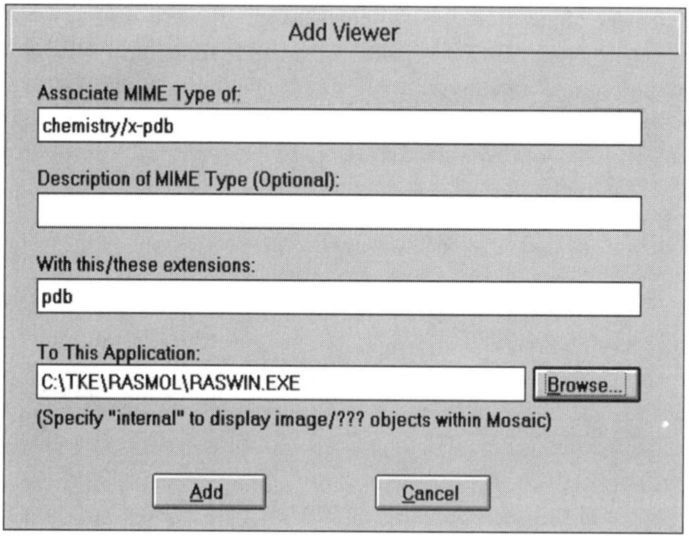

Add Viewer
Associate MIME Type of:
chemistry/x-pdb
Description of MIME Type (Optional):
With this/these extensions:
pdb
To This Application:
C:\TKE\RASMOL\RASWIN.EXE
Browse...
(Specify "internal" to display image/??? objects within Mosaic)
Add
Cancel

Figure 15.9. *NCSA Windows Mosaic viewer setup for raswin molecular modeling package.*

Once you've configured your PC or Macintosh Web browser to use the rasmol package, clicking a hyperlink pointing to a pdb file starts rasmol with a copy of the molecule loaded. From here, you have all the facilities of the rasmol package for viewing and manipulating the molecule in different ways. Figure 15.10 shows NCSA Mosaic for Microsoft Windows with raswin loaded.

RasMol Version 2.5
File Display Colours Options Export Help
File Edit Options Navigate Hotlists
NCSA Mosaic
Search Our Space
News and Announcements
World Wide Web Conference Information
Release Information
Bugs and Bug Like Features
http://www.ncsa.uiuc.edu/SDG/Software/Mosaic/NCSAMosaicHome.html

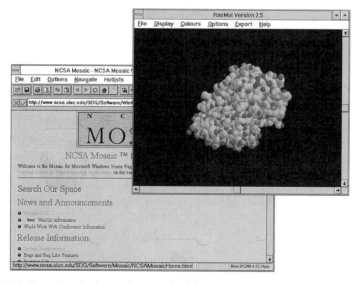

Figure 15.10. *NCSA Mosaic for Windows with raswin loaded.*

For more information about chemical MIME types, see the project's home page at http://chem.leeds.ac.uk/Project/MIME.html. Because this is a transatlantic link, you'll likely find accessing it from the United States slow. There you'll find detailed documentation, as well as links to other molecular modeling software, help in configuring Web browser helper applications for the other packages, and links to other chemistry resources on the Web.

> **Note:** Completely apart from the chemical MIME Project, you can find a number of Java applets for molecular modeling on the Web. Figure 15.11 shows one of them. Because Java applets are interactive, you can rotate or otherwise manipulate the model right in the Netscape window using your mouse or by clicking the plus and minus symbols at the bottom of the image to adjust the specifications. The difference between this and the previous modeling packages is that all interactivity with the model in Java is within your Web browser rather than in the externally running helper application.
>
> For more information about Java, which is taking the Web by storm (it's even brought together IBM, Sun, and Microsoft), see *Teach Yourself Java in 21 Days*, by Laura LeMay and Charles L. Perkins (ISBN 1-57251-030-4), also published by sams.net. You can get more information about this and other sams.net books at your local bookstore or the Macmillan Information SuperLibrary Web site at http://www.mcp.com.

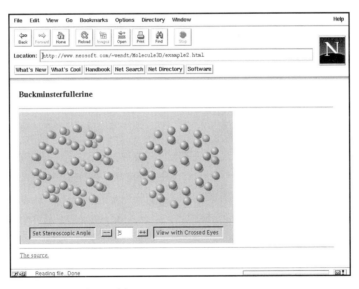

Figure 15.11. *Java applet for molecular modeling.*

Image Processing with Khoros

Computer-based image processing is a growing field, with strong interest in a number of technologies, including

Image morphology

Neural networks

Full-color image processing

Image data compression

Image recognition

Knowledge-based image analysis systems

Khoros is a freely available software integration environment from Khoral Research, Inc., featuring both information processsing and data exploration. Initially, Khoros was developed at the Electrical and Computer Engineering Department of the University of New Mexico. Khoral Research is now an independent company, supported by the Khoros Consortium, made up of 30 supporting and affiliate members from government labs and major U.S. and international companies interested in furthering the work of the project. Khoros is for scientists, engineers, data analysts, and explorers who need to perform a variety of domain-specific tasks and solve real problems. It is a complete data exploration and software development environment that reduces the time involved in solving complex problems, allows easy sharing of ideas and information, and promotes software portability. The package includes

A visual programming language

A suite of software development tools that extends the visual language and helps create new applications

An interactive user interface editor

An interactive image display package

2D/3D plotting

An extensive suite of image processing, data manipulation, scientific visualization geometry, and matrix operations.

Although Khoros is too complex a package to cover in any detail in this book, Figure 15.12 shows it running as a Netscape helper application. As with other Web browser helpers, the setup of this one is a matter of adding support in your Web server's `mime.types` file and of setting up the helpers themselves. In the screenshot, you see part of an online, Web-based training course from Khoral Research in the use of the Khoros package. This particular lesson deals with pseudocoloring, a technique to artificially assign colors to a gray scale image. You'll see more of this training course Chapter 21, "Web-Based Training and Presentations," when *Building an Intranet* focuses on using Web tools for training purposes. As with other helper applications about which you've learned in this chapter, this one is completely interactive once loaded from a Web page. In Figure 15.12, the Khoros application cantata has already been run. The glyphs in the main cantata window represent the process this workspace runs, and the smaller image in the upper left is one result of the workspace's run. A particularly interesting thing about cantata is that the onscreen glyphs represent the major elements of the specific program behind the GUI, with the connecting lines indicating program flow. As the program runs, each glyph changes color, giving the programmer and operator visual feedback about the process of each run.

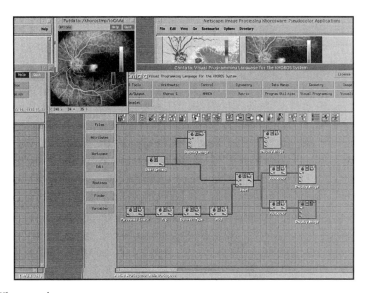

Figure 15.12. *Khoros workspace.*

Khoral Research's Web page, where you can view the training course pages and download the Khoros software, is at http://www.khoral.com/. You need to have installed Khoros before you can actually use the training course. Khoros runs on virtually all modern UNIX systems and requires X Windows. As with other X-based packages, PC users with X server software will be able to run it standalone from UNIX systems, including where it's started from CGI-bin scripts, but will not be able to set it up as a helper application.

Visualization of Complex Relationships

Most people have trouble making sense out of masses of statistical and other numerical data. It's even worse when the mass of information is nonnumerical, such as a massive pile of text documents or the relationships and dependencies of a large software development project. Our eyes seem better able to organize visual information than rows and columns of numbers, or other unorganized data. It's always better if you can somehow visualize the data, so you can see trends, relationships, and the like. This is, of course, why spreadsheet packages have graphing/charting capabilities, enabling you to turn your rows and columns of numbers into visual representations that are meaningful to people when they look at them on a computer screen or on an overhead visual at a business presentation. You've already seen how xgraph, gnuplot, PGplot, as well as your spreadsheet can make your life easier in this way. Sometimes, however, even these tools can't help you see all the trends and relationships in other kinds of highly complex data.

Visualization with Grok

Mentat Corporation's grok is a UNIX software package you can use for visualization of nonnumeric data. Figure 15.13 shows sample grok output. What you see is actually not the relationship of a lot of complex scientific or engineering data. Rather, this is a visual representation of a World Wide Web server home page and all of its subsidiary pages! The home page is represented by the large block at about 10 o'clock in the image's foreground. All the hyperlinks in the many pages are represented by the connecting lines between the source and destination of the link, and each page is represented by a block. You can see, then, not only the overall structure of the document tree and its organizational flow, but also the interrelationships among the documents themselves, such as which pages have hyperlinks to other pages.

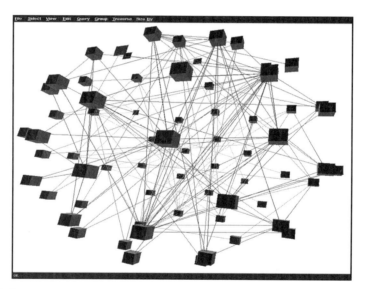

Figure 15.13. *Grok.*

Grok enables you to manipulate the visualization in a number of ways, rotating it to see it from different perspectives, exploding and imploding it, walking down the visual tree step by step, and the like; you can even have it display labels for each entity represented, although doing so on this one would obscure the whole graph. The package is a commercial one, available only on UNIX systems, and is controlled by one of those ubiquitous license-manager daemons that ensures not too many people are using it at any given time. Like gnuplot, grok is a mainly interactive application, since its primary advantages are the capability to manipulate the visualized data after it's drawn. Grok cannot be controlled with macro files or other command-line arguments or used in UNIX pipelines (as with gnuplot) to generate static images, as described earlier, because to do so would obviate all its interactivity.

The grok screenshot (Figure 15.13) was run from a CGI-bin script against a canned demonstration. As a CGI-bin script, it runs on the same machine where the Web server runs, with its X Windows display directed to the remote host that started the demo. You can also use grok as a Web browser helper application. Grok can take its data from plain-text resolver files containing object definitions. There's not a set file-naming rule for grok resolver files, so you can pick one, such as res. Whatever you pick, add it to your server's `mime.types` file, and modify your system mailcap file. The next lines show entries for these two files, respectively.

```
# grok entry for mime.types
application/x-grok     res
# grok entry for mailcap
aplication/x-grok;     /usr/local/bin/grok %s
```

Figure 15.14 shows grok running as an NCSA X Mosaic helper application, called simply by loading a URL containing the grok resolver file.

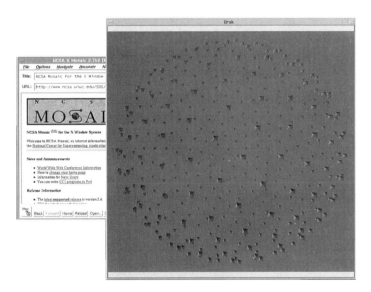

Figure 15.14. *Grok as a helper application.*

Note: Grok's Resolver application is a command-line utility that can be called in CGI-bin scripts to generate res files on the fly from current data. Your scripts, then, can read and resolve current data and pass it to grok for visual display. As with any CGI-bin script that generates data dynamically, the script needs to precede any data it sends to a Web browser with the appropriate MIME data type/sub-type header information.

Because grok is a UNIX-specific program, CGI-bin grok output can be viewed only on systems running X Windows, such as other UNIX systems or PCs running an X package such as DesQView X or Hummingbird's eXceed. Run as a Web browser helper application, grok requires both UNIX and an X Windows server on which to display its output. (One of X Windows' most important features is the capability to display graphics output of programs running on one computer on the X server running on a different, remote computer.) Consequently, use of grok may be limited on your Intranet to those technical customers using UNIX systems or PCs with X servers. There's usually a high correlation between technical users and high-powered workstations such as Sun, IBM, or SGI UNIX systems, so these customers may well be the primary people who need a tool like this; don't disregard the package for these reasons.

> **Tip:** As you work with grok, don't forget the presence of the license manager. Random, unexeplained failures of your CGI-bin scripts that call grok or the intermittent inability of customers to load grok as a helper application may be the result of all the available grok licenses being in use at the time the user tries to access it. In this connection, the Netscape browser has a nice feature of popping up a dialog box with standard output/error from helpers.

Visualization with GraphViz

AT&T's Graph Visualization (GraphViz), a freely available software package, contains programs for viewing and interacting with directed graph drawings, with emphasis on making readable layouts and offering graph layouts as an interface to other systems. One of its components, dot, quickly produces beautiful pictures of large abstract directed graphs on a personal workstation. GraphViz runs under X Windows on UNIX systems and on PCs running Microsoft Windows. As with grok, GraphViz can reduce large amounts of data to a graphical representation that shows the relationships among the data. Figure 15.15 shows a portion of a large directed graph produced by dot. The graph shows the cross references in a number of Internet Requests for Comments (RFCs). As you'll recall from Chapter 3, "Tools for Implementing an Intranet Infrastructure," RFCs are the vehicle by which much of the suite of TCP/IP networking protocols was defined, through public discussion and comment. Few RFCs are standalone documents, and most contain numerous cross-references to others. As Figure 15.15 shows, there are many interrelationships among them, some of which the grapher may not have suspected before generating the graph.

> **Note:** GraphViz is freely available software but is not included on the *Building an Intranet* CD-ROM because of AT&T's licensing requirements. You can download your own copy using your Web browser from http://www.research.att.com/orgs/ssr/book/reuse; there's an online license agreement you'll need to read and acknowledge as well as a Web form to fill out with identifying information about yourself and your company, before you're

allowed to do the actual download. You'll find both full source code for the package and binary versions for several UNIX systems, as well as for Windows PCs, along with full documentation. As a further note, when you access this Web site, you'll see GraphViz is part of a larger AT&T project called Practical Reusable Software, about which a book (of the same title) has been published. You can read about and download several other software packages that may be of interest here as well.

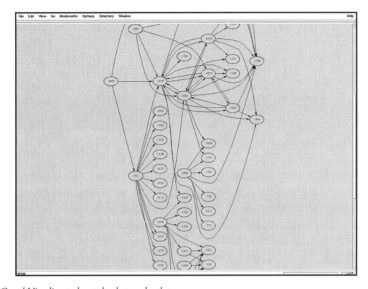

Figure 15.15. *GraphViz directed graph, drawn by dot.*

GraphViz's dot is a good candidate for your CGI-bin scripts because it can write its output in GIF format. (This is how the graph in Figure 15.15 was drawn; as you can see, it's displayed within Netscape.) dot reads plain-text files containing graph attribute specifications for your graphs. The format of the specifications files is well-defined. Here's a simple one, from the dot manual, which is rendered in Figure 15.16:

```
digraph G {
    main -> parse -> execute;
    main -> init;
    main -> cleanup;
    execute -> make_string;
    execute -> printf;
    init -> make_string;
    main -> printf;
    execute -> compare;
}
```

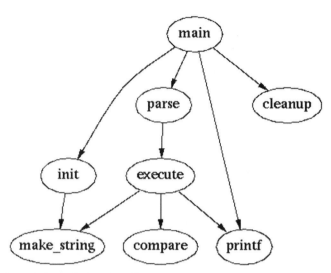

Figure 15.16. *Simple graph drawn by GraphViz dot.*

> **Tip:** Because the format of GraphViz specification files is precisely defined, you can use perl, Tcl, or other utilities to scan data using pattern-matching criteria and generate the specifications files on pretty much any plain-text data. This is how the specification file for the Internet RFCs was prepared, for instance. You really didn't think someone read through each one, jotting down all the cross-references, and then created a specification file by hand, did you? This ability can let you use CGI-bin scripts to dynamically generate new specification files at runtime. Fill-in forms can enable users to specify relationship criteria, with the backend script doing pattern-scanning on a live collection of data and then returning dot-generated graphs to the user's Web browser. This capability may not be a replacement for full-text or relational database indexing, but it can certainly complement the indexing tools about which you learned in Chapters 13, "Indexing and Searching Your Data," and 14, "Web Access to Commercial Database Applications," of *Building an Intranet*.

Once your specifications file is complete, you can turn it into a GIF image with dot for viewing in Web browsers with the following simple command

```
$ dot -Tgif simple.dot -o simple.gif
```

An example CGI-bin script using dot might use a Web fill-in form to prompt customers to enter, or select, the name of a file containing their attributed graph and then dynamically create the graph as a GIF image and return it to their Web browsers for viewing. In this case, the dot command line can be shortened to dispense with creation of the (temporary) output file, `simple.gif`. Here's a perl fragment to this end:

```
print "Content-Type: image/gif\n\n";
system("/usr/local/bin/dot -Tgif $filename");
```

The standard output of this fragment begins with the required MIME data type/sub-type header, followed by a blank line and the GIF image datastream created from the specification file (represented by $filename on the command line); no temporary file is created or needed. The customer's Web browser reads the incoming header information, recognizing the MIME data type/subtype as one it can handle directly, and displays the dynamically created image. The image is created once, with no cleanup afterward necessary. This is useful for *ad hoc* visualizations or when the data being graphed changes rapidly. In either case, there's no reason to keep the temporary image files around. Your customers benefit because your CGI-bin script runs faster, as it has one fewer step to perform, and with fewer file i/o operations.

Similarly, your CGI-bin script could retrieve a Web URL, from another Web server on your Intranet, just as easily as it could a file. Finally, to turn full circle to the first section of this chapter, dot can graph plain-text files containing columns and rows of numbers. Such files might be those generated by instruments or other data-gathering processes, or even your exported spreadsheet files. Whatever the data source, here you have yet another way of generating graphical representations of your numerical datasets. The advantage of dot over other graphing tools is its more refined data-visualization capabilities, including the capability of viewing the visually displayed data from different perspectives in different forms and to zoom in on parts of it.

dot can also function as a Web browser helper application for UNIX users, as shown in Figure 15.17. We've used the filename extension dot and added it the mime.types file in the usual fashion. Changes to the mailcap file, however, are a bit different from what you're accustomed to. Here's the example entry:

```
application/x-dot;      /usr/local/bin/dot -Tgif %s ¦ display
```

As you can see, the command-line invocation of dot is used in this example as well (with no temporary file being created), but the dot command's output is further processed by being piped to ImageMagick display. As the screenshot shows, the helper application your customer actually sees onscreen is display, not dot, which has merely done its thing in the background and gone away, passing its GIF-image output to display.

PC users won't be able to use dot as a helper application, even though it's available for Windows. The reason for this is the inability to do the sort of command pipelines shown in the UNIX mailcap example. Even though dot can directly produce GIF images that should be viewable in customers' Web browsers, the key MIME data type/sub-type header can't be generated by dot; this header must come from your CGI-bin scripts, which can call dot with the correct command-line arguments and pass the image data back to your customers' Web browsers for viewing.

Web Interface to Parallel Computing

Scientists and engineers often need to be able to harness the horsepower of multiple computer systems for large jobs. Often this involves parallel execution of pieces of the overall jobs across a range of networked computers. Such jobs can range from large software builds where several machines do parallel compilation of object code to other complex computations that can broken down and run in parallel on multiple CPUs. Besides the obvious value of such parallel execution, there's the less obvious value of being able to access underutilized computing resources on a network to speed up work. There are a number of these distributed job-scheduling packages available, a couple of which are described in following text. The particular package you might use, however, isn't important here. What is important is you can build Web-based interfaces to them using HTML forms markup and CGI-bin scripting. In fact, one vendor, CraySoft, has already come out with a Web interface to its product.

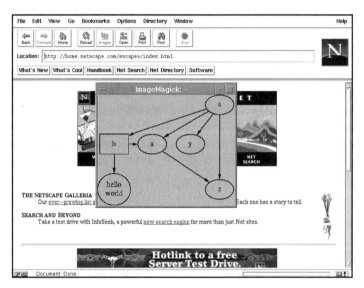

Figure 15.17. *dot as a helper application.*

CraySoft Network Queuing Environment

CraySoft's NQE is a job-management facility for integrating heterogeneous networks of UNIX workstations and servers. Users on client systems submit scripts to NQE batch-execution servers. Jobs are run under the control of a network load balancer, which sends them, or pieces of them, to the servers on the network, managing the load and coordinating the separate pieces of the running jobs. Besides network load balancing, which allows customers to treat multiple NQE servers as a single computational resource. NQE provides automatic job routing, event dependency, and guaranteed file transfers. Although most people think of massive, room-filling supercomputers when they hear the name Cray, both the NQE server and client products are available for even desktop UNIX systems from Sun, IBM, SGI, HP, and DEC.

Figure 15.18 shows CraySoft's Web front end to NQE, which is included with Version 2.0 of NQE. As you can see, it's a pretty standard looking Web page with a number of hyperlinks. Among them are the standard features of any distributed job scheduler, including job creation and submission, job status inquiries, and job management. One important practical result of this product is that now PCs can become NQE clients just as easily as UNIX systems. The form you see is merely the front end to a set of CGI-bin scripts that run on the Web server, which can submit users' jobs to the real NQE client software and return results to the user's Web browser. There's also online help, available in more Web documents. For more information about NQE, see CraySoft's technical paper at `http://www.cray.com/PUBLIC/product-info/craysoft/WLM/NQE/nqe.tech.paper.html`.

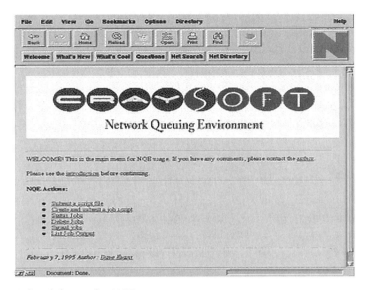

Figure 15.18. *CraySoft Web front end to NQE.*

Distributed Queueing System

Researchers at Florida State University's Supercomputer Computations Research Institute in the United States have developed the Distributed Queuing System (DQS) as freely available software. Available in UNIX source code form, you'll find DQS on the *Building an Intranet* CD-ROM and should have no trouble building it on your system. Although DQS has its own native graphical user interface, shown in Figure 15.19, you can certainly interpose a Web front end to the overall system, much like that shown previously for the CraySoft NQE product. In mid-February, 1996, in fact, the DQS team began work on CGI-bin interfaces to the package, so you may be able to get and install them by the time you read this book. Each one of the two rows of buttons across the top of the screenshot is a DQS utility that can be run standalone and to which instructions can be send using standard input. As a result, your customers can access them from a Web page to schedule jobs, check their status, and otherwise manage them. For more information about DQS, see the Florida State University Web page for it at `http://www.scri.fsu.edu/~pasko/dqs.html`.

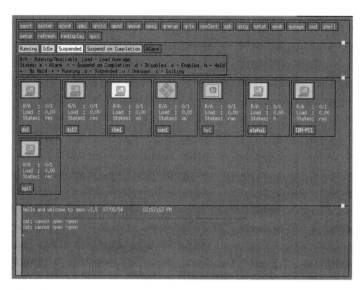

Figure 15.19. *Distributed Queuing System's qmon graphical interface.*

> **Note:** DQS is also available in a supported commercial version, called Codine, from the German company GENIAS Software GmbH. For more information, see the company's Web site at http://www.genias.de. No-cost 30-day demonstration versions of Codine for all the major UNIX platforms are available from the company. At the time this chapter was being written GENIAS did not have any Web-based interface to the product.

The DQS GUI is an X Windows package, limiting its use to UNIX users or those with X servers on PCs. This is not a critical factor in building your CGI-bin scripts as front ends for DQS. The package has a standard UNIX command-line interface as well, so your script can send commands to it via standard input and get back command results for reformatting into HTML for viewing in customers' Web browsers. This is essentially what's been done with the CraySoft DQE product's Web front end. The great value of using CGI-bin scripts to interface with DQS rather than using the package's own GUI is, as you've seen in so many other instances in *Building an Intranet*, users have access to the package's facilities using their Web browser. In a CGI-bin environment, it doesn't matter what kind of computer system customers are using. As long as they have an account on UNIX systems running DQS, they can use the system with Mosaic or Netscape as the graphical interface through your CGI-bin scripts.

Computer-Aided Drafting Packages

CAD is another so-far unmined area of Web applications. Depending on your particular CAD package, you may be able to use it as a Web helper application. A critical factor, particularly on

PC platforms, is how your package starts up. As you've probably figured out in setting up other Web browser helper applications, the key to any of them is the capability to start with a filename as a command-line argument. This is made quite clear in your UNIX mailcap files where you set up lines like:

```
application/pluperstat;    /usr/local/bin/pluper %s
```

Here the placeholder string %s represents the name of the file to be loaded by your helper application. In their efforts to be user friendly, though, some Windows applications forget to allow for starting them with a filename on the command line; even using the Program Manager's Run command to specify the command with a filename sometimes still brings up an empty application. In these cases, you have to use a pull-down menu or dialog box to load any file, and those particular applications can't be used as Web browser helpers. Check your CAD package's documentation to see whether it can be started with a filename as a command-line argument. If so, you're all set. Just modify your mime.types file to add your CAD package's standard filename extension and set up your package as a helper in the normal way.

Your company may use several different CAD packages, just as you may use different word processors or spreadsheets, so you'll want a way of sharing your drawings across platforms. The Initial Graphics Exchange Specification (IGES) and AutoCAD's Data eXchange format (DXF) are two CAD data-exchange formats many packages support in one way or another. Many of them also directly support the AutoCAD DWG (drawing) native format. Your package may be able to read one or more of these formats, either directly or via importing files in the foreign format. This is roughly analogous to word processors such as Word and WordPerfect being able to recognize and load documents in the other's format. Portability among CAD packages is not as widespread as in word processors or spreadsheets, but the DWG, IGES, and DXF formats are the nearest thing. Whether you can use your particular package as a helper application on these formats depends on whether it will automatically recognize and load them, or whether there's a manual import step you need to use first. Some packages may also provide standalone convertors that you can use to mass-convert a set of drawings. One such is Parametric Technology's Pro/ENGINEER, a UNIX package that includes a command-line utility, called proigsutil, for batch-converting IGES files into the Pro/ENGINEER native format. The package also has a Pro/BATCH utility for converting its native files into IGES, DXF, and several other less commonly used CAD exchange formats.

You may also want to consider using CGI-bin scripts that call standalone conversion utilities, such as Tailor Made Software's (http://www.serv.net/tms/) several conversion products for CAD datafiles. The company will also build your own custom package based on your particular mix of packages and exchange needs. Another company, SoftSource (http://www.softsource.com/softsource/), markets a package called DRAWING Librarian (DL), which supports exchange of AutoCAD DWG, DXF, and several other CAD formats (though not IGES). SoftSource also markets DXE (Data Exchange Engine), a programmer's toolkit for reading, writing, and displaying DWG and DXF files. With your CGI-bin scripts, you'll need to be able to run programs like DL (ordinarily an interactive application) in UNIX pipelines on your Web server to convert drawings on the fly and return them in a format the user's Web browser with a helper application is set up to handle. The DXE toolkit may come in handy if you need to build your own conversion utility.

> **Tip:** SoftSource has a Netscape Version 2 plug-in for dynamically viewing AutoCAD DWG and DXF files within Netscape; no helper applications are involved. The package, available from SoftSource's Web site, runs only on PCs running Windows 95 or Windows NT. For general information on Netscape plug-ins, see the Netscape home page at `http://home.netscape.com/`.

A Postscript on Scientific Data Formats

The National Center for Supercomputing Applications (NCSA), developer of NCSA Mosaic and the NCSA httpd Web server, has for some years been developing standard methods of storing and accessing scientific data of all kinds. Called the Hierarchical Data Format, or HDF, NCSA's work has led to development of an architecturally neutral, multi-object file format that facilitates the transfer of various types of data (text, images, n-dimensional datasets, and others) among computers and computer programs. HDF allows self-definition of data content (that is, the file contains its own data-format definition) and easy extensibility for future enhancements or compatibility with other data formats. Scientists know well the problems related to storing data electronically. Every project, it seems, generates a slightly different way of formatting electronic data for storage, along with the accompanying need to document the format so it can be extracted later. NCSA's HDF work is aimed at standardizing scientific data formats, so scientists can do science, not computer data-format programming and documentation.

Although this subject may seem at first to be more of a digression than an integral part of this chapter, unrelated even to the scientific aspects of your Intranet, stay with it for just a moment. NCSA Mosaic for X Windows (that is, for UNIX systems) has built-in support for HDF data. Figure 15.20 shows some example HDF data from the U.S. National Aeronautics and Space Administration's Distributed Active Archive Center (`http://daac.gsfc.nasa.gov`) viewed in X Mosaic. As you can see, the data includes not only plain text, but also graphics images showing numerical data; it looks, in fact, just like any other Web page, thanks to Mosaic's built-in HDF support. NCSA has plans to add HDF support to the PC and Macintosh versions of Mosaic and/or to develop more extensive, interactive helper applications with such support. You can read more about HDF, as well as downloading the HDF source code for your UNIX systems, at the HDF home page, `http://hdf.ncsa.uiuc.edu:8001/`.

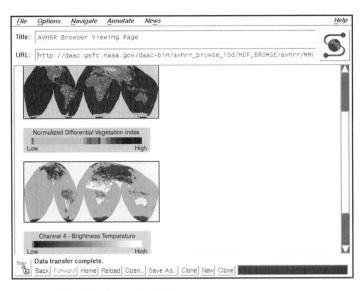

Figure 15.20. *NCSA Mosaic for X Windows and HDF data.*

Summary

Although earlier chapters of *Building an Intranet* have covered subjects of wide, general interest to Intranet builders, this chapter has focused on narrower, more technical ones. It's been a wide-ranging survey of how a number of scientific, technical, engineering, and related resources can be put in place on your Intranet. In the course of the chapter, you have

- ◆ Learned about dynamic graphing and data modeling, and applied both to a wide range of uses.
- ◆ Learned about the intensive Web-related activity in the field of chemistry.
- ◆ Learned about Web-based image processing.
- ◆ Learned how to use the Web for graphical visualization of complex relationships among numbers and other objects.
- ◆ Learned about using the Web for viewing and exchanging computer-aided drafting (CAD) drawings.
- ◆ Learned about existing and planned Web support for standardized scientific data formats.

This has been the final chapter of the fourth major section of *Building an Intranet*, in which you learned about setting up and using advanced applications on your Intranet. In the next section, you'll find a series of chapters giving practical examples of Intranet applications you can build, using the tools about which you've learned so far in this book and your imagination.

V

PART

Sample Applications

CHAPTER 16

Intranet Help Desk

Setting up your organization's Help Desk or Customer Service operation on your Intranet is a great way to enhance its efficiency, and an excellent practical use for your Intranet. In a Help Desk situation, it's important to get answers to customers quickly, whether the question is common or an out-of-the-ordinary one. Keeping your Help Desk files on your Intranet can help your employees and customers find the right answer to questions most efficiently. Your Intranet can also help track problem reports and generate historical information about their solutions, making it easy to deal with the frequently-occurring questions, and enhancing its management.

Setting up your Help Desk on your Intranet is likely to be one of your easiest Intranet jobs. Because you probably already have most of the pieces of an Intranet Help Desk already in place, all you have to do is creatively apply the information you've learned so far in this book. This chapter shows you how.

Chapter Objectives

As with the rest of the chapters in this book, let's begin by laying out some chapter objectives. This will help you get oriented to the material to be presented; you may want to refer back to this list as you work your way through the chapter. In this chapter, you will:

- ◆ Consider the nature, purpose, and substantive content of a Help Desk in the context of your Intranet
- ◆ Consider what existing Help Desk electronic information is available to put onto your Intranet

◆ Determine the form(s) of that information

◆ Learn how to put that information together so it's accessible to customers using a Web browser, putting what you've learned about MIME data types/subtypes and Web browser helper applications to work

◆ Put what you've learned about Intranet document indexing to work to streamline the search and retrieval of Help Desk information

◆ Think about maintaining Help Desk records for quality-control and related purposes

◆ Open up your Intranet Help Desk for direct access by your Intranet's customers

These objectives, as you can see, are the practical application of the information and tools found in the rest of this book. Your steps in putting your together Intranet Help Desk involve: analyzing and converting available data (Chapter 6); setting up MIME and helper applications information (Chapters 7 and 10-12); selecting appropriate network services and tools (Chapter 8) to implement your goals; and applying indexing and database tools (Chapters 13 and 14, respectively). You'll find this same general process of integration applied in this and each of the next seven chapters.

What Does a Help Desk Do?

Although the answer to that question may seem obvious to many readers, professionals know that it's still a good idea to lay out specifics. Doing so can help focus your Intranet Help Desk planning. Your first list may look like this:

◆ Receive and record telephone, e-mail, or other requests for help from customers

◆ Research customer questions and provide answers to the customers

◆ Track and update the status of trouble tickets (help desk terminology for the tracking records attached to trouble reports) for both internal and customer-reporting purposes

◆ Monitor the quality of the Help Desk's activities, including both accuracy and timeliness of answers

Intranet Context for Help Desk

Except for the physical taking of telephone calls, which can in large operations be partially automated by voice menuing systems, all of these steps can be performed using Web or Web-related tools about which you've learned in this book. Let's revise the above list to add some Intranet context; *italics* show what's been added to each item on the list.

◆ Receive and record, *using a Web fill-in-form front end to a trouble-ticket database*, telephone, e-mail, or other requests for help from customers

◆ Research customer questions *using a Web fill-in form that interfaces with a searchable index or other database system* and provide *located* answers to the customers, *possibly via your Web browser's e-mail capabilities*

◆ Track and update the status of trouble tickets, for both internal and customer-reporting purposes, *using a Web front end to your trouble-ticket database*

◆ Monitor the quality of the Help Desk's activities, including both accuracy and timeliness of answers, *using a Web front end to your trouble-ticket database*

Looking at this modified list, it'll probably occur to you that you can add one more item:

◆ Give your Intranet's customers direct access to the Web-based Intranet Help Desk, so they can use their Web browsers to enter their own questions and/or search for problem solutions themselves

What Is the Content of Your Help Desk?

Depending on the mission of your business or organization, your Help Desk may provide any of a wide variety of substantive information. What you provide is based on the perceived and expressed needs of your customers. Since you're probably involved with computers and networks (or you wouldn't be reading this book), it's no doubt easy for you to visualize a Help Desk for computer and network users; you probably already run one. Such an operation can provide answers to questions, such as how to use software packages, how to configure modems or printers, and so on. It can also take trouble reports on malfunctioning or inoperative computer or network hardware or software.

Help Desks are not limited to these narrow, though important, functions. Most large companies operate toll-free 800 numbers for customer support and questions about their products. You can call Proctor & Gamble, for example, with questions about toothpaste or other P&G products. Major furnace or air conditioner manufacturers will refer you to dealers in your area for sales or service. And, of course, computer and computer software manufacturers operate Help Desks for their customers. Of course, there are Help Desk databases of one kind or another underlying all of these operations.

Though quite simple, one of the most widely accessed Help Desk functions on the Internet is package delivery firm Federal Express's Web server. Here (`http://www.fedex.com/`) you can check the status of your delivery using a Web fill-in form and CGI-bin script back end. Figure 16.1 shows the FedEx Tracking Form; just type in your FedEx Air Bill number, and the system shows you the path of your package step-by-step through the delivery system, from pickup to final delivery, with date and time stamps. Even though this application does just one very narrow thing, it's one of the most widely accessed Help Desk/Customer Support sites on the Internet; all of FedEx's competitors have set up similar services on the Web.

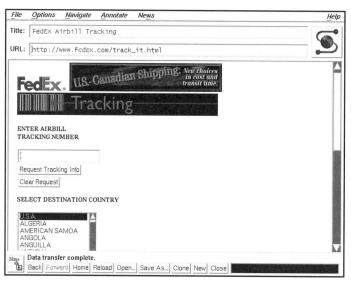

Figure 16.1. *Federal Express Package Tracking.*

Some organizations set up what might be called "Virtual Guy/Girl Friday" Web pages, with tips and information about doing odd jobs around the company. Such operations can cover a wide range of the kinds of miscellaneous questions that come up over and over again, such as who to call to get a broken desk repaired, how to ship an experimental widget, or how to get presentation booklets printed overnight. Your Intranet's Help Desk, then, can be just as expansive or as limited as you want, with the information available subject only to your own imagination.

> **Note:** The Virtual Guy/Girl Friday function might well be implemented using USENET news (see Chapter 22) or other means of communication and collaboration, such as Lotus Notes, Collabra, or other Intranet groupware (see Chapter 23).

Existing Help Desk Information

Help Desks get the same questions over and over again. These are your company's own Frequently Asked Questions, or FAQs. Your canned answers to these questions can form the foundation of your Intranet Help Desk.

In large part, the ease with which users can access the accumulated wisdom and experience of your Help Desk dictates how effective your operation is. Whether your Help Desk uses indexed file cabinets, shelves of tabbed, three-ring binders, a sophisticated database system, or some less formal method to store answers to previously asked questions, your first task is to get these answers online on your Intranet so they're easily accessible.

The main principles for getting your legacy data online are those outlined in Chapter 6, "Quick and Dirty Intranet." In that chapter, you learned how to convert your legacy data into Intranet-usable information. If you have electronic copies of Help Desk documents available, you'll want to use what you learned in that chapter to move this data quickly onto your Intranet, making it accessible via your Web server and browsers. Where you have legacy data that's not in plain text format, you may need to use the conversion tools about which you've learned. This may include using your applications' Save As features to convert data into easily usable formats like plain text. In addition, you may eventually want to use Rich Text format (RTF) as a waystation in converting legacy data into HTML documents for direct use on your Intranet. Also, with vendors like Microsoft and Novell having added direct HTML capabilities to their word processors, you'll be able to save some legacy documents directly to HTML.

As you've learned, it's quite simple to set up Web pages containing simple, clickable lists of available documents. To this end, you'll want to review basic HTML markup in Appendix B, "HTML and CGI Quick Reference," focusing on basic list markup.

Tip: Use your operating system's utilities to get a leg up on creating simple HTML listings of documents. Experienced UNIX vi and emacs editor users know that reading a directory listing into a document is a snap with *bang shell escapes*. DOS command-output redirection (for example, `DIR > skel.htm`) can help with the same thing. You can then add HTML markup to the skeleton files you've very quickly created.

As suggested in Chapter 8, "Adding Services to Your Intranet Adds Value," you can come back to your converted legacy documents once you have your Intranet Help Desk running. This will enable you to refine them and add value by cutting in hyperlinked cross references and the like. This done, your Help Desk staff can use their Web browsers to jump from one document to another, looking for answers to customers' questions by following promising threads. The more cross-references you're able to add, the more capabilities you'll give to your staff.

MIME Type/Subtype Setup

Even after you've successfully converted your legacy Help Desk documents, you'll no doubt end up with a variety of document formats, including plain text files, word processor files, HTML documents, spreadsheets, and others. This may seem a confusing mess. However, you can confidently deal with this situation, using what you learned in Chapters 7 and 10-12. After all, your purpose in building an Intranet was to pull together just such a wide variety of resources and make them accessible using a single interface. All the information about MIME data type/subtypes and helper applications you've learned earlier in this book will help you as you make your Help Desk information available.

As you'll recall, enabling the use of your word processor and other office software packages as Web browser helper applications is a simple, two-step process:

◆ Modify the `mime.types` file on your Intranet's Web server(s).

◆ Configure your customers' Web browsers to deal with the newly defined MIME types/subtypes by defining helper applications.

Chapter 7 provides a thorough grounding in the whole subject of MIME data types/subtypes, while Chapters 10-12 deal individually with common office software packages that you may need to set up as helper applications. Now that you are putting specific documents and other data in place for real work on your Intranet, you may want to review this material so you have the ticklish syntax of the `mime.types` file and the Web browser Helpers dialog boxes down pat. Figure 16.2, which shows WordPerfect being set up as a Netscape helper application, will no doubt bring this all back to you.

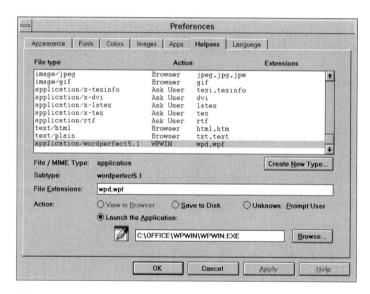

Figure 16.2. *WordPerfect as a Netscape helper application.*

Once you've taken these steps, your Intranet's Help Desk staff can simply use their Web browsers to retrieve and view your documents, regardless of their format. As needed, helper applications open to handle called-for documents. For example, clicking on a hyperlink pointing to a WordPerfect file opens WordPerfect to display the files onscreen. Having located the necessary document with which to respond to the customer's question, your Help Desk staff member is ready to close out the trouble ticket. It's just a couple of additional steps to provide not only the user's answer but also a copy of the document containing it right to the user, via your Intranet.

Indexing Your Help Desk Data

You're probably thinking this chapter has gotten ahead of itself. How, you're wondering, will the Help Desk staff locate answers to customer questions? Surely, they won't just have long onscreen lists of document names that they have to browse through? As with the conversion of your legacy data, the answers to these questions harken back to material we've covered earlier in this book. In Chapter 13, "Indexing and Searching Your Data," you learned about a variety of tools for indexing data on your Intranet and, equally important, tools for searching and retrieving data from the indexes. FreeWAIS-sf, glimpse, and the rest of the packages covered in that chapter give you several powerful means of indexing your Help Desk documents and other data. Equally powerful tools like SFgate and Harvest make it easy for your Help Desk staff to search out answers to customer inquiries by using Web fill-in forms of the sort you've seen earlier in this book.

In this connection, recall our tongue-in-cheek discussion of a search for Shakespeare's famous 'To thine ownself be true" line in Chapter 14. (The screen shown in Figure 16.3 should jog your memory.) The capability of searching for relatively complex text strings like that one is an important feature for a Help Desk to have. In this context, the Shakespearean example is a good deal more relevant. Note that the database here was built with the glimpse indexing tool, and the search engine being used is Harvest.

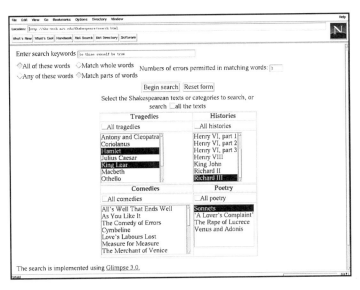

Figure 16.3. *A complex search in a Shakespearean text database.*

If your Help Desk data is bundled up into a commercial database application, you'll want to look at the Web-related relational database tools described in Chapter 14. The ability to create Web fill-in forms that interface with database engines via CGI-bin scripts (or other means) will enhance your Help Desk's ability to serve its customers.

If you have built a custom text-based database application for your Help Desk for which no tools are available, don't lose hope. You can probably dump the data out to plain text files, unless your database is locked up without standard capabilities. As long as the data has an identifiable format, it can be run through glimpse, freeWAIS-sf, or one of the other indexing tools mentioned in the last paragraph, to make it accessible via Web browsers using fill-in forms. This will enable you to continue to use the data you've accumulated in your application, while at the same time freeing you of proprietary data formats. Further, with the outstanding capabilities of these search engines, you may find search-and-retrieval performance better than you had with your custom database— plus, you get that nice, user-friendly Web interface.

Help Desk Record Keeping

Unless your Help Desk operation is quite small and managed out of one person's back pocket, you're probably interested in keeping records of questions and their resolutions, trouble reports, and the like. You want substantive information about your Help Desk calls, such as the answers to questions customers have asked, so you can have them available the next time the same question arises. You also want timeliness and quality-control information about the way the calls were handled. For example, was the answer provided on time, and with accuracy? Many Help Desks do this sort of tracking with paper forms, or with some sort of computer program, which may or may not be integrated with the Help Desk substantive database itself.

It has probably occurred to you by now to wonder if you can put a Web interface on your Help Desk management and record keeping itself. That is, if you can provide your Help Desk staff (or everyone in your Intranet) the capability to search and retrieve documents and other data using their Web browsers, shouldn't it be possible to do your housekeeping—assigning and tracking questions or trouble reports, getting quality-control information, and the like—using similar methods?

The answer is, of course, yes. You've already written CGI-bin scripts that interface with fill-in forms and the index of your substantive Help Desk data. The same techniques you've used to retrieve data can also be used to enter and track its progress, and to assign trouble reports to individual technicians. This can be done in as simple or as complex a way as you want or need.

For example, with the NCSA httpd server source distribution on the *Building an Intranet* CD-ROM, you'll find a directory of simple CGI-bin scripts. One of them, a perl script called `mail`, creates a fill-in form for sending e-mail to one or more of a pre-defined list of users. While this is part of a promised overall set of WebMonitor utilities from NCSA (see `http://hoohoo.ncsa.uiuc.edu/webmonitor/desc.html`), it's also something you can use almost right out of the box for your Help Desk.

As you can see from Figure 16.4, it's a simple fill-in form with a pull-down list of possible addressees. The user selects one or more addressee names, and fills in the subject, return address, and text of the message using the form. Clicking on the Send Email button fires the message off to the selected users. You can no doubt imagine many ways in which such a simple form can be used, but it can be particularly useful in the context of managing your Help Desk. Just fill in the form with the control information about a new call, question, or trouble report, select the person to whom the problem is to be assigned, and fire off the whole thing as e-mail. You'll find this mail script in the CGI-bin subdirectory of your main httpd directory.

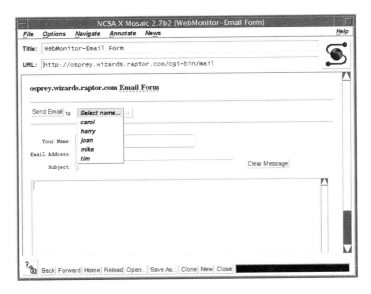

Figure 16.4. *NCSA WebMonitor mail fill-in form.*

This simple script should set your mind to overflowing with possibilities. Besides using it to assign support calls, here are some other uses (some of which might require the script to be modified, or other scripts written):

◆ Use it to send e-mail to people who are responsible for the tracking of calls themselves.

◆ Modify it to send a confirmation e-mail message to the original sender of the message, perhaps with tracking or Help-Desk staff assignment-control (that is, trouble ticket number) information.

◆ Use it to send mail, using UNIX standard input, to a back end program or other script that automatically updates your call-tracking database and/or makes trouble call assignments.

> **Note:** The WebMonitor mail script generates special e-mail headers (see Chapter 7, "MIME and Helper Applications," on the structure of Internet e-mail messages) that provide potentially useful information for your Help Desk. Here's what some of them look like:
>
> ```
> Received: (from nobody@localhost) by osprey.wizards.raptor.com (8.7.3/8.7.1)
> id VAA05477 for tkevans; Thu, 25 Jan 1996 21:14:00 -0500 (EST)
> Date: Thu, 25 Jan 1996 21:14:00 -0500 (EST)
> Message-Id: <199601260214.VAA05477@osprey.wizards.raptor.com>
> From: tkevans@dupont.com
> To: tkevans
> Subject: Test of WebMonitor mail Script
> X-Comments: NOTE: This message was sent through the WebMonitor mail form
> X-Comments: HOST: osprey.wizards.raptor.com (204.7.244.8)
> X-Comments: BROWSER: NCSA_Mosaic/2.7b2 (X11;SunOS 5.4 i86pc) libwww/2.12
> modified
> Content-Type: text
> Content-Length: 18
> Status: RO
> (message) This is a test message
> ```
>
> As you can see, the script uses an e-mail header X-Comments: to identify itself as having been generated by the script, as well as including useful hostname and browser name information. You'll recall from Chapters 13 and 14 how CGI-bin scripts can use this sort of information from Web browsers for decision-making and record-keeping purposes.

GNU Gnats, aka Problem Report Management System (PRMS)

The last bulleted item on the list in the preceding section (about using fill-in forms to generate Help Desk e-mail) suggests an even wider range of possibilities. In Chapters 13, "Indexing and Searching Your Data," and 14, "Web Access to Commercial Database Applications," you learned how complex fill-in Web forms can be front ends to sophisticated CGI-bin scripts for searching and/ or updating databases using UNIX standard input. Information entered into these forms is passed off to the database back end for processing by the CGI-bin scripts, with the results of searches or data entry passed back to the user's Web browser by the script. The *Building an Intranet* CD-ROM contains source code for a complete problem-tracking database system, the GNU Project's no-cost *Gnats Problem Management System*, sometimes also called PRMS.

> **Note:** GNU's Not UNIX. The Free Software Foundation's GNU (purposely mispronounced "GA-NU") Project is a volunteer project started by MacArthur Genius Grant winner Richard Stallman. The purpose of the project is nothing less than the development of a complete, no-cost replacement of the whole UNIX operating system. GNU places heavy emphasis on software-development tools, but there are a wide variety of packages in the GNU library. Whether the project, laden with Stallman's near-fanatic philosophies about the whole idea of patents for computer software, ever succeeds is still uncertain.

Nonetheless, the project has produced important major software packages, including the widely respected gcc compiler package (supporting both the C and C++ languages) and its supporting software-development packages, the GNU emacs text editor, and improved versions of many standard UNIX utilities. GNU software is distributed under the GNU General Public License (GPL), which states, generally, the software is copyrighted but free, that you can redistribute it for a fee, and that you may modify it and distribute the modification, as long as the redistribution is subject to the same GPL. For more information about GNU and the Free Software Foundation, see `ftp://prep.ai.mit.edu/pub/gnu`. Although all GNU project software, including gnats/PRMS, is free, you can purchase commercial-quality support for it from Cygnus Support; you'll find more information at `http://www.cygnus.com/`.

Gnats/PRMS is a complete problem-tracking database system. It provides for:

◆ Entering trouble reports

◆ Categorizing them by subject and severity for later reporting

◆ Automatic assignment and notification of incoming reports to gnats maintainers (individuals you have assigned to various areas of responsibility)

◆ Automated report tracking, including reminders about unresolved ones

◆ General relational database-reporting capabilities for extracting status and historical information about problem resolution

As distributed, gnats/PRMS has a bit of a torturous interface. You enter problems using a template form that you open in a text editor like vi or emacs. Basically, here's how it works: the problem reports you create using this interface are e-mailed to the gnats/PRMS program using UNIX standard input. The receiving program processes the reports based on the structure of the reporting template, enters the report into the database, issues a problem report tracking number, assigns the problem to a maintainer, and acknowledges the report's sender via e-mail.

Fortunately, Dan Kegel and Huy Le, of the California Institute of Technology, have developed (what else?) a perl CGI-bin script called wwwgnats, which provides a Web fill-in form interface to gnats. (Wwwgnats is on the *Building an Intranet* CD-ROM; more information at `http://alumni.caltech.edu/~dank/`.) Figures 16.5 and 16.6 show overlapping screenshots of an example wwwgnats data-entry form. The form includes not only check boxes and scrollable menus for identifying a problem, but also free-form text boxes for describing the problem in more detail.

Once the form is complete, the user clicks on a Submit button. Data on the form is passed off to the database back end via e-mail, then entered directly into the problem database. The problem is assigned to a maintainer, who is notified via e-mail of the new problem report. Help Desk staff members taking problem reports via telephone can fill in a form like this online as the problems come in. Perhaps more important, you can let your Help Desk customers access this form directly, so they can enter their own problem reports. Although it's often useful for call-takers to be able to question users reporting problems to focus the user's question, you may still find providing users direct access to a problem-reporting facility like this one useful and economical in many situations.

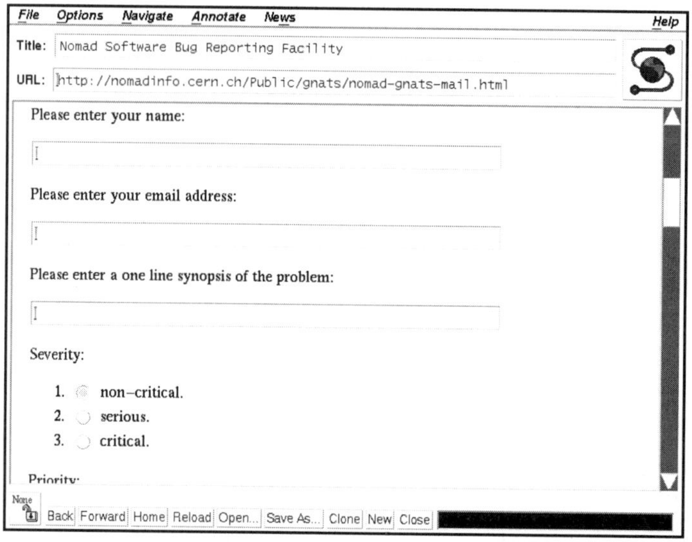

Figure 16.5. wwwgnats' problem reporting form (Part 1).

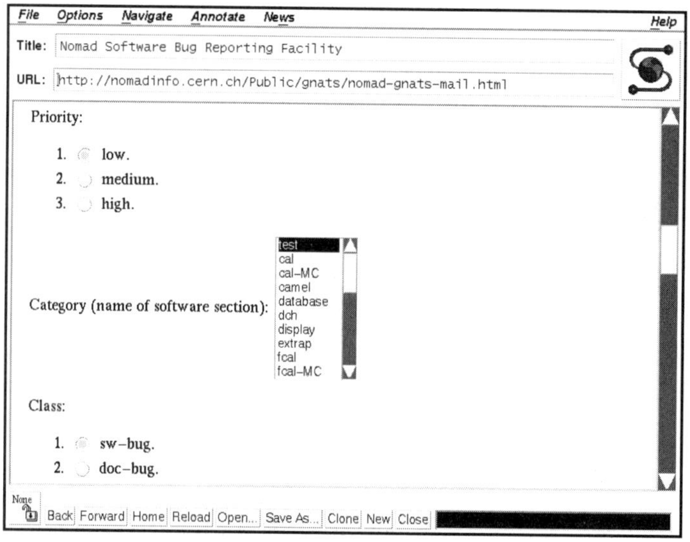

Figure 16.6. wwwgnats' problem reporting form (Part 2).

wwwgnats can also provide problem database management functions, enabling you to query the database by problem category, status, or maintainer, as well as for historical information about closed problems. Such functions are important for quality control and other purposes, of course. Figures 16.7 and 16.8 show a sample fill-in form for doing such database searches. There are several things to note about the form:

◆ You can either enter new problems or search for a specific existing problems, using the unique gnats/PRMS problem record (PR) number (Figure 16.7).

◆ You can get summaries of all active problems in the database (Figure 16.7).

◆ You can get summaries of active problems assigned to specific maintainers (Figure 16.7).

◆ You can restrict your search to specific fields of the problem database (Figure 16.8).

◆ You can select problem status and/or category for searches (Figure 16.8).

◆ You can select by the name of the problem originator.

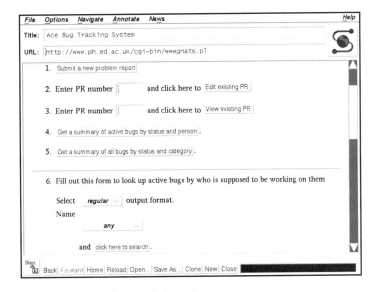

Figure 16.7. wwwgnats' problem database search (Part 1).

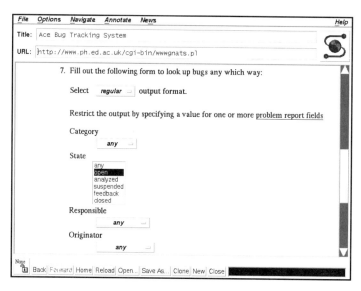

Figure 16.8. *wwwgnats' problem database search (Part 2).*

wwwgnats' co-author Dan Kegel maintains an extensive gnats/PRMS Web page at `http://alumni.caltech.edu/~dank/gnats.html`. Here you'll find, among other things, links to miscellaneous gnats-related subjects, including a link to a FAQ for the Usenet newsgroup `comp.software.config-mgmt`. This netnews group focuses on software configuration management, including problem-tracking software. Problem-tracking software is a critical part of software development and configuration, but is also useful in a generic sense for Help Desks. You'll want to look at the document's Problem Management Tools section (`http://www.iac.honeywell.com/Pub/Tech/CM/PMTools.html`), where you'll find lots of information about both free and commercial problem-tracking software. If you have access to Usenet news, you'll want to lurk in this newsgroup, watching for current useful information and discussion about software that may meet your Help Desk needs. The `comp.software.config-mgmt` FAQ lists a number of commercial vendors and tabulates mentions of them in the newsgroups. Most of the packages listed in the FAQ have graphical front ends, either for X Window or Microsoft Windows (or both), but few have Web interfaces, yet.

Most of the packages tracked in the newsgroup FAQ are software-development bug-trackers, so they may not be completely relevant to your Help Desk needs. Those more general problem-tracking packages receiving the most mentions include:

◆ Scopus Technologies' ProTEAM, an integrated set of packages (`http://www.scopus.com/`), supporting Sybase, Oracle, Informix, and Microsoft SQL database server back ends.

◆ Clarify's Customer Service Management System, supporting Sybase, Oracle, and Microsoft SQL database server back ends.

Neither of these two packages, however, has a Web-based user interface like wwwgnats, although both have e-mail interfaces. This being the case, you can toss out the vendors' graphical or text-based interfaces for creating problem reports and build your own Web fill-in forms and back end CGI-bin scripts to interface with the packages via e-mail. It shouldn't be difficult to capture one of the package's e-mail messages and take it apart. Recall what you learned in Chapter 7, "MIME and Helper Applications," about the Simple Mail Transport Protocol and the standard structure of Internet e-mail messages.

Remedy Corporation's ARWeb product provides one of the few Web interfaces to commercial problem-tracking software packages. Figure 16.9 shows one of Remedy's sample ARWeb forms, a front end to its Action Request product. Compared to the relational database Web interfaces you saw in Chapter 14, "Web Access to Commercial Database Applications," this is fairly crude, but Remedy's competitors don't have anything at all. You can expect this to change, possibly by the time you read this, if all the recent activity in the Relational Database market is any indication. Action Request supports Informix, Ingres, Oracle, Microsoft SQL, and Sybase database back ends, but can also create and use its own flat-file database for problem tracking.

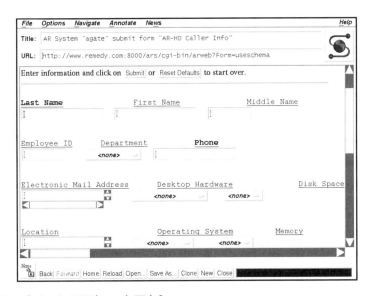

Figure 16.9. *Remedy Corp's ARWeb sample Web form.*

Dean Collins' freeware package Problem Tracking System (PTS) is in Alpha test, but it now has a (minimal) Web CGI-bin-based interface, called Web/PTS, shown in Figure 16.10. The package is so incomplete and support so spotty that it would not otherwise be mentioned, except for its Web interface. You'll find source code for the package on the *Building an Intranet* CD-ROM, but be sure to check out the PTS home page for a later, more stable release (http://www.halcyon.com/dean/pts/pts.html).

Collins has had a great deal of trouble porting the package to—of all UNIX systems—Suns. If you're a Sun shop, then, it may not pay you to get your hopes up. Happily, though, indications are the new Web/PTS interface is the focus of Dean's current attention. Use of Netscape, Mosaic, and other graphical Web browsers is widely supported on Sun systems, so problems with building the older PTS X Windows interface on Sun OpenWindows systems are probably irrelevant. PTS creates its own database for problem records; it does not interface with any commercial database.

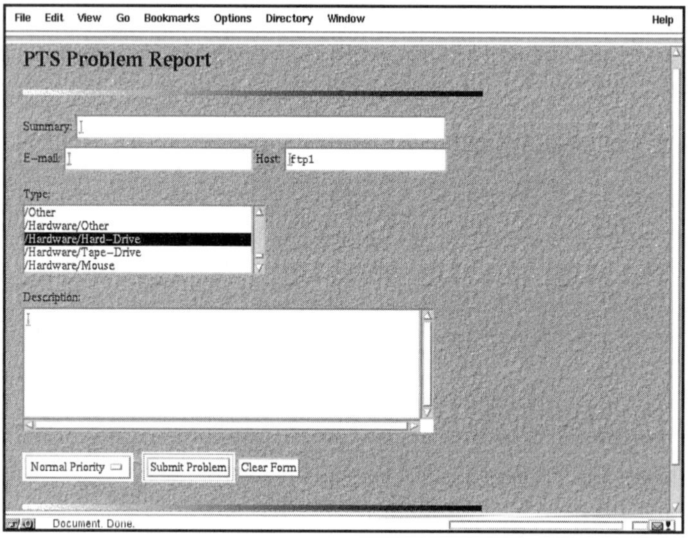

Figure 16.10. Web/PTS problem entry form.

The Connecticut consulting firm McGeary and Associates (http://www.mcgeary.com/) sells customized applications based on its electronic publishing/database package, Folio VIEWS. According to the company, VIEWS InfoBase databases can contain electronic information of all kinds, and the company can customize the package in a wide variety of ways, including as a Help Desk application. Figure 16.11 shows a Web-based, CGI-bin interface to a searchable VIEWS InfoBase of laboratories in the State of Connecticut. While the demo isn't a Help Desk by a long shot, it gives you a taste of what the package can do. Notice the table used as a fill-in form. (You may not be able to view this page with Mosaic or other browsers that don't support full HTML Table capabilities; Figure 16.11 shows Netscape Version 2, of course.)

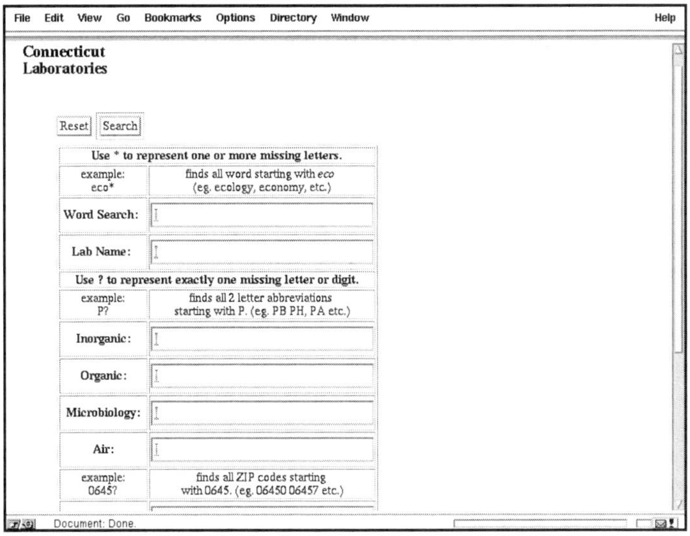

Figure 16.11. *Folio VIEWS InfoBase Web Interface.*

Give Your Customers Access

The preceding section on problem-tracking software for your Intranet was intended to do more than simply acquaint you with the available software and its capabilities. It was also intended to lead you to the notion of making your Intranet Help Desk system accessible to all of your customers via their Web browsers. Even in the largely non-Web-aware problem-tracking software environment, there's widespread support for making it possible for users to enter their own problem reports. Most of the vendor packages have some sort of graphical interface for users with which to enter problem reports. There are a number of reasons for this. Most of them are the same reasons that companies put voice-menu phone systems in place: to save time and staff costs.

Unlike the situation with such phone systems, however, which can make a customer feel depersonalized, direct user interface to problem-tracking systems can give customers more control over their problem reporting, and a better overall feel for the process. It may be true, for example, that a fill-in form on the customer's computer screen is the same one a Help Desk call-taker would fill in when answering the customer's telephone call. Still, there's a definite feeling of finality about clicking that Submit button, especially if the system gives you a confirmation message with a problem-tracking number, either onscreen or in an e-mail message.

Of the problem-tracking software packages described in the last section, only wwwgnats, ARWeb, and (just barely) Web/PTS have ready-to-use Web-based interfaces you can present to your Help Desk's customers. If you're interested in making your Help Desk application accessible across your Intranet, these packages are your best bet for a quick start. ARWeb's underlying application,

Action Request, is specifically a problem-tracking package, so you should expect to be able to use it as such pretty much out of the box, with minimal customization needed.

The Folio VIEWS InfoBase product, as a general database package, will no doubt require a good deal of customization to fit it to your needs. General-purpose products like Folio VIEWS InfoBase are sometimes too general to meet specific needs without massive, expensive customization. At the same time, while getting Folio VIEWS InfoBase customized for your operation may take more time (and consulting money) than the other packages, you may be able to get it customized to your own precise Help Desk specifications.

Of the two freeware packages, wwwgnats (and its gnats/PRMS infrastructure) seems most mature, having been around for several years in its text-based incarnation. It should be easy for you to build custom Web fill-in forms as front ends for the wwwgnats CGI-bin scripts, using Kegel and Le's basic form as a template. Check out the examples on Dan Kegel's wwwgnats page (cited earlier), where you'll find real-life implementations of the package. Also, since you can purchase commercial-grade support for gnats/PRMS from Cygnus Support, you may find that the combination of free software and commercial support will meet your Help Desk needs at the best price.

> **Tip:** You can locate more real-life gnats applications using one of the major Web search engines, such as Yahoo (`http://www.yahoo.com/`), Lycos (`http://www.lycos.com/`), or Digital's new Alta Vista (`http://altavista.digital.com/`).

The Web/PTS package is not for the faint of heart. It's almost completely unsupported, and at the time this chapter was written (March 1996), hadn't changed in more than eight months. It would appear, as is the case with many freeware software packages, this is a part-time project, not Dean Collins' day job. Further development of the package is therefore unlikely to move forward quickly, if at all. This is unfortunate, given the apparent business opportunities in problem-tracking software indicated by the lack of products with Web interfaces.

Summary

In this chapter, you've learned how the information and tools described in the rest of this book can be stitched together for purposes of your Intranet Help Desk. Specifically, you've:

◆ Considered the nature, purpose, and substantive content of a Help Desk in the context of your Intranet

◆ Considered what existing Help Desk electronic information, is available to put onto your Intranet

◆ Determined the form(s) of that information

◆ Learned how to put that information together so it's accessible using a Web browser, putting what you've learned about MIME data types/subtypes and Web browser helper applications to work

◆ Put what you've learned about Intranet document indexing to work to streamline search and retrieval of Help Desk information

◆ Thought about maintaining Help Desk records for quality-control and related purposes

◆ Opened up your Intranet Help Desk for direct access by your Intranet's customers

In the next chapter, we'll turn the same techniques used in this chapter to bear on making common organizational documents available on your Intranet.

17

CHAPTER

Intranet Company Practices/Procedures Manuals

Every organization, large or small, has hundreds of documents and other pieces of data that can be put on an Intranet for its customers. One major category of these is your company's practices and procedure manuals. Whether you have a formalized program of written standards for doing things or operate *ad hoc* much of the time, you undoubtedly have some documents that give instructions about how things are done. These instructions can range from the most mundane—how employees work, or how vacation and sick time are recorded and reported—to the practical, such as company purchasing procedures—to the sublime, as in overall organizational policy statements on such large matters as corporate goals, employee diversity, or safety in the workplace. In this chapter, you'll consider how to integrate the information and tools presented earlier in this book and to make many of these documents accessible on your practices/procedures Intranet.

Chapter Objectives

As with the rest of the chapters in this book, let's begin by laying out some chapter objectives. This helps you get oriented to the material; you may want to refer back to this list as you work your way through the chapter. In this chapter, you'll

◆ Consider what existing electronic practices/procedures information you have available to put onto your Intranet.

◆ Determine the form(s) of that information.

◆ Learn how to put that information together so it's accessible to customers using a Web browser, putting to work what you've learned about MIME data types/subtypes and Web browser helper applications earlier in this book.

◆ Put what you've learned about Intranet document indexing in this book to work, enabling search and retrieval of this information, also using Web browsers.

◆ Survey a wide range of possible corporate documents and other data for your practices/procedures Intranet.

◆ Use graphical images and HTML imagemaps to incorporate new special features in your Intranet.

These objectives, as you can see, are practical applications of most of the information and tools about which you've learned in the rest of this book. Your steps in putting your company's practices/procedures documents Intranet together involve analyses and conversion of available legacy data (Chapter 6, "Quick and Dirty Intranet"); MIME data type/subtype and helper applications information (Chapter 7, "MIME and Helper Applications;" Chapter 10, "Your Word Processor and the Web;" Chapter 11, "Spreadsheets and Data Warehouses;" and Chapter 12, "Other Common Office Applications"), selection of appropriate network services and tools to implement your goals (Chapter 8, "Adding Services to Your Intranet Adds Value"), and the use of indexing and database tools (Chapters 13, "Indexing and Searching Your Data," and 14, "Web Access to Commercial Database Applications," respectively). You'll also learn in this chapter about the use of graphical data and HTML *imagemaps* for your Intranet. You'll find this same general process of integrating the material from the rest of this book applies in the next several chapters.

Existing Electronic Practices/Procedures Information

If your company uses computers to create documents, you already have the foundation of your company's practices/procedures Intranet built. Your first task is identifying and locating these documents and getting them online on your Intranet so that they're easily accessible. You'll find these documents in personnel, materiel resources, and other corporate departments. You may also find them in filing cabinets. The fact that paper copies of employee manuals, for example, are distributed to all new employees probably means there is an electronic original somewhere in personnel. Similarly, if your shipping/receiving department has written procedures for handling dangerous or delicate shipments of various kinds, in all likelihood, you'll find those procedures on somebody's computer disk in word processor format. Although locating documents in this way may be a tedious, logistical problem, it's still possible, and what you find will provide the basis of your company's practices/procedures Intranet.

The main principles of this activity are those outlined in Chapter 8, with respect to the conversion of your legacy data for your Intranet. If you have electronic copies of documents available, you'll want to use what you learned in that chapter to move this data quickly onto your Intranet, making it accessible to your customers via your Web server and their browsers. Where you have legacy data that's not in plain-text format, you may need to use the conversion tools about which you've learned. This may include using your applications' *Save As* feature to convert data into easily usable formats such as plain text. You can also use some of the other conversion tools covered in Chapters 10–12. In addition, you may eventually want to use the Microsoft Rich Text format (RTF) as a way station in converting legacy data into HTML documents for direct use on your Intranet. Also, with more and more vendors, such as Microsoft, Frame Technologies, and Novell, adding direct HTML capabilities to their word processors and other packages, you'll be able to convert your legacy documents directly to HTML with almost no effort at all.

As you've learned, the basic setup of Web pages containing simple, clickable lists of available documents is quite easy. Adding a little subject-matter organization is simple, too, using hyperlinks to create nested menu listings. In just a few minutes, you can present a useful list of available documents to your customers. To these ends, you'll want to review basic HTML markup in Appendix B, "HTML and CGI Quick Review," focusing on basic list markup, hyperlinks to other documents, and the jump-to-spot features of the language.

> **Tip:** Use your operating system's basic utilities to get a leg up on creation of simple HTML listings of documents. Experienced UNIX vi and emacs editor users know reading a directory listing into a document is a snap with bang shell escapes (that is, reading the output of operating system commands, such as the `ls` command, right into the text of a document being edited). PC-DOS command-output redirection (for example, `DIR > skel.htm`) can help with the same thing, but it must be done ahead of time. You can then pop HTML markup into the skeleton files you've created. Add your basic required HTML markup, a couple of headlines, and some list markup and hyperlinks, and your new Web page is ready to be read with a Web browser, with access to all the listed documents just a mouse click away.

As suggested in Chapter 6, you can come back to your skeleton Web pages containing your converted legacy documents once you have your practices/procedures Intranet running. Then you can refine them and add value by cutting in hyperlinked cross references, graphics, and the like. Monthly reports, for example, can contain clickable cross references to other documents, statistical tables, spreadsheet data files, images, or even earlier months' reports (all with the same kinds of embedded links), for example. This done, your customers can use their Web browsers to jump from one document to another, looking for answers to questions by following promising threads. The more cross references and hyperlinks you're able to add, of course, the more capabilities you give to your customers. A little later, you'll learn about indexing your practices/procedures documents to give your customers even greater opportunities to locate documents and information.

MIME Type/Subtype Setup

Even after you've successfully converted your legacy practices/procedures documents and created skeleton Web pages for accessing them, you'll no doubt end up with a wide variety of document and data formats. You'll probably have plain text files, word processor files, HTML documents, spreadsheet datafiles, graphics images, datafiles created by other office software applications, and others. At first, this may seem a confusing mess to you. However, you can confidently deal with this situation using what you've learned earlier, particularly in Chapters 7 and 10–12, to organize the data and make it available in its native formats. After all, your purpose in building an Intranet was to pull together just such a wide variety of information resources and make them accessible using a single Web browser interface. All the information about MIME data type/subtypes and helper applications you've learned earlier in this book will help you as you make your practices/procedures information available.

As you'll recall from earlier chapters in *Building an Intranet*, enabling use of your word processor, spreadsheet, and such other office software packages as Web browser helper applications is a simple two-step process:

◆ Modifications to the `mime.types` file on your Intranet's Web server(s) to add your new document types

◆ Configuration of your customers' Web browsers to deal with the newly defined MIME types/subtypes by defining helper applications.

Chapter 7 provides a thorough grounding in the whole subject of MIME data types/subtypes. Chapters 10–12 deal individually with a variety of common office software packages you may need to set up as Web browser helper applications. Now that you are putting specific documents and other data in place for real work on your practices/procedures Intranet, you may want to review this material so that you have the ticklish syntax of the `mime.types` file and the Web browser Helpers dialogue boxes down pat. If your customers use more than one Web browser, you'll want to understand the slight differences between NCSA Mosaic and Netscape in this area, as well as knowing how to configure Helper Applications for your UNIX users. Figure 17.1, showing the setup of Microsoft Word as an NCSA Mosaic helper application, will no doubt bring this all back to you.

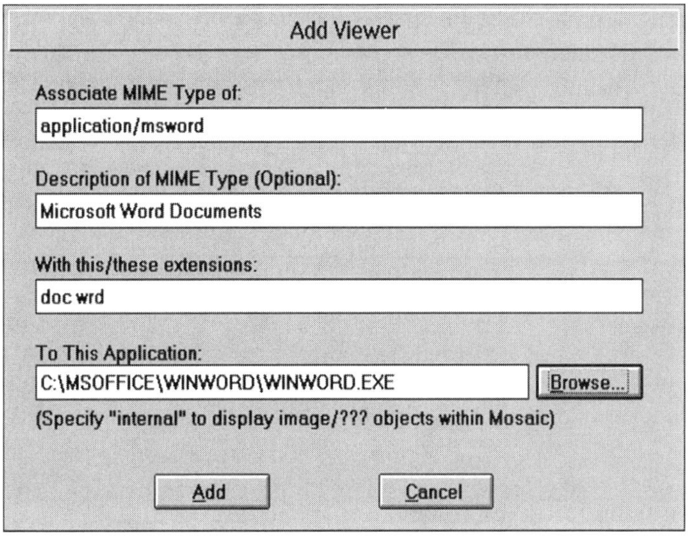

Figure 17.1. *Setting up Microsoft Word as a Mosaic helper application.*

> **Tip:** You'll also, of course, want to make sure the necessary helper application software packages are available to everyone, perhaps by setting up anonymous FTP (see Chapter 8, "Adding Services to Your Intranet Adds Value") services on your Intranet. This sort of infrastructure can save you a great deal of time that would otherwise be taken up with manual distribution of software around your Intranet. This way, if customers need a copy of some new helper application (or a new release of an old one), to download it, they can click on a Web page you've created.

Once you've taken these steps, your Intranet's customers can use their Web browsers to retrieve and view your practices/procedures documents as necessary, regardless of their actual document format. As needed, helper applications are fired off as documents are accessed. For example, clicking hyperlinks pointing to Word files opens Word to display the files; Lotus 1-2-3 spreadsheet files work the same way. Having located the necessary document with which to answer their questions, customers are just a couple of steps away from saving or printing a copy of the document, via your Intranet, all without a trip to the personnel or engineering department.

Kinds of Data for Your Practices/Procedures Intranet

There's virtually no limit to the kinds of information you can use on a corporate practices/procedures Intranet. You've already surveyed the legacy information you have available and put some of it up. You've only scratched the surface so far, so consider a few more ideas.

Personnel and Employee Benefits Information

Your personnel department can be a gold mine for your Intranet when it comes to supplying documents of the sort you're looking for. I've already mentioned the idea of an overall employee manual, but there are many other personnel-related documents that may be useful.

◆ Employee work-related expense and travel-expense reimbursement rules and procedures.

◆ Job vacancy announcements and application procedures/requirements.

◆ Procedural documents on time-keeping, health benefits claims, retirement and pensions, use of company vehicles and other company equipment, employee conduct, and a long list of others.

The first two of these items suggest possibilities far beyond mere static documents your customers can read. Simple fill-in Web forms can be used by employees to submit their travel expenses for reimbursement or apply for a job opening, to give a couple of simple examples. This sort of thing can turn your practices/procedures Intranet into something interactive, something that does something. Each of these items can be accomplished through simple CGI-bin scripts that take the information customers enter into fill-in forms and pass it via e-mail to appropriate other employees for some kind of processing. Although some security issues are involved in forms information processing (see Chapter 9, "Intranet Security"), you can implement this sort of thing quite easily. Employees won't have to deal with paper forms or spend work time for their pickup and delivery. Instead, customers' requests for expense reimbursements or job applications get sent off when they click the Submit button in their Web browser, all without the time and trouble usually attendant with such procedures, such as trips to the photocopy machine, interoffice mail delivery, and the like.

> **Tip:** A potentially valuable practices/procedures Intranet resource in the personnel area might be an interactive pension calculator. Your ordinary pension benefits information Web page would include static information about the rules of eligibility and the mathematical formula for computing pension benefit amounts. Based on an HTML fill-in form and CGI-bin script, such a calculator would enable employees to interactively enter their salary and years-of-service information and get back a pension estimate. Such a tool, easily implemented on your Intranet, can help an employee with retirement decisions, making multiple what-if-I-worked-just-one-more-year? calculations, without requiring time away from work to ask for the same calculations from a human resources specialist.

Other Corporate Department Information

You can easily extend this idea to other departments and activities in your organization. Here's a long, but by no means complete list of possible procedural documents:

◆ Purchasing and contracting procedures

◆ Equipment repair procedures

- On-the-job safety rules and regulations
- Building and grounds use and maintenance rules
- Physical plant security procedures
- Rules for telephone and fax machine use
- Parking and traffic regulations
- Procedures for operating manufacturing and other machinery
- Laboratory procedures
- Material Safety Data Sheets (MSDS) for chemicals and other potentially dangerous substances being used
- Procedures for handling dangerous materials and dealing with spills or releases of them
- Property-pass rules for employees and vendors taking company-owned equipment off site

You can probably come up with an equally long list of others to fit well here. Where appropriate, fill-in forms allow customers to use their Web browsers to perform job functions, such as ordering supplies or equipment repairs. Figure 17.2 shows the simple example order form you saw back in Chapter 2, "Designing an Intranet." Depending on how elaborate you'd like to get, your CGI-bin back end script to this form, or one like it, can e-mail the customer's order to data-entry personnel in your purchasing department for manual entry into your purchasing system, or actually place the order into your corporate purchasing database system for processing, untouched by human hands. Again, there are security issues here, explained in Chapter 9, which you'll want to consider to ensure accountability in the area of purchasing.

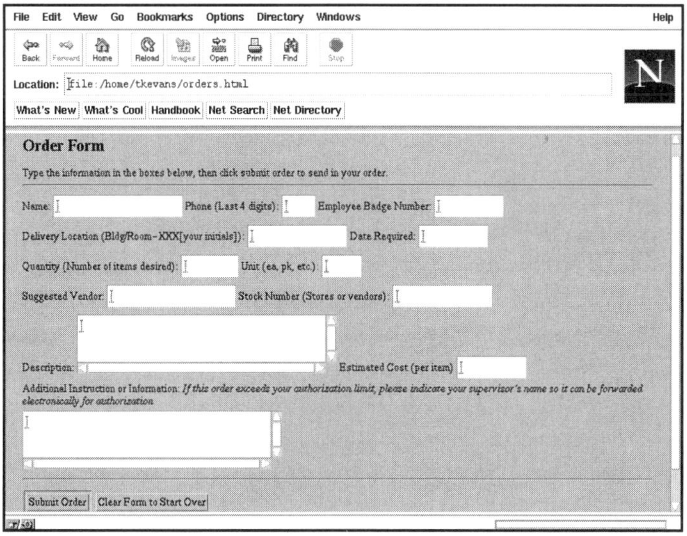

Figure 17.2. Order form.

Similar forms, using HTML menus, radio buttons, and check boxes, can be used for ordering normal office or other everyday supplies. (See Appendix B, "HTML and CGI Quick Review", or a book on HTML such as the author's *10 Minute Guide to HTML* for details on HTML forms markup.) Your CGI-bin scripts for all these kinds of forms can pretty much be the same script, with built-in options for sending the output of certain forms in one direction while others are being directed elsewhere. In Chapter 16, "Intranet Help Desk," you used the NCSA WebMonitor CGI-bin mail script for your Help Desk management, but you can find basic e-mail scripts you can modify to meet your needs in just about every book you'll find on setting up Web services; you probably already have one or more of them. See, for example, the e-mail feedback script in Chapter 12 of David M. Chandler's *Running a Perfect Web Site* (QUE Publishing, ISBN 0-7897-0201-X), or the more elaborate resume-processing script in Chapter 20 of *HTML & CGI Unleashed* (sams.net, ISBN 0-672-30745-6) by John December and Mark Ginsburg. Information on both these books can be found at the Macmillan Information SuperLibrary, `http://www.mcp.com/`.

Index Your Practices/Procedures Data

You're probably thinking this chapter has gotten ahead of itself. How will your customers locate answers to questions or locate specific documents? Surely, they won't just have long onscreen lists of document names they have to browse through? Subject-oriented menus aren't always a big help either. As with the conversion of your legacy data, the answers to these questions hearken back to material covered earlier in building an Intranet. In Chapter 13, "Indexing and Searching Your Data," you learned about a variety of powerful tools for indexing data on your Intranet and, equally important, flexible tools for searching and retrieving Intranet data from the indexes created by them. FreeWAIS-sf, glimpse, and the rest of the packages covered in that chapter provide powerful indexing for your practices/procedures documents, along with the rest of your Intranet. Equally powerful tools like SFgate and Harvest make it easy for your customers to search out answers to questions or look for specific documents using Web fill-in forms of the sort you've seen earlier in this book.

From Chapter 14 also, you'll recall our tongue-in-cheek discussion of a search (see Figure 17.3) for Shakespeare's famous line, "To thine ownself be true." The capability of searching for relatively complex text strings such as this one is an important feature of practices/procedures Intranet capabilities. Similarly, keyword searches, with Boolean capabilities are important also. Customers may not know exactly what it is they're looking for and even being able to view document names may not be enough. Text-string and keyword search becomes critical to customer searches for information. In this context, the Shakespearean example becomes a good deal more relevant to your Intranet. Note the database here is one built with the glimpse indexing tool, and the search engine Harvest. As you'll recall, several full-text indexing packages were covered in Chapter 13, including both freeware packages such as glimpse and freeWAIS-sf and commercial ones such as Fulcrum and Topic.

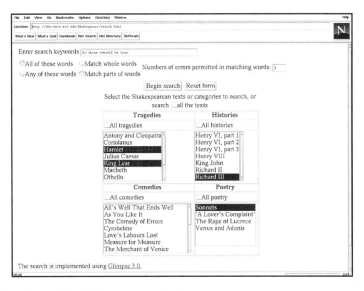

Figure 17.3. *Complex search in Shakespearean text database.*

Depending on the extent and nature of your library of practices/procedures documents (and other documents on your Intranet), you may want also to look at the Web-related relational database tools described in Chapter 14, "Web Access to Commercial Database Applications." This is particularly true because these packages are being extended to include many different kinds of data. The ability to create Web fill-in forms that interface with database engines via CGI-bin scripts (or other means) enhances your Intranet and its capability of serving its customers. Even if you have a pre-existing full-text or relational database, hope isn't lost. Unless it's locked up without standard capabilities, you can just dump the data out to plain text files. As long as the data has an identifiable format, it can be run through glimpse, freeWAIS-sf, or one of the other indexing tools mentioned in the previous paragraph, making it accessible via your Web browsers using fill-in forms. This enables you to continue to use the data you've accumulated in your application, and at the same time, frees you of proprietary data formats. With the outstanding capabilities of these search engines, you may find search-and-retrieval performance better than you had with your custom database. Not to mention that nice, user-friendly Web interface.

Imagemaps and Your Practices/Procedures Intranet

The HTML *imagemap* capability can be an important part of your practices/procedures Intranet, adding interactive features to otherwise static documents. As you probably know, imagemaps are graphical images embedded in Web pages that have *hot regions* marked off. Clicking such a hot region causes a pre-defined hyperlink to be accessed, taking the customer to another document or Web page. Clicking another hot region in the same image activates a different hyperlink, a third hot region, another, and so on. You'll find imagemaps on many Web pages, including the Netscape home page, shown in Figure 17.4. The image in the top center of the page is a clickable imagemap, with six hot regions defined (Exploring the Net, Company & Products, and so on). Moving your mouse cursor into the image causes the cursor to change from the standard arrow cursor to a pointing finger, giving you a tip-off that the image is an imagemap. Just click on any of the regions to access the underlying hyperlink. Not all Web page imagemaps are as well-defined as this one, with clear delineation, but all work the same way. You'll want to review Appendix B or your other HTML documentation for information on creating and using imagemaps.

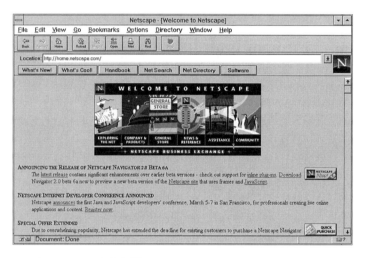

Figure 17.4. *Netscape home page with clickable imagemap.*

For creating your own imagemaps, try Thomas Boutell's mapedit software package, several versions of which are on the *Building an Intranet* CD-ROM. A sample mapedit session, using a graphics image you'll see later in this chapter, is shown in Figure 17.5. The package works by loading the graphics image, after which you select rectangles, circles, or polygons in the image for your hot spots. Once you've done that, you use your mouse to drag your hot spots to size, and mapedit generates the setup file to create the imagemap. In this screen shot, you can see Rectangle has been selected and a rectangular hot spot rubberbanded (using the mouse) in the upper center of the image. Once your hot spot is selected, mapedit prompts for the URL of the underlying hyperlink. Continue to define hot spots in your image, and then save it when you're done. Mapedit will create the necessary imagemap files for your Intranet.

Returning from the mapedit digression, let's continue the discussion of graphics imagemaps for your practice/procedures Intranet. Here, you can look at a couple of practical ideas for your Intranet.

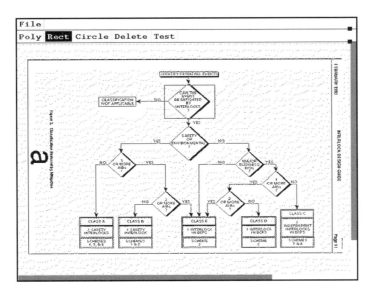

Figure 17.5. *mapedit.*

Graphics Campus Map/Phone Book

If your organization occupies a large campus or building complex, you may want to give your customers the ability to navigate around the place via your Intranet, as well as looking for employee locations. The United States National Aeronautics and Space Administration's Johnson Space Center in Houston, Texas, maintains such a service for NASA employees and visitors and that is accessible on the World Wide Web. Figure 17.6 shows a portion of a large graphics map of the Space Center campus (although maximized, this map is still too large for even high-resolution displays). The map is useful in itself, because it shows where building, roads, parking lots, and the like are located. Both visitors to and employees of large organizations like NASA can use locator maps to find their way around, and more and more organizations are setting up such interactive, wherever-your-cursor-is-there-you-are maps on their Web servers.

In addition to the obvious value of this map, the image has additional value because it's an imagemap. It provides direct, hyperlinked Web-browser access to a great deal of additional information about the Space Center. Clicking any building on the map, for example, takes you to a Web page specific to that building. On the building Web pages, you'll find a photo of the building (good for helping the visitor identify the building), along with information about activities and NASA organizations in that building. Figure 17.7 shows part of the Web page for a randomly selected building from the imagemap (Building 32, the Space Environment Simulation Laboratory). Many of the building Web pages accessible from this imagemap contain photos or other graphical images of building-related activities or facilities.

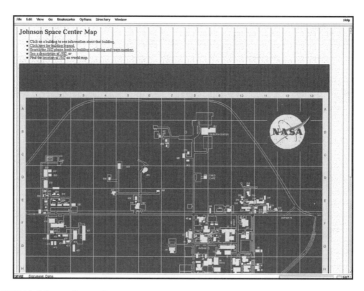

Figure 17.6. *NASA's Johnson Space Center campus imagemap.*

Figure 17.7. *NASA JSC Building 32 Web page.*

But there's more information here. On each one of these NASA JSC building Web pages, you'll find a hyperlink labeled "Click here for building occupants." Selecting this hyperlink brings up a scrollable onscreen telephone directory for the people in that building. From here, you can use your Web browser's find feature (Mosaic File|Find in Current; Netscape Edit|Find) to locate an individual's name on the directory. In Chapter 13, you learned about the ph phonebook database server, which enables you to use your Web browser and a fill-in form to search your corporate phonebook by name. Ph is a general search facility, but you might also want your customers to be able to search for people by their physical location on your campus. Figure 17.8 shows part of the phone listing for JSC Building 32. Note at the top of the page the hyperlink to the JSC's campus-wide telephone directory, which provides access to more general phonebook search capabilities.

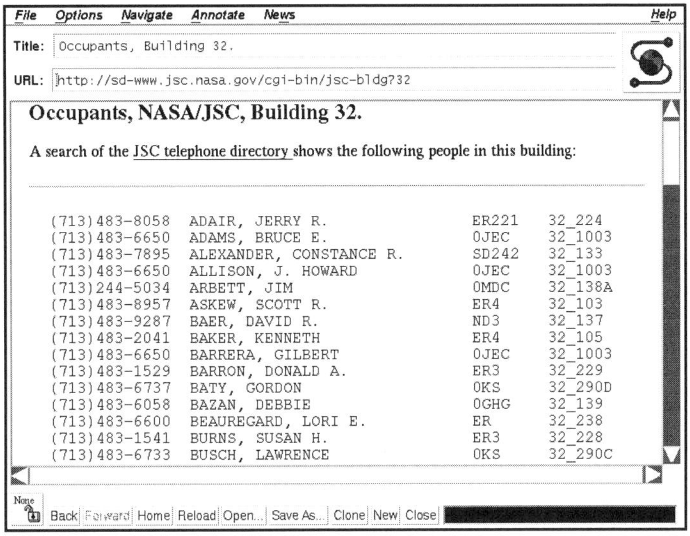

Occupants, NASA/JSC, Building 32.

A search of the JSC telephone directory shows the following people in this building:

(713)483-8058	ADAIR, JERRY R.	ER221	32_224
(713)483-6650	ADAMS, BRUCE E.	OJEC	32_1003
(713)483-7895	ALEXANDER, CONSTANCE R.	SD242	32_133
(713)483-6650	ALLISON, J. HOWARD	OJEC	32_1003
(713)244-5034	ARBETT, JIM	OMDC	32_138A
(713)483-8957	ASKEW, SCOTT R.	ER4	32_103
(713)483-9287	BAER, DAVID R.	ND3	32_137
(713)483-2041	BAKER, KENNETH	ER4	32_105
(713)483-6650	BARRERA, GILBERT	OJEC	32_1003
(713)483-1529	BARRON, DONALD A.	ER3	32_229
(713)483-6737	BATY, GORDON	OKS	32_290D
(713)483-6058	BAZAN, DEBBIE	OGHG	32_139
(713)483-6600	BEAUREGARD, LORI E.	ER	32_238
(713)483-1541	BURNS, SUSAN H.	ER3	32_228
(713)483-6733	BUSCH, LAWRENCE	OKS	32_290C

Figure 17.8. Individual NASA JSC building phone listing.

Blueprints, Engineering Drawings, CAD Drawings

As the NASA imagemap example shows, there are many ways you can implement this tool on your own Practices/Procedures Intranet and many services you can provide with it. Campus maps like the NASA map shown previously can contain links to individual building imagemaps, with the individual maps further explodable to show individual floors or even individual rooms. Your building services department might have imagemaps containing building blueprints—showing electrical, HVAC, and plumbing infrastructure—for use in building repairs or other service. Engineering drawings of industrial equipment or company products can be made available in the same way, with imagemap hot regions allowing for enlargements of individual portions of the drawings. Even your computer-aided design (CAD) drawings can be turned into imagemaps.

Getting your paper blueprints or engineering drawings into electronic format may require a scanner; be sure to save your scanned drawings in `GIF` or `JPEG` format, if it's possible. If you already have electronic CAD drawings available, you'll want to see whether your CAD software can export your drawings to one of the standard, Web-supported image formats, such as `GIF`, `JPEG`, PostScript, or Adobe Portable Document Format (PDF). Even if this is not the case, check the quite long list of image formats supported by the ImageMagick package (on the *Building an Intranet* CD-ROM) shown in Chapter 6, "Quick and Dirty Intranet." You may find that your particular CAD package's image format is supported directly, and that you can use ImageMagick's convert utility to turn your CAD drawings into a standard format for your Intranet. If all else fails, there are still more ways to skin this cat; fall back on the screen-snapshot software described in Chapter 6, some of which is free, with ImageMagick a leading package. You can use this software to capture and manipulate onscreen displays of your CAD drawings and then save them to standard image format. From here, creation of imagemaps is a simple next step.

In this connection, you'll want to look at the FAQ document for the USENET newsgroup `comp.lsi.cad`, where you'll find descriptions of a wide variety of free and commercial CAD-related software that might be of use, especially if you're using an older CAD package. Possibilities include software to convert your existing CAD drawings to new formats, including those supported by Web browsers. You'll find this at `http://www.cis.ohio-state.edu/hypertext/faq/usenet/lsi-cad-faq/top.html`.

Your practices/procedures Intranet need not be limited to blueprints and building maps. Figure 17.9 shows a schematic diagram for an electrical lock-out device (a device for preventing use of defective electrical equipment or equipment under repair). Here, you see a practical use for your practices/procedures Intranet. If you have electricians in your company, this and other procedural standards documents can be Web-accessible with little work on your part. Although your graphics images can be in any format supported by your Web browsers, this diagram is in the Adobe Portable Document Format (PDF), and is shown displayed in the Adobe Acrobat Reader. Acrobat Reader is free software you can download from Adobe's Web site, `http://www.adobe.com/`. The package is available for Windows 3.1, PC-DOS, the Macintosh, and several UNIX systems. You'll also find a new PDF reader for Windows 95/NT, Adobe Amber, which was in pre-release at the time this chapter was written. Latest releases of the GNU ghostscript package (`ftp://prep.ai.mit.edu`) also support PDF documents, as does the ImageMagick package.

> **Tip:** You'll need to define Adobe Acrobat Reader, Amber, or ghostscript as a Web Browser helper application before you can view PDF files found on Web pages. See Chapter 10, "Your Word Processor and the Web," for details on setting up helper applications.

> **Note:** In late 1995, Adobe Systems acquired Frame Technologies, makers of the FrameMaker desktop publishing package. It seems logical to expect that Frame's products may incorporate direct support for Adobe PDF documents in the future. As you learned in Chapter 10, the no-cost FrameReader package can be set up as a read-only helper application for viewing native FrameMaker documents. In addition, Version 5 of FrameMaker includes direct HTML support for creating, saving, and viewing Web documents. Everything that rises must converge.

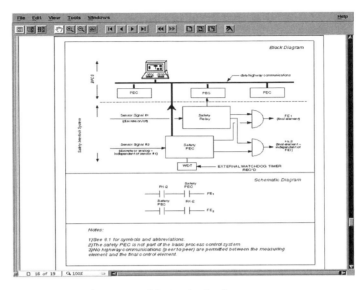

Figure 17.9. *Electrical schematic diagram in Adobe Acrobat Reader.*

Figure 17.10 shows yet another example of the sort of document you can place on your practices/ procedures Intranet. From the same document as the electrical schematic diagram shown previously, this screen shot shows a decision-making flowchart. (You saw part of this image above, in the discussion of the mapedit software package.) Although this particular image applies, again, to electrical devices, flowcharts are widely used in many endeavors, including computer programming, and you'll surely find uses for them on your Intranet. As with the imagemap example above, you can explode portions of such flowcharts to reveal underlying details of the process.

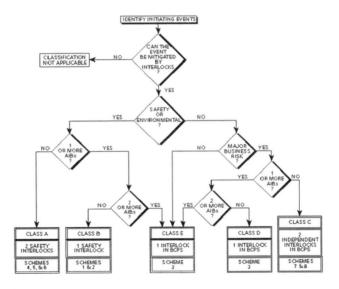

Figure 17.10. *Flowchart.*

You can see how you can make wide use of graphics images and HTML imagemaps on your practices/procedures Intranet. Web browsers' ease-of-use, together with your graphics presentations, can add substantial value to your overall Intranet. Having these sorts of documents and graphics available will help your customers meet their own job needs. This is particularly helpful, because many of these kinds of documents are accessed only rarely. Having them immediately accessible saves the time that would otherwise be used in locating them, ensuring the located copy is a current version, and the like.

Summary

Chapter 17 has focused on the use of Web and Web-related technology to create a practices/procedures Intranet, incorporating much of what you've learned from the rest of this book. The chapter has focused on organizational documents and other information that spells out how your company does things. Large or small, every organization has its standard operating procedures for a myriad of activities, just a few of which have been listed in this chapter. Documentation of those practices and procedures is a rich source of data for your Intranet, and you can easily put it at your customers' fingertips. Here's what you've done in this chapter:

◆ Considered the existing electronic practices/procedures information available for your Intranet

◆ Determined the form(s) of that information

◆ Learned how to put that information together so it's accessible to customers using a Web browser, putting what you've learned about MIME data types/subtypes and Web browser helper applications to work

◆ Put what you've learned about Intranet document indexing to work to enable search and retrieval of this information, also using Web browsers

◆ Surveyed a wide range of possible documents and other data for your practices/procedures Intranet

◆ Used graphics images and HTML imagemaps to incorporate new special features in your Intranet

In the next chapter, we'll cover spreadsheet data warehouses, repositories of ready-made what-if data for number crunchers in your Intranet. As with this chapter, the next one provides concrete examples of how you can integrate what you've learned in this book into useful and valuable features for your Intranet.

18

Numbers for Number Crunchers

Expensive data warehouse software packages are available from a number of vendors. These packages accumulate information from a variety of sources around an organization and provide database-like front ends, allowing searches for mostly numerical data. Data sources can include a number of different corporate databases running on different platforms. Once located, even the data from different sources can be downloaded for local number crunching to users' PCs or workstations, usually in a spreadsheet package. In this chapter, you'll learn about using your Intranet as a data warehouse, making full-blown, ready-to-run spreadsheet datafiles available to your customers. Although less capable than true data warehouse packages, your Intranet data warehouse shares many features with its larger cousins and at a much smaller price. You may find the trade-off worthwhile.

Chapter Objectives

As with the other chapters in this book, let's begin by laying out some chapter objectives. This will help you get oriented to the material to be presented; you may want to refer back to this list as you work your way through the chapter. In this chapter, you'll

- ◆ Survey the available existing spreadsheet data in your organization.
- ◆ Identify its datafile format.
- ◆ If necessary, convert spreadsheet datafiles into a common format or formats.
- ◆ Learn how to put your spreadsheet data together so that it's accessible to customers using a Web browser, putting to work what you've learned about MIME data types/subtypes and Web browser helper applications earlier in this book.
- ◆ Learn how to use the indexing tools about which you've learned in this book to create searchable indexes of your Intranet spreadsheet datafiles.
- ◆ Understand how the use of interactive helper applications such as spreadsheets constitutes important enabling technology for your customers.
- ◆ Using spreadsheets as an example, understand how your Intranet can stimulate and support collaboration among your customers.
- ◆ Identify techniques for using your Intranet spreadsheet data to do ongoing, daily work.

These objectives are practical application of most of the information and tools about which you've learned in rest of this book. Your steps in putting your Intranet spreadsheet data together involve analyses and conversion of available legacy data (Chapter 6, "Quick and Dirty Intranet"); MIME data type/sub-type and helper applications information (Chapters 7, "MIME and Helper Applications," 10, "Your Word Processor and the Web," 11, "Spreadsheets and Data Warehouses," and 12, "Other Common Office Applications"); selection of appropriate network services and tools to implement your goals (Chapter 8, "Adding Services to Your Intranet Adds Value"); and the use of indexing and database tools (Chapters 13, "Indexing and Searching Your Data," and 14, "Web Access to Commercial Database Applications," respectively). You'll find this same general process of integration of the material from the rest of this book applies in the next several chapters.

Existing Spreadsheet Data

Cliché has it the spreadsheet was the first personal computer killer application, so it's no surprise use of PC spreadsheet software is widespread in many organizations. Individual users create and maintain their own spreadsheets, sometimes for personal use, sometimes shared. Often, the numbers used in the spreadsheets are company-wide data on sales, production, and other statistically measurable information. Collectively, your customers probably already have a great deal of useful data in spreadsheet format that could be quite valuable on your Intranet. You'll probably not want to go snooping on your Intranet's customers' PCs, or in their private fileserver directories for candidate spreadsheet files. At the same time, though, as discussed in Chapter 5, "Skill Sets", you should encourage your customers to contribute information for your Intranet. (As you'll learn while reading the chapter, the collaborative aspects of making spreadsheets available on your Intranet will encourage customers to contribute.) Here is a great opportunity for them to do so. While locating documents in this way may be a tedious logistical problem, it's still possible, and what you find will provide the basis of your Intranet spreadsheet data.

The main principles of this activity are those already outlined in Chapter 8, "Adding Services to Your Intranet Adds Value," with respect to the conversion of your legacy data for your Intranet. Where you have spreadsheet data available, you'll want to use what you learned in that chapter to move this data quickly onto your Intranet, making it accessible to your customers via your Web server and their browsers. If you have multiple spreadsheets in use in your company, you'll have to determine how to make datafiles widely usable. You can do this by selecting a common spreadsheet datafile format, such as standard Lotus format, which most other spreadsheets can read, or the exportable SYLK format. (See your spreadsheet documentation for its capabilities in this area.) This may include using your spreadsheet's Save As feature to convert data from one format to another. Even though many, or even most, of your customers have the necessary spreadsheet software available to them, you'll probably also want to make plain-text versions as well so the data are available to customers without the software. If you have Microsoft Excel spreadsheet data, you can also use the XL2HTML converter, described in Chapter 11 to save your Excel spreadsheets in the form of HTML tables for the same purpose.

As you've learned, the basic setup of Web pages containing simple, clickable lists of available documents is quite easy. Adding a little subject-matter organization is simple, too, using hyperlinks to create nested menu listings and adding explanatory text to the pages. In just a few minutes, you can present a useful list of available spreadsheet datafiles to your customers. To these ends, you'll want to review basic HTML markup in Appendix B, "HTML and CGI Quick Reference," focusing on basic list markup and hyperlinks to other documents.

Tip: Use your operating system's basic utilities to get a leg up on creation of simple HTML listings of spreadsheet datafiles. Experienced UNIX vi and emacs editor users know reading a directory listing into an open document is a snap with bang shell escapes (that is, reading the output of operating system commands, such as the ls (list) command, right into the text of a document being edited). For example, typing the following command sequence in vi will read a list of the Lotus files in a directory right into the active document:

```
ESC :r !ls *.wks
```

PC-DOS command-output redirection can help with the same thing, but it must be done ahead of time. Try this at the PC-DOS prompt, or with the Run command on the Windows File menu:

```
DIR /w *.wks > skel.htm
```

You can then pop HTML markup into the skeleton files you've created. Add your basic required HTML markup, a couple of headlines, and some list markup and hyperlinks, and your new Web page is ready to be read with a Web browser, with access to all the listed spreadsheet datafiles just a mouse click away.

As suggested in Chapter 8, you can come back to your skeleton Web, pages containing your converted legacy spreadsheet data once you have your basic Intranet data up. At that time, you can refine your Web pages and add value by cutting in hyperlinked cross references, graphics, additional explanatory text, and the like. For example, monthly reports can contain clickable cross references to other documents, statistical tables, live spreadsheet data files, images, or even earlier months' reports (all with the same kinds of embedded links). This done, your customers can use their Web browsers to jump from one document to another, looking for answers to questions by following promising threads. Where they come across spreadsheet data, they'll be able to look at it and even manipulate it using their own spreadsheet software as Web browser helper applications. The more cross references and hyperlinks you're able to add, of course, the more capabilities you'll give to your customers. We'll talk about indexing the contents of your spreadsheet datafiles a little later to give your customers even more options for searching for specific information.

MIME Type/Subtype Setup

Except where you've successfully converted your legacy spreadsheet datafiles into plain text or HTML and created Web pages for accessing them, you'll need to configure your customers' Web browsers to use their own spreadsheet software as helper applications. You've already learned how to do this earlier in this book, particularly in Chapters 7 and 10–12. Thus, you can easily organize the data and make it available to your customers in its native formats. After all, your purpose in building an Intranet was to pull together just such a wide variety of information resources, organize them, and make them accessible using a single Web browser interface. All the information about MIME data type/subtypes and helper applications you've learned earlier in this book will help you as you make your spreadsheet information available.

As you'll recall from earlier chapters of *Building an Intranet*, enabling use of your word processor, spreadsheet, and other office software packages as Web browser helper applications is a simple two-step process:

1. Modifications to the `mime.types` file on your Intranet's Web server(s) to add your new document types; and

2. Configuration of your customers' Web browsers to deal with the newly defined MIME types/subtypes by defining helper applications to handle each.

Chapter 7 provides a thorough grounding in the whole subject of MIME data types/subtypes, and Chapters 10–12 deal individually with a variety of common office software packages you may need to set up as Web browser helper applications. Chapter 11 deals particularly with spreadsheet helper application setup. Now that you are putting specific spreadsheet data in place for real work on your Intranet, you may want to review this material so that you have the ticklish syntax of the `mime.types` file, the Web browser Helpers dialog boxes, and the UNIX `mailcap` file down pat. If your customers use more than one Web browser, you'll want to understand the slight differences between NCSA Mosaic and Netscape in this area, as well as knowing how to configure helper applications for your UNIX users. Figures 18.1 and 18.2, showing setup of Lotus 1-2-3 as a Netscape helper application and Microsoft Excel as a Mosaic helper, respectively, will no doubt bring this all back to you.

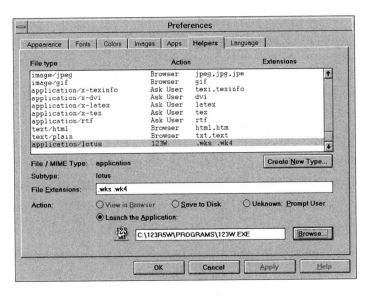

Figure 18.1. *Configuring Lotus 1-2-3 as a Netscape helper application.*

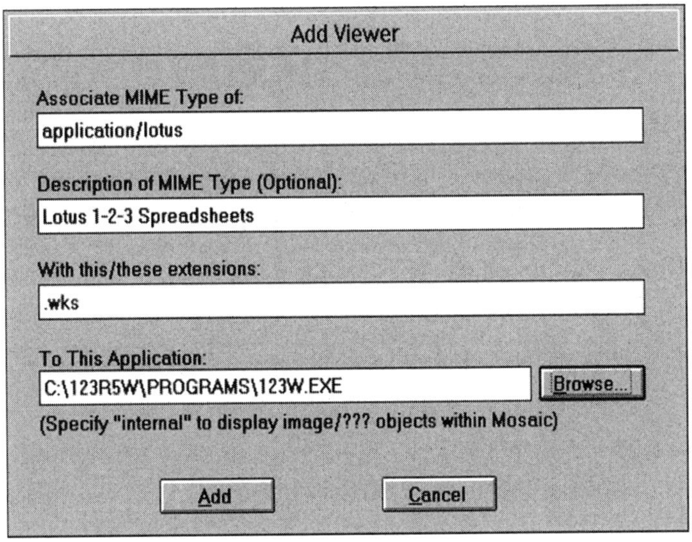

Add Viewer

Associate MIME Type of:

application/lotus

Description of MIME Type (Optional):

Lotus 1-2-3 Spreadsheets

With this/these extensions:

.wks

To This Application:

C:\123R5W\PROGRAMS\123W.EXE   Browse...

(Specify "internal" to display image/??? objects within Mosaic)

Add   Cancel

Figure 18.2. *Configuring Microsoft Excel as a Mosaic helper application.*

Once you take these steps, your Intranet's customers can use their Web browsers to retrieve, view, and interact with your spreadsheet data as necessary, just as they would with any other hyperlink. Customers' spreadsheet helper applications are enabled as spreadsheet datafiles are accessed. For example, clicking hyperlinks pointing to Lotus 1-2-3 files causes 1-2-3 to start with a copy of the datafile loaded. Having located the necessary document with which to answer customers' questions, they're just a couple of steps away from saving, printing, recalculating, graphing, or doing any other spreadsheet function with the data.

> **Note:** Helper applications, like your customers' spreadsheet, always operate on a copy of the original spreadsheet datafile. Your original remains unchanged on your Web server until you change it. Customers can freely change the data in spreadsheet or other datafiles they've opened with a Web browser helper application for their own needs, all without touching the original. This is directly analogous to the data warehouse situation, where copies of corporate data are downloaded for local processing without changing the original source data. The whole idea is, of course, the provision of raw corporate data, sales numbers, or production numbers, for example. Customers who download the data are free to do all sorts of what-if and other spreadsheet analyses, but can't change the original data. Even where individual users make spreadsheet datafiles available from a desktop PC Web server, or from their UNIX Home Directory, the same thing applies; the original isn't changed.

Index Your Spreadsheet Data

You're probably thinking this chapter has gotten ahead of itself. How, you're wondering, will your customers locate spreadsheet data they want? Surely, they won't just have long onscreen lists of filenames they have to browse through? Even subject-oriented menus aren't always a big help. As with the conversion of your legacy data in earlier chapters, the answers to these questions hearken back to material you've covered earlier in *Building an Intranet*. In Chapter 13 you learned about a variety of powerful tools for indexing data on your Intranet and equally important flexible tools for searching and retrieving Intranet data from the indexes created by them. FreeWAIS-sf, glimpse, and the rest of the packages covered in that chapter give you powerful means of indexing your spreadsheet datafiles, along with the rest of your Intranet. Equally powerful tools like SFgate and Harvest make it easy for your customers to search out specific datafiles using Web fill-in forms of the sort you've seen earlier in this book.

You probably wonder how binary files such as spreadsheet datafiles can be indexed with tools like freeWAIS-sf and glimpse. After all, the detailed descriptions of these tools in Chapter 13 suggested they can only index plain-text files. You probably concluded from reading that chapter these indexing tools could index the filename and a few command-line keywords of binary files such as spreadsheet datafiles at best. This is what both packages' documentation indicates.

Experimentation with freeWAIS-sf and glimpse index, however, reveals useful indexes can be created by both when reading Excel and Lotus 1-2-3 datafiles. In fact, both packages can root out character strings in spreadsheet files (and other binary files, such as word processor documents as well). Of course, virtually all spreadsheet files contain some character strings, primarily as column and row labels; they would not be worth much without these labels to identify the data the columns contain. As the example Lotus 1-2-3 spreadsheet shown in Figure 18.3 indicates, spreadsheets may contain significant amounts of text in individual cells as well as in column or row labels. Both freeWAIS-sf and glimpse index will create searchable indexes of your spreadsheet datafiles using the character strings they're able to find among the binary data. This means your Intranet spreadsheet files, carefully indexed with one of your indexing tools, are nearly as searchable as your plain-text data. Searching these indexes will be quite fast because they'll be small compared to the indexes created for all-text files. This is because the actual word counts of text in most spreadsheet files is quite small and from a limited vocabulary. Adding spreadsheet datafiles to your existing freeWAIS-sf or glimpse index indexes will add but little to their size, and search time, for the same reason. Of course, your revised freeWAIS-sf or glimpse index is subject to use with the Harvest distributed indexing mechanism described in Chapter 13.

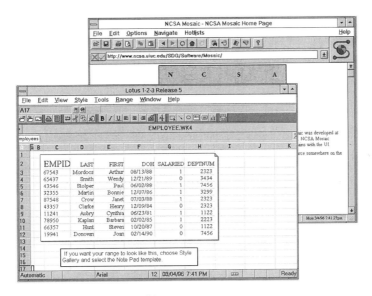

Figure 18.3. *Text strings in Lotus 1-2-3 spreadsheet.*

> **Note:** As Figure 18.3 indicates, Mosaic gives the downloaded spreadsheet datafile a temporary filename (`mos2.wk4`). Netscape generates a completely random temporary filename for spreadsheet files you open (see Figure 11.9 in Chapter 11, where the temporary filename used for an Excel spreadsheet is `V0OCKBMO.XLS`). If you want to save the file, you'll want to give it a meaningful name and save it in a permanent place in your system.

You saw in Chapter 13 how your indexed Web server data can be retrieved using the glimpse, Harvest, or SFgate search engines across your Intranet. Results of your searches show as lists of clickable Web browser hyperlinks, showing the hits on your search keywords (and, with freeWAIS-sf indexes, each hit's relevance ranking). Just as selecting such a hyperlink pointing to a text or HTML document brings the document up for viewing in your browser, so does selecting a spreadsheet datafile hyperlink. The difference is the spreadsheet datafile is handed off to your customer's spreadsheet helper application for viewing. And, of course, once loaded, the spreadsheet is an interactive entity your customer can use, not a static Web page that just sits there.

Depending on the extent and nature of the overall library of documents on your Intranet and your customers' indexing needs, you may want also to look into the commercial full-text indexing tools described in Chapter 13. There, you learned about

♦ The OpenText 5 distributed indexing product from OpenText (`http://www.opentext.com/`) claims support for more than 40 file formats, specifically including Microsoft Excel spreadsheets. OpenText 5 is the underlying search engine for the company's Latitude network search-and-retrieval product.

♦ Fulcrum's SearchServer product, the full-text database that underlies its Web Surfboard package, claims to support 50-odd document formats, though no list can be found on its very poorly organized Web site (`http://www.fulcrum.com`). With this large a number of supported file formats, you would reasonably expect common spreadsheet formats to be included.

♦ Verity's Topic Enterprise Server full-text indexer supports multiple file formats, explicitly including both Excel and Lotus 1-2-3. More information, including information on the related product, Topic Internet Server, is at `http://www.verity.com/`.

♦ The Illustra object relational database enables all sorts of nontext data to be included in its relational databases, allowing for transparent search and retrieval using its Web DataBlade add-in. Although the company's literature (`http://www.illustra.com/`) isn't specific, its claim that "all kinds" of nontext data can be indexed should extend to spreadsheet datafiles.

Use Spreadsheets on Your Intranet

Assuming you've made spreadsheet datafiles available on your Intranet, let's look at how they might be used by your customers. First, some perspective.

Intranet Spreadsheets Versus Data Warehouses

Because of the generic nature of data accessible from standard data warehouse applications, the numerical data customers retrieve is not in spreadsheet format, ready for them to use. Rather, it's in raw, plain text, columns of numbers or text, with the entries on each line separated by some field separator. Spreadsheet packages have the capability of importing such raw data, including both numerical data and text row and column headings, provided the customer tells it about the format of the incoming data. Microsoft Excel for example, uses its TextWizard feature to prompt the customer through the importation of the incoming data. Lotus 1-2-3 accepts only a few standard field separators and also requires row and column labels to meet a specific format. UNIX spreadsheets are much the same. Thus, even though customers can bring rows and columns of text and data into their spreadsheet package, the resulting spreadsheet isn't of much more value than a plain tabular listing of numbers and text. Customers have to take the time to add formulae and other spreadsheet-specific features. For the imported data to be immediately useful, each customer needs to have spent time building spreadsheet templates containing the necessary housekeeping that allows imported raw data to be dealt with.

Negative-sounding comparisons between commercial data warehouse applications and the use of spreadsheets on your Intranet shouldn't be taken too far. Data warehouse packages have many strong features not present in the more limited situation described in this chapter. For instance, a strong feature is the ability to browse a variety of sources, including multiple corporate databases, picking and choosing data from here, there, and yon and then integrating the chosen data into a single spreadsheet for *ad hoc* manipulation. Canned Intranet spreadsheets can't match this capability, though it can be roughly replicated through saving and combining individual downloaded spreadsheets. As with using your Intranet to replicate the services of other software packages (see the discussion of Lotus Notes in Chapter 24, "Web Groupware: Collaboration on Your Intranet," for example), your tradeoff is between cost and features. (Cost includes more than purchase price; it also includes staff time.) If you need the advanced features an industrial-strength data warehouse package provides, you'll want to get one. Nevertheless, you don't want to ignore the ability to replicate and improve on some of these packages' features on your Intranet at very low cost. If you can get 75 percent of the features of a data warehouse package for five percent of its cost, integrating your replication into your Intranet, you may be still ahead of the game, even taking into account staff costs. Only you can decide on the value of the remaining 25 percent.

This is especially true because Web interfaces to the major data warehouse packages haven't shown up. Because your overall objective in using Web technology for your Intranet is to enable use of your customers' Web browsers as front ends to as much organizational data as possible, this is a critical point. Each vendor's data warehouse has its own user interface, and although these can be perfectly good, user-friendly graphical interfaces, each one is different. Customers have to learn to use the interface before it's much good to them. On the other hand, your customers already know how to use their Web browser: see a hyperlink and click it.

The critical difference between the generic data-warehouse approach and the Intranet-spreadsheet approach becomes clear in this context. The spreadsheet your Intranet customers accesses by clicking a Web page hyperlink is already a live, ready-to-run spreadsheet, in their own spreadsheet packages' formats. Formulae, spreadsheet layout, and all the other housekeeping are already in place. If you provide, for example, spreadsheet datafiles containing corporate revenue, expense, and inventory information, together with appropriate formulae linking the information, customers can do quick what-if analyses by changing some of the numbers in their temporary copy of the spreadsheet or by resorting the data to get different views of it. Similarly, interactive macro commands can be built into commonly accessed spreadsheets. Thus, customers can run their spreadsheets' statistical-analysis tools (frequency distribution, regression analysis, data matrices, and so on) on a range of spreadsheet cells they interactively select.

What Can You Do with an Intranet Spreadsheet?

The quick and easy answer to this question is, of course, anything you can do with any other spreadsheet. Although this answer is obvious, it's not a sufficient answer to the question. Let's look, then, at the question in the context of your Intranet, seeing how your customers might use the spreadsheets you make available to them. First, though, the central unifying motif of this book needs to be repeated here.

You've already learned the most fundamental lesson about this. The World Wide Web is revolutionary, enabling technology. It provides new, easy-to-use ways for people to view and use information using their computers. Your customers use their Web browsers, not their standard operating system or windowing interface or data warehouse graphics front end to access your Intranet spreadsheet data. Among all the other information you've made available on your Intranet, accessible by simple point and click, are your spreadsheet datafiles. Let's take another look at a figure you saw in Chapter 13, shown in Figure 18.4. Clicking one of these otherwise ordinary looking hyperlinks dynamically starts the customer's own spreadsheet package with a copy of the data.

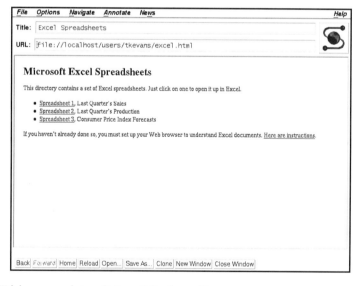

Figure 18.4. *Web browser rendering of Microsoft Excel spreadsheets page.*

This is probably the most critical notion in this chapter; in fact, it is the reason for this chapter. This is something truly new and potentially revolutionary. Figure 18.4 looks no different from many another everyday Web page. It has neither cool graphics nor anybody's stamp of approval. In fact, there's nothing special at all about the way it looks, but this simple page can integrate statistical and other numerical data about your organization and its activities in your Intranet. Having done this, you have given powerful new tools to your customers who use that data. Moreover, the audience of potential users of the data is also vastly increased. Customers who might never use the corporate data filed away in filing cabinets or in annual stockholders' reports, now might begin to use it, potentially benefiting themselves and your company. Putting that data in the form of Web page hyperlinks makes it accessible to everyone in your Intranet. While doing so might lead on occasion to unqualified people acting as junior actuaries, there's much to be said for making nonconfidential organizational statistical information widely available to the members of the organization.

Collaborative Aspects of Spreadsheet Sharing via Your Intranet

Further, as we'll discuss in more detail in Chapter 24, spreadsheet data is yet another way in which you can enable your customers to collaborate using your Intranet. You'd never want to detract from the value of having the sort of information described in Chapter 17, "Intranet Company Practices/Procedures Manuals," your company's practices/procedures documents, available on your Intranet. Still, most of that information is static, reference information; people use it to look up things. Intranet spreadsheets, like some of the scientific data discussed in Chapter 15, "Scientific, Mathematical, and Technical Applications on Your Intranet," can be used by customers to do things. Even more important, a spreadsheet is an original creation, aimed at making it possible to view statistical data in some unique way, with the additional ability of refining or changing that view through what-if and other analysis. This is much like the scientist who publishes the results of an experiment on your Intranet, together with the program he wrote to perform the experiment. The data and methodology, and the means of rerunning the experiment (that is, the spreadsheet itself) is made available to others who can attempt to replicate the results, possibly refine the view of them, and, of course, use them.

The facility with which PC Web servers can be put together or customer-created HTML documents served from their home directories on UNIX systems, together with the simplicity of HTML markup, makes this kind of customer data sharing easier. Customer-created spreadsheets, with results based on their unique views of common data, can be made readily accessible by their creators to rest of your Intranet. Other customers who use these grassroots spreadsheets are likely to offer comments and improvements to them, stimulating and feeding a collaborative process, generating new ideas, solving research or production problems, and increasing your organization's overall body of knowledge.

Here's a scenario: Frank, a salesman for Amalgamated Enterprises can't understand why his clients have started complaining about slow delivery of the flovats he's sold them. Using his laptop, Frank plays with corporate figures in a Lotus 1-2-3 spreadsheet, discovering there's plenty of flovat inventory. He probes further and hits on what he thinks might be the problem, although he isn't sure. Deciding to use the Amalgamated Enterprises Intranet to share his analysis, Frank creates a simple Web page (he's not an HTML expert, so it's pretty plain) and uploads it to the Web server in the home office using his laptop from his motel room in Boise. Figure 18.5 shows Frank's Web page, with a very big message. He's identified a potentially dangerous trend in the delivery of flovats, which portends production and inventory problems. Frank has put his analysis into spreadsheet form, made the spreadsheet accessible on the Amalgamated Enterprises Intranet, and asked for comments.

The HTML markup is too trivial to reproduce; it's just a couple of paragraphs of text with hyperlinks to two versions of the spreadsheet datafile and a mailto hyperlink (see Appendix B). Flip back to Figure 18.3 and imagine the Frank's flovat production-shipping-inventory spreadsheet onscreen, called up by clicking one of the hyperlinks while viewing the document in Mosaic or Netscape. With this simple stroke, Frank has brought everyone's attention to a problem that may threaten the business. All who want to look at Frank's data need only click with their mouses to do so. If they want to contact Frank, who's on the road, all they need do is click the mailto hyperlink to send him e-mail.

Figure 18.5. *Intranet collaboration via spreadsheet.*

Now, it's true this same sort of collaboration could have been accomplished through any of several other means. Frank could have sent a group e-mail message, with the spreadsheet(s) attached or entered it in a Lotus Notes forum. He might well have gotten a good deal of response to either and possibly solved his problem. Nevertheless, Frank's simple, direct Intranet presentation is quite effective. Anybody on the Amalgamated Enterprises Intranet can independently view the spreadsheet data, using their own spreadsheet software (notice both Lotus and Excel formats are provided), refine or change the view of the data, recalculate/reanalyze it, and otherwise seek to verify or disprove Frank's conclusions. Other customers may in turn generate new spreadsheet views of the original data, supporting or disproving Frank's conclusions, and make their own revised versions available on the Intranet as well, for still further collaboration and discussion by the group. Frank will be able to see the new spreadsheet versions and read his e-mail by the time he gets to Seattle the next afternoon. By the following day, the shipping bottleneck having been traced to Denver, Amalgamated personnel locates 50 flatcars of flovats sitting forgotten on a railroad siding and Frank's been given a fat bonus.

Bolts and Nuts

Continuing the discussion of the flovat crisis, we can see some of the actual possibilities for use of spreadsheet data on your Intranet. We've already discussed the collaborative nature of such a situation, with the ability of many Intranet customers to view and verify data in a spreadsheet available through a hyperlinked Web page. Let's probe that idea further for some detailed possibilities.

◆ Numerical spreadsheet data can be quickly turned into charts and graphs to further assist in visualizing the data the spreadsheet contains.

◆ The data, including the graphs and charts, can be saved or printed locally.

◆ The spreadsheet's data can be combined with other data in new spreadsheets as a means of verifying or amplifying the original data.

◆ The original or modified spreadsheet data and the graphics can be exported to other applications. Excel spreadsheets and graphics can be popped right into Word documents, for example.

◆ Related corporate databases can be queried for supporting information, and new date can also be imported either into new, more elaborate spreadsheets or other documents.

◆ The generated graphics can be saved as slides for a later presentation.

◆ All the resulting documents, datafiles, slides, and supporting information can be fed right back onto your Intranet for customer viewing and further collaboration if desired.

Again, each of these separate activities, even for a single overall situation such as Amalgamated's flovat crisis, could have been taken completely outside the context of your Intranet. Certainly, the importation of spreadsheet data and graphics into word processing documents isn't anything new nor is the creation of slides from the data using something like PowerPoint, nor the querying of databases using the spreadsheet software. This is one of the primary strengths of integrated office packages such as Microsoft's or Novell's. What's new about this scenario is that it arose and played completely out on Frank's Intranet, with one customer initiating the collaboration and others participating in the process. And the entire process used Web browsers and browser helper applications. If Frank was right in identifying shipping bottlenecks as the culprit, he helped his own sales by keeping his own clients happy, and he helped Amalgamated Enterprises by moving inventory to make room for urgent plant expansion—all using an Intranet.

Admittedly, this is a contrived example; not everyone can save their company from disaster wearing only a Web browser as a loincloth. Nonetheless, it shows important possibilities for collaboration on your Intranet using lowly spreadsheet data. In a more practical sense, certainly data from multiple hyperlinked spreadsheets on your Intranet can be combined to form altogether new spreadsheets. This is analogous to, though probably a clumsier process than, the data-warehouse browsing process described earlier, where data from various sources is combined into new spreadsheets for analysis. Spreadsheet numbers also can be turned into charts, graphs, or presentation slides or incorporated into documents, each of which can be plugged right back into your Intranet for more customer viewing and collaboration using Web browsers and helper applications.

Realtime Intranet Data Feed with a Spreadsheet

Users of high-end UNIX spreadsheet packages, including stockbrokers and other Wall Street types, along with a lot of engineers, need access to continuously changing information. Spreadsheet packages such as Advanced Information Systems' Xess (http://www.ais.com/) Lotus' Realtime (http://www.lotus.com/corpcomm/2f0a.htm), and UniPress' Q-Calc Realtime (http://www.unipress.com/cat/exclaim.html) can be connected to live stock market ticker and other live data feeds. Perhaps more widely useful than a stock-market ticker, realtime spreadsheets can monitor data generated by computer controlled instruments in a manufacturing facility, refinery, or laboratory. In such a process control setting, the realtime spreadsheet monitors the instrument's datafile as it grows, continuously loading incoming new data into the spreadsheet as it arrives. Whenever your Intranet customers click the link to that process-control spreadsheet, the spreadsheet package fires up as a helper application to display the latest set of data. Through the use of automatically executing macro commands, if available, your spreadsheet could automatically graph the new data first thing on loading by a customer. Figure 18.6 is a simulation of such a setup, using a stand-alone X Windows grapher, rather than a spreadsheet graphing tool, but it's illustrative nonetheless. Here, a clickable HTML imagemap (see Appendix B) represents an overall process, with process control sensor icons in the imagemap being the hot spots. Clicking one of the sensors reads the latest spreadsheet datafile containing data points that are dynamically passed to the graphing tool, called as a Mosaic helper application. The whole process is shown in Figure 18.6. Here is a truly interactive Intranet application.

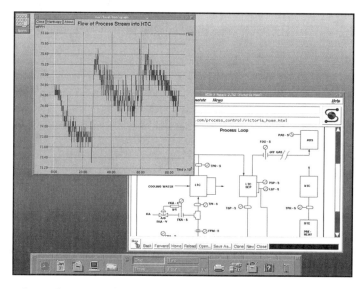

Figure 18.6. *Simulation of realtime spreadsheet process control monitor.*

If your UNIX spreadsheet package can accept commands via standard input, you'll be able to create additional realtime features using CGI-bin scripts. Assume, as in the previous example, your spreadsheet is monitoring the data created by several lab instruments. Using an HTML fill-in form, your customer selects which instrument's data he or she wants to see. Your CGI-bin script can send a command to the spreadsheet package to extract and, if necessary, recalculate the data from the range of cells used for the instrument's data, and then graph it. Your script can take the graphed data as standard input and pass it through a filter such as ImageMagick's convert to produce a GIF or JPEG image. At the end of the pipeline, the GIF or JPEG image is passed back to your customer's Web browser for direct viewing. No helper application is involved. Your customer never even sees the spreadsheet application itself onscreen, seeing just the initial fill-in form and the final graphed results in his or her Web browser.

Summary

You've learned some practical applications of spreadsheet data for your Intranet in this chapter. Use of spreadsheets as Web browser helper applications adds to your Intranet an important feature of interactivity that was heretofore lacking. This interactivity enables your customers to do their work in a completely new way. In addition, you've learned the potential value of collaboration on your Intranet using spreadsheet data as an example. Here's a review of what you've done in this chapter.

- ◆ Surveyed the available existing spreadsheet data in your organization.
- ◆ Identified its datafile format.
- ◆ Converted spreadsheet datafiles, if necessary, into a common format or formats.
- ◆ Learned how to put your spreadsheet data together so that it's accessible to customers using a Web browser, putting what you've learned about MIME data types/subtypes and Web browser helper applications earlier in this book to work.
- ◆ Learned how to use the indexing tools about which you've learned in this book to create searchable indexes of your Intranet spreadsheet datafiles.
- ◆ Understood how the use of interactive helper applications such as spreadsheets constitutes important enabling technology for your customers.
- ◆ Understood how, using spreadsheets as an example, your Intranet can stimulate collaboration among your customers.
- ◆ Identified techniques of using your Intranet spreadsheet data for ongoing, daily work.

In the next chapter, we'll consider how you can use Web fill-in forms and CGI-bin scripts to handle merchandise ordering and inventory in your Intranet. Some of what's in that chapter builds on the material in this one.

Ordering and Inventory

The last several chapters and this one are about putting several of the things you've learned in this book together to create something altogether new on your Intranet. In fact, most of this book is about the use of imaginative elbow grease to create wonderful things on your Intranet; there's more imagination than rocket science involved. Like the UNIX operating system, which is made up of hundreds of little programs, each of which does one small thing well, but which can be combined by imaginative users to do big, new things, the tools you've been learning in this book can be put together to bring off near miracles for your Intranet. We'll talk about using some of the tools in this chapter to create an ordering and inventory application for your Intranet. Keep in mind while reading this chapter that these techniques are generally useful on an Intranet, so don't focus too closely on the ordering and inventory application.

Chapter Objectives

Let's begin by laying out some chapter objectives, as have the other chapters in this book. The objectives will help you get oriented to the material to be presented; you may want to refer to this list as you work your way through the chapter. You'll review the several pieces that will, when you put them together, creatively build your ordering and inventory application.

- ◆ HTML forms markup, focusing on specifics for setting up order forms, with details in Appendix A, "Setting Up a Web Server."
- ◆ The basics of CGI-bin scripting, about which you learned in Chapter 5, "Skill Sets," along with some general CGI-bin tips you can generalize to other applications on your Intranet.
- ◆ Interfacing your application with your ordering and inventory database in the context of the information you learned in Chapters 13, "Indexing and Searching Your Data," and 14, "Web Access to Commercial Database Applications."

These objectives, as you can see, are practical applications of much of the information and tools about which you've learned in rest of this book. You'll find this same general process of integration of the material from the rest of this book applies in the next couple of chapters as well.

> **Note:** Although this chapter is nominally about creating a specific order and inventory application for your Intranet, the ideas and techniques, including some important CGI-bin scripting tips, aren't limited to this application. You'll be able to use them in other Intranet applications you build, even if you don't build this particular one.

Visualize Your Intranet Ordering and Inventory Application

Before going into a lot of implementation details, let's get a bird's-eye view of the application. We'll look first at its basic purpose, then at the customer's view of it, and finally at the component parts of the application.

Purpose of the Application

Your Intranet ordering and inventory application's purpose is to provide your customers with Web-browser access to the underlying company ordering and inventory database. Specifically, your application will

- ◆ Allow customers to place orders for in-house store items using fill-in forms and their Web browser
- ◆ Generate e-mail acknowledgments of orders, including availability and delivery information on ordered items

◆ Allow customers to query the underlying ordering and inventory database for order status and availability of items

◆ Use customer account number information, entered by the customer in the Web order form, to debit accounts for the costs of ordered items

◆ Consider the security aspects of the overall system

◆ Update the inventory database when items are delivered

We won't include specific information about the design of the database application underlying your Intranet application nor any product-specific recommendations. It's assumed, however, that your in-place database is a full-text or relational database application capable of accepting input from HTML forms using the standard CGI-bin mechanism. In addition, it's assumed that the database tracks your inventory, accepts and verifies orders using user account numbers, debits user accounts for orders, and updates inventory once orders are delivered using predefined procedures.

This sort of database application is fairly typically required in the corporate world, so details on setting one up aren't provided. If you don't already have such a database in place, refer to Chapters 13, "Indexing and Searching Your Data," and 14, "Web Access to Commercial Database Applications," for specifics on how a number of free and commercial databases work in a World Wide Web environment. It's not required there be a specific Web interface to your particular database, though you'll agree it's nice if there is, as you'll use the CGI-bin mechanism to access it. What sort of database you'll need to implement the application described in this chapter depends on your organization's needs, anticipated level of use, and other factors. Small operations may be able to use a PC-based database, such as Microsoft Access, accessed using Visual Basic CGI-bin scripts from a Web server running on the same PC. Others may require a full-featured UNIX relational database package, such as Oracle or Sybase.

What the Application Might Look Like to the Customer

The primary view of your Intranet ordering and inventory application your customers will have is the one they see through their Web browser, of course. Figure 19.1, which is another look at something you saw in Chapter 2, "Designing an Intranet," shows a simple HTML fill-in form for placing orders. As you can see, the form has spaces for, among other things: customer name, account information, delivery information, and product and vendor information. There are also a couple of free-form text boxes for entering unformatted information. Later in this chapter, you'll see modified versions of this form with additional features to make ordering things easier in your Intranet ordering and inventory application. The form interfaces with a CGI-bin script that processes what the customer enters, and then accesses the underlying database application to place the order.

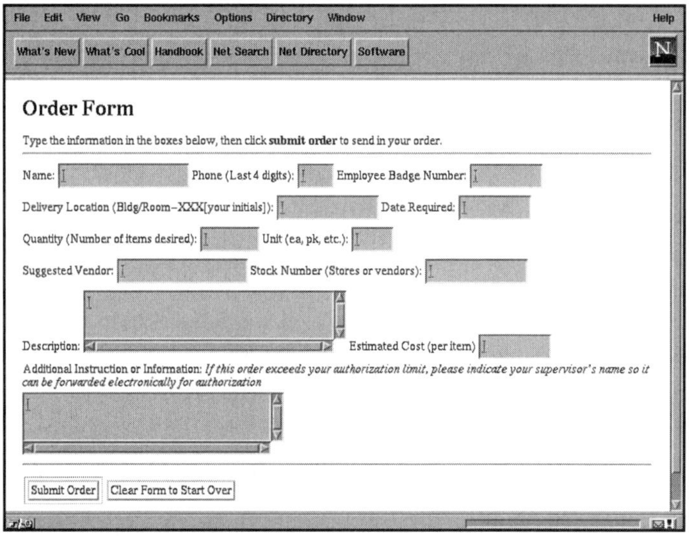

Figure 19.1. *Web order form.*

Pieces of the Application You'll Create

There are several discrete parts of your Intranet ordering and inventory application. The first is the underlying database application, which we've assumed is already in place. You'll need to create the rest of these parts. Your first step should be the creation of your HTML fill-in forms for each of the major functions of the application. These functions include simple ordering, order status inquiry, and inventory search, so you'll want to build forms for each.

Next, you'll create the CGI-bin scripts that underlie your fill-in forms. Although it's possible to write a single script with multiple options, you may want to follow the KISS! (Keep it Simple, Stupid!) principle, at least at the outset, by creating separate, simple scripts for each of your forms. Doing so makes debugging substantially easier, and you can always steal from one script when you work on another. It's critical in crafting CGI-bin that interface with database applications that you have an intimate understanding of the way your database accepts and outputs data. As a result, your scripts need to reflect your knowledge of the database itself.

Finally, you'll want to put together an overall Web page (or set of pages) that neatly provides a single, easy-to-access interface to the application. Because HTML markup allows hyperlinks among documents, you can provide a top-level entry point, with branches to each major form accessible with a customer mouse click. Don't forget to provide a way back to the top from each major point in the application.

Forms, Forms

Although detailed HTML authoring is beyond the scope of this book, let's take a look at the code that creates the form shown in Figure 19.1. (For more information on HTML, see Appendix B, "HTML & CGI Quick Reference," or an HTML reference work, such as the author's book, *10 Minute Guide to HTML*, published by Que Publishing; information at http://www.mcp.com/.) HTML markup is shown in all uppercase letters; you should be able to pick out the essential form markup and what it means by comparing the code with its rendering in Figure 19.1.

```
<HTML><HEAD><TITLE>Order Form</TITLE></HEAD><BODY>
<FORM METHOD="post" ACTION="http://intranet.yourcompany.com/cgi-bin/order.pl">
<H1>Order Form</H1>
Type the information in the boxes below, then click <STRONG>submit
order</STRONG> to send in your order.<HR>
Name:
<INPUT TYPE="text" SIZE=20 NAME=yourname>
Phone (Last 4 digits):
<INPUT TYPE="text" SIZE=4 NAME="phone">
Employee Badge Number:
<INPUT TYPE="text" SIZE=10 NAME="sitepass"><BR>
Delivery Location (Bldg/Room-XXX[your initials]):
<INPUT TYPE="text" SIZE=15 NAME="location">
Date Required:
<INPUT TYPE="text" SIZE=10 NAME="datereq"><BR>
Quantity (Number of items desired):
<INPUT TYPE="text" SIZE=8 NAME="quantity">
Unit (ea, pk, etc.):
<INPUT TYPE="text" SIZE=5 NAME="unit"><BR>
Suggested Vendor:
<INPUT TYPE="text" SIZE=20 NAME="vendor">
Stock Number (Stores or vendors):
<INPUT TYPE="text" SIZE=15 NAME="stockno"><BR>
Description:
<TEXTAREA NAME="descript" COLS=40 ROWS=3></TEXTAREA>
Estimated Cost (per item)
<INPUT TYPE="text" SIZE=10 NAME="cost"><BR>
Additional Instruction or Information:
<EM>If this order exceeds your authorization limit, please indicate
your supervisor's name so it can be forwarded electronically
for authorization</EM><BR>
<TEXTAREA NAME="moreinfo" COLS=40 ROWS=3></TEXTAREA><BR><HR>
<INPUT TYPE="submit" VALUE="Submit Order">
<INPUT TYPE="reset" VALUE="Clear Form to Start Over">
</FORM></BODY></HTML>
```

Analysis of HTML Form Example

Despite its length, this form is quite simple, with repeated use of just a couple of HTML forms tags. Several fixed-size fill-in boxes are created using the <INPUT> tag, with the <TYPE> and <SIZE> attributes setting the type of input (text) and the displayed box's size. In addition, the <TEXTAREA>

tag is used, with the <COLS> and <ROWS> attributes spelling out the dimensions of the free-form text box. Finally, the special <INPUT TYPE> attributes submit and reset are used for form housekeeping.

Also notice that the <VALUE> tag is used many times. In each case, the word inside the double quotes is used as a name for the information that is entered into the form. Read these into a mental array, as you'll learn more about them later in this chapter, when we consider the CGI-bin scripting that underlies your fill-in forms. For the time being, just think of the <VALUE> tag as a label for each piece of information requested by the form; the labels will be retained and passed to the CGI-bin script when the customer submits the form.

As for the rest of the form, please note

◆ The <METHOD="post"> tag specifies one of two methods for sending data to the server via the script (the other is get). There is virtually no situation with respect to fill-in forms that you would use get; using post should be your standard method.

◆ The back end CGI-bin script for the form is specified using the <ACTION> tag, as a Web URL, in this case http://intranet.yourcompany.com/cgi-bin/order.pl. (The filename extension .pl should tip you off to the fact this is a perl script.)

◆ Standard HTML markup, with overall housekeeping tags (<HTML>, <HEAD>, etc.), as well as general text formatting, line-break, and horizontal rule tags.

◆ The actual text to be displayed to the customer when viewing the form.

Modify the Form to Add Choices

This form is quite generic, and is a good all-purpose form for ordering any number of things. Although this is quite generic, because your Intranet order and inventory application is limited to a specific inventory, you may want to give customers access to a predefined set of choices, rather than requiring them to manually type in a text box the name of the item(s) they want to order. This makes customers' lives easier. It also makes the creation of your CGI-bin scripts a lot less troublesome, because customers are not able to make typographical errors in text boxes (see below). Let's look at Figure 19.2, which is a modified version of the form shown previously.

The first thing you'll notice about the modified form is the presence of a drop-down list of available items, shown already pulled down in the right center of the screen. Although the example shows a list of just a few office items, the illustration indicates you can provide any menu of choices to your customers, who can select the item they want just by clicking on it. The menu is implemented using the HTML <SELECT> tag, with the <OPTION> attribute. You saw this same pop-up menu feature with respect to the NCSA WebMonitor mail script in Chapter 16, "Intranet Help Desk." You'll want to read the details of the <SELECT> tag and its several attributes in your HTML reference. Here's the HTML fragment which sets this up; it replaced the Description entry in the HTML previous document.

```
Description:
<SELECT NAME="descript">
<OPTION>File folders
```

```
<OPTION>Letterhead, 8.5x11
<OPTION>Letterhead, Legal
<OPTION>Notepads, 5x7
<OPTION>Notepads, 8.5x11
<OPTION>Paperclips
<OPTION>Pencils
<OPTION>Pens, ballpoint
<OPTION>Pens, felt tip
<OPTION>Scotch Tape</SELECT>
```

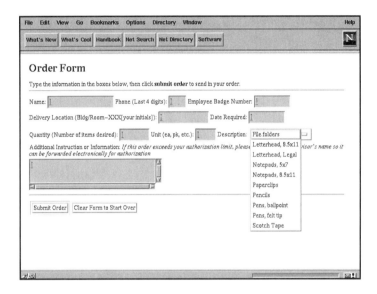

Figure 19.2. Modified order form with pull-down item selection.

As you can see from Figure 19.2, this is a substantial improvement over the previous form (Figure 19.1). Customers no longer have to type the name of the item they want. Instead, they can just select it from the pop-up menu by clicking the item. You'll also notice that the form has been simplified by removing the Suggested Vendor and Estimated Cost text-entry boxes. Presumably, when ordering office supplies, as this form does, you'll get all of them from a single source with known pricing, so you needn't trouble the customer for these two pieces of information. We've also gotten rid of the Stock Number box, because the customer need not know it when selecting from the pop-up menu. Already, this first revision of the order form is much more useful.

There's at least one major remaining problem with this form, however. Suppose customers want to order more than one item at a time. The current form allows only one item to be selected from the pop-up menu. If customers want to order something else, they'll have to reload the form, retype all the identifying information and select the next item. Another attribute of the HTML <SELECT> tag, however, resolves this limitation with a three-word change to the HTML code. Just change the <SELECT NAME="descript"> line to read like this:

```
<SELECT NAME="descript" MULTIPLE SIZE=5>
```

This quick and easy change generates a substantially different-looking order form, as shown in Figure 19.3. Note that we have also added some customer instructions to the form, since it's not immediately apparent that multiple selections can be made. As you can see from the product selections already made in the screenshot, the customer can now select multiple items from the scrollable menu; notice the scrollbar on the right. (Incidentally, the menu created using the <MULTIPLE> attribute is no longer a pop-up, as in Figure 19.2, but rather is now integrated right into the page, sized, in lines, according to the <SIZE=5> attribute.)

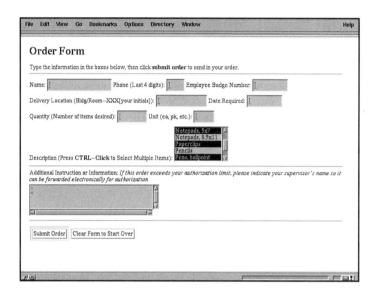

Figure 19.3. *Modified order form with scrollable item selection.*

> **Note:** You'll also want to look at the <SELECTED> HTML forms attribute, which enables you to specify preset, default selections on pop-up and scrolling menus of the sort used in this form. In addition, as you'll learn from detailed HTML forms documentation, there are a number of other features you can use, including checkboxes, radio buttons, and hidden information useful for session tracking. Hidden information can be useful when the customer needs to fill in more than one form.

Advantages of the Modified Form to the WebMaster

The advantages of the modified form, with its scrollable menu of choices, to the customer are quite obvious. The advantages of the form to you as WebMaster are not so readily apparent but are possibly even more important. The main benefit, besides the adoration of your customers, is your CGI-bin script back end for the form can now be much simpler. By removing the requirement that customers type the name of the item(s) they want and replacing it with clickable menu selections, you've eliminated customers' typographical and spelling errors. Because dealing with mis-entered data is the bane of programmers everywhere, this change makes your scripting easier. You now have a set, predictable list of possible entries for the Description field of the form and no longer have to anticipate and deal in your script with every possible misspelling or typographical error customers might enter in the form. Also, as you learned in Chapter 9, "Intranet Security," a preset list of selections avoids potential efforts by the malicious to subvert your Intranet's security by sending shell metacharacters or other dangerous text strings to a CGI-bin script from a Web form.

Note: While you're considering the security aspects of your fill-in forms and CGI-bin scripts, you may want to look at the <PASSWORD> tag in HTML forms markup. It works much like an ordinary HTML form text box, but echoes a string of asterisks when customers enter their passwords (to escape the prying eyes of over-the-shoulder onlookers) rather than the actual password. The password entered by the customer is passed on to the CGI-bin script by the form for processing, which can verify that customers are who they say they are.

Further, as explain in Chapter 9, "Intranet Security," your CGI-bin script can use the network hostname of the computer from which the customer is entering information as another verification check by associating customer name, password, and/or computer hostname and checking them against an internal list of allowed matches. (Recall that one of the standard CGI-bin environment variables, listed in Chapter 14, "Web Access to Commercial Database Applications," is the network hostname of the customer's computer.) Finally, you may want to limit access to the form itself, requiring a username and password before bringing up the form in the first place. For more security considerations and related information, refer to Chapter 9.

Creating Forms on the Fly and Making Them Smart

So far, the discussion of HTML forms has focused on pre-set HTML documents containing your forms. These are static HTML documents you create with a text editor and serve with your Web server, just like other static documents. Your CGI-bin scripts, however, can create forms dynamically, and the ability to do so can be important to you. On-the-fly forms creation with a CGI-bin script is done, essentially, by having the script generate valid MIME data type/sub-type headers (see Chapter 7, "MIME and Helper Applications"), followed by a stream of HTML markup. In perl, for example, use the print statement to generate the necessary header and HTML output.

It may be difficult at first to distinguish a reason for preferring a static HTML document over a CGI-bin script (or vice versa) that generates the same fill-in form. In this context, however, recall from the descriptions of several of the Web interfaces to commercial database packages (in Chapter 14) the capability of CGI-bin scripts to make intelligent decisions about what to return to a customer and in what form. Most everyone knows Web browsers differ in their capabilities of rendering nonstandard HTML markup. Netscape, for example, has developed a set of semi-proprietary extensions to HTML its browsers support; in addition, the company has integrated advanced features of HTML table formatting to its browsers. If you've used another browser, such as NCSA Mosaic, you've no doubt encountered Web pages with such Netscape-isms and found these pages difficult, if not impossible, to view. A growing number of Web pages, however, are based on smart CGI-bin scripts that ferret out the name of the user's Web browser and return an HTML document appropriate to the browser. This is done simply. One of those standard CGI-bin environment variables, HTTP_USER_AGENT, contains the name and release number of the user's Web browser. The return might be something like NCSA_Mosaic/2.7b2 (X11;SunOS 5.4 i86pc) libwww/2.12 modified, indicating NCSA Mosaic for X Windows, Release 2.7 Beta 2, running on a PC under SunOS 5.4 (that is, x86 Solaris 2.4).

Intelligent CGI-bin scripts can use the HTTP_USER_AGENT environment variable with each run to identify each customer's Web browser and then return a document or form the browser can display properly. Similarly, you can use other CGI-bin environment variables in your scripts to make decisions and provide the appropriate document or form back to the customer. Recall that among these variables is the customer's computer hostname (REMOTE_HOST), numerical IP address (REMOTE_ADDR), and possibly, username (REMOTE_USER), as well as several others. Because your Intranet is by definition a closed group, with access limited to customers inside your organization, you can use prebuilt lists of users and hostnames in combination with these CGI-bin environment variables to customize the documents, including fill-in forms, returned to customers by your Intranet order and inventory application.

CGI-Bin Scripting for Your Intranet Ordering and Inventory Application

The last couple of paragraphs jumped the gun on this section's subject matter, introducing some advanced smart CGI-bin scripting techniques in the context of dynamically generating custom HTML forms and other documents for different Web browsers. Before we get too far ahead of ourselves, let's take a few steps back and look at the CGI-bin mechanism from a larger perspective and then return our focus to your Intranet ordering and inventory application.

CGI-Bin Basics Revisited

Reduced to its most basic level, the CGI-bin mechanism does two things.

- ◆ It passes the information entered by a customer into a Web fill-in form to a back-end script or other computer program for processing
- ◆ It returns the results of the script's run, in the form of HTML markup, to the initiating customer's Web browser for viewing.

For the most part, CGI-bin scripts use variables to pass and receive data using UNIX standard output and standard input. Each piece of information a customer enters into a fill-in form is assigned to a variable for easy handling. The values represented by the variables are passed to the back-end script for processing, and results generated by the script are processed by the script and sent back to the customer's browser.

CGI-bin scripts can pass the variable information they get from the customer to application packages on your computer system, such as your ordering and inventory relational database package. For example, as you learned in Chapter 14, full-blown Structured Query Language (SQL) queries can be built from Web fill-in forms. Customers enter or select SQL search criteria using their Web browsers. All the features of HTML forms markup are useful here, including text boxes, pop-up or scrolling menus, checkboxes, radio buttons, and free-form text areas. The back end CGI-bin script receives the customer's entries from the form as variables, reformatting the information into a legitimate SQL query. Next, the script passes the query off to the database engine using standard output and waits for a response. When the database engine returns the query results, the script receives them as standard input. Recognizing the structure of the database engine's output, the script takes that data and reformats it into HTML. Finally, the HTML-formatted output of the results of the customer's query is returned to his Web browser for viewing.

Along the way, the CGI-bin mechanism provides a handy set of standard environment variables for each transaction. You can use and manipulate these variables in your CGI-bin scripts to smarten them up further, allowing them to make decisions about Web-browser capabilities, user authentication, and a long list of other matters. Such decision making enables you to customize the presentation of your Intranet ordering and inventory application. The very same CGI-bin script might, for example, serve clerical staff ordering office supplies and scientists ordering lab supplies. Based on the customer's userid, computer hostname, or other information from the list of standard CGI-bin environment variables, the form previously shown (Figure 19.3) can be dynamically generated, displaying a different list of available supplies for each customer.

For more detailed information on CGI-bin programming, check out the NCSA Common Gateway Interface tutorial at http://hoohoo.ncsa.edu/cgi/overview.html where you'll find an archive of example scripts. In addition, there's tremendous list of CGI-related resources, with access to many more example scripts, at http://www.yahoo.com/Computer_and_Internet/Internet/World_Wide_Web/CGI_Common_Gateway_Interface/. Also, you may want to get one of Sams.net's recent book-length treatments of CGI, *Teach Yourself CGI Programming with Perl in a Week*, by Eric Herrmann (ISBN 1-57521-009-6) or *HTML and CGI Unleashed*, by John December and Mark Ginsburg (ISBN 0-672-30745-6). Information about both is available at the Macmillan Information SuperLibrary Web site, http://www.mcp.com/.

Forms, CGI-Bin Scripts, and Your Intranet Ordering and Inventory Application

Let's now trace the process of a transaction on your Intranet ordering and inventory application, looking at your forms, how the CGI-bin script processes the data entered into it, and the results.

The Order Form

Having covered this background, let's fill out the example order form and go over those parts of the HTML markup not analyzed earlier in this chapter. We deferred discussion of the numerous <VALUE> tags in the form's HTML markup. Let's now turn to these items. Take a look at Figure 19.4, which is the same order form as that shown previously but with specific order information filled in. All the data-entry boxes are filled in and a product selected.

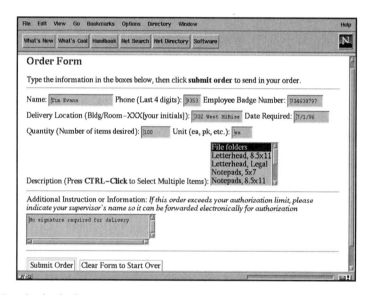

Figure 19.4. *Completed order form.*

Each of the data-entry boxes in the order form is now filled in. Let's look once again at the HTML document that creates this form, in its final modification.

```
HTML><HEAD><TITLE>Order Form</TITLE></HEAD><BODY>
<FORM METHOD="post" ACTION="http://intranet.yourcompany.com/cgi-bin/order.pl">
<H1>Order Form</H1>
Type the information in the boxes below, then click <STRONG>submit
order</STRONG> to send in your order.<HR>
Name:
<INPUT TYPE="text" SIZE=20 NAME=yourname>
Phone (Last 4 digits):
<INPUT TYPE="text" SIZE=4 NAME="phone">
Employee Badge Number:
```

```
<INPUT TYPE="text" SIZE=10 NAME="sitepass"><BR>
Delivery Location (Bldg/Room-XXX[your initials]):
<INPUT TYPE="text" SIZE=15 NAME="location">
Date Required:
<INPUT TYPE="text" SIZE=10 NAME="datereq"><BR>
Quantity (Number of items desired):
<INPUT TYPE="text" SIZE=8 NAME="quantity">
Unit (ea, pk, etc.):
<INPUT TYPE="text" SIZE=5 NAME="unit"><BR>
Description:
<SELECT NAME="descript" MULTIPLE SIZE=5>
<OPTION>File folders
<OPTION>Letterhead, 8.5x11
<OPTION>Letterhead, Legal
<OPTION>Notepads, 5x7
<OPTION>Paperclips
<OPTION>Pencils
<OPTION>Notepads, 8.5x11

<OPTION>Pens, ballpoint
<OPTION>Pens, felt tip
<OPTION>Scotch Tape
</SELECT>Description:
Additional Instruction or Information:
<EM>If this order exceeds your authorization limit, please indicate
your supervisor's name so it can be forwarded electronically
for authorization</EM><BR>
<TEXTAREA NAME="moreinfo" COLS=40 ROWS=3></TEXTAREA><BR><HR>
<INPUT TYPE="submit" VALUE="Submit Order">
<INPUT TYPE="reset" VALUE="Clear Form to Start Over">
</FORM></BODY></HTML>
```

Table 19.1 shows each piece of information the customer entered in this order form, associated with the HTML <VALUE> label for that information used in the HTML form.

Table 19.1. Order form processing of user entered information.

Label	Value
yourname	Tim Evans
phone	9353
sitepass	734638797
location	3202 West HiRise/TE
datereq	7/1/96
quantity	100
unit	ca
descript	File folders
moreinfo	No signature required for delivery

The heart of your CGI-bin script for ordering these file folders is the manipulation and use of these nine chunks of information. The information from the fill-in form is passed by the script to the httpd server, then to the script, as a set of variables via standard input. Your script, then, should expect to receive as standard input these nine discrete pieces of information. Whether you're writing your script in perl, tcl, the UNIX shell, Visual Basic, or a high-level programming language like C, you'll need to have it accept this information and deal with it. You can do this piece by piece, or by reading the standard input into an array. In either event, your script can use these variables to generate a database SQL query/update or a request for a canned database procedure to run. Finally, the script sends your request, containing the variable data in SQL format, via standard output, to your database engine for execution.

> **Tip:** Because several of these pieces of information are text strings containing white space, with more than one word in them, but sure to use appropriate quoting in your CGI-bin script to handle them properly.

Your script needs also to expect to get data back from the database engine. Based on the input from the form, which is sent on to the database engine, the script expects a specifically formatted response to the query, containing a specific number of chunks of data. Your script must know precisely how the output of the database engine looks, including record and field separators, to be able to parse it. Again, your script can read this information into an array for easy handling or deal with each piece of data individually. Whichever choice you make, the script now must reformat this variable information into HTML, with appropriate MIME type/subtype header information. At this point, it's useful to recall the Shakespeare search example from Chapter 14, in which the CGI-bin script fragment (minus the comments included in the earlier version, to make it a little shorter and easier to read) outputs the results of the search in HTML:

```
print "Content-type: text/html\n\n";
print "<HTML><HEAD><TITLE>Query Response</TITLE></HEAD>";
print "<BODY><H1>Results of Your Query</H1>";
print "In Shakespeare's <EM>$play</EM>, Act $act, Scene $scene, Speaker $speaker said
\"$line\"\n";
print "</BODY></HTML>";
```

Here you see the variables (signified by the dollar signs) play, act, scene, speaker, and line returned by the database engine being inserted right into the dynamically created HTML using variable substitution. (Note the line variable is quoted to deal with multiword information.) The final stage in the CGI-bin process is the return of the output to the httpd server for relay to the customer's Web browser. You can easily modify the perl script fragment shown previously to acknowledge your customer's order. Here's what it might look like:

```
print "Content-type: text/html\n\n";
print "<HTML><HEAD><TITLE>Order Response</TITLE></HEAD>"\n;
print "<BODY><H1>Thanks for Your Order, $yourname</H1><HR>\n";
print "Your order for $quantity \"$descript\" has been placed;\n"
print "It will be delivered to \"location\" and charged to your account $sitepass on
or before \"$datereq\"<HR>"\n;
print "For information about your order, call the Help Desk"\n;
print "</BODY></HTML>\n";
```

As you can see, the script has echoed back the customer's order essentials with some acknowledgment text and some cosmetic HTML markup to dress up the output. In the user's Web browser it looks like Figure 19.5.

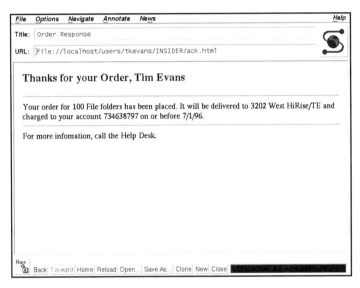

Figure 19.5. Order acknowledgment.

Bells and Whistles

Now you've gotten your basic CGI-bin script to process orders, you'll want to add some useful features. There are any number of them, but here are a few ideas to consider. You'll undoubtedly think of others.

◆ Change the acknowledgment to a confirmation dialog by making your script output another HTML form with a single clickable Confirm Order button. This will change your CGI-bin script so that its initial output is the acknowledgment/confirmation form. The customer's order would not actually be placed until she has confirmed it.

◆ Prompt the customer for a password and/or verify his name, account number and/or computer hostname against an approved list before accepting the order.

◆ Automatically route the order to the customer's supervisor via e-mail if the cost of the order exceeds a pre-set authorization limit.

◆ Generate e-mail to store personnel, actually placing the order.

You can apply these and other similar extra features as you develop additional forms and CGI-bin scripts for other functions in your Intranet order and inventory application. These can provide your customers with the ability to query the database for the status of an order, ask for inventory information on particular items or categories of items, browse the overall catalogue of supplies, and the like. You can also create and use fill-in forms that are accessible only to store staff for use in updating inventory and customer account information.

Summary

In this chapter, you've applied much of the information you've learned in other chapters of this book to the practical task of creating an Intranet order and inventory application. This combination of HTML forms and CGI-bin scripting is a widely useful technique, so you'll want to consider its general lessons in creating other Intranet applications, not limiting your imagination to this particular application. In this chapter, you have focused on

◆ HTML forms markup, with specifics for setting up order forms

◆ The basics of CGI-bin scripting for your application, including some general CGI-bin tips you can generalize to other applications on your Intranet

◆ Interfacing your Intranet ordering and inventory application with your ordering and inventory database

In Chapter 20, you'll see a similar process of integration of the information and techniques scattered throughout *Building an Intranet*, this time for the creation of boilerplate document libraries.

CHAPTER

Intranet Boilerplate Library

Experienced word processors know one of the most valuable features of their word processing software is the ability to reuse documents, and parts of documents, without retyping them. For even the fastest typists, copying a paragraph, page, or an even-larger part of one document to another makes words-per-minute measurements obsolete. Although virtually everyone who uses a word processor can profit from its copy, cut, and paste features to save time and typing, organizations that generate large volumes of documents using stock language, or boilerplate, will find it invaluable. In this chapter, we'll look at how two such organizations—the Public Inquiries Department of a Government agency and a law firm—can build an Intranet Boilerplate Library.

Chapter Objectives

As with the rest of the chapters in this book, let's begin by laying out some chapter objectives. This will help you get oriented to the material to be presented; you may want to refer back to this list as you work your way through the chapter. In this chapter, you'll

- ◆ Create a library of boilerplate documents on your Intranet's Web server using your existing word processing documents
- ◆ Convert documents to a common format usable in several different word processing programs, if necessary

◆ Make your boilerplate library accessible to customers using their Web browsers, putting what you've learned about MIME data types/subtypes and Web browser helper applications earlier in this book to work

◆ Enable your customers to use their Web browsers to search for and retrieve documents from your Intranet Boilerplate Library, bringing up retrieved documents directly in their word processor for editing and document assembly

◆ Use the indexing tools about which you've learned in this book to create searchable indexes of your Intranet Boilerplate Library documents

These objectives, as you can see, are practical applications of most of the information and tools about which you've learned in the rest of this book. Your steps in putting your Intranet boilerplate library together involve assembly, analyses, and conversion of available legacy word processing documents (Chapter 6, "Quick and Dirty Intranet"); MIME data type/subtype and helper applications information (Chapters 7, "MIME and Helper Applications" and 10, "Your Word Processor and the Web," 11, "Spreadsheets and Data 'Warehouses,'" and 12, "Other Common Office Applications"); selection of appropriate network services and tools to implement your goals (Chapter 8, "Adding Services Adds Value"); and the use of indexing and database tools (Chapters 13, "Indexing and Searching Your Data," and 14, "Web Access to Commercial Database Applications," respectively) to make your document collection searchable. You've found this same general process of integrating material from the rest of this book in the last several chapters of *Building an Intranet*.

Existing Word Processing Documents

Because you're interested in creating an Intranet boilerplate library, your organization is probably already running some sort of operation that reuses the same documents. Our example organizations—the Department of Public Inquiries (DPI) and a law office—do. The former answers letters from the public or from legislators about this or that government agency's program, often answering the same questions again and again. The latter assembles legal briefs and other legal documents, much of which are made up of boilerplate language. In both cases, it's likely a large number of reusable documents are already available for your Intranet boilerplate library. Your organization may or may not have organized this into a formalized process, so you may have to search out documents that can be used. Although you probably won't want to search customers' hard disks or fileserver directories for candidate documents, you'll want to encourage your customers to contribute information for your library. Here, then, is a great opportunity for them to do so. Although locating documents in this way may be a tedious, logistical problem, it's still possible, and what you find will provide the basis of your Intranet boilerplate library.

The main principles of this activity are those already outlined in Chapter 8, with respect to the conversion of your legacy word processing documents and other data for your Intranet. Where you have word processing documents available, you'll want to use what you learned in that chapter to move this data quickly onto your Intranet, making it accessible to your customers via your Web server and their browsers. If you have multiple word processors in use in your company, you'll have to determine how to make datafiles widely usable across two or more application platforms. You can do this in a couple of ways:

Doing mass conversions of all your documents, using the word processor Save As feature, into each of the necessary document formats, resulting in two or more copies of each converted document.

Selecting a common document format, such as the Microsoft Rich Text Format, or RTF (see your word processor documentation for its capabilities in this area). This, too, involves using your word processor's Save As feature but limits the conversions to just one format.

As you've learned, the basic setup of Web pages containing simple, clickable lists of available documents is quite easy. Adding a little subject-matter organization is simple, too, using hyperlinks to create nested menu listings and adding explanatory text to the pages. In just a few minutes, you can present a useful list of available word processing documents to your customers. To these ends, you'll want to review basic HTML markup in Appendix B, "HTML & CGI Quick Review," focusing on basic list markup and hyperlinks to other documents.

Tip: Use your operating system's basic utilities to get a leg up on creating simple HTML listings of spreadsheet datafiles. Experienced UNIX vi and emacs editor users know reading a directory listing into an open document is a snap with bang shell escapes (that is, reading the output of operating system commands, such as the ls (list) command, right into the text of a document being edited). For example, typing the following command sequence in vi will read a list of the Microsoft Word files in a directory right into the active document:

```
ESC :r !ls *.doc
```

DOS command-output redirection can help with the same thing, but it must be done ahead of time. Try this at the DOS prompt, or with the Run command on the Windows File menu:

```
DIR /w *.doc > skel.htm
```

You can then pop HTML markup into the skeleton files you've created. Add your basic required HTML markup, a couple of headlines, and some list markup and hyperlinks, and your new Web page is ready to be read with a Web browser with access to all the listed word processing documents just a mouse click away.

As suggested in Chapter 8, you can come back to your skeleton Web pages containing your converted legacy word processing documents, once you have your basic Intranet Boilerplate Library up. This enables you to refine your Web pages and add value by cutting in hyperlinked cross references, graphics, additional explanatory text, and the like. Your Web pages, for example, can contain clickable cross references to other documents, statistical tables, live spreadsheet data files, and images. This done, your customers can use their Web browsers to jump from one document to another, looking for the particular stock language they need by following promising threads. The more cross references and hyperlinks you're able to add, of course, the more capabilities you give to your customers. We'll talk about indexing the contents of your word processing documents a little later to give your customers even wider abilities to search for specific information.

MIME Type/Subtype Setup

Having converted your legacy word processing documents into your chosen common format and created Web pages for accessing them, you still need to configure your customers' Web browsers to use their own word processing software as helper applications. You've already learned how to do this earlier in *Building an Intranet*, particularly in Chapters 7 and 10. All the information about MIME data type/subtypes and helper applications you've learned earlier helps you create your Intranet boilerplate library.

As you'll recall from earlier chapters of *Building an Intranet*, enabling use of your word processor, spreadsheet, and many other office software packages as Web browser helper applications is a simple, two-step process.

1. Modifications to the `mime.types` file on your Intranet's Web server(s) to add your new document types.
2. Configuration of your customers' Web browsers to deal with the newly defined MIME types/subtypes by defining helper applications to handle each.

Chapter 7 provides a thorough grounding in the overall subject of MIME data types/subtypes, and Chapter 10 deals particularly with your word processor helper application setup. Now that you are putting specific word processing documents in place for real work on your Intranet, you may want to review this material so that you have the ticklish syntax of the `mime.types` file, the Web browser helper applications dialog boxes, and if necessary, the UNIX mailcap file down pat. If your customers use more than one Web browser, you'll want to understand the slight differences between NCSA Mosaic and Netscape in this area, as well as knowing how to configure helper applications for your UNIX users. Figures 20.1 and 20.2, showing setup of WordPerfect as a Mosaic helper application and Microsoft Word as a Netscape Helper, respectively, will no doubt bring this all back to you.

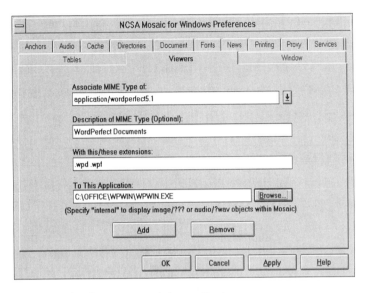

Figure 20.1. *Configuring WordPerfect as a Mosaic helper application.*

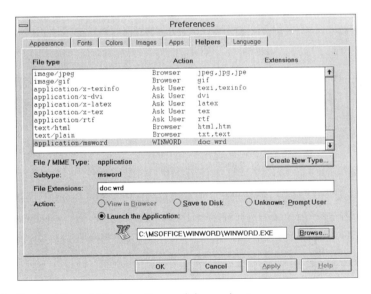

Figure 20.2. *Configuring Microsoft Word as a Netscape helper application.*

Once you have taken these steps, your Intranet boilerplate library's customers can use their Web browsers to retrieve, view, and interact with documents as necessary, just as they would with any other Web-page hyperlink. Customers' word processor helper applications are fired off as documents are accessed. For example, clicking hyperlinks pointing to WordPerfect files causes that program to start with a copy of the retrieved document loaded. Having located the necessary document, customers are all set to save, print, and edit the document for their own purposes. More importantly, for purposes of the Intranet boilerplate library, customers are able to use the downloaded documents as the framework for new ones, with boilerplate language intact. They'll even be able to assemble documents from multiple original source documents. Figure 20.3 shows WordPerfect as a Netscape helper application.

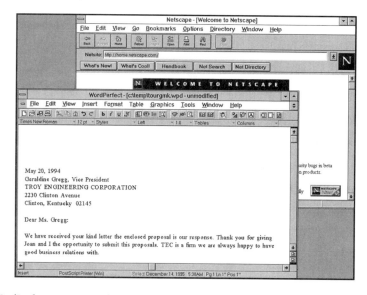

Figure 20.3. *WordPerfect as a Netscape helper application.*

Note: Web browser helper applications, like your customers' word processors, always operate on a copy of the original document. Your original document on your Web server remains unchanged until you change it. Customers can freely change the documents they've opened with a Web browser helper application for their own needs, all without touching the original.

Tip: As Figure 20.3 indicates (see the WordPerfect title bar), Netscape places the downloaded document in a temporary location on your hard disk, rather than in your current directory. (Where temporary files are stored by Netscape is a settable user Preference, incidentally.) NCSA Mosaic handles the temporary files in the same way. If you want to save the file, you'll want to remember to save it in a permanent place in your system. Otherwise, when you exit from Word or WordPerfect, your document is gone. Although you can always retrieve it again, any changes you may have made in the temporary copy are also lost unless you save the document permanently.

Use of Your Intranet Boilerplate Library

Government agencies receive a lot of mail, including letters from the public, from legislators exercising constituent service and general legislative oversight, and from other government agencies. As does your Help Desk (see Chapter 16, "Intranet Help Desk"), your DPI gets repeated, similar questions and probably has a large library of canned responses to these common questions. You don't want to send an often-photocopied form letter in response to such questions, particularly to an influential legislator who may have control over your agency's budget. As a result, your DPI finds itself creating what it wants to appear to be original responses to these inquires. In many cases, such responses are nothing more than a cobbling together of several off-the-shelf, stock paragraphs, with a few personalizing edits to make the letter look original. Your word processor's copy-and-paste function is a critical part of this process, but you may not have a way of easily finding the particular stock paragraphs you want or an easy way of assembling those paragraphs into a completely new document.

Law firms are like DPIs in that they generate loads of documents consisting largely of standard, off-the-shelf language and also develop altogether new documents that often include lengthy quotations from legal opinions, court cases, and other existing documents. Attorneys give scissors-and-paste documents to clericals for typing, with text from prior briefs, photocopied pages from court decisions, and the like. Much of the text may have come from existing documents already online as word processor document files, and some court systems are making electronic copies of court documents available. It goes without saying that it profits the firm if the scissors-and-paste documents can be assembled by the clerical staff from available electronic boilerplate.

High-volume DPI organizations, such as large government agencies, for example the U.S. Social Security Administration, which receives hundreds of thousands of inquiries a year, may be able to contract for an industrial-strength document management system to meet these needs. Depending on its size and way of doing business, a law firm may need to do the same thing. Like other custom applications, such as custom numerical data warehouse applications, discussed in Chapter 18, "Numbers for Number Crunchers," these systems may come at very high cost but may also have capabilities you need. Although very large operations may require such custom document management systems, your Intranet boilerplate library can replicate most of their features at substantially lower costs. As with the data warehouse packages, you have trade-off choices between costs and capabilities.

Home Page

Your first task in setting up your Intranet boilerplate is the creation of what you might call its home page. This is just like any other Web home page, consisting of ordinary HTML markup, introductory text, graphics (if you want to include them), and a top-level set of clickable hyperlinks. For your word-processing staff, you may want to configure their Web browsers to start with this home page; if not, be sure to include a link to your home page on whatever startup page they use. The hyperlinks on the home page may be organized in several ways. The best may be an organization by subject, with the home page main links leading down a hierarchy of subject matter that enables customers to perform a top-down search for documents matching their needs. For example, you might provide just five or 10 broad top-level subjects with branches leading to more specific subjects. Although it's not a boilerplate operation by any means, take a look at the Yahoo Search Engine home page, shown in Figure 20.4, for such a hierarchical organizational approach. See also Netscape's Net Search page, shown in Figure 20.5, with essentially the same method of subject-matter layout.

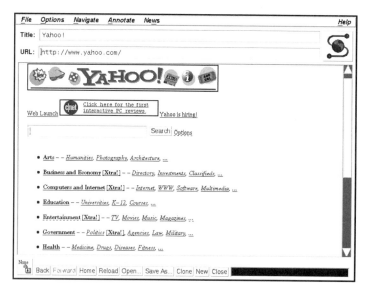

Figure 20.4. *Yahoo top-level subject layout.*

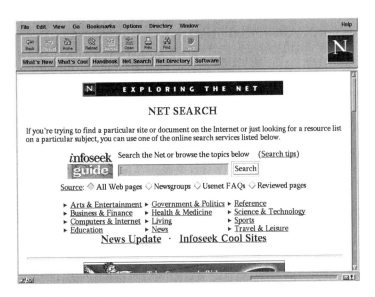

Figure 20.5. *Netscape Net Search subject layout.*

Walk Down the Subject Tree to Live Documents

Each of these search engine pages presents a dozen or so very broad subject categories, such as Science & Technology or Business and Economy. (We'll defer discussion of the search text boxes in both screenshots until later in this chapter; as you probably can guess, these are about searchable indexes.) Selecting one of these links takes you to progressively more specialized subjects within the general subject matter tree, finally leading you to individual Web pages and documents you can view with your Web browser. Your Intranet boilerplate library can be laid out in just the same way, with subject matter breakdown based on the documents in your own library. In fact, you can almost certainly port your existing paper file cabinet subject-matter organization over, with top-level links representing, say, drawers, each one of which contains organized folders containing individual documents. The only difference between your Intranet boilerplate library and these search engine pages is that when you reach the individual-document level and select a hyperlink, the document pops up in your customers' word processors, rather than in their Web browser, looking something like Figure 20.6. At this point, customers have a live document with which they can do more than just look at.

> They can edit, save, or print it with their word processors or do anything else the software is capable of.

> They can customize the stock language to personalize the boilerplate and to focus it toward the specific incoming inquiry.

Perhaps more importantly, they can open entire new documents from here and then use the word processor's copy-and-paste facility to clip paragraphs of the stock language and paste them into it. The new document ultimately becomes the final response to the constituent's letter or the new legal brief. (Recall that the boilerplate documents they have downloaded are temporary copies.) Further, they can continue to open more boilerplate documents to grab additional text for insertion into the final document.

They can use all the other facilities of the word processor software, including global search-and-replace, macro commands, capability of inserting graphics, tables, spread-sheet data, and the like, to further customize the new document to its intended purpose.

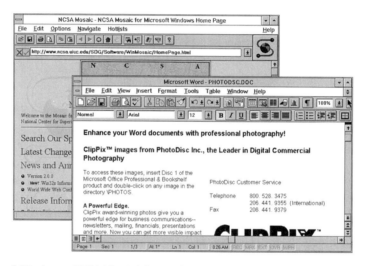

Figure 20.6. *Microsoft Word as an NCSA Mosaic helper application.*

The last item in the preceding list deserves a bit more attention here. Your word processor can be custom-tailored to the needs of your Intranet boilerplate library operation. Besides the actual library of reusable documents you've created on your Intranet, you can also configure and share document style sheets and formatting templates, macro commands for inserting pieces of boilerplate too short to put in your library, custom spelling-checker dictionaries, and many other word-processing-specific facilities. Doing so not only adds efficiency to your operation, but it also brings about uniformity in the look of your documents and in the way they are produced. Although it's true these things are not really part of your Intranet, they're common sense means of streamlining the work a boilerplate operation like a DPI or law firm does.

> **Note:** You'll recall the discussion, in Chapter 18, of commercial data warehouses with reference to retrieving spreadsheet datafiles from a World Wide Web server and pasting them directly into customers' Web browser helper application spreadsheet packages. We discussed the critical difference between raw rows and columns of numbers and live spreadsheets, with formulae, macros, and the like already built-in. This same reasoning applies to custom document management systems. Being able to retrieve the text of a boilerplate document on-screen may be one thing; being able to retrieve it directly into your word processor and use it immediately is something else altogether.

Documents and More Documents

Customers' Web browsers are still active after having retrieved a document into their word processors (notice the background of Figure 20.6 where NCSA Mosaic still lurks, active and ready to use). As a result, there's nothing to stop them from popping back into the Web browser window and locating and retrieving additional documents. Unless your boilerplate library has all its stock paragraphs in just a few large documents (which would defeat many of your purposes), it's likely customers will need to open several documents to retrieve all the necessary stock language to assemble their final documents. Continued browsing and retrieving documents, however, can result in multiple copies of the customer's word processor running all at once. Unfortunately, each new retrieval loads a new copy of customers' word processors. This can result, as Figure 20.7 shows, in a badly cluttered screen (and possibly badly confused customers!); it can also result in out-of-memory errors on PCs. It's, of course, possible to manage this multiple-document situation in several ways.

Closing the first downloaded document before loading another, as well as saving the new document (into which customers have inserted boilerplate material) in a permanent location.

Designating one of the retrieved documents as a master document and then copying and pasting from the others into it. The master document can ultimately be saved as a permanent file.

Saving the several retrieved boilerplate documents to separate temporary files and then closing them all and opening a new, blank document into which they can be inserted; this document, containing all the stock language from the several others, can then be customized as needed.

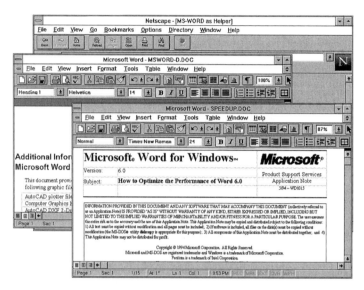

Figure 20.7. *Multiple copies of Word with Netscape.*

Manage Your Boilerplate Library

Even the longest-lived, largest boilerplate operations will occasionally generate a completely original document. More frequently, though, incremental changes in stock language are made. In either case, it's important to ensure new and revised documents get placed in your library so that they're retrievable by everyone. Keeping your library up to date is important, and how you go about doing it goes back to some of the organizational choices you considered back in the early chapters of *Building an Intranet.*

If your boilerplate operation is a large and/or critical one, with frequent document changes that must be put in place quickly, you'll probably want a Web server right in the department, with a local WebMaster to update the documents promptly rather than relying on a central MIS department to maintain one for you.

Supervisors or others with the authority to update documents on your Intranet boilerplate library Web server, can use facilities such as the TCP/IP file-transfer protocol (FTP) to upload files to the Web server from their PC or workstation. As you learned in Chapter 8, because you have the TCP/IP networking infrastructure to support World Wide Web services, you also have FTP and many other networking capabilities with which to supplement the Web services on your Intranet. Version 2 of Netscape even has FTP-upload capabilities built in, so customers don't need to learn to use a standalone FTP tool. Access this feature when browsing an FTP server—you'll need to specify a username in the URL, such as `root@ftp.yourcompany.com`—by pulling down the File menu and selecting Upload File. The Netscape file-upload dialog box is shown in Figure 20.8.

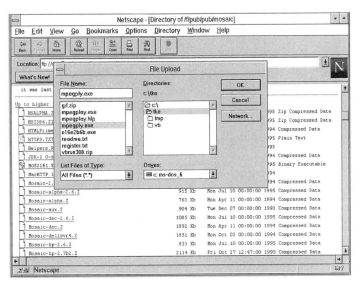

Figure 20.8. *Netscape FTP file upload.*

> **Tip:** Because government staff work is often reviewed by managers and legal documents by paralegals and other attorneys, you can use the FTP-upload facility in Netscape or manual FTP uploads to make draft documents accessible to reviewers, also using their Web browsers. Setting up a publicly writable, shared review directory on an FTP server enables reviewers to download the drafts for review and edit them using their Web browsers, just as your customers download boilerplate documents. Pointing and clicking with a Web browser, the document is loaded right into your word processor.

Network drives can also be a way of keeping your Intranet boilerplate library up to date. If the system running the Web server, where your files are located, makes its filesystem available for network mounting via the Network File System (NFS) facility, supervisors with NFS client capabilities can mount the remote file systems as network drives and then just copy new documents over.

Index Your Boilerplate Library

How, you're wondering, will your customers locate the boilerplate documents they want? Surely, they won't just have long onscreen lists of filenames they have to browse through? Even nested, subject-oriented menus like those shown in Figure 20.8 are tedious and aren't always a big help, either. As with the conversion of your legacy data in earlier chapters, the answers to these questions refer to material you've covered earlier in *Building an Intranet.* In Chapter 13, "Indexing and

Searching Your Data," you learned about a variety of powerful tools for indexing data on your Intranet and equally important, flexible tools for searching and retrieving Intranet data from the indexes created by them. FreeWAIS-sf, glimpse, and the rest of the packages covered in that chapter give you powerful means of indexing your word processing documents, along with the rest of the data on your Intranet. Equally powerful tools, like SFgate and Harvest, make it easy for your Intranet customers to search out specific documents using Web fill-in forms of the sort you've seen earlier in this book for keyword search. Figure 20.9 shows a sample SFgate search form; notice the multiple-field search capabilities.

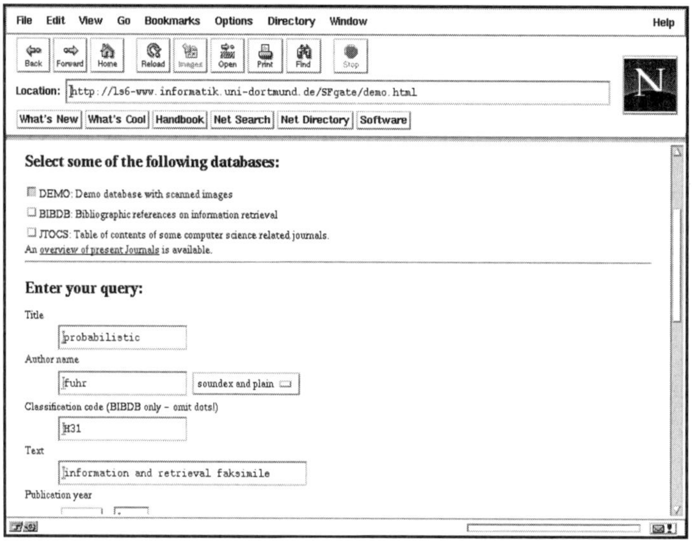

Figure 20.9. SFgate fielded search form.

You probably wonder how binary files such as word processing documents can be indexed with tools like freeWAIS-sf and glimpse. After all, the detailed descriptions of these tools in Chapter 13 suggested they can only index plain-text files. You probably concluded from reading that chapter these indexing tools could, at best, index the filename and a few command-line keywords of binary files such as spreadsheet datafiles. Indeed, this is what both packages' documentation indicates.

You could use a workaround, maintaining parallel plain-text copies of all your documents just for indexing. In such a situation, you'd index only the plain-text versions but somehow contrive to retrieve the original documents with custom CGI-bin scripts. This, however, would be quite clumsy. Experimentation with both freeWAIS-sf's waisindex and glimpseindex, however, reveals useful indexes can be created by both when reading WordPerfect and Word documents; your word processing documents should work the same way. In fact, both packages root out character strings in these document files (and other binary files, such as spreadsheet datafiles). Both waisindex and glimpseindex create searchable indexes of your word processing documents, using the character strings they're able to find among the binary data. Of course, your word processing documents are mostly text, so your indexes will reflect the full content of your documents, minus only the formatting codes, on which you most likely won't want to search anyway. This means your Intranet Boilerplate Library documents are just as searchable as your plain-text data. Of course, your waisindex or glimpse database index is subject to use with the Harvest distributed indexing mechanism described in Chapter 13 as well.

You can also index your RTF documents, if you're using RTF as a means of document portability among different word processors. RTF is a plain-text file format, much like PostScript or the Adobe Portable Document Format (PDF), with plain-text markup commands included right in with the document's text. As such, the full indexing power of waisindex and glimpseindex will be available to you to index all your RTF documents (as well as PostScript and PDF ones). You may want, however, to create your own waisindex stop files to exclude RTF-specific markup, such as font names and the like, from your indexes. Take a look at the bit of RTF that follows this paragraph, which is just one line from the top of a document, declaring the document to be RTF and specifying the available fonts:

```
{\rtf1\defformat\mac\deff2 {\fonttbl{\f0\fswiss Chicago;}{\f2\froman New
York;}{\f3\fswiss Geneva;}{\f4\fmodern Monaco;}{\f5\fscript Venice;}{\f6\fdecor
London;}{\f8\fdecor San Francisco;}{\f11\fnil Cairo;}{\f16\fnil
Palatino;}{\f20\froman Times;}{\f21\fswiss Helvetica;}
```

As you can see, there are a number of RTF-specific commands, such as the opening {\rtf1\defformat\mac\deff2, along with several font names, roman New York, modern Monaco, and the like. Because these font names contain words that might otherwise appear in your document text, you'll want to craft your stop list carefully. Otherwise, searches for words such as *New York* or *Cairo* generate hits on the font names rather than on the substantive text; a search for New York, for example, might bring you back every single RTF document in your index. As an alternative to extending your stop files, you can create waisindex document format description files that exclude the RTF or PostScript markup. As you'll recall from Chapter 13, these define the structure of your documents so you can do fielded indexing. You can then build SFgate search forms that exclude all RTF markup codes from customer searches.

You saw in Chapter 13 how your indexed Web server data can be retrieved across your Intranet using the glimpse, Harvest, or SFgate search engines. As shown in Figure 20.10, the results of your searches show up as lists of clickable Web browser hyperlinks, showing the hits on your search keywords (and, with freeWAIS-sf indexes, each hit's numerical relevance ranking). Selecting such a hyperlink pointing to a text or HTML document brings the document up for viewing in your browser, and so does selecting a word processing document hyperlink. The difference is the document is handed off to your customer's word processor helper application for viewing. And once loaded, the document is an interactive entity your customer can use to do his or her job, not a static Web page which just sits there.

Figure 20.10. *Results of SFgate search on the WAIS document index.*

Depending on the extent and nature of the overall library of documents on your Intranet and your customers' indexing needs, you may want also to look into commercial full-text indexing tools, some of which are described in Chapter 13. There you learned about

The OpenText 5 distributed indexing product from OpenText (`http://www.opentext.com/`) claims support for more than 40 file formats, specifically including Word and WordPerfect. OpenText 5 is the underlying search engine for the company's Latitude networked search-and-retrieval product. Check with the company for support of your particular word processor. If you're using RTF as a common word processing format for your Intranet boilerplate library, to support multiple word processors, you'll want to check for RTF support as well.

Fulcrum's SearchServer product, the full-text database that underlies its Web Surfboard package, claims to support 50-odd document formats, though no list can be found on its very poorly organized Web site (`http://www.fulcrum.com`). With this large a number of supported file formats, you would reasonably expect common word processor formats to be included. Check with the company for support of your specific word processor and/or for RTF support.

Verity's Topic Enterprise Server full-text indexer supports multiple file formats, explicitly including both Word and WordPerfect. More information, including information on the company's related product, Topic Internet Server, for indexing documents across your Intranet, is at `http://www.verity.com/`. Check with the company for support of your specific word processor and/or for RTF support.

The Illustra object relational database allows all sorts of nontext data to be included in its relational databases, allowing for transparent search and retrieval using its Web DataBlade add-in. Although the company's Web site documents (http://www.illustra.com/) aren't specific, its claim that "all kinds" of nontext data can be indexed should extend to word processing documents. Because RTF is a plain-text file format, it, too, should be supported, if only as plain text, though you'd hope for better, RTF-specific support.

> **Tip:** With any commercial full-text indexing product, if you need RTF support, be sure to ask for specific details about how the product's RTF support works. As described previously with respect to waisindex and glimpse, you'll want the package to exclude, or otherwise work around, all the RTF markup in your documents, so as not to get false hits in your customer searches.

Summary

In this chapter, you've seen a practical application for your Intranet, again combining several of the facilities about which you've learned in *Building an Intranet*. As you've seen in the several previous chapters, this flexibility, used in combination with your imagination, can result in significant added value for your Intranet. Creating an Intranet boilerplate library like the ones described in this chapter involves

- Using your existing word processing documents to create a library of boilerplate documents on your Intranet's Web server

- Converting documents to a common format usable in several different word processing programs, if necessary

- Making your boilerplate library accessible to customers using a Web browser, putting what you've learned about MIME data types/subtypes and Web browser helper applications earlier in this book to work

- Enabling your customers to search for and retrieve documents from your library using their Web browsers, bringing up retrieved documents directly in their word processor for editing and document assembly

- Using the indexing tools about which you've learned in this book to create searchable indexes of your Intranet boilerplate library documents

In the next chapter, you take the ideas discussed and illustrated in the past several chapters and create a completely standalone Intranet application, one that is wholly self-contained and accessed through Web browsers.

CHAPTER

Web-Based Training and Presentations

This chapter contains another series of exemplary Web-based applications for your Intranet. In it, you learn about enabling your customers to conduct computer-based training courses and business presentations using World Wide Web technology. You'll be able to use the information in this chapter in numerous ways, including setting up training for your customers in the use of your Intranet itself. As with the other examples shown, your customer's home base is his Web browser. In some cases, the customer's Web browser itself will be the means of the training or presentation; in others, Web browser helper applications will be called to perform the task, with the Web browser as the supervisor of the process. Overall, your Intranet can be an important part of your company's training and business presentation program.

Chapter Objectives

As with the rest of the chapters in this book, let's begin by laying out some chapter objectives. This will help you get oriented to the material to be presented (you may want to refer back to this list as you work your way through the chapter). In this chapter, you'll

◆ Learn about simple, leader-presented or self-paced *slide shows* that can be shown on one or more customers' Web browser screens for corporate seminars, lectures, or business presentations

◆ Learn about playing back *prerecorded training sessions*, complete with mouse movements and clicks, using Web browser helper applications much like you use your home VCR, for individual or classroom training

◆ Learn how you can use HTML to incorporate all the multimedia aspects of World Wide Web and related technology to organize effective Web training and presentation pages for your Intranet

◆ Learn about *interactive*, self-paced training sessions that allow customers to actually use the software about which they're learning

◆ Consider all the capabilities of your Intranet as fodder for use in your training curricula

In Chapter 24, "Web Groupware: Collaboration on Your Intranet," you'll see some of the same facilities discussed in this chapter put to use in a different context. As you've seen frequently in *Building an Intranet*, your Web-based tool kit is a versatile one, allowing you to use individual pieces of it in new and changing combinations to develop completely new ways of using your Intranet. What you learn about in this chapter is no exception to this.

Simple Slide Shows

The overhead projector and a stack of transparencies are the everyday tools of the professor, the salesperson, and the corporate executive. Laptop computers outfitted with special hardware and software to replicate the transparency are dragged to presentations. While the art of the slide show is advanced by such hardware and software, participants are still left sitting in the dark looking at transparencies that are all-too-often hard to see and paper printouts of the slides they can't read in the dark. Wouldn't it be better if your customers could sit at workstations, or at their own desks, and see the presentation or training slides onscreen as they were meant to look? And, because *Building an Intranet* is all about using Web and related technology for everyday work purposes, wouldn't it be great if they could do all this using their Web browser? Let's take a look at how you can have slide show presentations on your Intranet, using simple tools and your customers' Web browsers.

Slide Shows with UNIX Netscape and Mosaic

Both Netscape and NCSA Mosaic have slide-show capabilities in their UNIX implementations. PC versions of the two packages take different approaches. Let's look at the UNIX approach first, starting off with Netscape.

Netscape Slide Shows

Before we go into Netscape slide-show specifics, we'll need to take a short side trip for some important background information about the X Window graphical user interface under which Netscape runs on all UNIX systems.

X Window (often shortened to just X) is a graphical user interface (GUI) for UNIX systems that works in a client/server relationship. This relationship seems confusing at first, with the definition of clients and servers a little tricky. The best way to keep this relationship straight is to remember that individual programs, like Netscape, are X Window clients. All X clients must connect to an X server. In order to run Netscape, for example, you must already have an X server running for it to communicate with. Now, your X server is usually, but not always, running on your own computer. It's your overall GUI with a window manager and one or more X clients, like Netscape, running on it. Your X server displays the running clients in individual windows on your graphical desktop. A special X client, your *window manager*, manages all your other clients. In Figure 21.1, think of the whole screen as being the X server, while Netscape, the Console window, the Xterm (where you can see the command used to make the screenshot), the Icon box, and the Common Desktop Environment dashboard (at the bottom of the screen) are all X clients.

Figure 21.1. X Window server and clients.

All this is fairly straightforward once you get the idea of the X server and clients both running on the same computer. Suppose, however, you want to run an X client from some other computer. You still have to have that client communicate with some X server. Obviously, you don't want your remote client to display on the remote computer's screen where you can't use it. Instead, you want the client to communicate with the X server running on your own computer. Here's where X can get a little confusing, playing fast and loose with the traditional definition of client/server computing. In such a situation, the X program running on the remote machine is the client, while your computer's X server is the server, exactly backwards it might seem. In other situations, you may want to run an X client on your machine with the graphical output going to the X server on a different computer. For example, you can show a friend a screenshot, sending it to his computer's screen using something like ImageMagick display, like this:

```
$ display -display myfriend:0 myslide.gif &
```

Here, we've used the standard X Window `-display` command-line argument to tell our client program (also, just coincidentally, named `display`) to run with its output directed to the X server on the remote computer named `myfriend`. The GIF image pops up on the remote screen (the X server), not yours, even though the display program itself (the X client) is running on your computer.

> **Note:** As you might guess, you must have permission to throw your X clients onto a remote X server. Things could get quite confusing, to say the least, if just anyone could pop up the display of graphical applications on anyone else's screen. Check your system manual for the `xhost` command for details on how to exercise control over who can display things to your X server, as well as for the potentially serious security implications of doing so. Note in particular that opening your X server to just anyone is a very dangerous thing to do if your computer is on the Internet and it's not protected by a firewall system. (See Chapter 9, "Intranet Security.")

This brings our digression back to our original topic: UNIX Netscape slide shows. Your objective is to display your slide(s) on one or more other computer screens, not your own. Based on what you've just learned, you've probably figured you can do this by running Netscape with its display directed to the X server on the other computer(s). And you can certainly run Netscape in this way; something like this will surely work:

```
netscape -display myfriend:0 file://myslide.gif &
```

Netscape pops up on your friend's screen with your image displayed. This leaves you in a bit of a fix, however. First, with Netscape's display redirected to the other X server, you now have no way of controlling it. It's running on the other X server across the hall or across the country. All the pull-down menus and other ways of running Netscape are no longer accessible to you. Instead, they're accessible to your friend; if you want her to do anything with Netscape, you'll have to dictate instructions over the phone. While you presumably trust your friends, you still may not want them to be able to edit your Netscape bookmarks, for example, or retrieve and look at files in your personal directories. In this situation, the remote user can operate Netscape under your user account; you gave over control of the program when you started it remotely. Anything you can do with your account is now in the hands of your friend. Your only recourse to limit this access is to kill the running Netscape process from your own workstation.

Fortunately, you don't need to go to all this trouble and risk access to your private files just to show a slide on someone else's screen with UNIX Netscape. X Window Netscape has a special remote-control capability you can use to display your slides, or any other Web documents, in a remote Netscape session on another computer whose owner has given you permission to access its X server. Here's how it works.

1. Place in your Web server's filetree a copy of the slide you want to display.

2. Ask your friend to give permission for you to access his X server by entering this command:

   ```
   $ xhost yourhostname
   ```

3. Have your friend start up his own local copy of UNIX Netscape if it's not already running.

4. On your workstation, enter this command:

```
$ netscape -display myfriend:0 -remote "openURL(http://www.yourcompany.com/
path/to/myslide.gif)"
```

Having taken these four steps, your slide now pops up in your friend's already running Netscape window. What you've done with this command is to instruct your friend's running Netscape program to retrieve, for itself, your slide from your Web server using its URL. In other words, you're remotely controlling your friend's copy of Netscape. You won't see the slide in your own Netscape window; see below for how you can include yourself. It's important to note the `-display` argument must precede the `-remote` argument on this command line; otherwise, the command will fail with a most unhelpful error message.

> **Note:** Netscape's `-remote` option has a number of additional features that can enable other kinds of Intranet collaboration. You learn more about them in Chapter 24. If you're really curious right now, check out Netscape's own documentation for the remote-control capability, at `http://home.netscape.com/newsref/std/x-remote.html`. Here you'll find not only more detail on using the facility, but also detailed specifications of the protocol used by Netscape and reference source code you can use to build your own applications. Note the limitation on commercial use of the source code, however.

So, you've displayed one slide in one remote Netscape session. Your next step, no doubt, is displaying the slide on several remote sessions at once. While the above command line can't include multiple `-display` options, you can repeat it several times, each time using a different remote computer's hostname. You can retype the command for each remote host, but this is tedious and prone to typographical errors, and is therefore not a good idea for a training session or business presentation. A much better idea is to put several such commands in a UNIX *shell script* so you can automate this process. You can try out a script that goes something like this one, connecting to three different remote Netscape processes and displaying your slide on each in turn.

```
#!/bin/sh
# display slide on multiple displays with Netscape -remote
for HOST in student1 student2 student3
do     netscape -display $HOST:0  -remote "openURL(http://www.yourcompany.com/path/
to/myslide.gif)"
done
# show me a copy, too, also using remote control of my own
# running Netscape
netscape -remote "openURL(http://www.yourcompany.com/path/to/myslide.gif)"
```

This simple looping script executes the `netscape` command with both the `-display` and `-remote` arguments three times, once each for the three training room hosts `student1`, `student2`, and `student3`. On each computer, your slide is displayed in turn in the currently running Netscape window. As you can see, we used the shell loop to substitute the actual hostname of the student workstation in each iteration of the basic command. Of course, there is a small delay while each command in your script executes. The script has been extended an extra step and it also displays the same slide to the script operator's own Netscape session; notice the last `netscape` command does not include the `-display` option, though it does require the `-remote` argument even though the Netscape session is local to the instructor's computer.

You can use the same technique to display a series of slides by adding a second loop to your script for the slides themselves. Here's a modified version of the shell script that displays three slides on each of three workstations in turn.

```
#!/bin/sh
# display slides on multiple displays with Netscape -remote
# first, the outer loop with the three slides
for SLIDE in slide1.gif slide2.gif slide3.gif
# now an inner loop for the three student workstations
do for HOST in student1 student2 student3
   do    netscape -display $HOST:0  -remote "openURL(http://www.yourcompany.com/
path/to/$SLIDE)"
   done
   # show me a copy, too
   netscape -remote "openURL(http://www.yourcompany.com/path/to/$SLIDE)"
   # pause for 5 minutes to let everybody look
   sleep 300
done
```

As you can see, each slide is sent to each of the three remote hosts' Netscape sessions and also displayed on the instructor's Netscape session, after which the script pauses for five minutes (300 seconds) before going on to the next slide. The five-minute pause allows everyone plenty of time to view the slide while the instructor or presenter expounds on its content.

Note: Double quotes (") are used in the above Netscape `-remote` commands to make sure the `$SLIDE` variable is handled correctly. The Netscape documentation for remote control (see the previously listed URL) uses single quotes (') in all its examples. However, basic UNIX shell quoting rules hold that strings surrounded with single quotes are treated as *literals*. As a result, enclosing the `openURL` command in single quotes in our script would cause the program to try to locate the actual file with the literal name $SLIDE, not the one assigned to the variable *$SLIDE* by your script. Using the double quotes resolves this problem.

You may want to introduce into the script more flexibility for your instructor or presenter. A hard-coded five-minute pause between slides may be either too short or too long depending on the nature of the presentation unless the presentation is on a strict time schedule, as you might want under some circumstances. To make the script more interactive so the instructor can control the slide show, replace the last three lines of the above script with these three:

```
# pause until instructor wants the next slide
/bin/echo "Press RETURN for Next Slide"
read PRESS < /dev/tty
```

Now, the script pauses indefinitely after displaying each slide on the three remote workstations. The instructor's console prompts him for the display of the next slide with the message built into the script. Simply pressing the Return key ends the pause and brings up the next slide in the presentation on all student workstations.

Finally, it's important to note each student's Netscape session has a history of each slide having been accessed. Because you're remotely controlling the students' copy of Netscape, all the capabilities of Netscape are available to the student anytime during the presentation. Through use of the Back and Forward buttons on the Netscape toolbar, for example, or the history list (accessed from the Go button), the student can page back and forth among the previously displayed slides, adding bookmarks, saving or printing the slides, or using any other Netscape feature.

NCSA X Mosaic Slide Shows

Although UNIX Mosaic is also an X Window program, you needn't be concerned about accessing remote X servers to do Mosaic slide shows, even to remote computers' screens. Since version 2.5 (2.7 beta Release 2 was the current release at the time this chapter was written), NCSA Mosaic for X Window has supported a feature called the *Common Client Interface*, or *CCI*. CCI is a general application programming interface (API) from NCSA that allows CCI-compatible external applications to communicate over the network with a running Mosaic session. You can build CCI applications that instruct a remotely running copy of Mosaic to load a local file or grab a Web URL and display it in the Mosaic window. Although the CCI protocol is different from that used by Netscape Remote, the effect of using it is the same, then. As a result, you can use CCI to create X Mosaic slide shows.

In fact, NCSA distributes source code for sshow, a simple slide-show program written by Alan Braverman that uses CCI. You'll find a copy on the *Building an Intranet* CD-ROM. You'll need to compile it on a UNIX host using one of the included makefiles (or one of your own if there's not one included one for your particular version of UNIX). As with the Netscape remote-control examples above, let's start with a simple one here and work our way up. The first step in using sshow, or any other CCI application, is to ask the running Mosaic program to listen for CCI requests over the network. This is done from the pull-down X Mosaic File menu. Select CCI (see Figure 21.2). This opens the NCSA Mosaic CCI dialog box shown in Figure 21.3. Here the customer enters a CCI Port Address and clicks on the Accept Requests radio button. The port number can be any number between 1024 and 65535; in Figure 21.3, the port number 5555 has been selected as one that's easy to remember. If you plan to use CCI on a regular basis on your Intranet, you'll probably want to adopt a standard port number to use; check with your TCP/IP network administrators to make sure you don't pick a port number being used for some other purpose on your network.

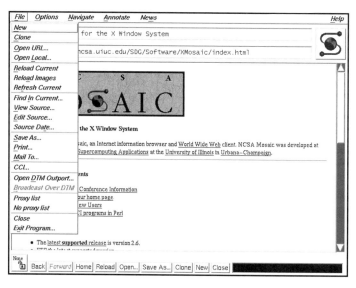

Figure 21.2. *NCSA X Mosaic File menu with CCI selection.*

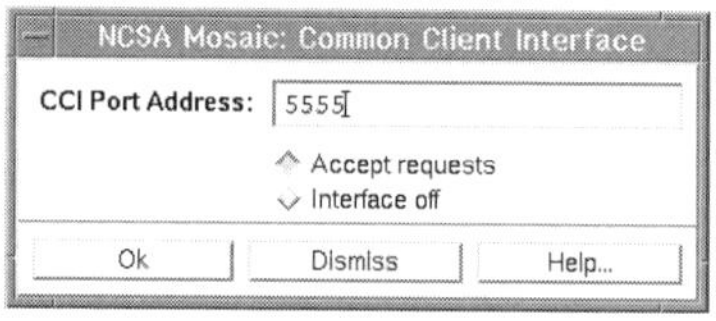

Figure 21.3. *NCSA X Mosaic CCI dialog box.*

Every participant in your X Mosaic slide show must go through this process of enabling CCI on the port number you're going to use for the show.

Now you've enabled X Mosaic to listen for CCI requests on port address 5555, here's an sshow command to display a single slide from your Web server in a single remote X Mosaic session.

```
$ sshow -host student 1 -port 5555 -url http://www.mycompany.com/path/to/myslide.gif
```

This command line is pretty clear and is in some respects similar to the one used with Netscape remote control. You've specified the remote host named student1 with the -host argument, the CCI port address 5555 with -port, and the URL with the -url of your slide. The copy of X Mosaic running on the student workstation will retrieve and display the URL you've specified: your slide. As with Netscape Remote, you're actually controlling the student's X Mosaic program remotely with the sshow commands you issue.

So, you've displayed one slide on one remote X Mosaic session. Your next step, obviously, is displaying the slide on several remote sessions at once. While the previous command line can't include multiple -host options, sshow provides a mechanism that's considerably simpler than the shell-script approach used above with Netscape Remote. You can tell sshow to take its input from a *script file* you create. The script file contains sshow commands that replace the command-line options in the example and which allows for more flexibility in running your slide shows. Here's a simple example of an sshow script file displaying your one slide to each of three remote systems' X Mosaic sessions in turn:

```
# sshow.list
# run through a list of machines, displaying URL on each
port 5555
host student1
url http://www.mycompany.com/path/to/myslide.gif
host student2
url http://www.mycompany.com/path/to/myslide.gif
host student3
url http://www.mycompany.com/path/to/myslide.gif
```

As you can see, having set the CCI port number to 5555 (at the top of the script), each subsequent section of the file merely repeats what the previous one did, except for changing the hostname of the destination computer. Now you can use the script, by running sshow with this command line to display your slide on each of the three student computers in turn.

```
$ sshow -f sshow.list
```

As you might expect from this sample script, sshow allows multiple URLs to be retrieved just by adding new url lines to the script file. Also, pauses can be inserted after each slide, using the sshow sleep command. The following code shows the three-host, three-slide example you saw previously with Netscape Remote, implemented in a sshow script file, showing each slide then pausing for five minutes before going on to the next one.

```
# sshow.list
# run through a list of machines, displaying URL's on each
port 5555
host student1
url http://www.mycompany.com/path/to/slide1.gif
host student2
url http://www.mycompany.com/path/to/slide1.gif
host student3
url http://www.mycompany.com/path/to/lide1.gif
sleep 300
host student1
url http://www.mycompany.com/path/to/slide2.gif
host student2
url http://www.mycompany.com/path/to/slide2.gif
host student3
url http://www.mycompany.com/path/to/slide2.gif
sleep 300
host student1
url http://www.mycompany.com/path/to/slide3.gif
host student2
url http://www.mycompany.com/path/to/slide3.gif
host student3
url http://www.mycompany.com/path/to/slide3.gif
```

As with the Netscape Remote example, you'd like more flexibility here with the pause between slides. sshow also supports adding an indefinite pause to your script file. Just replace each of the sleep lines in the preceding script with the following two lines:

```
exec /bin/echo "Press RETURN for Next Slide"
exec read PRESS < /dev/tty
```

The sshow exec command executes ordinary UNIX shell commands as part of the script. Here, as with the Netscape Remote shell script, this one prompts the instructor (on the initiating computer's console) to press Return before the script continues with the next iteration of slides. The script sits and waits indefinitely until the instructor presses Return.

Finally, it's important to note each student's X Mosaic session has a history of each slide having been accessed. Because you're remotely controlling the student's copy of Netscape, all the capabilities of X Mosaic are available to the student at anytime during the presentation. Through use of the Back and Forward buttons on the X Mosaic toolbar, or the history list accessed from the Navigate button, the student can page back and forth among the previously displayed slides, adding *hotlist* entries, saving or printing the slides, or using any other X Mosaic feature.

> **Note:** The Common Computer Interface protocol is described in some detail at `http://www.nsca.uiuc.edu/SDG/Software/XMosaic/CCI/cci-spec.html`. There you'll also find information about other CCI-compatible applications that are available.

Driving Slide Shows from CGI-bin Scripts

Under the right circumstances, you can drive Netscape Remote or X Mosaic CCI-based slide shows from your Web server using CGI-bin scripts. Customers with UNIX systems or X Window server software installed on their PCs can access the scripts and view the slides. Recall from your earlier work with CGI-bin scripts one of the standard CGI environment variables is the network hostname of the computer accessing the script. Having this piece of information makes it possible for you to include in your CGI-bin scripts calls to Netscape with the -display and -remote command-line flags or the sshow program with the -host flag set to the hostname of the initiating user's computer. If you develop CGI-bin scripts to do this sort of thing, you'll need to make sure users are told what they need to do before trying to run your slide show scripts. Specifically

- ◆ Netscape users will need to have executed the xhost program to give permission for the CGI-bin script to access their X server.
- ◆ X Mosaic users will need to have opened their browser sessions to incoming CCI connections using a standard port number used on your Intranet for all CCI connections.

Be sure your Intranet slide show Web pages provide these instructions to customers, including, possibly, image files with instructive screenshots on what they need to do before they can view your slide shows.

Important Considerations about Slide Shows

It's probably apparent from this section that both Netscape Remote and the CCI program sshow operate by accessing Web URLs. While the discussion has been cast in terms of a set of slides you'd use in a classroom or business-presentation context, it should be clear these two approaches to creating and sharing slide shows can be used for any Intranet purpose involving Web URLs, and need not be limited to slide shows. For example, you can mix in your presentation slides with real live URLs from your Intranet as a means of illustrating points made in the slides. If you want to show a customer group how to use their Web browsers to search and retrieve text data (see Chapter 13, "Indexing and Searching Your Data"), for example, you can prepare a slide show that runs through sample searches with your explanatory slides written in HTML, and with hyperlinks to your Intranet's real fill-in search forms. The heretofore static slide show then becomes *interactive*. By using the indefinite-pause features described, together with your training slides containing hyperlinks, your class has the opportunity to actually use the services on which they're being trained, live and right in the classroom. The instructor always has the ability, by controlling the return to the fixed part of the slide show or presentation, to bring students back from their interactive wanderings.

Both Netscape and NCSA have published detailed specifications of their respective remote-access protocols. If you believe the sorts of slide shows described in this section can be important to your Intranet, you'll want to look at the specifications with a view toward using them to develop your own applications. You should be aware, though, it appears from recent developments on the Web, particularly the explosive growth of Java now underway, these remote control methods may soon turn out to be relics of earlier days. (In fact, NCSA doesn't seem to be making much progress with CCI applications.) As you'll see later in this chapter, widely available Web browser helper applications for Windows PCs can provide high-quality slide shows and presentations for your PC users.

X Web Teach—Slide Shows Extended

After he wrote sshow, NCSA's Alan Braverman extended the basic idea of Web-based slide shows by developing another CCI application he called X Web Teach. Though the package (and sshow, for that matter) are a couple of years old by now and may be overtaken by forthcoming Java applets that do the same thing, it's worth a look, just to see what might be possible. The basic idea behind X Web Teach is to link students' Web browsers to that of the instructor. When the instructor accesses a hyperlink, or executes any other command in the browser, all the student browsers, controlled via CCI, follow along. Figure 21.4 shows the administrative interface to X Web Teach. By using the Setup button, the instructor defines the master X Mosaic session with hostname and CCI port number, then adds one or more student computers to the session, and clicks on Broadcasting to start the shared X Mosaic session. From then on, all activities in the instructor's X Mosaic session are transmitted to the student sessions, which, one at a time, retrieve the same URLs the instructor's does. As a result, each student's session is kept synchronized with the instructor's session.

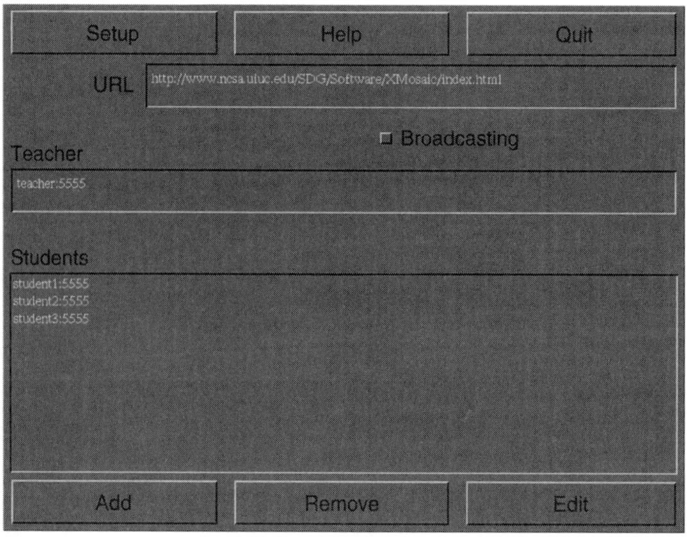

Figure 21.4. X Web Teach.

Helper Applications for Training and Presentations

You can use a wide range of helper applications for Intranet training and presentation purposes, with your Web pages providing smooth access to various kinds of information that might be included in an overall curriculum. We'll first look separately at a couple of very useful PC Helpers, Microsoft PowerPoint and Lotus ScreenCam. Both are excellent packages you can use for your purposes, but, as you'll learn a little later, your Intranet presents quite flexible training and presentation opportunities, and you won't want to limit yourself to just these two packages, or any other single package, regardless of how great they might be.

PowerPoint

In Chapter 12, "Other Common Office Applications," you learned how to set up the Microsoft PowerPoint presentation slide applications as a Web browser application on Windows PCs and Macintoshes. For your training and presentation purposes, PC users can access and view PowerPoint slide shows easily, provided they have access to PowerPoint itself, or the read-only PowerPoint viewer now available at Microsoft's Web site, `http://www.microsoft.com`. You may need to refer back to Chapter 12 for specifics on setting up PowerPoint datafiles as a new MIME data type/subtype on your Web server. Also, you'll find detailed instructions on configuring both Netscape and NCSA Mosaic to call PowerPoint as a helper application to view and manipulate downloaded slide presentations. Figure 21.5, showing PowerPoint setup as a Netscape helper application will no doubt jog your memory on this subject.

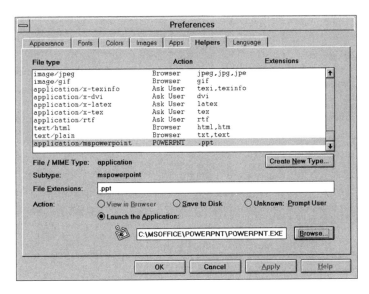

Figure 21.5. *Setting up PowerPoint as a Netscape Helper Application.*

Once a customer has downloaded a PowerPoint slide show data file and the application has started, she can view the slide show just as if it had been created on her own PC or as if she were sitting in a conference room. (To start a PowerPoint slide show, pull down the View menu and select Slide Show to bring up the dialog box shown in Figure 21.6.). Slide show presentations using PowerPoint as a Web browser helper application are an excellent means of self-paced training exercises. Customers can download and run them at their convenience, page through them, save or print individual slides, and so on. Using this mechanism in a group training room can, however, be a bit difficult to coordinate. In such a situation, each student independently downloads a copy of the same slide presentation and views it on their own workstation. Keeping everyone on the same page might present problems, but no more so than those that occur when presenters provide paper handouts of slides.

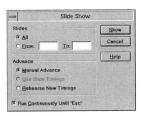

Figure 21.6. *PowerPoint Slide Show dialog box.*

Tip: A bonus to using PowerPoint as a helper application for presentations and training classes is that customers can use PowerPoint interactively during the presentation. While some users might get distracted by this capability, the ability to view the overall structure of a presentation in PowerPoint's Outline view mode can be useful. In addition, class or presentation participants have the ability to save or print the slides for permanent reference, or to steal for use as models for other slide shows.

Lotus ScreenCam

As you may know, ScreenCam is a Windows software package which can be likened to your home VCR. Like a video camera, the ScreenCam recorder software records all on-screen activity on your PC, including mouse movements and clicks, the opening and closing of programs, and so on. It's frequently used to produce software demos and training sessions. The ScreenCam player plays back previously recorded ScreenCam sessions, using the VCR metaphor, with start, stop, rewind, and fast-forward buttons. Lotus has made the ScreenCam player freely available; you'll find it at Lotus' Web site, `http://www.lotus.com/intrprod/2142.htm`. (The ScreenCam recorder itself is not, however, freely available, but must be purchased from Lotus; it costs about $100.) Figure 21.7 shows the ScreenCam player in action in a demonstration of the Collabra Share groupware package from Collabra, Inc. (a company now owned by Netscape Communications and which, not coincidentally, you'll learn more about in Chapter 24). The ScreenCam controller window has VCR-like buttons to allow the demo to be played, paused, rewound, new demos loaded, and so on. The running ScreenCam session was, of course, paused while the screenshot was taken.

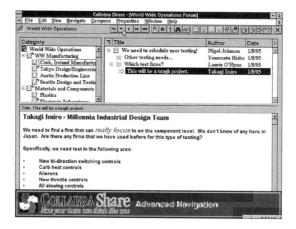

Figure 21.7. ScreenCam.

While ScreenCam can be run as a standalone application, as you probably expect, you can set up the ScreenCam player as a Web browser helper application for your customers. Doing so allows you to use the package as a part of your Intranet training program to display sessions you record with the ScreenCam recorder or obtain from vendors. Helper application setup for the ScreenCam player is much the same as that for other helpers.

1. Add a new entry for the SreeenCam player application to your Web server's `mime.types` file, like this:

```
application/x-screencam     scm
```

2. Set up your customers' Web browsers to use the new MIME data type/sub-type (`application/x-screencam`) and filename extension (scm) to call the ScreenCam player.

Figure 21.8 shows the ScreenCam player helper application set up in Netscape; the setup is similar in Mosaic. You'll probably have installed the package in a different directory than the one shown, so be sure to enter the right one for your installation, or just use the Browse button to locate your copy.

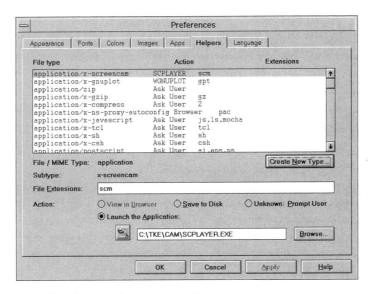

Figure 21.8. *ScreenCam Player helper application setup in Netscape.*

As with Microsoft PowerPoint slide shows, ScreenCam presentations and training sessions can be self-paced, run at customer convenience right from the customer's own Web browser. ScreenCam has important features not present in any slide show package, because the customer is viewing a complete session rather than frozen slides with screenshots. Every mouse movement and click and screen change are shown; slides have a completely different purpose, of course. In a group training session, ScreenCam adds its advantages to those described with respect to PowerPoint, and your overall training program can profit from using it. As suggested above with the X Web Teach package, you can use the ScreenCam recorder to provide training to your customers on the use of the various parts of your Intranet itself, recording sample Netscape or Mosaic sessions for playback by customers, or in training sessions. The ability to pause, rewind, fast-forward, and the like using the VCR buttons is quite important because customers can go back to see earlier parts of the recording.

ScreenCam has, however, some features that might be considered both advantages and disadvantages compared to the other helper applications your customers might use. Most importantly, ScreenCam recordings are read-only. They can be viewed again and again but not changed in any way. Customers who view them can't save them to review later (although they can reload them with their Web browser) nor modify them for their own presentations as they can with word processor, spreadsheet, or PowerPoint datafiles. ScreenCam, too, is subject to the whims of meeting participants or trainees, in that each customer, having downloaded his own copy of the demo recording, is free to fast forward, rewind, and otherwise ignore the progress of the meeting or training class. Again, this happens in every presentation or training class ever conducted, regardless of the presentation media, and there's nothing at all you can do about it. Finally, you should note that, with a room full of students downloading a ScreenCam recording from your Web server all at once, getting everyone's viewing of the demo synchronized can be a slight problem. ScreenCam recordings can be quite large, and download time over your Intranet may be affected by multiple simultaneous downloads in a classroom setting. Each session will start separately and may well do so at different times. The stage of the demo customers see can therefore differ unless you're able to get them all to pause the demo at the same place and restart it together.

Simple Web-Based Training

As it did with the first graphical Web browser and the leading freeware httpd Web server, NCSA has also led the way in Web-based training with its outstanding Web-related tutorials. You'll find a list of them at http://www.ncsa.uiuc.edu/SDG/Software/Mosaic/docs/web-index.html#Tutorials. You'll no doubt use these extensively as you set up and refine your Intranet and its capabilities, but you'll want to look at them in the context of this chapter's subject matter as well. Completely apart from their (very important) subject matter, the NCSA tutorials are great examples of how to use the Web as a training mechanism. A good place to start is the NCSA httpd server tutorial, at http://hoohoo.ncsa.uiuc.edu/docs/, one page of which is shown in Figure 21.9. Although the page is mostly text, you'll notice it's arranged in a logical sequence with each page containing hyperlinks to the next steps in the process of installing and configuring the *httpd* server. The customer can simply follow the logical steps laid out at the top level to work his way through the course systematically.

As you work your way through the NCSA httpd setup tutorial, you'll find this nice, logical organization is followed consistently throughout. For example, you'll recall the discussion of setting up access controls on your Web server's filetree from Chapter 9. Detailed information, with step-by-step setup instructions, is available on all the directives of the NCSA httpd server's access.conf file within this tutorial, with access to each one of them via a hyperlink from this page. You'll recall from Chapter 9, for example, the discussion of many of the directives shown in Figure 21.10, as you learned how to control access to your Web pages using username/password authentication, as well as hostname/IP address authentication.

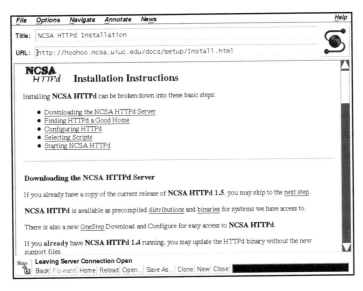

Figure 21.9. NCSA httpd server setup tutorial.

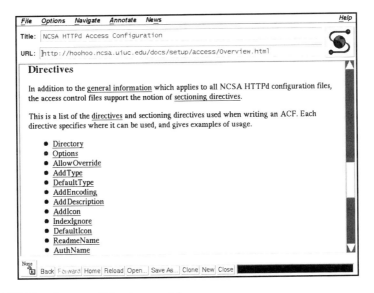

Figure 21.10. NCSA httpd access.conf directives tutorial page.

Multimedia, Multi–Helper Application Presentations

The NCSA tutorials are great as a starting point, because they show you the basics of how the Web can be used for training purposes. Your Intranet, however, is a multimedia system with plain text, graphical images, sounds, video, and various other kinds of data accessible using the Web browser helper applications you've set up for your customers. This being the case, you won't want to limit your Intranet-based training and presentations to a single, text-based method as with the NCSA tutorials. Plain-text HTML markup with logically arranged hyperlinks, PowerPoint, Netscape Remote, Mosaic CCI, ScreenCam, and others are all great tools, but the overwhelming value of an Intranet like yours, as *Building an Intranet* has hammered home repeatedly, is the ability to combine all these tools into something uniquely suited to your organization's needs. Using your Intranet as a training resource is no exception. There's absolutely no reason you can't use all of these tools as part of a single training session or presentation, picking and choosing each one based on its strengths at presenting the particular information you need to show at a given point in your presentation. Here are some things to keep in mind in putting together your Intranet-based training.

◆ While a plain-text slide may be good at one point in your presentation, a spreadsheet with a graph in it (see Chapter 11, "Spreadsheets and Data Warehouses") will be better than a slide with boring columns of numbers at another presentation. Why limit yourself to slides, or go to the trouble of importing your spreadsheet into a slide, when you can just show the spreadsheet on your Intranet?

◆ If you're measuring process control in a factory, you may want to show in real time both video or graphical images of the process and a graphical visualization (see Chapter 15, "Scientific, Mathematical, and Technical Applications on Your Intranet") of the data being collected.

◆ A ScreenCam recording of an application being operated is great, but so is the ability for the trainee to get his hands on the application and run it himself. Use the wide array of tools you've implemented on your Intranet to give him both.

Khoros Digital Image Processing Training Course

Khoral Research, Inc., maintainer of the Khoros image processing software introduced in Chapter 15, has developed an online, Web-based, comprehensive training course in the use of the Khoros software. Even if your organization has no need for the sort of scientific image analysis and processing Khoros makes possible, you'll want to look at the course as an example of how you can integrate many of the tools on your Intranet to create an outstanding training mechanism. The Khoros *Digital Image Processing* (*DIP*) course works best if you've installed the Khoros software (download it from the Khoral Research home page, http://www.khoral.com/), but you can get a flavor of it by taking a look at it without installing the software.

Start at the Khoral Research home page or go directly to the top-level DIP course welcome page at http://www.khoral.com/dipcourse/Welcome.html. Run through the *Course Overview* to get your bearings, then come back to the welcome page and select *List of Experiments*. Figure 21.11 is a screenshot taken from one of the experiments (Item 5, Point Operations (Single Operand), subitem 9 (Pseudocolor Applications)). Only part of the page is shown in the screenshot, so you may want to access it yourself to see the whole thing and get a better idea of what the experiment is actually about. You'll definitely want to access this page if you've installed Khoros and want to try things out.

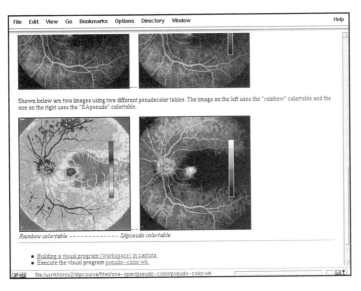

Figure 21.11. *Khoros Digital Image Processing online training course.*

Note: If you're planning on running the DIP course, you'll need not only to install the Khoros software, but also modify your *mailcap* files to accommodate the course. Here are your new entries:

```
application/x-cantata; cantata -wksp %s
application/x-editimage; editimage -i %s
application/x-editcmap; edicmap -i %s
application/x-putimage; putimage -i %s
application/x-putplot2; putplot2 -i %s
application/x-putplot3; putplot3 -i %s
application/x-xprism; xprism -i1 %s
application/x-preview; preview -i %s
application/x-puticon; puticon -i %s
application/x-putpalette; putpalette -i %s
application/x-putanimate; putanimate -i %s
```

Finally, you also need to make sure your login environment sets a *command-search path* that will pick up the Khoros executable programs you've just listed. The Khoros executables also like to have a KHOROS_HOME environment variable set, pointing to the top level of the Khoros software tree on your system.

As you can see, this appears to be an ordinary Web page with several graphical images and a couple of ordinary looking hyperlinks at the bottom of the page. To give you a better look, Figure 21.12 is a blow-up of the bottom of Figure 21.11. In particular, notice the second hyperlink, Execute the visual program pseudo-color.wk, which points to the file named pseudo-color.wk. (This is shown in the Netscape status bar at the very bottom of the screenshot, next to the broken key icon.)

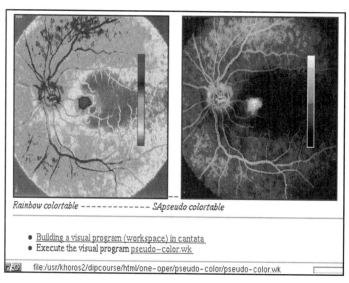

Rainbow colortable ----------- *SApseudo colortable*

- Building a visual program (workspace) in cantata
- Execute the visual program pseudo-color.wk

file:/usr/khoros2/dipcourse/html/one-oper/pseudo-color/pseudo-color.wk

Figure 21.12. *Enlarged detail from Figure 21.11.*

You've probably already put two and two together, picking up on the wk filename extension and figuring it's tied to a Khoros helper application that will fire up if you select the link. This is, in fact, exactly right. The mime.types file on the Khoral Research Web server is set up to define filenames ending in wk as Khoros *cantata* workspaces (cantata being the visual programming part of the overall Khoros package). If you've installed the Khoros package and set it up properly, you're all set to try out this experiment. Clicking on the hyperlink in question downloads the cantata workspace to your own computer and starts up the cantata program to run the workspace, processing the images from the page. Figure 21.13 shows a partial result of this workspace's run. Again, as with the ScreenCam demo discussed above, it's difficult to show an active, running program with a static screenshot. If you run this workspace on your own system, you'll be able to watch the program's flow, as each *glyph* in the workspace lights up, and a series of images are generated by the process.

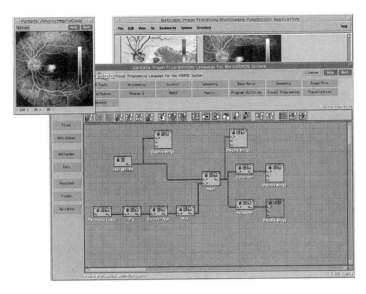

Figure 21.13. *Active cantata workspace from DIP training course.*

Designing Your Intranet Training

We've jumped the gun a bit with Figure 21.12 to show you how helper applications can be built directly into multimedia training courses on your Intranet. It's easy to get lost in the details of setting up a complex helper application like the Khoros package and lose sight of the basics of training design for your Intranet. The glue that holds the DIP training course together, and any other one you might set up, is, of course, the HTML documents that contain it. While this fact may be implicit in the last few paragraphs, it needs to be underscored here.

Like your training curriculum itself, your Web training pages need to be well thought out. Moreover, your planning needs to be done from a point of view that takes into account the important idea of using appropriate Intranet tools throughout a course. While this requires you to use an expanded horizon in planning your Intranet-based training, it also gives you incredible flexibility. Using Web technology for training is superior to any other single technology, simply because you can use all those other technologies as you need them to form an overall Intranet training curriculum. If you need to show a picture to illustrate a point, for instance, add an image to your training page; a sound or movie, add an audio or video link; or a complex scientific application, add the application itself as a helper application as you did with Khoros. If you have a corporate training staff, get them involved in your Intranet training. Professional instructors know, from being on their feet in front of students, how to design training curricula. You and they should put your collective heads together to develop training which use the capabilities of your Intranet to their fullest extent.

Summary

Training and business presentations using your Intranet have been the focus of this chapter. Your Intranet is an enormous potential source of training resources for your customers. Moreover, the nature of an Intranet, with all its multimedia capabilities, makes completely new ways of creating and executing training and presentations possible, because you can stitch together a wide range of training components. You'll want to give free rein to your imagination in putting together your Intranet's tools for these purposes. As a review, here's what you've done in this chapter:

♦ Learned about simple leader-led or self-paced slide shows for seminars, lectures, or business presentations

♦ Learned about playing back recorded training sessions for individual or classroom training

♦ Learned how HTML can be used to organize effective training Web pages for your Intranet

♦ Learned about interactive training which allows customers to actually use the software about which they're learning

♦ Considered all the capabilities of your Intranet for use in your training curricula

In Chapter 22, you turn your attention to USENET news, an old but still vibrant Internet tool (discussed in Chapter 8), which you can use to facilitate collaboration and cooperation among your Intranet's customers.

CHAPTER

22

Newsgroups for Group Discussions and Collaboration

In Chapter 8, "Adding Services to Your Intranet Adds Value," you learned the basics of Usenet news. Reference was made to using netnews as a means of group discussion and collaboration in your Intranet. Usenet's post-and-follow-up process is well suited to continuing online discussions. Your Web browser is great for following and participating in these discussions. In this chapter, you'll explore specific examples of how you can put Usenet to work in your company. You'll also learn how to use other tools about which you've learned in *Building an Intranet* to piggyback onto your Usenet setup to provide more value for your customers. In all cases, your customers will be able to access the services described in this chapter using their Web browsers.

Chapter Objectives

As with the rest of the chapters in this book, let's begin by laying out some chapter objectives to help you get oriented to the material to be presented; you may want to refer back to this list as you work your way through the chapter. In this chapter, you'll

◆ Learn more about how Usenet newsgroups work

◆ Learn about newsgroup management on your netnews server

◆ Learn how to create local newsgroups your customers can use for communication and collaboration

◆ Learn how your customers can use their Web browsers to post and respond to news articles

◆ Learn how to archive newsgroup articles for future reference

◆ Learn how to index your archived newsgroup articles

◆ Learn how to give your customers the ability to search the newsgroup indexes you've created and retrieve articles from them

The discussion, descriptions, and examples in this chapter are based on use of the INN Usenet news server package, the freeWAIS-sf WAIS server package, and the SFgate CGI-bin WAIS gateway package in conjunction with your Web browser. All these packages were introduced in Chapter 8. It's assumed you have these packages installed on your Intranet. If you haven't already installed these packages (all three are on the *Building an Intranet* CD-ROM) you may want to do so now. This will allow you to follow and try out the examples on your own system. Where necessary, you'll find instructions for reconfiguring these packages to implement the examples in this chapter, based on your Intranet's specific setup.

How Usenet Newsgroups Work

Because you're running (or considering running) a netnews server on your Intranet, you need to know some basics about how Usenet works, including how newsgroups work and how INN manages newsgroups. This background will allow you to set up Usenet-related facilities in your Intranet.

Newsgroup Names

You'll recall the list of the seven major netnews newsgroup categories from Chapter 8 (comp, sci, rec, soc, talk, news, and alt). Besides these major categories, there are many others, including regional newsgroups and, most important for your Intranet, local newsgroups. Before going into the details of creating and using local newsgroups, though, let's look at the way newsgroups in general work, using the seven major categories as examples.

Each of the seven major newsgroup categories is the tip of a massive iceberg of newsgroups. Within each are major subcategories, and many of the subcategories are recursively subdivided into more categories. Eventually, the subdivision stops and individual newsgroups begin. There are more than 10,000 newsgroups, not counting local ones. Given the penchant among netnews readers to want more and more specifically focused groups, you can imagine the near infinite subdivision of subject matter. Let's take a look at just one subcategory of the comp newsgroup category, newsgroups dealing with the World Wide Web. You'll find this subcategory within the comp.infosystems category (one of 70-odd first-level subdivisions of the comp category. Its name is comp.infosystems.www. You're probably already catching onto netnews' nomenclature, with newsgroup categories and subcategories named using periods to separate the levels. Thus www is a subcategory of the infosystems category of the comp top-level newsgroup category. Within the www newsgroup subcategory, there are as of January 1996 eight further subdivisions (advocacy, announce, authoring, browsers, misc, providers, servers, and users).

Let's follow the comp.infosystems.www subcategory down one more step into the browsers category, where you'll find yet another four subdivisions, mac, misc, ms-windows, and x. Here, you've finally touched bottom and reached the last subdivision of this branch of the comp.infosystems.www newsgroup tree. Each of these is an actual newsgroup, devoted to Macintosh, Miscellaneous, Microsoft Windows, and X Window World Wide Web browsers, respectively.

Your customers' view of the Usenet system reflects the way newsgroups are named. Figure 22.1 shows NCSA Mosaic's display of the newsgroup comp.infosystems.www.browsers.ms-windows. As you can see, this is pretty plain, mostly text display of a list of news articles. Each article entry is a hyperlink, so clicking on one selects the article for display. A sample article is shown in Figure 22.2. (We'll come back to the clickable selections at the top of the screen later.)

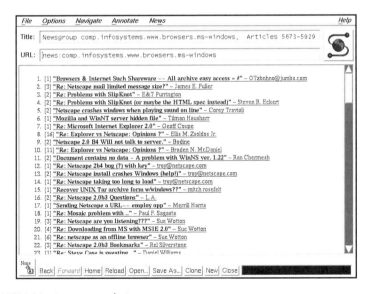

Figure 22.1. *NCSA Mosaic newsgroup listing.*

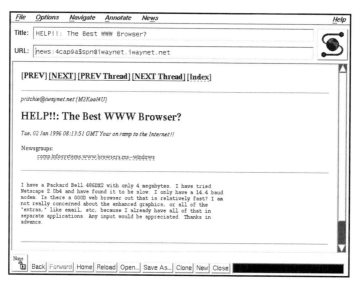

Figure 22.2. *NCSA Mosaic News article display.*

Rather than using a separate window to display a selected article, Netscape attempts to display everything you see in the two previous figures in a single screen, as shown in Figure 22.3. This very busy screen is divided into three panes. The panes show

A scrollable, graphical display of the news server you've selected and its available newsgroups, in the upper left, that has a faint resemblance to the Microsoft Windows File Manager

A scrollable list of the articles in the currently selected newsgroup, on the upper right, also with a suggestion of the File Manager

The actual text of a selected article, in the lower half of the screen, with a scrollbar to move through the article

Although Netscape uses a separate window for Usenet news so the main Netscape window is free for other use, the news window is difficult to understand and use. The list of newsgroups in the newsgroup pane shortens the (often very long) newsgroup names, placing ellipses in the names. Unfortunately, the contraction method is so brutal as to make most newsgroup names unrecognizable, even to experienced readers. Even though you can resize the newsgroups window (click on the double vertical line, just to the right of the scroll bar and drag it to the right), the newsgroup names aren't expanded. There's just too much information crammed onto this one screen.

> **Note:** You can resize the other two panes of the Netscape News window by grabbing the double lines with your mouse and sliding left or right, or up or down.

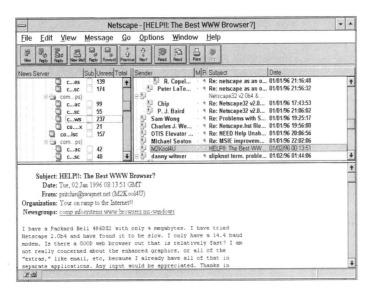

Figure 22.3. *Netscape Navigator news window.*

The Usenet News Server File Structure

Your Usenet news server stores news articles in a file tree that parallels these newsgroup subdivisions, with subdirectories for each category, subcategory, and individual newsgroups. Thus, the filesystem path to the `comp.infosystems.www.browsers` newsgroups, beginning at the top of your Usenet news spool, is `comp/infosystems/www/browsers`. As you can see, the tree-structured system of directories and subdirectories parallels the subdivision of Usenet newsgroups. Within the bottom-level subdirectories, you find the actual netnews articles. Files are named with a consecutive numbering mechanism, so when you do a directory listing of one of your netnews article subdirectories, you'll just see a list of numbers. The first article that was created on your local system was placed in a file named 1, the second, in file 2, and so on. These filenames are unique to your system, as they're created when users post articles or your system receives articles from other systems. The file named 7835 on your system will most likely not correspond with the file 7835 on any other system.

Newsgroup Management

If you asked for a directory listing on one of your netnews server's article subdirectories, you probably noticed the numbers used for filenames there start somewhere beyond 1. This is because INN (and all other netnews server software) continuously manages your news server, adding new articles and expiring (removing) old articles once they have reached a given age. (Numbers are not reused.) If there were no means of expiring articles, you couldn't buy enough disk space to keep every one of them indefinitely, and probably wouldn't want to anyway. (Later on in this chapter, you'll learn how to archive important newsgroups for permanent retention.)

Newsgroup management, including the expiration of old articles, is controlled by several files on your netnews server, with which you'll want to be familiar. The normal place for these is in the /usr/lib/news directory, although you may have installed your NEWSLIB directory elsewhere. The most important of these files, along with short descriptions of what they do follow:

active	Master list of all newsgroups and articles you've ever received
newsfeeds	Controls which newsgroups your system subscribes to and which ones you forward on to to other systems
expire.ctl	Controls the expiring of news articles

The active File

Although you'll rarely change the active file, you'll want to know what it looks like. It contains one line for each newsgroup on your system. That line looks like this:

```
comp.infosystems.www.servers.ms-windows 0000002132 0000001135 y
```

The format of the file is fairly obvious. There are four fields, including the newsgroup name, the highest article number that has been used in the newsgroup, and the lowest numbered article that's still present on the system. The last field is a flag that sets permissions on posting to the group. These permissions are

y	Local postings are allowed to the newsgroup.
n	No local postings are allowed.
m	The group is moderated.
j	Articles in this group aren't kept on the local system.
x	All articles are blocked for this newsgroup.

Tip: You can use newsgroup permissions to block unwanted newsgroups, such as those with inappropriate content, or prevent outgoing postings to inappropriate groups. Most news media and political attention to hate groups, pornography, and other controversial areas on the Internet are actually referring to Usenet newsgroups. Many people have strong views about what is appropriate on the Internet, but just as many have strong feelings about net.censorship. More important, perhaps, newsgroup censorship can become the proverbial Tar Baby, taking more of your time and effort than it's really worth. Like TCP/IP itself, Usenet generally interprets censorship as damage, and routes around it. Still, organizations have an interest in making sure their computing facilities aren't misused, so you may want to employ the last field of the active file in some way.

> From a practical viewpoint, some of the newsgroups drawing the most political attention are also those that can eat up the most disk space on your netnews server. Binary images posted to newsgroups, sexually oriented or not, are big consumers of disk space. Accordingly, you may want to block newsgroups that contain large numbers of binary postings, just to preserve disk space, if for no other reason.

You may have wondered about the m, or moderation, flag. Some newsgroups are moderated, meaning users can't post articles directly to them. Only the moderator can actually post articles to the group. When an attempt to post to a moderated newsgroup occurs, the posting is sent via e-mail to the designated moderator, who can approve and post it, or reject it.

The newsfeeds File

The newsfeeds file determines "where netnews articles get sent," according to its man page. This is a little misleading, because news articles are "sent" not only to other Usenet servers, but also to programs on the local system that do the news article posting and housekeeping. As a result, you need to know about and deal with this file, even if you're using Usenet only as a local communications media and don't exchange netnews with any other systems. At the very least, the newsfeeds file must contain an entry for your local system, which tells INN what to do with news articles it gets. This entry is labeled ME. A ME entry in newsfeeds for a netnews server that accepts all incoming newsgroups except the alt groups and the group named junk would look like this:

```
ME\
    :*,!alt.*,!junk\
    ::
```

Each entry in the newsfeeds file has four colon-separated fields. This example places the four of them on two separate lines for ease of reading. The backslash character is a line-continuation character. Also, whitespace is used on each subsequent line until the entry is finished. The first field is, of course, the name of the entry, ME. The second field is the list of newsgroups to be dealt with. For purposes of newsgroup naming, the newsfeeds files use a special kind of shorthand newsgroup name matching, documented on INN's wildmat man page. Wildmat matching is very much the same as the wildcard matching done by the UNIX shell in filename expansion. If you're accustomed to UNIX regular expressions, note that wildmat matching is not the same, so the meaning of the asterisk is not what you might expect. Here, we've specified all groups (the initial asterisk) that will be accepted, but modified this with the next two entries. The !alt.* entry says no newsgroups in any of the major newsgroup category alt will be accepted; the !junk entry says no articles in the one newsgroup named junk will be accepted. The newsfeeds file has its own man page; be sure to read it and the wildmat man page carefully to make sure you understand how to specify newsgroups.

The last two fields newsfeeds entries are for specification of miscellaneous flags and parameters for the entry. In this example, none are specified, which is normally the case for the ME entry, so the fields are empty. The flags and parameters are described in detail on the newsfeeds man page.

> **Tip:** Many people with Usenet administration experience confuse aspects of the newsfeeds file with the sys file used by older netnews server software, such as B News or C News. The ME entry in newsfeeds doesn't control which newsgroups you get from your upstream newsfeeds; if a newsgroup appears in your active file, it's likely to appear. To make sure unwanted newsgroups don't appear, make sure the upstream feed isn't sending them. Also, just in case they manage to show up anyway, block them in the active file with the x flag. Be sure also to note the syntax of the newsfeeds file is very different from the old sys file, with a special wildcard syntax for matching newsgroup names.

The expire.ctl File

The last major control file for Usenet news is expire.ctl. As noted, netnews flows ever onward in an increasing flood. Without expiring old news articles, you'd soon run out of disk space. How hard-nosed you need to be on expiring netnews depends on how much news you receive and how much disk space you have. If, for example, you're getting an outside netnews feed, you'll need to pay careful attention to disk space and run expire frequently (regularly, using the UNIX cron daemon). Also, you'll want to set a default expiration period, as well as an expiration period for specific groups you want to keep longer (or expire sooner) than the default. Expire.ctl has single-line entries matching one or more newsgroups. For example, you may want to set up a default entry like this one:

```
*:A:14:14:14
```

This one says all newsgroups not otherwise specified in the file should be kept for 14 days and then expired. The last three fields need not be the same. They refer to the keep, default, and purge periods, explained in the expire.ctl man page. Normally the next-to-last or default field is your main concern, but you can use the others with articles like FAQ postings, which have their own expiration date, to keep them around longer than the default. If you have created local newsgroups on your Intranet, for local discussion/collaboration, you'll want to keep them longer, using an entry something like this:

```
mycompany*:A:60:60:60
```

Here, all newsgroups in the mycompany category are expired only after 60 days. Other newsgroups are controlled by either the default or other specific entries in expire.ctl.

> **Note:** The expire.ctl file uses wildmat newsgroup name matching, in the same way the newsfeeds file does. See the INN wildmat man page for details.

Local Usenet Newsgroups for Your Intranet

In Usenet, local newsgroups are much the same as regular ones. Normally, netnews articles get sent out to the outside world via your upstream newsfeed, from where they are sent on to netnews systems all over the Internet. Since you're using netnews as a local communication and collaboration mechanism on your Intranet, however, you'll agree it's not appropriate for your purely local newsgroups to get handled this way. Instead, you want them to stay inside your Intranet, where confidentiality and privacy is protected.

> **Tip:** If you're using Usenet news in isolation and don't have communications with the outside world, this is not a concern, but you should still follow the procedures outlined here in the creation of local newsgroups. As with companies that installed TCP/IP networks with no plans to connect to the outside world and now have to readdress all their systems before connecting to the now-essential Internet, don't make decisions now you'll have to undo later. When you install Usenet news software, create truly local groups. You never know; you may change your mind and want to have outside Usenet access two or five years from now.

Creating Local Newsgroups

Local newsgroups are created in exactly the same way normal newsgroups are created; the difference is in what's done with them after they're created. With INN, netnews management, including creation of new newsgroups, is handled with the INN superutility, ctlinnd. This complex program handles all of the nuts and bolts of netnews management, including updating such files as the active file for new or deleted groups. Check out ctlinnd's man page, but the basic syntax for creating a newsgroup is

```
$ ctlinnd newgroup name-of-group [flag] [creator-name]
```

Let's look at this command piece by piece. First, items in square brackets aren't required. You're calling ctlinnd with the newgroup argument, signaling that you're creating a new group. The third item on the command line is the name of the group being created. Refer back to the discussion of the active file for what you'll put in place of flag. This is the flag you want to go in the active file for this newsgroup. If you leave out the flag argument, the effect is to use the y flag (permit anyone local to post to the newsgroup). If you want to moderate the newsgroup, you must include the m. The last item on the previous command line, creator-name, also optional, is the name of the person who created the newsgroup. Usually, this will be the name of the Usenet account (that is, news). Because you can put anything here, though, you may want to use real usernames, especially if more than one person manages your netnews server. All ctlinnd commands are logged, so you'll have a record of who has created new groups. ctlinnd newgroup commands add new entries to the active file, so it's not necessary for you to edit the file directly.

> **Note:** Because the creation of a new newsgroup changes the `active` file, you'll want to make sure you don't use this command while the news system is active. Some other part of the system may also be working on the `active` file (or system's history files) at the same time. To avoid this, use the throttle option to ctlinnd first, like this:
>
> ```
> $ ctlinnd throttle newgroup
> ```
>
> Next, run your `ctlinnd newgroup` command as shown previously and then release the throttle:
>
> ```
> $ ctlinnd go newgroup
> ```
>
> In both of these commands, the last argument (*newgroup*) is a placeholder, indicating the reason for running the command. Although you can put just anything here, it's better to use something meaningful, because `ctlinnd` commands are logged for future reference. In this example, the last argument must be the same in both the throttle and go commands.

Managing Local Newsgroups

Once you've created your local newsgroups, be sure to edit your `newsfeeds` file to ensure they're handled properly. First, add them to the *ME* entry. You may have multiple netnews servers in your Intranet and want your local newsgroups to be distributed to all of them. Also, if you have Usenet news connectivity with the outside world, you'll want to make sure your local groups don't get sent outside, where they might get propagated across the Internet. If you want to archive your local newsgroup traffic, you'll also want to add a stanza to the `newsfeeds` file to do so as illustrated later in this chapter. (Don't forget to run the `ctlinnd reload newsfeeds` command after editing `newsfeeds`.) If you're not archiving your local newsgroups, you still may want to set a lengthy expiration time in the `expire.ctl` file for them. Doing so enables you to keep your local newsgroup articles around for a longer-than-normal period.

Reading, Posting, and Responding to Usenet News Articles

Earlier in this chapter, you saw several screenshots of the NCSA Mosaic and Netscape netnews interfaces. Let's now turn to the specifics of how your Intranet's customers use their Web browsers to read, post, and respond to netnews articles.

Web Browser Setup for Usenet News

All Web browsers require some initial setup for netnews. First, users need to define the Usenet news server to which they'll connect. Second, users need to select the newsgroups they want to read. The first of these is a quick, one-time thing, but the second is a potentially tedious process.

Configuring Your Usenet News Server in Your Web Browser

Except for NCSA Mosaic on UNIX systems, both Mosaic and Netscape use an essentially similar process for defining your netnews server. Let's cover the similarities using Mosaic and Netscape for Microsoft Windows and then turn to how UNIX Mosaic differs.

Both Netscape and Mosaic have Options pull-down menus that are the starting point for your Usenet setup. In Mosaic, pull down Options and then select Preferences. This brings up Mosaic's main Preferences window, shown in Figure 22.4. Along the top of the window are two rows of Tabs. In the second row, click News, to bring up the News Dialogue Box. There are several configuration items here, but you're concerned for the moment with only one of them, the box on the right, about halfway down, labeled NNTP Server. (NNTP is an acronym for Network News Transport Protocol.) In Figure 22.5, the NNTP Server box has been filled in with the example server name Usenet.mycompany.com. Fill in the hostname of your Intranet's Usenet news server and click OK. This will return you to the main Preferences window; click OK again to exit.

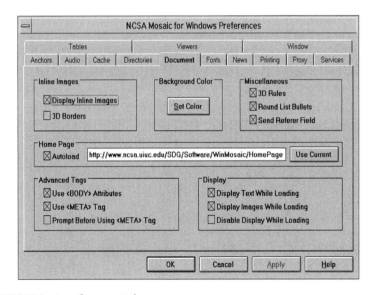

Figure 22.4. *NCSA Mosaic preferences window.*

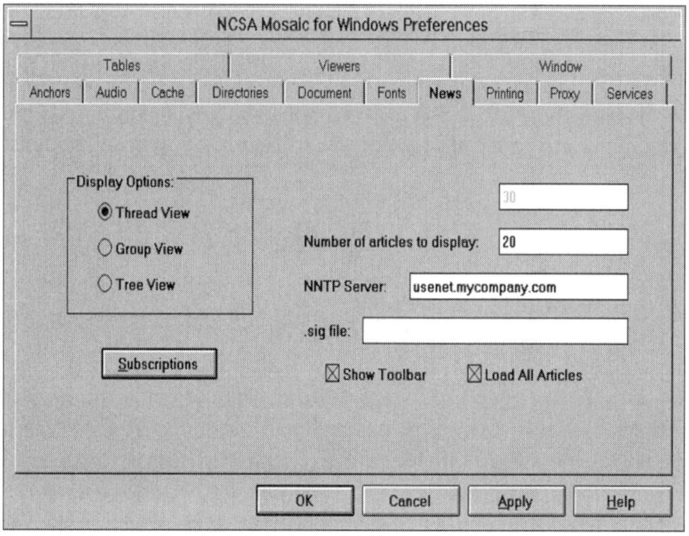

Figure 22.5. *NCSA Mosaic news dialog box (example).*

Netscape's process is quite similar. Pull down the Options menu, select Mail and News Preferences, and then click on the Servers tab to bring up the screen shown in Figure 22.6. This dialog box is for setting up both Usenet news and Netscape's e-mail. (UNIX Netscape's Mail and News Preferences box is essentially the same as that for Windows, but the e-mail section is a bit different.) For our purpose here, focus on the News box in the lower quarter of the screen showing the sample Usenet server name Usenet.*mycompany*.com in the News (NNTP) Server box in figure 22.7. Click OK to commit your change.

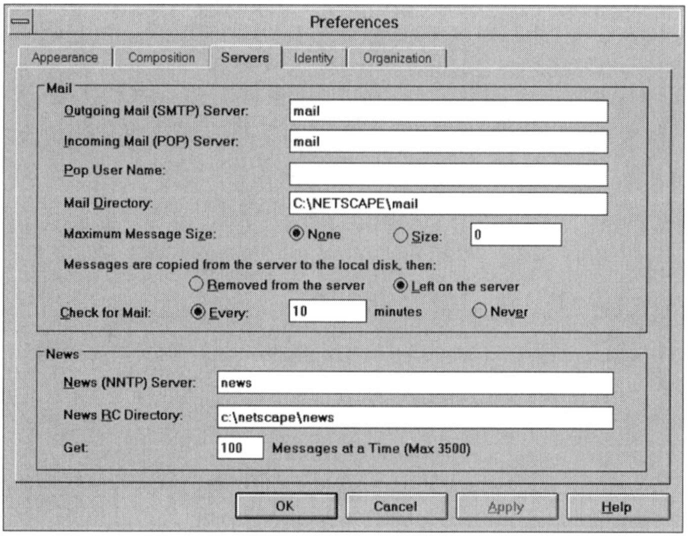

Figure 22.6. *Netscape Mail and News dialog box (full).*

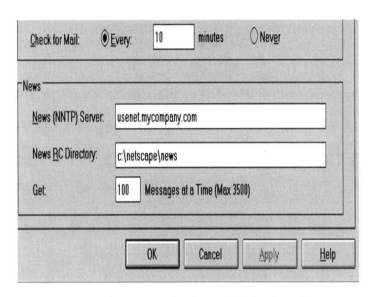

Figure 22.7. Note the News section of Netscape Mail and News dialog box (example).

NCSA Mosaic on UNIX systems gets its Usenet news configuration in a different way. Rather than having a dialog box for setting its configuration up, Mosaic will use a UNIX environment variable. Just set the variable NNTPSERVER to point to your Usenet news host before starting Mosaic. This can be done in one of several ways:

◆ Set it manually from your shell prompt using NNTPSERVER=usenet.*mycompany*.com (Bourne and Korn shells) or setenv NNTPSERVER usenet.*mycompany*.com (C shell).

◆ Add this environment variable to your .profile, .cshrc, or .login file, so it's set automatically each time you log in.

◆ Use a shell script wrapper, which sets up your environment to start Mosaic.

The third of these options is probably your best choice. A little shell script like this can do the trick:

```
#!/bin/sh
NNTPSERVER=usenet.mycompany.com
export NNTPSERVER
Mosaic
```

Make this script, which you might call Mosaic, executable with the chmod command. You then can start Mosaic by running this script rather than the real Mosaic executable. The script sets the NNTPSERVER environment variable and then calls the real executable.

> **Note:** Be sure to replace usenet.*mycompany*.com in these examples with the hostname of your Intranet's Usenet news server.

Tip: You'll want to use a shell script wrapper like this across the board on your UNIX systems so all users have access to it. To do so, put the script someplace in users' normal command search path. A customary place for local programs and scripts like this is the directory /usr/ local/bin.

NCSA Mosaic understands several other environment variables, which you may want to add to this wrapper script. For example, you can set users' default home page using WWW_HOME. If you're behind a network firewall and need to use Mosaic's capability of contacting a proxy server to reach outside Web services (see Chapter 9, "Intranet Security"), you can set several proxy-related environment variables here as well.

When users start Mosaic using your shell script wrapper, their environment is always set properly. Moreover, any changes you need to make in users' environments are picked up automatically when you use the wrapper method.

Selecting and Subscribing to Newsgroups

Both UNIX and Windows NCSA Mosaic make it easy for you to view and select newsgroups. The latter has the additional capability of letting you subscribe to groups you want to see on a regular basis. On a UNIX system, pull down the Mosaic News menu and select List Groups, as shown in Figure 22.8, to get a list of all newsgroups available from your Usenet news server. Figure 22.9 shows a sample listing of newsgroups; as you can see from the aspect of the scroll bar on the right, the list is quite long. You'll also note each newsgroup listed in Figure 22.9 is a clickable hyperlink. Selecting one of these takes you directly to the newsgroup for a list of available articles. From this list, you can display individual articles.

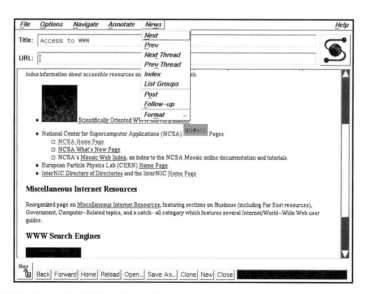

Figure 22.8. *NCSA Mosaic for UNIX pull-down News menu.*

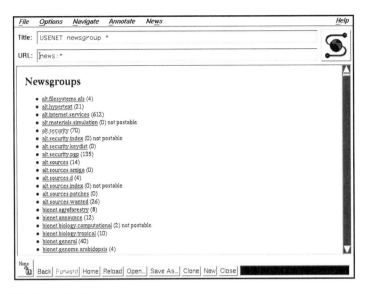

Figure 22.9. *NCSA Mosaic for Usenet newsgroup listing.*

NCSA Mosaic for Windows goes about listing newsgroups in a different way. Pull down the Options menu and select Preferences, and then click on the News tab. Next, click the Subscriptions button to bring up the News Subscriptions window. This window is divided into two panes, as shown in Figure 22.10. The upper pane is a complete, scrollable list of newsgroups available from your netnews server. Clicking any newsgroup brings up a list of the articles in that group, from which you can select and read articles of interest. The lower pane in this Window shows any newsgroups to which you may have subscribed. Initially, this pane will be empty. To subscribe to a group, highlight it by clicking its name and then click the Subscribe button. (You can select multiple newsgroups to which to subscribe using Ctrl-Click; once done selecting newsgroups, click Subscribe to add all of them to your subscription list at once.) Note also the Search, Unsubscribe, Select All, and Unselect All buttons, as well as the Update button, which contacts your netnews server for an updated list of available newsgroups.

Netscape provides the same set of features for listing and subscribing to newsgroups. Pull down the Window menu and select Netscape News to open a separate window for Usenet news purposes. (Note that your main Netscape window stays open and that you can switch back and forth.) Netscape's Usenet news reader is highly capable, with more features than Mosaic's, but it is also much more complex and its user interface is very confusing. Let's try to sort it out. First, as Figure 22.11 shows, the window is divided into three panes.

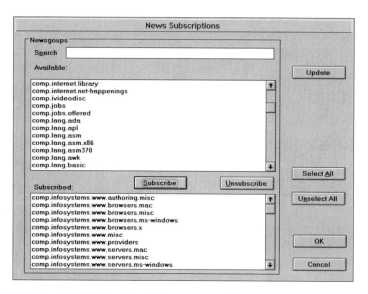

Figure 22.10. *NCSA Mosaic for Windows News Subscriptions window.*

◆ In the upper left, occupying about one third of the upper half of the screen, one or more available Usenet news servers is listed. Selecting one of them displays your list of newsgroup subscriptions. In Figure 22.11, the Netscape default subscription list (three newsgroups) is shown. To select a newsgroup for reading, click its name. Also displayed is the number of unread articles in each subscribed group. Note that this pane has a faint resemblance to the Microsoft Windows File Manager, with file folder icons representing newsgroups.

◆ In the upper right, occupying the other two thirds of the upper half of the screen, a scrollable list of articles in your selected newsgroup appears.

◆ In the lower half of the screen, individual news articles are displayed. Here also is a scrollbar for moving through the article.

Each of the three panes in the Netscape News window can be resized. Use your mouse to grab the vertical bar, just to the right of the scrollbar in the left pane, and pull right or left to resize the two top panes. Similarly, use the horizontal bar separating the lower pane from the others up or down to resize the lower pane. Of course, as you resize one pane, the others are affected as well. The truncated newsgroup names (shortened with ellipses) shown in the upper left pane don't get expanded, however, as you increase the width of the pane. This is an unfortunate problem, because many of the truncated names appear identical and it's almost impossible for you to identify the group names in deciding whether to subscribe.

Getting a list of available newsgroups in Netscape is a two-step process. From the News window, click your netnews server (in the upper left pane). Next, pull down the Options menu. (Be careful to get the one from the news window, not from your main Netscape window, which may still be displayed onscreen.) This menu contains a long list of newsgroup-related functions, including Show All Newsgroups. (See Figure 22.12.)

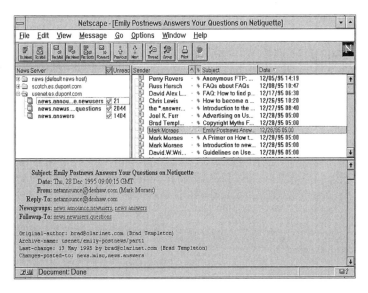

Figure 22.11. *Netscape News window.*

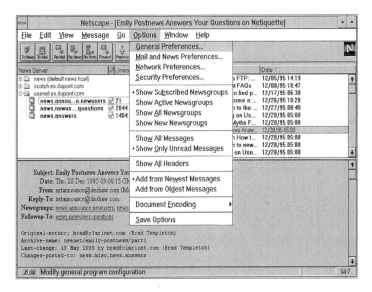

Figure 22.12. *Netscape News window's Options menu.*

You've finally reached the place where you can display the list of available newsgroups. Select Show All Newsgroups to generate a full listing. Doing so clears the News window, except for the upper-left pane, where the display now shows a listing of the top-level newsgroup categories. The display is graphical, with icons indicating categories and individual newsgroups. Selecting one of the top-level categories generates a tree-like display of subcategories and/or individual newsgroups within the category, still in the upper-left pane of the windows. You progressively work your way down through newsgroup categories and subcategories until you reach individual newsgroups. With each step down the hierarchy, the graphical display in the upper-left pane changes, retaining the File Manager–like display of folder and document icons and also displaying tree-like lines grouping the newsgroup categories. Selecting a newsgroup from this display pops up a list of articles in the upper-right pane. Figure 22.13 shows the display of the newsgroup comp.infosystems.www.browsers.ms-windows. Clicking an individual article entry brings up that article in the lower pane. Refer back to Figure 22.11 for display of an article.

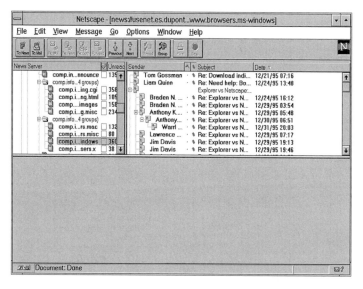

Figure 22.13. *Netscape newsgroup display.*

Posting and Responding to Usenet News Articles

You've just learned how to set up your Usenet news subscriptions and, along the way, seen how to read netnews articles. Let's now turn to using your Web browser to post your own articles. A little later, we'll delve into ways to respond to others' articles. Together, these two subjects will give you all you need to know to enable your customers to use netnews as a means of group discussion and collaboration.

Posting Original News Articles

Both Netscape Navigator and NCSA Mosaic allow the direct posting of netnews articles. Doing so is pretty direct: Specify a newsgroup and use a simple editing window to create your posting and then click an onscreen button to send your article. Let's look at Netscape first.

Both UNIX and Windows Netscape work the same for posting news articles. Pull down the Window menu and open a Netscape News window. To post a new article, click the To: News icon in the toolbar (first on the left) or pull down the Netscape News window's File menu and select New News Message. In either case, a new window like that shown in Figure 22.14 pops up. This screenshot shows UNIX Netscape's Compose Window; the Microsoft Windows Netscape Compose Window differs slightly, though both have the same function. Just enter one or more newsgroup names in the box labeled Newsgroups: enter a subject, and type your posting in the main pane. Use the Attach button if you'd like to attach a file or a Web URL to your posting. If you'd like, you can e-mail a copy of your posting as well. Just fill in the Mail CC: box, either with a typed address or from your Netscape Address Book (accessible by clicking the Address button). When you're finished, click the Send button.

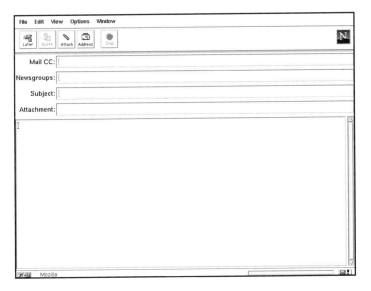

Figure 22.14. Netscape News posting window.

> **Tip:** If you're already reading netnews, clicking To: News brings up your news posting window with the name of the newsgroup you're currently reading already filled in. If this is the newsgroup to which you want to post, you're all set. Otherwise, just edit the Newsgroups box to enter the newsgroup you want.

To post a Usenet news article in NCSA Mosaic for Windows, you must already be reading news. That is, you must have selected Newsgroups from the Mosaic File Menu and then opened a newsgroup for viewing. Next, click the Post icon (first icon to the right of the down directional arrow icon; see Figure 22.15, where the Mosaic Usenet news toolbar has been enlarged to show detail not readily apparent in the full window). This opens the popup shown in Figure 22.16. Your newsgroup name is already filled in, as is your name. Fill in your Subject: and e-mail address for a mailed copy (in the Mailto: box), and then type your posting in the main window. There are several other items of note in this window. First, you can turn word wrap on or off in the posting editor by clicking the Auto word wrap button; if you turn it off, be sure to press Return or Enter at the end of each line of text. Also, the Append .sig button will automatically append your signature file (if you've defined one in your News Preferences) to your posting. When you're finished with your posting, click the Post button to send it off to your Usenet news server for posting.

Figure 22.15. *NCSA Mosaic for Windows news Post icon (detail).*

The UNIX Mosaic news posting window is substantially simpler. Access it by pulling down the News menu and selecting Post. This brings up a very simple editing window into which you enter your newsgroup name and subject. Create your posting and then click Post to send your posting. Note there is an Insert File button that enables you to read a file into your posting.

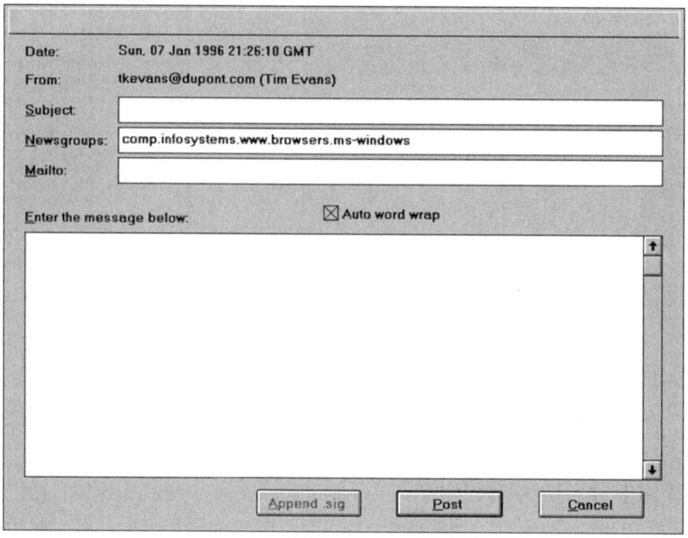

Date:	Sun, 07 Jan 1996 21:26:10 GMT
From:	tkevans@dupont.com (Tim Evans)
Subject:	
Newsgroups:	comp.infosystems.www.browsers.ms-windows
Mailto:	

Enter the message below: ☒ Auto word wrap

[Append .sig]   [Post]   [Cancel]

Figure 22.16. *NCSA Mosaic News post editing window.*

Responding to Others' Usenet News Articles

Because the whole purpose of this chapter is to show you how to use netnews as a means of group communication and collaboration on your Intranet, the ability to respond to others' news postings is critical. Let's get to it then.

There are two ways of responding to posted netnews articles:

◆ Responding privately using e-mail
◆ Posting a follow-up news article

Except for NCSA Mosaic for UNIX, our sample Web browsers each allow private e-mail to be sent to the original poster of a netnews article. In Mosaic for Windows, once you've opened an article for reading, click the Mail icon (two icons to the right of the Post icon) to start the Mosaic e-mail editor. It comes up preaddressed to the original poster and with the subject line taken from the subject of the initial posting. If you'd like to include all or part of the first posting, click Include Text, answer the prompt about prepending the > character, and then edit the message. Figure 22.17 shows the Windows Mosaic Mail editor with a sample netnews article follow-up. Part of the original posting is included (marked off with the > characters in the left margin) and a short question is asked. Click Send to send the e-mail reply. Your message is sent directly to the original poster and is not posted as a netnews follow-up article.

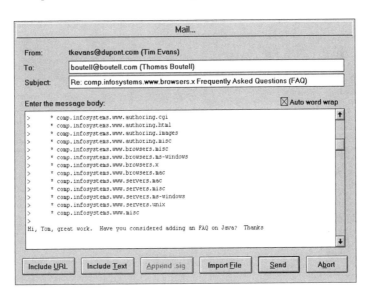

Figure 22.17. *NCSA Mosaic for Windows e-mail reply to a netnews posting.*

Tip: UNIX Mosaic doesn't have a direct way of replying to a news posting, but you can work around this, albeit in a terribly Rube Goldbergian way. Here's how. Once you've opened an article you want to reply to, use your left mouse button to highlight the posting's subject line, and then pull down the File menu and select Mail To. This pops up a dialog box asking for an e-mail address and subject. Click your middle mouse button in the Subject: box to paste the subject line and put your own e-mail address in the Mailto: box. Use your left mouse button once more to grab the poster's e-mail address and then click Mail. When you receive the e-mail you sent to yourself, containing the text of the posting, use your mail package's Forward feature to send the message to the original poster, using your middle mouse button to paste in the address. Edit the message to add your response and then send it off. This isn't elegant, but it'll work. Maybe NCSA will add a Reply To feature soon.

Netscape's private e-mail reply works in much the same way. Once you've opened an article for reading, click Re: Mail to initiate an e-mail reply to the original poster. As with Mosaic, the e-mail editor pops up pre-addressed and with an appropriate Subject line. If you would like to include part or all of the initial posting, click the Quote icon. Edit your message and then click Send to deliver it directly to the original poster's e-mail box. Your reply is not posted as a netnews follow-up article. See Figure 22.18 for a Netscape filled-in sample private e-mail reply to a netnews article.

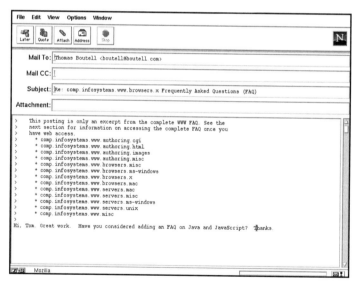

Figure 22.18. *Netscape e-mail reply to a netnews posting.*

While it's sometimes appropriate to use private e-mail replies as part of a Usenet communication/collaboration mechanism on your Intranet, it's likely that posted follow-up articles will be used more often. With a follow-up news article, users are able to respond to posted articles with new articles of their own. The follow-up articles are posted where others can read them and possibly post their own follow-ups. The process, then, becomes an online dialog or group conversation. Let's look at how Netscape and Mosaic Netnews follow-ups work.

To post a follow-up article in Netscape, you must (as you might expect) be reading the article to which you want to respond. Click the Re: News icon to bring up the follow-up screen shown in Figure 22.19. As you can see, it's essentially the same as that in Figure 22.18. The difference is the Newsgroups box appears, filled in with the current newsgroup name. Otherwise, the two windows work in the same way. In UNIX Netscape, click Quote to include the text of the original article. Windows Netscape automatically quotes the article. Use the built-in text editor to compose your response and then click Send to ship it off for posting as a netnews article

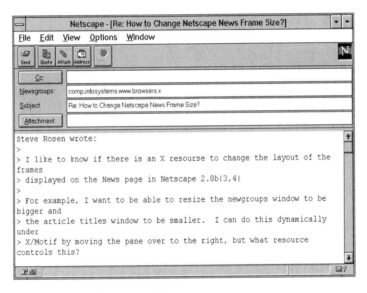

Figure 22.19. Netscape Usenet post follow-up article..

To post a follow-up article using Mosaic, open the article to which you want to respond and then click the follow-up icon (second to the right of the down arrow icon). This brings up the screen shown in Figure 22.20, which is similar to the e-mail screen shown in Figure 22.17. Note the newsgroup name is filled in, as is the subject. You may quote the original posting by clicking Include Original Posting. You can also send a copy of your follow-up via e-mail by filling in the Mailto: box. There's a potentially useful additional button on this screen, labeled Include Author in Mailto. Clicking this button generates an e-mail copy of your follow-up posting for the original poster of the article. You can use this to ensure the author sees your follow-up. As with the Mosaic private e-mail window, you may turn word wrap on and off in the editor. Finally, you can also have your signature file appended, if you've defined one in your News Preferences, by clicking Append .sig.

Once you've made all your selections, you can edit your follow-up message and then click Post to
send your follow-up article to your netnews server for posting. At the same time, any e-mail copies
of your follow-up posting (including, if you selected it, the copy to the original author of the
posting) are sent directly to the addressees' mailboxes.

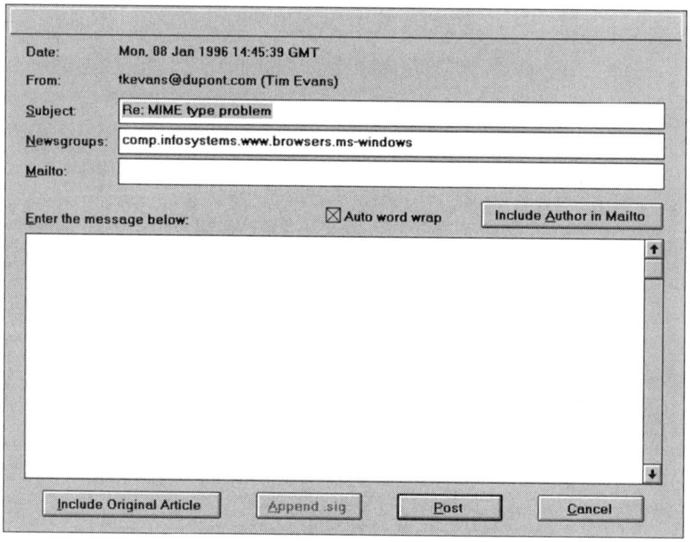

Figure 22.20. *Windows Mosaic News follow-up screen.*

Archiving Usenet Articles

If you're using netnews as a local communications and collaboration mechanism on your Intranet
with local newsgroups, you may want to keep the articles indefinitely for future reference. You'll
want to treat these articles specially because you don't regard them as transitory (or even
ephemeral), the way normal Usenet news articles are treated. With both older news software and
with INN, you retain articles permanently. Just use the word never in place of a number of days
in the expire.ctl file, so your local articles will never expire. This leaves the articles in place in your
news spool, which is something you may not want to do.

If you'd rather archive news articles in a special location on your system away from the transitory
news spool directory, older news server software enables you to archive news articles with special
flags in its article-expiration setup files. As articles were expired, those you want to archive are
placed in your archive for retention and then removed from the original news spool. INN includes
a standalone program called, interestingly enough, *archive*, to accomplish the same thing for you.
You can run archive manually or via the cron daemon to archive articles. (If you use *cron*, be sure
to run *archive* before you run normal newsgroup expirations, so the articles you want archived are
saved before expire runs.) You may find both these ways of archiving articles unsatisfactory for the

simple reason that your archive is, by definition, always out of date, because you can't know when new articles and follow-ups get posted. Running `archive` via the `cron` daemon will always leave you with an archive that's potentially out of date, especially if your customers use netnews heavily for collaboration and discussions.

The best way to run archive is to have it place each new article directly into your archive the moment it's posted. You can do this with INN, by creating a special entry in your `newsfeeds` file to do your archiving. This entry can be something like this:

```
archive\
    :!*,mycompany*\
    :Tc,Wn\
    :/usr/usenet/bin/archive -a /mycompany-archive -f -i \
        /usr/spool/news/news.archive/INDEX
```

See the newsfeeds man page for specifics on the formatting and syntax of this file, as well as the meaning of the `Tc` and `Wn` flags. Here, you're archiving all articles in the `mycompany` newsgroup category (and no others, signified by the leading `!*`) to the directory location `/mycompany-archive` and keeping an index of what gets archived in the file `/usr/spool/news/news.archive/INDEX`. As you learned earlier in this chapter, the last field of a newsfeeds entry can contain what the man page calls parameters. Here, the parameters are a complete command line to execute the archive program, with appropriate command-line options to create your archive.

Every new article posted on your system is tested against the entries in newsfeeds. When an article matching your specification (anything in the `mycompany` newsgroup category in this example) is posted, INN immediately calls `archive`. As a result, your archived articles are available immediately and are always current. In the next section of this chapter, you'll learn how to make searchable indexes of your archived articles.

Note: Anytime you edit the `newsfeeds` file, you need to signal the INN software to put your changes into effect. This is done using the INN superutility `ctlinnd`. Once you've edited `newsfeeds`, issue the following command:

```
$ ctlinnd reload newsfeeds add archive
```

In this example, the `add archive` character string is the reason for the reload. You can put anything as the reason on `ctlinnd` command lines, but you'll want to put something meaningful so INN's logfiles will make sense. Thus, `add archive` was used to indicate that the `newsfeeds` file was edited to add the archiving feature.

Indexing Your Archived Usenet Articles

So far in this chapter, you've learned about the creation and management of netnews, including the creation of local newsgroups for your Intranet's customers. You've learned about how news articles are posted and how private e-mail replies and follow-up articles can be used to create a means of group discussion in your Intranet. Finally, you've learned how to save the articles posted to your local newsgroups using INN's archive program. Let's now turn away from INN and use another of the tools you've learned about in *Building an Intranet* to create a searchable index of the news articles you've archived. (We'll use the term *index* in this section, although you may want to create more than just one.) Once you've created your index, your customers will be able to use their Web browsers to search and retrieve archived articles based on key words and phrases.

Indexing in this chapter is done using freeWAIS-sf. As noted earlier, it's assumed you've compiled and installed this package, preferably on the same computer system that runs INN or on the system where you've archived your articles. (freeWAIS-sf indexing will work using NFS-mounted filesystems, but it's much faster when run on local ones.)

Creating Your Initial Index

Your first step in creating an index with freeWAIS-sf is the preparation of a list of files to be indexed. (It's assumed in this section and the next you're using the news user account on your system, the same account under which INN runs and that creates your archive.) Based on the previous example for archiving the mycompany local newsgroup category, the archived files all reside in the directory /mycompany-archive. It's easy to create a list of the files in your archive, with a command like this:

```
$ find /mycompany-archive -type f -print > /tmp/filelist
```

This command creates a list of all the regular files (not directories) in the /mycompany-archive file tree with the full pathname to each file listed individually. Before you go any further, run this command; it'll be explained a bit later in this section:

```
$ touch /mycompany-archive/mycompany.stamp
```

Next, locate a directory on your system that has sufficient free space available to handle your index. It's assumed you're using the directory /mycompany-wais. You're now ready to use the waisindex command (part of the freeWAIS-sf package) to generate your searchable index.

```
$ waisindex -d /mycompany-wais/mycompany -export -T Mycompany -t netnews -stdin < \/
tmp/filelist
```

You'll want to read the waisindex man page for details, as well as other command-line options, but let's parse this command. Reading the command from left to right, here's what the pieces of it mean:

-d /mycompany-wais/mycompany	Defines the name and location of the database or index you're creating. This will create the index files in the directory /mycompany-wais and the name of the index will be mycompany.
-export	Means you want to make the index searchable on your network.

-T Mycompany	Puts a label on the Type of documents in your index. This is a completely arbitrary character string that you can use to put a meaningful label on your index. Use double quotes if you want the type to be more than one word.
-t netnews	Tells waisindex the files to be indexed are Usenet news articles, a file format waisindex understands.
-stdin	Tells waisindex to take the list of files from the UNIX standard input.
< /tmp/filelist	Indicates that the standard input comes from the file you created using the find command.

Depending on how many files you have in your archive, waisindex may take several minutes to complete its work. During the run, you'll see lots of screen output from the program as it's working. When the run completes, you'll find several files in the /mycompany-wais directory, all of them with names beginning with mycompany. These include mycompany.src, the database description; mycompany.fn, the list of filenames index, mycompany.hl, the headlines file; mycompany.cat, the database catalog file; mycompany.dct, the data dictionary; mycompany.inv, an inverted index file; and, possibly, mycompany.stop, a file of words to be ignored in future updates of the index.

> **Note:** The .cat file is not essential and can be very large. If you're limited on disk space, add -nocat to the previous waisindex command line to suppress creation of the .cat file.
>
> The .stop file consists of words that occur so frequently that it makes no sense to index them; it may or may not get crated.

You'll want to test your new index next. The freeWAIS-sf distribution includes standalone WAIS client software. You can test your index quickly with the plain-text client waissearch. Here's a sample invocation of this command on the same system as the WAIS server software:

```
$ waissearch -d mycompany keyword1 keyword2
```

This will return one or more lines like this:

```
1: Score: nnn, lines: nnn 'Subject Line from Article'
```

Except for the score field, this is fairly self-explanatory. freeWAIS-sf assigns a score to each article it finds containing some or all of your keywords; the higher the score, generally speaking, the more frequent the occurrence of your keywords.

You'll want to do network testing of your index as well, particularly from the system where your Web server software is running if it's not the same machine as your netnews server. (This may mean you need to compile and install freeWAIS-sf on your Web server as well as on your Usenet news server.) To test WAIS network searches, change the waissearch command line to this one:

```
$ waissearch -h hostname_of_wais_server -d mycompany keyword1 keyword2
```

If all goes well, you'll get back the same results as on the local machine.

Updating Your Index

As more articles are archived by INN, you'll need to update your index so it's current. Although you can repeat the initial indexing on a regular basis, it's inefficient because you're reindexing much of the same data repeatedly. The waisindex program has the capability to append to an existing index, and this is what you'll use to update yours. As with the initial indexing, your first step in updating your index is finding the new files. For this purpose, you can use a modified version of the find command in combination with the *mycompany*.stamp file you created earlier with the touch command.

```
$ find /mycompany-archive -type f -newer /mycompany-archive/mycompany.stamp -print >
/tmp/filelist
```

This is a one-line command. Once it's completed, immediately run the touch command, as shown earlier, again. What you've done is to create a list of all the files in your archive area that have been created or modified since the *mycompany*.stamp file was touched and then redate-stamped the stamp file. Now, you can rerun waisindex to update your database, using the new list.

```
$ waisindex -a -d /mycompany-wais/mycompany -t netnews -stdin < /tmp/filelist
```

This command differs from the one used previously in several respects. Most importantly, the -a option is used to signify the command is to append to the existing index. In addition, because the index already exists with the type label Mycompany, the -T Mycompany option has been omitted, as has the -export option for the same reason.

Keeping Your Index Up-to-Date

One of the most important features of the UNIX operating system is the capability of putting frequently run commands and series of commands into shell scripts for future use. Keeping your archive index up to date is a perfect candidate. Here's a script that'll do this for you; its separate commands are described with comments (the lines beginning with the # symbol):

```
#!/bin/sh
# keep 'mycompany' WAIS index up to date
# set some variables for short-hand use later
ARCHIVEDIR=/mycompany-archive
WAISDIR=/mycompany-wais
# find the files that have been created since the last run
find $ARCHIVEDIR -newer $ARCHIVEDIR/mycompany.stamp -print > /tmp/filelist
# immediately retouch the time stamp file for the next run
touch $ARCHIVEDIR/mycompany.stamp
# now run waisindex to update the index
waisindex -a -d WAISDIR/mycompany -t netnews -stdin < /tmp/filelist
```

```
# get rid of the temporary file
rm -f /tmp/filelist
```

Create this script, with your localizations, save it, and make it executable using the chmod command. Now, you can run the script whenever you need to update your index.

Automating Your Index Updates

Let's take your index-update process one step further and have the computer do it for you automatically. Add an entry to the news user's crontab file to have your script run on a regular, automated basis via the UNIX *cron* daemon. Check your crontab man page if you're not familiar with using cron. Many modern UNIX systems support the -e option to the crontab command. If yours does, you can edit the crontab file directly like this (assuming you're logged into the news account):

```
$ EDITOR=vi;export EDITOR
$ crontab -e
```

This brings up the news user's crontab file in the vi editor. (Change the first command above if you prefer another editor.) Add an entry like this:

```
0 0,12 * * * /path/to/shell/script
```

Save the file and exit your editor. This entry will run your archive index script (you, of course, need to change this entry to point to the location and name of your script) at midnight and noon each day to update your index. Depending on how busy your local newsgroups are, you may want to run this more or less frequently.

Tip: For systems that don't support the -e option to crontab, use the following sequence to implement this change:

Make a copy of the crontab file using this command:

```
$ crontab -l > tmpcrontab
```

Edit the tmpcrontab file with your favorite editor to add the entry shown above and then resubmit the changed file to cron.

```
$ crontab tmpcrontab
```

Now you're all set. You've created an initial index of your local newsgroup archive and set in motion regular, automated updates of the index. In the next section, you'll set up your Intranet's customers to search your index and retrieve the documents in it using their Web browser.

Searching Your Netnews Archive

The final task for this chapter is to make it possible for your Intranet's customers to search the local newsgroups archive you've created and to retrieve news articles from it. You'll do this with the freeWAIS-sf companion program SFgate. As you'll recall from Chapter 8, "Adding Services to Your Intranet Adds Value," SFgate is a CGI-bin gateway script that interfaces your Web server to WAIS indexes, including, naturally, those created by freeWAIS-sf. If you haven't already installed this package from the *Building an Intranet* CD-ROM, you'll want to do so before you go any further in the chapter.

Customizing SFgate to Your Intranet

Once you've installed Sfgate, there's some minor customization required to make it search the index you've created. You do this on your Web server in a couple of places. First, in your Web server's cgi-bin directory, you'll want to edit the perl script named Sfgate. As distributed, the Sfgate script has several specific WAIS indexes hardwired in. The script also assumes you have multiple local indexes. Even if you're not a perl hacker, this is pretty easy to change. Bring up the Sfgate script in your favorite editor and locate, fairly near the top of the file, the section that looks similar to this one:

```
# settings for your default waisserver
$default_wais_server    = 'webserver.mycompany.com';
$default_wais_port      = 210;
$default_wais_db        = 'directory-of-servers';
```

This file was created at the time you built the Sfgate software on your system, and it has your own Web server's hostname in it (the example uses webserver.mycompany.com). What you need to change here is the fourth line, where the variable default_wais_db is set. Replace *directory-of-servers* with the name of your WAIS index; we've used *mycompany* in the examples of this chapter, so you'd change this line to read:

```
$default_wais_db        = 'mycompany';
```

Be sure to include the single quotes and the line-ending semicolon, as required in perl.

Next, you'll need to edit the index.html file the Sfgate installation placed in your Web server's document tree. Unless you told it otherwise, this will be in a subdirectory named Sfgate at the top level of your Web document tree. If, for example, your Web server's DocumentRoot is /usr/local/web-docs, you'll find the Sfgate HTML files in /usr/local/web-docs/SFgate. There are a couple of changes you need to make in the index.html file. First, locate the following section of this file, which is, of course, written with HTML:

```
<H2>Select some of the following databases:</H2>

 <INPUT NAME="database"
  TYPE="checkbox"
  VALUE="webserver.mycompany.com/directory-of-servers" CHECKED>
  Default WAIS server: WAIS source descriptions in the
  directory-of-servers database on  webserver.mycompany.com<BR>
```

Change directory-of-servers to *mycompany* (or the actual name of your index).

Your second change to the index.html file is not required, but you'll want to make it to avoid confusing your Intranet's customers. The file, an HTML fill-in form, provides a menu of several WAIS servers to which the user might connect. All except for the default server are outside your Intranet; they may not even be accessible if your network is not connected to the Internet. Because you're using Sfgate to access your own private WAIS index on your Intranet, you'll want to delete the remote WAIS servers listed in this file. The menu is part of the same section of the file you just edited, a couple of lines down. Delete the additional choices here, leaving only the default index, your own. Figure 22.21 shows the Mosaic rendering of the index.html file, as edited according to these instructions.

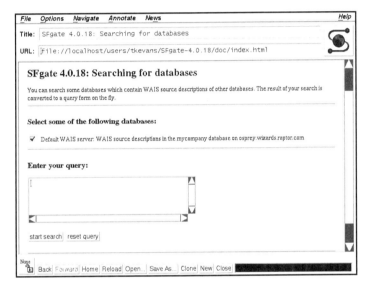

Figure 22.21. SFgate default fill-in form, as edited.

As you can see from the screenshot, the form shows a one-item menu of WAIS servers under the heading Select some of the following databases. Because you've just edited out all the other servers, your menu now contains only one item, and the heading may be confusing to your customers. Unless you have multiple WAIS indexes on your Intranet, you may want to do away with this menu business altogether and just set the default index name using a hidden value in this form. For more information on HTML forms, see the author's *10 Minute Guide to HTML* (ISBN 0-7897-0541-9) published by Que Publishing. You can find this book in most bookstores, or you can order it and get more information at the Macmillan Information SuperLibrary at URL http://www.mcp.com/.

Using SFgate on Your Intranet

You'll probably want to further customize the Sfgate startup form (the index.html document you've just edited), or even create a new one of your own, tailored to your Intranet and its searchable index. Whatever the case, you're now ready to turn your customers loose with SFgate. Of course, you don't have to tell them it's called SFgate, or even explain it's based on WAIS and the index you've created. All you need to do is provide a hyperlink on one of your Web pages pointing to your customized form. Users simply fill in the blanks using their Web browsers and then run their searches. Figure 22.22 shows a customized SFgate form. (In fact, it's the official SFgate demonstration form, from the University of Dortmund, at URL `http://ls6-www.informatik.uni-dortmund.de/SFgate/demo.html`.)

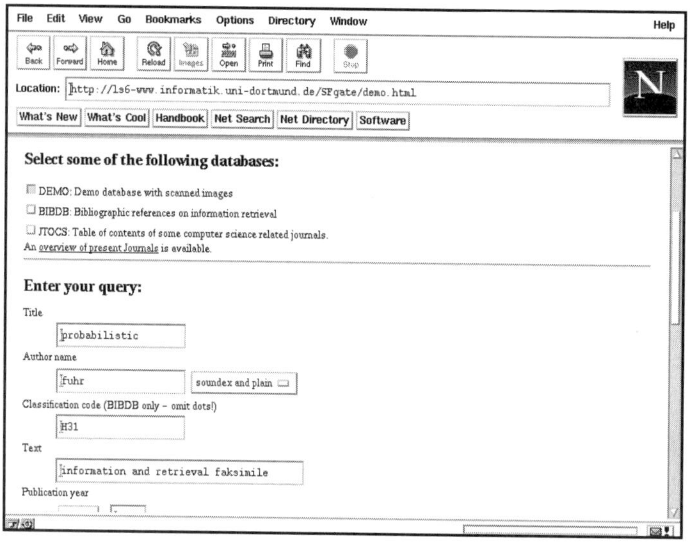

Figure 22.22. *Sample SFgate fill-in form.*

Behind the scenes, the SFgate CGI-bin script contacts your Intranet's WAIS server and uses the CGI-bin script of the same name to search its index for the keywords typed into the fill-in form by your customers. The script then returns the results of its search in dynamically created HTML. Your customer's Web browser receives the results, renders the HTML, and presents a list of documents containing the keywords, ranked according to the weighted scoring you learned about earlier. Each document on the list users get back from their queries is a clickable hyperlink, so they can retrieve any one of them just by clicking its entry in the list. Figure 22.23 shows a sample search result from the SFgate demonstration page shown in Figure 22.23.

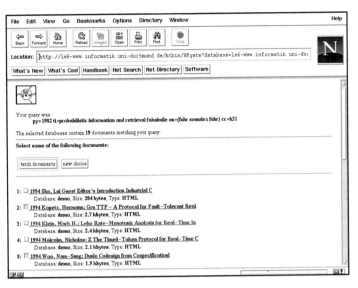

Figure 22.23. *SFgate search results in HTML.*

Chapter Summary

In this chapter, you've learned how to put Usenet news to work on your Intranet. In addition, you've learned how to integrate netnews with the WAIS service adding value to both. In summary, here's what this chapter has covered

- ◆ How Usenet newsgroups work
- ◆ Managing newsgroups on your netnews server
- ◆ Creating local newsgroups for local communication and collaboration
- ◆ Using Web browsers to post and respond to news articles
- ◆ Archiving newsgroup articles for future reference
- ◆ Indexing your archived newsgroup articles
- ◆ Searching the newsgroup indexes you've created and retrieving articles from them using a Web browser

In Chapter 23, "Web Front End for Custom Applications," you'll learn how you can wrap an entire application program up inside a Web interface.

CHAPTER

23

Web Front End for Custom Applications

In the preceding seven chapters of *Building an Intranet*, you've learned how to use your Intranet to create a series of specific, real-life applications. In describing these applications, we've slid right past the important high-level concepts of putting them together into a single, coherent, full-blown Intranet application. It's like we're sitting around on Christmas Eve with bicycle parts strewn all over the garage floor, with no instructions for assembling them, and no shortcuts for doing so. In this chapter, we'll revisit some of those sample applications and discuss building a framework around them that turns them into a self-contained, custom Intranet application. You'll also pick up a number of tips and tricks to facilitate building and using your applications.

Chapter Objectives

As with the rest of the chapters in this book, let's begin by laying out some objectives. This will help you get oriented to the material to be presented. (You may want to refer back to this list as you work your way through the chapter.) In this chapter, you'll do the following:

◆ Revisit an exemplary Web site you saw in Chapter 21 and consider it as a complete, self-contained application.

◆ Revisit the sample, but fragmentary, Intranet applications you saw in Chapters 16-22 and consider how they can be turned into finished ones.

◆ Learn some simple tools and techniques that will lessen the work of putting together Intranet applications.

The Khoros DIP Training Course Revisited

In Chapter 21, you were introduced to Khorosware, the Khoros Digital Image Processing (DIP) training course on the Web. Our objective in looking at the course at that point was fairly narrow, focusing on it as a *training mechanism*. However, Khorosware can also be seen as a complete, self-contained application (much like you'd buy off the shelf at Computer City), the object of which is training. As such, Khorosware *the application* can provide important examples of how to take Web services and turn them into something more than just pretty Web pages. Let's analyze Khorosware, then, from that point of view. (You may want to access the Khorosware startup page at `http://www.khoral.com/dipcourse/Welcome.html` and follow along to see what we're talking about here.) As you look at it, you'll see four major touchstones, worthy of emulation in your own Intranet applications:

◆ Attractive packaging subtly encourages users to try the product.

◆ Good internal design and organization of material into a logical sequence allows both logical progression through the course and *ad hoc* browsing.

◆ Visual aids illustrate important points about digital image processing.

◆ Hands-on interaction throughout the course gives the user frequent opportunities to actually use the Khoros applications with real image data.

A Package Without Shrink Wrap

Like other self-respecting software application programs, Khorosware comes wrapped in a nice, attractive package. There's no shrink wrap (and no price tag) on the Web, but, as Figure 23.1 shows, the package has a visually pleasing shelf appearance. You can also see, even in the relatively small window used to fit *Building an Intranet* screen shots on the page, there are immediately useful hyperlinks, accessible right from the start. Among the ones shown in the screen shot are answers to all a customer's most immediate questions. What is this package? What is it for, and how do I learn to use it? What if I need more information about it? And what if something goes wrong? If you've ever thumbed through a software package's reference manual, looking for Tech Support's toll-free telephone number (knowing full well the manufacturer has deliberately hidden it to cut down on calls), you can appreciate all that Khorosware has made available in this small window, before you ever open the package.

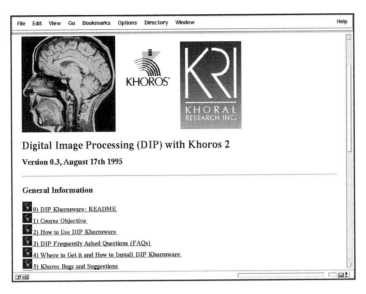

Figure 23.1. The Khorosware welcome page.

Attractive, Utilitarian Design Inside the Package

Khorosware's authors have also devoted attention to the internal design of the application to make it effective, useful, and aesthetically pleasing. Pages decorated with attractive, clickable thumbnail photographs of interesting places provide restful breaks in the course; thus the package invites you to turn its pages, even if you're not really interested in digital image processing or equipped to understand it. Simple, uncluttered pages present the course syllabus, with strategic icons providing visual cues to content along the way. The hammer-and-screwdriver icon in the left center of Figure 23.2, for example, tips the reader off to the availability of an introduction to the component tools of the software package itself. Further down the page, the cool blue-and-green Earth icon marks off the first of a list of interactive demonstrations of the software, with hyperlinks leading to each major experiment. Online help is available virtually anywhere you go in the course.

Visual Aids Enhance Understanding

In its introductory material (click on the "Khoros 2: Data Model, Programming and Visualization Tools" hyperlink on the Khorosware startup page), Khorosware shows us what its cantata visual programming language is all about. (See Figure 23.3.) Even though it's a still screen shot, you can almost see the program flow by looking at the cantata glyphs and their connecting lines. Better than a flow chart, and surely better than lengthy text explanations, this important visual aid stands out as an example of how you can use the Web's multimedia capabilities to dress up your applications with critical, intuitively clear information. The image also gives even the casual reader a good idea of how the cantata visual programming environment operates.

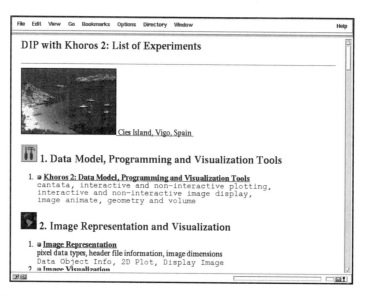

Figure 23.2. Khorosware main start page.

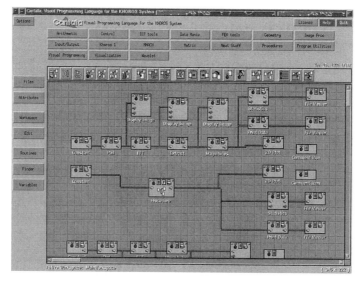

Figure 23.3. Cantata visual programming environment, from Khorosware.

Hands On, Interactive Demonstrations

Lastly, Khorosware doesn't just tell you about digital image processing with pages of gray text; nor does it just show you a picture or two as an afterthought. The course actually lets you run example image-processing experiments, using your own computer and your installed copy of the Khoros software. As explained in detail in Chapter 21, "Web-Based Training and Presentations," Khorosware experiment pages contain hyperlinks to real data files which, when clicked on in a properly configured Khoros environment, actually kick off Khoros helper applications on your own computer to process the digital image data pointed to by the links. Figure 23.4 shows just such an interactive run of cantata, running a hot-linked pseudocolor experiment. Embedding live data in the application lets customers use the application immediately, just by clicking on hyperlinks. (Recall our process-control data modeling example from Chapter 18, "Numbers for Number Crunchers.") You'll want to do the same thing with your spreadsheet, your boilerplate document libraries, your Web-based help desk, or other custom Intranet applications.

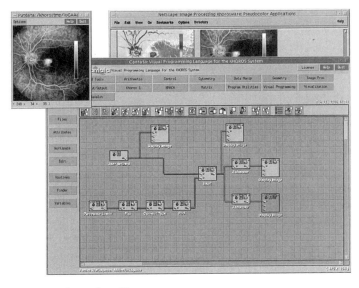

Figure 23.4. *Active cantata workspace from Khorosware.*

Welcome to the Help Desk

Chapter 16, "Intranet Help Desk," was about using your Intranet to automate your computer or other help-desk/customer-support operations. You'll recall having learned about both no-cost and commercial database software applications that can allow both search and retrieval of help-desk data and aid in help-desk management. The main thing left out of that chapter was some sort of high-level organization for the application, including a main Web startup page for your help desk. Figure 23.5 shows a very simple example of such a help-desk home page. (It's assumed you have your relational database or other help-desk data resource already up and running). Although the home page has no graphics, it's a good, minimalist model, providing access to the main functions of most help desks in a straightforward, intuitive fashion. While you can certainly add your own corporate logo or other images to dress it up as much as you want, there are few if any other substantive features you'll need to add to this basic approach. You'll want to check Appendix B, "HTML and CGI Quick Reference," for the basic HTML markup tags you can use to create pages like this one.

Tip: Do your customers a favor and go easy on the graphics on your Intranet application Web pages. For an analogy, think of the most overdeveloped, busy, garish commercial strip in your city, with all its neon and other visual overcrowding. Try to keep your Web pages from looking like that.

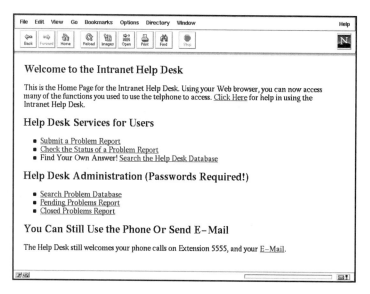

Figure 23.5. Intranet help desk page.

Despite the page's simplicity, there are quite a few significant observations to make.

◆ The page is divided functionally, with user and help-desk administrator sections (although you may want to have completely separate startup pages for these two main functions).

◆ A Help link is provided to assist customers in using the application.

◆ The third bulleted item under Help Desk Services for Users suggests *search-and-retrieval* functions are available for self-service, in case customers want to try finding their own problem solutions.

◆ The headline for the Help Desk Administration section indicates username/password authentication will be applied.

◆ There's a *mailto* URL at the bottom of the page, allowing customers to contact the help desk via e-mail, as well as a phone number.

On the whole, then, here's a good beginning for your Intranet help desk, which follows the four principles illustrated above with respect to the Khorosware application. Add a fill-in form like the one show in Figure 23.6, which customers can use for making problem reports and/or the help-desk staff can use for extracting status information and management reports from the problem database, and add a CGI-bin back end for it, like the wwwgnats script featured in Chapter 16, and your Intranet help desk is ready for business.

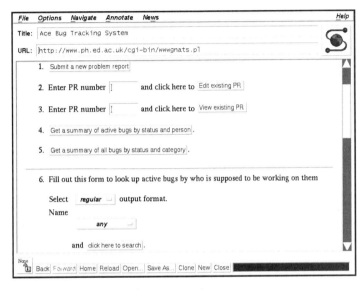

Figure 23.6. Help desk problem-report form (from wwwgnats).

Intranet Corporate Practices/Procedures Manuals Application

Figure 23.7 shows a skeleton home page for an organization's Practices and Procedures Intranet, an application about which you learned in Chapter 17. Here we use the same minimalist approach we took with the help-desk home page, and many of the same general features as well. Some different HTML markup has been used in this page, however, to vary the typefaces used and to create a different kind of list (called an *ordered list*; see Appendix B). Also, a standard page footer (or *trailer*), with an embedded *mailto* URL hyperlink and a visual separator, has been added to the bottom of the page; you may want to continue using such a footer throughout your application.

Other additions to the Practices and Procedures home page include access to a graphical campus imagemap and searchable telephone directory database, two non-text Web resources, built right into your Practices and Procedures Intranet application. Here's another instance of one of *Building an Intranet*'s leitmotifs: integrating different services into a single, seamless application, with all the services available to customers right from their Web browsers. As you can see, a hyperlink to the help-desk page is provided, providing access to a completely different Intranet application from this one. Each of the major information categories has links to a category home page, where you'd expect to find links to documents and other resources for that category. For example, within the Materiel and Logistics Department's pages, you'll probably find a fill-in form for obtaining a campus parking permit, along with traffic rules and information and more graphical maps, showing you the parking lots. The Safety section might contain a searchable database of standard Material Safety Data Sheets on dangerous substances in use around the campus, as well as a hyperlinked, and possibly searchable, manual of corporate- and government-required safety procedures and regulations.

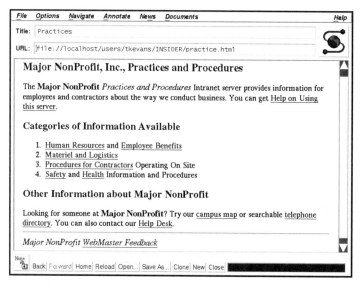

Figure 23.7. *Practices and Procedures home page.*

Numbers for Number Crunchers

Low-cost Intranet data warehouses were discussed in Chapter 18. There you learned about serving live spreadsheet data files from your Web server. Customers retrieving the data files with their Web browsers saw them pop directly into their waiting spreadsheet application for manipulation, analysis, and graphing. You'll want to wrap your data warehouse in a nice, unified package, possibly starting out with something like Figure 23.8.

Our page has now grown too large to fit in a single screen shot without using a smaller font size. You don't need to be able to read all the text of the page, however, to see what's new about it. Graphics have been added to jazz up the page. But they're useful graphics, too, because (though you may not quite be able to make it out in the screen shots) each image is a clickable hyperlink. (See Appendix B for details on including images as hyperlinks in HTML documents.) Inserting the visual element adds an extra, intuitive feature to the page, making it easier for customers to interpret and use it. Customers can load the spreadsheet data file by clicking on the appropriate image in the page, getting the 1-2-3, Excel, or Xess version, as appropriate for their own package. Besides the addition of the graphical images, note these other features of the data warehouse page:

◆ A hyperlink leads to instructions on setting up spreadsheets as Web browser helper applications, ensuring customers know what they need to do to make things work. (Presumably, this link will contain not only written instructions, but also screen shots like you saw in Chapter 18.)

◆ The link to the help desk has been compacted by integrating it right into one of the page's headlines. (See Appendix B for specifics.)

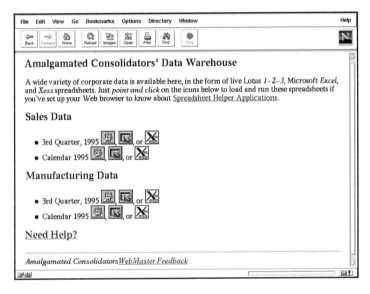

Figure 23.8. *Data warehouse home page.*

Naturally, your own Intranet data warehouse pages will provide access to many more data files than this simple example can show in a single screen shot. Still, you get the idea of how the application becomes more full-featured as new elements (such as graphics) are added—without it becoming any more complex. Indeed, as you judiciously apply the tools you learn in this book, your applications become more and more intuitive—and therefore more useful—to your customers, even as the applications do more things.

Intranet Ordering and Inventory Application

You've seen enough top-level or application home pages for the moment. Let's start looking at Chapter 19, "Ordering and Inventory," at a lower level, then come back up for air later. You'll recall the several generations of the fill-in order form from that chapter. Let's modify it once more, as shown in Figure 23.9. The change and its meaning are obvious: If the customer needs help, it's as easy to find now as the customer's finger.

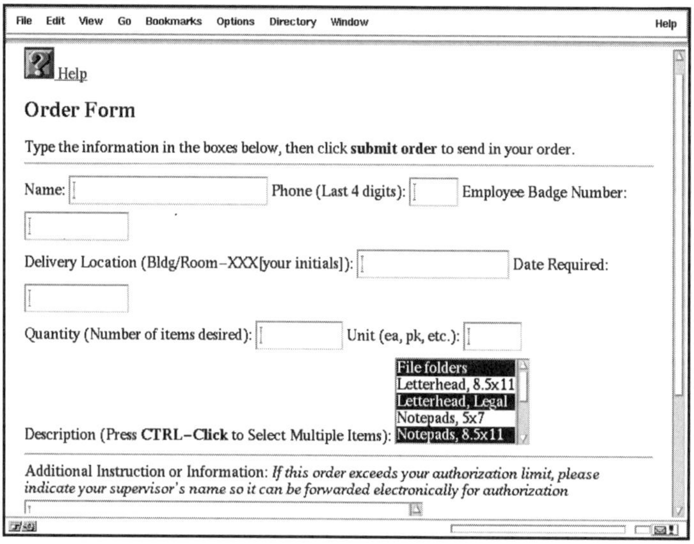

Figure 23.9. *Modified order form.*

The example form is quite simple, with only a handful of office-supply items orderable. This doesn't mean it's unusable. Smart webmasters steal from themselves as often as possible. There's no reason you can't recycle this form for each major category of supplies carried by your in-house store, then link each copy onto an overall Orders page, from which the customer selects a category of supply and receives the fill-in form for that category. All your forms are virtually identical, because you cloned them, merely changing the list of supplies available from each one. Your back-end CGI-bin script won't need to be changed at all, because all the forms are the same as far as it's concerned, and shipping the orders off to the database back end is, too.

To allow customers to order multiple items using multiple forms, you'll want to develop a *shopping cart* (sometimes also called *shopping bag*) CGI-bin script. Such scripts maintain state across a series of Web transactions, so the customer's identifying information doesn't have to be entered for each new item being ordered. Instead, the customer identifies himself just once at the start, then browses the online store, selecting items and dropping them into his virtual shopping cart. Only when he's finished picking things out does he finally click on the Order button.

Freelance CGI scripter Eric Tachibana's online alter ego, Selena Sol, maintains a library of no-cost shopping cart (and other CGI-bin) scripts at http://www.eff.org/~erict/Script/. The page has a number of potentially useful scripts, as well as links to many other CGI-bin resources on the Web. You'll find shopping cart, or shopping bag, CGI-bin scripts running almost anywhere you can shop on the Web. For example, Figure 23.10 shows an information page for the author's earlier book, *10 Minute Guide to HTML*, from Macmillan Computer Publishing's online bookstore (http://www.mcp.com/). Using the three icons at the lower left center of the window, customers can order a copy of the book (Add to Bag), take a look back at what they've already selected (Review Bag), and finally, head for the electronic cash register to pay for their books (Checkout).

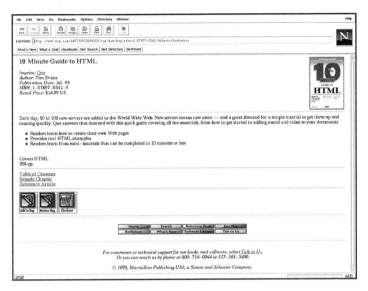

Figure 23.10. *Online bookstore shopping bag.*

Boilerplate Library

You'll no doubt recall the Department of Public Inquiries from Chapter 20, "Intranet Boilerplate Library," where you learned about putting together a library of canned, reusable word processing documents. The DPI has a massive library of documents from which staffers cut and paste to create new responses to its own list of FAQs. One of DPI's major problems is locating the right stock language with which to answer questions from the public or from legislators. As a result, the indexing tools about which you learned in Chapter 13, "Indexing and Searching Your Data," become important. Let's work the need for search-and-retrieval into a Department of Public Inquiries home page and, as usual, throw in something additional as well. Have a look at Figure 23.11 to start.

Since we just mentioned document indexing and retrieval, let's first discuss the fill-in box at the top of the screen. Here we've used the HTML <ISINDEX> tag (see Appendix B) to generate this simple fill-in form automatically. Our back-end search script isn't defined, but it could be any of the search-and-retrieve tools described in Chapter 13 for which you've created an index. If you need more complex search capabilities, which you undoubtedly do, <ISINDEX> won't be enough, so you'll need to use a CGI-bin script, such as SFgate or one that uses the glimpseHTTPD search engine. Our favorite full-text index database, the Shakespeare search from Chapter 13, shown again in Figure 23.12, is based on a glimpse index, with the form created by the glimpseHTTP CGI-bin script. It seems particularly well-suited for the DPI, because it allows for full-text search by category and sub-category (or combinations thereof), searches with Boolean logic, and across-the-board searches of the entire database.

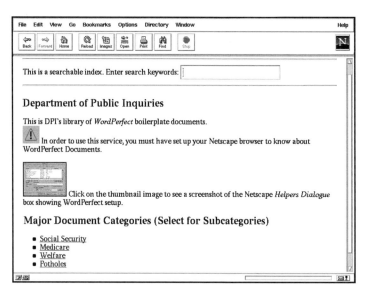

Figure 23.11. *The Department of Public Inquiries home page.*

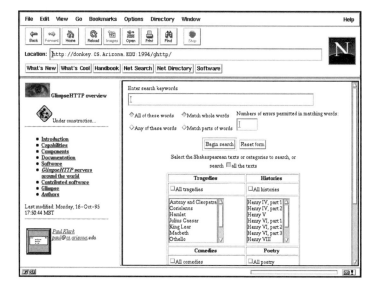

Figure 23.12. *The glimpseHTTP search form.*

Tip: Figure 23.12 shows the use of Netscape 2.0's Frames feature. The left side of the screen holds constant as the links in it are selected, keeping the list of links visible. See below for more discussion of Netscape Frames.

The DPI home page has yet another important new feature. There's a small, thumbnail-sized graphical image in the left center of the page. Look closely and you'll see that the thumbnail is itself a hyperlink. Clicking on it brings up a full-size version of the same image. Here it's used as a way of providing context-sensitive help on setting up WordPerfect as a Netscape helper application. Opening the full-size image shows the Netscape Helpers dialog box, all filled in for WordPerfect. Note also the warning icon that's been thrown in as an attention-getter on this home page.

Tools and Tricks for Building Your Custom Intranet Applications

Besides the text editor or specialized HTML document editor you use to create your Intranet Web pages, you can use a number of tools to help put your applications together. These can range from screen shot tools that make it easy to get documents or data from their original source to your Web server to tools for customization of customer Web browsers. These tools can make your life as an Intranet application builder much easier.

Screen Shot Tools

Throughout *Building an Intranet*, we have turned to the ImageMagick package of tools for image-related examples. You've seen how the display and convert utilities can be used for image display and image-format conversion for a wide variety of formats, as well as how these ImageMagick utilities can be called in your CGI-bin scripts. The package also has integrated utilities for capturing screen shots (import), combining separate images into new ones (montage and mogrify), and for animating series of images (animate). Display also allows interactive image editing, allowing resizing, rotation, and addition of special effects and text annotations, and other modifications. Figure 23.13 shows display's interactive menu, with one submenu (Transform) having been selected. ImageMagick is on the *Building an Intranet* CD-ROM in both source code and compiled versions for several UNIX systems, VAX/VMS systems, and (in a limited version, with no working *display* or *animate*) for the Macintosh. For other image-capture/modification packages, including packages for non-UNIX platforms, see the examples in Chapter 4, "Content Development Tools."

> **Tip:** A port of ImageMagick to Microsoft Windows may be available by the time you read this. Check the ImageMagick home page at `http://www.wizards.dupont.com/cristy/ImageMagick.html`.

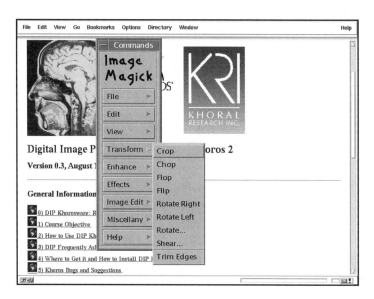

Figure 23.13. *ImageMagick's Convert Menu.*

In Chapters 21 and 24, "Web Groupware: Collaboration on Your Intranet," screen shots from the Lotus ScreenCam product are featured. While the ScreenCam playback tool is available at no cost (`http:/www.lotus.com/`), the ScreenCam recorder is a commercial, though quite inexpensive, package. It's a useful tool to add lifelike demonstration features to your Intranet, giving customers the ability to watch a program being run, right down to the mouse movements and clicks.

Moving Your Intranet Data Around

Building an Intranet has frequently sidestepped the question of moving your HTML documents and other Intranet data files around your network, implicitly assuming you know how to use networking tools such as FTP or the Berkeley R-commands and can use them to transfer files from one computer to another. Let's take a few minutes to look at some alternatives to these command-line tools you might be able to use for moving data.

Network File Systems/Drives

One way to make data transfer on your Intranet completely transparent is to use your UNIX httpd server computer's Network File Systems (NFS) server capability to export your httpd server file tree for remote mounting over the network. NFS allows networked computers to treat a remote file system as if it were local. Virtually all UNIX systems now have both NFS client and NFS server capabilities, so there's a good chance you can do this. Using NFS, you can transparently transfer new or updated HTML documents from your own computer to your Intranet's Web server simply by copying them from one directory to another or just editing them in place. NFS client software is also available for Microsoft Windows, MS-DOS, and Macintosh computers, which treat remote NFS filesystems as *network drives* (or, as on the Macintosh, *shared folders)*, accessible for drag and drop.

> **Note:** If you're running a Macintosh httpd server, you may want to create and export shared folders in the server's file tree to allow drag-and-drop file transfers between client machines and the server. This is a good way not only of making data transfer transparent and easy for yourself but also of enabling customers to create their own home pages.

FTP File Transfers

While you can use command-line FTP to move data around on your Intranet, there are a number of other tools that can make your life a little easier. Virtually all TCP/IP networking packages for Windows PCs now include a graphical FTP tool that enables you to point and click your way through file uploads and downloads. Figure 23.14 shows an FTP session using ftp Software, Inc.'s OnNet graphical FTP tool. Other GUI FTP tools use the Windows File Manager metaphor. Sun UNIX users may want to try out Sun's unsupported ftptool, shown in Figure 23.15; you'll find source code to ftptool on the *Building an Intranet* CD-ROM.

If you use Netscape 2.0, you may want to skip over the tools just mentioned and just use Netscape itself for FTP uploads. This is a new capability. Earlier versions of Netscape have long been able to do FTP downloads, using both anonymous FTP and username/password authentication, but the upload facility is new. Whenever Netscape 2.0 is connected to an FTP server, the standard Netscape pull-down File menu changes to add a new Upload File selection, as shown in Figure 23.16. Selecting this item opens a typical Windows file-browsing dialog box, which allows you to select the file to be uploaded. Assuming you're authenticated and have permission to upload the file to the FTP server, your file will get transferred.

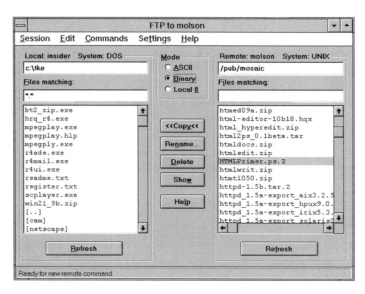

Figure 23.14. *Example Windows FTP client.*

	Date	Size	Filename
	Feb 6 10:31	330739	18inw06.pcx
	Jan 30 1995	294994	HSALPHA.ZIP
	Jan 30 1995	192905	HSI386.ZIP
	Jul 23 1994	971481	HTMLPrimer.ps.Z
	Jan 30 1995	3801	HTTPS.TXT
	Nov 12 1993	537	Helpers.README
	Jan 25 20:16	4595974	JDK-1_0-solaris2-sparc.tar.Z
	Dec 30 17:31	2354206	MOS21B1.EXE
	Mar 2 1994	3965	MacHTTP_1.2.3_updater
	Jun 3 1994	1333996	Mosaic-2.0.VMS-10.tar.Z
	Jul 10 1995	936964	Mosaic-alpha-2.6.Z
	Apr 11 1994	781841	Mosaic-alpha.Z
	Dec 7 1993	926357	Mosaic-aux.Z
	Jul 10 1995	1111311	Mosaic-dec-2.6.Z
	Apr 11 1994	1938358	Mosaic-dec.Z
	Oct 4 1994	1895945	Mosaic-dellsvr4.Z
	Jul 10 1995	853351	Mosaic-hp-2.6.Z
	Oct 27 16:47	2165329	Mosaic-hp-2.7b2.Z
	Jul 10 1995	797705	Mosaic-ibm-2.6.Z
	Oct 27 16:54	3042581	Mosaic-ibm-2.7b2.Z
	Jul 10 1995	915718	Mosaic-indy-2.6.Z
	Oct 27 16:59	1787423	Mosaic-indy-2.7b2.Z
	Jul 10 1995	903973	Mosaic-linux-2.6.Z
	Dec 7 1993	445725	Mosaic-sco-odt.tar.Z
	Jul 10 1995	648431	Mosaic-sgi-2.6.Z

Defaults saved to /p/home/tkevans/.ftptooldefaults.   130 items, 2 selected.

Figure 23.15. *ftptool on the SunOS 4.1.4 system.*

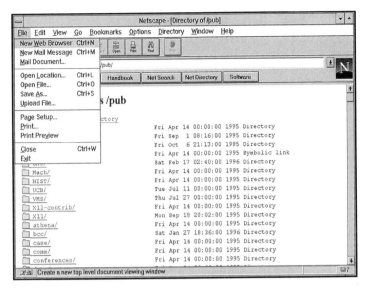

Figure 23.16. Netscape 2.0 File menu with Upload File selection.

You can't usually upload files to anonymous FTP sites, even with the new Netscape functionality, unless you authenticate yourself first. A little-known fact about FTP URLs on the Web is that they can contain not only the hostname and directory path of the destination server but also a non-anonymous username. To access a computer on which you have an account for FTP purposes using Netscape, just click the Open button on the Toolbar and enter a URL such as this:

```
ftp://myname@mycomputer.mycompany.com/path/to/directory
```

As you can see, what's new about this URL is the addition of your account name, with the @ symbol as a separator between it and the hostname. Clicking OK brings up an authentication dialog box, like the one shown in Figure 23.17, where you're prompted to enter your password on the remote host. Once you've done this correctly, you're connected to the FTP server on the host with your own username, with all its normal permissions, and you can both download and upload files.

> **Note:** NCSA Mosaic supports username/password authentication with FTP URLs of the type shown herein, for access to non-anonymous FTP accounts, but it doesn't allow files to be uploaded.

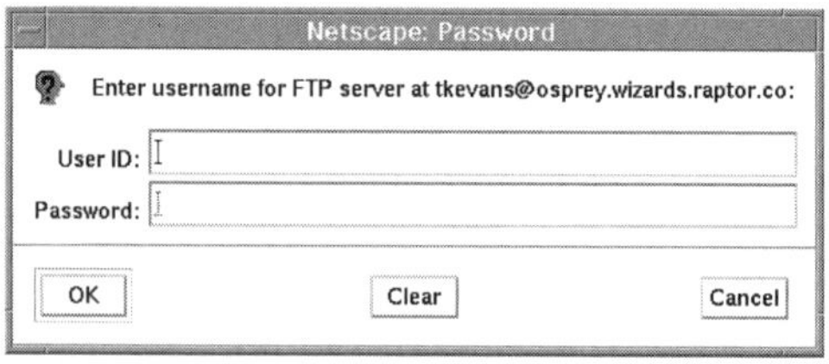

Figure 23.17. *Netscape FTP user authentication dialog box.*

NCSA WinMosaic AutoSurf Builds Cache

Like most Web browsers, Mosaic stores recently accessed Web pages in a local disk cache for quick access when the document is accessed a second time. You can take advantage of this feature with NCSA Windows Mosaic's unique AutoSurf capability, accessible from the pull-down Navigate menu. AutoSurf starts at the currently loaded document, such as the customer's home page, then works its way automatically through the page, opening each hyperlink it finds in turn, possibly recursively. Although AutoSurf is fun and interesting to watch, it's not meant to be used as a demonstration or training mechanism. Pages are fetched and loaded in too rapid a succession for customers to read them. (A running AutoSurf can be stopped at any time with a mouse click.)

The purpose of running AutoSurf, rather, is to populate the customer's disk cache for later access. Having a rich cache of documents speeds up access to them, so you can streamline your Intranet application by ensuring all or most of the documents it might need are already locally cached on each customer's PC. If you have a busy help desk, for example, you won't want document retrievals from the help desk Web server to bog down ongoing customer support calls. Instead, when your agents have local copies of commonly accessed documents cached locally, document look-ups run faster, giving customers better response and making help-desk staff more efficient.

One possible way to use AutoSurf is to have your customers start it up as they leave for the day at the top level of the document tree you want them to cache locally. The feature will run without need for user intervention until it has fetched all the documents linked to the starting one. By the next day, customers will have a fresh local disk cache of documents for ready access. Mosaic's disk-cache feature must be turned on before it can be used, and you may need to do some tinkering with its set-up to tailor it to your needs. Both are done from the Mosaic pull-down Options Menu. Select Preferences, then click on the Cache tab to access the Cache dialog box shown in Figure 23.18.

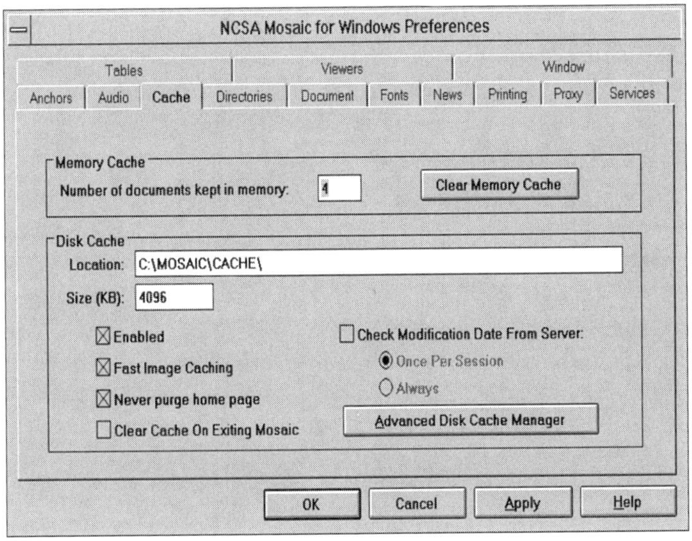

Figure 23.18. NCSA WinMosaic cache dialog box.

Look for the Enabled checkbox and select it if necessary. The amount of disk space devoted to the cache controls how many documents can be held there. The disk space set aside, therefore, indirectly controls how long documents stay in the cache before being purged; when space is needed for new documents, the oldest ones are removed. Notice you can specify how frequently documents are to be checked for updates, and you'll want to check the box labeled Check Modification Date from Server and the subsidiary button, Once Per Session. On the lower right, the Advanced Cache Manager button opens a new dialog box for more detailed cache configuration, including flagging documents that are never to be purged from the cache, such as a static home page, and the like. The default Mosaic cache disk space is 4MB, but you can increase it if necessary.

Note: Netscape Navigator, while it has no comparable feature to WinMosaic's AutoSurf, does maintain a similar document cache on local disk. You can control its size and behavior from a similar, though less extensive, dialog box. From the Options menu, select Network Preferences, then Cache. Here you can control the amount of disk space set aside for the cache and tell Netscape how frequently to check for document changes.

As you might imagine, AutoSurf has the potential to run out of control if you point it toward a page with loads of links to other pages and those other pages also have lots of links. To limit how far AutoSurf will go in these situations, use its own configuration dialog, shown in Figure 23.19, to select how many levels deep into an HTML document tree the package should go. You can also control some other details, such as the following:

◆ How many documents to retrieve;

◆ Whether to follow links to other Web servers or stay local (a potentially important consideration in your application);

◆ Whether to log retrievals, and, if so, in what format;

◆ Whether to traverse a page's hyperlinks by depth or breadth first

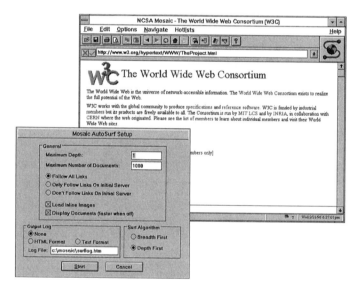

Figure 23.19. *NCSA WinMosaic AutoSurf Setup dialog box.*

> **Warning:** Be sure not to allow AutoSurf to retrieve URLs that cause Web browser helper applications to be called, such as word processor documents or spreadsheet data files. Failing to limit the facility using the AutoSurf Setup dialog could result in a real mess in the morning, with customer PCs having fired up multiple copies of Word or Lotus 1-2-3.

Custom Pull-Down Documents Menus in X Mosaic

NCSA Mosaic for X Windows doesn't have AutoSurf, but it has a nifty feature you can use to replicate the AutoSurf function. The UNIX version allows you to add quick-reference documents to your applications. If you compare Figure 23.20 with Figure 23.21, you'll see an important difference. Obviously, there's a pull-down menu open in Figure 23.21, but if you look a little closer, you'll see that the big difference is the latter doesn't even have a Documents menu to pull down from its menu bar.

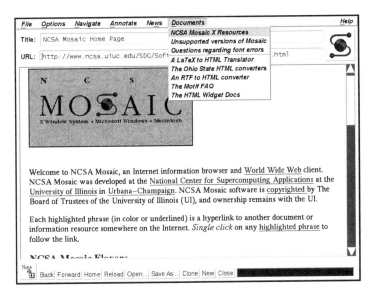

Figure 23.20. NCSA X Mosaic with custom Documents menu.

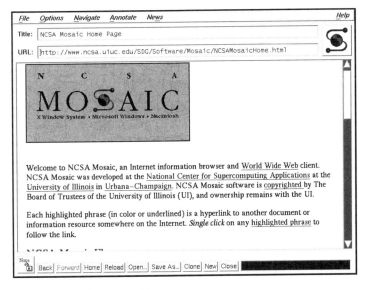

Figure 23.21. NCSA X Mosaic without custom Documents menu.

Setting up a Custom Documents Pull-Down Menu

The X Mosaic Documents menu is a custom pull-down you can add to the browser's main menu bar. You've probably noticed it closely resembles the Help pull-down in the upper right. The primary difference between the two is you can include any local or remote Web or other documents you want on your Documents pull down; NCSA controls what appears on the Help menu. Creating the Documents menu is easy; it uses a plain text file. Let's take a look at the one file that created the pull-down in Figure 23.12 (this is the example file NCSA distributes with the X Mosaic source code):

NCSA Mosaic X Resources
```
http://www.ncsa.uiuc.edu/SDG/Software/Mosaic/Docs/resources.html
```
Unsupported versions of Mosaic
```
http://www.ncsa.uiuc.edu/SDG/Software/Mosaic/Docs/faq-machines.html#contribs
```
Questions regarding font errors
```
http://www.ncsa.uiuc.edu/SDG/Software/Mosaic/Docs/faq-interface.html
--
```
A LaTeX to HTML Translator
```
http://cbl.leeds.ac.uk/nikos/tex2html/doc/latex2html/latex2html.html
```
The Ohio State HTML converters
```
http://www.cis.ohio-state.edu:80/hypertext/about_this_cobweb.html
```
An RTF to HTML converter
```
ftp://ftp.primate.wisc.edu/pub/RTF
```
The Motif FAQ
```
http://www.cis.ohio-state.edu:80/hypertext/faq/usenet/motif-faq/top.html
```
The HTML Widget Docs
```
http://www.ncsa.uiuc.edu/SDG/Software/Mosaic/Docs/htmlwidget.html
```

Comparing the preceding source listing to the pull-down menu shown in Figure 23.20, you can see this file consists of simple pairs of lines. The first line of each pair contains the character string you see on the menu (NCSA Mosaic X Resources, for example). The second line in each pair is easily recognizable as a Web URL. Selecting one of the items from the Documents pull-down immediately opens the corresponding URL. You'll also see the dashed line (only two dashes are needed, beginning immediately on the left), in the Documents menu source file creates a visible separator in the on-screen pull-down menu. In our example Documents menu, you'll see the separator between the third and fourth items. The example source document is just that—an example. You'll want to include your Intranet's local documents in place of those shown. Up to 80 lines may be included in the Documents menu file, including those with dashed line separators. Thus, you can have a total of 40 readily accessible documents listed on a Mosaic Documents menu, if you don't use any separators.

Different Documents Menus for Different Customers

You can even cause different customers to see a different list of documents on their pull-down list, giving each one a custom Documents listing based on their individual needs. To do so, you need to understand a bit more about how the Documents menu source file works with X Mosaic. By default, the Documents menu source is contained in the file /usr/local/lib/mosaic/documents.menu. If this file is present, the extra Documents pull-down appears on the menu bar; if not, there's no menu. To customize Documents menus for different customers on your Intranet, you want to override the default location of the source file, and you can do this in a couple of different ways:

◆ Set the customer's Mosaic X Windows Resource named documentsMenuSpecfile to point to a different filename. See the X Mosaic online *User's Guide,* `http://www.ncsa.uiuc.edu/SDG/Software/Xmosaic/UserGuide/`, for specifics about this and other Mosaic X Resources. (If you're not familiar with the concept of X Resources, see your X Windows, or other system documentation, such as Sun's OpenWindows documentation, CDE manuals, or AnswerBooks, HP-UX's LaserRom, SGI's Insight, or your system's manual pages for more information); or

◆ Set your customers' environment variable `MOSAIC_DOCUMENTS_MENU_SPECFILE` to point to a different Documents menu source file.

These two options for setting the Documents menu give you the ability to create customized Documents menus for different groups of users, or even for individual users, based on their work responsibilities and needs. For example, your help-desk staff might need a different list of quickly accessible documents than human resources or sales personnel.

Immediately Accessible Documents

The key phrase in the previous paragraph is *quickly accessible documents.* While your Web application pages should always have online help for customers, basic ready-reference documents can always be accessible in the customer's Mosaic window from the Documents menu—sort of like a group hotlist. Regardless of how far they may have scrolled down into a document, your customer's Documents menu always remains available, right at the top center of any window, for the customer to grab. The Documents menu is, thus, like the notebook, manual, or other ready reference that customers keep on their desk, always accessible, no matter what else they're doing.

> **Tip:** Use X Mosaic's CCI feature (described in Chapter 21) and the UNIX cron daemon to keep your staff's local disk cache up to date with these ready reference and other frequently accessed documents. Via shell scripts of the sort shown in Chapter 21, you can run customers' copy of X Mosaic via remote control to load and cache your desired documents, all in the middle of the night.

Netscape Frames

In the last couple of sections, you've learned about ways to make and keep ready reference documents immediately accessible to customers using the two versions of NCSA Mosaic. Not to be outdone, Netscape's come up with a different way of accomplishing essentially the same purpose, using new HTML capabilities they call *frames*. Figure 23.22 shows the new home page (`http://home/netscape.com/`) Netscape unveiled in February 1996, right after the official release of Netscape Navigator 2.0.

Figure 23.22. *Netscape 2.0 frames.*

The frames capability had been in beta versions going back several months before that date. This new feature consists of having portions, or panes, of your overall Netscape window, remain fixed, even when you follow hyperlinks within the central pane. Thus, in Figure 23.22, the strip of frames across the bottom of the screen don't change as you access different pages at Netscape's Web site. While this page and many other frames pages on the Web use the new capability primarily to provide navigational bars or banners, you can use them in your Intranet applications to make your ready reference pages available to your Netscape customers at all times. Just as Netscape's done in the two panes in the lower left corner of the screen, you can keep a list of important pages on your Intranet constantly visible—and clickable—regardless of where else in your applications your customer wanders.

> **Note:** Once you leave a frames page and access a page that doesn't have them (whether it's on another Web site or the same one), your frames disappear.

Tip: When you're viewing Web pages with frames, the Netscape toolbar's Back button doesn't act as you're accustomed. Hitting it takes you back to the last *non-frames* page you've visited. To get back your Back capability in a frames document, press your right mouse button (on a Mac, press and hold your only button). A small pop-up menu will appear with options for moving backward and forward within the frames.

Summary

In this book, you've learned about many separate Web and Web-related tools and capabilities and the techniques of using them. This chapter has shown you how to put these disparate pieces together into complete Intranet applications. With a clear understanding of the capabilities of these tools, you can build Intranet applications that use just the right ones, exactly where your customers need them. In this chapter, you've done the following:

◆ Revisited the Khorosware training application you saw in Chapter 21 and looked at it as a complete, self-contained application;

◆ Revisited the sample, but fragmentary, Intranet applications you saw in Chapters 16-22 and considered how they can be turned into finished ones;

◆ Learned some tools and techniques that will ease the work of putting together Intranet applications

In Chapter 24, the last chapter of *Building an Intranet*, you'll again supplement the material you've learned in earlier chapters as you consider how your Intranet can be used to foster and facilitate collaboration and communications among your customers.

VI PART

New Intranet Possibilities

CHAPTER

Web Groupware: Collaboration on Your Intranet

In Chapter 22, you learned about using local USENET newsgroups as a means of group collaboration and discussion on your Intranet. That sample application barely scratched the surface of what we might call *Web groupware*. Along with the much-discussed Java, group collaboration using World Wide Web technology is one of the Web's most exciting possibilities. This is attested to not only by the fact that IBM's Lotus Notes product has been dragged kicking and screaming into Web integration, but also by the emergence of completely new products, built specifically for Web collaboration. After reviewing some simple, and immediately available, means of using your Intranet for group collaboration, this chapter will survey the world of Web groupware and give you some ideas of how you can put it to work on your Intranet.

Chapter Objectives

As with the rest of the chapters in this book, let's begin by laying out some chapter objectives. This will help you get oriented to the material to be presented. (You may want to refer back to this list as you work your way through the chapter.) In this chapter, you'll

- Learn to distinguish broad categories of Web-based collaboration
- Learn about using personal and group home pages on your Intranet as a means of knowledge and information sharing
- Learn about using hyperindexed USENET news and e-mail archives as a means of collaboration
- Learn about free-for-all Web resources that allow customers to post their own URLs or other information for all to see
- Learn about Web-based annotation and conferencing systems
- Learn to use what you learned about Web-based training and presentations in Chapter 21, "Web-Based Training and Presentations," to do group presentations in real time across your Intranet using Web technologies
- Learn about major commercial groupware packages and how they can integrate into your Intranet
- Learn about miscellaneous Web groupware, including workflow management, collaborative writing and art, and other multi-user activities that may be directly or indirectly useful

The Different Means of Collaboration

It may be useful to begin this discussion by broadly categorizing the means of Web-based collaboration. Several may be defined (although in practice, Web services more often than not cross these neat category boundaries), as follows:

- Simple, one-way information sharing, primarily through the posting of information on Web pages, including individual user home pages
- Free-for-all Web resources, in which anyone is free to add comments and/or hyperlinks
- Multi-directional conferencing systems of various kinds, such as USENET newsgroups, e-mail distribution lists, bulletin board systems, and the like
- True groupware applications, such as Lotus Notes and the newly important Collabra Share product, in which the preceding categories may be combined into a single monolithic application

Simple One-Way Collaborative Activities on Your Intranet

Leaving aside fancy groupware computer applications for now, let's remember the most basic means of human collaboration and cooperation is simple, straightforward information sharing. People tell other people what they are doing, what they've learned, and so on. Learning by listening to what other people say about themselves and their activities is one of the most fundamental means by which we are educated and socialized—and by which we grow in our professional lives. Scholars and scientists write books to share information, and information distribution is the reason journalism exists. Simple information sharing can form the collaborative core of your Intranet, and its value should not be overlooked in the glittery world of groupware. Indeed, online information exchange may be your most important tool. Let's therefore take a look at some simple but potentially powerful means of Intranet information sharing, beginning with user home pages.

User Home Pages on Your Intranet

In the introductory chapters of *Building an Intranet*, we emphasized the need for customer input in the design and content of your Intranet. As you'll recall from Chapter 2, "Designing an Intranet," one criticism of the centralized model of Intranet administration is that a bureaucratic process of Web-page approval places obstacles in the way of customers getting their own information out onto your Intranet. Looking at your Intranet from a high-level viewpoint, you've perhaps not focused on how individual users' home pages can contribute significantly to its overall value.

> **Note:** Perhaps at this point you're thinking of some of the personal home pages you've seen on the World Wide Web, full of adolescent bravado, bandwidth-eating images of CD covers, song lyrics purporting to state a philosophy of life, self-indulgent posturing, and hyperlinks pointing to similar drivel, and you probably wonder how such things can be a useful part of your Intranet. They can't. But what a 20-year-old college sophomore thinks appropriate for his university home page and what a working scientist, engineer, or other professional might put on a professional page are two completely different matters, and we're interested in the latter.

Basic HTML markup can be learned in half an hour. Users' Web pages can be served right out of their home directories on UNIX Web servers, so they don't need to learn anything about Web servers to make their pages available. This makes the language an excellent vehicle for information sharing on an organization's Intranet. Figure 24.1 shows a simple, yet effective user home page, that of NCSA staff member Briand Sanderson. This author doesn't know Sanderson (though he's given permission to reproduce his home page), but the page shows, in a no-nonsense fashion, basic information about Sanderson's professional activities and academic background. Substantive content is highlighted by hyperlinks, leading to detailed information on Sanderson's work. As you can see, Briand's projects include the Hierarchical Data Format, about which you learned in Chapter 15, "Scientific, Mathematical, and Technical Applications," and the development of NCSA Mosaic for Microsoft Windows.

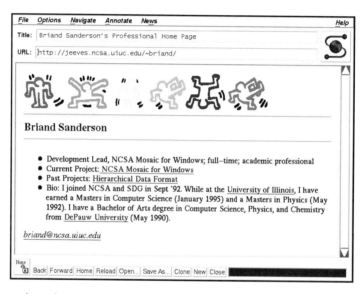

Figure 24.1. *A sample user home page.*

Virtually any computer-literate individual can put together a home page with this sort of information about himself and his work. The HTML document source for the home page shown above is only 20 lines long. We've included it herein because it's a great model, containing just about everything necessary to put together a useful home page.

```
<TITLE>Briand Sanderson's Professional Home Page</TITLE>
<H1><IMG SRC="khbord2.gif"><HR>Briand Sanderson<HR></H1>
<UL><LI>Development Lead, NCSA Mosaic for Windows; full-time; academic
professional
<LI>Current Project:<A HREF="http://www.ncsa.uiuc.edu/SDG/Software/WinMosaic/
HomePage.html">
NCSA Mosaic for Windows</A>
<LI>Past Projects:  <A HREF="http://hdf.ncsa.uiuc.edu:8001/">Hierarchical
Data Format</A>
<LI>Bio:  I joined NCSA and SDG in Sept '92. While at the
<A HREF="http://www.uiuc.edu">University of Illinois</A>, I have
earned a Masters in Computer Science (January 1995) and a Masters in
Physics (May 1992). I have a Bachelor of Arts degree in Computer Science, Physics,
and Chemistry from <A HREF="http://www.depauw.edu">DePauw University</A> (May 1990).
</UL>
<ADDRESS>
<A HREF="mailto:briand@ncsa.uiuc.edu">briand@ncsa.uiuc.edu</A>
</ADDRESS>
```

While you'll want to look at Appendix B, "HTML and CGI Quick Review," for more information on the HyperText Markup Language, you can readily see how simple, yet effective this home page is. There's little fluff, just a single included image and a bulleted list of substantive hyperlinks. Whether they're office support staff or engineers, paraprofessionals or scientists, your customers can easily create home pages of this sort to share their work with others in your company. Fancy graphics don't usually add much to Web Page substance. Here are some possibilities:

◆ Scientists can share the results of their work with colleagues across the company, placing descriptions of their research on their home pages, together with underlying data in a format accessible with a helper application. Word processing documents containing article or book manuscripts can be made available for viewing (see Chapter 10, "Your Word Processor and the Web"), while numerical data can be graphed on the fly, and other data can be seen with other helper applications. (See Chapter 15.)

◆ Engineers and draftsmen can place their CAD drawings on your Intranet for organization-wide viewing/sharing, as outlined in Chapter 15.

◆ Researchers of all kinds can provide links to summaries of their work, or to its details, regardless of its format.

It's hard to overstate the potential value to an organization of this sort of simple information sharing. In a business research environment, for example, the linking of a few important ideas can lead to breakthrough products or services. One researcher, stuck on a project, may find just the thing she needs on some other researcher's home page. Moreover, once the collaborative ball is rolling, customers will add hyperlinks pointing to other customers' home pages on their own pages, making the combined resources of many available to all.

Multi-Directional Collaboration and Information Sharing via USENET News and E-Mail

In Chapter 8, "Adding Services to Your Intranet Adds Value," you were introduced to a wide range of common Internet services that can be integrated into your Intranet. USENET news and e-mail were two of those services. Let's look at them in the context of Intranet collaboration; as you read this section, you may want to flip back to Chapter 8 for reference.

USENET News

You already saw in Chapter 22, "Newsgroups for Group Discussions and Collaboration," how an organization can set up local USENET newsgroups for in-house discussions and collaboration. Such free-for-all, online discussion groups can be invaluable as threaded discussions develop consensus on problem resolution or other matters. (Later in this chapter, you'll learn about several other kinds of Web-based conferencing resources.) You can do the same thing with (expensive) commercial groupware software on your Intranet, but netnews, the original groupware dating back to the 1970s, remains both free and viable today. Figure 24.2 shows a portion of the articles in the newsgroup bionet.immunology in February 1996; note the indentation, showing the discussion threads. You may want to refer back to Chapters 8 and 22 for detailed information on the installation, setup, and use of USENET news in your Intranet. Note in particular the sections on archiving, indexing, and search/retrieval of your netnews articles, subjects that will inevitably become important to you if you implement USENET news collaboration.

Figure 24.2. *USENET news.*

Electronic Mail as a Collaborative Resource

As with USENET news, you're already familiar with the potential collaborative value of e-mail in your Intranet. E-mail distribution lists, run manually or with automated list servers, can be an important adjunct to your Intranet by providing another means of group discussions. And since both Mosaic and Netscape now have e-mail interfaces, it's easy to integrate e-mail into your Intranet. (For details on the use of e-mail lists and list servers, refer to Chapter 8.)

If you expect e-mail to become a major part of your Intranet's collaborative efforts, you'll want to set up a means of retaining and retrieving messages, just as you've done with your USENET news articles. This will enable your customers to go back to mailing list archives and search for old messages that might have current relevance. There are several ways you can archive e-mail messages:

◆ Charge someone with the responsibility of manually saving each and every message on your mailing list(s)

◆ Create a special user account on your system whose only purpose is to receive the mailing list traffic, then configure that account to automatically save all incoming mail in mailbox folders (a good tool for doing this is the filter utility program that comes as part of the popular freeware UNIX e-mail package called elm, available at ftp:// ftp.virginia.edu/pub/elm)

◆ Use an e-mail-to-netnews script that will route all e-mail messages to a local newsgroup for posting as ordinary news articles

In the latter example, you can simply use the USENET news-indexing tools described in Chapter 22 to index everything, since your e-mail traffic and netnews traffic will be merged into a single database. The elm filter program is a useful one that can be set up to read all incoming mail to a user and automatically dispose of it in some way. In this situation, you'd want a filter to automatically save all incoming messages on a mailing list to a file or directory, which can later be indexed.

> **Note:** Despite sharing a common name and software ancestor, the version of elm that comes with the HP-UX operating system on Hewlett-Packard UNIX workstations and the freeware version are vastly different. Dave Taylor's original code has developed in substantially different directions under the separate elm development projects. Most importantly in this context, HP's version doesn't include the filter utility. You can build the freeware elm package under HP-UX with little trouble.

However you manage to save your e-mail list traffic, indexing it for future search and retrieval is your next task. Here you have a couple of choices. First, as you'll recall from Chapter 13, the freeWAIS-sf package has the capability of doing fielded indexing. Because (as you learned in Chapter 7, "MIME and Helper Applications") all Internet e-mail messages have a standard format, consisting of headers and a body, it'll be easy to generate a freeWAIS-sf format file for e-mail messages so you can do fielded indexing. In fact, the freeWAIS-sf FAQ document includes just such a format file. Here it is, in all its simplicity:

```
record-sep: /^From /
layout:
headline: /^From: / /\J/ 20 /^From: ./
headline: /^Subject: / /\J/ 80 /^Subject: ./
region: /^From: /
from SOUNDEX LOCAL TEXT BOTH
end: /$/
region: /^Subject: /
subject stemming TEXT BOTH
end: /$/
```

Once you've done your e-mail traffic indexing, your customers can use the freeWAIS-sf companion package SFgate to do fielded searches on your mailing list database, using the From and Subject fields of messages for search criteria. Figure 24.3 shows a fielded SFgate search form. You'll want to refer back to Chapters 8 and 13 for more information about installing and using the freeWAIS-sf and SFgate packages, both of which are included on the *Building an Intranet* CD-ROM.

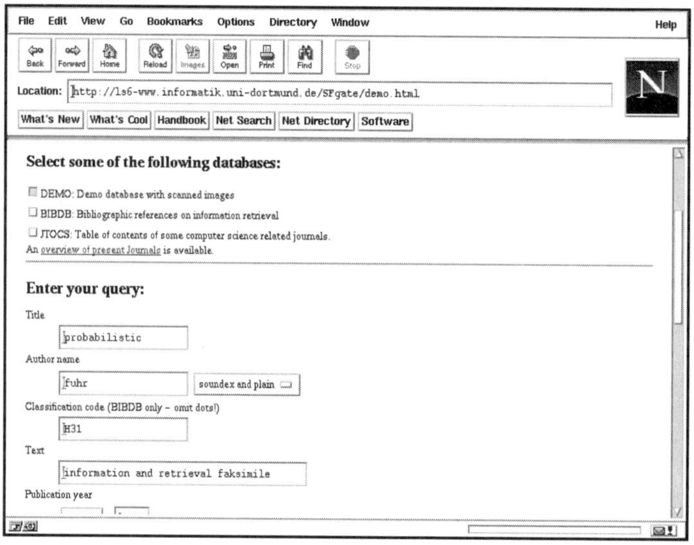

Figure 24.3. *SFgate fielded search form.*

Unless you're already familiar with freeWAIS-sf's fielded-indexing capabilities, you may want try Hypermail instead to index your e-mail list's archives. Also included on the *Building an Intranet* CD-ROM, this package (written by Tom Gruber and Kevin Hughes of Verifone's Enterprise Integration Technologies) converts a standard UNIX mailbox file containing multiple messages into a set of cross-referenced, hyperlinked HTML documents. All the new documents produced by Hypermail contain links to other messages in the archive, so messages in a thread (that is, those which share a Subject line) show up as hyperlinks when you view messages in your Web browser. You can sample a Hypermail archive (which EIT maintains) at `http://www.eit.com/www.lists`, which is an indexed database of e-mail messages from a couple of World Wide Web-related Internet mailing lists.

Figure 24.4 shows a partial listing of the Hypermail Subject database of the www-talk mailing list for early 1996. As you can see, the user interface to Hypermail databases is not a fill-in form, but is, rather, in plain, scrollable HTML, with the individual messages shown as clickable hyperlinks. In fact, it looks a lot like the USENET news article listing in Figure 24.2. (If you scroll all the way to the bottom of the page, however, you'll find a fill-in search form as well for doing keyword searches on the database.) The Hypermail package also indexes and creates hyperlinks based on message authors' e-mail addresses and the creation date of the message, giving you additional search capabilities.

> **Tip:** You can, of course, use both Hypermail and freeWAIS-sf (or any of the other indexing tools described in Chapter 13, such as glimpseindex) for your archived e-mail, giving your Intranet's customers the capabilities of both kinds of searches. Integrate your e-mail indexes with your Harvest information gathering service (see Chapter 13) and you're well on your way to having a truly useful Intranet.

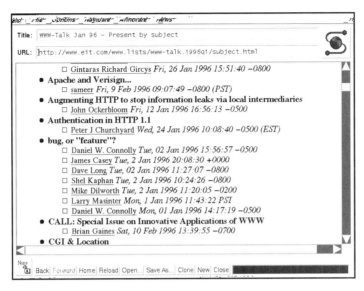

Figure 24.4. *Sample hypermail index.*

Free-for-All Collaboration

The popularity of the World Wide Web, with thousands of new pages coming on line every day, has generated the need for individual users to share new Web resources they've found or created. Since most webmasters are busy people, often having job responsibilities over and above their webmastering, ordinary users need a way to post hyperlinks to useful Web resources in a public place for others to see, without having to rely on a webmaster or other system administrator to do it for them. (This is quite a different thing, of course, from users placing new hyperlinks on their own home pages.) However, it doesn't take much thinking to come up with several significant reservations about implementing such a *free-for-all* Web resource. Leaving questions of appropriate content aside for the moment, the idea of a Web page that allows *just anyone* to add *anything they want* should bring shudders to anyone with the faintest sense of network security. Nonetheless, a large number of such services (and the CGI-bin scripts to implement them) have sprung up across the Web. Even the major Web search services (such as Lycos, Yahoo, eXcite, and the others) allow users to fill in forms to have URLs added to the service. Figure 24.5 shows a sample free-for-all page.

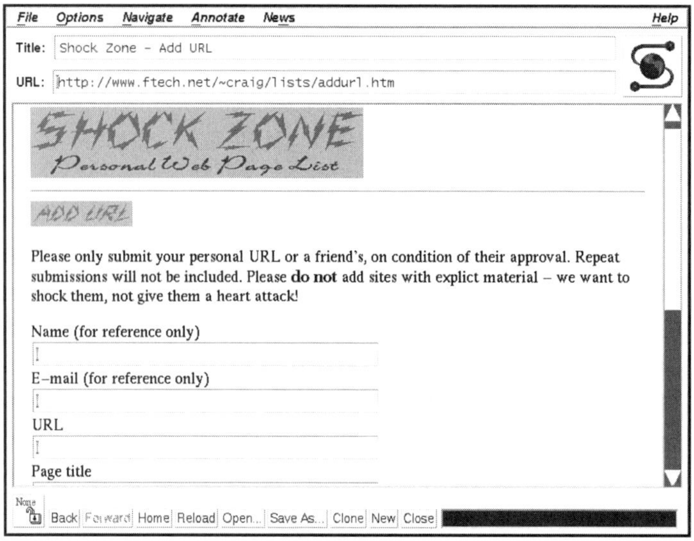

Figure 24.5. *A Web free-for-all page.*

Even taking these security concerns into account, though, there are good reasons for implementing a free-for-all page on your Intranet. Not everyone wants to create a home page of their own, but such people may still find useful resources they want to share with other customers. The ability to add URLs to such a page may, in fact, inspire these people to eventually create Web pages of their own as a contribution to your Intranet; certainly, these people shouldn't be discouraged from doing so. From a collaborative point of view, browsing customers may want to be able to suggest links to those who do have home pages, complementing the information already there. If these folks can add a URL to a free-for-all page easily, they'll do so; if they can't, they may not bother to share their ideas. In any case, giving your customers free rein to add URLs to a free-for-all page can improve overall collaboration and communication on your Intranet. The question of appropriate content on a free-for-all Web page is, in the author's opinion, a management issue, not a technical one, and should be dealt with as such.

You'll find a long list of Web free-for-all links at `http://union.ncsa.uiuc.edu/HyperNews/get/www.collab/free.html`. This and several other such lists mentioned in later sections of this chapter are maintained by Daniel LaLiberte of NCSA, who may be the Web's foremost collaboration guru; he's also the author of the HyperNews software mentioned in Chapter 22.

> **Note:** Web pages that collect *votes* of some kind or take *surveys* are a special kind of free-for-all page, as are pages that allow you to access some service or enter in a raffle after you've filled in a form with personal information such as your e-mail address or phone number. Many of them are thinly disguised marketing ploys, aimed at generating sales leads.

Web-Based Training and Presentations

As indicated frequently in *Building an Intranet*, neat dividing lines between Web technologies may look good in a book's table of contents or back-cover bulleted listing, but the reality is the many technologies you've learned about here often overlap. Chapter 21 provided extensive coverage of using Web technologies for training and business presentations. It goes almost without saying there's heavy crossover between those subjects and the subject of this chapter, Intranet collaboration and communication. You may want to refer back to Chapter 21 at this point, re-reading it in the context of this chapter's emphasis. You'll find tools there you can use as general collaborative mechanisms, as well as tools in this chapter that'll apply to your Intranet training and presentations. Note in particular the sections on remote control of Web browsers and the use of the ScreenCam player as a Web browser helper application.

Web-Based Annotation and Conferencing

Almost as soon as the first World Wide Web server and browsers came into use, people wanted some way to use these new tools for interactive conferencing. Being able to post documents is one thing; being able to respond to them in some way is quite another. Let's look at a couple of the results.

Web Interactive Talk

One of the earliest efforts at developing such a resource was the Ari Luotonen/Tim Berners-Lee project called Web Interactive Talk, or WIT, which was developed when both were at CERN. In WIT, discussions proceed according to traditional dialectic methods, with general topics and subsidiary proposals. The way it works, someone posts a document proposal, then others are invited to post comments about the proposal in the form of agreements or disagreements. WIT is primarily valuable as a pioneering work in the area of annotation and conferencing (and it's no longer being maintained by the authors, both of whom have left CERN), but you may want to look at it anyway. You can do so at `http://www.w3.org/hypertext/WWW/WIT/User/Overview.html`. Early on, NCSA Mosaic for X Windows also had a built-in group annotation feature, which allowed the collection and sharing of group annotations to Web pages. The feature was removed from the package, apparently due to problems with it, and unfortunately it has not yet reappeared.

Stanford's ComMentor

Group annotation has reappeared, however, in a more recent annotation system, Stanford University's ComMentor. The package is described as a generalized form of shared annotations, built on top of the existing Web infrastructure. According to the project's Web page (`http://www-pcd.stanford.edu/COMMENTOR/`), it supports shared comments on Web documents, along with collaborative filtering and seals of approval, guided tours of Web sites, usage indicators, and several other more esoteric features. Figure 24.6 shows an example ComMentor screen with an annotation in a pop-up box; there's an indication of additional annotations as well. As you can see, the package uses a modified NCSA X Mosaic as its browser, with additional/changed pull-down menus at the top and new navigational buttons at the bottom. You can download the binary versions of the ComMentor server and client software for IBM RS/6000's and Sun UNIX systems, as well as the source code for both, at `ftp://www-pcd.stanford.edu/pub/pcd/brio/`.

AEX About Server

The commercial About Server product (`http://www.aex.com/`) provides forums for group discussions, much like USENET news and other commercial groupware packages such as Lotus Notes, but at lower cost and with what AEX calls "tighter integration" with the World Wide Web. About forums are

◆ Accessible from Web browsers

◆ Searchable by keyword, in both document title and text, author name, and date

◆ Immediately accessible, in that your postings and responses to postings are made right away and are not queued for posting/propagation as in USENET news

◆ Subject to quite flexible security, allowing you to restrict access to all or portions of forums by username/password and other means

◆ User configurable, so each user can customize his view of the available forums, much like traditional USENET news kill files

◆ Administered using a Web browser

Demonstration versions of About Server for several UNIX systems are available from the AEX Web site. Figure 24.7 shows a sample About forum. The user interface appears quite self-explanatory, with individual article hyperlinks, and indentations indicating article threads.

Open Meeting on the National Performance Review

A discussion of Web-based conferencing/annotation systems would not be complete without a brief look at the United States government's Open Meeting on the National Performance Review, reachable on the Web at `http://www4.ai.mit.edu/npr/user/root.html`. Here you can read various findings and recommendations of the NPR, which has been led by Vice President Al Gore, a major influence in the federal government's all-out plunge into the Internet/World Wide Web in the past four years. As shown in Figure 24.8, the service is interactive, and you can add your own comments and questions. It's a bit clumsy, though, requiring you to enter your Internet e-mail address in a fill-in form, after which you're e-mailed a comment form to fill in and send back, also via e-mail. Moderators review submitted comments and questions and not all of them are posted.

You'll find links to Daniel LaLiberte's long list of other Web conferencing/collaboration links at `http://union.ncsa.uiuc.edu/HyperNews/get/www/collab/conferencing.html`.

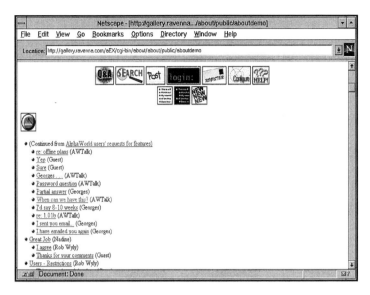

Figure 24.6. *About discussion forum.*

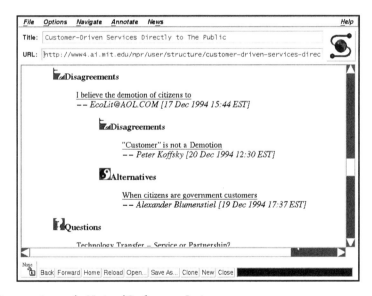

Figure 24.7. *Open meeting on the National Performance Review.*

Full-Blown Groupware for Web Collaboration and Communication

The demarcation lines among free-for-alls, conferencing/annotation systems, and the more full-featured Web groupware are indistinct. Nonetheless, let's take a look at the latter. As with the previous sections, we'll start with some very simple ones (and a seemingly not-very-useful one) and work our way up to the more complex, full-featured groupware packages.

Collaborative Art and Games

There's a large number of collaborative groupware art services on the Web. The basic idea of them is that anyone can add Web resources to the picture, the work of fiction, or some other creative work-in-progress. Image collages, for example, can be augmented by adding the URL to your own image on the Web; the next user will see the modified collage with your image added. Figure 24.9 shows the start-up page for an interactive literary endeavor; it's interesting in that you can enter the novel at any page, using the clickable HTML imagemap. Once you're in, you can browse about the work or contribute to it by inserting your own text. Other collaborative groupware on the Web comes in the form of interactive single- or multi-user games or other creative *add-a-link* pages. The latter are modified free-for-all pages that have a theme of some sort; users are free to add URLs for images, other Web pages, and so on, which somehow advance the interactive fiction, enhance the art object, or otherwise contribute to the evolving entity that is that particular Web page. The beauty, if any, is in the eye of the beholder.

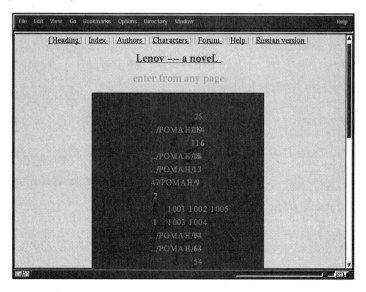

Figure 24.8. *An interactive fiction Web site.*

These examples, and others like them are useful not so much in their substantive content as in the possibilities they represent. After all, the World Wide Web is the world's largest vanity press, where anyone can post anything they want with no evaluation of its actual value (and often no check of the spelling). While you or your customers might not be interested in these particular endeavors, there is a wide range of possibilities for collaborative groupware for your Intranet, and these may be instructive as examples.

Lotus Notes

Almost from the beginning, the World Wide Web has been called, among many other things, "the Lotus Notes Killer." You can see from the examples given so far in this chapter how this quip derived. After all, many of the Web tools about which you've learned in this book replicate some feature(s) of Notes. Whether it's simple information sharing via home pages, conferencing with USENET news using a Web browser, Web-based e-mail, or Web-based annotation systems like ComMentor, artful webmasters can in fact provide their customers with most of Notes' features, at a tiny fraction of that package's not inconsiderable cost. The downside of this replication is the lack of Notes' tight integration; but being able to access the wide range of services Web browsers support may be integration enough for many. Making the choice between home-grown collaborative and commercial groupware on your Intranet can boil down to the choice we mentioned in Chapter 14, "Web Access Commercial Database Applications": Is the 10-15 percent of Notes' capabilities you miss with a homegrown set of applications worth the very substantial cost of the package?

IBM (the new owner of Lotus) thinks not. In early 1996, version 4.0 of Lotus Notes was released, outfitted with a whole raft of new capabilities, including World Wide Web browsing and authoring support, USENET news access, and a lower (though still pricey) per-seat cost. Let's take a look at Notes R4, as it's called; you can be the judge of its potential value on your Intranet.

Notes R4 is, in essence, a document database. Users can search the database according to everyday criteria and can also browse the database. Browsing can be done based on different views of the database, with the ability to step back and see high-level organization or dig in and see the details. Notes R4 databases can be replicated across an organization, over multiple servers, so everyone in a far-flung company, including those on the road, has access to the same consistent information. Integrated e-mail, group document annotations, collaborative functions, workflow-management, and group calendaring/scheduling are also featured. Built-in security controls access to authorized users at all levels of the database. Links in documents can be followed to other, related documents with point-and-click. Users can create altogether new Notes applications using a set of graphical tools. Figure 24.10 shows a sample Notes R4 front end, taken from a ScreenCam demo on the Lotus Web site, http://www.lotus.com/.

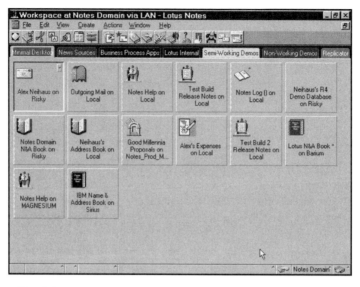

Figure 24.9. *Lotus Notes R4.*

Finally, Notes R4, IBM/Lotus jumped into the World Wide Web with what it hopes will be a "Notes-killer killer." Consider these features:

◆ Notes R4 databases are now browsable using ordinary Web browsers like Mosaic or Netscape, because the httpd protocol is now part of the Notes R4 server package.

◆ IBM plans to add Java support to Notes R4 in the future, while maintaining compatibility with its own scripting language, LotusScript.

◆ Even when viewing Notes R4 databases with a standard Web browser, Notes R4 document links work as Web hyperlinks.

◆ Notes R4 forms and database search facilities are also available when viewing Notes R4 databases from a Web browser.

◆ Web documents can be created and managed using Lotus InterNotes Web Publisher, then browsed with both the InterNotes Web Navigator Web browser and a standard Web browser. As shown in Figure 24.11, if you didn't know it had been created with InterNotes Web Publisher, you'd think AT&T's Web page was just an everyday one.

◆ The InterNotes Web Navigator client supports the httpd protocol, so it can be used to browse non-Notes Web pages as well as Notes R4 databases.

◆ InterNotes News integrates with USENET news services via the Internet-standard NNTP protocol, but it adds support for Notes R4 database replication, hypertext links and embedded objects, giving users enhanced news-browsing capabilities.

◆ The e-mail capability in Notes R4 supports the Internet-standard SMTP and MIME protocols to provide universal e-mail connectivity for Notes users.

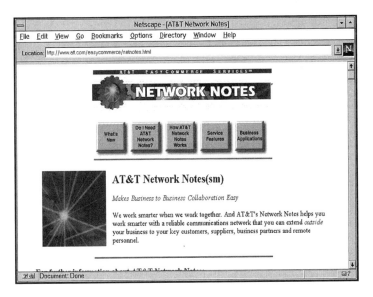

Figure 24.10. *AT&T Network Notes Web site.*

Note: You may want to look at Lotus' Web site, `http://www.lotus.com/`, where you'll find several detailed white papers about Notes R4, as well as some ScreenCam recordings. Interestingly, though, as of late February 1996, none of the available ScreenCam recordings on the site featured any of the Web-related features of Notes R4.

Collabra Share

Among Lotus Notes R4 competitors, Collabra Software, Inc.'s Collabra Share stands out. Despite the fact the package is a direct Notes competitor—providing integrated, collaborative groupware, with document-databases, e-mail, database replication, access to USENET newsgroups, and even a Notes-compatible client for both Windows and the Macintosh—this isn't the real reason the product has become important in the past year. See Figure 24.12 for a sample Collabra Share screenshot, viewed within Netscape Navigator, from the company's Web site, `http://www.collabra.com`.

Note: From the Collabra Web site you can download Lotus ScreenCam recordings of Collabra Share in action as well as evaluation copies of the Collabra Share client software itself.

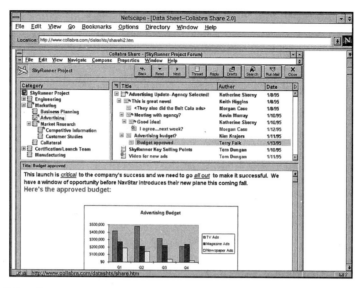

Figure 24.11. *Collabra Share.*

The real reason this upstart company has suddenly become worth mentioning here is not even that Collabra Share won the *PC Magazine* Editor's Choice award in late 1995 (although that must have been a big boost for the product). No, what's really important is Collabra Software, Inc., has been acquired by the Netscape Communications Corporation juggernaut, which has announced plans to integrate all of Collabra Share's features directly into the Netscape Navigator Web browser. Although Netscape says there will continue to be a stand-alone Collabra Share product for Windows and the Macintosh, and a Collabra server, and those products will continue to evolve, the next major release of Netscape Navigator will "incorporate fully the Collabra Share functionality." Given Netscape's dominance of the Web browser market, building on Collabra Share client support will undoubtedly provide a major boost to the Collabra server products, potentially to the detriment of Lotus Notes R4.

The acquisition should also help Netscape itself. As you'll recall, this book has been critical of Netscape's e-mail and USENET news-reading interfaces, primarily because they attempt to cram too much information onscreen at once, rendering most of it virtually unreadable. Collabra Share supports integration with both Microsoft Mail (see Figure 24.13, which is a snapshot of a ScreenCam demo of Collabra Share, viewable from Collabra's Web site) and Lotus cc:Mail. The ability to use these popular and mature e-mail products within the Netscape environment should go a long way to meet these criticisms. It can be hoped Collabra's USENET news reader will be a similarly major step forward from Netscape's unusable netnews interface.

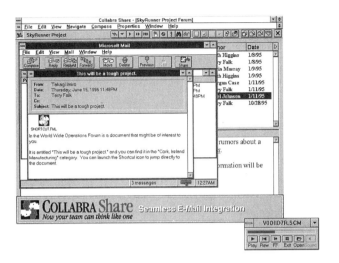

Figure 24.12. *Collabra Share with Microsoft Mail interface.*

Summary

This final chapter of *Building an Intranet* has covered the World Wide Web's collaborative waterfront. Along the way, you've seen Web groupware ranging in capability from simple, one-way information sharing on user home pages to elaborate and expensive integrated groupware application suites. Here's a review of what we've covered in this chapter:

- ◆ A breakdown of broad categories of Web-based collaboration
- ◆ The use of personal and group home pages as a means of knowledge and information sharing
- ◆ The use of hyperindexed USENET news and e-mail archives as a means of collaboration
- ◆ Free-for-all Web resources that allow customers to post their own URLs or other information
- ◆ Web-based annotation and conferencing systems
- ◆ Using what you learned about Web-based training and presentations in Chapter 21 to do group presentations in real time across your Intranet using Web technologies
- ◆ Major commercial groupware packages and how they can integrate into your Intranet
- ◆ Miscellaneous Web groupware, including workflow management, collaborative writing and art, and other multi-user activities that are potentially instructive

Setting Up a Web Server

by Billy Barron

Setting up a new World Wide Web Server generally isn't hard but can be a little challenging at times. This appendix covers some of the general issues such as selecting a platform and a server package and then shows you how to set up a couple of sample Web servers.

Platforms

Web servers exist for just about every computing platform currently in use. The most popular platforms are UNIX, Windows (especially NT), and the Mac. None of these platforms is the perfect Web server platform; each has its pluses and minuses. I will discuss all of these platforms. In addition, I will briefly discuss OS/2, as it is another viable, though less popular choice.

UNIX

The first Web servers were written for UNIX machines. Even today, UNIX may be the most popular Web server platform. UNIX is unique because there are several different popular, high quality, free Web servers, such as NCSA and CERN, available for it that include the source code. The benefits are that not only the server is free but you can make your own custom changes if you are so inclined. Also, you can fix server bugs on your own without waiting for the vendor to come out with a release. On the other end of the spectrum, expensive, well-supported commercial Web servers with advanced features, such as the Netscape Commerce Server and OpenMarket SecureWeb, are available for purchase for UNIX machines.

One additional choice you have to make with UNIX is which UNIX to run on your Web server. Several vendors (for example, SGI and DEC) want you to believe that their UNIX is the best for Web service. Not only that, they may tell you that you need an expensive, state-of-the-art machine to handle all the Web requests you'll get in. However, I have found that every UNIX platform is pretty much equally capable of running a Web server. Also, unless you are going to handle more than 100,000 hits a day, which few sites do, I wouldn't worry too much about what machine you buy. Even an old SPARCstation 2, which is down to PC prices on the used market, can handle tens of thousands of hits every day without a problem. If you don't have much money, but want UNIX, another good alternative is Linux, which can run on most PCs.

> **Note:** Linux is a popular version of UNIX that can run on most Intel-based PCs. Linux is unique because it's a free, well-developed version of UNIX. It's surprisingly stable and full-featured. Unless you run precompiled commercial packages, you'll find just about everything you need or want from a UNIX system with Linux.
>
> Though Linux is free if you download it from the Internet, you may want to pay for one of the many CD-ROM distributions. They are easier and quicker to install. The cost will be more than made up by the time savings.

If your load is going to be several hundred thousand hits a day or greater, I recommend benchmarking machines to decide which has the best price-performance for your needs. SGI has put out a benchmark suite called WebStone that you can use. However, I feel uneasy about that suite because it may (or may not) be optimized for SGI Web servers.

If you aren't sure which UNIX system to buy, I recommend going with the one you are most familiar with or can get the best service for in case it breaks. However, if expense is your major concern, use Linux or find a used UNIX machine.

Windows 3.1

Windows 3.1 is the world's most popular operating environment. This means that many people know how it operates in great detail, which is useful when running a Web server if you are having problems and looking for some help. However, this is its major advantage.

On the negative side, it has many painful limitations as a Web server. First, you have to acquire a TCP/IP (Winsock) package and then find a Web server package. The problem is that some of the Winsock packages have minor bugs that can be exorcised by certain Web servers. This means you can never be sure if a particular Web server will work with your particular Winsock without testing them yourself unless they are made by the same vendor.

Windows 3.1 has very weak multitasking, which has several effects. First, running a Web server while trying to use the machine as a workstation does not generally work well. Second, under high load, especially with CGI scripts, the server will perform poorly. Finally, the "8.3" filenames are limiting for making meaningful directory names and filenames. With bad directory names and filenames, your URLs may be difficult for people to remember because they are cryptic.

My advice is to avoid Windows 3.1 as a Web server platform and instead to use Windows 95, Windows NT, or OS/2 if you want a Windows type environment. If you must use Windows 3.1, though, it can work adequately for a low-volume Web server.

OS/2

From IBM, OS/2 is another Windows-like operating system that can run a Web server. In a lot of ways, OS/2 is similar to Windows NT from a feature standpoint. From a technical standpoint, OS/2 is a fine choice for a Web server. However, its future is somewhat cloudy because IBM seems to be in some ways supporting OS/2 fully and in other ways seems to be backing away from it.

Windows 95

First of all, it's important to separate Microsoft's hype for and the reality of this product. Yes, long file names are allowed in Windows 95. However, if you go into a DOS window, you will see the good old "8.3" filenames of yesteryear. Windows 95 has a hidden translation table to convert the "8.3" names into what you see when you are using a graphical interface. Yes, Windows 95 has better multitasking than Windows 3.1, but that is only true if you use only 32-bit applications. When using any 16-bit applications, the multitasking works similarly to the way it did under Windows 3.1.

The good news is that the networking support in Windows 95 is far superior to Windows 3.1, and it is built-in. Also, Windows 95 is a much more robust system than 3.1 and crashes less often. Windows 95 is a fairly decent operating system to run a Web server on. One of its best attributes is that it is relatively inexpensive. However, it works best if you use it as either a dedicated Web server or you upgrade to all 32-bit applications.

Windows NT

NT is the next step up from Windows 95. It is even more robust, has better multitasking, and, of course, is much more expensive. If money is no object and you want a Windows-based Web server, NT is the OS of choice.

However, there are two versions of NT. There is a workstation version and a server version. For Web serving, the major difference is really the price (NT Workstation is much cheaper). Most NT Web servers will run on either one. One important exception to this rule will be the Microsoft Gibraltar Web server. Supposedly, when it is released, it will be free, but require NT server. NT makes on excellent Web server platform.

> **Note:** If you are using NT Workstation, you should select the Foreground & Background Applications Equally Responsive option in the Tasking menu under the Control Panel. If you do not and use the NT machine as a workstation as well as a Web server, your Web server won't get many CPU resources and will perform very poorly.

Macintosh

The Macintosh is a unique platform for a Web server, as it is the only one without a command line. Web servers for the Mac are generally easy to install, though. The Mac does make an adequate Web server. However, I don't know any high-volume Web sites that use Macs as their platform. Though there has been much talk recently about Apple's instability, they should be around for a few more years at least. If you are a Mac person and will be running a low-volume web site, by all means, go ahead and use your Mac.

Deciding

After looking at all the platforms, you now have to decide which one to use. My general advice is to use UNIX or Windows NT for the Web server if at all possible. These are the premier Web server platforms. However, there are times to go with the other platforms, especially if you already own one and know how to use it well.

Web Server Software

Unfortunately, there are many more Web servers in existence than I can possibly discuss here. I have picked out a few that are the most popular to talk about.

NCSA HTTPD

```
URL: http://hoohoo.ncsa.uiuc.edu/
Platforms: UNIX
```

NCSA is probably the most popular Web server package in the world. It is free, has good performance, and a nice set of features. Its major omission is the lack of support for Web encryption protocols.

Apache

URL: http://www.apache.org/
Platforms: UNIX

Apache is a popular derivative of the NCSA server. One of the major differences is that there are patches available to support SSL (Secure Socket Layer).

Netscape Communications Server

URL: http://home.netscape.com/comprod/netscape_commun.html
Platforms: UNIX, Windows NT

This is a feature-laden, high-performance server. It is expensive, however.

Netscape Commerce Server

URL: http://home.netscape.com/comprod/netscape_commerce.html
Platforms: UNIX, Windows NT

This product is the same as the Netscape Communications Server except that it supports SSL and costs more.

EMWAC HTTPS

URL: http://emwac.ed.ac.uk/html/internet_toolchest/https/contents.htm
Platforms: Windows NT

A good and free Web server. However, its security features are minimal.

Purveyor

URL: http://www.process.com/prodinfo/purvdata.htm
Platforms: Windows NT, Windows 95

A very good, full-featured commercial Web server.

WebSite

URL: http://gnn.com/gnn/bus/ora/news/c.website.html
Platforms: Windows NT, Windows 95

A very powerful, popular, but non-intuitive Web server. It is a commercial product.

MacHTTP

URL: http://www.starnine.com/machttp/machttpsoft.html
Platforms: Macintosh

A commercial but somewhat low-end Web server.

OpenMarket WebServer

URL: `http://www.openmarket.com/products/webserver.html`
Platforms: Unix

OpenMarket is a high-performance and feature-rich server including encryption features. It is commercial and appears to compare fairly well with Netscape Communications Server.

OpenMarket SecureWeb

URL: `http://www.openmarket.com/products/secureweb.html`
Platforms: Unix

The same as the OpenMarket WebServer but supports SSL and S-HTTP (Secure HTTP). Also, it is more expensive.

CERN

URL: `http://www.w3.org/pub/WWW/Daemon`
Platforms: UNIX

This is the original Web server. It is free and has some interesting features. However, it is a little unusual in the way it does certain things.

HTTPD for Windows

URL: `http://city.net/win-httpd/`
Platforms: Windows 3.1

This server is free for personal and nonprofit use. Others must pay to use it.

Actually Setting Up the Server

In the descriptions for setting up the various Web servers, I made many simplifying assumptions. First, I picked out just a few of the most popular servers. Second, I kept the steps to an absolute minimum to get the servers up. (The advanced features of these Web servers are outside of the scope of this appendix.)

Also, I picked two free servers to use as installation examples. Each server runs on one of the two platforms that I recommended earlier: UNIX (NCSA HTTPD) and Windows NT (EMWAC HTTPS).

NCSA HTTPD

These instructions were written for version 1.5 of the NCSA server, but other versions should be similar. To keep matters as simple as possible in this section, I only discuss the precompiled binary release of NCSA httpd and not the source release.

Step 1: Download the software.

Pick the correct release for your operating system from `ftp://ftp.ncsa.uiuc.edu/web/httpd/ncsa_httpd/current/` and download it. Be sure to download it into the directory you wish to install your Web server in.

Step 2: Uncompress the software.

The files come in a compressed tar (tape archive) file and must be extracted before you can use them. Use the following commands to extract them:

```
uncompress <filename>.tar.Z
tar xvf <filename>.tar
```

Step 3: Copy the configuration files.

Go into the configuration directory (`conf`). You will find files called `access.conf-dist`, `httpd.conf-dist`, and `srm.conf-dist` there. Issue the following commands to copy the distribution configuration files to the filenames that are actually used by the server:

```
cp access.conf-dist access.conf
cp httpd.conf-dist httpd.conf
cp srm.conf-dist srm.conf
```

Step 4: Configure the main HTTPD configuration file.

Edit the `httpd.conf` file. What follows is the simplest possible configuration. If a particular configuration parameter is not mentioned here but you see it in the configuration file, leave it at the default setting.

ServerType—This variable can be set to either `inetd` or `standalone`. `inetd` starts a new server for every request that comes in and can be quite a performance drain. Most of the world uses `standalone`, which reuses the same server(s) over and over again. This is what I strongly recommend. If you prefer to use `inetd`, the rest of this configuration will differ somewhat from what I describe.

Port—This is the TCP port number that the server listens on. Usually, this is set to 80. Leave it at 80 unless you have a good reason to change it. Changing it will make your URL look worse.

User—This defines which `userid` on the sytem httpd runs as. Never set this to `root` or any regular user can log in. Good choices, for security reasons, are to set it to `nobody` or to create a password entry for a dummy user just for the Web server and use that.

Group—This defines which UNIX group httpd runs as. Using the default `#-1`, which is a group with little access to the system, is a good choice. Otherwise, I recommend you create a new UNIX group just for the Web server.

ServerAdmin—This should be followed by the e-mail contact address for someone who takes care of your Web server.

ServerRoot—This specifies the root directory of httpd where the executable, configuration, and log files live. This probably should be the directory you unpacked the Web server into in most cases.

ServerName—This is not needed if your machine's actual hostname is the same as the Internet hostname of the Web server. However, many of us have a hostname for a machine and then use a DNS alias such as www.utdallas.edu for the Web server. If you do this, follow the ServerName directive by the alias name.

StartServers—This is used to determine how many child Web servers will be started by httpd when it first comes up. This number should be set based on how much Web traffic you think you will have. On a small Web server, you may want to set it as low as 1. On an average setup, 5 may be a good number. On high volume, just set it anywhere you want. Probably 20 or so is a practical upper limit, though.

MaxServers—This is used by httpd to determine the maximum number of child Web servers that can possibly run. If more requests come in at once than the number of StartServers, httpd will determine if more servers can be started to help handle the load. My advice is to set this to as high a number as you can without causing RAM problems on your system. A number between 10 and 20 is fairly common on average-sized Web sites.

Step 5: Configure the resource configuration file.

To configure the resource configuration file, edit the file srm.conf. Only two variables need to be changed for a minimal configuration.

DocumentRoot—This parameter sets the directory in which the files you are serving up with your Web server will be stored.

ScriptAlias—This is used to determine where CGI scripts can be stored on the Web server. It takes two parameters. The first is the virtual pathname in which the CGI scripts will appear in URLs. The second is the real path of the CGI scripts on the system. For example, if you put ScriptAlias /cgi-bin/ /usr/httpd/cgi-bin/ and you have a CGI script called finger.pl, you would place it on the system as /usr/httpd/cgi-bin/finger.pl and then reference it via a URL like http://www.utdallas.edu/cgi-bin/finger.pl.

Step 6: Configure the access configuration file.

To set up the correct access control, edit the file access.conf. In this part, we are going to branch off from our simplest Web server possible configuration so that you can set up a reasonably secure Web server. The default configuration offers the least security.

Directory—This is a block that starts with <DIRECTORY dirname> and ends with </DIRECTORY>. In the middle of these tags, you can put some directive that applies to that directory and all its subdirectories. In our simple Web server, specify the directory to be the same as the DocumentRoot you specified in the resources configuration.

One of the directives that goes inside the directory block is Options. Options can be followed by a set of server features that are enabled for that directory. The default is Options All, which enables all features. This setup is fine if you fully trust all the people who are writing Web documents on your servers. If you can't, you'll want to change the setup. The list of options is

None	No options are allowed
All	All options are allowed
ExecCGI	Allow CGI scripts
FollowSymLinks	Allow symbolic links
Includes	Allow server side includes
IncludesNoExec	Allow server side includes but turn off the exec feature
Indexes	Allow the server to send server-generated indexes for directories
SymLinksIfOwnerMatch	Allow symbolic links if the link and the real file have the same owner

If you are unsure of what setup to use, I would recommend starting with `Options IncludesNoExec SymLinksIfOwnerMatch` until you know your needs better. The setup I've listed is a good balance between server security and functionality.

Another important directive within the directory block is `AllowOverride`. The default is `AllowOverride All`, which is fine if you can trust all the users who can post documents to your Web server; with this setup, they can override your global settings. I recommend setting this to `AllowOverride None` until you fully understand the implications of allowing users to override settings.

Let's tie together the directory block now. Assume that the `DocumentRoot` is `/usr/local/webdocs` and you use the settings I recommended. The directory block will look like

```
<DIRECTORY /usr/local/webdocs>
Options IncludesNoExec SymLinksIfOwnerMatch
AllowOverride None
</DIRECTORY>
```

Step 7: Start the server.

Your Web server program is called `httpd` and it should reside in your ServerRoot directory. Suppose that your ServerRoot is `/usr/httpd`. Then the program would be `/usr/httpd/httpd`. To start the Web server, you must use the `-d` flag followed by the server root directory. In this example, you would type `/usr/httpd/httpd -d /usr/httpd` to start the Web server.

Step 8: Add HTTPD to system startup.

Unfortunately, this step is very system dependent. You will need to read your system's documentation to make sure how this is done for your particular system. I will give a brief overview for a couple of popular systems, but you will still need to look at the documentation and understand your particular setup.

On most BSD-based UNIX systems, you will need to add a line to the file `/etc/rc.local` that reads something like `intr /usr/httpd/httpd -d /usr/httpd`. Normally, it will go somewhere near the end of the file, but it depends on your system.

On many System V-based UNIX systems, you will need to create a file called `/etc/init.d/httpd`. In that file, you will need to create start and stop routines for your Web server. Look at other files in the /etc/init.d directory for some examples of how to do it. Then you need to symbolically link this file to a file in the /etc/rc2.d directory called something like S95httpd, which will be called to start the Web server when the system boots. Also, you will need to link the file to a file called something like K95httpd in the /etc/rc0.d directory, which will be used to shut down the Web server when the system shuts down.

Step 9: Test the server.

At this point, you should test the server to make sure it works correctly. Create an HTML file in the DocumentRoot named index.html. Then point your Web browser at your Web server and see whether you can view the HTML file. If you can, congratulations! Your Web server works. If you can't, something is wrong with the setup and you will need to debug it. Please note that this just tests very basic funtionality and does not mean that every part of the Web server works correctly.

EMWAC HTTPS for Windows NT

As I mentioned previously, HTTPS is a popular, free Web server for Windows NT. One of its best features is that it is easy to install. As I did in my previous example, I'll keep the installation instructions down to the minimum necessary to get the server going.

Step 1: Acquire HTTPS.

Go to http://emwac.ed.ac.uk/html/internet_toolchest/https/software.htm. On that page, select the version of the software for your CPU architecture and download it.

Step 2: Uncompress the software.

The file you downloaded is a ZIP file. You need some kind of ZIP decompression program, such as WinZip or PKUNZIP to decompress the files. Get such a utility and then decompress the ZIP file you downloaded.

Step 3: Move some files.

You will need to move the files HTTPS.EXE, HTTPS.CPL, and HTTPS.HLP to the \WINNT\SYSTEM32 directory.

Step 4: Check TCP/IP setup.

Type https -ipaddress. If it reports the wrong hostname or IP Address for your machine, you need to fix your TCP/IP setup before continuing.

Step 5: Install HTTPS.

Type https -install to register HTTPS with the Event Logger and the Service Manager. To verify that the installation worked, start the Services item in the Control Panel and see if the HTTP Server is listed.

Step 6: Configure HTTPS.

Start HTTPS from the Control Panel. A dialog screen appears. In the Data Directory field, enter the directory where the files your Web server will be serving up are. Leave all other options alone for a simple setup. Click OK when you're done.

Step 7: Set up an account and start the server.

Create a new account with General User privileges. Do not add it to the Administrators group. This account is the one that HTTPS will run under. Then go back to the Services menu of the Control Panel. Highlight HTTP Server and click Startup. A dialog screen will appear, enter the account you just created in the `his Account` field. Enter the account's password in the Password field. Then click OK.

Step 8: Test server.

Create an HTML file in the Data Directory named `default.htm` you specified in Step 6. Point a Web browser at your server. If you can see the HTML file, your server works.

HTML & CGI Quick Reference

by Lay Wah Ooi & Billy Barron

HTML

This reference guide marks the origin of all tags. Most, but not all, browsers fully implement the HTML 2.0 tags correctly, which are marked in this guide as *HTML 2.0*. If a tag is marked as *HTML 3.0*, it's in the 3.0 release of HTML. However, the HTML 3.0 release isn't finalized and is subject to change. We used the latest draft available, which is dated March 28, 1995. Apparently, this single draft will eventually be a series of separate documents that will as a whole compromise the HTML 3.0 specification.

Netscape HTML Extensions means that the tag was invented by Netscape. Netscape Navigator may or may not be the only browser that supports these particular tags. *Sun* means that the tag was invented by Sun Microsystems for use with Java. Currently, HotJava and Netscape Navigator are the only browsers that support them. Netscape has created its own JavaScript specific tags that currently can be used only by Netscape Navigator. More browsers probably will be available before the end of 1996. *Internet Explorer* means that Microsoft invented this tag and it's currently supported only by Microsoft's Internet Explorer.

Also, this is a quick reference guide, so only commonly used tags and attributes will be listed. We have also added a few recently created tags that we expect will be popular in the future.

For more information on other HTML tags, see the following list:

Client-Side Image Map Draft	`http://ds.internic.net/internet-drafts/` `draft-seidman-clientsideimagemap-02.txt`
HTML 2.0	`http://www.w3.org/pub/WWW/MarkUp/html-spec/`
HTML 3.0 Draft	`http://www.w3.org/pub/WWW/MarkUp/html3/` `CoverPage.html`
Internet Explorer Extensions	`http://www.microsoft.com/windows/ie/` `ie20html.htm`
Netscape Extensions to HTML 2.0	`http://home.netscape.com/assist/net_sites/` `html_extensions.html`
Netscape Extensions to HTML 3.0	`http://home.netscape.com/assist/net_sites/` `html_extensions_3.html`
Netscape Frames Extensions	`http://home.netscape.com/assist/net_sites/` `frames.html`

Netscape JavaScript Extensions

`http://home.netscape.com/eng/mozilla/ Gold/handbook/javascript/`

Special Characters

The following are the commonly used special characters The full list can be found at `http://www.w3.org/hypertext/WWW/MarkUp/html-spec/html-spec_13.html`.

&	`&amp`
<	`&lt`
>	`&gt`
"	`&quot`

Structure

These tags define the structure of an HTML document. Although most browsers don't require the use of these tags, they're recommended for ensuring that HTML documents are always parsed correctly.

`<html>..</html>`

Purpose: Contains the entire HTML document.

Version: HTML 2.0.

Additional Details: These tags are used at the beginning and the end of the HTML codes in a particular page.

`<head>..</head>`

Purpose: Contains other tags that describe the document in general.

Version: HTML 2.0.

Details: These tags should always come before `<BODY>` and `<FRAMESET>` tags.

`<title>..</title>`

Purpose: The title of the document goes within the tags.

Version: HTML 2.0.

Details: This is usually displayed in the title bar of the Web browser. However, a few browsers don't display this tag at all. This tag is highly recommended for all HTML documents and required according to the HTML 2.0 specification, though most browsers don't enforce this requirement.

`<base>`

Purpose: References the absolute URL of the document itself, goes within the `<head>..</head>` tags.

Version: HTML 2.0, `TARGET` is a Netscape Frame Extension.

Attributes:

`HREF="URL"`	Specifies the absolute URL of the document itself.
`TARGET="window_name"`	Specifies the frame to which links in this document will be targeted.

Details: It's useful when you view the document with a `file://` URL because the `<base>` tag will reference the document to the correct absolute URL of the document.

`<body>..</body>`

Purpose: Contains the actual displayable part of the HTML document.

Version: HTML 3.0, `BACKGROUND` attribute is HTML 3.0, `ALINK`, `BGCOLOR`, `LINK`, `TEXT`, and `VLINK` are Netscape HTML 3.0 Extensions; `BGPROPERTIES` is an Internet Explorer Extension.

Attributes:

`ALINK="#rrggbb"`	Specifies the color of an active link.
`BACKGROUND="URL"`	Specifies a background image.
`BGCOLOR="#rrggbb"`	Specifies the background color if there is no background image.
`BGPROPERTIES=FIXED`	Specifies the properties related to the background. `FIXED` is the only one currently available, which means that the background shouldn't be scrolled.
`LINK="#rrggbb"`	Specifies the color of a link.

| TEXT="#rrggbb" | Specifies the color of the text. |
| VLINK="#rrggbb" | Specifies the color of a link that has been previously visited by the user. |

Details: It should come after the </HEAD> tag. It should never be used in the same document as a <FRAMESET> tag. "#rrggbb" is an RGB (Red-Green-Blue) value in Hex.

Style

These are logical style tags. It is recommended that these are used instead of the hard formatting tags in the next section.

<A>..</A>

Purpose: Specifies an anchor.

Version: HTML 2.0, TARGET attribute is a Netscape Frame Extension.

Attributes:

HREF="URL"	Specifies a link to another document. The other document is at the URL location.
NAME="ANCHOR-NAME"	Creates an anchor within this document so that a URL exists that can go to this exact location in the document.
TARGET="window_name"	Specifies which frame in a frameset will load the new URL.

Details: Other attributes exist but are very infrequently used. Between the opening and closing tags, text that appears on the screen and describes the anchor goes there. In the case of the HREF attribute, this text is then highlighted as a link. If two or more shapes overlap, the one with a center closest to the point clicked will be selected. Valid shape specifications are listed in the following table.

default	Specifies the default link that is used when a spot on an image doesn't have a shape defined.
circle x, y, r	A circle with center at x, y, with radius r.
polygon x1, y1, x2, y2, ...	A polygon with sets of x,y coordinates that are the vertices of the polygon.
rect x, y, w, h	A rectangle with an upper-left corner at x,y with width w and height h.

<address>..</address>

Purpose: Contains any kind of address.

Version: HTML 2.0.

Details: It is typically displayed in italics and may be indented also.

`<blockquote>..</blockquote>` and `<bq>..</bq>`

Purpose: Contains a block of text quoted from another source.

Version: HTML 2.0, `<bq>` is HTML 3.0.

Details: Typically displayed in an italic font and/or with larger right and left margins. Both `<blockquote>` and `<bq>` are valid under HTML 3.0. However, use of the first is recommended because more browsers should know about it since it is in HTML 2.0.

`<br>`

Purpose: Specifies a line break.

Version: HTML 2.0.

Details: There is no closing tag.

`<cite>..</cite>`

Purpose: Contains a citation.

Version: HTML 2.0.

Details: Typically displayed by an italic font, `<cite>` is usually for short citations. Use `<blockquote>` for long citations.

`<code>..</code>`

Purpose: Contains a segment of a computer program (code).

Version: HTML 2.0.

Details: Typically displayed in a monospaced font such as Courier.

`<em>..</em>`

Purpose: Contains words that need to be emphasized.

Version: HTML 2.0.

Details: Typically displayed as italics.

`<fn>..</fn>`

Purpose: Contains a footnote.

Version: HTML 3.0

Attribute:

`ID="identifier"` Places an anchor associated with the footnote so that you can link to it.

Details: The HTML 3.0 specification recommends that these be displayed as pop-up notes whenever possible.

`<hr>`

Purpose: Specifies a horizontal line (rule) goes at this location.

Version: HTML 2.0, ALIGN, NOSHADE, SIZE, and WIDTH are Netscape HTML 2.0 extensions attributes; SRC is a HTML 3.0 attribute.

Attributes:

ALIGN=LEFT ¦ RIGHT ¦ CENTER	Specifies the alignment of the line if the WIDTH attribute is used.
NOSHADE	Make a solid colored line and don't do fancy shading.
SIZE=n	Specifies the thickness of the line.
SRC="URL"	Specifies the URL of an image to be used as the rule.
WIDTH=n ¦ n%	Specifies the length of the line in pixels or a percentage of the screen width.

Details: There is no closing tag.

`<kdb>..</kdb>`

Purpose: Contains text typed by a user from a keyboard.

Version: HTML 2.0.

Details: Usually displayed in a monospaced font such as Courier. Used primarily in computer user manuals.

`<marquee>..</marquee>`

Purpose: Contains a marquee.

Version: Internet Explorer Extensions.

Attributes:

ALIGN= BOTTOM ¦ MIDDLE ¦ TOP	Specifies the alignment of the text around the marquee.
BEHAVIOR=ALTERNATIVE ¦ SCROLL ¦ SLIDE	Specifies how the marquee will move. SCROLL will scroll the text repeatedly across the screen like a stock ticker. SLIDE will slide the text in one side until it reaches the other side and then it stops. ALTERNATIVE causes the text to bounce back-and-forth.
DIRECTION=LEFT ¦ RIGHT	Specifies which side of the screen the marquee enters from.

HEIGHT=n ¦ n%	Specifies the marquee height in either pixels or percent of the screen height.
HSPACE=n	Specifies a horizontal margin in pixels.
LOOP=n ¦ INFINITE	Specifies the number of loops the marquee goes through.
SCROLLAMOUNT=n	Specifies how many pixels the marquee moves per redraw.
SCROLLDELAY=n	Specifies how many milliseconds between redraws.
WIDTH=n ¦ n%	Specifies the marquee width in either pixels or percent of the screen width.
VSPACE=n	Specifies the virtual margin in pixels.

Details: To do this feature, instead of Java-aware browsers, use `tickertape.java` or `ticker.java`.

`<note>..</note>`

Purpose: Contains an important note for the reader.

Version: HTML 3.0.

Attributes:

CLASS=CAUTION ¦ NOTE ¦ WARNING	Specifies the classification of the note.
SRC="URL"	Specifies an image to use along with the note.

Details: Without a CLASS attribute, the HTML 3.0 document recommends indenting the warning.

`<p>..</p>`

Purpose: Contains a paragraph.

Version: HTML 2.0, attributes are HTML 3.0.

Attributes:

ALIGN= CENTER ¦ JUSTIFY ¦ LEFT ¦ RIGHT	Specifies the alignment of the paragraph.
NOWRAP	Specifies that the paragraph should be automatically word wrapped. Line breaks should occur only at ` ` tags.

Details: Under HTML 1.0, the `</p>` wasn't required. We strongly recommended that you use the closing tag.

`<pre>..</pre>`

Purpose: Contains preformatted text.

Version: HTML 2.0.

Details: Contains text that shouldn't be reformatted automatically by the browser. The text is displayed in a monospaced font, usually Courier, by browsers.

`<q>..</q>`

Purpose: Contains a short quote.

Version: HTML 3.0.

Details: Long quotes should use `<blockquote>`.

`<samp>..</samp>`

Purpose: Contains sample characters.

Version: HTML 2.0.

Details: Usually displayed in a monospaced font such as Courier.

`<strong>..</strong>`

Purpose: Contains text that should be strongly emphasized.

Version: HTML 2.0.

Details: Usually displayed in bold.

`<sub>..</sub>`

Purpose: Contains a subscript.

Version: HTML 3.0.

`<sup>..</sup>`

Purpose: Contains a superscript.

Version: HTML 3.0.

`<var>..</var>`

Purpose: Contains a variable.

Version: HTML 2.0.

Details: Usually displayed in italics.

Formatting

HTML purists recommend trying to use the style tags described previously and to avoid these tags whenever possible because they specify a fixed layout. The problem with this is that some browsers may not be able to display these. For example, the italics tag mentioned doesn't work with Lynx.

`<b>..</b>`

Purpose: Contains bold text.

Version: HTML 2.0.

Details: If bold is unavailable, the browser may select another representation.

`<big>..</big>`

Purpose: Contains text that should be displayed with a big font.

Version: HTML 3.0.

Details: Netscape's `<font>` tag can accomplish this, but this appears to be the standard.

`<blink>..</blink>`

Purpose: Makes text blink.

Version: Netscape HTML 2.0 Extensions (undocumented).

Details: This is possibly the world's most hated tag because it is irritating to many users. Its use isn't recommended.

`<center>..</center>`

Purposes: Contains items that need centering.

Version: Netscape HTML 2.0 Extensions.

Details: This is a much hated tag by much of the HTML community that recommends using the `ALIGN=center` attribute on other tags instead.

`<font>`

Purpose: Changes the font size.

Version: Netscape HTML 2.0 Extensions.

Attributes:

> `SIZE=n`   Specifies the font size. This can also accept a relative font size change with `-n` or `+n`.

Details: Font sizes range from 1 to 7. The default is 3.

`<i>..</i>`

Purpose: Contains italicized text.

Version: HTML 2.0.

Details: If italics are unavailable, the browser may select another representation.

`<nobr>..</nobr>`

Purpose: Contains text that must be on the same line.

Version: Netscape HTML 2.0 Extensions.

Details: To be used sparingly but can be helpful at times.

`<small>..</small>`

Purpose: Contains text that should be displayed with a small font.

Version: HTML 3.0.

Details: Netscape's `<font>` tag can accomplish this but this appears to be the standard.

`<tt>..</tt>`

Purpose: Contains teletype (monospaced) text.

Version: HTML 2.0.

Details: If a monspaced font is unavailable, the browser may select another representation.

`<wbr>`

Purpose: Specifies where a word break can go.

Version: Netscape HTML 2.0 Extensions.

Details: Only for use within a `<NOBR>` element. It tells the browser where it can break if it needs to.

Headings

HTML has six different sizes of headings available. Some people recommend using them progressively in your document. However, most HTML documents use them randomly without following a pattern.

`<h1>..</h1>,<h2>..</h2>,<h3>..</h3>,<h4>..</h4>,<h5>..</h5>,<h6>..</h6>`

Purpose: Contains headings within the text.

Version: HTML 2.0.

Details: `<h1>` is the largest size heading. They get progressively smaller with `<h6>` being the smallest.

Lists

HTML supports quite a bit of flexibility in list types. They can handle anything from a simple numbered list to building an entire dictionary.

`<dl>..</dl>`

Purpose: Contains a definition list.

Version: HTML 2.0.

Details: A definition list contains terms as specified by the <DT> tag and definitions by the <DD> tag.

`<dd>`

Purpose: Gives a definition.

Version: HTML 2.0.

Details: Usually follows a <DT> tag and a term. <DD> has no closing tag.

`<dt>`

Purpose: Identifies a definition term.

Version: HTML 2.0.

Details: Usually followed by a term and then a <DD> tag with a definition of that term. There is no closing tag.

`<lh>..</lh>`

Purpose: Specifies a list header.

Version: HTML 3.0.

Details: This is placed after a <ul> or <dl> tag and before the <li> tag.

`<li>`

Purpose: Specifies the start of a list item.

Version: HTML 2.0, TYPE and VALUE are Netscape HTML 2.0 Extensions attributes, SKIP and SRC are HTML 3.0 attributes.

Attributes:

SKIP=n	In an ordered list, specifies that n sequence numbers be skipped in the list.
uSRC="URL"	Specifies an image to use as a bullet for this item.
TYPE=xxx	Specifies a change of type in the list type. xxx can be any of the choices from the TYPE attributes of <ol> and <ul>.

VALUE=n	Specifies the start element number of the list. For example, to start with 4 instead of 1. For ordered lists only.

Details: `<LI>` has no closing tag.

`<ol>..</ol>`

Purpose: Contains an ordered list.

Version: HTML 2.0, START and TYPE are Netscape HTML 2.0 Extension Attributes, CONTINUE and SEQNUM in HTML 3.0

Attributes:

CONTINUE	Specifies that sequence numbers should continue where the last ordered list ended.
SEQNUM=n	Specifies the starting sequence number of the list. For example, to start with 4 instead of 1.
START=n	Specifies the starting sequence number of the list.
TYPE=A ¦ a ¦ I ¦ i ¦ 1	Specifies the type of enumerators used. 1 is the default, which is Numbers. A is capital letters. a is lowercase letters. I is large roman numerals. i is small roman numerals.

Details: An ordered list is displayed as a numbered list by default. `<LI>` tags are used to specify where list items start.

`<ul>..</ul>`

Purpose: Contains an unordered list.

Version: HTML 2.0, The TYPE attribute is a Netscape HTML 2.0 Extension. PLAIN, SRC, and WRAP are HTML 3.0 attributes.

Attributes:

PLAIN	Specifies that no bullets be used.
SRC="URL"	Specifies an image to use for bullets.
TYPE=circle ¦ disc ¦ square	Specifies the type of bullet to use.
WRAP = horiz ¦ vert	Specifies a multicolumn list. horiz and vert tell the browser whether to add items horizontally or vertically first. The browser determines how many columns are appropriate.

Details: An unordered list is usually displayed as a bulleted list of items by default. `<LI>` tags are used to specify where list items start.

Images and Sounds

HTML has quite a bit of support for images but relatively little for sound (and none for smell and taste!). There is quite a bit of debate over the future of image-related tags. In some ways, HTML 3.0 is heading one direction, but Netscape and some other companies are heading another. Much debate is sure to ensue. In this section, we lean toward using the Netscape tags because they are more widely used at the current time.

`<area>`

Purpose: Defines an area of a client-side image map.

Version: Netscape HTML 3.0 Extension, Also in Client-Side Image Map Draft.

Attributes:

`COORDS="x,y,.."`	Specifies the vertices of the shape.
`HREF="URL"`	Specifies the URL that should be linked to.
`NOHREF`	Specifies that no action should be taken.
`SHAPE=CIRCLE ¦ DEFAULT ¦ POLY ¦ RECT`	Specifies whether the shape is a circle, polygon, or rectangle.
`TARGET="window name"`	Specifies the frame in which the URL being linked to should be displayed.

Details: Must be used with a `<map>` block.

`<bgsound>`

Purpose: Specifies a background sound should be played.

Version: Internet Explorer Extensions.

Attributes:

`SRC="URL"`	Specifies the URL of the sound file.

Details: Currently supports au, midi, and wav file formats.

`<caption>..</caption>`

Purpose: Contains a caption for a figure.

Version: HTML 3.0.

Attributes:

`ALIGN= BOTTOM ¦ LEFT ¦ RIGHT ¦ TOP`	Specifies the alignment of the caption in relation to the figure.

Details: Only used within a `<FIG>` block.

`<img>`

Purpose: Specifies an inline image in the document.

Version: HTML 2.0, the BORDER, HEIGHT, WIDTH, HSPACE, VSPACE, and the second version of the ALIGN attribute shown are Netscape HTML 2.0 extensions; the HEIGHT and WIDTH attributes are in HTML 3.0; USEMAP is a Netscape HTML 3.0 Extension and also in the Client-Side Image Map Draft.

Attributes:

ALIGN=TOP¦MIDDLE¦BOTTOM	Specifies how the image will be aligned compared with the text. TOP aligns the top of the image with the tallest item in the line. MIDDLE aligns the bottom of the text with the middle of the image. BOTTOM aligns middle of the text with bottom of the image.
ALIGN=LEFT ¦ RIGHT ¦TOP ¦ TEXTTOP ¦ MIDDLE ¦ ABSMIDDLE ¦ BASELINE ¦ BOTTOM ¦ ABSBOTTOM	Specifies how the image will be aligned compared with the text. LEFT puts the image on the left margin and flows text around to the right. RIGHT does the opposite of LEFT. TEXTTOP is like TOP but uses the tallest text not the tallest item. ABSMIDDLE is like MIDDLE but uses the middle of the text. BASELINE is the same as BOTTOM. ABSBOTTOM aligns the bottom of the image with the bottom of the text.
ALT="text"	Specifies text that can be used as an alternative to the image if the image cannot be displayed.
BORDER=n	Specifies the thickness of the image border.
HEIGHT=n	Specifies the height of the image. Allows the browser to leave space for the image and go ahead and display the text.
HSPACE=n	Specifies how much of a horizontal margin to leave around the image.
ISMAP	Indicates that the image is a server-side image map.
SRC="URL"	Specifies the URL of the image.
USEMAP="URL"	Specifies the URL of the client-side image map.
VSPACE=n	Specifies how much of a vertical margin to leave around the image.
WIDTH=n	Specifies the width of the image. Allows the browser to leave space for the image and display the text.

Details: GIF is the most commonly implemented image format in browsers. JPEG is commonly supported (though not as much as GIF) and is a good alternative choice because it saves disk space and bandwidth. For an imagemap to work, the `<IMG>` tag must be surrounded by an `<a>..</a>` pair.

`<map>..</map>`

Purpose: Defines a client-side image map.

Version: Netscape HTML 3.0 Extension; also appears in Client-Side Image Map Draft.

Attributes:

> `NAME="anchor"`   Specifies the anchor that can be linked to for this image map.

Details: The anchor needs to be linked to by a `<img usemap="#anchor">` tag.

Forms

All HTML forms require a CGI program to be written to process the form. This means the use of these tags alone isn't sufficient to have a working form. HTML forms are primitive because it's not possible, without using JavaScript or Java, to check the validity of input while it's being typed.

`<form>..</form>`

Purpose: Contains a form.

Version: HTML 2.0.

Attributes:

> `ACTION="URL"`   Specifies a URL that will process the form when completed.
>
> `METHOD=GET¦POST`   Specifies the data exchange method with the action URL.

Details: With the opening and closing tags, there should be some other tags such as `<input>` or `<textarea>` to specific the fields of the form.

`<input>`

Purpose: Specifies a field for user input.

Version: HTML 2.0 (first TYPE attribute shown), HTML 3.0 (second TYPE attribute shown), all attributes except for TYPE are Netscape JavaScript extensions.

Attributes:

> `onBlur="function"`   Specifies a JavaScript function to call when the field loses focus.
>
> `onChange="function"`   Specifies a JavaScript function to call when the field loses focus and the data in the field has changed.
>
> `onClick="function"`   Specifies a JavaScript function to call when this field has a mouse click.
>
> `onFocus="function"`   Specifies a JavaScript function to call when this field gets focus.

onLoad="function"	Specifies a JavaScript function to call when all frames are loaded.
onMouseOver="function"	Specifies a JavaScript function to call when the mouse pointer is over this field.
onSelect="function"	Specifies a JavaScript function to call when the user selects some text in a text or textarea field.
TYPE=TEXT ¦ PASSWORD ¦ CHECKBOX ¦ RADIO ¦ IMAGE ¦ HIDDEN ¦ SUBMIT ¦ RESET	Specifies the type of field to be used.
TYPE=CHECKBOX ¦ FILE ¦ HIDDEN ¦ IMAGE ¦ PASSWORD ¦ RADIO ¦ RANGE ¦ RESET ¦ SCRIBBLE ¦ SUBMIT ¦ TEXT	Specifies the type of field to be used.

Details: Because the explanation of these attributes is complex, we have broken them out separately below. A few of the uncommon ones aren't covered below. There is no closing tag.

<input type=checkbox>

Purpose: Specifies a checkbox that represents a true-false choice.

Version: HTML 2.0.

Attributes:

CHECKED	Specifies that the checkbox is checked by default.
NAME="name"	Specifies the name of the field. Required.
VALUE="value"	Specifies the value of the field. Required.

Details: You can have several type=checkbox items that have the same field name as specified by the NAME attribute. When you do this, you can create an n-of-many selection field.

<input type=hidden>

Purpose: Allows the HTML document to specify fields and values that the user cannot change.

Version: HTML 2.0.

Attributes:

NAME="name"	Specifies the name of the field. Required.
VALUE="value"	Specifies the value of the field. Required.

Details: A hidden field is not displayed to the user.

<input type=image> 2.0 - p41

<input type=radio>

Purpose: Specifies a radio button representing a true-false choice.

Version: HTML 2.0.

Attributes:

CHECKED	Specifies that the radio button is checked by default.
NAME="name"	Specifies the name of the field. Required.
VALUE="value"	Specifies the value of the field. Required.

Details: You can have several type=radio items that have the same field name as specified by the NAME attribute. Only one of these may be checked at any time. This is how you can create a 1-of-many selection field.

<input type=range>

Purpose: Specifies that the user must pick a numeric value within a range.

Version: HTML 3.0.

Attributes:

MAX=n	Specifies the upper limit of the range.
MIN=n	Specifies the lower limit of the range.
NAME="name"	Specifies the name of the field. Required.

Details: If either MAX or MIN are real numbers, real numbers are accepted as input. Otherwise, only integers are accepted.

<input type=reset>

Purpose: Specifies a button that resets the form to its initial state.

Version: HTML 2.0, SRC is an HTML 3.0 attribute.

Attributes:

SRC="URL"	Specifies an image to be used as the reset button.
VALUE="value"	Specifies the label for the reset button.

<input type=submit>

Purpose: Specifies a Submit button.

Version: HTML 2.0, SRC attribute is HTML 3.0.

Attributes:

NAME="name"	Specifies the name of the field.
SRC="URL"	Specifies an image to be used as the Submit button.
VALUE="value"	Specifies the value of the field. If present, this also is the label for the button.

Details: The value of the NAME and VALUE attributes is that if you have multiple Submit buttons, the ACTION URL can figure out which one was pressed.

<input type=text> and <input text=password>

Purpose: Specifies a field for the input of textual data.

Version: HTML 2.0.

Attributes:

MAXLENGTH=n	Specifies the maximum length of the field. The default is infinite.
NAME="name"	Specifies the name for the field.
SIZE=n	Specifies the size of the field on the screen. If the number of characters entered is greater than SIZE but less the MAXLENGTH, the field will scroll. The browser chooses its own default size if one is not specified.
VALUE="value"	Specifies the default value of the field.

Details: The NAME attribute is required but all other attributes are optional. The only difference between type=text and type=password is that the users' keystrokes are displayed on the screen with type=text and aren't displayed with type=password.

<option>

Purpose: Specifies a list item in a selection list.

Version: HTML 2.0.

Attributes:

SELECTED	Specifies that the item is selected by default.
VALUE="value"	Specifies the value of the item.

Details: <OPTION> tags may only appear with a <select> block. Each <option> tag is followed by text that is displayed as in the list and also used as the value if a VALUE attribute isn't specified.

<select>..</select>

Purpose: Specifies a selection list.

Version: HTML 2.0, DISABLED is an HTML 3.0 attribute.

Attributes:

DISABLED	Specifies that the select list should be displayed, but not to allow the user to change it.
MULTIPLE	Specifies that multiple options may be selected at the same time. If it isn't specified, only one option may be selected at any given time.

| NAME="name" | Specifies the name of the field. |
| SIZE=n | Specifies the name of options that are visible at any one time. If this is not specified, the browser chooses its own size. |

Details: This is typically displayed as a scrolling list. List items are defined with the <OPTION> tag.

<textarea>..</textarea>

Purpose: Specifies a multiline text field.

Version: HTML 2.0, DISABLED is a HTML 3.0 attribute, WRAP is a Netscape HTML 3.0 Extension, the first set of attributes are Netscape JavaScript Extensions.

Attributes:

onBlur, onChange, onClick, onFocus, onLoad, onMouseOver, onSelect	See <input> for the meaning of these attributes.
COLS=n	Number of columns to be displayed on-screen.
DISABLED	Specifies that the text area should be displayed but no changes to it are allowed.
NAME="name"	The name of the field.
ROWS=n	Number of rows to be displayed on-screen.
WRAP=OFF ¦ PHYSICAL ¦ VIRTUAL	Specifies how word wrapping should be handled. PHYSICAL means word wrap on display and transmission. VIRTUAL means word wrap on display, but transmit line breaks only where the user typed them.

Details: If text appears between the opening and closing tags, it's the default value of the field. The COLS and ROWS attributes are used to determine the display size only. If the text is larger than the display size, scroll bars should be used.

Java and JavaScript

Java and JavaScript are languages that enhance the Web by making it more interactive. Sun and Netscape have invented their own tags for these languages. There has been some talk in the HTML community about replacing some of these tags by a new tag called <insert> but no formal proposal has been made public yet.

<app>..</app>

Purpose: Includes an Alpha Java applet in a document.

Version: Sun HTML Extensions.

Details: This works only for the Alpha release of Java and is obsolete. Use <applet> instead.

`<applet>..</applet>`

Purpose: Includes a Java applet in the document.

Version: Sun HTML Extensions.

Attributes:

CODEBASE	Specifies the base URL or the directory that contains the applet.
CODE	A required attribute that contains the name of the applet class file.
ALT	Alternate text that will be displayed if the browser does not know how to interpret the `<applet>` tag.
NAME	Name or an anchor for the applet so that other applets on the same page will be able to communicate with the named applet.
WIDTH, HEIGHT	Required width and height in pixels of the area where the applet is going to be displayed.
ALIGN	Alignment of the applet with the same attributes as the `<IMG>` tag.
VSPACE, HSPACE	Blank vertical (above and below the applet) and horizontal (right and left sides of the applet) space in pixels around the applet. It's the same as VSPACE and HSPACE in the `<IMG>` tag.

`<param>`

Purpose: User-defined parameters that go within the `<applet>..</applet>` tags.

Version: Sun HTML Extension.

Attributes:

NAME="attribute of the applet"	Applet programmer-defined attribute.
VALUE="value"	Value of the attribute NAME.

`<script>..</script>`

Purpose: Contains a script.

Version: Netscape JavaScript Extension.

Attributes:

LANGUAGE=JAVASCRIPT	Specifies the language the script is in. JavaScript is the only current option.

Tables

Tables are currently the most widely implemented part of HTML 3.0. They are powerful and extremely useful. The only negative is that table documents look very bad on browsers that do not support tables.

`<table>..</table>`

Purpose: Main table tag that wraps around all other table tags.

Version: HTML 3.0, `BORDER=n`, `CELLSPACING`, `CELLPADDING`, and `WIDTH=percent` are Netscape HTML 3.0 Extensions.

Attributes:

`ALIGN= BLEEDLEFT ¦ BLEEDRIGHT ¦`	Specifies the alignment of the `CENTER ¦ JUSTIFY ¦ LEFT ¦ RIGHT` table. The difference between `BLEEDLEFT` and `LEFT`, and `BLEEDRIGHT` and `RIGHT` is that the regular versions are flush with the margins. The `BLEED` versions are flush with the window border. `JUSTIFY` scales the figure to cover from left to right margin.
`BORDER`	Specifies that the table should have a border displayed.
`BORDER=n`	Specifies that the table should have a border of the given width.
`CELLPADDING=n`	Specifies the amount of space between the edge of the cell and its contents.
`CELLSPACING=n`	Specifies how much space should be placed between cells.
`COLSPEC="column spec"`	Specifies column widths and alignments.
`NOFLOW`	Specifies that text should not flow around the table.
`NOWRAP`	Specifies that the browser should not automatically break lines.
`UNITS= EN ¦ PIXELS ¦ RELATIVE`	Specifies what kind of units are used for `COLSPEC` and `WIDTH`. `EN` is a half of a point size. `PIXELS` is the number of pixels. `RELATIVE` is that each column is relative to the others.
`WIDTH=n`	Specifies the width of the table. Netscape allows this to be a percentage of the document width.

Details: A column specification is a set of column widths and alignment from left to right. Each column is made up of a letter specifying the alignment (C for center, D for decimal alignment for floating point numbers, J for justified, L for left, and R for right) and then a number specifying the width in the UNITS specified.

`<td>..</td>` and `<th>..</th>`

Purpose: Specifies table data and table header cells respectively.

Version: HTML 3.0.

Attributes:

ALIGN=CENTER ¦ DECIMAL ¦ JUSTIFY ¦ LEFT ¦ RIGHT	Specifies the horizontal alignment within the cell DECIMAL makes sure that decimal points are aligned.
COLSPAN=n	Specifies that this cell should span n columns.
NOWRAP	Specifies that the cell should not wrap the text within it.
ROWSPAN=n	Specifies that this cell should span n rows.
VALIGN= BASELINE ¦ BOTTOM ¦ MIDDLE ¦ TOP	Specifies the vertical alignment within the cell. BASELINE guarantees that all cells in the same row share the same baseline. The meaning of the others are obvious.

Details: `<td>` and `<th>` must occur within a `<tr>` block. The major difference between `<td>` and `<th>` cells are that `<th>` cells are given a darker or larger font.

`<tr>..</tr>`

Purpose: Specifies a table row.

Version: HTML 3.0.

Attributes:

ALIGN=CENTER ¦ DECIMAL ¦ JUSTIFY ¦ LEFT¦ RIGHT	Specifies the horizontal alignment within the row. DECIMAL makes decimal points are aligned between rows.
VALIGN=BASELINE ¦ BOTTOM ¦ MIDDLE ¦ TOP	Specifies the vertical alignment within the cell. BASELINE that all cells in the same row share the same baseline. The meaning of the others are obvious.

Details: Must occur with a `<table>` block.

Frames

Frames are a Netscape invention. They break the browser screen in multiple windows each of which contain a different HTML document. Unfortunately, navigation in Frames can be confusing and are disliked by many people.

`<frame>`

Purpose: Defines the size of a single frame in a frameset.

Version: Netscape Frame Extensions.

Attributes:

`MARGINHEIGHT=n`	Specifies a fixed top/bottom margin for the frame.
`MARGINWIDTH=n`	Specifies a fixed right/left margin for the frame.
`NAME="window_name"`	Specifies a name for a frame. This can be used to link to this frame from other documents.
`NORESIZE`	Specifies that the user isn't allowed to resize this frame.
`SCROLLING= YES ¦ NO ¦ AUTO`	Specifies whether or not the frame should have a scrollbar. AUTO means that the browser gets to decide whether there is a scrollbar.
`SRC="URL"`	Specifies the URL of the document to be displayed in this frame.

Details: There is no closing tag. Must be used within a `<frameset>` block.

`<frameset>..</frameset>`

Purpose: Defines a document as being a set of frames instead of an HTML document.

Version: Netscape Frame Extensions.

Attributes:

`COLS="columns_spec"`	Specifies the width of columns in a frameset. The specification is a comma-delimited list. Each element of the list can be a percentage, a pixel value, or a relative value. Relative values are specified as `*` (meaning 1), `2*` (meaning 2), and so on.
`ROWS="rows_spec"`	Specifies the height of rows in a frameset. See COLS for syntax.

Details: May not be used in the same file as the `<body>` tag.

`<noframes>..</noframes>`

Purpose: Contains an alternative view for browsers that don't support frames.

Version: Netscape Frame Extensions.

Details: Must be used within a `<frameset>` block.

Comments

A comment starts with `<!--` and ends with `-->`. Unfortunately, some browsers (for example, certain versions of Lynx) don't recognize comments. Therefore, though useful, the use of comments isn't recommended.

CGI

Common Gateway Interface (CGI) is an interface for external programs or applications to interact with information servers like the Webservers. CGI programs are commonly used to process forms, and they can be written in any language that can be executed on the Webserver such as C, C++, shell scripts, Visual Basic, Perl, Tk/Tcl. CGI programs normally only reside in a special directory designated by the webmaster due to security reasons. But some Webmasters use wrapper programs such as cgiwrap (UNIX) to safely allow Web authors to write and run CGI programs in a special directory under their home directories.

This section serves as a reference guide for commonly used CGI environment variables and headers. Version 1.1 of the CGI standard was used as the basis for this section.

Environment Variables

These are environment variables that are passed into CGI scripts. The last three involving REDIRECTs are specific to the NCSA HTTPD server and may not work with other services.

SERVER_SOFTWARE	The name and the version number of the server.
SERVER_NAME	The server's full hostname, IP address, or an alias.
GATEWAY_INTERFACE	Revision of the CGI specification.
SERVER_PROTOCOL	The name and revision of the service protocol.
SERVER_PORT	The port where the server is running.
REQUEST_METHOD	The method of the request.
PATH_INFO	Extra information at the end of the path of the executing CGI script.
PATH_TRANSLATED	A translated version of PATH_INFO that has removed any virtual mappings.
SCRIPT_NAME	The full virtual path of the executing CGI script.
QUERY_STRING	Anything that goes after the ? in the URL that referenced this CGI program.
REMOTE_HOST	The hostname of the machine making the request to the Webserver.
REMOTE_ADDR	The IP address of REMOTE_HOST or the machine making the request.
AUTH_TYPE	The authentication method used if the script was protected.
REMOTE_USER	Login name of the user from REMOTE_ADDR if the user logged in via user authentication.
REMOTE_IDENT	Login name of the user from REMOTE_ADDR if the remote host supports user identification.

CONTENT_TYPE	Content type of the data.
CONTENT_LENGTH	Length of the content given by the client.
HTTP_ACCEPT	The MIME type that the client accepts.
HTTP_USER_AGENT	The browser from the client.
HTTP_REFERER	The page that refers the client to this CGI program.
REDIRECT_REQUEST	The request for a redirect as sent to the server.
REDIRECT_STATUS	The status the server would have sent if it hadn't been redirected.
REDIRECT_URL	The URL that caused the redirect.

Headers for the Output of a CGI Program

These headers are HTTP headers. Your CGI program can return them to the browser as meta information about the document being returned.

Allowed	Lists the requests that the user is allowed to use on this URL.
Content-Encoding	Encoding method.
Content-Language	ISO3316 language code with an optional ISO639 country code.
Content-Length	The length of the returning document.
Content-Transfer-Encoding	The MIME encoding method used on the returning document.
Content-Type	MIME type of the returning document.
Date	Creation date in GMT format.
Expires	Expiration date.
Last-Modified	Last modification date.
Location	Virtual path or the URL of the returning document.
Message-Id	Message identifier.
Public	Lists all requests that anyone can use.
Status	Returned status of the request.
URI	URI of the document.
Version	Version of the document.
Title	Title of the document.

Index

SYMBOLS

A

Teach Yourself the Internet in a Week, Second Edition

— *Neil Randall*

The combination of a structured, step-by-step approach and the excitement of exploring the world of the Internet make this tutorial and reference perfect for any user wanting to master the Net. Efficiently exploring the basics of the Internet, *Teach Yourself the Internet* takes users to the farthest reaches of the Internet with hands-on exercises and detailed instructions. Completely updated to cover Netscape, Internet-works, and Microsoft's Internet Assistant.

Price: $25.00 USA/$34.99 CDN   User Level: Beginner-Inter
ISBN: 0-672-30735-9   622 pages

Tricks of the Internet Gurus

— *Various Internet Gurus*

Best-selling title that focuses on tips and techniques that allow the reader to more effectively use the resources of the Internet. A must-have for the power Internet user, *Tricks of the Internet Gurus* offers tips, strategies, and techniques for optimizing use of the Internet. Features interviews with various Internet leaders.

Price: $35.00 USA/$47.95 CDN   User Level: Inter-Advanced
ISBN: 0-672-30599-2   809 pages

Teach Yourself More Web Publishing with HTML in a Week

— *Laura Lemay*

Ideal for those people who are ready for more advanced World Wide Web home page design! The sequel to *Teach Yourself Web Publishing with HTML*, *Teach Yourself More* explores the process of creating and maintaining Web presentations, including setting up tools and converters for verifying and testing pages. Teaches advanced HTML techniques and tricks in a clear, step-by-step manner with many practical examples. Highlights the Netscape extensions and HTML 3.0.

Price: $29.99 USA/$39.99 CDN   User Level: Inter-Advanced
ISBN: 1-57521-005-3   480 pages

The Internet Business Guide, Second Edition

— *Rosalind Resnick & Dave Taylor*

Updated and revised, this guide will inform and educate anyone on how they can use the Internet to increase profits, reach a broader market, track down business leads, and access critical information. Updated to cover digital cash, Web cybermalls, secure Web servers, and setting up your business on the Web, *The Internet Business Guide* includes profiles of entrepreneurs' successes (and failures) on the Internet. Improve your business by using the Internet to market products and services, make contacts with colleagues, cut costs, and improve customer service.

Price: $25.00 USA/$39.99 CDN   User Level: All Levels
ISBN: 1-57521-004-5   470 pages

Teach Yourself Netscape Web Publishing in a Week

— Wes Tatters

Teach Yourself Netscape Web Publishing in a Week is the easiest way to learn how to produce attention-getting, well-designed Web pages using the features provided by Netscape Navigator. Intended for both the novice and the expert, this book provides a solid grounding in HTML and Web publishing principles, while providing special focus on the possibilities presented by the Netscape environment. Learn to design and create attention-grabbing Web pages for the Netscape environment while exploring new Netscape development features such as frames, plug-ins, Java applets, and JavaScript!

Price: $39.99 USA/ $47.95 CDN   User Level: Beginner-Inter
ISBN: 1-57521-068-1   450 pages

Teach Yourself CGI Programming with Perl in a Week

— Eric Herrmann

This book is a step-by-step tutorial of how to create, use, and maintain Common Gateway Interfaces (CGI). It describes effective ways of using CGI as an integral part of Web development. Adds interactivity and flexibility to the information that can be provided through your Web site. Includes Perl 4.0 and 5.0, CGI libraries, and other applications to create databases, dynamic interactivity, and other enticing page effects.

Price: $39.99 USA/$53.99 CDN   User Level: Inter-Advanced
ISBN: 1-57521-009-6   500 pages

Teach Yourself Java in 21 Days

— Laura Lemay and Charles Perkins

The complete tutorial guide to the most exciting technology to hit the Internet in years—Java! A detailed guide to developing applications with the hot new Java language from Sun Microsystems, *Teach Yourself Java in 21 Days* shows readers how to program using Java and develop applications (applets) using the Java language. With coverage of Java implementation in Netscape Navigator and Hot Java, along with the Java Development Kit, including the compiler and debugger for Java, *Teach Yourself Java* is a must-have!

Price: $39.99 USA/$53.99 CDN   User Level: Inter-Advanced
ISBN: 1-57521-030-4   600 pages

Presenting Java

— John December

Presenting Java gives you a first look at how Java is transforming static Web pages into living, interactive applications. Java opens up a world of possibilities previously unavailable on the Web. You'll find out how Java is being used to create animations, computer simulations, interactive games, teaching tools, spreadsheets, and a variety of other applications. Whether you're a new user, a project planner, or developer, *Presenting Java* provides an efficient, quick introduction to the basic concepts and technical details that make Java the hottest new Web technology of the year!

Price: $25.00 USA/$34.95 CDN   User Level: All Levels
ISBN: 1-57521-039-8   207 pages

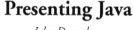

Netscape 2 Unleashed

— *Dick Oliver, et. al.*

This book provides a complete, detailed, and fully fleshed-out overview of the Netscape products. Through case studies and examples of how individuals, businesses, and institutions are using the Netscape products for Web development, *Netscape Unleashed* gives a full description of the evolution of Netscape from its inception to today, and its cutting-edge developments with Netscape Gold, LiveWire, Netscape Navigator 2.0, Java and JavaScript, Macromedia, VRML, Plug-ins, Adobe Acrobat, HTML 3.0 and beyond, security and Intranet systems.

Price: $49.99 USA/$61.95 CDN   User Level: All Levels
ISBN: 1-57521-007-X   Pages: 800 pages

The Internet Unleashed 1996

— *Barron, Ellsworth, Savetz, et. al.*

The Internet Unleashed 1996 is the complete reference to get new users up and running on the Internet while providing the consummate reference manual for the experienced user. *The Internet Unleashed 1996* provides the reader with an encyclopedia of information on how to take advantage of all the Net has to offer for business, education, research, and government. The companion CD-ROM contains over 100 tools and applications. The only book that includes the experience of over 40 of the world's top Internet experts, this new edition is updated with expanded coverage of Web publishing, Internet business, Internet multimedia and virtual reality, Internet security, Java, and more!

Price: $49.99 USA/$67.99 CDN   User Level: All Levels
ISBN: 1-57521-041-X   1,456 pages

The World Wide Web Unleashed 1996

— *December and Randall*

The World Wide Web Unleashed 1996 is designed to be the only book a reader will need to experience the wonders and resources of the Web. The companion CD-ROM contains over 100 tools and applications to make the most of your time on the Internet. Shows readers how to explore the Web's amazing world of electronic art museums, online magazines, virtual malls, and video music libraries, while giving readers complete coverage of Web page design, creation, and maintenance, plus coverage of new Web technologies such as Java, VRML, CGI, and multimedia!

Price: $49.99 USA/$67.99 CDN   User Level: All Levels
ISBN: 1-57521-040-1   1,440 pages

Teach Yourself Web Publishing with HTML in 14 Days, Premier Edition

— *Laura Lemay*

This book teaches everything about publishing on the Web. In addition to its exhaustive coverage of HTML, it also gives readers hands-on practice with more complicated subjects such as CGI, tables, forms, multimedia programming, testing, maintenance, and much more. CD-ROM is Mac- and PC-compatible and includes a variety of applications that help readers create Web pages using graphics and templates.

Price: $39.99 USA/$53.99 CDN   User Level: All Levels
ISBN: 1-57521-014-2   804 pages

Teach Yourself Web Publishing with HTML 3.0 in a Week, Second Edition

— Laura Lemay

Ideal for those people who are interested in the Internet and the World Wide Web—the Internet's hottest topic! This updated and revised edition teaches readers how to use HTML (HyperText Markup Language) version 3.0 to create Web pages that can be viewed by nearly 30 million users. Explores the process of creating and maintaining Web presentations, including setting up tools and converters for verifying and testing pages. The new edition highlights the new features of HTML, such as tables and Netscape and Microsoft Explorer extensions. Provides the latest information on working with images, sound files, and video, and teaches advanced HTML techniques and tricks in a clear, step-by-step manner with many practical examples of HTML pages.

Price: $29.99 USA/$34.95 CDN   User Level: Beginner-Inter
ISBN: 1-57521-064-9   518 pages

Web Page Construction Kit (Software)

Create your own exciting World Wide Web pages with the software and expert guidance in this kit! Includes HTML Assistant Pro Lite, the acclaimed point-and-click Web page editor. Simply highlight text in HTML Assistant Pro Lite, and click the appropriate button to add headlines, graphics, special formatting, links, etc. No programming skills needed! Using your favorite Web browser, you can test your work quickly and easily without leaving the editor. A unique catalog feature allows you to keep track of interesting Web sites and easily add their HTML links to your pages. Assistant's user-defined toolkit also allows you to add new HTML formatting styles as they are defined. Includes the #1 best-selling Internet book, *Teach Yourself Web Publishing with HTML 3.0 in a Week, Second Edition,* and a library of professionally designed Web page templates, graphics, buttons, bullets, lines, and icons to rev up your new pages!

PC Computing magazine says, "If you're looking for the easiest route to Web publishing, HTML Assistant is your best choice."

Price: $39.95 US/$46.99 CAN   User Level: Beginner-Inter
ISBN: 1-57521-000-2   518 pages

HTML & CGI Unleashed

— John December & Marc Ginsburg

Targeted to professional developers who have a basic understanding of programming and need a detailed guide. Provides a complete, detailed reference to developing Web information systems. Covers the full range of languages—HTML, CGI, Perl C, editing and conversion programs, and more—and how to create commercial-grade Web Applications. Perfect for the developer who will be designing, creating, and maintaining a Web presence for a company or large institution.

Price: $49.99 USA/$53.99 CDN   User Level: Inter-Advanced
ISBN: 0-672-30745-6   830 pages

Web Site Construction Kit for Windows NT

— Christopher Brown and Scott Zimmerman

The Web Site Construction Kit for Windows NT has everything you need to set up, develop, and maintain a Web site with Windows NT—including the server on the CD-ROM! It teaches the ins and outs of planning, installing, configuring, and administering a Windows NT–based Web site for an organization, and it includes detailed instructions on how to use the software on the CD-ROM to develop the Web site's content—HTML pages, CGI scripts, imagemaps, and so forth.

Price: $49.99 USA/$67.99 CDN   User Level: All Levels
ISBN: 1-57521-047-9   430 pages